THE CONSTITUTION OF 1789

The Constitution of 1789 is a new introduction to the Constitution written on the semiquincentennial of American Independence, packed with novel and surprising insights about the Constitution's original meaning. The book takes readers on an in-depth tour of the Constitution's structure and separation of powers, starting with the nature of written constitutions and the compound nature of the American Union. The book also explores the enumeration of legislative powers and its relation to the historic royal prerogatives, the meaning of executive power, and the distribution of foreign affairs and war powers between Congress and the President. It investigates the nature of judicial power and the Constitution's complex relationship with slavery, before addressing federalism and the scope of national powers. *The Constitution of 1789* dismantles several common misconceptions and conventional wisdoms and is suitable for all readers interested in the law, politics, and history of the American Republic.

Ilan Wurman is the Julius E. Davis Professor of Law at the University of Minnesota. He is also the author of *The Second Founding: An Introduction to the Fourteenth Amendment* (2020) and *A Debt against the Living: An Introduction to Originalism* (2017), as well as a leading casebook on administrative law. He splits his time between Saint Paul, Minnesota, and rural Arizona.

The Constitution of 1789

A NEW INTRODUCTION

ILAN WURMAN

University of Minnesota

CAMBRIDGE
UNIVERSITY PRESS

Shaftesbury Road, Cambridge CB2 8EA, United Kingdom

One Liberty Plaza, 20th Floor, New York, NY 10006, USA

477 Williamstown Road, Port Melbourne, VIC 3207, Australia

314–321, 3rd Floor, Plot 3, Splendor Forum, Jasola District Centre, New Delhi – 110025, India

Cambridge University Press is part of Cambridge University Press & Assessment,
a department of the University of Cambridge.

We share the University's mission to contribute to society through the pursuit of
education, learning and research at the highest international levels of excellence.

www.cambridge.org
Information on this title: www.cambridge.org/9781009485715

DOI: 10.1017/9781009485708

First published 2026

Cover image: The inauguration of Washington as first president of the United States.
(Photo by Heritage Art/Heritage Images via Getty Images)

A catalogue record for this publication is available from the British Library

A Cataloging-in-Publication data record for this book is available from the Library of Congress

ISBN 978-1-009-48571-5 Hardback
ISBN 978-1-009-48569-2 Paperback

To Ze'ev Wurman,

1950–2023.

And to Irena, his mother,

who had nothing after the war,

and who trained as a lawyer

when so few women did;

1914–1976.

Contents

Detailed Contents

Figures

Acknowledgments

This book has been eight years in the making, since the day I began teaching constitutional law. There was then no convenient, single-volume work introducing the original Constitution from a historical and textual perspective. The book has changed numerous times as my own views have evolved over nearly a decade of teaching and conversations on the subject. I owe an unpayable debt to many colleagues as well as students at the University of Minnesota (my current institution) and at Arizona State University (my first academic institution) for helping shape my perspective over the years. I have learned much from them. A debt is also owed to my many previous teachers and mentors. I rank among them my late father, to whom this volume is dedicated.

I owe specific thanks to several academic colleagues who read parts of the manuscript within their areas of expertise: William Baude, Curtis Bradley, Jean Galbraith, Stephen Griffin, Gary Lawson, Bradley Rebeiro, and Samuel White. Bradford Clark, Paul Rahe, and Lorianne Updike Schulzke read the manuscript in its entirety or in substantial part. I also presented chapters at the University of Minnesota faculty workshop, the Originalism Works-in-Progress Conference at the University of San Diego in 2024, and a conference on executive power (virtually) at the University of Adelaide, in Australia. Stephanie Barclay and Randy Barnett also hosted a book workshop on the late-stage manuscript at the Georgetown University Law Center in which several other professors participated to provide comments, including Aditya Bamzai, Jud Campbell, Bradford Clark, Jean Galbraith, Christopher Green, Yonatan Green, Tara Grove, Christina Mulligan, Nicholas Parrillo, Michael Ramsey, Michael Rappaport, and Marton Sulyok. I thank all the readers, commentators, and participants for their insightful comments.

Finally, I owe thanks to my research assistant at the University of Minnesota, Benjamin Ayanian, as well as the following army of students from the Harvard Law School for helping to cite-check the manuscript in its later stages: Susannah Cray, John Erskine, Monroe Harless, Jacob Meech, Jorge Plaza, Paige Proctor, Jin Qiu, Will Randolph, Jon Suh, Aidan Turley, Katherine Wang, Bryden Wright, and Jack Wroldsen. All errors, substantive or otherwise, remain my own.

A Note on the Cover

The book is entitled, "The Constitution of 1789: A New Introduction." The date 1789 was chosen because although the Constitution was drafted and approved by the Constitutional Convention in 1787, it had no legal effect until ratified by the people of the United States. Some might still ask why not the Constitution of 1788 – the year the ninth state ratified the Constitution?

Although some parts of the Constitution may have gone into effect in 1788, particularly those provisions binding on the states, the date is not as commonly associated with the American Constitution as is 1787 or 1789. Moreover, this study is concerned with the separation of powers. The "Constitution" with which it deals is the one implemented in 1789 with the inauguration of the first national executive, the convening of the first congress, and the establishment of the national judiciary. I hope readers who feel the date 1789 is imprecise will forgive the author this license.

The cover illustration depicts the inauguration of George Washington as the first president of the United States on April 30, 1789, as illustrated by Nathaniel Currier and James Merritt Ives in 1876 on the centennial of American Independence. This book comes out on the semiquincentennial, and it seemed appropriate for that reason, too, to reproduce the image.

Introduction

This July 4, the United States turns 250 years old. Its current constitution, drafted in 1787 and carried into effect in 1789, is the oldest in the modern world; it follows closely behind at 237 years. The government structure that constitution creates has been remarkably enduring, yet today very few Americans understand how it works. Many have some awareness of its key elements of representation, separation of powers, checks and balances, federalism, and the Bill of Rights. But many remain unaware of, or confused about, how the U.S. Constitution creates this structure and the enduring questions surrounding it. This book introduces that structure and those questions and seeks to equip sophisticated readers – from law students and law professors to everyday Americans – to analyze and answer them.

Some of these enduring questions include: Did the states or the people create the federal government? Was secession unconstitutional? Did the Framers intend to create a government of limited, enumerated powers or to give the national government "sweeping" and "elastic" powers over the general welfare? Who has power over foreign affairs? Can presidents engage in undeclared military actions around the world? Do they enjoy any inherent powers? Did the Supreme Court invent judicial review? What role should that institution play in our constitutional order? Was the Constitution proslavery? Do the states retain any power to regulate interstate commerce? Can Congress use its taxing and spending powers to circumvent the enumeration of powers?

These are just some of the questions this book seeks to answer as it introduces the basic structure of the Constitution: how the document frames the legislative, executive, and judicial powers of the national government and distributes power between the national and state governments. It tracks much of the material a first-year law student might encounter in a constitutional law course, and such students will benefit from this book. But so will any readers interested in understanding the original structure of the Constitution and how it operates today. Its most fundamental motivation is the author's considered view that the Constitution's original structure is worth recovering and preserving.

In introducing the original Constitution, this book will canvas the latest historical and legal scholarship on many constitutional questions. It will dispel common myths about the Constitution, challenge several conventional wisdoms, and take on some fashionable academic opinions. For example, the book will demonstrate that the Constitutional Convention likely did not enumerate power to limit the national government's powers – although that may have been the effect – but rather to limit executive power by assigning historically royal prerogatives to Congress. It will establish that the Necessary and Proper Clause permits the exercise only of implied powers, which are small and relatively unimportant powers. It will show that many contemporary academics are wrong about the "general welfare clause" because there is no such clause in the Constitution. And the chapters on the presidency, contra many "originalists," will argue that there is no inherent presidential power but also that "living constitutionalists" are equally, if not more, responsible for the rise of the imperial presidency.

On these and many other questions, this study will examine and challenge the conventional wisdom among both originalists who believe the Constitution should be interpreted with its original meaning and living constitutionalists who believe interpretations of its text should evolve. It will explore different perspectives within these camps. It will also, however, generally advance the author's own considered views of the problems it addresses. These views, it should be noted, reflect the author's current, studied understanding of the Constitution's meaning, and are liable to change in the future. The author has yet to encounter another constitutional scholar who agrees with everything in this book. It is intended to be a starting point for debate and discussion of America's founding document.

PART I: CONSTITUTIONAL UNION

This study consists of seven parts and eighteen chapters. The first part, "Constitutional Union," examines in Chapter 1 the nature and purposes of written constitutions generally and of the American Constitution particularly. It investigates the differences between the British unwritten constitution from the written constitutions the Americans developed after Independence; such differences will have implications, including for the validity of judicial review. It explores the settlement functions that constitutions play and the tension between self-government and liberty that constitutions for free societies must reconcile.

Chapter 2 addresses the compound nature of the American Union. The Framers had studied Montesquieu's "old science of politics," which maintained that republics had to be small and that the solution to common defense was a confederation of independent states. The American Revolution and the critical period between 1776 and 1787, however, demonstrated the inadequacies of a mere confederacy. The Framers thus established a "new science of politics." Part of the innovation of the new politics was a vision of a compound republic. The central government would be partly federal because the states retained independent existences and partly national because the central government would itself be established by the people and operate directly on them as individuals. The direct operation of federal laws on everyday citizens was the key innovation over the Articles of Confederation and will set the background for at least some questions of constitutional interpretation, such as nullification and secession; this innovation also partly explains why the early Supreme Court declined to give a strict construction to the Constitution. The national government had limited and defined powers, but within its sphere it was supreme and had all the subordinate powers reasonably necessary to effectuate its objectives.

PART II: THE LEGISLATIVE POWER

Chapters 3 and 4 introduce the structure of legislative power in Article I of the Constitution. Chapter 3 addresses how the Constitution creates an enumeration of power and the relationship between that enumeration and the subsequent addition of an enumeration of rights. It explores why the Committee of Detail that drafted the Constitution during the Constitutional Convention may have enumerated power despite the Convention having rejected a proposal to do so. It is likely that the leading drafter sought to assign historically royal prerogative powers to Congress. But that the result was a national government of limited and enumerated powers cannot seriously be questioned. The chapter investigates some modern revisionist scholars who argue "enumerationism" is not a necessary understanding of the Constitution's original meaning and rejects such revisionism.

Chapter 4 turns to the Necessary and Proper Clause, which gives Congress the power "to make all Laws which shall be necessary and proper for carrying into Execution the foregoing Powers, and all other Powers vested by this Constitution in the Government of the United States, or in any Department or Officer thereof." It has become fashionable among modern revisionist scholars to argue that this clause allows Congress to legislate in the general interest of the Union. Although much of this study will reject conventional wisdom, here it seeks to maintain the conventional view. Properly understood, the clause was merely a grant of implied or incidental powers. It excludes the exercise of any great, substantive, or independent power because such powers are unlikely to have been left to implication. Here, the reader shall encounter Chief Justice John Marshall's famous and oft misinterpreted dictum that "it is *a constitution* we are expounding," which was nothing more than a statement about implied powers.

This study next turns to the structure of executive power and returns to the scope of the national government's powers only in the final part. This organization may seem odd to those accustomed to thinking about the enumeration of power and the Necessary and Proper Clause together with other federalism topics such as commerce, taxing, and spending. Yet, establishing the structure of legislative power is essential to any discussion of the separation of powers because the Necessary and Proper Clause authorizes Congress to make laws necessary and proper for carrying into execution not only its own powers but also the powers the Constitution vests in any other "department or officer." It is this clause, then, that gives Congress at least some power to structure the other branches. The debates over executive power in particular cannot be understood without first understanding Congress's powers under this clause.

PART III: THE EXECUTIVE POWER

Part III consists of three chapters on the presidency. Chapter 5 introduces the debates over the presidency at the Convention and the resulting structure of presidential powers. The fundamental problem confronting the Convention was how to create an executive with sufficient energy to execute the laws and protect such a large nation while avoiding the risk of tyranny; the objective was to give energy to the executive, but only "as far as republican principles will admit."

The chapter then explores the debates over the meaning of the executive power. Unlike the vesting clause of Article I, which vests in Congress "all legislative powers herein granted," the vesting clause of Article II vests in the President "the executive power." This slight difference in language has led to major consequences and debates over the past two centuries. Some scholars argue that this linguistic variation means all powers executive in nature, even if nowhere mentioned in the Constitution, belong to the President. The conventional view among most academics, in contrast, is that Article II's vesting clause is no grant of power at all, but merely identifies who is to exercise the powers subsequently enumerated in Article II. It is likely that neither view is correct. Rather, as a handful of scholars have recently begun to argue, the executive vesting clause is likely a grant of power, but only a single power: the power to execute law.

Even if the executive power means only the power to execute law, there is a great debate over the scope of that power. Chapters 6 and 7 address the President's control over law execution and whether the President can direct and remove executive officers at pleasure. These questions go to the heart of the modern administrative state and in particular the constitutionality of the so-called headless fourth branch of government comprising "independent" agencies and commissions. Many originalists believe the President must have the power to control all officials in the executive branch through direction and removal. Other scholars maintain that the President has no constitutional right to direct or remove officers at all, and that Congress may structure the executive branch accordingly. These scholars argue that the President's only power to control the executive branch is the "power to persuade," elevating to constitutional status what the political scientist Richard Neustadt famously described as the President's practical power.

Chapter 6 disagrees with both schools of thought and seeks to recover a lost understanding of presidential power, one according to which the President can remove principal officers but cannot directly control them. At least, there is no constitutional obligation on the part of principal officers to obey the President; the only inducement is the threat of removal. The Opinions Clause – the clause in Article II empowering the President to demand written opinions from the principal officers in the executive branch about their duties – then assures the President the power to acquire information intelligently to exercise the power to remove. In addition to this account's textual and structural virtues, historical evidence for it abounds. Chapter 7 then gives a brief account of the modern cases involving independent agencies and addresses the academic arguments defending them.

PARTS IV AND V: SEPARATION OF POWERS

The next several chapters investigate disputes about the Constitution's relative distribution of powers between the legislative and executive departments. Parts II–VI all involve the Constitution's distribution of powers among Congress, the executive branch, and the judiciary, and could fall under the description of "separation of powers." Nevertheless, these two parts deal specifically with disputes and subjects in which that distribution is uncertain or contested.

Chapter 8 begins this investigation with a study of inherent or emergency presidential powers. It examines the famous *Steel Seizure Case* in which the Supreme Court rejected President Truman's seizure of steel mills without statutory authorization during the Korean War. The case is celebrated for Justice Robert Jackson's tripartite framework for analyzing separation of powers disputes. That framework, however, is not tethered to constitutional text or history, and moreover makes little conceptual sense. It is an invitation to emergency power. The chapter offers a more conceptually and historically sound framework for thinking about presidential power and proceeds to examine and reject several claims of inherent or emergency presidential power.

Chapter 9 takes up foreign affairs. It disagrees with scholars of all methodologies who claim that the Constitution is laconic on foreign affairs, or that there are missing foreign affairs powers. Originalists tend to argue that the President, because so many foreign affairs powers are otherwise missing, must have a residuum of executive powers. More functionalist scholars, who take a pragmatic approach to the separation of powers, agree that the President must have broad power over foreign affairs. They argue, however, that the President's power depends on historical accretion, contestation between Congress and the President, and functional considerations. Both sets of scholars take an unduly narrow view of the Constitution's assignment of foreign affairs powers and an unjustifiably broad view of inherent, residual, or unwritten presidential powers. The chapter demonstrates that many "missing" powers are not missing at all: "Setting" foreign policy is rarely an act of power in the constitutional sense; both Congress and the President can "recognize" nations for their own purposes; and the power to send ambassadors and to make treaties with foreign nations, which necessarily includes the power to "treat" with them, encompasses the general conduct of foreign affairs. The chapter concludes with an explanation of the differences between executive agreements and treaties.

Chapter 10 pivots to the closely related topic of war. It demonstrates that as a historical matter, the President's warmaking power was, in the absence of congressional authorization, at most the power to defend against attacks on the United States and to protect U.S. persons abroad. This power does not come from a residuum of executive powers, but rather from the President's status as commander in chief. That status includes the power to conduct war when a state of war exists. A state of war can exist in the absence of a congressional declaration when the United States is attacked, and moreover a state of war can be "imperfect" or "partial" rather than perfect or total. The President's power to repel invasions derives from the commander-in-chief power to use the armed forces to engage in a state of imperfect war thrust upon the United States by others. It is limited to defensive actions or limited offensive actions necessary to meet only that existing state of imperfect armed conflict. There is no historical support for the proposition, adopted by modern presidential administrations of both political parties, that presidents may order military actions short of war anywhere in the world so long as doing so is, in their opinion, in the national interest.

Chapters 11 and 12, comprising the book's fifth part, raise a different set of separation of powers disputes. Chapter 11 examines whether the President can exercise legislative power delegated from Congress. At least since the middle of the last century, Congress has delegated power to the executive branch in increasingly broad terms. Originalists have for decades decried this practice as violating the nondelegation doctrine, the idea that Congress cannot constitutionally delegate its power to the executive. Several new scholars have waded into the historical debate to argue that there is no evidence for a nondelegation doctrine and that Congress delegated extremely broad powers from the beginning. Yet, there is significant evidence of a nondelegation principle at the Founding, although it may not have been as robust as some modern originalists would like. This chapter goes through that evidence.

Chapter 12 then pivots to an analysis of the famous *INS v. Chadha* case in which the Supreme Court invalidated the innovation of the "legislative veto" that Congress had invented to retain more control over policymaking as it delegated increasingly broad authority to the executive branch. The chapter offers a fresh analysis of the case to make a broader point about the separation of powers. "Formalists" tend to divide all government power into three parts – legislative, executive, judicial – and maintain that all separation of powers disputes are simply about identifying the kind of power at issue and who must exercise that power. "Functionalists," on the other hand, believe that balance among the branches is the touchstone of separation of powers analysis and argue that government power is "chameleon like": It takes the shape of whatever institution is exercising it and it is therefore too hard to characterize as legislative, executive, or judicial.

This chapter advances a different theory: that of nonexclusive powers, or, more precisely, nonexclusive functions. It turns out that many governmental activities partake in both legislative and executive (or judicial) qualities, and therefore can be reached by an exercise of more than one type of power. Thus, there are many government functions that are not exclusive to the province of any one branch of government. This theory of nonexclusive functions explains many important administrative law concepts that are otherwise difficult to explain, as well as many separation of powers disputes.

PART VI: JUDICIAL POWER

Chapter 13 introduces the structure of judicial power and judicial review in Article III. It briefly describes the structure of the federal courts and Congress's ability to control the existence of lower courts and the jurisdiction of the Supreme Court. Such issues are usually left for an advanced course in federal jurisdiction. But it is worth introducing this basic structure if for no other reason than it clarifies the underlying dispute in the 1803 case *Marbury v. Madison*. Here, the chapter demonstrates how Chief Justice Marshall likely got almost everything wrong in his famous opinion, but he was right about the Court's power of judicial review. The Court did not invent judicial review, which follows from basic conflict-of-laws principles and the nature of written constitutions.

Chapter 14 turns to *Dred Scott v. Sandford*. It goes through that infamous and terrible 1857 decision for a few reasons. It is the first major exercise of federal judicial review of congressional legislation since *Marbury*. It raises important methodological questions about how the Constitution should be interpreted. It raises the even more explosive question whether Chief Justice Taney, the opinion's author, was right that the Constitution and the Founders were proslavery. The chapter analyzes the understudied and underappreciated dissent of Justice Benjamin Curtis and argues that Chief Justice Taney was wrong about the Founders and the Constitution. He anachronistically projected the prejudices and ideological biases of his own time and place back onto the founding generation.

This decision is also useful to examine because it leads to the next line of inquiry: the role of the Supreme Court in the constitutional order. Chapter 15 explores Abraham Lincoln's response to the *Dred Scott* decision. In his famous debates with Stephen Douglas, he argued that the Supreme Court was not the final arbiter of the Constitution's meaning. In contrast to Lincoln's departmentalism, whereby each branch interprets the Constitution in pursuance of its own duties, the modern Supreme Court has acted and is treated as though it is the ultimate arbiter of constitutional meaning. With talks of court packing and court reform, understanding the differences between departmentalism and judicial supremacy may go a long way to resolving contemporary disagreements over the role of the courts. The chapter concludes with *executive* supremacy: whether the President can refuse to enforce laws the President believes to be unconstitutional. The chapter casts doubt on that proposition.

PART VII: FEDERALISM

This part of the study returns to the subject of the book's earliest chapters: federalism and the compound nature of the American Republic. It investigates the scope of Congress's most important enumerated powers. It addresses the interstate commerce power and revisits the Necessary and Proper Clause before concluding with the taxing and spending powers.

Chapter 16 reconstructs the original structure of the Commerce Clause. Contrary to what many originalists claim today, there is much historical evidence for the proposition that the interstate commerce power was exclusive to Congress. Therefore, a "dormant commerce clause doctrine" that prohibits the states from regulating interstate commerce is a legitimate part of the Constitution's original meaning. The states retain their police powers over health, safety, welfare, and morals, which sometimes affect interstate commerce. Historically, courts would uphold state regulations that incidentally affected interstate commerce so long as they genuinely advanced a police-power purpose. The states could not, however, directly regulate interstate commerce.

On the "active" side of the interstate commerce power, Congress did not historically have power over subjects that preceded commerce such as production or agriculture. But Congress could exercise its power over interstate commerce to close the channels of commerce to the interstate traffic in goods, even if it did so with the aim of discouraging certain state practices (such as child labor) that it could not have regulated directly.

Chapter 17 turns to the Supreme Court's "state sovereignty" cases. It addresses whether Congress may apply its laws under the Commerce Clause to state employees, may commandeer state officials, or may abrogate a state's sovereign immunity. The Supreme Court's anti-commandeering and sovereign immunity cases have been much maligned, and rightfully so. But this chapter argues that the outcomes in these cases are likely correct under a Necessary and Proper Clause analysis. Although the Court has made a muddle of its sovereign immunity cases, those cases follow from the basic text, structure, and logic of the Constitution.

Chapter 18 addresses Congress's powers to tax and to spend. The relevant clause – the first in the eighth section of Article I – states that "Congress shall have power to lay and collect taxes, duties, imposts, and excises, to pay the debts and provide for the common defense and general welfare of the United States." There is a historical debate over whether that clause gave Congress one power or two: a single power to tax for certain purposes, or a power to tax for any purpose and a power to spend for certain purposes. There is also a modern debate over whether the clause might be three powers: the power to tax, the power to pay the debts, and the power to regulate for the general welfare of the United States.

The weight of the evidence suggests that the clause is a single power: the power to tax. That does not mean Congress has no power to spend; it can do so by virtue of the Necessary and Proper Clause. Spending in pursuance of an enumerated power is not a great, substantive, independent power requiring specific enumeration. Taxing is. The taxing power is therefore enumerated, and limited: Congress may raise taxes, but only for the purposes of raising revenue to provide for the common defense and general welfare and to pay the debts of the United States. Chapter 18 establishes the evidence for this original meaning of what is often incorrectly referred to as the General Welfare Clause, and which should more accurately be called the Taxing Clause.

The chapter then addresses how the taxing power works under modern doctrine. Congress can raise taxes for any purpose, so long as it is genuinely imposing taxes and not penalties. Just as Congress may close the channels of interstate commerce to affect state practices, it can tax for the same purpose, so long as it is genuinely exercising its taxing power rather than a forbidden regulatory power.

The chapter concludes the study with an analysis of the spending power. Although the best reading of the first clause of the eighth section of Article I is that there was no independent spending power, there is some evidence for the contrary proposition; and the Supreme Court adopted the independent spending power interpretation in 1936. The chapter therefore examines the scope of this independent spending power. Congress's spending under this power must first and foremost be "for the general welfare" and not merely for local welfare. And as with its commerce and taxing powers, Congress can use the spending power indirectly to achieve regulatory objectives. It can offer states money to spend on textbooks that must meet certain curricular standards. It can tell the states how to spend the money. Contrary to what the modern Supreme Court has held, however, it cannot promise the states money on condition that they undergo regulatory changes. Congress cannot, for example, promise South Dakota highway funds but only if it raises its drinking age first. One is an exercise of the spending power, the other is a usurpation of regulatory power reserved to the states.

As should be evident, readers on the left and the right, functionalists and formalists, living constitutionalists and originalists, will find much here with which to disagree. The book will, it is hoped, contribute significantly to modern scholarly debates over the structure of the Constitution and its original meaning. But it also aims to introduce that structure to a wider audience, and to persuade the reader that, even 250 years after American Independence, that structure is worth recovering and preserving.

PART I

Constitutional Union

1

The Written Constitution

An introductory study of the Constitution ought to begin with its purposes and functions. What, exactly, is a constitution, and why have one? What is the Constitution of the United States specifically, and what purposes does it serve? Why is it worth studying? This chapter addresses these questions through a series of topics. It explores the differences between Britain's unwritten constitutional system from which Americans broke in 1776 and the written constitutional systems they developed. It examines the functions of written constitutions, the ends of free government, and whether the American Constitution meets those ends. It asks whether that constitution creates a republican or, as some have alleged, an undemocratic form of government. Chapter 2 analyzes the unique, compound nature of the American constitutional union. These topics are not only interesting in themselves but also relevant to the interpretation of specific provisions of the Constitution examined in later chapters.

1.1 WRITTEN CONSTITUTIONS

The British constitutional system from which the American colonists separated in 1776 was not what Americans today understand as a written constitutional system. It was "unwritten": There was no superintending written constitution that limited the power and controlled the acts of the legislature. In eighteenth-century Britain, Parliament was supreme. Whatever Parliament enacted with royal assent was the supreme law, which Parliament could always undo. "[T]he legislature, being in truth the sovereign power, is ... of absolute authority," William Blackstone wrote in his influential eighteenth-century *Commentaries on the Laws of England*. "[I]t acknowledges no superior upon earth."[1] "The power and jurisdiction of parliament ... is so transcendent and absolute," he reiterated, that Parliament "hath sovereign and uncontrollable authority in the making, confirming, enlarging, restraining, abrogating, repealing, reviving, and expounding of" all the laws of the realm.[2]

Many of Britain's constitutional principles were, however, written down.[3] The Magna Carta of 1215, establishing principles of due process, is one example of how

England's (and later Britain's) constitutional principles were reduced to writing. The Habeas Corpus Act of 1679; the Bill of Rights of 1689, enacted following the Glorious Revolution; and the Act of Settlement of 1701, granting lifetime tenure to judges, are other examples. Those writings contributed to a body of "constitutional law" because they were understood to derive from certain fixed principles and to advance fundamental ends.[4] The system was unwritten principally in the sense that Parliament was the final arbiter of what those principles and ends were and could revise the constitutional rules at any time.[5]

Because Parliament could always alter the British constitution, the term "constitution" was also understood as the arrangement of government institutions that happened to exist and the distribution of power among them. Blackstone described the British constitution as the distribution of power among the King, Lords, and Commons. But because Parliament could alter the institutional arrangements, there was no guarantee that those arrangements at any given time would advance liberty, the common good, or any of the other fundamental ends of civil government. "[I]f by any means a misgovernment should any way fall upon it [Parliament]," Blackstone wrote, "the subjects of this kingdom are left without all manner of remedy."[6]

Some Americans also thought of the constitution as did the English, as whatever arrangement and distribution of power happened to exist.[7] Charles Inglis, an American Tory and royalist, argued in 1776 that the constitution was merely "that assemblage of laws, customs, and institutions, which form the general system; according to which the several powers of the state are distributed and their respective rights are secured to the different members of the community."[8] The historian Bernard Bailyn summarized this understanding: Parliament was "itself part of the constitution, not a creature of it."[9]

Americans saw the dangers of such an unwritten constitutional system in which the legislative power was supreme. The "heart" of the problem faced by the colonists in the 1760s, Bailyn has explained, was to determine in what sense the "'constitution' could be conceived of as a limitation on the power of lawmaking bodies."[10] The colonists were presented with "the continuing need, after 1764, to distinguish fundamentals from institutions and from the actions of government so that they might serve as limits and controls."[11]

This mode of thinking was not entirely new: Americans were steeped in seventeenth-century English constitutional thinking in which even Parliament was limited by prescriptive rules rooted in immemorial custom. The emerging eighteenth-century British constitution of legislative sovereignty and supremacy created an irreconcilable conflict between the older and this newer constitutional model, which led directly to the American Revolution.[12] What was new, however, was the importance of establishing written constitutions as a solution to that conflict between those two constitutional models.

According to the historian Gordon Wood, the pamphleteer Thomas Tudor Tucker wrote the "conclusive statement" on the nature of the new American conception of constitutionalism.[13] Tucker wrote that Americans should frame their constitutions "on the firm and proper foundation of the express consent of the people, unalterable by the legislative, or any other authority but that by which it is to be framed."[14] Contrary to British subjects, most of whom "could not conceive of the constitution as anything anterior and superior to government and ordinary law, but rather regarded it as the government and ordinary law itself," American colonists began to conceive of a constitution as "a written superior law set above the entire government against which all other law is to be measured."[15] "Something must exist in a free state," wrote Thomas Paine, "which no part of it can be authorised to alter or destroy, otherwise the idea of a constitution cannot subsist."[16] It was "inconceivable," writes Wood, quoting Paine, "that the liberties of the people should depend 'upon nothing more permanent or established than the vague, rapacious, or interested inclination of a majority of five hundred and fifty eight men.'"[17]

There would be implications of this new view of constitutionalism. Most significantly, it supplied an argument for judicial review, upon which a subsequent chapter will elaborate. If a written constitution was to be antecedent and superior to the constituted government, including its legislature, then it was widely understood that it would be enforceable against the legislature. Even before the famous case of *Marbury v. Madison*,[18] many Americans assumed that courts would exercise the power of reviewing legislation for constitutionality.[19] Written constitutions do not compel judicial review, to be sure, but they do suggest that if the system otherwise provides for such review, then the written constitution supersedes contrary laws.

Later chapters explore in more depth the implications of having a written constitution for questions of judicial power. The present point is that written constitutions are intended to control not only the executive but also the legislative power. They are intended to superintend and limit the actions of all government actors. The question that naturally follows is why such actions should be limited or controlled at all.[20]

1.2 SETTLEMENT FUNCTIONS

At the most basic level, the content of a written constitution can be morally neutral. The constitution must, at a minimum, establish the machinery of government. It settles structural questions, which then allows the people to engage in ordinary politics. David Strauss has explained this function of constitutions as follows, focusing on America's:

> The written Constitution is valuable because it provides a common ground among the American people, and in that way makes it possible for us to settle disputes that might otherwise be intractable and destructive. Sometimes, in a familiar formulation, it is more important that things be settled than that they be settled right, and the provisions of the written Constitution settle things. The Constitution tells us the qualifications for various offices, how long a president's term will be, how many senators each state will have, whether there must be jury trials in criminal cases, and

many other things. Even if the rules the Constitution prescribes are not the best possible rules, they give us good enough answers to important issues, so that we do not have to keep reopening those issues all the time. This is an immensely valuable function.[21]

Mark Graber has explained that constitutions "creat[e] a framework" for making and enforcing laws, establish the "rules of [the] game," and serve as precommitments that make ordinary politics possible. Although a constitution written in the past may seem constraining – why be bound by the "dead hand" of past generations? – it is also empowering. "Just as persons cannot compose music if no rules define the significance of various musical notations," Graber writes, "so persons cannot ban abortion or run for Congress if no rules establish how one enacts statutes or runs for public office."[22] The rules of grammar may similarly seem constraining, Stephen Holmes has written, but these rules allow people "to do many things they would not otherwise have been able to do or even have thought of doing."[23]

These functions, it should be noted, do not require that a constitution be reduced to writing. The unwritten British constitution served many similar functions.[24] The written nature of a constitution itself serves important functions, however. As Randy Barnett has written, relying and expanding on the work of others, writing serves evidentiary, cautionary, channeling, and clarification functions.[25] To start, writing is evidence that a certain transaction took place. "Like a written contract, a written constitution provides good evidence of what terms were actually enacted when later they might be disputed."[26]

Writing also serves a cautionary function by requiring an opportunity for deliberation and reflection on the wisdom of the agreement. "[I]t seems to have been reserved to the people of this country, by their conduct and example," Alexander Hamilton famously wrote in the first essay of The Federalist, "to decide the important question, whether societies of men are really capable or not of establishing good government from reflection and choice, or whether they are forever destined to depend for their political constitutions on accident and force."[27] The written constitution is what allowed such reflection and choice back in 1787–1788 and continues to create opportunities for reflection and choice today.

Writing also serves a channeling function by focusing the parties', the public's, or a court's attention on a given agreement and its intended results. In the case of a written constitution, it channels disputes so that contenders focus on what that constitution says, or where the constitution says to look.[28] Finally, writing serves a clarification function because written agreements are usually more detailed than oral ones;[29] that is certainly true of the American Constitution, although some of its provisions are underdetermined.

In sum, constitutions generally serve important settlement functions, including setting up the basic structure of government. In the case of America's constitution, it was particularly important to settle the pressing question of the distribution of power between two levels of government – a subject Chapter 2 will address. And writing down constitutions enhances their settlement value because doing so channels and clarifies the debates over the constitution's rules and its answers to questions that need settlement. As suggested previously, however, it remains the case that the most important point settled by writing down America's constitution was the conflict created between a constitution of customary practices and a competing constitution of legislative supremacy and sovereignty. A written constitution can commit customary constitutional principles to writing and make them binding on the legislature. The most important point that America's written constitution "settled," in other words, was that the people were sovereign.

1.3 FREE GOVERNMENT

Most of the settlement functions that written constitutions serve apply to many different constitutions. These functions say little about what purposes constitutions for free societies ought to serve. Even very illiberal regimes can have constitutions that establish the rules of the game. That is not to say this functions is unimportant; it is the minimum that constitutions must do. Rather, it is to say that settlement values only advance the ball so much. Some other rule or principle is needed to know whether a particular constitution ought to be adopted or preserved. The settlement functions and the values of writtenness do not establish what the American Constitution is about, what its ends and objectives are. What kind of questions did the American Constitution settle – beyond that it would be binding even on the legislature – and why? More broadly, what are the ends of free societies? What function ought constitutions to serve in such societies?

Some scholars argue that the principal end of constitutional government is to secure natural rights.[30] Others say that it must enable democratic self-government.[31] The Founders themselves indicated their understanding of the ends of free government and in what ways the British government acted inconsistently with those ends. "[A]ll men are created equal," the Declaration of Independence insisted, and are "endowed . . . with certain unalienable rights," among which "are life, liberty and the pursuit of happiness." And "to secure these rights, Governments are instituted among men, deriving their just powers from the consent of the governed." These words suggest the two ends of a free constitution: It must secure unalienable rights, and it must "derive its power from the consent of the governed."

This latter requirement refers not only to the original contract but also to the ongoing consent of the present generation. That is, the constitution for a free society, at least as the Founders seem to have understood matters, must enable continuing rule by self-government. It must constitute a democratic or republican form of government. The long chain of usurpations and abuses listed in the Declaration – the acts that justified separating from Great Britain – included King George III's attempts to force colonists to "relinquish the right of Representation in the Legislature" and his having "dissolved Representative Houses repeatedly." The Declaration went on to accuse the king of having refused to cause other legislatures to be elected, and thus the legislative powers "have returned to the People at large for their exercise." The king also kept standing armies and taxed the people without their consent.[32] Thus, protecting natural liberty is one end of free government, but so is enabling ongoing democratic governance.

The Constitution expressly declares its purposes in its preamble. "We the People of the United States," it begins, "in Order to form a more perfect Union, establish Justice, insure domestic Tranquility, provide for the common defence, promote the general Welfare, and secure the Blessings of Liberty to ourselves and our Posterity, do ordain and establish this Constitution for the United States of America." Many of these objectives do not necessarily require representative democracy; nondemocratic regimes could conceivably establish justice, order, defense, and general welfare. In a free society, however, these objectives are achieved through democratic self-government. The people govern themselves so that they can better establish justice, order, defense, and welfare.

These objectives, however, can only be achieved through coercion and the exercise of government power. Achieving them will often require restraints on liberty. The two principal ends of free government are therefore in considerable tension. A constitution for a free society such as that which Americans have enjoyed for over two centuries, in summary, requires carefully balancing self-government, order, and coercion on the one hand and liberty on the other. Edmund Burke expressed the heart of the matter in the following reflection on the French Revolution:

> To make a government requires no great prudence. Settle the seat of power; teach obedience; and the work is done. To give freedom is still more easy. It is not necessary to guide; it only requires to let go the rein. But to form a *free government*; that is, to temper together these opposite elements of liberty and restraint in one consistent work, requires much thought, deep reflection, a sagacious, powerful, and combining mind.[33]

In examining the Constitution in this study, the reader might ask whether the Constitution achieves these objectives successfully, whether its separation of powers and its division of national and state powers help to secure a free government suitable for the modern age.

1.4 OVERVIEW OF THE CONSTITUTION

An overview of the Constitution's key provisions and features can assist in beginning to form an answer to that question. An overview will also illustrate what this study examines and what parts of the Constitution it leaves for others. The Constitution's provisions generally account for who can exercise power; what powers those officials are allowed or prohibited to exercise; and how they may exercise those powers. As noted previously, America's Constitution is also particularly concerned with distributing power between two levels of government, a distribution the Founding generation thought instrumental to achieving the ends of free government.

Much of the Constitution is dedicated to the first question of who may wield coercive governmental authority at the national level. Members of the House of Representatives who exercise part of the legislative power are elected by the people, now universally in districts within states, every two years. Members of the Senate, who also exercise part of the legislative power, were historically elected by the state legislatures until the Seventeenth Amendment superseded that provision of the Constitution; now the people of an entire state elect senators for six-year terms. And every four years the entire nation elects the President through a series of elections in all the states. Each of these three constitutional actors represents a different constituency and for a different length of time. The national government generally cannot enact any laws unless all three actors align, ensuring that nationally transformative change has enduring rather than ephemeral, and geographically distributed, majority support.[34] Having three different constitutional actors in the legislative process also serves to slow the legislative process and ensure due deliberation.

The Constitution also specifies what powers the national government may exercise. It does so through an overlapping set of features. First, the eighth section of the Constitution's first article – examined in more detail in Chapter 3 – enumerates the national government's legislative powers. That has historically been understood as limiting the national government to the exercise of those powers. The original Constitution also contained a kind of bill of rights in the ninth section of that first article, which enumerates specific prohibitions on Congress and possibly on the other branches of the national government, and the tenth section of the same article, which imposes prohibitions on the state governments. The first ten amendments, what are today called the Bill of Rights, were not added until 1791, a few years after the Constitution was first ratified. These amendments also impose limits on the national government, and the Fourteenth Amendment has been interpreted to impose nearly identical limits on the state governments.

Some introductions to constitutional law might include materials on the Bill of Rights, such as the First Amendment or the Second Amendment. Studies of criminal procedure are likely to examine the Fourth, Fifth, Sixth, and Seventh Amendments. This study focuses instead on the structural components, one of which is the scope of the national government's powers.

The Constitution, after establishing who can exercise national government power and what they can and cannot do, also specifies how that power is to be exercised. Specifically, it establishes a separation of powers between three branches of the national government – the Congress, the President, and the courts. The Constitution does not, however, create a complete separation of powers. The powers of the three branches overlap so that they may also check and balance each other. Hence the President has a role in the legislative process through the veto power; the Senate has a role in executive power through advising and consenting to appointments; both the House and Senate exercise some judicial power through the impeachment process; and Congress generally, through the Necessary and Proper Clause, can regulate and structure the executive branch and the judiciary. This study is concerned with these features, too: the Constitution's separation *and interrelation* of powers.

1.5 REPUBLICAN REMEDIES

These structural mechanisms – in particular, the separation and interrelation of powers – have led some to assert that the American Constitution is undemocratic. For example, Sanford Levinson argues in his book, *Our Undemocratic Constitution,* that the Constitution is not sufficiently democratic in light of the disproportionate Senate, in which even the smallest of states has two votes on par with the larger states; the Electoral College, which gives the same voting boost to the people of smaller states in presidential elections; the presidential veto power, which can clog the legislative process; the lifetime tenure of Supreme Court justices, who presently wield significant power in the American system; and the ability of a mere thirteen states to block a constitutional amendment, which requires approval of three-quarters of the states.[35]

The Founders had a very different understanding of their handiwork, however.[36] As James Madison wrote in *Federalist* No. 39:

> The first question that offers itself is, whether the general form and aspect of the government be strictly republican. It is evident that no other form would be reconcilable with the genius of the people of America; with the fundamental principles of the Revolution; or with that honorable determination which animates every votary of freedom, to rest all our political experiments on the capacity of mankind for self-government. If the plan of the convention, therefore, be found to depart from the republican character, its advocates must abandon it as no longer defensible.[37]

John Adams, in his Thoughts on Government, likewise declared that "principles and reasonings ... will convince any candid mind, that there is no good government but what is Republican."[38] As Gordon Wood has written, "For most Americans ... this was the deeply felt meaning of the Revolution: they had created a new world, a republican world. No one doubted that the new polities would be republics."[39]

Yet, many in the Founding generation were skeptical of mankind's capacity for democracy. Elbridge Gerry, one of the most Whiggish delegates to the Constitutional Convention, said, "The evils we experience flow from the excess of democracy. The people do not want virtue; but are the dupes of pretended patriots."[40] George Mason agreed, "admitt[ing] that we had been too democratic," though he "was afraid we [should] incautiously run into the opposite extreme."[41] Edmund Randolph observed that the general object of the Senate "was to provide a cure for the evils under which the U.S. laboured; that in tracing these evils to their origin every man had found it in the turbulence and follies of democracy: that some check therefore was to be sought for [against] this tendency of our Governments."[42] And Alexander Hamilton commented in *Federalist* No. 78 on the "ordinary depravity of human nature."[43]

As Madison summarized, human beings quite evidently have a capacity for virtue and self-government, and for the opposite. "As there is a degree of depravity in mankind which requires a certain degree of circumspection and distrust," he wrote in *Federalist* No. 55, "so there are other qualities in human nature which justify a certain portion of esteem and confidence. Republican government presupposes the existence of these qualities in a higher degree than any other form." If it were otherwise and there were "not sufficient virtue among men for self-government," then "nothing less than the chains of despotism can restrain them from destroying and devouring one another."[44]

The key, then, was to establish a republican regime, but one that did not easily fall victim to the follies and problems incident to democratic rule. The objective, Madison wrote in *Federalist* No. 10, was to find "a republican remedy for the diseases most incident to republican government."[45] What was needed was popular rule, but not rule by popular passions. Although Madison made that observation in the context of representation and the federal nature of the Union, addressed in more detail in Chapter 2, it applies equally to the other structural features of the Constitution.

1.6 A NOTE ON INTERPRETATION

This study is not about how to interpret the Constitution, at least not directly. It will explore the text, structure, and history of various constitutional provisions. These interpretive tools are relevant to all theories of constitutional interpretation. The study will also note where the modern Supreme Court, or modern historical practice, has deviated from the original, historical meaning of the text. Whether such are positive developments will be for the reader to determine.

Although this book will not explicitly defend any interpretive theory,[46] it is important to understand the basics of the two predominant ones. Many scholars and judges misunderstand the distinction between them. Originalism is the idea that the Constitution should be interpreted with its "original meaning," the meaning the words of the text had to the Framers who wrote it and the public that ratified it. Some scholars dispute whether interpreters should value the original public meaning, the original intent of specific Framers, or how a hypothetical reasonable observer would have understood the text at the time of adoption. What role historical practices play, especially if they appear inconsistent with the text, is also contested. And some authors, this one included, have emphasized how much of the Constitution is written in legal language. These disputes need not detain the reader for purposes of this study. All these tools – intent, public understanding, historical practice, and legal terminology – generally align for most constitutional provisions and questions. On one or two occasions, differences might be noted.

Living constitutionalism, in contrast, maintains that modern-day interpreters should not treat the original meaning of the text as binding. Rather, the constitutional rules that ought to govern and constrain the people and their legal officials today can be updated even outside the formal amendment process provided in Article V of the Constitution. Who does this amending is a somewhat complicated question. The most common answer is that judges will do so; that in cases that come before them they will interpret the Constitution's provisions in accord with the "evolving standards of decency that mark the progress of a maturing society."[47] But the judges will often look to contemporary practices, too. The Supreme Court adapted its jurisprudence under the Commerce Clause in response to repeated congressional assertions of authority.

The debate between living constitutionalism and originalism is not, however, strictly speaking a debate over "original meaning." It is hard to find serious scholars or judges who dispute the proposition that texts intended as public instructions have original public meanings. If it were otherwise, human communication would be impossible. When modern-day Americans interpret a non-originalist Supreme Court decision, they do so by seeking the original public meaning of the Court's opinion. Only that way can they understand what the Court allows, requires, or prohibits them to do. The dispute between originalism and living constitutionalism is thus not over original meaning, but instead over the source of the constitutional rules that will govern America. It is over whether those constitutional rules shall be supplied by the parchment under the glass at the National Archives, by modern-day judicial opinions, or by something else besides. The dispute is over where American constitutional law comes from, not over the meaning of legal texts.

As to where that law should come from, that is a question only the people today can answer. If the people today still believe that the Constitution, interpreted with its original public meaning, continues to secure the ends of free government and that it therefore should remain the nation's "constitution," then it shall continue to be treated as such by the people and their legal officials. To have any serious position in the contemporary debates over constitutional interpretation, it is therefore essential to understand what the original Constitution in fact does and accomplishes. That is the task the rest of this work begins.

2

The Compound Republic

One of the most important structural features of the American Constitution is the compound nature of the American republic, the union over which the Constitution governs. To this day, the very nature of the American union remains contested. There are still occasional rumblings of secession.[1] Politicians adhere to the idea that the states created the federal government when making assertions of government overreach.[2] Perhaps the South, although wrong about slavery, was correct that the Constitution was ratified by the states and therefore any state can withdraw from the union.

This view is mistaken. The Constitution does not create a league of states. Its key innovation over the Articles of Confederation that preceded it was that it would be ratified by the people of the states and all national laws made pursuant to the new Constitution would be directly binding on them. Thus, the national government may act without the intervening agency of the state governments. Yet, the national government is not a consolidated government; it does not have plenary power to act in all matters where governments may legitimately act. The national government is one of limited and enumerated powers, as Chapter 3 will demonstrate; but within its assigned sphere, the national government acts directly on the people and its acts cannot be abrogated by the states. This regime – which Madison described as partly federal, partly national – was an innovation that Hamilton claimed was part of a new and improved "science of politics."[3]

2.1 THE OLD SCIENCE OF POLITICS

The Framers who convened at the Constitutional Convention of 1787 had studied the old science of politics.[4] If their legal bibles were Blackstone and Coke,[5] and their philosophical bibles Locke and Sidney,[6] their political bible was unquestionably Montesquieu.[7] In the *Spirit of the Laws*, published in French in 1748 and translated into English in 1750, Montesquieu divided regimes into three categories. Aristotle had also classified regimes into three types, based on who ruled: the one, the few, or the many. All such regimes could govern for the public good or for private interests.[8]

Montesquieu, with another 2,000 years of history behind him, divided regimes instead into type and territory: Republics could only exist in small territories; monarchies could successfully govern territories of medium extent; and only despotisms could govern territories of a large, or imperial, extent.[9]

The reason republics could not long persist over any serious extent of territory, Montesquieu wrote, was because in "a large republic, there are large fortunes, and consequently little moderation in spirits"; ambitious and powerful individuals have interests of their own. The public good is also less obvious in a large republic. "In a large republic, the common good is sacrificed to a thousand considerations . . .. In a small one, the public good is better felt, better known, lies nearer to each citizen; abuses are less extensive there and consequently less protected."[10] A large territory, moreover, required speed and efficiency to govern; otherwise, the central government would be unable to control far-flung provinces: "A large empire presupposes a despotic authority in the one who governs. Promptness of resolutions must make up for the distance of the places to which they are sent; fear must prevent negligence in the distant governor or magistrate . . .."[11]

The problem is that small republics cannot long subsist because they will be overcome by more powerful foreign enemies.[12] "Thus, it is very likely," Montesquieu observed, "that ultimately men would have been obliged to live forever under the government of one alone if they had not devised a kind of constitution that has all the internal advantages of republican government and the external force of monarchy. I speak of the federal republic."[13] "This form of government," Montesquieu explained, "is an agreement by which many political bodies consent to become citizens of the larger state that they want to form. It is a society of societies that make a new one, which can be enlarged by new associates that unite with it."[14]

A federation, or what is more commonly described as a confederation or league of states, would allow small republics to avoid the internal defects of large ones but also the external weakness of small ones. The confederated states could pool their resources together, have a common foreign policy, and share in the common defense. That is why, in 1776, it was obvious to many Americans that the thirteen states would form one large confederated republic, that is, a confederation of thirteen reasonably small republics.[15] The Articles of Confederation largely focused on matters of common defense and foreign policy, providing that the Congress "shall have the sole and exclusive right and power of determining on peace and war," "sending and receiving ambassadors" and "entering into treaties and alliances," establishing rules for "captures on land or water," "granting letters of marque and reprisal in times of peace," and "appointing courts for the trial of piracies and felonies committed on the high seas" and for determining appeals in "cases of captures."[16]

The Articles of Confederation that defined the Union during and immediately after the Revolutionary War was thus nothing more than a treaty among the several states. It was adopted by the states as states, and only the unanimous consent of all thirteen could alter it.[17] The intent behind the Articles was to give a national body powers over those matters that the individual states were incompetent to handle. The most pressing objective was to provide for common defense and a uniform foreign policy.

2.2 THE NEW SCIENCE OF POLITICS

But this old science of politics, this combination of small republics and a confederated league for matters of common defense, proved unworkable. Taxes and troops were the two most essential ingredients for fighting and winning the ongoing Revolutionary War; yet, because the Confederation Congress could only act through the individual states, it had to requisition such taxes and troops from the states. The confederated government thus had to rely on the states' good graces to provide the money and the soldiers, and several states were not quite willing to pay their fair share.[18] Between 1782 and 1789, Georgia did not make a single payment to the Confederation government.[19] A single state, Rhode Island, thwarted the efforts of the twelve others to impose a minimal national impost tax to help finance the war, and other states also insisted on problematic conditions.[20]

The central government was also unable to protect against domestic upheavals such as Shays's Rebellion, a taxpayer revolt in Massachusetts.[21] And Americans discovered that the states discriminated against one another's commerce and engaged in other commercial rivalries, which not only hampered economic prosperity but also risked creating more violent encounters.[22] The states also threatened the national honor, routinely passing legislation in violation of the 1783 peace treaty with Great Britain.[23]

Just before the delegates were to meet at the Constitutional Convention of 1787, James Madison wrote *Vices of the Political System of the United States*, where he laid out some of these principal defects. One critical defect of the Articles, Madison explained, was the "want of sanction to the laws, and of coercion in the Government." "The federal system," he argued, "being destitute of both, wants the great vital principles of a Political Cons[ti]tution." It is "nothing more than a treaty of amity of commerce and of alliance, between so many independent and Sovereign States." The national government could not count on "a unanimous and punctual obedience of 13 independent bodies, to the acts of the federal Government" because every national act will "bear unequally hard" on some members of the Union and the states are partial "to their own interests and rights." And if one state did not voluntarily comply with its federal obligations, why should the others?[24]

A related defect was the compact-based nature of the Articles and the want of popular ratification by the people. Because the Articles of Confederation was adopted by the legislatures of the several states, whenever there was a conflict between federal and state authority, naturally the states would tend to favor their own laws. Moreover, because the Union was a "league of sovereign powers," it would seem to "follow from the doctrine of compacts, that a breach of any of the articles of the confederation by any of the parties to it, absolves the other parties from their respective obligations, and gives them a right if they chuse [sic] to exert it, of dissolving the Union altogether." A league of states could be dissolved by any member of the compact.[25]

The delegates to the Constitutional Convention immediately turned their attention to these twin problems. On May 29, Edmund Randolph of Virginia observed that the Articles "had its ratification not by any *special appointment* from the people, but from the several assemblies," and hence "[n]o judge will say that the *confederation* is paramount to a State constit[ut]ion." As a result, "the confederation is incompetent to any *one* object for which it was instituted." He hinted at the difficulties of relying on "[r]equisitions for men and money."[26]

A week later on June 5, the delegates debated the proposition that the new constitution they were framing ought to be ratified by the people. Roger Sherman thought the process of amendment established by the Articles sufficient, but Madison "thought this provision essential," repeating the two points from his *Vices* essay: "The articles of Confedn. themselves were defective in this respect, resting in many of the States on the Legislative sanction only," and hence state laws will always be favored over federal laws and one party to the compact could always dissolve it.[27] Weeks later he added, "All the examples of other confederacies prove the greater tendency in such systems to anarchy than to tyranny; to a disobedience of the members than to usurpations of the federal head. Our own experience had fully illustrated this tendency."[28]

When taking up the issue again in July, George Mason argued that the Convention had to resort to "the people with whom all power remains that has not been given up in the Constitutions derived from them." He observed that were the state legislatures to ratify the Constitution, then "succeeding Legislatures having equal authority could undo the acts of their predecessors."[29] Gouverneur Morris added that under the Articles of Confederation, the unanimous consent of all thirteen states was necessary to make amendments, meaning that a single state (like Rhode Island) could prevent the new constitution from taking effect. "Whereas in case of an appeal to the people of the U. S., the supreme authority," Morris explained, "the federal compact may be altered by a *majority of them*."[30]

Madison concluded the discussion with the observation that "[h]e considered the difference between a system founded on the Legislatures only, and one founded on the people, to be the true difference between a *league* or *treaty*, and a *Constitution*." Madison warned, "The doctrine laid down by the law of Nations in the case of treaties is that a breach of any one article by any of the parties, frees the other parties from their engagements. In the case of a union of people under one Constitution, the nature of the pact has always been understood to exclude such an interpretation."[31]

The motion to have the new Constitution ratified by the state legislatures was then decisively defeated.

In The Federalist, Madison argued that ratification, although it would occur via constitutional conventions in the respective states, was ultimately rooted in popular sovereignty. Ratification, he wrote, appears to be both a federal and a national act: "the Constitution is to be founded on the assent and ratification of the people of America, given by deputies elected for the special purpose," but it is also derived from "the assent and ratification of the several States" whose powers are themselves derived from "the authority of the people themselves." The Constitution ultimately depended on the authority not of the state governments acting through state legislatures but "of the people themselves."[32]

Later in this series of essays, Madison repeated his argument from his prior *Vices* essay. "A compact between independent sovereigns, founded on ordinary acts of legislative authority, can pretend to no higher validity than a league or treaty between the parties," he explained, and "a breach, committed by either of the parties, absolves the others, and authorizes them, if they please, to pronounce the compact violated and void."[33] Ratification by the people would supply the defect: "The express authority of the people alone could give due validity to the Constitution."[34] The proposed Constitution is "of no more consequence than the paper on which it is written, unless it be stamped with the approbation of those to whom it is addressed," he wrote in another number.[35] The Convention bore in mind that the "plan to be framed and proposed was to be submitted to *the people themselves*, the disapprobation of this supreme authority would destroy it forever; its approbation blot out antecedent errors and irregularities."[36]

Hamilton agreed that popular ratification by the people was a distinct advantage of the Constitution over the Articles of Confederation:

> It has not a little contributed to the infirmities of the existing federal system that it never had a ratification by the PEOPLE. Resting on no better foundation than the consent of the several legislatures, it has been exposed to frequent and intricate questions concerning the validity of its powers, and has in some instances given birth to the enormous doctrine of a right of legislative repeal. Owing its ratification to the law of a State, it has been contended that the same authority might repeal the law by which it was ratified.
>
> However gross a heresy it may be, to maintain that a *party* to a *compact* has a right to revoke that *compact*, the doctrine itself has had respectable advocates. The possibility of a question of this nature proves the necessity of laying the foundations of our national government deeper than in the mere sanction of delegated authority. The fabric of American empire ought to rest on the solid basis of THE CONSENT OF THE PEOPLE. The streams of national power ought to flow immediately from that pure, original fountain of all legitimate authority.[37]

In the Pennsylvania ratifying convention, James Wilson – who had been a delegate to the Constitutional Convention and was a future justice of the

Supreme Court – responded to charges that the Convention exceeded its authority by proposing an entirely new constitution. "I think the late Convention has done nothing beyond their powers," he argued. The Constitution "is laid before the citizens . . . to be judged by the natural, civil, and political rights of men. By their *fiat*, it will become of value and authority; without it, it will never receive the character of authenticity and power."[38] Although there were some alternative and confused voices,[39] the general writings of the advocates of the Constitution confirmed that its central innovation was that it would be ratified by the people. After all, the preamble began "We the People of the United States," which signaled to numerous Anti-Federalists this very point.[40] Some key thinkers appear to have thought that the states were also a party to the constitutional compact, but they did not deny that so were the people themselves; they argued the Constitution created a kind of "tripartite" contract among the people, the states, and the United States.[41]

One key feature of this new science of politics was therefore that the confederated portion of the government would itself be authorized and approved by the people themselves; it would not be a mere league of states from which any one could secede at any time. The second key innovation was that the laws enacted by the new national government would operate directly on the people themselves. "[I]f we are in earnest about giving the Union energy and duration," Hamilton wrote in *Federalist* No. 23, "we must abandon the vain project of legislating upon the States in their collective capacities; we must extend the laws of the federal government to the individual citizens of America; we must discard the fallacious scheme of quotas and requisitions as equally impracticable and unjust."[42] In *Federalist* No. 15 he generalized the point, arguing that "we must extend the authority of the Union to the persons of the citizens – the only proper objects of government."[43] "It is essential to the idea of a law that it be attended with a sanction"; but when the law operates on states in their collective capacities, sanction can only be achieved by "coercion of arms." To replace coercion of arms with the "coercion of the magistracy," the laws must "apply only to men."[44]

Madison summarized eloquently in *Federalist* No. 39. "The difference between a federal and national government, as it relates to the *operation of the government*," Madison agreed with opponents of the proposed Constitution, is "that in the former the powers operate on the political bodies composing the Confederacy in their political capacities; in the latter, on the individual citizens composing the nation in their individual capacities."[45] The "operation of the [new] government on the people, in their individual capacities, in its ordinary and most essential proceedings, will, . . . on the whole, designate it, in this relation, a *national* government."[46]

2.3 NATIONAL BUT LIMITED

Although the national government would have the legitimacy that comes from the authority of the people themselves, and would operate on the people themselves, it would still retain a key feature of the old science of politics: Its powers would be limited to subjects requiring the common action of all the states. As Madison reminded his readers, "[I]f the government be national with regard to the *operation* of its powers, it changes its aspect again when we contemplate it in relation to the extent of its powers," for "its jurisdiction extends to certain enumerated objects only, and leaves to the several States a residuary and inviolable sovereignty over all other objects."[47] "If the circumstances of our country are such as to demand a compound instead of a simple, a confederate instead of a sole, government," Hamilton agreed, "the essential point which will remain to be adjusted will be to discriminate the *objects*, as far as it can be done, which shall appertain to the different provinces or departments of power."[48]

The key features of the new Constitution, then, were first that the national government would be limited to objects of common concern, as a confederated government would be. That national government, however, would be authorized by the people themselves, rather than the states as states, and that government would operate directly on the people. The Constitution, Madison thus summarized, is "neither wholly federal nor wholly national," but rather "a composition of both."[49] By "national," Madison meant those powers today associated with the federal government as opposed to the states, and by federal he meant the powers of the states. This combination of national and state power, each approved by and operating directly on the people themselves, but each limited to its respective sphere, is what the term federalism has come to mean.

Even though the national government would operate on the people themselves, the states as states would have an essential role in establishing the laws of the national government that would operate in this manner. The Great Compromise at the Constitutional Convention proposed a Senate in which each state would have equal suffrage and whose state legislatures would choose the senators to represent them – the first of which mechanisms the Framers thought so important that they made it unamendable.[50] The Senate, designed in this manner to represent the states, would have a say in passing national laws, in making treaties, and in approving executive appointments, allowing the states to exert their influence throughout the machinery of the national government. And the Supremacy Clause ensured that only national laws made "in Pursuance" of the Constitution – pursuant to the bicameral process, which required the Senate's consent – would supersede contrary state laws.[51]

These features marked the Framers' new science of politics. They would give the national government necessary energy and legitimacy, but only over certain objects. The national government would not operate through the states, but the states would exert their influence in the machinery of the national government. These features would ensure a robust common defense against foreign enemies, while simultaneously avoiding the defects of the Articles of Confederation but also preserving the importance of the states. They would solve the problems of the old science of politics.

The compound republic, Madison famously argued in *Federalist* No. 10, would also solve the problem of territory. Montesquieu had argued that an extensive republic would fall under the weight of personal ambitions and private interests. But a compound republic could turn personal ambitions and private interests into an advantage. In the larger territory over which a compound republic could govern, Madison argued, factional impulses will rarely obtain majority support across the entire nation; many will remain localized and factional interests throughout the Union can counteract one another.[52] The Founders' new science of politics could advance beyond Montesquieu's proposition that republics could only subsist in small territories. Thomas Jefferson thus observed that "no constitution was ever before so well calculated as ours for extensive empire & self government," and to hope for an "empire for liberty."[53]

2.4 DEBATING THE NATURE OF THE UNION

The relatively clear assertions of the leading Founders notwithstanding, the nature of the Union remained contested until the Civil War.[54] The nullification and secession controversies in the antebellum period would put the Union, and free government itself, to the ultimate test. The debate over "interposition" and the Alien and Sedition Acts from 1798 to 1800 also put the nature of the Union in question. It is helpful to begin with nullification and secession to establish clearly what states may not do under the compound republic that the American Constitution creates before exploring what role the states might still have in interpreting and enforcing the Constitution. It is somewhat risky as a methodological matter to work backward in this manner; one risks seeing themes or distinctions that may not have been so clear at the time.[55] In this case, while acknowledging these limitations, it may be fruitful to take that risk.

The principles of the new science of politics were tested in an 1830s prelude to the Civil War. In 1828, Congress enacted and President John Quincy Adams signed into law what became known as the "tariff of abominations." The tariffs on foreign manufactures, intended to help northern industrial interests, would increase prices in the South. In 1832, new tariffs replaced the set from 1828, but they were still odious to the South, leading the South Carolina legislature to declare that the tariffs were "nullified" and unenforceable in the state. Such talk had been common since shortly after the 1828 tariffs went into effect; John C. Calhoun had written an "exposition" arguing that the states could nullify federal laws, although, he had cautioned, it was not the time to do so.[56]

A great unplanned debate took place on the floor of the United States Senate in 1830 on this very question between Senators Robert Hayne and Daniel Webster as well as other prominent senators. The bill in discussion was not about the tariffs, but rather the sale of public lands in the West, yet it turned into a wide-ranging discussion on the nature of the Union. The most famous of the exchanges took place between January 25 and 27 and has become known as the Second Webster–Hayne Debate.[57]

Why, Senator Hayne asked, should the federal government have the final say over the scope of its own power? "[T]he doctrine that the Federal Government is the exclusive judge of the extent as well as the limitations of its powers . . . seems to be utterly subversive of the sovereignty and independence of the States." If the federal government is "to prescribe the limits of its own authority; and the States are bound to submit to the decision, and are not to be allowed to examine and decide for themselves, when the barriers of the Constitution shall be overleaped," then "this is practically 'a Government without limitation of powers;' the States are at once reduced to mere petty corporations, and the people are entirely at your mercy."[58]

In response, Senator Webster "inquire[d] into the origin of this Government and the source of its power." "Whose agent is it?" asked Webster:

> Is it the creature of the State Legislatures, or the creature of the People? If the Government of the United States be the agent of the State Governments, then they may control it, provided they can agree in the manner of controlling it; if it be the agent of the People, then the People alone can control it, restrain it, modify, or reform it. It is observable enough, that the doctrine for which the honorable gentleman contends leads him to the necessity of maintaining, not only that this General Government is the creature of the States, but that it is the creature of each of the States severally, so that each may assert the power for itself of determining whether it acts within the limits of its authority. It is the servant of four-and-twenty masters, of different will and different purposes and yet bound to obey all.

"This absurdity," Webster continued in words that Abraham Lincoln would later echo, "arises from a misconception as to the origin of this Government and its true character. It is, sir, the People's Constitution, the People's Government, made for the People, made by the People, and answerable to the People."[59] The people have declared the Constitution and federal laws to be supreme; the states are sovereign within the large sphere left to them by the Constitution, but they are not sovereign insofar as they are affected by the supreme law. Webster continued:

> We are all agents of the same supreme power, the People. The General Government and the State Governments derive their authority from the same source. Neither can, in relation to the other, be called primary, though one is definite and restricted, and the other general and residuary. The National Government possesses those powers which it can be shown the People have conferred upon it, and no more. All the rest belongs to the State Governments, or to the People themselves . . . .
>
>   The People, then, sir, erected this Government. They gave it a Constitution, and in that Constitution they have enumerated the powers which they bestow on it. They have made it a limited Government. They have defined its authority. They have restrained it to the exercise of such powers as are granted; and all others, they declare, are reserved to the States or the People . . . . Sir, the very chief end, the main

design, for which the whole Constitution was framed and adopted, was to establish a Government that should not be obliged to act through State agency, or depend on State opinion and State discretion. The People had had quite enough of that kind of Government under the Confederacy.[60]

Webster went on to say that the judicial tribunals of the United States were established to resolve definitively conflicts that might arise between the general government and the state governments.[61]

President Andrew Jackson agreed. In response to South Carolina's purported nullification of the tariff two years later, Jackson declared, "I consider, then, the power to annul a law of the United States, assumed by one State, incompatible with the existence of the Union, contradicted expressly by the letter of the Constitution, unauthorized by its spirit, inconsistent with every principle on which it was founded, and destructive of the great object for which it was formed."[62] It does not follow that revolution is impossible, but such a revolution would have nothing to do with the Constitution. "Secession," Jackson said, "like any other revolutionary act, may be morally justified by the extremity of oppression; but to call it a constitutional right is confounding the meaning of terms."[63]

The logic of Webster's and Jackson's argument seems unimpeachable. If the states could judge for themselves the constitutionality of all federal laws, the implication must be that Americans had never abandoned the Articles of Confederation, under which the states decided whether or not to comply with the national laws. And if that were true, then every state might have a different opinion about any number of federal laws, leaving the Constitution subject to "four-and-twenty [today, fifty] masters." The national government may be one of limited, enumerated powers; but within the sphere assigned to it, it is supreme and uncontrollable by state power.

The implication for secession is unmistakable. Secession was an unconstitutional act.[64] This should be clear also from the Framers' discussions in the Constitutional Convention and in The Federalist essays. "However gross a heresy it may be, to maintain that a *party* to a *compact* has a right to revoke that *compact*, the doctrine itself has had respectable advocates," Alexander Hamilton had written (see preceding text). "The possibility of a question of this nature proves the necessity of laying the foundations of our national government deeper than in the mere sanction of delegated authority."[65] The New York Anti-Federalists sought to ratify the Constitution on condition that the state could subsequently secede from the Union if amendments were not secured; Hamilton and others emphatically rejected the idea as unconstitutional under the new governing framework.[66] A right of secession, Justice Joseph Story later wrote, would bring back "all the evils of the old confederation."[67] James Buchanan, who was president during the Secession Winter of 1860–1861, agreed that secession was unconstitutional because the Union was not "a mere voluntary association of States, to be dissolved at pleasure by any one of the contracting parties."[68]

President Buchanan, however, refused to do anything about the seceding states because he believed the federal government was without power to compel the states back into the Union even though secession was unconstitutional. This position, it should be stated, was absurd. The eighth section of the first article of the Constitution expressly gives Congress and the President the power to call forth the militia both to suppress insurrection and to execute the laws of the Union.[69] And the President has the duty to take care that the laws be faithfully executed.[70] The loyal people of the Southern states were entitled to the benefit of federal law, and the national government had sufficient constitutional authority to ensure those laws would not go unexecuted.[71]

2.5 INTERPOSITION

An episode closely connected to nullification and secession, and which was repeatedly invoked by Calhoun and Hayne during the nullification crisis, is the famous "interposition" of Virginia and Kentucky over the Alien and Sedition Acts of 1798. The constitutionality of these laws was contested. The Alien Enemies Act gave the President almost plenary authority to remove foreigners from the United States if they were from a country with which the United States was at war. The statute was almost certainly constitutional under Congress's war powers. The Alien Friends Act, however, was more problematic: It allowed the President to remove lawfully present aliens from friendly countries on mere suspicion that they were a threat to the peace and safety of the United States.[72]

The Sedition Act allowed the federal government to prosecute seditious speech, defined to include any untrue and malicious statement with a tendency to bring the government into disrepute.[73] At the time, the act was also almost certainly constitutional under the First Amendment, which prohibits Congress from making any law "abridging the freedom of speech, or of the press."[74] At common law, the freedom "of the press" was understood to be a prohibition only on prior restraints.[75] The government could not prohibit the subject from making or publishing a statement, but the subject was still liable to be punished for that statement under a variety of common law rules. (Even today, one can be punished for defamation, incitement, and obscenity.) The more serious question was whether Congress had an enumerated power to punish speech. The only plausible hook was Congress's power to enact all laws necessary and proper to carry into execution the President's law-execution power.[76]

Thomas Jefferson and James Madison rallied the state legislatures of Kentucky and Virginia to publish resolutions in opposition to these acts. The Kentucky Resolutions announced the view of the Kentucky legislature that Congress had no power delegated to it in the Constitution to enact these laws; that the power of the President to imprison and remove aliens on mere suspicion violated a variety of procedural protections in the Fifth and Sixth Amendments; and that the sedition law violated the First Amendment.[77] The Virginia Resolutions further argued that the Alien and Sedition Acts reflected unconstitutional "exercises [of] power no where delegated to the federal government," unconstitutionally "unit[ed] legislative and judicial powers to those of [the] executive," and sought to accomplish that which was "expressly and positively forbidden by one of the amendments."[78]

In their resolutions, Jefferson and Madison reintroduced the question of the nature of the union. In the Virginia Resolutions, Madison was relatively cautious. He stated that the Constitution was a "compact to which the states are parties." The states, as parties to the Constitution, "have the right, and are in duty bound, to interpose for arresting the progress of the evil, and for maintaining within their respective limits, the authorities, rights and liberties appertaining to them," he wrote.[79] The reader will recall that Madison had argued in 1788 that "the Constitution is to be founded on the assent and ratification of the people of America," but also on "the assent and ratification of the several States."[80] Madison was suggesting that, unlike the Articles of Confederation, which was merely a compact among the states, the Constitution reflected a kind of tripartite contract among the people, the states, and the national government. As such, perhaps the states could not secede or nullify federal laws, but they had some role in helping to enforce this national contract.

The Kentucky Resolutions were more incautious. They declared that the Constitution was a "compact" to which "each state acceded as a state," and that the general government "was not made the exclusive or final *judge* of the extent of the powers delegated to itself," but rather "as in all other cases of compact among parties having no common Judge, each party has an equal right to judge for itself, as well of infractions as of the mode and measure of redress."[81] Jefferson's earlier draft of the resolutions even included a reference to the right of nullification – a reference stripped by the legislature before publication.[82] It is not surprising that Senator Robert Hayne claimed his doctrine of nullification was supported by the "republican doctrine of '98."[83] Madison found himself embarrassingly trying to distinguish nullification in the 1830s from the "interposition" he and, especially, Jefferson had sought to accomplish in 1798.[84]

Although Jefferson's resolutions in particular did have some embarrassing statements – it implied the Union was a mere compact of states – understood in their best light, such resolutions could serve a useful constitutional function. In *Federalist* No. 46, Madison had claimed that the federal government's exercising unconstitutional power would signal "general alarm," and committees of correspondence would be opened among the states.[85] Hamilton had made a similar point in *Federalist* No. 26.[86] So did the Virginia legislature in 1790, when it remonstrated against the proposal to assume the state debts. "As the guardians, then, of the rights and interests of their constituents; as sentinels placed by them over the ministers of the Federal Government, to shield it from their encroachments, or at least to sound the alarm when it is threatened with invasion," the legislature declared, "they can never reconcile it to their consciences silently to acquiesce in a measure which" exceeds Congress's enumerated powers.[87]

That is arguably the extent of what Virginia – and possibly Kentucky – did in 1798, even opening correspondence with other states by transmitting their resolutions to their executives.[88] The states may not have the final say over interpretation of the Constitution, but they can use their prominent positions in the constitutional system of the compound republic to warn the people themselves about danger from the federal head. And the people themselves can engage in their own acts of constitutional interpretation, as they arguably did in the election of 1800, when they swept the Federalists out of power and ushered in decades of Democratic–Republican rule.[89] The sedition law was thereby swept into the ash heap of history.[90]

Nullification and secession may have been unconstitutional, but that conclusion is not incompatible with the states' serving a role in sounding the general alarm and educating the citizenry. Many states already take on a similar role by, for example, banding together to sue the federal government in court. The states have historically played a role in constitutional interpretation, in educating the citizenry, and in helping to ensure that the federal government stays within its proper sphere. They can exercise those same functions today.

PART II

The Legislative Power

3

Enumeration

The most significant way in which the Constitution has long been understood to create a compound or federal republic is through the enumeration of national legislative powers. That is by no means a necessary understanding. The delegates to the Constitutional Convention rejected a proposal to enumerate power; they approved instead a resolution granting Congress power to legislate on all subjects over which the separate states were incompetent. Yet, the Committee of Detail tasked with drafting the proposed constitution proceeded to enumerate power. As a few scholars have suggested, it is possible they did so not because they sought to limit the powers of the national government but because they sought to limit the power of the chief executive. The effect, however, was both to ensure that the President would not exercise a suite of historically royal prerogative powers and to limit the national government's jurisdiction to certain enumerated objects.

This chapter begins with the widespread evidence that advocates of the Constitution understood the enumeration of powers to limit Congress to those specified powers. It explores the debates over whether to include a bill of rights and the relationship between an enumeration of powers and an enumeration of rights. It then assesses some revisionist claims by modern scholars who argue that limiting Congress to its enumerated powers was not a necessary understanding of the original Constitution and that some in the Founding period held other views. Such revisionism is largely unpersuasive. The chapter concludes with an investigation of the connection of the enumeration of powers to the royal prerogative, which might partly explain why the Committee of Detail enumerated powers despite a resolution not to do so. Chapter 4 turns more specifically to the Necessary and Proper Clause and implied powers under the Constitution.

To those accustomed to thinking about the enumeration of powers and the Necessary and Proper Clause together with other grants of national legislative power such as those over interstate commerce or taxing and spending, it may seem unusual to discuss the former topics presently while deferring the latter to the end of this study. The choice is deliberate. One can understand neither federalism nor the separation of powers without a clear understanding of Congress's power under the

Necessary and Proper Clause. That clause grants Congress implied powers to carry into execution not only its own enumerated powers but also those of the executive and judicial departments. Many observers have also made much (possibly too much) of the difference between the vesting clauses of Articles I and II. And, as this chapter will show, Article I has much to do with historically royal powers. One simply cannot study the separation and interrelation of powers without first examining the enumeration of powers generally and Congress's implied powers specifically.

3.1 THE ENUMERATION OF POWERS

The first operative sentence of the Constitution appears to establish a national government of limited powers: "All legislative Powers herein granted shall be vested in a Congress of the United States, which shall consist of a Senate and House of Representatives."[1] Not all legislative powers, but only those "herein granted," are vested in the national Congress. After the Constitution sets up the composition of the House and Senate, these powers are listed in the eighth section of the first article: "Congress shall have Power" to tax (and possibly to spend) for the general welfare;[2] to borrow money;[3] to regulate interstate and foreign commerce, and commerce with the Indian tribes;[4] to establish uniform rules of naturalization and bankruptcy;[5] to coin money and punish counterfeiting;[6] to establish post offices and post roads;[7] to provide for patents and copyrights;[8] to create inferior federal courts;[9] to define and punish offenses against the law of nations;[10] to declare war, grant letters of marque and reprisal, and make rules concerning wartime captures;[11] to raise and support armies and to provide and maintain a navy;[12] to make rules for the government of the military;[13] to provide for calling forth the militia to execute the laws, suppress insurrection, and repel invasions;[14] to organize the militia;[15] to exercise exclusive legislation over what is now the District of Columbia, as well as over forts and other needful buildings;[16] and to "make all Laws which shall be necessary and proper for carrying into Execution the foregoing Powers, and all other Powers vested by this Constitution in the Government of the United States, or in any Department or Officer thereof."[17]

Article IV of the Constitution, which deals with interstate relations, further grants Congress, in its first section, the power to pass laws to enforce the requirement that states give full faith and credit to the public acts, records, and judicial proceedings of other states.[18] Its third section grants Congress the power to admit new states into the Union and "to dispose of and make all needful Rules and Regulations respecting the Territory or other Property belonging to the United States."[19] And its fourth section makes it the duty of the "United States" to guarantee to the states a republican form of government, to protect each of them against invasion and, upon application of the legislature or the state executive when the legislature is not in session, against domestic violence.[20] Article V of the Constitution empowers Congress, by a two-thirds vote of each chamber, to propose amendments to the Constitution, which become effective upon ratification by three-quarters of the states.[21]

The Founding and succeeding generations understood the Constitution to create a government of limited and enumerated powers. In his debate with Robert Hayne, Daniel Webster summarized that in the Constitution the people "have enumerated the powers which they bestow on" the national government: "They have made it a limited Government. They have defined its authority. They have restrained it to the exercise of such powers as are granted; and all others, they declare, are reserved to the States or the People."[22] As Webster indicated, the Tenth Amendment to the Constitution, adopted in 1791 along with the other amendments that have become known as the Bill of Rights, reiterates that "[t]he powers not delegated to the United States by the Constitution, nor prohibited by it to the States, are reserved to the States respectively, or to the people."[23]

The Federalist essays articulated that same understanding well before the Tenth Amendment was adopted. In *Federalist* No. 14, James Madison explained that the general government's jurisdiction "is limited to certain enumerated objects, which concern all the members of the republic."[24] In *Federalist* No. 39, he reiterated that national jurisdiction "extends to certain enumerated objects only, and leaves to the several States a residuary and inviolable sovereignty over all other objects."[25] In a series of subsequent essays, Madison went through the "several" – that is, separate and independent – powers proposed to be vested in the national government.[26] At the end of the discussion, in *Federalist* No. 45, he wrote:

> The powers delegated by the proposed Constitution to the federal government are few and defined. Those which are to remain in the State governments are numerous and indefinite. The former will be exercised principally on external objects, as war, peace, negotiation, and foreign commerce; with which last the power of taxation will, for the most part, be connected. The powers reserved to the several States will extend to all the objects which, in the ordinary course of affairs, concern the lives, liberties, and properties of the people, and the internal order, improvement, and prosperity of the State.[27]

To be sure, these statements are merely those of one person. Deferring for the moment other evidence, it is worth observing that there was likely an early consensus that The Federalist essays, although surely not correct in every respect and written to achieve a particular political result, reflected at least the general understandings of the Constitution. Thomas Jefferson, in adopting the essays as part of the curriculum for the University of Virginia, declared in 1825 that they were "an authority to which appeal is habitually made by all, and rarely declined or denied by any, as evidence of the general opinion of those who made and of those who accepted the constit[utio]n of the US. on questions as to its genuine meaning."[28] By 1802, certainly, the collection of essays was "in the hands of every one," according to one member of Congress who referenced them in a debate on the judiciary.[29] The Federalist was translated into French earlier, in 1792, and the introduction by the French translator suggested that the work reflected the "opinion of a nation."[30] There is other evidence of influence.[31]

There is also evidence beyond The Federalist. Other pro-ratification writers corroborated the limitations on and definitions of the national government's powers. Noah Webster wrote, for example, that "the powers of the Congress are defined, to extend only to those matters which are in their nature and effects, *general.*"[32] A different Webster – Pelatiah Webster, writing as "A Citizen of Philadelphia" – wrote that the states were "confederated . . . for certain defined national purposes only," leaving "all the dignities, authorities, and internal police of each State in free, full, and perfect condition."[33] The federal powers "are *defined* in the new constitution, as minutely as may be, in their principle; and any detail of them which may become necessary, is committed to the wisdom of Congress" – a reference to the Necessary and Proper Clause.[34]

Convention delegates Roger Sherman and Oliver Ellsworth of Connecticut, writing to their state's governor with an enclosed copy of the new draft constitution, stated: "Some additional powers are vested in congress, which was a principal object that the states had in view in appointing the convention. Those powers extend only to matters respecting the common interests of the union, and are specially defined, so that the particular states retain their sovereignty in all other matters."[35] Numerous other advocates for the Constitution agreed,[36] and no pro-ratification writer openly stated that the national government would have a reservoir of undefined powers.[37] All seem to have understood that Congress would have power over national objects, and that the enumeration of powers empowered Congress over as well as limited Congress to those objects.[38]

Future Supreme Court Justice James Wilson, who had also been a delegate to the Constitutional Convention, is an important source of evidence of constitutional meaning. Wilson was one of the two key Framers who drafted much of the Constitution and was a proponent of extensive national powers.[39] He is often cited by revisionist scholars in support of the proposition that the national government has a power to regulate for the general welfare of the nation. Yet, in the Pennsylvania ratifying convention, he commented on "the *accuracy* with which the *line is drawn* between the powers of the *general government* and those of the *particular state governments.*" These powers are "limited and defined." They "are as minutely enumerated and defined as was possible." He argued that the Necessary and Proper Clause granted "nothing more than what was necessary to render effectual the particular powers that are granted."[40]

Wilson confirmed these views in his Lectures on Law. The lectures were delivered after ratification when there was no incentive to diminish the powers of the national government to convince skeptical Anti-Federalists. On the subject of the powers of Congress, "we discover a striking difference between the constitution of the United States and that of Pennsylvania," Wilson said. "By the latter, each house of the general assembly is vested with every power necessary for a branch of the legislature of a free state. In the former, no clause of such an extensive and unqualified import is to be found. The reason is plain. The latter institutes a legislature with general, the former, with enumerated, powers."[41]

Wilson then grouped the various powers of Congress under the categories of ends described in the preamble. Modern-day revisionists claim Wilson believed that Congress had implied powers to pass any legislation in furtherance of the ends listed in the preamble.[42] Yet, in the Lectures on Law one sees very clearly, and consistently with what others had written,[43] that the enumerated powers effectuate the great ends of the preamble. "One great end of the national government is to 'provide for the common defence,'" Wilson stated. All the powers "naturally connected with the power of declaring war," including the powers over the military establishment, "therefore, are vested in congress."[44] Wilson then listed the other ends of government described in the preamble, along with the specific powers enumerated in the eighth section of the first article that empowered Congress to accomplish those ends.[45] At least here, there was no indication that Congress had any power to legislate for the general interests of the Union or any of the other preambulatory ends beyond what the remainder of the Constitution granted specifically for those purposes.[46]

3.2 DEBATING A BILL OF RIGHTS

During the ratification period, Americans also debated the need for a bill of rights. The Federalists who successfully argued for ratification without one claimed that a bill of rights was unnecessary because the national government had only enumerated powers. The national government had no power over the press, for example, and hence there was no need to guarantee press freedom. Including a bill of rights might even risk the implication that rights not enumerated were intended to be assigned into the hands of the general government. The Federalists eventually acquiesced in the desire for a bill of rights, but James Madison proposed an amendment – what would become the Ninth Amendment – that negated any such implication and reiterated that the national government's powers were enumerated.

Immediately, skeptics of the proposed Constitution asked why there was no bill of rights. In late September 1787, delegates to the Confederation Congress debated whether to submit the draft constitution to the states for ratification [47] According to the notes of some of the participants, Madison and another delegate to the Convention, Nathaniel Gorham, were asked about the absence of a bill of rights. Both defended on the ground that a bill of rights was unnecessary in a government of enumerated powers. Gorham reportedly stated, "[N]o necessity of a Bill of rights, because a Bill of rights in state Govts. was intended to retain certain powers, as [the] Legis[lature] had unlim[ite]d. Powers." Madison agreed that "a Bill of rights" was unnecessary "because [the] powers are enumerated and only extend to certain cases."[48]

Discussing the proposed draft constitution in the old Congress, Richard Henry Lee responded to the point by observing that the Articles of Confederation had restricted the Confederation Congress to powers "expressly" delegated, "and therefore no constructive power can be exercised"; a like provision was missing in the proposed Constitution.[49] One modern-day revisionist has argued that after Lee's statement, Madison did not repeat the argument against a bill of rights except in rare circumstances.[50] Contrary to this scholar's suggestion, however, nothing about the exchange or its aftermath suggested that either Lee or Madison believed Congress could exceed its enumerated powers. Lee was almost certainly observing that the Necessary and Proper Clause was a grant of implied powers, and the Constitution thus diverged from the Articles of Confederation in not limiting Congress to expressly specified powers. The grant of implied powers was itself, of course, enumerated. Lee was merely arguing that the grant of implied powers in the Constitution made a bill of rights necessary; Madison made the precise point when introducing the proposed bill of rights in the First Congress.[51] And to that we might add George Mason's argument that without a bill of rights, Congress could infringe fundamental rights in the District of Columbia or other territories where it had plenary power.[52] It does not follow that they or anyone else believed Congress could exceed its enumerated powers.[53]

James Wilson soon fleshed out the pro-ratification position. In a prominent speech at the Pennsylvania State House Yard on October 6, 1787, which was the first public defense of the Constitution by a delegate to the Convention,[54] Wilson proclaimed that the people in the States "invested their representatives with every right and authority which they did not in explicit terms reserve." But "congressional authority is to be collected, not from tacit implication, but from the positive grant expressed in the instrument of union." Therefore, under the state governments "every thing which is not reserved is given," but in the national government "every thing which is not given is reserved."[55] This speech was reprinted in thirty-four newspapers in twenty-seven different towns all the way from Maine to Georgia.[56] Pauline Meier, the late and distinguished historian of ratification, wrote that Wilson's speech "would become a basic text for defenders of the Constitution as well as a major target for its critics."[57]

In the speech, Wilson used the example of freedom of the press. If a power "had been granted to regulate literary publications, it would have been ... necessary to stipulate that the liberty of the press should be preserved inviolate."[58] But the Constitution grants Congress no such power. In contrast, because the Constitution grants Congress the power to regulate interstate commerce, Wilson observed, it also specifically provides that duties must be uniform.[59] Indeed, the ninth section of the first article provided a kind of bill of rights, restricting Congress from prohibiting the international slave trade for twenty years;[60] from suspending the privilege of the writ of habeas corpus unless in times of rebellion or invasion the public safety may require it;[61] from passing bills of attainder or ex post facto laws;[62] from laying direct taxes without apportionment according to population;[63] from laying duties on exports from states;[64] from giving the ports of one state preference over those of other states;[65] from drawing money from the treasury without appropriations;[66] and from granting titles of nobility.[67] The Constitution specifies several of these restrictions because they otherwise would fall within Congress's enumerated powers.[68]

"[I]n a government consisting of enumerated powers, such as is proposed for the United States," Wilson reiterated in the Pennsylvania ratifying convention, a bill of rights would be "unnecessary."[69] But in this speech, Wilson went further; a bill of rights would also be "highly imprudent," even dangerous. That is because if "we attempt an enumeration" of rights, Wilson explained, then "every thing that is not enumerated is presumed to be given." The consequence would be that "an imperfect enumeration would throw all implied power into the scale of the government, and the rights of the people would be rendered incomplete."[70] In other words, an enumeration of rights risks implying that anything not enumerated was thrown into the hands of the national government. That would undermine the enumeration of powers. Better to enumerate the powers than the rights, he said.[71] He repeated the point a few weeks later.[72]

Hamilton made similar arguments in *Federalist* No. 84. Hamilton, like Wilson, was one of the greatest proponents of national power. Yet, he, too, like Wilson, believed in an enumeration of powers. "[B]ills of rights," Hamilton wrote, echoing Wilson, "are not only unnecessary in the proposed Constitution but would even be dangerous" because "[t]hey would contain various exceptions to powers which are not granted," and would therefore "afford a colorable pretext to claim more than were granted." He illustrated with freedom of the press: "[W]hy declare that things shall not be done which there is no power to do? Why, for instance, should it be said that the liberty of the press shall not be restrained, when no power is given by which restrictions may be imposed?"[73] Still others made the point, too.[74]

The Federalists eventually acceded to the Anti-Federalists' desire for a bill of rights. "My own opinion has always been in favor of a bill of rights," Madison wrote in a letter to Jefferson in 1788, "provided it be so framed as not to imply powers not meant to be included in the enumeration."[75] And Madison, who served in the First Congress, made sure that the Bill of Rights would be framed appropriately. In particular, he drafted what would become the Ninth Amendment: "The enumeration in the Constitution, of certain rights, shall not be construed to deny or disparage others retained by the people."[76]

The Ninth Amendment is often thought to be an independent bar against both national and state legislation over unenumerated liberties.[77] There is little evidence for this robust view of the amendment. It does protect liberty, but it does so by reiterating that the national government is one of specifically enumerated powers. The Ninth Amendment was a rule of construction intended principally to prevent the implications against which Wilson and Hamilton warned. It meant that the existence of a right in the Bill of Rights should not be "construed" to suggest that somehow the government had power to infringe other rights. That is just another way of saying the enumeration of rights should not be construed to enlarge the government's powers – which is what Madison's first draft of the Ninth Amendment had said explicitly.[78] Just because a right is not listed does not mean the government must have the power to infringe it. The government only has such power if it can point to a specific enumeration.[79]

When introducing the amendments, Madison explained that he included what is now the Ninth Amendment in response to the Federalist opposition of 1788:

> It has been objected also against a bill of rights, that, by enumerating particular exceptions to the grant of power, it would disparage those rights which were not placed in that enumeration; and it might follow by implication, that those rights that were not placed in that enumeration, that those rights which were not singled out, were intended to be assigned into the hands of the General Government, and were consequently insecure. This is one of the most plausible arguments I have ever heard urged against the admission of a bill of rights into this system; but, I conceive, that it may be guarded against. I have attempted it, as gentlemen may see by turning to the last clause of the fourth resolution [Madison's draft of the Ninth Amendment].[80]

The Ninth Amendment, in summary, goes further than the Tenth Amendment. The Tenth Amendment affirms that any powers not delegated to the national government are reserved to the states. The Ninth Amendment is then principally about the scope of the national government's powers; it explains that the enumeration of rights should not be construed to expand by implication any grants of power elsewhere in the Constitution.

This discussion is not intended to deny that the Ninth Amendment might do additional interpretive work. If Congress does have an enumerated power to act, then the enumeration of rights are, of course, exceptions to the powers that are granted. The Ninth Amendment might then be a reminder that other rights exist, and that Congress ought to protect such rights by declining to interfere with them even if such rights are not judicially enforceable. Or perhaps courts should not presume that Congress intended to interfere with such rights absent clear language in its laws to the contrary; in that sense, the Amendment would serve as an additional rule of construction. Scholars have made both points.[81] One could go further and maintain that Congress cannot, under its necessary and proper authority, interfere with such rights absent clear necessity. That would be consistent with its principal function of the Amendment to negate an inference about the scope of enumerated powers, especially in light of the grant of implied powers.

During the Sedition Act controversy, some Federalists attempted a construction of the enumeration of rights at odds with what they had argued during ratification. These Federalists tried to argue that the very existence of the First Amendment was evidence that the national government had at least some authority over the press. "[The First Amendment] would have been certainly unnecessary thus to have modified the legislative powers of Congress concerning the press, if the power itself does not exist."[82] Madison criticized them for their inconsistency. It was "painful to remark," Madison understated, "how much the arguments now employed in behalf of the sedition act, are at variance with the reasoning which then justified the constitution, and invited its ratification."[83] Not only were the Federalists contradicting themselves but the Ninth Amendment was also intended to negate precisely such an implication.

This history may explain other puzzles about the Bill of Rights that have long perplexed scholars and judges. One of the more contested issues of the present time is whether the Second Amendment right to keep and bear arms guarantees an individual right or a collective right.[84] The puzzle originates in the prefatory clause: "A well regulated Militia, being necessary to the security of a free State, the right of the people to keep and bear Arms, shall not be infringed."[85] Advocates of the collective view emphasize the prefatory clause, and limit the operative clause to that purpose;[86] advocates of the individual view argue that the operative clause is not limited to the prefatory clause because operative provisions of law frequently accomplish both more and less than what their drafters may have intended.[87]

There may be another explanation. The prefatory clause of the Second Amendment helps to avoid precisely the implication that the Ninth Amendment also guards against. If the amendment had merely provided that the right to bear arms shall not be infringed, that might have raised the implication that Congress had the power to regulate such arms in the first place. Putting aside modern and ahistorical interpretations of the Commerce Clause, discussed in Chapter 16, there is no clause in the Constitution that gives Congress such a power directly outside the territories or the District of Columbia (where it has plenary legislative jurisdiction). The only possibility is Congress's power to regulate the militia. By including a prefatory clause connected to the militia, the language of the Second Amendment made clear that Congress's only power to regulate arms, if any, would have come from its power over the militia.[88]

3.3 REVISIONIST SCHOLARSHIP

Before turning to the royal prerogative and what is perhaps the true reason the Constitution enumerates power – to limit executive power – a brief examination of recent revisionist scholarship is in order. As the introduction to this study indicated, several scholars now claim that the best reading of the Constitution is that Congress is not limited to its enumerated powers; at least, these scholars argue that what they call enumerationism is not a necessary understanding of the original Constitution.

Not all of their arguments can or must be addressed here in detail. They vary in the degree of their seriousness and constructive ingenuity. Some scholars argue that there is no textual reason to think that listing Congress's powers means Congress was in fact limited to the powers listed; that is unpersuasive.[89] Others rely on expansive interpretations of the various powers granted to Congress, such as the first clause of the enumeration or the Necessary and Proper Clause; these discussions shall be deferred to the appropriate chapters. Some suggest that the Constitution's preamble is a grant of power.[90] Other scholars rely on the role James Wilson and Gouverneur Morris played in drafting the Constitution.[91] As previously noted, Wilson was the lead drafter on the Committee of Detail; Morris was likely the lead drafter on the Committee of Style, which finalized the language of the Constitution.[92] What is remarkable about these particular efforts is the degree to which they rely on unenacted proposals at the Constitutional Convention or the secret intentions of these two individuals. The reader may consult the notes for an initial assessment of these claims.[93] Suffice it to say the better evidence is what Wilson said.

The evidence that shall be examined here comprises the actual statements of prominent individuals who are supposed to have maintained after ratification that the national government was not limited to its enumerated powers. The temporal qualification is important. As two leading revisionist scholars have acknowledged, "Much … of the evidence against enumerationism[] consists of Anti-Federalist interpretations reading the Constitution to grant Congress effectively unlimited power."[94] These scholars recognize that, like pro-ratification arguments, such interpretations "were offered in the heat of political battle" and the Anti-Federalists "had incentives to exaggerate the scope of the powers [the Constitution] conferred to rally support for their cause."[95]

These scholars give no persuasive reason why these statements should be given much weight;[96] but in all events, they seem to misunderstand the evidence. The Anti-Federalists worried about the possible constructions of powers actually granted, such as the Necessary and Proper Clause or the first clause of the eighth section; very few stated anything approximating an anti-enumerationist principle.[97] But even if these scholars' interpretations were correct, the proponents of ratification won the argument, and the people who ratified the Constitution depended on their representations. After ratification, those who had opposed adoption had an incentive to diminish the scope of national powers, and those who had supported it might have had an incentive to exaggerate them. Yet, there is remarkably little evidence that anyone on either side retreated from the principle of enumeration advanced by the pro-ratification faction.

Richard Primus and William Treanor do, however, rely on what prominent members of Congress said in the First Congress when debating whether Congress had the power to establish a national bank. Chapter 4, which deals with the Necessary and Proper Clause, examines that debate in more detail because it elucidates how that clause and implied powers work. For present purposes, Primus claims to have discovered several members of Congress who believed Congress was not constrained by its enumeration of powers, some focusing on the preamble.[98] Treanor similarly claims that several members of Congress argued over the course of this debate that the preamble was a grant of power to regulate for the general welfare.[99] Their evidence, however, is thin, and many of the cited statements do not support the precise propositions for which they are advanced.

As an initial matter, Primus recognizes that most of the participants argued in enumerationist terms. The writings of the "four famous participants" in the debate, Madison, Jefferson, Attorney General Edmund Randolph, and Hamilton – whose writings on the bank the next chapter investigates – all started with the proposition that Congress was limited to enumerated powers.[100] And several members of the House of Representatives specifically responded to Madison's speech in the House (he was then an elected representative from Virginia) in terms of Congress's enumerated powers.[101] Still, Primus argues, "[s]everal representatives who spoke in support of the Bank rejected the premise that Congress could legislate only on the basis of some express specification of its powers in the Constitution."[102]

One of the strongest pieces of evidence comes from Representative Elias Boudinot. Primus argues that Boudinot "read the list of constitutional purposes specified in the Preamble as an enumeration of the purposes for which Congress could legislate," and any law that advanced those purposes "qualified as a law expressly authorized by the Constitution."[103] That is not a persuasive reading of Boudinot's speech, which began with the statement "[t]hat whatever implication destroys the principle of the Constitution ought to be rejected" – the principle being that "whatever powers . . . not granted by this instrument, are still in the people" of the states.[104] That statement is not necessarily inconsistent with the proposition that the preamble is a grant of powers, but it has enumerationist overtones. Boudinot continued:

> Mr. B[oudinot] then took up the Constitution, to see if this simple power [of establishing a Bank] was not fairly to be drawn by necessary implication from those vested by this instrument in the Legislative authority of the United States. It sets out in the preamble with declaring the general purposes for which it was formed: – "the insurance of domestic tranquility, provision for the common defence, and promotion of the general welfare."
>
> These are the prominent features of this instrument, and are confirmed and enlarged by the specific grants in the body of it, where the principles on which the Legislature should rest their after proceedings are more fully laid down, and the division of power to be exercised by the general and particular Governments distinctly marked out. By the eighth section, Congress has power "to levy taxes, pay debts, provide for the common defence and general welfare, declare war, raise and support armies, provide for and maintain a navy;" and as the means to accomplish these important ends, "to borrow money," and, finally, "to make all laws necessary and proper for carrying into execution the foregoing powers."
>
> Let us, then, inquire, is the constituting a public bank necessary to these important and essential ends of Government?[105]

Boudinot then proceeded to demonstrate why a bank was necessary and proper to "these important and essential ends of Government" by going through several of Congress's enumerated powers.[106] The entire thrust of the passage is consistent with what James Wilson said in the Lectures on Law: The preamble establishes the purposes of the Constitution, and the enumeration of power is what gives Congress the great powers to effectuate those purposes. To be sure, Boudinot may have misinterpreted the scope of these granted powers, but it is to those powers that he turned.

Treanor cites other statements for the proposition that the preamble "played a central role in the first great debate in Congress involving the scope of congressional authority,"[107] but none asserted that the preamble is a grant of power.[108] At best, advocates suggested that the enumerated powers of Congress should be interpreted in light of the purposes established in the preamble, which is not a particularly controversial proposition.[109] That is what Gouverneur Morris, the preamble's author, believed: It was a "declaration of the motives, which induced the American people to bind themselves by this compact."[110] He used the preamble to aid his interpretation of specific textual provisions.[111]

Primus, however, argues that some representatives went even further; they "not only rejected the idea that the federal government needed specific textual warrants in order to act but also showed no sense that federal legislation requires some special kind of justification that state legislation does not," he asserts. "On the contrary, they seem to have assumed that the principles determining what legislative powers the federal government could exercise were the same as those applicable to states."[112] Yet, for this proposition, Primus cites only two representatives, Boudinot and Theodore Sedgwick.[113]

Neither representative supplied strong support for the proposition. As for Sedgwick, Primus writes that he "was willing to assert that if state legislatures could exercise nonenumerated powers, Congress must be able to do so as well."[114] The only support for this proposition is Sedgwick's argument "that Congress had implicit powers" because "the state legislatures have such implicit powers."[115] Yet, no one denied that Congress had implied powers pursuant to the Necessary and Proper Clause; the question was whether incorporating a national bank could be left to implication. There is nothing whatsoever in his reported statement that questions the principle of enumeration.[116] For good measure, Sedgwick's next reported sentence was that in construing Congress's powers, "it was no doubt their duty to be careful not to exceed those limits to which it was intended they should be restricted."[117]

Returning to Boudinot, Primus writes that Boudinot thought that Congress should be able to incorporate a bank even if doing so fell outside the scope of the Necessary and Proper Clause.[118] After going to great lengths to show how the bank was necessary and proper for various enumerated powers, Boudinot is reported to have said that even if the establishment of a bank were a "high act of power" – something that could not be left to implication – "who so proper as the Legislature of the whole Union to exercise such a power for the general welfare?"[119]

Boudinot's stray statement in this long speech could certainly be interpreted as supporting a general power to legislate for the general welfare. But that is the only statement adduced to support an otherwise quite astonishing and unorthodox position.[120] Moreover, one must also recall that these are transcriptions from stenographers and not exact facsimiles of what was said. If one reads Boudinot's speech as a whole, it is remarkable for the degree to which it supports the enumerated powers position. The same is true of all the other representatives, such as Sedgwick, who supposedly espoused a nonenumerationist view of Congress's power.

As the reader will soon discover, this study undermines the conventional wisdom on several important points of constitutional law. But on this most fundamental question of constitutional structure, the revisionists give insufficient reason to do so.[121]

3.4 ROYAL PREROGATIVE

It was not a foregone conclusion that the Constitution would contain an enumeration of power. The actual resolution adopted by the Constitutional Convention in the debates during the summer of 1787, the sixth resolution of the Virginia Plan proposed early in the Convention, stated that in addition to the legislative powers of the Confederation Congress, the national legislature would have the power "to legislate in all cases to which the separate States are incompetent."[122] A proposal to specify the powers that this general and vague provision contemplated was defeated by an equally divided 5–5 vote.[123] After an addition by Gunning Bedford, the resolution adopted by the Convention was

> [t]hat the Legislature of the United States ought to possess the legislative Rights vested in Congress by the Confederation; and moreover to legislate in all Cases for the general Interests of the Union, and also in those Cases to which the States are separately incompetent, or in which the Harmony of the United States may be interrupted by the Exercise of individual Legislation.[124]

The Convention tasked a Committee of Detail, also known as the Committee of Five, with drafting a constitution conformable to the adopted resolutions. John Rutledge, Edmund Randolph, Oliver Ellsworth, Nathaniel Gorham, and James Wilson staffed the committee. It was out of this committee that the initial draft of the Constitution with a specification of legislative powers emerged. From that moment, the delegates debated the specific grants and proposed additional ones, but no one questioned the enumeration of powers.[125]

That raises the question: Why did the Committee of Detail apparently ignore the instruction not to specify the legislative powers of the national government? It is certainly possible that the members of the committee wanted a second bite at the apple; three of its five members, Rutledge, Gorham, and Randolph, had all expressed a desire to enumerate power.[126] It is also possible to interpret the Committee as not violating the instructions of the Convention. Although the motion to enumerate lost by an evenly divided vote, Gorham's state of Massachusetts, which voted against the enumeration, may have done so because of Gorham's understanding that the Convention was merely "establishing general principles, to be extended hereafter into details which will be precise & explicit."[127] Thus, there might have been six states favoring specification and only four against.

There might be an additional explanation for why the Committee proceeded to enumerate the specific powers of the legislature. James Wilson, likely the leading drafter,[128] was highly concerned with the royal prerogative powers of the British monarch. Early in the Convention, Wilson pointed out that the powers enjoyed by the British executive should not guide Americans about executive power: He "did not consider the Prerogatives of the British Monarch as a proper guide in defining the Executive powers."[129] In particular, the powers of "war & peace" and other royal prerogatives "were of a Legislative nature."[130] In his Lectures on Law, Wilson boasted that the Constitution restored part of the ancient constitution of England from before the Norman Conquest, in which these powers belonged to the witenagemote, the Anglo-Saxon assembly.[131] Several of the powers that the Committee of Detail enumerated, and not just the power to declare war, were historically royal prerogative powers. The committee, if indeed led by Wilson, might have enumerated Congress's powers to assign to Congress these historically royal powers and thereby diminish the power of the President.[132]

If we compare a list of these powers to famous accounts of the royal prerogative, the parallel is striking. William Blackstone's *Commentaries on the Laws of England* was very influential in the Founding period.[133] Certainly, Wilson, in his law lectures, cited Blackstone dozens of times. In his chapters on the royal prerogative, Blackstone examined "those branches of the royal prerogative, which invest . . . our sovereign lord . . . with a number of authorities and powers; in the exertion whereof consists the executive part of government."[134] These powers related either to "th[e] nation's intercourse with foreign nations, or it's* own domestic government and civil polity."[135] The former category included the powers to send and receive ambassadors;[136] to make treaties, leagues, and alliances;[137] to make war and peace;[138] to issue letters of marque and reprisal;[139] and to grant safe-conduct and admit strangers (foreigners) into the country.[140]

The latter, domestic prerogatives include the power to veto legislation; act as the commander in chief (or "generalissimo"); raise and regulate fleets and armies; and erect forts and similar buildings.[141] The king was also the "fountain of honour, of office, and of privilege," by which he could, for example, grant titles of nobility.[142] This prerogative included the power to naturalize aliens and to erect corporations.[143] The king was the arbiter of commerce, regulated weights and measures, and could coin money.[144] He was also the head of the Church of England.[145] Blackstone also wrote that he was the "fountain of justice and general conservator of the peace of the kingdom."[146] This meant that the king was the "proper person to prosecute for all

---

* Although odd to modern readers, the possessive form of the word "it" contained an apostrophe until sometime in the nineteenth century. The Oxford English Dictionary has several examples of this usage between 1611 and 1802. 8 Oxford English Dictionary 150–51 (2d ed. 1989).

public offenses and breaches of the peace," to grant pardons, and to nominate judges.[147] The king had the power to make proclamations as to the "manner, time, and circumstances of putting [the] laws in execution."[148] And he could create judicial tribunals to assist him in carrying into execution the "executive power of the laws."[149]

The Constitution assigns almost every one of these prerogatives: to send ambassadors (President and Senate);[150] to receive ambassadors (President);[151] to make treaties, leagues, and alliances (President and Senate);[152] to make war and peace (Congress has the power to declare war, the President to wage it and conclude peace);[153] to issue letters of marque and reprisal (Congress);[154] to veto legislation (President subject to override);[155] to be commander in chief (President);[156] to raise and regulate fleets and armies (Congress);[157] to erect forts and similar buildings (Congress);[158] to grant titles of nobility (specifically forbidden);[159] to naturalize aliens (Congress);[160] to regulate commerce and weights and measures, and to coin money (Congress);[161] to institute judicial tribunals (Congress);[162] and to nominate and appoint judges (President and Senate).[163] It was also determined soon after the Constitution was adopted that Congress could erect corporations via the Necessary and Proper Clause.[164] And although Congress has no explicit power over immigration, it is highly probable that its power to "define and punish . . . Offences against the Law of Nations"[165] included this power. Blackstone had written that without grants of safe-conduct, "by the law of nations no member of one society has a right to intrude into another."[166]

We shall come back to this point because the Constitution's assignment of a variety of traditionally royal powers to other departments of government – the Senate, for example, participates in the appointment and treaty powers – clarifies how the Constitution structures executive power. For present purposes, the distribution of royal prerogatives may very well explain why the Committee of Detail enumerated Congress's powers despite having approved the sixth resolution of the Virginia Plan.[167]

In summary, it appears that the enumeration of powers in the eighth section of the first article had a dual purpose. It empowered the national government over, and limited it to, certain enumerated and national objects but also limited executive power by assigning many historically royal prerogatives to Congress. None of that is necessarily inconsistent with the adopted resolution. It is entirely possible, in fact likely, that the delegates accepted the enumeration of powers because they believed it granted Congress all the powers necessary to effectuate national purposes. As Mark Graber has written, "Federalist rhetoric during the ratification debates . . . indicates that few notables thought the Committee on Detail had altered the original constitutional design."[168] Many thought, along with John Jay, who would become the first Chief Justice of the United States, that the Constitution created a "national government, competent to every national object."[169] The only conclusion that fits all of the data is that the enumeration of power covered every national object for which the Framers thought it necessary to provide.

4

Implied Powers

The first enumerated power with which the student of constitutional law must contend is the Necessary and Proper Clause, sometimes called the "sweeping" or "elastic" clause. This final grant in the eighth section of the first article authorizes Congress "[t]o make all Laws which shall be necessary and proper for carrying into Execution the foregoing Powers, and all other Powers vested by this Constitution in the Government of the United States, or in any Department or Officer thereof."[1] There are two principal reasons now to address this clause. First, the clause gives Congress power to make laws "necessary and proper" for carrying into execution not only its own powers but also the powers of the other government departments and officers, including the President and the executive branch. The President's role as the head of the executive branch can only be understood in relation to Congress's power to make necessary and proper laws for the regulation of that branch. How Congress can do so under its necessary and proper power will be examined in the next part of this study. Second, notwithstanding the enumeration of powers, some revisionist scholars argue that Congress may effectively accomplish anything it desires by virtue of this clause, and that the clause effectuated the sixth resolution of the Virginia Plan. These claims must also be examined.

This chapter demonstrates that the Framers and ratifying public understood the Necessary and Proper Clause as a grant of implied or incidental powers. Incidental powers are related to specified powers but are sufficiently less important that they can be left to implication. Under the Articles of Confederation, Congress could only exercise powers "expressly delegated" by the states.[2] The object of the Necessary and Proper Clause was to eliminate that restriction and, more affirmatively, to put Congress's authority to exercise incidental powers beyond doubt.

Thus, early on, Congress established the form of oath its members would take,[3] provided that census takers shall record the sex and age of those counted,[4] erected the first executive departments,[5] divided the army into units and provided salaries and pensions,[6] made it a crime to bribe federal judges or commit perjury or interfere with the delivery of the mails,[7] purchased a building to house the U.S. Mint,[8] and authorized a national flag, presumably necessary and proper for executing various martial powers.[9] The reason the Founders included a Necessary and Proper Clause is that it would have been impossible to list in the Constitution all the minor, detail-oriented powers such as these that Congress might exercise. Had they done so, the Constitution would have had the "prolixity of a legal code,"[10] an undesirable quality in a constitution by and for the people. This clause, however, did not implicitly grant Congress a power to regulate in the general interest of the Union; such a power would have been far too important to be left to implication.

The chapter begins in 1791 with the great debate in Congress and in President Washington's cabinet over whether Congress had power under the Necessary and Proper Clause to incorporate a national bank. The four great players in the debate, Madison, Jefferson, Randolph, and Hamilton, agreed not only on the principle of enumeration but also on the higher-order question of how the Necessary and Proper Clause operates. To these distinguished individuals one may add Chief Justice John Marshall, who adopted the same framework in the landmark case *McCulloch v. Maryland* nearly thirty years later. Here, the reader will encounter Marshall's famous and often misinterpreted dictum that "it is a *constitution* we are expounding"; he meant no more than to explain why the Convention could not have enumerated all the incidental, lesser powers Congress might exercise to effectuate its granted powers. That all five agreed on the proposition that the clause was merely a grant of implied or incidental powers, even though they disagreed on its application to the Bank of the United States, is great evidence of the clause's original meaning.

As noted, however, some modern scholars have questioned whether the incidental powers reading was the necessary original meaning of the clause. The previous chapter examined some evidence for the proposition that, during the bank debate, certain members of Congress did not believe themselves limited to enumerated powers. Much of that evidence has already been discounted. John Mikhail of Georgetown University's law school, however, has carefully argued that the Necessary and Proper Clause does not confine Congress to lesser powers incidental to granted powers but rather implements the sixth resolution of the Virginia Plan and grants Congress power to legislate for the general interests of the Union.[11]

The chapter therefore examines whether the views of Madison, Jefferson, Randolph, Hamilton, and Marshall were invented in service of a contemporary constitutional debate. It concludes that their distinction between incidental and principal powers was consistent with what both proponents and opponents of ratification said in 1787–88. The distinction also appears to have been well established in other areas of law and confirmed by several decades of subsequent practice. The chapter then considers the various arguments that revisionist scholars, Mikhail most prominent among them, have made in support of the notion that the clause implies the existence of inherent national powers of great importance. It rejects those arguments.

4.1 THE BANK DEBATE

In 1791, members of Congress debated whether they had power to incorporate a national bank. The Constitutional Convention had considered but rejected including an express provision granting such a power of incorporation.[12] The eastern and northern merchant and commercial classes supported a national bank but the western and southern agrarian interests largely opposed financial institutions.[13] Was such a power nevertheless necessary and proper for carrying into execution Congress's other enumerated powers in the Constitution's first article or any other power the Constitution vested in the United States or in any department or officer thereof? Madison, Jefferson, and Randolph on the one hand, and Hamilton and Marshall on the other, agreed on the principle but disagreed over its application to a national bank.[14]

Beginning with then-Representative Madison, the architect of the constitutional argument against incorporating a national bank, he argued that the Necessary and Proper Clause was a grant of implied powers only. In his speech in the House of Representatives, Madison asserted the following interpretive principle: "In admitting or rejecting a constructive authority, not only the degree of its incidentality to an express authority, is to be regarded, but the degree of its importance also; since on this will depend the probability or improbability of its being left to construction."[15] On the merits, Madison argued, "It cannot be denied that the power proposed to be exercised is an important power" because "the bill creates an artificial person previously not existing in law."[16] "It confers important civil rights and attributes, which could not otherwise be claimed," he explained. "It is, though not precisely similar, at least equivalent, to the naturalization of an alien, by which certain new civil characters are acquired by him. Would Congress have had the power to naturalize, if it had not been expressly given?"[17]

Madison here argued that incorporation of a bank is an important power, similar to the naturalization power, and one would not lightly presume that Congress had the latter power without express authorization. Later in his speech, he added, "Had the power of making treaties, for example, been omitted, however necessary it might have been, the defect could only have been lamented, or supplied by an amendment of the Constitution."[18] Important powers are generally not left to implication.

Madison added that the power to incorporate a bank was important because it involved "the power to make bye laws," which was "a sort of legislative power" and "unquestionably an act of a high and important nature."[19] The proposed bill "gives a power to purchase and hold lands," which even Congress could not do within a state "without the consent of its legislature."[20] And the bill "involves a monopoly, which affects the equal rights of every citizen."[21] "From this view of the power of incorporation exercised in the bill," Madison concluded:

> [I]t could never be deemed an accessary or subaltern power, to be deduced by implication, as a means of executing another power; it was in its nature a distinct, an independent and substantive prerogative, which not being enumerated in the

constitution, could never have been meant to be included in it, and not being included, could never be rightfully exercised.[22]

Attorney General Edmund Randolph similarly opposed the bank in two written opinions to President Washington. Randolph's first opinion is a bit opaque but can be read to support Madison. Randolph described the attributes of the corporation, and wrote that "their importance strikes the eye."[23] He went on to write, "Governments, having no written Constitution, may perhaps claim a latitude of power, not always easy to be determined. Those, which have written Constitutions, are circumscribed by a just interpretation of the words contained in them."[24] He gestured to the doctrine of implied powers when he quoted the Necessary and Proper Clause and observed, "To be necessary is to be incidental, or . . . the natural means of executing a power."[25] In his second paper, he elaborated that powers "are either incidental, or substantive, that is independent powers," the latter of which are "capable of being used[] independently of what is called the principal power."[26] Randolph thus appears to have agreed that it would be improper to interpret the words of a written constitution to authorize important powers by implication.

Secretary of State Jefferson also agreed that the clause authorized Congress to legislate regarding "means" but not "ends." In his opinion for President Washington, he used those terms in pointing out that the very power under discussion was rejected by the Convention: "It is known that the very power now proposed *as a means* was rejected *as an end* by the Convention which formed the Constitution."[27] Jefferson's argument about the Convention proceedings was of dubious validity; the power might have been rejected because the Convention believed it to be incidental and, as Hamilton responded, the meaning of a legal instrument is to be gathered from the instrument itself.[28] For present purposes, though, Jefferson agreed that the clause granted incidental powers only; his concern was to avoid interpreting the clause in a way that rendered useless the enumeration of powers. The alternative construction, he argued, "would swallow up all the delegated powers, and reduce the whole to one power."[29]

Secretary of Treasury Hamilton led the defense of the bank bill and did not dispute the applicable principles. He began with the proposition that the Necessary and Proper Clause explicitly granted Congress implied powers. "It is conceded that implied powers are to be considered as delegated equally with express ones," he wrote in his written opinion for President Washington.[30] And the power to erect a corporation was an "incident to" Congress's various regulatory powers.[31] The dispute was one of application: "An incorporation seems to have been regarded as some *great independent substantive thing*; as a political end of peculiar magnitude and moment; whereas it is truly to be considered as a *quality, capacity*, or *means* to an end."[32] Corporations are never established for the sake of their own existences; they are always erected for some other purpose.

Thus, "the importance of the power of incorporation has been exaggerated," Hamilton emphasized,[33] before proceeding to argue that a national bank would be useful, expedient, and convenient for laying and collecting taxes, borrowing money, regulating trade, and raising and supporting armies.[34] The contrary argument, he concluded, "is founded upon an exaggerated and erroneous conception of the nature of the power" in question, and that "viewed in a just light," incorporating a national bank "is a means which ought to have been left to implication, rather than an end which ought to have been expressly granted."[35] He summarized: "[T]he power to erect corporations is not to be considered as an independent or substantive power, but as an incidental and auxiliary one, and was therefore more properly left to implication, than expressly granted."[36] Congress, agreeing with Hamilton and (as Chapter 3 detailed) Representative Boudinot and the other proponents of a bank, enacted the bank legislation, which President Washington signed.

4.2 *MCCULLOCH V. MARYLAND*

When Chief Justice Marshall upheld the constitutionality of the Second Bank of the United States almost three decades later in the 1819 case *McCulloch v. Maryland*,[37] he was treading old ground. Maryland had sought to tax the bank's Maryland branch. The cashier refused to pay the tax and was sued. The questions thus arose whether Congress had constitutional authority to create the national bank and, if so, whether the states could tax its branches. Marshall's conclusion that the "power to tax involves the power to destroy," and that the states could not tax the instrumentalities of the federal government, is often studied and is consistent with the principles of a compound republic established in Chapter 2. Allowing the states to tax the bank would completely change "the character of" the Constitution, arrest "all the measures of the government," and prostrate the government "at the foot of the states." "This was not intended by the American people. They did not design to make their government dependent on the states."[38]

As to the constitutionality of the bank, Marshall began with these same principles. Counsel for the state of Maryland had argued that the Constitution was a compact and therefore its powers should be construed strictly.[39] Marshall corrected the record. "The convention which framed the constitution was indeed elected by the state legislatures. But the instrument, when it came from their hands, was a mere proposal, without obligation, or pretensions to it." It was then "submitted to the *people*." It is true, Marshall acknowledged, that the people "assembled in their several states – and where else should they have assembled?" "But the measures they adopt do not, on that account, cease to be the measures of the people themselves, or become the measures of the state governments," he explained.[40] "The government of the Union, then … is, emphatically and truly, a government of the people. In form, and in substance, it emanates from them. Its powers are granted by them, and are to be exercised directly on them, and for their benefit."[41]

That hardly meant the government had unlimited powers. "This government is acknowledged by all, to be one of enumerated powers," Marshall wrote. But within its domain it is supreme: "[T]he government of the Union, though limited in its powers, is supreme within its sphere of action."[42] Marshall further acknowledged that "[a]mong the enumerated powers, we do not find that of establishing a bank or creating a corporation"; but unlike in the Articles of Confederation, which included a provision declaring that the national government could only exercise those powers "expressly" delegated by the states, "there is no phrase" in the Constitution which "excludes incidental or implied powers[,] and which requires that everything granted shall be expressly and minutely described."[43]

Marshall went on to explain why a clause authorizing implied powers was critical to the Constitution's success. The Framers surely could not have drafted "an accurate detail of all the subdivisions of which its great powers will admit, and of all the means by which they may be carried into execution." If they had done so, Marshall wrote, the Constitution "would partake of the prolixity of a legal code." The Constitution's nature required "that only its great outlines should be marked, its important objects designated, and the minor ingredients which compose those objects, be deduced from the nature of the objects themselves." Therefore, in considering Congress's implied powers, Marshall insisted, "we must never forget that it is a *constitution* we are expounding."[44]

Marshall then turned to the bank itself. Marshall observed that the enumeration of powers in the eighth section, first article included "the great powers[] to lay and collect taxes; to borrow money; to regulate commerce; to declare and conduct a war; and to raise and support armies and navies."[45] The Constitution, however, "does not profess to enumerate the means by which the powers it confers may be executed; nor does it prohibit the creation of a corporation, if the existence of such a being be essential, to the beneficial exercise of those powers."[46] The power to create a corporation, Marshall wrote, "is not, like the power of making war, or levying taxes, or of regulating commerce, a great substantive and independent power, which cannot be implied as incidental to other powers, or used as means of executing them." A corporation "is never the end for which other powers are exercised, but a means by which other objects are accomplished." The power to create such a corporation "is never used for its own sake, but for the purpose of effecting something else."[47]

Marshall next addressed the argument that incidental powers had to be absolutely necessary to the exercise of an enumerated power. He quickly dispatched the argument. The word "necessary," he observed, "is often connected with other words, which increase or diminish the impression the mind receives of the urgency it imports"; thus "[a] thing may be necessary, very necessary, absolutely or indispensably necessary."[48] Marshall pointed to the clause in the tenth section of the first article that prohibited a state from laying "imposts, or duties on imports or exports, except what may be absolutely necessary for executing its inspection laws." If the word "necessary" meant strictly and absolutely necessary, as the opponents of the national bank argued, then the word "absolutely" in this other provision would have been superfluous.[49] Marshall ultimately concluded, almost certainly correctly, that the word "imports no more than that one thing is convenient, or useful, or essential to another."[50]

Thus, one arrives at another famous passage. It cannot be the case that the Framers, through the Necessary and Proper Clause, intended to confine "the choice of means to such narrow limits as not to leave it in the power of congress to adopt any which might be appropriate" and "conducive to the end." "This provision" – the Necessary and Proper Clause – "is made in a constitution intended to endure for ages to come, and consequently, to be adapted to the various *crises* of human affairs."[51] Despite what many modern commentators and judges have suggested,[52] Marshall did not say the Constitution itself must be adapted to the various crises of human affairs or that judges must reinterpret its great enumerated powers. He said only that the *means* Congress chooses to effectuate its enumerated powers – the implied, incidental powers it may exercise – are flexible and adaptable. He continued:

> To have prescribed the means by which government should, in all future time, execute its powers, would have been to change, entirely, the character of the instrument, and give it the properties of a legal code. It would have been an unwise attempt to provide, by immutable rules, for exigencies which, if foreseen at all, must have been seen dimly, and which can be best provided for as they occur.[53]

Marshall thus concluded with the following interpretation of the Necessary and Proper Clause, parroting Hamilton's opinion on the bank: "Let the end be legitimate, let it be within the scope of the constitution, and all means which are appropriate, which are plainly adapted to that end, which are not prohibited, but consist with the letter and spirit of the constitution, are constitutional."[54] Under this standard, it is "not now a subject of controversy" that a bank "is a convenient, a useful, and essential instrument" in the administration of the government's finances,[55] and therefore to carry into execution the national government's powers.[56]

All the leading players in the bank controversy thus agreed with the proposition that the Necessary and Proper Clause was a grant of implied powers. Congress had a choice of means as to which of these lesser and incidental powers it would deploy to effectuate its enumerated powers and the other powers the Constitution grants. This choice of means could not be construed too narrowly because the Constitution was meant to be adaptable to the various crises of human affairs. Whether or not incorporating a national bank was a lesser and incidental power that Congress could exercise, or was instead a great, substantive, and independent prerogative that Congress could not exercise without an express enumeration, was a lower-order dispute.[57]

4.3 BEFORE AND AFTER

The distinction between incidental and important or substantive powers also featured in salient legal sources and discourses before and after the bank debate.

Starting with ratification, Madison explained in *Federalist* No. 44 that the Necessary and Proper Clause was inserted precisely to avoid the problems under the Articles of Confederation with its provision disabling the Confederation Congress from exercising any power not "expressly" delegated. If the new Constitution had contained a like provision, it would "disarm the government of all real authority whatever." "It would be easy to show," Madison explained, "that no important power delegated by the Articles of Confederation has been or can be executed by Congress, without recurring more or less to the doctrine of *construction* or *implication*."[58]

Hence, Madison acknowledged that the clause granted only implied powers. Had the Convention attempted to enumerate all such implied powers, "the attempt would have involved a complete digest of laws on every subject to which the Constitution relates."[59] And if the Convention had taken the approach of not including the Necessary and Proper Clause at all, Congress would still have had implied powers because "[n]o axiom is more clearly established in law, or in reason, than that wherever the end is required, the means are authorized."[60]

James Wilson agreed. He stated in the Pennsylvania ratifying convention that the Necessary and Proper Clause granted "nothing more than what was necessary to render effectual the particular powers that are granted."[61] In responding to various Anti-Federalist attacks on the clause, he emphasized in relation to the enumeration:

> I leave it to every gentleman to say whether the powers are not as accurately and minutely defined, as can be well done on the same subject, in the same language.... [E]ven the concluding clause, with which so much fault has been found, gives no more or other powers; nor does it, in any degree, go beyond the particular enumeration; for, when it is said that Congress shall have power to make all laws which shall be necessary and proper, those words are limited and defined by the following, "for carrying into execution the foregoing powers." It is saying no more than that the powers we have already particularly given, shall be effectually carried into execution.[62]

In his Lectures on Law, he reiterated: "The powers of congress are, indeed, enumerated; but it was intended that those powers, thus enumerated, should be effectual, and not nugatory."[63]

On the whole, the Anti-Federalist writers did not think that the clause on its own would work much mischief; the risk depended instead on the scope of the specific enumerated grants of power. Centinel acknowledged that the clause only authorized laws "necessary and proper for carrying into execution any of the powers vested in them."[64] The Federal Farmer agreed.[65] Brutus argued that the necessary and proper clause and Article VI's supremacy clause would give the national government "absolute and uncontroulable power, legislative, executive and judicial, *with respect to every object to which it extends*."[66] That is a truism; the question is the scope of those referenced objects.

Brutus argued that the clause in combination with the preamble created the *inference* "that the legislature will have an authority to make all laws which they shall judge necessary for the common safety, and to promote the general welfare."[67] Brutus also interpreted the first grant of power in the eighth section as a power "to provide for the common defence, and general welfare," rather than as a power to tax for such purposes (or to appropriate funds); he feared such a power in combination with the Necessary and Proper Clause.[68] A Countryman similarly stated the Necessary and Proper Clause "gives [Congress] power to do any thing at all, if they only please to say, it is for the common welfare."[69] The revisionist scholars cited in the prior chapter have pointed to a handful of other Anti-Federalist writers who made this interpretation of the so-called "general welfare clause."[70]

What is remarkable is how few (if any) Anti-Federalists worried about the Necessary and Proper Clause in isolation. The revisionists have cited none and the present author could not locate any.[71] The merits of their claims about the meaning of the first clause of the eighth section will be addressed in Part VII of this study when the specific powers of Congress are examined. The present point is that not even the Anti-Federalists disputed that Congress's laws under the Necessary and Proper Clause required a connection to some other vested power, or that it extended only to implied or incidental powers.[72] The doctrine of implication could be abused, and that appears to have been the Anti-Federalist concern; but that the clause was a grant of implied powers does not seem to have been doubted.

Perhaps the Anti-Federalists understood along with the proponents of ratification that implied powers were a well-established feature of many areas of law. As four modern scholars have argued, the clause in some form captures earlier doctrines.[73] The clause "has a rich history, with numerous antecedents that would have been readily knowable (and were almost certainly known) by informed eighteenth-century drafters and ratifiers," they write. The clause's origins "are found in principles of agency law, administrative law, and corporate law that infused founding-era constitutionalism."[74] Many founding-era and pre-founding-era legal instruments involving a principal–agent relationship included "necessary and proper clauses" or their equivalents as a means of giving "fiduciary agents incidental powers beyond those expressly described in the instruments."[75] Similar clauses also appeared in corporate charters "to ensure that an organization with limited powers and purposes would not be frustrated in the essential conduct of its governmentally authorized activities but would still be confined to its assigned functions."[76]

The reader may consult the work of these scholars for a more detailed treatment; a few examples will suffice here. Blackstone wrote in his *Commentaries* in the context of a land grant that "[a] subject's grant shall be construed to include many things, besides what are expressed, if necessary for the operation of the grant."[77] Sir Edward Coke's influential *Institutes on the Laws of the England* from a century earlier referenced incidental powers several times. In the context of one statute, for example, Coke wrote that although the Act was "general," "all necessary incidents are to be supplied."[78] Elsewhere, he wrote that "they that have Conusance [jurisdiction] of any thing are to have Conusance also of all Incidents and Dependants thereupon, for an Incident is a thing necessarily depending upon another."[79] The central insight is that grants of implied or incidental powers did not authorize important or extraordinary actions. Coke wrote that an "incident" was "a thing appertaining to or following another as a more worthy or principal."[80] Giles Jacob's law dictionary, which was the most prominent law dictionary in America at the Founding,[81] similarly explained that an "incident" was "a thing necessarily depending upon, appertaining to, or following another that is more worthy or principal."[82]

Another example is found in the English case *Howard v. Baillie* from 1796, a few years after the Founding.[83] The executrix of an estate authorized two others "to act for her in collecting and getting in the estate of the deceased, and paying his debts."[84] The question was whether that authorization included the power to make the executrix personally liable for a debt on condition that the creditor wait twenty months for payment.[85] Although this may seem like an important power by modern lights, Lord Chief Justice Kenyon explained that such a procedure was not unusual in the administration of estates.[86] The critical point is that the Lord Chief Justice recognized that the grant of a general, principal power to pay the debts "necessarily includes...all the means necessary to be used, in order to attain the accomplishment of the object of the principal power";[87] that is, "subordinate powers, though not expressly given, ... must be understood to be included in this power to pay debts."[88] "Subordinate" powers can be left to implication, but "principal" powers cannot.

These sources all tend to show that implied powers, authorizations, and grants were accepted in several areas of law. Such grants were in service of specified objects, and the incidental powers were therefore subordinate to and less important than those objects. If it were otherwise, the clause would supersede the specification and make the specification nugatory. That is consistent with the many other examples of the phrase "necessary and proper" prior to the Constitution.[89]

The evidence from the bank debate, ratification, and pre-ratification legal sources all point to the distinction between great powers and incidental ones. William Baude has further studied subsequent practice under the Constitution in the context of eminent domain, the power to take land from a private citizen without that citizen's consent. He has demonstrated that until 1864, Congress relied on states to exercise their powers of eminent domain and to transfer the land to the national government when it needed to condemn land.[90] Not until 1875 did the Supreme Court hold that the national government had its own eminent domain power by implication,[91] and in so doing it reversed a prior Supreme Court decision[92] as well as decades of prior practice.

In that prior decision, the Court had explained that "the United States have no constitutional capacity to exercise municipal jurisdiction, sovereignty, or eminent domain, within the limits of a state or elsewhere, except in the cases in which it is expressly granted," namely, in the District of Columbia and the national territories.[93] The Necessary and Proper Clause was not even invoked. This practice regarding eminent domain is useful because unlike the bank, it was a power widely understood to be denied to the national government under the doctrine of implied powers, confirming that some powers were too great or important to be left to implication.

4.4 "ALL OTHER POWERS"

Some revisionist scholars insist, however, that the Necessary and Proper Clause allows Congress to exercise great powers beyond those that the Constitution expressly grants. These scholars focus on the second part of the clause, authorizing laws necessary and proper for carrying into execution "all other Powers vested by this Constitution in the Government of the United States." These scholars argue that the clause presumes there is power vested in the undifferentiated government of the United States as a whole, in contrast to those vested "in any Department or Officer thereof." And because the Constitution does not otherwise vest "the United States," as opposed to specific departments or officers, with any power, such power must be implied, or rather inherent, in the very fact of nationhood.

These scholars argue, for example, that this part of the clause could authorize a national immigration power or any regulations for the general welfare of the United States.[94] Although these scholars often use the term "implied" national powers, such powers should not be confused with incidental powers. Both inherent powers and incidental powers might be "implied" by some fact or granted power, but incidental powers are limited to lesser powers and are related to granted powers. Inherent powers are not necessarily lesser powers, and they do not even need a connection to any of the enumerated powers.

There are some possible explanations for the middle part of the Necessary and Proper Clause that do not depend on the existence of inherent powers in the government as a whole.[95] But even if the Constitution does not otherwise expressly grant powers to the undifferentiated "United States," it does not follow that the clause must necessarily imply the existence of inherent powers of great significance. Corporate bodies, including political corporations, were understood to have incidental powers such as the right to sue and hold property; but these were "incidental" and not great and important powers.[96]

Moreover, a double implication would be a troubling and roundabout way to grant government powers of significance. The argument, to put it another way, takes the following form: The United States as a whole has inherent, unenumerated powers, and that proposition is itself derived from implication, insomuch as the middle part of the Necessary and Proper Clause would otherwise refer to an empty set. But recall what Madison stated in the debate over the bank: "In admitting or rejecting a constructive authority, not only the degree of its incidentality to an express authority is to be regarded, but the degree of its importance also; since on this will depend the probability or improbability of its being left to construction."[97] If Madison's dictum reflected a shared understanding of how language (legal or otherwise) worked, then it is highly improbable that great and important powers would have been left to such a double implication.

Still another argument against the inherent powers reading is that it would undermine the entire enumeration of powers. If the federal government had power to regulate for the general welfare, the Constitution could simply have said that. And if it does have such power despite no written authorization, the entire enumeration becomes irrelevant. If the evidence examined in Chapter 3 was persuasive, then surely it would take more than two layers of implication to refute it.

Finally, the "all other powers" provision was often referred to as a "sweeping" clause, and such clauses were intended to capture omitted details. Mikhail explains that sweeping clauses were common "in wills, contracts, corporate charters, and other legal instruments at the time, both in England and in the United States," and their "well-established function" was "[t]o negate the inference that a given list of items is exhaustive."[98] Here, the sweeping clause would negate the inference that Congress only had implied powers to carry into execution the "foregoing" powers in the first article.[99] But even if the sweeping clause somehow implied Congress had powers not specified in the Constitution, legal sources show that such clauses were not used to capture powers of great substantive importance.

Mikhail, for example, cites to a pair of 1774 English cases authored by Chief Justice Mansfield. In one of these cases, Mansfield explained that by "sweeping clauses, conveyancers often take in every thing relative to what had been before recited, and which it was possible they might have omitted to enumerate precisely."[100] Mansfield's clause ended in a semicolon, after which he added: "but they never mean to pass any thing new."[101] The entire case concerned the meaning of a sweeping clause in a land grant in which the grantor minutely described two pieces of land, and then ended "with all my other estates in the kingdom of Ireland." The estates were of considerable value. Lord Mansfield asked, "Now is it credible this would have passed by so few general words, when such an immense detail was made of the others?"[102]

So far, the linguistic argument in favor of implied national powers of great importance is plausible but weak. Mikhail's most sophisticated argument, however, turns on his understanding of the intent of James Wilson, who drafted the "all other powers" portion of the Necessary and Proper Clause. The argument, as best as the present author understands it, is as follows. James Wilson believed that the united, national government had implied powers the day the states declared independence. He defended the chartering of the Bank of North America in 1781 on such grounds, even though the Articles of Confederation did not grant Congress any such explicit power. If Wilson still believed that such powers existed in the national government, then the "all other powers" portion of the Necessary and Proper Clause would give Congress the power to make all laws necessary and proper for carrying such powers into execution.[103]

Mikhail summarizes his conclusions: "[I]t seems probable that Wilson's primary purpose in drafting the All Other Powers Provision was to ensure that the Constitution would expressly recognize the implied and inherent powers of the United States that he and the nationalists had labored so extensively to defend under the Articles of Confederation."[104] Wilson of course said nothing about this; the reason, Mikhail suggests, is that specifying the regulatory power over the general interests of the Union, per the sixth resolution of the Virginia Plan, "would have been to raise a red flag."[105] Nevertheless, "[b]y adding a sweeping clause to the other enumerated powers," Mikhail concludes, "Wilson and the other framers laid the groundwork for ensuring that the Government of the United States would possess all of the other necessary and proper powers it needed to provide for the general interests of the United States at any point in the future, as unforeseen circumstances and new contingencies arose."[106]

These conclusions amount to conjecture as to what Wilson's motives might have been. A much surer guide is what Wilson said time and again: The national government was limited to enumerated powers, and the Necessary and Proper Clause was intended to make those powers effectual. Not only do Mikhail's conclusions depend on conjecture but they also require one to believe that Wilson kept his intentions secret to fool opponents of ratification. Even if plausible and admissible as evidence of meaning, such secret intent cannot take precedence over the actual text of the Constitution. The Necessary and Proper Clause is simply not worded in a way that would give Congress all powers to regulate for the general interest of the Union.

Which leads to the merits of Mikhail's claims about Wilson and whether he believed there were inherent national powers vested in the government of the United States. In 1785, Wilson did in fact argue, as Mikhail observes, that the Confederation Congress had authority to incorporate the Bank of North America despite no express provision authorizing such an incorporation.[107] He argued that the United States had power as a Union when the states declared independence: "The United States have general rights, general powers, and general obligations . . . resulting from the union of the whole."[108] "To many purposes," he argued, "the United States are to be considered as one undivided, independent nation; and as possessed of all the rights, and powers, and properties, by the law of nations incident to such."[109] "Whenever an object occurs," he continued, "to the direction of which no particular state is competent, the management of it must, of necessity, belong to the United States in congress assembled."[110] These powers vested in the Union when the Declaration announced the independence of "these United Colonies."[111] Wilson provided two examples of inherent national powers: the sale and government of lands "not within any state," and the formation of new states.[112]

There is every reason to believe, however, that Wilson abandoned this position in 1787, or at least no longer relied on it. In his 1785 essay, he was defending the Bank of North America against state legislation that would repeal the bank's state charter in Pennsylvania. Wilson lost; the legislature repealed the charter.[113] Apparently they did not agree with his arguments about implied powers, although they of course also had political reasons to oppose the bank.

Wilson's draft of the Constitution strongly suggests that he changed his strategy. He drafted the clause that would allow Congress the power to create new states,[114] and the final language of the Constitution authorized Congress to make needful rules and regulations respecting the property and territories of the United States.[115] The Constitution thus expressly provided for the two powers Wilson had argued were implied in the nation as a whole. And the Necessary and Proper Clause negates the effect of the "expressly delegated" provision of the Articles of Confederation. The clause also made clear that there were powers vested in the United States "by this Constitution," whereas Wilson's earlier argument was that some powers were vested inherently by the act of becoming an independent nation. Together, these changes suggest Wilson no longer relied on the inherent powers argument he had unsuccessfully deployed a few years earlier.

4.5 MISSING POWERS

One final argument for why the Constitution must allow for great national powers by implication is that the government simply could not exist without them. Andrew Coan and David Schwartz propose a non-exhaustive list of such implied powers the national government has been held to possess:

> The Constitution fails to enumerate certain essential powers that were widely recognized at the founding as inherent in any sovereign government. The Supreme Court has long recognized several of them, despite the fact that they cannot properly be cabined as subordinate means to carry into effect any enumerated power. These include but are not limited to the powers to regulate immigration, conduct foreign affairs, acquire territory, exercise eminent domain, regulate noncommercial Indian affairs, and issue paper money.[116]

This already lengthy study cannot examine all of these issues in great detail. But one should be skeptical. Although it is true that the Supreme Court relied on inherent powers to justify national power over immigration,[117] it hardly needed to do so. The clause prohibiting the abolition of the slave trade until 1808 presumed that Congress had power over the "migration or importation of ... persons."[118] Where that power comes from has been somewhat of a mystery; Christopher Green proposes the foreign commerce clause, on which the Supreme Court has relied in the past.[119] More plausible, however, is Congress's power to define offenses against the law of nations. As Chapter 3 noted, Blackstone had written that without grants of safe-conduct, "by the law of nations no member of one society has a right to intrude into another."[120] Robert Natelson has recently canvassed other writers on the law of nations and argues that the immigration power comes from this clause.[121]

The conduct of foreign affairs will be addressed in a future chapter; it is not a "missing" or "implied" power at all. The power to send ambassadors to other countries surely means the ambassadors are to do what ambassadors have always done, namely, manage relations with foreign countries.[122] Acquiring territory is also an odd power to claim is missing.[123] As Chief Justice Marshall stated, if Congress has the power to declare war, surely that includes the power under the laws of war to acquire territory by conquest. Congress also has the power to make treaties, which would seem to include the types of treaties into which nations have always entered.[124] Or put another way, if Congress can acquire by conquest, and can make peace by treaty, surely it can also acquire territory by treaty rather than conquest.

It is true that Congress does not have an enumerated power over noncommercial Indian affairs. That is why Congress treated with the native tribes for the first several decades of the Republic. It is an open question whether the Indian Appropriations Act of 1871, eliminating this treaty practice, was in fact constitutional.[125] It is also not obvious that the national government must have a power of eminent domain. As noted earlier, Baude has shown that for the first several decades Congress exercised this power in coordination with state governments.[126]

Finally, it may be that, as an originalist matter, Congress has no power to issue paper money. But even if that power were desirable, it hardly follows that it is an inherent power of government. And supposing it is, one example is insufficient to establish that the national government has, or must have, inherent powers beyond those granted in the Necessary and Proper Clause or which follow from other clauses under the doctrine of implication. The overwhelming weight of the evidence confirms that the national government is limited to the powers enumerated in the Constitution, including all incidental powers necessary or convenient for carrying those great powers into execution.

PART III

The Executive Power

5

Creating the Presidency

Article I creates a national government of limited and enumerated legislative powers, principally through its first sentence: "All legislative Powers herein granted shall be vested in a Congress of the United States." Article II creates the executive branch. It is formulated differently: "The executive Power shall be vested in a President of the United States of America."[1] The Vesting Clause of Article II does not say only those executive powers "herein granted" shall be vested in the President; it says "the executive power" shall be vested in the President.

This formulation has caused much controversy over the past 230 years. Its meaning is not immediately clear because there is a subsequent enumeration of powers in the remainder of the article. The first paragraph of the second section declares the President to be commander in chief of the armed forces and grants the President the power to demand the opinions in writing of the principal officers of the executive departments and to grant reprieves and pardons.[2] These appear to be powers the President can exercise independently. The second paragraph of this section gives the President certain powers to be shared with the Senate, namely, the power to make treaties and appointments, although Congress may vest the appointment of inferior officers in the President alone, the heads of departments, or the courts.[3] The President also has the power to make recess appointments.[4]

Article II's third section then involves the President's relationship and duties to Congress as well as more general duties. The President must from time to time give Congress information about the state of the union and recommend legislative measures; may convene Congress on extraordinary occasions and may adjourn them in the event the House and Senate disagree about adjournment; and "shall take Care that the Laws be faithfully executed, and shall Commission all the Officers of the United States." This paragraph also gives the President the duty to "receive Ambassadors and other public Ministers."[5]

What is the purpose of this enumeration? Does the enumeration imply that the President, like Congress, has only specifically enumerated powers? If so, why is Article II's Vesting Clause written differently than its equivalent in Article I? "Article II is the most loosely drawn chapter of the Constitution," Edward Corwin wrote in the mid twentieth century.[6] "To those who think that a constitution ought to settle everything beforehand it should be a nightmare; by the same token, to those who think that constitution makers ought to leave considerable leeway for the future play of political forces, it should be a vision realized."[7]

Over the past two and a third centuries, those political forces have generally moved in one direction: toward more presidential power. Despite the enumeration of powers in Article II, many scholars (not to mention a few presidents) have asserted that the Vesting Clause is a general grant of all conceivable executive powers. Former president and then-Chief Justice Taft held in a famous opinion that this grant of power was general, and in the remainder of Article II the grant was "strengthened by specific terms where emphasis is appropriate, and limited by direct expressions where limitation is needed."[8] (Based on his other writings, however, as Chapter 6 explains, President Taft seems to have had in mind a residuum of law-execution authorities only.)

President Theodore Roosevelt supplied an even more forceful articulation of executive power. "My view was that every executive officer, and above all every executive officer in high position, was a steward of the people bound actively and affirmatively to do all he could for the people."[9] Roosevelt "declined to adopt the view that what was imperatively necessary for the Nation could not be done by the President unless he could find some specific authorization to do it." He believed it was "his duty to do anything that the needs of the Nation demanded unless such action was forbidden by the Constitution or by the laws." He acted for the "public welfare" and "common well-being of all our people, whenever and in whatever manner was necessary, unless prevented by direct constitutional or legislative prohibition."[10]

The next several chapters explore whether modern understandings of the presidency have deviated from the original conception of the office. Roosevelt's "stewardship theory" of executive power may be a positive development, or inevitable. Whether it is justified by the grant of "the executive power" in Article II is more doubtful. The material to follow will attempt to give as fair an account as possible of the competing views, but skepticism of such claims about executive power is warranted. Not only are these broad understandings of presidential power likely incorrect as an originalist matter, but, more controversially, they are also largely the product of progressive and functionalist constitutionalism. To restrain the presidency (or, the corollary, to restore Congress to its proper role) requires a more formalist conception of the presidency.

This chapter unfolds as follows. It begins with a brief account of the Constitutional Convention and its work on the presidency. As will become clear, the "unitary executive theory" is a misnomer for the legal theory at the core of the modern legal debates over presidential power. There was no question that the executive would be "unitary." The debate is entirely different: It is over the scope of that unitary President's powers. In this regard, "the executive power" was likely a substantive grant of power, but a rather limited one: It was only the power to oversee the execution of the laws and nothing more. The remaining chapters in this part of the study will then examine the President's relationship to subordinate officers in the executive branch, sometimes known as the administrative state. The next part will address "inherent" or "emergency" executive power and will create a framework for analyzing separation of powers disputes between the President and Congress. It will then address some of those disputes, including those involving foreign affairs and war.

5.1 BEFORE THE CONSTITUTION

The modern legal debates over the presidency focus on what is often called "unitary executive theory." This label is a misnomer. It is better to start afresh. There is no genuine debate over whether the President is a unitary executive. There is only one President. The work of the Constitutional Convention and the text of the Constitution make clear that the presidency was to be unitary: The Framers explicitly rejected the idea of a plural executive that would enervate the executive branch and a privy council that would obscure the President's responsibility. The contested questions are instead over the scope of the President's powers.

The work of the Convention and the events leading up to it are instructive because, although nothing dispositive can be gleaned for many contemporary debates, the discussions do strongly suggest that the President's powers were to be carefully cabined precisely because the executive was to be unitary. Put somewhat differently, even though unitary executive theorists are often accused of believing in great presidential powers (and some do), the opposite proposition is more sensible: The Constitution carefully defines the scope and sweep of presidential power because the President is unitary.

The fundamental problem confronting the Convention was how to create a presidency with sufficient energy to execute the laws and defend a large nation while minimizing the risk it would develop into a tyranny. The need for energy was pressing; as Gouverneur Morris declared in the Convention, in an extensive country such as that of the United States, "We must either then renounce the blessings of the Union, or provide an Executive with sufficient vigor to pervade every part of it."[11] The immediate examples the Convention had of executive power were the weak governors in the states and the central government under the Articles of Confederation, which had no independent executive at all. Most delegates agreed that these models were out of the question for the future national executive.

Both examples were, however, historically explicable. After fighting a revolution against a king the Americans thought to be a tyrant, the Americans revolutionized their own state constitutions and "made of the gubernatorial magistrate a new kind of creature, a very pale reflection indeed of his regal ancestor."[12] "In Pennsylvania," Gordon Wood has explained, "where radical Whig thought found its fullest expression, the governor was actually totally eliminated, and replaced by an Executive Council of twelve."[13] And even in most of the states with a single president or governor, all executive powers had to "be exercised with the advice and consent" of councils, which were intended to be "more controllers than servants of the governors."[14]

As for the scope of these executives' powers, "all of the states destroyed the substance of an independent magistracy."[15] This was accomplished through stripping the governors of any powers beyond the reach of the legislature. The typical formulation specified that the governor, with advice of the council, was to exercise any executive powers "according to the laws," and forbade the exercise of any "power or prerogative" rooted in the customs of England. Thus, the Virginia Constitution of 1776 provided that the governor "shall, with the advice of a Council of State, exercise the executive powers of government, according to the laws of this Commonwealth; and shall not, under any pretence, exercise any power or prerogative, by virtue of any law, statute or custom of England."[16] Numerous state constitutions had similar provisions.[17]

The problems with this arrangement soon became apparent. Americans had gone too far in the other extreme. The historian Forrest McDonald describes the results, particularly in Rhode Island and Massachusetts. In the former state, which many came to call "Rogue's Island," the legislature enacted various debtor relief laws and paper money schemes; eventually the state's currency "depreciated until it was worth no more than seven or eight cents on the dollar."[18] It was the experience of Massachusetts, though, that tended to confirm prevailing perceptions regarding the combination of strong legislative assemblies and weak executives. Although Massachusetts had a stronger separation of powers than most other states, McDonald explains how the "demagogic" governor, the famous John Hancock, "induced the legislature" to provide generously to public creditors who financed the state during the Revolutionary War, but then declined to collect any of the necessary taxes.[19] When the next governor finally had to collect, the taxpayers revolted in what is known as Shays's Rebellion.[20] Although the rebellion was suppressed, the general "misunderstanding" of the events, McDonald argues, led many Americans to believe that they had gone too far in the direction of democracy; they needed stronger executives to check legislative excesses.[21]

As James Madison explained in the Constitutional Convention, "The Executives of the States are in general little more than Cyphers; the legislatures omnipotent."[22] "Experience had proved," he added, "a tendency in our governments to throw all power into the Legislative vortex."[23] Elbridge Gerry asserted in the Convention, "The evils we experience flow from the excess of democracy. The people do not want virtue; but are the dupes of pretended patriots."[24] According to Rufus King's notes, James Wilson stated, "The people of Amer[ica] did not oppose the British King but the parliament – the opposition was not ag[ainst] an Unity but a corrupt multitude."[25] And Gouverneur Morris declared, "One great object of the Executive is to controul the Legislature. The Legislature will continually seek to aggrandize & perpetuate themselves; and will seize those critical moments produced by war, invasion or convulsion for that purpose. It is necessary then," he continued, "that the Executive Magistrate should be the guardian of the people . . . ."[26]

If the experience of the state constitutions led the delegates to believe that a stronger executive was necessary, so too did their experience under the Articles of Confederation. The reader will recall that the Articles were nothing more than a treaty or league and depended on the good will of the states. The central government could not directly requisition troops or taxes for the Revolutionary War. "The confederation . . . had a right to propose certain things to their sovereigns, and to require a compliance with their resolution; but they could, by their own power, execute nothing," Chief Justice John Marshall would later say.[27] As not a few prominent constitutional law scholars have observed, "This failure of execution soon became evident. The commands of the Articles of Confederation were . . . frequently disregarded. No state paid all that it owed for keeping up the government under the Articles, and one state, Georgia, never paid a cent."[28] One of the central differences between the Articles and the subsequent Constitution was that the latter would operate directly on the people.

The absence altogether of a national executive under the Articles provided a second demonstration of need. Executive duties were vested in the Confederation Congress itself. "In the early days of its existence Congress attempted to pass on everything while acting as a corporate whole," Charles Thach explained over 100 years ago. "Having reached a decision, it entrusted its execution to whatever agency seemed at the moment most convenient, perhaps a committee of its own membership . . . . There was neither plan nor organization. Congress was primarily itself the executive, the administrator."[29] Congress routinely busied itself with unnecessary details and meddled with nonlegislative business. "It is common knowledge that this system failed, and failed lamentably," Thach observed. "Inefficiency and waste, if not downright peculation and corruption, were as sure to follow as the night the day. In the wake of the inefficiency came discontent, a discontent which seized upon certain features of the system as the causes of the general administrative debacle, and demanded reformation."[30] Among the generally suggested reforms were separating execution from the work of Congress, departmental integration, and unitary control at the head.[31]

5.2 THE CONSTITUTIONAL CONVENTION

It is not surprising that the Constitutional Convention settled on a separate and unitary executive department. The Convention did not settle on this course immediately. In the opening debate, James Wilson and Charles Pinckney moved that the executive consist in a single person. John Rutledge argued that a single executive "would feel the greatest responsibility and administer the public affairs best," although, importantly, he was against giving the executive the historically royal prerogatives of war and peace.[32] Wilson also "preferred a single magistrate, as giving most energy dispatch and responsibility to the office," and generalized the point about royal powers; he "did not consider the Prerogatives of the British Monarch as a proper guide in defining the Executive powers."[33] Despite these assurances, Edmund Randolph argued that he opposed unity in the executive because "[h]e regarded it as the foetus of monarchy."[34]

James Madison then proposed to "fix the extent of Executive authority" – to settle on the executive's powers – before "determining how far" such powers "might be safely entrusted to a single officer."[35] He moved and the Convention subsequently agreed that the executive have "power to carry into effect[] the national laws [and] to appoint to offices in cases not otherwise provided for."[36] This statement will become particularly relevant: It suggests that "the executive power" was understood to be only the power to execute law.

A few days later, the Convention resumed the question of a single executive and voted in favor, seven states to three.[37] Wilson was reassuring: "All know that a single magistrate is not a King."[38] In addition to the "vigor" that a single magistrate would bring, it would avoid the "uncontrouled, continued, & violent animosities" that would occur among multiple executives sharing power.[39] Roger Sherman pointed out that at least in the states, the constitutions affixed councils to the governors; but Wilson argued that a council would obscure responsibility and give cover for malpractices.[40] Elbridge Gerry added that a three-member executive would be like "a general with three heads," which would be "extremely inconvenient in many instances, particularly in military matters."[41] That appears to have clinched the argument, and the delegates then voted in favor of unity.

One might summarize the proceedings: The President was not to have the prerogative powers of the king. At least, those powers were not to serve as a guide. And if the President's only power was to oversee the execution of the law and to appoint officers to assist in that task, the people could safely entrust the President with the necessary energy.

Nevertheless, delegates continued to worry about the potential for this energetic, unitary executive to develop into a monarchy. These worries manifested in the discussion over a veto power. After having voted for a unitary executive, the delegates granted the President a qualified veto over legislation subject to congressional override, as opposed to the absolute but rarely used veto of the British monarch.[42] Several delegates argued against an absolute veto, again highlighting the risk that a unitary executive could develop into monarchy. Pierce Butler observed that he had favored unity in the executive but would have changed his vote if he had known an absolute veto would be granted. "It had been observed that in all countries the Executive power is in a constant course of increase."[43] George Mason similarly warned that an absolute veto combined in the hands of a sole magistrate would "pave the way to hereditary Monarchy."[44] Benjamin Franklin delivered the more famous warning, gesturing toward George Washington, who was presiding over the Convention: "The first man, put at the helm will be a good one. No body knows what sort may come afterwards. The Executive will be always increasing here, as elsewhere, till it ends in a monarchy."[45] The Convention voted in favor of a qualified veto subject to congressional override rather than an absolute veto.

There was one other question related to the executive that absorbed much of the delegates' time: the mode of selection. The delegates rejected selection by state executives, worrying that that would favor the powerful, big-state governors.[46] Despite exhortations by Wilson, Madison, and Morris in favor of popular election,[47] several delegates also worried about direct election by the people. Elbridge Gerry, who already had warned of the "excess of democracy," did not trust the people "to act directly" because they were "too little informed of personal characters in large districts, and liable to deceptions."[48] Roger Sherman agreed that the people "will never be sufficiently informed of characters."[49] George Mason more colorfully asserted that "it would be as unnatural to refer the choice of a proper character for chief Magistrate to the people, as it would, to refer a trial of colours to a blind man"; he thought "[t]he extent of the Country renders it impossible that the people can have the requisite capacity to judge of the respective pretensions of the Candidates."[50]

Thus, time and again the delegates voted in favor of appointment by the national legislature.[51] However, the problems with such a mode became apparent when discussing reeligibility. If the executive were to be reappointable by the legislature, the obvious consequence would be obsequiousness to the legislative will. That would result in still more power gravitating toward the impetuous legislative vortex. Several members of the Convention, exasperated, suggested a lifetime appointment if the choice remained with the legislature.[52]

The eventual solution was the electoral college. This mechanism solved several problems. It was not a direct election by the people, nor an election by the legislature. Although it should be mentioned that state electors never thwarted the popular will by choosing someone other than the choice of a state's voters, at least some of the Framers expected the possibility of an interposition between the electors and the people as an additional safeguard against tyranny. As Hamilton defended the system in The Federalist, "It was desirable that the sense of the people should operate in the choice of the person to whom so important a trust was to be confided," but "[i]t was equally desirable, that the immediate election should be made by men most capable of analyzing the qualities adapted to the station, and acting under circumstances favorable to deliberation."[53] Although the legislature was left out of this process altogether, it would still have a say in holding the President accountable through the possibility of impeachment.[54]

The electoral college solved an additional problem: If there had been a direct popular election, the different suffrage rules in the different states posed a serious obstacle. Madison, who came from slaveholding Virginia, pointed out that a national popular election would advantage the northern states where more people could vote.[55] Without an electoral college today, any state could increase its voting power in national elections by allowing sixteen-year-olds to vote. The electoral college was an ingenious solution: The states themselves would decide their suffrage rules, but that would not affect their votes in the electoral college, which was to be determined by population. (Even today, one can therefore be in favor of lowering the voting age in particular states or abolishing the electoral college, but not both.) No one disputed the brilliance of the electoral college solution. "The mode of appointment of the Chief Magistrate of the United States," Hamilton began *Federalist* No. 68, "is almost the only part of the system, of any consequence, which has escaped without severe censure or which has received the slightest mark of approbation from its opponents."[56]

That is where matters stood, more or less, when the Committee of Detail began the task of drafting the Constitution.[57] The Committee's work is important for assessing the scope of the President's powers. The delegates had decided to fix the extent of the President's authority before deciding on unity; and they determined that the only powers the executive should have were to carry into effect the national laws and to appoint officers to assist in that function. When the Committee of Detail produced its draft, however, the President had several additional powers; the reader will also recall that the Committee enumerated Congress's powers despite the sixth resolution of the Virginia Plan. It is now easy to see why. It is one thing to vest Congress with the legislative power, the President with the executive power to carry law into execution, and the courts with judicial power to adjudicate cases under existing law. But what was to be done with the historically royal prerogatives, such as those over war and peace, raising and regulating fleets and armies, regulating coin and commerce, and the like?

Particularly because many of these prerogatives were not obviously executive in nature – as Wilson said, the prerogatives were not a proper guide to executive power – these historic powers had to be enumerated and assigned somewhere. The Constitution assigns almost all of them to Congress. That may explain the enumeration, which, as noted previously, may have resulted more from a desire to check executive power than to curb the power of the states. The draft then also limited in various ways those prerogatives assigned to the President, for example, allowing the President to adjourn Congress only if the two houses could not agree on the matter. And it authorized the President to issue pardons, but not in cases of impeachment; and eventually the treaty and appointment powers would be shared with the Senate. This strongly suggests that the Committee was faithful to the Convention's desire carefully to circumscribe the President's powers precisely because the President was to be a sole magistrate.

5.3 "AS FAR AS REPUBLICAN PRINCIPLES WILL ADMIT"

To summarize the problem at hand, and the Convention's solution: Energy in the executive was of paramount importance. As Morris had argued, an extensive republic could not long persist without an executive power with sufficient energy to pervade throughout. The examples of weak state governors and a central government without an independent executive were stark demonstrations. That is why the Convention adopted an independent and unitary executive with minimal dissent. The problem with unity, however, was that it risked devolving into tyranny; a unitary executive was "the foetus of monarchy."[58] A unitary executive is not necessarily a monarch, but has the potential to develop into one.

The question thus became, how was the Convention to keep a unitary executive from becoming a monarch?[59] The task, as Alexander Hamilton put it in both the Convention and The Federalist, was to give energy to the executive, but only "as far as republican principles will admit."[60] Or as Madison said after he observed the excesses of legislatures, "The preservation of Republican Govt. therefore required some expedient" to check the legislature, but "required evidently at the same time that in devising" such a check "the genuine principles of that form should be kept in view."[61] One recalls Madison's similar statement in *Federalist* No. 10: The problem the Convention addressed overall was how to create "a republican remedy for the diseases most incident to republican government."[62] Here, unity in the executive was one important remedy; but the executive itself had to remain republican in form. This was to be accomplished through the mode of selection and through carefully circumscribing the President's powers.

5.4 VESTING CLAUSE (I): CROSS-REFERENCE THEORY

To return to the question with which this chapter began, and which may now be seen in a new light: The first clause of Article II does not provide that all "executive powers herein granted" shall be vested in a President, but only the singular "executive power." Yet, there is a subsequent enumeration of presidential powers elsewhere in Article II. The first paragraph of the second section grants powers the President can exercise unilaterally; the second paragraph those the President must share with the Senate (to make treaties and appointments); and the third section delineates various presidential duties, and responsibilities toward Congress. There are at least three ways to interpret the clause and the scope of power that it confers in light of the enumeration.[63]

The first, "cross-reference" theory maintains that the Executive Vesting Clause simply establishes who is to exercise the subsequently enumerated executive powers and is not a substantive grant of power at all. Justice Robert Jackson advanced this view in a famous concurrence in the *Youngstown* steel seizure case, examined in Chapter 8: "I cannot accept the view that [the executive power] clause is a grant in bulk of all conceivable executive power but regard it as an allocation to the presidential office of the generic powers thereafter stated."[64] The cross-reference theory remains the most prominent view in the academy.[65] The view makes a great deal of sense. The subsequent enumeration of presidential powers would not be superfluous. And it appears to be how James Wilson intended all of the vesting clauses to operate in his draft for the Committee of Detail.[66]

The cross-reference theory does not fit the data perfectly, however, for two reasons. First, if Article II's Vesting Clause merely identifies who is to exercise the subsequently granted powers, then the Take Care Clause – the President "shall take care that the laws be faithfully executed" – must be a grant of power to execute the laws. But that clause is framed as a duty and not a power. It is not implausible to think that a duty implies the necessary power; James Madison made the point in the famous removal power debates discussed in the next chapter. Still, the clause reads more like a limitation on power, a limitation on how the laws are to be executed. It suggests that that power comes from somewhere else.

Second, the Vesting Clause in Article III – "The judicial Power of the United States, shall be vested in one supreme Court, and in such inferior courts as the Congress may from time to time ordain and establish" – is formulated in the same manner as the parallel clause in Article II. And some scholars have argued that Article III's clause must be a grant of substantive power to judges. Otherwise, it is not clear what else in that article would allow judges to exercise any powers at all.[67]

An astute former student of this author has observed, however, that legal dictionaries defined "jurisdiction" to be "an authority or power" to act.[68] For example, Giles Jacob's law dictionary – the reader will recall it was the most prominent law dictionary at the Founding[69] – defined jurisdiction as "an authority or power, which a man hath to do justice in causes of complaint brought before him."[70] Article III does grant the Supreme Court "original jurisdiction" in certain cases and "appellate jurisdiction" in others, implying that if Congress creates inferior courts those courts will have original jurisdiction. Still, the power of the inferior courts would derive from this implication, and it is more natural to read "judicial power" as giving authority to both the supreme and inferior courts; the subsequent jurisdictional division simply further allocates that authority. To be sure, James Wilson's draft for the Committee of Detail supports the argument that the judiciary was to have power through grants of "jurisdiction."[71] But the language was changed by the Committee of Style, perhaps because Gouverneur Morris understood each of the relevant vesting clauses to grant power.[72]

Whatever one thinks of the arguments for or against the cross-reference theory, there is significant evidence that prominent Americans soon after adoption of the Constitution understood "the executive power" to be a substantive grant of authority. In their pseudonymous debates over the President's foreign policy power, examined in Chapter 9, both James Madison and Alexander Hamilton assumed it was a substantive grant of power although they disagreed over its scope.[73]

5.5 VESTING CLAUSE (II): RESIDUUM THEORY

The prevailing view among originalists may be termed the "residuum" or "residual" theory. According to this view, Article II's Vesting Clause is a substantive grant of power, and a relatively broad grant. It vests all executive-type powers in the President, including those traditionally exercised by the British monarch. The subsequent enumeration in Article II – and elsewhere in the Constitution – is then largely a limitation on the President's ability to exercise specific executive powers, or perhaps a confirmation of them.[74]

Michael W. McConnell explains the view as follows: The Vesting Clause "vests all national powers of an executive nature in the President, except for that portion of the executive power that is vested elsewhere (mostly in Congress in Article I, Section 8), and except for the limitations and qualifications on the particular executive powers that are set forth in the text."[75] Article I, for example, assigns a number of traditionally royal prerogative powers to Congress, such as the powers to declare war, issue letters of marque, coin money, and regulate fleets and armies; as discussed in Chapter 3, these powers all appear as royal prerogatives in English legal treatises. Article II assigns some of this "executive" power (over treaties and appointments) to the President and the Senate together. And historically, the king could prorogue Parliament,[76] but the American President may only adjourn Congress in the event of a disagreement between the two houses.

It is sometimes thought this theory makes the Take Care Clause superfluous. As suggested earlier, however, the Take Care Clause is framed as a duty, not a power; thus, it could still serve as a limitation on the President's exercise of the law-execution power, which itself derives from the opening grant. The President must carry the laws into execution in a particular way, namely, faithfully. This requirement may have been intended to address the historically royal prerogatives of "suspending" the laws altogether for a period of time, or "dispensing" with it on particular occasions by authorizing actions that would otherwise violate the law.[77] The Stuart monarchs, unsurprisingly, abused this power.[78] The Declaration of Rights of 1689, and subsequently the Bill of Rights of 1689, provided "[t]hat the pretended power of suspending the laws or the execution of laws by regal authority" and "the pretended power of dispensing with laws or the execution of laws by regal authority" were "illegal."[79] Blackstone summarized these provisions in his *Commentaries*: "[T]he suspending or dispensing with laws by regal authority, without consent of parliament, is illegal."[80] McConnell has observed that after the American Revolution, three states, Virginia, Delaware, and Vermont, explicitly rejected these prerogatives in their constitutions.[81]

It seems likely that the Take Care Clause, which borrowed from some other state constitutions, was intended to negate the suspending and dispensing powers. There is no definitive proof. In the Constitutional Convention, the delegates resoundingly rejected a power to suspend laws even for a brief period in lieu of a veto power. After rejecting the absolute veto, but before approving the qualified veto, Pierce Butler moved "that the National Executive have a power to suspend any legislative act for the term of _____."[82] Only Elbridge Gerry made a comment: "a power of suspending might do all the mischief dreaded from the negative [veto] of useful laws;

without answering the salutary purpose of checking unjust or unwise ones."[83] All ten states represented at the Convention then voted resoundingly to reject "this suspending power."

One cannot read too much into this episode because this power was proposed instead of a veto; it appears that the proposal would have allowed the President to suspend any legislative act only upon its initial enactment. It was likely rejected because a qualified veto better served the Convention's purposes. But it does suggest the delegates would have been cautious of allowing the President to suspend laws; if the President had such a general power, presumably that would include precisely the more limited suspending power that was rejected. The Convention's rejection of the lesser power to suspend temporarily when legislation is enacted would seem to be a rejection of the greater power to suspend more generally. The grant of a qualified veto power to the President was a determination that the President was not to have a suspending power at all; the only power to stop the operation of congressional laws was to be the qualified veto. The Take Care Clause bolsters that interpretation.[84]

The intuitive appeal of the residuum theory is that it can account for several actions that presidents have undertaken whose source of power is thought to be difficult to locate in the Constitution. As McConnell writes in defense of this theory, "it would be impossible to conduct foreign policy" with only the Constitution's three specifically enumerated foreign affairs powers.[85] Elsewhere, he writes that Article II is "silent" about "all the other foreign affairs powers such as entering international agreements, supporting or opposing foreign insurrections, forming or breaking alliances, voting in bodies like the United Nations, recognizing foreign regimes, locating embassies, or abrogating treaties[.]"[86] Louis Henkin similarly argued that many foreign affairs powers are "missing" from the Constitution, which was "laconic" on the question of foreign policy.[87] The proponents of the residuum theory argue that the Vesting Clause can accommodate these missing powers.[88]

This theory raises a whole set of questions, many of which Chapter 9 will revisit. But for now, two points of skepticism. The first is that, even on the assumption that many foreign affairs powers are "missing," it is unclear why the President would get to exercise the balance of such powers. As John Hart Ely observed, "[V]irtually every substantive constitutional power touching on foreign affairs is vested in Congress," and therefore "[t]he Constitution gives the president no general right to make foreign policy."[89] And Edward Corwin observed years earlier that although there may be "unallocated" foreign affairs powers, the Constitution leaves it to Congress and the President "to struggle for the privilege of directing American foreign policy."[90]

The second point, defended also in Chapter 9 in more detail, is that many foreign affairs powers are not in fact missing. For example, the power to "make treaties" presumably included the power to "treat" with foreign nations.[91] And as the Convention delegates were debating the Committee of Detail draft, which at that point had given the Senate the power over treaties and ambassadorial appointments,[92] Charles Pinckney observed that "the Senate is to have the power of making treaties & managing our foreign affairs."[93] Apparently, the power to appoint ambassadors and to make treaties was all that was believed necessary for "managing foreign affairs." That would be consistent with Blackstone's *Commentaries*, which listed the "principal prerogatives of the king, respecting" Britain's "intercourse with foreign nations," each one of which was assigned somewhere in the Constitution.[94]

To be sure, not all actions presidents have undertaken can be explained under this account of the various foreign affairs prerogatives. But maybe those actions were unconstitutional. Scholars have a tendency to justify much presidential action that otherwise little coheres with the constitutional text. In any event, if many of the foreign affairs powers are not missing, the differences between the residuum view and the other possible theories of executive power greatly diminish.

5.6 VESTING CLAUSE (III): LAW-EXECUTION THEORY

The third theory is that "the executive power" simply meant the power to execute law. On this account, the Executive Vesting Clause is a substantive grant of power, but a single power: to carry into execution the national laws. The source of power for other presidential actions would have to be found in other clauses, such as the Commander-in-Chief Clause or the power to make treaties. On this account, the Take Care Clause does the same work it does under the residuum theory: It is a limitation on how the President is to carry laws into execution.

There is much to commend this view. Start with the Constitutional Convention. Before voting on executive unity, the delegates resolved that the only powers the President should have were "to carry into effect[] the national laws[and] to appoint to offices in cases not otherwise provided for."[95] A residual grant of power, particularly if many executive powers are otherwise "missing," would go plainly beyond that decision. McConnell openly acknowledges that on his understanding, the Committee of Detail audaciously exceeded its authority. "On the one hand," he writes, "the Committee jettisoned the Convention's general authorization for Congress to 'legislate in all cases for the general interests of the Union' in favor of a specific and exclusive enumeration of legislative powers"; on the other hand, it "augmented what had been a narrow and exclusive enumeration of presidential powers by adding a general grant of 'the Executive Power of the United States.'"[96] Yet, if "the executive power" is merely a power to carry law into execution, then the Committee did not exceed the Convention's instruction at all.

John Locke and William Blackstone, two critical influences on the Founders, further support the law-execution view.[97] Locke described an "executive power" in the domestic sphere and a "federative" power in the foreign sphere. After discussing the legislative power, Locke wrote that because the laws "need a perpetual Execution, ... [it is] necessary there should be a Power always in being, which should see to the Execution of the Laws that are made, and remain in force. And thus the Legislative and Executive Power come often to be separated."[98] Here, "the executive power" is defined as "the execution of the laws that are made." Locke then wrote that there was "another" power involving the relations between members of one political community and those of another; "[t]his therefore contains the Power of War and Peace, Leagues and Alliances, and all the Transactions, with all Persons and Communities without the Commonwealth, and may be called Federative, if any one pleases."[99]

Locke explained that although "[t]hese two Powers, Executive and Federative," are "really distinct in themselves, . . . they are always almost united" in a single person because both require "the force of the Society for their exercise."[100] Saikrishna Prakash and Michael Ramsey write of Locke's discussion that "[a]lthough the powers were distinct as a theoretical matter, Locke could cite the powers interchangeably, because he had stated that they were inseparable."[101] Yet, some of the specific powers that Locke described as federative – war and peace and leagues and alliances – were distinctly given to Congress or the Senate in coordination with the President. The Framers rejected Locke's very proposition that these powers are "always almost united" in a single magistrate; decisions to go to war and to enter into treaties require just as much policymaking, if not more policymaking, than they require the application of any force. Hence James Wilson in the Constitutional Convention observed that "the great qualities in the several parts of the Executive are vigor and dispatch," but "[m]aking peace and war are generally determined by Writers on the Laws of Nations to be legislative powers."[102]

Instead of treating Locke's executive and federative powers as united in a single person, then, the Framers appear to have maintained the distinction and assigned the bundle of federative powers away from the chief magistrate. Or, as John Harrison has put it, "The strongest indication that the Constitution does not employ Locke's typology is that it vests three powers, [the legislative, executive, and judicial,] not four."[103] It excludes the federative power.

As for Blackstone, when he turned to the second part of the king's prerogatives "which invest . . . our sovereign lord . . . with a number of authorities and powers; in the exertion whereof consists the executive part of government,"[104] he described powers that almost all appear somewhere in the Constitution. These powers dealt either with "th[e] nation's intercourse with foreign nations, or it's own domestic government and civil polity."[105] Blackstone then described the executive power of the laws as a subset of these various powers. Although the king has "the whole executive power of the laws, it is impossible, as well as improper, that he should personally carry into execution this great and extensive trust," and so "courts should be erected, to assist him in executing this power."[106]

The case should not be overstated. There is evidence to suggest that "the executive power" included more than merely the power to execute law.[107] But it bears repeating that the various federative powers were largely assigned to Congress or otherwise specifically enumerated, leaving only Locke's "executive power" in the hands of the President by virtue of Article II's opening grant. That would also have been consistent with the Convention's instruction.[108]

5.7 CONCLUSION

The law-execution account makes sense of the three vesting clauses together. Congress is granted the legislative power to make laws, relating to the subjects in the eighth section of the first article of the Constitution. The President then has the executive power to carry those laws into execution. There is no need to say "herein granted" because the President can only execute such laws as Congress enacts; and Congress is limited to legislative powers "herein granted." The judicial power, examined in more detail later in this study, is the power to apply those same laws to resolve existing disputes. Every other power of government, such as the power to pardon or of military command, is given separately and specifically.

Treating each of the three major powers as a single function is logical and appears to be the way some prominent individuals used the terms.[109] As Montesquieu wrote, "All would be lost if the same man or the same body of principal men ... exercised these three powers: that of making the laws, that of executing public resolutions, and that of judging the crimes or the disputes of individuals."[110] It seems likely that the Constitution deploys each power in the opening grants of the first three articles in the sense of its respective function: the power to make law, to execute the law, or to adjudicate disputes under the law.

The differences among these accounts of executive power should not, however, be overstated. The more robust view one has of the President's own enumerated powers, the less significant the difference becomes between the residuum theory of executive power and the other theories. And the more robust view one has of congressional prerogatives, the less will be left in the residuum of presidential powers. Perhaps not too much rides on the question. The reader can decide whether these differences matter after analyzing the President's textually enumerated prerogatives – and Congress's related prerogatives – over law execution, foreign affairs, and war and peace. That is the project of the next several chapters.

6

Overseeing Law Execution

Whatever the scope of the grant of "the executive power," all agree that by virtue of either the Vesting Clause or the Take Care Clause the President has the power to oversee the execution of the national laws. Judges and scholars disagree over just how much control the President must have over the other officers of the government, including whether the President has a constitutional power to remove them. That power is not explicitly mentioned in the Constitution. In 1789, Congress debated the question and appears to have concluded that the power to remove at least principal officers belonged to the President as a matter of constitutional right.

Some scholars have contested this interpretation of those debates and argue that Congress has discretion to grant or structure the removal power. Since 1887, Congress has created many so-called independent agencies, such as the Federal Trade Commission and Securities and Exchange Commission, whose commissioners are removable only "for cause." The idea behind the creation of such agencies is that the President should not be able to control the exercise of their discretion or to fire their administrators merely for disagreeing on matters of policy. This and the next chapter explore these questions about the President's role in administration.

There are two prevailing understandings of the President's constitutional power to execute the laws.[1] The more formalist, originalist academics argue that any time Congress vests duties in subordinate officers, the President has a constitutional right to direct those officers in the exercise of their duties and can fire them for insubordination. This view is misleadingly called "unitary executive theory."[2] It is often thought to create some puzzles. The most prominent has to do with the Opinions Cause, the clause in Article II that provides that the President "may require the Opinion, in writing, of the principal Officer in each of the executive Departments, upon any Subject relating to the Duties of their respective Offices."[3] Many have observed that if the President can control officers in the exercise of their duties by virtue of the second article's opening grant, presumably that includes the power to obtain information from them relating to those duties.[4]

The second prevailing conception of executive power, favored by more progressive scholars and judges, maintains that the President has the constitutional right neither to direct and control nor to remove officers; at least, Congress can structure the executive branch under the Necessary and Proper Clause to limit the President's ability to do either.[5] The Supreme Court partly adopted this view in 1935 when approving independent agencies.[6] The proponents of this view take the political scientist Richard Neustadt's memorable phrase that the President's power is merely the "power to persuade," and elevate it to constitutional status.[7] The President can do no more than "offer advice."[8] The problem with this "persuader-in-chief" conception of executive power, however, is that there is no historical support for it.

These next two chapters will recover another conception of executive power, remarkably consistent with the historical record, that has been lost. According to this conception, absent statutory language to the contrary, the President has no constitutional right directly to interfere with the duties Congress vests in subordinate officers; but the President always has the right to demand information about those duties and the right to remove the officers. The distinction between direction and removal may seem trivial, but it has real political and structural bite. And it appears to have been the view shared by many early presidents.

Edward Corwin observed several decades ago that an "unqualified" adoption of either of the two standard accounts of presidential power "would invite startling results." If one adopts the formalist position, that "would make all questions of law enforcement questions of discretion, the discretion moreover of an independent and legally uncontrollable branch of the government." Such a view "would render it impossible for Congress ... to leave anything to the specially trained judgment of a subordinate executive official with any assurance that his discretion would not be perverted to political ends for the advantage of the administration in power." Yet, an unqualified adoption of the persuader-in-chief view "would hold out consequences equally unwelcome," allowing Congress to "divide and transfer" control of law execution into a "parliamentary despotism."[9] An account of executive power that distinguishes control and removal solves the dilemma Corwin posed.

There is much ground to cover. This chapter addresses whether the President has a right to execute the laws personally; how the power of appointment was an essential component of the power to execute law and how the Constitution's Appointments Clause works; how the power to remove was understood to be an incident of the power to appoint; how the First Congress resolved the question of the President's removal power in 1789; and how inferior officers fit within this scheme. Chapter 7 then addresses the rise of the modern administrative state, the use of "for-cause" removal restrictions, and the President's ability to direct and control administrative discretion.

6.1 PERSONAL EXECUTION

There is little question the Framers expected the President to superintend the execution of the laws. It was not expected, however, that the President would personally execute them. The President's duty to "take care that the laws be faithfully executed" was a recognition that other officers would do most of the execution. When writers spoke of this clause, or of the importance of unity in the person charged with executing the laws, they tended to confirm that the relevant power was to "superintend" or "see to" law execution.

At the Virginia ratifying convention, for example, Edmund Randolph said the President was vested with an uncontroversial prerogative: "[t]o see the laws executed," a power that "every Executive in America has."[10] James Wilson said in the Pennsylvania ratifying convention that a power "of no small magnitude" with which the President was entrusted was the power to "take care that the laws be faithfully executed."[11] William McClaine of North Carolina similarly explained that the President's power was to "take[] care to see the laws faithfully executed."[12] James Iredell said in the North Carolina ratifying convention: "The office of superintending the execution of the laws of the Union is an office of the utmost importance."[13] And in Charles Pinckney's speech on the draft constitution, Pinckney argued that the President was empowered when necessary "to inspect" the various executive departments "as a check upon those Officers." The President would keep them "attentive to their duty," "prevent[] and correct[] errors," and "detect[] and punish[] mal-practices."[14] Most of these speakers suggested the power to execute derived from the take care duty rather than the opening clause of Article II.[15]

That seems to have been the view across the board. The Anti-Federalist writer Federal Farmer wrote that in every state "the execution of" the laws was left "to the direction and care of one man," because one man "seems to be peculiarly well circumstanced to superintend the execution of laws with discernment and decision, with promptitude and uniformity."[16] Here, the power was described as the power to "superintend." And even Hamilton, one of the greatest proponents of executive power, described that power as one of superintendence. Officers to whom "different matters are committed" – implying it is they who must exercise discretion left to them by law – "ought to be considered as the assistants or deputies of the Chief Magistrate, and on this account, they ought to derive their offices from his appointment, at least from his nomination, and ought to be subject to his superintendence."[17] It would seem that most knowledgeable American lawyers understood that the President would not have the power to execute the law personally, at least not without congressional authorization. The President's power was one of superintendence.

That understanding was consistent with English practice. In 1607 or 1608, King James I asserted the power personally to sit in judgment of judicial cases at a time when the judicial power was still part of the executive power. James summoned the common law judges for their opinions, and, though it is not entirely clear what transpired, Sir Edward Coke wrote an account of the encounter published posthumously in 1656. In what he described as the "Case of Prohibitions of the King," Coke reported that "the Judges informed the King, that no King after the [Norman]

Conquest [of 1066] assumed to himself to give any judgment in any cause whatso-ever, which concerned the administration of justice within this realm, but these were solely determined in the courts of justice."[18]

It is likely that this confrontation helped lead to the Act of Settlement of 1701, which provided that the commission of judges shall be *quamdiu se bene gesserint*, "during good behavior."[19] That Act effectively separated the judicial power – the power to adjudicate the kinds of cases that Coke described, namely, the power to divest a subject of life, liberty, or property – from the more general executive power. But the point is nevertheless that the executive could not personally sit in execution of the laws, at least not in the kinds of cases that have since been understood to be judicial in nature.

Coke broadened the point to other components of executive power. He explained that the king could not personally arrest anyone: "[T]he King cannot arrest any man ... for the party cannot have remedy against the King."[20] Because the king enjoyed sovereign immunity and could do no wrong, there was no recourse against him if he made a wrongful arrest. The king's officers executed the laws in his stead; they could do wrong and against them legal remedies did exist. These principles remained so ingrained in the eighteenth century that Blackstone wrote that it was not only impossible but also "improper" that the monarch "should personally carry into execution" what he described as "the executive power of the laws."[21]

None of this is to say that Congress cannot assign duties to the President directly, which it has done on many occasions. But there is unlikely to be a right of personal execution in the absence of such statutory authority.[22] What is more, the general doctrine in American constitutional law is that even when Congress delegates authority to the President personally, the President may subdelegate that power to the appropriate subordinate officer unless Congress has prohibited doing so.[23]

6.2 APPOINTMENTS BEFORE THE CONSTITUTION

If the President cannot personally execute the law, how then to carry into effect the national laws? How did the king do so if he could not personally carry them into execution? The answer is that the executive power included the authority to appoint subordinate officers to assist with the task. Even if the President could personally execute the laws, this power would still have been essential. As Representative Fisher Ames said in 1789, "[C]ould [the President] personally execute all the laws, there would be no occasion for establishing auxiliaries; but the circumscribed powers of human nature in one man, demand the aid of others." The President "must therefore have assistants."[24]

Certainly, the English monarch had this power. Blackstone wrote that although "the constitution of the kingdom hath entrusted [the king] with the whole executive power of the laws, it is impossible, as well as improper, that he should personally carry into execution this great and extensive trust." It was "necessary, that courts should be erected, to assist him in executing this power."[25] The king nominated the judges.[26] As to "officers," Blackstone wrote that "the law supposes, that no one can be so good a judge of their several merits and services, as the king himself who employs them," from which principle "arises the prerogative of erecting and disposing of offices."[27] Charles I had argued that "[h]e cannot perform the Oath of protecting His people if He abandon" the appointment power, "and assume others into it."[28]

In the 1782 edition of his popular law dictionary, and in editions dating back at least to 1736, Giles Jacob wrote that the king "names, creates, makes and removes the great officers of the government."[29] He wrote an identical passage in his popular treatise *Every Man His Own Lawyer*.[30] In another treatise, he wrote that the king "hath alone the Choice and Nomination of all Commanders, and other Officers at Land and Sea, the Nomination of all Magistrates, Counsellors, and Officers of State."[31] The power of appointing was part and parcel of the executive power.

The same was true in America. Julian Mortenson has canvassed numerous early American sources to conclude that "the executive power was often viewed as either logically entailing or functionally implying the appointment of 'assistances.'"[32] For example, George Mason thought that the Senate should have no role in "the appointment of publick officers" because it was an executive power.[33] James Wilson thought similarly: "there can be no good Executive without a responsible appointment of officers to execute."[34] In the Constitutional Convention, Wilson and Madison both argued that the "extent of the Executive authority" was the "power to carry into effect[] the national laws" and "to appoint to offices in cases not otherwise provided for."[35] The Anti-Federalists agreed. Hampden wrote that "the most important and most influential portion of the executive power" was "the appointment of all officers."[36] Brutus, Centinel, and Richard Henry Lee, among others, made similar points.[37] As did Publius: "the appointment to offices . . . is in its nature an executive function."[38] For an executive that could not execute the law personally, the appointing power was essential.

6.3 THE APPOINTMENTS CLAUSE

A broad appointment power, and certainly a broad power of office creation, could easily lead to abuses. The Declaration of Independence alleged that the king had "erected a multitude of New Offices, and sent hither swarms of Officers to harrass our people, and eat out their substance." Royal governors did the same; offices were the greatest source of patronage and influence. "With the unforeseen and prodigious multiplication of offices, places, favors, and perquisites," Gordon Wood has written, it appeared by the eighteenth century that the Crown "had been given nothing less than the power to structure the society as it saw fit." And in the colonies, eighteenth-century royal governors "continually sought to use their authority as the source of honor and privilege in the community to build webs of influence."[39] As a result, "Americans in 1776 were resolved to destroy the capacity of their rulers ever again to put together such structures of domination," and they took this power away from the governors acting alone. In most of the revolutionary constitutions, "the appointing power was lodged in the legislatures, either exclusively, or concurrently with the governor."[40]

As with other revolutionary era reforms, the reaction could lead to the other extreme. If the executive is to oversee faithful execution of the laws, that requires the ability to put in place people in whom the executive has confidence. The U.S. Constitution's solution to the problem of either extreme is twofold. First, it assigns to Congress the power to establish offices. The Appointments Clause in the second paragraph of the second section of Article II, quoted in full below, refers to offices "which shall be established by law." Thus, Congress, under the Necessary and Proper Clause, establishes the executive departments.

As for the appointment of persons to those offices, the clause gives the President the appointment power but the Senate a check:

> [The President] shall nominate, and by and with the Advice and Consent of the Senate, shall appoint Ambassadors, other public Ministers and Consuls, Judges of the supreme Court, and all other Officers of the United States, whose Appointments are not herein otherwise provided for, and which shall be established by Law: but the Congress may by Law vest the Appointment of such inferior Officers, as they think proper, in the President alone, in the Courts of Law, or in the Heads of Departments.

The Senate is thus given a check on the appointment of all officers by default, but Congress may choose, by law, to vest the appointment of "inferior officers" in the President alone, the heads of departments (such as the Secretary of Treasury or Defense), or in the courts.

It is important for both appointment and removal purposes to understand the distinction the clause makes between different classes of officers. There are inferior officers whose appointments Congress can choose to vest (for example) in the department head, but whose appointments are otherwise by and with advice and consent of the Senate. Then the clause implies there are non-inferior officers, who must always be appointed by and with advice and consent of the Senate. The courts call such non-inferior officers "principal officers," and so there are two categories of officers, principal and inferior.[41]

Modern doctrine more or less correctly maintains that an inferior officer is one whose work is at some level supervised by another officer under the President.[42] Inferior officer status can be demonstrated if another officer has the ability to fire the officers in question for any reason or to countermand or reverse their decisions.[43] Some officers, such as an army captain or Federal Bureau of Investigation (FBI) agent in the field, will make irreversible decisions; but they can always be fired for failing to follow general directions. Others, such as administrative law judges, are less easily removable, but their decisions are subject to review and reversal by principal officers.[44]

The modern doctrine also distinguishes between officers and non-officers. Only those individuals occupying an ongoing office "established by law," and who exercise "significant authority," are officers subject to the Appointments Clause.[45] Once this significant authority test is met, a court must then decide whether the officer is principal or inferior. The test for distinguishing officers from non-officers is intended to exempt mere "employees" like janitorial staff or typists; they (naturally) do not need to be appointed by the President or a department head.

The test distinguishing non-officers from officers had taken on a life of its own, however, such that it was recently questioned whether administrative law judges are officers of the United States, which they quite evidently are.[46] It also seems likely that at the Founding, any individual exercising government duties of any significance was understood to be an officer who required appointment.[47] That would, for example, include all modern-day agents of the Transportation Security Administration present at American airports. That may seem absurd because it would require the head of the department to appoint all of these agents. It is not absurd, however, because the Secretary can easily approve a slate of preselected individuals. The Secretary would then have one final back-end check. That is precisely how Congress provided for the appointment of steamboat inspectors in the 1852 Steamboat Act, one of the earliest regulatory statutes.[48]

Congress put the Appointments Clause to the test even more dramatically in 2020. In the Horseracing Integrity and Safety Act, Congress purported to empower a private, nonprofit corporation that had incorporated itself under the laws of Delaware as the Horseracing Integrity and Safety Authority to promulgate and enforce rules relating to the national horseracing industry. Even though the Authority's governing board exercised the same governmental powers as any administrative agency, its members were not appointed under the Appointments Clause. Instead, the incorporation documents selected the initial boards, which then could select future boards.

The government astonishingly defended this arrangement by arguing that the Authority was not "established by law," but rather established by their private incorporation documents. Of course, that is absurd. The relevant question is whether the duties of the office are established by law; it is the duties that create the office. If Congress cannot directly appoint an individual to execute a statute – all agree that would violate the Appointments Clause – then Congress cannot appoint a group of individuals to execute that same statute.[49]

6.4 REMOVALS BEFORE THE CONSTITUTION

It cannot seriously be doubted that the President's power, at a minimum, is one of superintending the execution of the laws; that this power includes the right to appoint officers to assist in that task; and that the Constitution modifies this right by giving the Senate a check on its exercise. The more controversial question is whether this power of law execution includes the power to remove officers once appointed.

There is some explicit evidence for that proposition. Giles Jacob's prominent law dictionary stated: The king "names, creates, makes *and removes* the great officers of the government."[50] And Blackstone's chapter on the removal and tenure of inferior officers suggested these removal and tenure protections did not apply to the high officers of state.[51] There is, however, admittedly little direct discussion of the removal power in Founding-era sources; and certainly it was not discussed in the Constitutional Convention. That has led Michael W. McConnell to make the following observation: "The Committee of Detail and the Convention addressed and allocated every other significant royal prerogative, but not the Removal Power. Yet it is hard to see how it could have been neglected; it is crucial to the structure of the executive branch."[52]

There is an explanation. It was widely understood that the power to remove followed from, and was an incident to, the power to appoint. Jed Shugerman has canvassed numerous authorities for the proposition in common law, and even in Roman law. As Shugerman explains, this tradition was "enshrined in Latin" maxims, "[u]numquoque dissolvitur, eodem modo, quo ligatur" and "[c]ujus est instituere ejus abrogate [sic]," translating to "[e]very obligation is dissolved by the same method with which it is created" and "whose right it is to institute, his right it is to abrogate." Shugerman found the former formulation or closely related phrases "in many eighteenth-century legal sources." The latter formulation "is in dozens of eighteenth-century treatises."[53] Other sources provide further support. Dalton's treatise on Justices of the Peace was widely distributed in Founding-era America.[54] It stated as to high constables that "[a]lso in such manner as they are to be chosen, in the same manner, and by the like Authority are they to be removed; for, *eodem modo quo quid constituitur, dissolvitur.*"[55]

This maxim was so well engrained in the law that, in 1779, Thomas Jefferson wrote that "Lawyers know," as to "offices held during will," that "issuing a new commission" terminates the old one.[56] That explains why the power of appointment implied the power to remove; the possessor of the power could always make a new appointment. There are numerous examples from colonial Virginia of the governor-in-council removing individuals in the very commissions appointing new officers.[57] And in 1780, Thomas Jefferson wrote in a private note: "The power of appointing and removing executive officers inherent in Executive. Executive inadequate to every thing. Appoint deputies . . . . He who appoints may remove."[58]

This maxim explains why removal was not mentioned in the Constitutional Convention. When Madison and Wilson and others agreed that the only power strictly executive in nature was the "power to carry into effect[] the national laws" and "to appoint to offices in cases not otherwise provided for," that included removal. That is because one who appoints also removes. The initial drafts of the

Constitution to come out of the Committee of Detail assigned the appointment power over ambassadors and judges of the Supreme Court entirely to the Senate, and the appointment of other officers to the President alone.[59] There was no need to think about removal at all; the Senate, acting alone, would remove ambassadors, and the President, acting alone, would remove other officers. Each could accomplish such removals simply by making new appointments. The appointment power was not shared between President and Senate until the Committee of Postponed Matters altered the appointment provisions in the final days of the Convention on September 4.[60] The delegates had no time to think about the implications that sharing the appointment power might create for removals.

6.5 THE DECISION OF 1789

It was therefore only in the early days of the First Congress, tasked with establishing the first departments of the national government, that the issue arose. The draft statutes creating the departments of foreign affairs, war, and treasury provided for a principal officer to be appointed by and with advice and consent of the Senate, and "to be removable by the President." The House of Representatives first struck the appointment provision as being already provided for in the Constitution itself.[61]

The Representatives then debated the provision "to be removable by the President." Some argued that the principal officers had to be removed by the President with the advice and consent of the Senate, the same way they were appointed (the "senatorial" faction); others that the Constitution vested that power in the President alone (the "presidentialist" group); and still others maintained that Congress in its discretion could delegate that power to the president under the Necessary and Proper Clause (the "congressionalists").[62]

The congressionalist position – the view that Congress could decide that matter under the Necessary and Proper Clause – is problematic for at least two reasons. First, it begs the question at issue. Congress can only pass laws that are necessary and proper for carrying into execution Congress's own powers, or those of another department or officer of the government (such as the President's). One thus has to know whether the President does or does not possess the removal power. If answered in the affirmative, then giving the Senate a veto on that power would be a hindrance to, not in furtherance of, the President's power. And alternatively, if the Constitution requires the Senate and President together to remove, then assigning it to the President alone would be a hindrance to the Senate's powers.

Second, it is not clear where a discretionary veto power would end. Why could Congress give the Senate a role, but not Congress as a whole, or the House, or even a Committee of a House? As James Madison stated in the debates:

> [W]hen I consider, that, if the Legislature has a power, such as is contended for, they may subject and transfer at discretion powers from one department of our Government to another; they may, on that principle, exclude the President

altogether from exercising any authority in the removal of officers; they may give it to the Senate alone, or the President and Senate combined; they may vest it in the whole Congress, or they may reserve it to be exercised by this House. When I consider the consequences of this doctrine, and compare them with the true principles of the Constitution, I own that I cannot subscribe to it.[63]

Madison may have overstated the case: Perhaps placing the removal power either with the Senate or the President, but not with some other institution, could be considered necessary and proper. That would still beg the question and require an analysis of what else the Constitution says about removal. The point is that invoking the Necessary and Proper Clause alone is insufficient to answer the question of which institution possesses the removal power to begin with. Once that question is answered, Congress could perhaps invoke the clause to condition the President's (or the Senate's) exercise of the removal power, for example with for-cause protections for officers. That question is at the heart of the modern administrative state and the status of independent agencies, addressed in Chapter 7.

Taking the congressionalist view off the table leaves the "senatorial" and "presidentialist" camps. The common law maxim sheds light on these alternatives. If ordinarily a removal was effected through a new appointment and commission, the "senatorial" position made good sense; presumably only the Senate and President together can effect a removal through making a new appointment. Madison agreed with this reasoning; or at least he would have. But, he argued, there were other provisions of the Constitution at play. "[T]he power to annul an appointment is, in the nature of things, incidental to the power which makes the appointment," he conceded. "[I]f nothing more was said in the Constitution than that the President, by and with the advice and consent of the Senate, should appoint to office, there would be a great force in saying that the power of removal resulted by natural implication from the power of appointing."[64]

But the Constitution did say more. As Madison pointed out, it included both the Vesting Clause and the Take Care Clause. Madison stated that the duty the latter clause imposed implied that the President "should have that species of power which is necessary to accomplish that end."[65] It seems rather obvious that a legislative veto on the power of removal would interfere with this duty. Although Justice Brandeis argued in dissent in the 1926 case *Myers v. United States* that the President could always suspend the officer pending removal,[66] as did some representatives in 1789,[67] that does not solve the problem if the Senate disagrees with the President on the ultimate removal. That would be giving the Senate the final say over whether the laws have been faithfully executed, a duty the Constitution assigns to the President.

Madison also relied on the Vesting Clause. He explained that "the executive power" was vested in the President, but that the Constitution had assigned some of that power to the Senate. "[T]he Constitution ... declares that the Executive power shall be vested in a President of the United States. The association of the Senate with the President in exercising that particular function, is an exception to this general rule; and exceptions to general rules, I conceive, are ever to be taken strictly."[68] Madison thus argued that all of the executive power not assigned elsewhere belonged to the President. The question according to Madison was therefore, "Is the power of displacing, an Executive power?" "[I]f any power whatsoever is in its nature Executive," he argued, "it is the power of appointing, overseeing, and controlling those who execute the laws."[69] "[I]f any thing in its nature is executive," he added later in the debates, "it must be that power which is employed in superintending and seeing that the laws are faithfully executed."[70]

It is useful to consider the implications of Madison's statements for the different theories of the Vesting Clause. They are sometimes taken as evidence for the residuum theory. That is not correct. There is no indication in these debates that anyone in Congress understood Madison to be referring to the entire suite of royal authorities when he said "the executive power." The discussion was entirely in the context of "appointing, overseeing, and controlling those who execute the laws." That is perfectly consistent with the view that the executive power is the power to execute law, but that that power entails the right to appoint and therefore also to remove officers to assist in that task. A residual grant of executive powers is simply not necessary for the argument.[71]

To summarize Madison's position: The power to remove may follow from the power to appoint, but the power to appoint, and therefore the power to remove, are ultimately incidents of the executive power. And the "association of the Senate with the President in exercising" the appointment function "is an exception to this general rule" that the executive power is vested in the President, which exception does not apply to removal. The Take Care Clause further supports this proposition, implying the President has the power "necessary to accomplish" the duty of faithful execution. A senatorial veto would interfere with that duty.

With the various arguments on the table, the House of Representatives devoted over five full days of debate to the question. After the first day, a majority agreed to retain the clause that the principal officer would be "removable by the President,"[72] and further rejected a proposal to include the modifying phrase "by and with the advice and consent of the senate."[73] After the fifth day, the House altered the bill to ensure that its language would not be construed as a *conferral* of the removal power. The amended provision stated that "whenever the said principal officer shall be removed from office by the President," the departmental papers would then be under the control of the department's clerk.[74] Representative Egbert Benson, the sponsor of this amendment, explained that the alteration was intended "so that the law may be nothing more than a declaration of our sentiments upon the meaning of a Constitutional grant of power to the President."[75] The amendment passed by a vote of 30–18,[76] and the Senate agreed by a vote of 10–10, with Vice President John Adams breaking the tie.[77]

Despite the close nature of the vote in the Senate, Madison thought that Congress's decision on this question, which has come to be known as the "Decision of 1789,"[78] would become the "permanent exposition of the Constitution."[79] Alexander Hamilton and Chief Justice John Marshall wrote that Congress's decision reflected its constitutional interpretation that the removal power was constitutionally vested in the President.[80]

Scholars today continue to debate whether Congress truly resolved the constitutional question in 1789, noting that the final Benson amendment was approved by representatives in both the presidentialist and congressionalist camps.[81] Not even these scholars claim, however, that the senatorial position was correct, even though in some ways that was the most plausible view in light of the common law maxim. Rather, these scholars maintain that Congress has discretion whether to grant the removal power or not. But for the reasons noted earlier – Congress would then be transferring the take care duty away from the President – that cannot possibly be correct (putting aside for now the question of for-cause restrictions). In any event, what matters more than the mere fact of this precedent is the force of the arguments that appear to have carried the day.

6.6 THE REMOVAL OF INFERIOR OFFICERS

The final piece of the Appointments Clause puzzle is whether the President must be able to remove inferior officers. The answer is "no." If Congress chooses to vest the appointment of an inferior officer in the head of department, the head may also remove that inferior officer. That is because the power to remove is incident to the power to appoint; one who appoints also removes, if for no other reason than the ability to make a new appointment. Thus, the "inferior officer exceptions clause" allows Congress to take away the President's power of appointment and removal of inferior officers. The President's overall responsibility, however, stays intact: If the President wishes to remove an inferior officer whose appointment has been vested in the department head, the President may request as much from the latter. The department head could always refuse; but the President could always remove that officer.

Controversial removals have been effected this way throughout American history. In the "Saturday Night Massacre," President Nixon could not simply fire special prosecutor Archibald Cox. He had to demand that his Attorney General fire the special prosecutor. The Attorney General refused, and resigned; the Deputy Attorney General, then acting as Attorney General, also refused and resigned. When President George W. Bush sought to remove a number of United States Attorneys, his Attorney General had to do the firing; the reputational damage to the Attorney General was significant. Thus, the vesting of the appointments of inferior officers in the department heads gives inferior officers some additional degree of insulation from the President. They can be fired, but only through the actions of an additional agent, the department head.

Can such officers be further insulated with civil service protections, that is, with tenure protections that secure them against at-will removal by the department head?

It was decided in the nineteenth century that such protections were constitutional. *United States v. Perkins* (1886) is the leading case for the proposition that Congress can restrict the ability of a head of department to remove an inferior office whose appointment Congress vests in that head of department.[82] The case involved a naval cadet engineer whose services were no longer required; the secretary of the navy thus wrote to the cadet that he was honorably discharged with a year's sea pay, as provided by an act of Congress.[83] The cadet sued for pay subsequently accruing on the ground that he was not lawfully discharged because the statute also provided that no officer in military service could be discharged in peacetime except by a sentence of court-martial.[84]

The Supreme Court ruled for the cadet, holding that Congress's power to vest the appointment in the department head included the power to "limit and restrict the power of removal as it deems best for the public interest."[85] The Court thus rejected the position of the department of navy that the secretary had inherent authority to remove inferior officers at will.

The Court may have erred. If the power to remove is incident to the power to appoint, it seems equally plausible that Congress's power to vest the appointments in the heads of department necessarily brings along with it the power to remove freely. But given the definition of inferior officer, it does not seem to matter whether or not the power to remove is restricted. If Congress protects the inferior officer from at-will removal, that officer's decisions must be subject to review and reversal by a superior officer, or at least that officer must follow orders. No one doubts that the navy cadet had to follow the orders of the secretary, and a refusal would have made the cadet liable for court-martial.

The conclusion that follows is that Congress may restrict the ability of the department head to remove so long as there are adequate alternative means of control. In the modern administrative state, the work of most civil servants – including administrative law judges – are reviewable and reversible by presidentially appointed and removable personnel.[86] To the extent they are not, President Donald Trump's executive order seeking to make all administrative regulations subject to approval by a department head – an executive order that President Joseph Biden revoked – was salutary and may have even been constitutionally compelled.

6.7 *MYERS V. UNITED STATES*

That is how matters stood as of 1926 when the Supreme Court decided *Myers v. United States*.[87] That decision, to which some critical scholars trace the "unitary executive theory," is much maligned in the academy but obviously correct as a matter of text and structure for the reasons explained in this chapter. The case involved a first-class postmaster whom President Woodrow Wilson had removed. The problem was the statute provided that the removal of first-class postmasters was to be with the "advice and consent" of the Senate. Former president and then-Chief Justice William Howard Taft's opinion for the Court held that, because the first-class postmaster was appointed by and with advice and consent of the Senate, the President could remove him at will without senatorial interference.

Taft relied on precedents like *Perkins* to conclude that if Congress vests the appointment of inferior officers in the department heads, then Congress can protect those officers from removal. But unless and until Congress does so, all officers, whether principal or inferior, appointed by and with advice and consent are subject to the President's removal authority. The dissenters' invocation of the Necessary and Proper Clause cannot overcome the arguments noted earlier against the congressionalist position. Whether the officer is principal or inferior, a senatorial veto unconstitutionally transfers the take care duty from the President (and the department heads) to the Senate.

Importantly, Chief Justice Taft did not rely on the residuum theory to arrive at his conclusions. In 1916, ten years before Taft published the opinion in *Myers*, he had published a book on the powers and duties of the President. He argued that Presidents James Garfield and Theodore Roosevelt's "ascribing an undefined residuum of power to the President is an unsafe doctrine and that it might lead under emergencies to results of an arbitrary character."[88] He elaborated on his own view:

> The true view of the Executive function is, as I conceive it, that the President can exercise no power which cannot be fairly and reasonably traced to some specific grant of power or justly implied and included within such express grant as proper and necessary to its exercise. Such specific grant must be either in the Federal Constitution or in an act of Congress passed in pursuance thereof. There is no undefined residuum of power which he can exercise because it seems to him to be in the public interest . . .. The grants of Executive power are necessarily in general terms in order not to embarrass the Executive within the field of action plainly marked for him, but his jurisdiction must be justified and vindicated by affirmative constitutional or statutory provisions, or it does not exist.[89]

Nothing in *Myers* suggests that Taft's views had evolved. Quite the opposite. "The vesting of the executive power in the President was essentially a grant of the power to execute the laws," Taft wrote. "But the President alone and unaided could not execute the laws. He must execute them by the assistance of subordinates. This view has since been repeatedly affirmed by this court."[90] The Court's "conclusion on the merits," Taft summarized, "is that article 2 grants to the President the executive power of the government – i.e., the general administrative control of those executing the laws, including the power of appointment and removal of executive officers – a conclusion confirmed by his obligation to take care that the laws be faithfully executed."[91] These passages were about law execution and do not imply or require a residuum of royal prerogative powers.[92]

6.8 SUMMARY

The basic structure of presidential supervision of the executive branch is relatively clear. Whether the President's power of law execution comes from the Vesting Clause or the Take Care Clause, the President must at a minimum oversee the execution of the laws by others. This must include the ability to remove principal officers without a senatorial veto. Whatever other power the Vesting Clause might grant in terms of law execution authority, a senatorial veto would give the Senate the final say over whether the laws are being faithfully executed. The better understanding of the Vesting Clause is that it grants the President the power to oversee the execution of the laws; that this power necessarily includes the power to appoint and remove assistants; and that the Constitution modifies the appointment power but not the removal power.

As for inferior officers, they too are subject to the President's removal power if appointed by and with advice and consent. But Congress can vest their appointments and removals in the heads of department if it wishes to do so. In that case, the President cannot control or remove them directly, but the department heads can, and the President can always remove the department head. Congress's greater power to vest such appointments and removals in the head of department may perhaps include the power to supply removal protections for the inferior officers. But if so, then Congress must ensure other adequate means of control. Without the ability of the department head to direct the inferior officers or countermand their decisions, such officers would effectively be principal officers who must be appointed by and with advice and consent. The civil service would thus be constitutional, so long as heads of department have adequate means of control.

Several pressing questions remain. If inferior officers can be secured in their tenure because they must in any event follow orders, why can the same not be said of principal officers? Do they not have to obey the President and, if so, can they not be protected from removal? Can Congress condition the President's exercise of the removal power by granting principal officers for-cause removal protections? These are the questions at the heart of the debate over the modern administrative state.

7

The Fourth Branch

Myers v. United States stood, and still stands, for the proposition that the removal power is the President's. The Senate cannot retain a role for itself. But can Congress, while not retaining a role, place restrictions on the President's exercise of that power? The Supreme Court answered that question in the affirmative in *Humphrey's Executor v. United States*,[1] a judicial cornerstone of the modern administrative state. Although the Supreme Court likely erred in *Humphrey's Executor* – and as this book goes to press, the Court appears poised to overturn the decision – Congress may nevertheless have power to establish some degree of agency independence. Such independence is strongly correlated with the bipartisan, multimember structures that Congress has sometimes created. More importantly, Congress's vesting of duties in the commissioners or other administrators also allows for a measure of independence. It turns out that neither prevailing conception of presidential supervision – total control or total balkanization – is constitutionally compelled or even desirable.

7.1 *HUMPHREY'S EXECUTOR*

When Congress created the Federal Trade Commission (FTC), it provided that five commissioners would serve as its head, no more than three of whom could be from the same political party.[2] It provided for staggered, seven-year terms and that "any commissioner may be removed by the President for inefficiency, neglect of duty, or malfeasance in office."[3] The removal power still belonged to the President, but Congress purported to restrict the President's use of that power to specified causes. The idea was that the President should not be able to remove these officers for mere disagreements over policy, so long as the agency acts within the scope of its statutory authority. For example, the FTC Act required the Commission to prohibit "unfair methods of competition in commerce."[4] If the commissioners believed that a particular practice was unfair but the President disagreed, that would not be cause to remove; such a disagreement would not reflect "inefficiency" or "malfeasance."

Nor would it be "neglect of duty" because the agency would be following the statute's commands as it understood them.

President Franklin Roosevelt nevertheless sought to remove a commissioner, whom President Herbert Hoover had appointed, over a mere policy disagreement. "You will," Roosevelt wrote the commissioner, "realize that I do not feel that your mind and my mind go along together on either the policies or the administering of the Federal Trade Commission, and, frankly, I think it is best for the people of this country that I should have a full confidence."[5] Commissioner Humphrey sued for his salary, and the Supreme Court had to decide whether Roosevelt's removal was inconsistent with the statute and, if so, whether the statute was constitutional.

The Court first held that the statute by its terms precluded the President from removing a commissioner for reasons other than those specified in the statute. "The commission is to be non-partisan," the Court reasoned, "and it must, from the very nature of its duties, act with entire impartiality."[6] The "general purposes of the legislation ... demonstrate the Congressional intent to create a body of experts who shall gain experience by length of service – a body which shall be independent of executive authority, except in its selection, and free to exercise its judgment without the leave or hindrance of any other official or any department of the government."[7] Allowing the President to remove for reasons other than the specified causes would defeat Congress's purposes in creating such independence.

The Court held this arrangement constitutional. The Court concluded that the reach of *Myers* affirming the Decision of 1789 "goes far enough to include all purely executive officers," but "goes no farther; – much less does it include an officer who occupies no place in the executive department and who exercises no part of the executive power vested by the Constitution in the President."[8] The presidential removal power was inapplicable to the FTC, which was "an administrative body created by Congress to carry into effect legislative policies embodied in the statute in accordance with the legislative standard therein prescribed, and to perform other specified duties as a legislative or as a judicial aid."[9] Thus, the FTC "acts in part quasi-legislatively and in part quasi-judicially."[10] The Court stated elsewhere, "Its duties are neither political nor executive, but predominantly quasi-judicial and quasi-legislative."[11] In sum, the Court concluded, an unfettered presidential removal power "threatens the independence of a commission, which is not only wholly disconnected from the executive department, but which, as already fully appears, was created by Congress as a means of carrying into operation legislative and judicial powers, and as an agency of the legislative and judicial departments."[12]

Many have observed that the Court's holding is inconsistent with the Constitution's text and structure. As an initial matter, the Court's description of the agency's function as "carry[ing] into effect legislative policies embodied in the statute" would be an apt description of "executive power." The whole Constitutional Convention agreed that the extent of executive authority should be to appoint officers and "to carry into effect the national laws."[13]

More fundamentally, the Constitution recognizes only three types of power: legislative, executive, and judicial. The Constitution also provides specific procedures for the exercise of each of these powers. Only Congress can exercise legislative power, and only through bicameralism and presentment (both House and Senate must agree and the President must sign); only judges with lifetime tenure and salary protections can exercise judicial power (per Article III); and only the President can exercise the executive power, whatever that is. "Formalism," a term occasionally used in this study, stands for the propositions that the Constitution recognizes only three powers, that all government functions can be characterized as one of these powers, and that those powers must be exercised according to the constitutional requirements for each type.

The recognition of new "quasi powers" in *Humphrey's Executor* was inconsistent with this formalist understanding of the Constitution. There is no such thing as legislative-like or judicial-like power that need not be exercised by Congress or the judiciary, but which also is not part of "the executive power." Either the power in *Humphrey's Executor* was legislative, in which case its exercise by the FTC was unconstitutional because the commission was not Congress; or it was judicial, in which case its exercise by the commission was unconstitutional because the commission was not a federal court; or it was executive power, in which case it had to be exercised in accordance with the Vesting Clause and the Take Care Clause.

To decide the case properly, then, the Court would have had to decide what those two clauses establish with respect to executive power. The Court might have said that the *Myers* decision applied only to a senatorial veto on removals, but that for-cause restrictions do not interfere with the President's duty to ensure faithful execution. Or it might have concluded that *Myers* was based on the general "administrative control" the President enjoys over administration. The following sections propose possible formalist answers to the question in *Humphrey's Executor* and continue the examination of presidential supervision under the original meaning of the Constitution. It is the kind of analysis a Court attuned to the text and structure of the Constitution might have undertaken. The first part of the analysis considers whether granting for-cause restrictions might exceed Congress's power under the Necessary and Proper Clause by, among things, creating property interests in officeholding that are incompatible with republican government. The second distinguishes the power to remove from the right to control.

7.2 NECESSARY AND PROPER

Assuming the President's only law-execution power is the power to oversee the execution of the laws by others, it may seem consistent with such oversight to impose for-cause restrictions at least if faithless execution would be grounds for removal. Yet, such restrictions are likely also unconstitutional under the best original meaning of the Constitution. The question is whether Congress can create for-cause removal protections consistently with the Necessary and Proper Clause because such restrictions carry into execution one of Congress's own powers or one of the President's. Congress almost certainly cannot, for a few reasons.

First, once it is acknowledged that the President has the power to remove, it is not clear why Congress would have any more ability to limit the President's exercise of that power than it has the ability to limit the President's exercise of the pardon power. In other words, it is often said that Congress's greater power under the Necessary and Proper Clause to establish offices includes the lesser power to structure the tenure, duties, qualifications, and even the removal of the officers. But Congress establishes federal crimes, too; yet, no one would say that Congress therefore has the "lesser" power to restrict the reasons why the President could pardon individuals convicted of those crimes.

Another reason such restrictions are constitutionally problematic is that, at least if they are to be judicially enforceable, they would transfer the take-care duty to the judiciary. Giving final say to courts over whether a removal is proper would seem no better than giving the Senate final say.

It is possible to conceive of for-cause restrictions without judicial review, however, in which such restrictions might still do some work. Perhaps they force the President to provide reasons for the removal, which reasons Congress can then scrutinize. Congress would be aided in that scrutiny if the President had to engage in an executive-branch adjudication to establish cause for the removal. That appears to be how then-President Taft understood the imposition of such restrictions.[14] And if the President was abusing the removal power, impeachment would be a remedy; as Madison said in 1789, the "wanton removal of meritorious officers would subject [the President] to impeachment and removal from his own high trust."[15] On this account, such restrictions would not too seriously interfere with presidential supervision, but would have much less teeth than traditionally believed.

A third reason why for-cause restrictions are problematic is that they create some degree of property rights in federal offices. If Congress can create a type of good-behavior tenure for a period of seven years, it is not clear what would prevent it from establishing such tenure for thirty years, or for life. If Congress can prohibit removal except for specified causes for a period of time, then it can create such tenure protections for any period of time. It is doubtful whether such offices would be "necessary and proper" for carrying into execution the President's power or any of Congress's powers. In a republican government where all officeholders are to derive their authority directly or indirectly from the people, creating property rights in offices would seem inconsistent with the spirit of the Constitution and would amount to the exercise of a great and important prerogative. The American revolutionary generation rejected the idea of property rights in office.[16] As the Supreme Court would eventually say, "The decisions are numerous to the effect that public offices are mere agencies or trusts, and not property as such."[17] Where the Constitution deviates from this principle, with respect to judges, it does so expressly.

7.3 INDEPENDENT DUTIES

For-cause removal restrictions, at least as to officers appointed by and with advice and consent,* are likely unconstitutional. It follows, then, that the "persuader-in-chief" view of executive power is wrong: The President must *at least* be able to remove officers appointed by and with advice and consent. Does it follow, however, that the strongest version of what has been called "unitary executive" theory is correct and the President must be able to direct and control all such officers, including those at the heads of independent commissions?

As noted, many have argued that such a view would make the Opinions Clause superfluous. Why empower the President to demand the opinions of the principal officers of the executive departments if the President can already threaten to remove them? Would not the greater power to remove include the lesser power to demand information? There is, however, a non-superfluous reading of the Opinions Clause that could cohere with a view of presidential control. The President may have a right to demand obedience and to remove subordinate officers, but nothing compels an officer to *speak*. Better to require such officers to give the President information so that the latter can make informed decisions, rather than require the President to rely on threats of removal without the relevant information at hand.

Still, the objection has some bite. The Opinions Clause does not seem to do much work under the traditional formalist view. There is, however, another possibility that makes more sense of the clause: Merely because the President must be able to remove officers does not mean the President has a constitutional right to interfere with their duties. In other words, principal officers perhaps do not have a constitutional obligation to obey the President's instructions, *except* for a demand to provide opinions in writing. The President can always remove for disobedience, but removing an officer comes at a political cost; and that cost is even higher if the President does not have a constitutional right to interfere. This distinction between interference and removal may seem too fine or trivial, but it is crucial and has significant ramifications.[18]

The following material presents some of the more prominent historical evidence supporting this account of presidential power, starting with the Decision of 1789. The reader will recall that Congress went out of its way to alter the language of the bill to make it appear as though the President's removal power was a matter of constitutional right and did not derive from congressional grant. Congress did the

---

* The reader will recall that if Congress vests the appointment of an inferior officer in the head of department, it can restrict the ability of the head of department to remove; but the inferior officer must in any event follow orders. Thus, the inferior officer would have to follow the policy preferences of the department head. Nevertheless, the argument presented here about property rights and officeholding would seem to apply to inferior officers, too, casting at least some doubt on the *Perkins* decision. The conclusion of this chapter will revisit this question.

same with respect to the appointment process. Initially, the bill provided that "at the head" of the department "there shall be an officer, to be called the Secretary of the Department of Foreign Affairs, who shall be appointed by the President, by and with the advice and consent of the Senate; and to be removable by the President."[19] The House agreed to the establishment of the department, "but when they came to the mode of appointing the officer," Representative Smith of South Carolina moved to strike the relevant words as "unnecessary," and because "it looked as if they were conferring power, which was not the case, for the Constitution has expressly given the power of appointment in the words there used."[20] The language was struck.[21]

Despite the House having altered both the appointment and removal language to avoid the impression of a congressional grant, the statute contained the following provision: The Secretary "shall conduct the business of the said department in such manner as the President of the United States shall from time to time order or instruct."[22] Identical language was included in the bill establishing the War Department[23] and similar language was included in the bill temporarily establishing the postal department.[24] These provisions are telling. It would be surprising if after the efforts to ensure that Congress would not appear to be conferring either an appointing or a removal power, the representatives would say nothing at all about appearing to confer an instructional power. The more likely explanation is that the President had a constitutional power of removal, but perhaps not a constitutional right of control.

This distinction between the power to remove and a right to control an officer while still in office often arose in the context of legal claims against the United States. Congress could resolve such claims directly by legislation ordering the payment of government funds.[25] But Congress also assigned such claims to the Comptroller of the Treasury. The question thus arose whether the President could interfere with the duties of the Comptroller. Many presidents, including Washington, Jefferson, Madison, and even Taft, argued there was no such constitutional right of interference.

James Madison, despite his prominent role in the removal power debates, thought the President should not be able to interfere. Madison "question[ed] very much whether [the President] can or ought to have any interference in the settling and adjusting the legal claims of individuals against the United States."[26] He thus proposed that "the Comptroller should hold his office during ___ years, unless sooner removed by the President."[27] By establishing a term of years, that would guarantee that the officer would remain accountable to Congress, too, because the Senate would have to consent to the reappointment after the expiration of the term. Importantly, Madison's proposal accepted that the President could always remove the officer sooner. Madison thus recognized a difference between the power to remove and a right to interfere.

Both Presidents Washington and Jefferson treated the Comptroller in precisely the manner Madison suggested. Washington wrote to one supplicant that "my public situation forbids any interference in questions of individual claims otherwise than as they may come before me officially in the form of an act of Congress – This will be satisfactory to you for my declining to direct any investigation of the vouchers which you mention."[28] In another letter, he wrote, "I have no power, nor would there be any propriety, in my interfering with the settlement of accounts; unless it be in cases of mal-practice in the Officer."[29] And in an 1808 letter, President Jefferson wrote, "[W]ith the settlement of the accounts at the Treasury I have no right to interfere in the least" because the Comptroller "is the sole & supreme judge in all claims for money against the [United States] and would no more receive a direction from me as to his rules of evidence than one of the judges of the supreme court."[30]

Attorney General William Wirt wrote an oft-cited opinion for President James Monroe on the Comptroller's duties. Wirt concluded that Monroe could not interfere with those duties and generalized the point beyond legal claims against the government. "[I]t could never have been the intention of the constitution, in assigning this general power to the President to take care that the laws be executed, that he should in person execute the laws himself," Wirt wrote. "To interpret this clause of the constitution so as to throw upon the President the duty of a personal interference in every specific case of an alleged or defective execution of the laws, and to call upon him to perform such duties himself," Wirt added, "would be not only to require him to perform an impossibility himself, but to take upon himself the responsibility of all the subordinate executive officers of the government – a construction too absurd to be seriously contended for." Wirt explained how he understood the general rule:

> [T]he requisition of the constitution is, that he shall take care that the laws be executed. If the laws, then, require a particular officer by name to perform a duty, not only is that officer bound to perform it, but no other officer can perform it without a violation of the law; and were the President to perform it, he would not only be not taking care that the laws were faithfully executed, but he would be violating them himself. The constitution assigns to Congress the power of designating the duties of particular officers: the President is only required to take care that they execute them faithfully.[31]

And the President could do so, Wirt concluded, through displacing the officer and appointing a new one.[32]

Even Chief Justice Taft in *Myers* recognized this distinction. "Of course there may be duties so peculiarly and specifically committed to the discretion of a particular officer as to raise a question whether the President may overrule or revise the officer's interpretation of his statutory duty in a particular instance," he wrote.[33] And "there may be duties of a quasi judicial character imposed on executive officers and members of executive tribunals whose decisions after hearing affect interests of individuals, the discharge of which the President cannot in a particular case properly influence or control."[34] But, he explained, "even in such a case he may consider the decision after its rendition as a reason for removing the officer, on the ground that the discretion regularly entrusted to that officer by statute has not been on the whole intelligently or wisely exercised."[35] That is consistent with what Taft wrote prior to *Myers* in his book on presidential powers: The President may remove the Comptroller of the Treasury "but under the act of Congress creating the office, the President cannot control or revise the decisions of this officer."[36]

7.4 THE SECOND BANK DEBATE

A famous debate between Senator Daniel Webster and President Andrew Jackson elucidates this distinction between removal and control and expands it beyond legal claims. President Jackson wanted to abolish the Second Bank of the United States, but the Bank was not due to expire for another few years. Thus, he sought instead to withdraw all U.S. government deposits. The law authorized only the Secretary of the Treasury to make such a withdrawal and the Secretary would have to supply Congress with reasons for doing so. Jackson's Treasury Secretary, Louis McLane, was against the removal of deposits, so Jackson had him reassigned to the State Department. He then appointed William Duane as the new secretary; but Duane did not withdraw the funds, and Jackson fired him. He then appointed as acting secretary Roger B. Taney, who promptly withdrew the funds.[37]

Even here, it is interesting to observe that in his message to the Cabinet about his views about the removal of the deposits, Jackson emphasized that he was in effect hoping to persuade the Secretary of the Treasury rather than to direct him. "In the remarks he has made on this all-important question he trusts the Secretary of the Treasury will see only the frank and respectful declarations of the opinions which the President has formed on a measure of great national interest deeply affecting the character and usefulness of his Administration," Jackson stated, "and not a spirit of dictation, which the President would be as careful to avoid as ready to resist. Happy will he be if the facts now disclosed produce uniformity of opinion and unity of action among the members of the Administration."[38]

Nevertheless, Jackson's removal of the Secretary (and of the deposits) caused an uproar in the Senate, which censured Jackson, maintaining that "the President had assumed a power not conferred by the constitution and laws, but in derogation of both."[39] Jackson, in turn, published a "protest" arguing that the censure was improper and justifying his actions.[40] On May 7, 1834, Daniel Webster delivered a speech in the Senate on the President's protest, defending the Senate's action in censuring the President.[41]

Webster first granted the President's constitutional power to remove. "I did not vote for the resolution on the mere ground of the removal of Mr. Duane from the office of Secretary of the Treasury. Although I disapprove of the removal altogether," Webster insisted, "yet the power of removal does exist in the President, according to the established construction of the constitution; and, therefore, although, in a particular case, it may be abused, and, in my opinion, was abused in this case, yet its exercise cannot be justly said to be an assumption or usurpation."[42]

The charge against the President was different. The public moneys were "in their proper place," a place "fixed by the law of the land," and the law "conferred" only on the Secretary of the Treasury the power to change the place of the deposits. "On him the power of change was conferred, to be exercised by himself, if emergency should arise."[43] The power to change the location "was a trust confided to the *discretion* of the Secretary, and to *his discretion alone*."[44] "The President had no more authority to take upon himself this duty," Webster argued, "than he had to make the annual report to Congress, or the annual commercial statements, or to perform any other service which the law specially requires of the Secretary."

"The consideration of the propriety, or necessity of removal," Webster stated, must therefore "be the consideration of the Secretary; the decision to remove, his decision; and the act of removal, his act."[45] Although technically the acting secretary had removed the deposits, the President had made known to all that the acting secretary was doing his bidding. "The act of removal, to be lawful, must be the *bona fide* act of the Secretary; *his* judgment, the result of *his* deliberations; the volition of *his* mind."[46]

Webster then drew the critical distinction. "All are able to see the difference between the *power to remove* the Secretary from office, and the *power to control him*, in all or any of his duties, while in office," he declared. "The law charges the officer, whoever he may be, with the performance of certain duties. The President, with the consent of the Senate, appoints an individual to be such officer, and this individual he may remove, if he so please," Webster continued; "but, until removed, he is the officer, and remains charged with the duties of his station; duties which nobody else can perform, and for the neglect or violation of which he is liable to be impeached." The President, Webster concluded, "may terminate his political life; but he cannot control his powers and functions, and act upon him as a mere machine, while he is allowed to live."[47]

Webster then explained why the "visible and broad" distinction "between the power of removal and the power to control an officer not removed" made sense.[48] He responded to the point – similar to the point many today make – that the power "of control and direction," although "no where given ... by any express provision of the constitution," is "derived ... from the right of removal." Webster argued the reasoning is precisely the opposite: If the President did not have a power to remove, a power to control would be even more necessary if the President was to have oversight of law execution. But if the President can, in fact, remove, "there would appear to be less necessity to give him also a right of control."[49]

7.5 IMPLICATIONS

This account of presidential power has many virtues. It makes the most sense of the Opinions Clause. Even if that clause is not superfluous under the traditional view, it does far more work under the account presented here: It ensures that principal officers always obey the President in at least that one respect, so that the President may obtain information to exercise intelligently the power to remove. It also makes more sense of the pardon power, which does more work in a system in which prosecutions might be conducted independently of the President's commands. And unlike the "persuader-in-chief" conception of the presidency, for which there is no historical evidence, there is significant historical support for a conception that distinguishes between the power to remove and a right of control.

This distinction, as noted, may seem rather too fine. But it is not. Many scholars have observed that the political cost of firing officers is much higher than simply ordering them around.[50] As Webster proclaimed, "All are able to see the difference between the power to remove the Secretary from office, and the power to control him, in all or any of his duties, while in office."[51] In this sense, the removal power is very much like the pardon power: It is widely understood that the political costs of pardoning someone after the fact is much greater than not prosecuting in the first place.[52] The exact same principle applies to the distinction between control and removal.

There are many examples of the serious political costs that can come with removing an officer. Modern readers will recall the firing of James Comey, the director of the Federal Bureau of Investigation.[53] Roger Taney, who finally agreed to remove the U.S. deposits, was subsequently denied a permanent appointment to the post of Secretary of the Treasury and was even denied an appointment as Associate Justice on the Supreme Court.[54] Another example is the high-profile resignations of the Attorney General and the Deputy Attorney General when President Richard Nixon asked them to fire special prosecutor Archibald Cox during the "Saturday Night Massacre."[55] In the past few years alone, there are ample examples of numerous appointees who may have been kept on because the political costs of firing them were too high; at least, the press has recognized these political costs as among the reasons to retain such officials.[56] President Donald Trump specifically stated that he did not fire Special Counsel Robert Mueller because of the political consequences that Nixon had experienced.[57]

Not only is the political cost of removal greater than the cost of merely directing or personally executing the law but the political cost goes up even more if it is understood that the President does not have the constitutional right of interference. In other words, if one believes officers must always follow the President's orders, then the political cost of removing an officer diminishes. Insubordination would always be a good reason to remove. But if there is no right to interfere, then the removal becomes even more politically damaging. Consider one of the proposed articles of impeachment against President Nixon. It provided that, "[i]n disregard of the rule of law," Nixon "knowingly misused the executive power by interfering with agencies of the executive branch ... in violation of his duty to take care that the laws be faithfully executed."[58] This critique has salience only if "interfering" is constitutionally improper.

7.6 CAVEATS AND CONCLUSIONS

A few caveats are in order. The first is that nothing about this analysis necessarily applies to inferior officers. The civil service system does create at least a kind of property interest in holding office. As noted in Chapter 6, nineteenth-century cases had held that inferior officers can be protected from removal at the hands of their principals; but the textual argument in favor of that arrangement is that inferior officers must obey orders. The only constitutional obligation of obedience on the part of principal officers, in contrast, derives from the Opinions Clause. Without a constitutional obligation to obey, the President's only constitutionally guaranteed power of supervision over the principal officers is removal.

The second caveat is that other constitutional provisions may supersede this general understanding in more specific instances. For example, the President's commander-in-chief status might empower the President both to direct and control as well as to remove all principal officers involved in military matters;[59] the treaty power might also require the President to have the control and direction of diplomats. Hence, Secretary of State Henry Clay flatly but respectfully wrote to a diplomat under the administration of John Quincy Adams: "With respect to the nature of instructions which may be sent to you, and of orders to the commanders of our public vessels, that must rest with the President, where the Constitution has placed it."[60]

One must admit, finally, the significant evidence in favor of the traditional "unitary executive" view. Alexander Hamilton argued the Opinions Clause was superfluous.[61] Attorney General Caleb Cushing thought Wirt was wrong.[62] Scholars have uncovered strong statements in favor of presidential direction.[63] For example, both the Anti-Federalist Federal Farmer and future Justice James Wilson explained that the President would "direct" all subordinate officers.[64]

Blackstone also described a "proclamation power": The king's proclamations have "binding force, when ... they are grounded upon and enforce the laws of the realm."[65] Although lawmaking is the work of the legislative branch, "yet the manner, time, and circumstances of putting those laws in execution must frequently be left to the discretion of the executive magistrate."[66] Therefore, the king's "proclamations, are binding upon the subject, where they do not either contradict the old laws, or tend to establish new ones; but only enforce the execution of such laws as are already in being, in such manner as the king shall judge necessary."[67] This prerogative power does seem to imply that any discretion left by law is for the king – or the President – to exercise. Proclamations would presumably be binding on subordinate officers equally with subjects. Michael McConnell argues that the proclamation power reflects "the President's power to direct executive officers to exercise power they already have, by virtue of statutes, in a particular way."[68] The present author has previously argued the same.[69]

The "proclamation power" may very well be part of the executive power to execute law, and its description in Blackstone should give one pause about the distinction between removal and control. Nevertheless, an account of presidential power that does distinguish the two fits much of the historical data, including the First Congress's statutes and the various statements of Washington, Jefferson, Madison, Webster, Wirt, and, later, Taft. There is therefore a range of plausible explanations for the Opinions Clause, and a range of plausible accounts of presidential power. The idea that the President can remove but not always directly interfere is a possibility that accords with much of the evidence.

To conclude with the exhortation with which the present investigation began: An "unqualified" adoption of either of the two standard accounts of presidential power "would invite startling results," according to Corwin. If one adopts the standard formalist position, that "would make all questions of law enforcement questions of discretion, the discretion moreover of an independent and legally uncontrollable branch of the government." Yet, an unqualified adoption of the persuader-in-chief view "would hold out consequences equally unwelcome," allowing Congress to "divide and transfer" control of law execution into a "parliamentary despotism."[70] The middle path presented in this chapter provides an account of executive power consistent with the text, structure, and history of the Constitution, and that also solves Corwin's dilemma. It would, in short, allow for an independent administrative state – Congress could create multimember agencies who must exercise independently the discretion Congress has conferred – but one over which the President has an important check through the power to remove.

PART IV

Separation of Powers (I)

8

Emergency Powers

That the President's executive power is essentially a grant of law-execution authority does not immediately answer all questions involving the separation of powers between President and Congress. This Part considers disputes between these two great departments of government, and particularly those in which the President's power to act is not entirely clear and may encroach on Congress's prerogatives. The framework for addressing such cases is often thought to be Justice Robert Jackson's famous concurring opinion in the *Steel Seizure Case* decided during the Korean War, with which this chapter begins. The chapter then addresses more broadly the claim, presented in that case, that the President has inherent or emergency powers to act beyond the law. Notwithstanding the Supreme Court's rejection of President Truman's actions, the Court has often upheld presidential actions of dubious constitutionality, or upheld such actions on rather dubious grounds.

Chapters 9 and 10 address more specific areas in which both Congress and the President have power, and in which they sometimes clash: foreign affairs and war. An overarching theme of the coming chapters is that a more formalist, originalist understanding of the Constitution would create a more restrained presidency and a correspondingly more robust Congress. Functionalists and living constitutionalists share a large measure of responsibility for the rise of what has been called the imperial presidency.

8.1 THE *STEEL SEIZURE CASE*

Youngstown Sheet & Tube Co. v. Sawyer, sometimes referred to as the *Steel Seizure Case*, arose during the Korean War in 1952.[1] The nation's steelworkers were about to go on strike, but President Truman needed steel for the war effort. Truman ordered his commerce secretary to seize and operate the steel mills. There was no statute expressly prohibiting the President's actions; however, Congress had explicitly provided for seizures in different circumstances, and had even considered and rejected providing that power to resolve the kind of labor dispute at hand.[2]

The case is celebrated for Justice Jackson's concurrence, in which he elaborated a tripartite framework for thinking about separation of powers disputes.
In the first category, the President is merely executing Congress's laws, and so
presidential power is at its maximum. In the second category, Congress has been
silent on the matter; here, the President "can only rely upon his own independent powers, but there is a zone of twilight in which [the President] and Congress
may have concurrent authority, or in which its distribution is uncertain." In this
zone, "any actual test of power is likely to depend on the imperatives of events
and contemporary imponderables rather than on abstract theories of law." In the
third category, Congress has expressly forbidden an action, and the President's
power is at its "lowest ebb," depending in that situation solely on the President's
"constitutional powers minus any constitutional powers of Congress over the
matter."[3]

Two of the three categories make intuitive sense. In category one, the President is
merely executing law. There is no question of the President's power to do so, unless
Congress's law is unconstitutional for some other reason, such as exceeding the
enumeration of powers. In category three, the President can only act against
Congress's wishes if its law violates the Constitution by infringing on some independent presidential prerogative. These cases should be, at least theoretically, quite
rare. A statute that deprives the President of command of the armed forces, interferes
with the removal power, nullifies the effect of presidential pardons, or purports to
direct the appointment of specific persons to office would be an example. Assuming
the President can refuse to enforce unconstitutional laws that interfere with presidential prerogatives (an issue examined later in this study), the President would be
justified in ignoring these laws because they impinge on the President's own
prerogatives. Otherwise, the President must do as Congress says.

These two categories sufficed to address the dispute at hand. Justice Jackson
concluded that the Truman administration was effectively operating in the third
category because Congress had legislated specifically about how to resolve labor
disputes and had therefore not left these matters an "open field." In other words,
although no law specifically prohibited the President from seizing the steel mills,
that point was immaterial. Every law does not specifically prohibit an infinite
number of things. What laws do – at least those related to the executive branch –
is authorize specific actions; everything else is not authorized.[4]

This is rooted in common linguistic conventions reflected in the *expressio unius
est exclusio alterius* canon of legal interpretation, which stands for the proposition
that the expression of certain items implies the exclusion of other, similar items not
mentioned. By thus specifying how labor disputes are to be resolved and not
providing for the seizure of property, Congress effectively prohibited the
President's actions. That Congress had provided for seizure in two circumstances
not applicable to Truman's situation and had even considered but rejected authorizing seizure in such a situation buttressed this conclusion.[5]

Did the President have independent presidential authority to seize the steel mills despite Congress's prohibition? A comparison of the President's powers with those of Congress settled the question. The President's law-execution power did not apply because, as both the majority and Justice Jackson argued, Congress had prohibited the action in question. A moment's reflection suggested also that the core commander-in-chief power was inapplicable because, as Justice Jackson explained, "[w]hile Congress cannot deprive the President of the command of the army and navy, only Congress can provide him an army or navy to command."[6] It is up to Congress to supply the armed forces through its enumerated powers to "raise and support Armies" and to "provide and maintain a Navy."[7] And as Justice Douglas argued in his concurrence, any taking of private property for public use would require just compensation, for which only Congress could appropriate funds.[8] These arguments are conclusive that the commander-in-chief status did not authorize Truman's actions.

That left one final source of potential presidential authority: an inherent, residual executive power to act in emergencies. It would be quite dramatic to claim that the President has unwritten, unenumerated, inherent powers to act in certain situations in the absence of statutory or other constitutional authority. It would be positively astonishing to claim that any such inherent power is indefeasible to the point that the President can ignore Congress.

Justice Jackson seemed to reject the existence of any such power.[9] Despite having somewhat awkwardly asserted emergency powers on behalf of President Franklin Roosevelt when he had been his attorney general, Jackson refused to "declare the existence of inherent powers *ex necessitate* to meet an emergency."[10] The Founders knew, Jackson elaborated, "what emergencies were, knew the pressures they engender for authoritative action, knew, too, how they afford a ready pretext for usurpation." He added, "We may also suspect that they suspected that emergency powers would tend to kindle emergencies."[11] The Constitution already provided for emergencies by authorizing the "suspension of the privilege of the writ of habeas corpus in time of rebellion or invasion, when the public safety may require it"; otherwise, the Framers "made no express provision for exercise of extraordinary authority because of a crisis."[12] With the Weimar Republic and World War II firmly in view, Jackson exhorted:

> I do not think we rightfully may so amend their work, and, if we could, I am not convinced it would be wise to do so, although many modern nations have forthrightly recognized that war and economic crises may upset the normal balance between liberty and authority. Their experience with emergency powers may not be irrelevant to the argument here that we should say that the Executive, of his own volition, can invest himself with undefined emergency powers.[13]

Or as Justice Douglas wisely put it, although the Korean War may have created an "emergency," that "emergency did not create power; it merely marked an occasion when power should be exercised. And the fact that it was necessary that measures be taken to keep steel in production does not mean that the President, rather than the Congress, had the constitutional authority to act."[14]

The case could therefore have been resolved entirely through a recognition of two categories of presidential action: those authorized by statute or those authorized by some other constitutional power. The opinion for the Court resolved the case that way: "The President's power, if any, to issue the order must stem either from an act of Congress or from the Constitution itself."[15] No statute or constitutional provision authorized the President's actions.

8.2 REVISING THE FRAMEWORK

There remains the question of category two, when Congress is silent and so the President is neither executing the law nor violating the law. What work does this category do? Would the analysis in the *Steel Seizure Case* have been any different had Truman's actions fallen into this category? If Congress had been silent, then there would be no law to carry into execution. Nor would the President's commander-in-chief power do any additional work; it would still have been Congress's prerogative to supply an army and navy for the President to command. And if one rejects emergency powers altogether, then such powers also cannot be invoked in the face of congressional silence. Such powers either exist or they do not.

Justice Jackson rejected such powers outright; yet, what he took away with one hand, he seemed to give back with the other. The President's powers in the second category, he said, "depend on the imperatives of events and contemporary imponderables." What could such dictum possibly be if not an invitation to exercise power that would otherwise not exist? Justice Jackson seemed to recognize this possibility: "congressional inertia, indifference or quiescence may sometimes, at least as a practical matter, enable, if not invite, measures on independent presidential responsibility."[16] Yet, the President either has a statutory power to act or a constitutional power to act; it is not clear what imperatives of events and contemporary imponderables have to do with the question. Jackson's second category dangerously invites presidential assertions of emergency authority that other parts of his opinion reject.

There is, nevertheless, important insight to be gleaned from this category. As Jackson explained, Congress and the President may have "concurrent authority." To be more specific, Congress and the President have their respective powers, and functionally those powers sometimes overlap. That is, in at least some situations, both Congress and the President can exercise their respective powers to achieve the same result. Thus, if Congress has been silent, the President may have independent constitutional authority to accomplish the result in question. But Congress might also have some relevant constitutional authority. The President can therefore act until Congress does; but once Congress stakes out a position, the President must conform to Congress's wishes and faithfully execute the laws.

There are several examples of such overlapping or concurrent authority. Congress has the power to "make Rules for the Government and Regulation of the land and naval Forces."[17] But the President is commander in chief. In the absence of congressional legislation, perhaps the President can make rules for the government of the army and navy; but as soon as Congress legislates pursuant to its more specific power, the President must conform. And the President can manage the public lands until Congress "dispose[s] of" or "make[s] . . . Rules and Regulations respecting the Territory or other Property belonging to the United States."[18] Perhaps the President can also close embassies or appoint ambassadors without legislation; but it is not at all obvious that Congress could not direct and appropriate for the maintenance of embassies or consulates in specific locations. The President has authority to engage in defensive war until Congress specifies otherwise, and perhaps both the President and Congress have power over troop movements and military bases in peacetime. These and other examples will be explored in subsequent chapters.

Another highly significant example of overlap is the function of filling in the details of a legislative program.[19] Congress often omits details necessary for implementation. An obvious example comes from *Chevron v. Natural Resources Defense Council*, the famous administrative law case that once stood for the proposition that courts should defer to the executive branch when it fills statutory gaps.[20] In that case, Congress required the Environmental Protection Agency (EPA) to regulate "stationary sources" of certain pollutants. But it defined a "stationary source" as "any building, structure, facility, or installation which emits or may emit any air pollutant."[21] The statute did not address the possibility that there could be a power plant – a facility or installation – with multiple buildings or structures that emitted pollution. The question thus arose whether the entire plant should be treated as a stationary source, or each emitting unit within the plant should be so treated. Answering that question one way or another in the face of congressional silence was surely in execution of Congress's law. But had Congress provided a specific answer to that question, the President and EPA would have had to conform.[22]

The present point is that the President may have power that can be exercised in the absence of congressional legislation even if Congress also has power over the matter in question. But the President must still have some independent basis of authority to act. The absence of a prohibition on presidential action is irrelevant, except in the trivial sense that the President must conform to Congress's laws as soon as Congress does act. An affirmative grant of power, whether from statute or a constitutional provision, is always necessary no matter in what category the President's actions fall. All of this is to say that Justice Jackson's framework poses some dangers by inviting assertions of emergency power and also overcomplicates the matter.

It is important to emphasize that if Congress has been silent, the President can act either if the President has concurrent power with Congress or if there is an independent basis of power that Congress can never infringe. Thus, the President is commander in chief whether or not Congress has said anything on the matter. Congress can be silent, or it can express itself; it simply does not matter. The President gets to command the armed forces either way. If Congress is silent, then, the President may have concurrent authority; but the President can always exercise any exclusive and preclusive powers. In category three, however, the President can only rely on the latter type of power; concurrent power is not enough.

One can therefore think of a better three-part framework in terms of congressional action (Figure 8.1).

It might be better to reconceptualize the three-part framework altogether from categories of congressional action to sources of presidential authority. That is because a statute alone does not authorize the President to act; it is the statute in combination with the Constitution's grant of a law-execution power to the President that allows the action. Thus, the President's actions can stem from the following *constitutional* sources: (1) the law-execution power, if there is specific statutory authorization; (2) independent constitutional authority in which the President's powers are concurrent with Congress, so the President can act until Congress does; and (3) independent and exclusive constitutional authority, such that the President can act whether or not Congress has said anything on the matter (Figure 8.2).

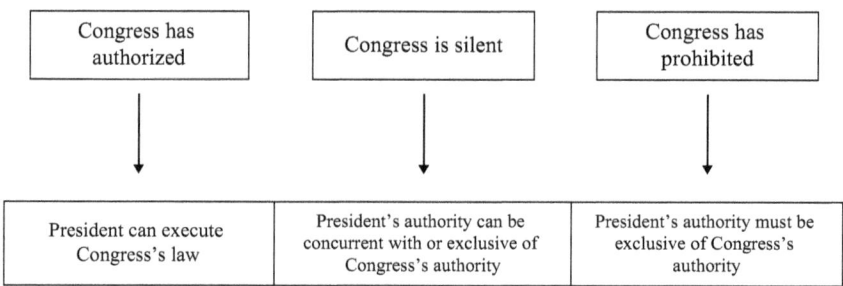

FIGURE 8.1 The President's power depending on congressional action.

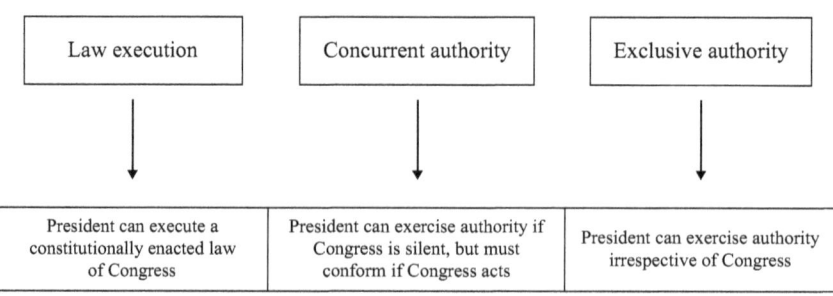

FIGURE 8.2 The President's constitutional sources of power.

This schema still lacks some relevant information, namely, the actual clauses of the Constitution granting the President power. These grants of power might give the President some exclusive authority and some concurrent or overlapping authority. The Commander-in-Chief Clause, for example, might grant the President the exclusive authority of battlefield command, but also some concurrent authority such as over military discipline or base deployments. The grant of law-execution power to the President is relevant to all three conceptual boxes. It empowers the President to execute a statute (box one). It is also the grant of power that authorizes the President to fill statutory gaps, which is a "concurrent authority" in that the President can act until Congress does (box two). And the grant of law-execution power also entails some exclusive presidential prerogatives, such as the ability to remove principal officers (box three). The important point is that each clause in the Constitution granting the President power may be a source of both concurrent or exclusive authority. Concurrent authority may be exercised in the face of congressional silence. Exclusive authority can always be exercised.

Applying this framework to Truman's actions makes the constitutional answer clear. There was no statute, and there was no constitutional grant of power – neither a concurrent grant nor an exclusive grant. Justice Black's opinion for the Court discounted, as the concurrences did, the commander-in-chief power because the United States itself was not a "theater of war."[23] As for the "several constitutional provisions that grant executive power to the President," Justice Black explained, these too were insufficient because "[i]n the framework of our Constitution, the President's power to see that the laws are faithfully executed refutes the idea that he is to be a lawmaker."[24] By seizing the steel mills, the President was not purporting to execute the laws, but rather to make a new law.[25]

The dissenters, led by Chief Justice Vinson, disagreed that the President was making new law. Rather, they argued that the President's seizure of the mills was in execution of various congressional statutes. They observed that the Senate had ratified various defense treaties and Congress had enacted defense and anti-inflationary legislation, including legislation granting the President power "to stabilize prices and wages and to provide for settlement of labor disputes arising in the defense program."[26] "The President has the duty to execute the foregoing legislative programs," the dissenters argued, and "[t]heir successful execution depends upon continued production of steel and stabilized prices for steel."[27]

Put another way, the dissenters relied on the President's concurrent power to fill in the details of a legislative scheme until Congress acts. The question in the *Steel Seizure Case* thus boiled down to a lower-order dispute: whether President Truman's seizure of the steel mills was merely a "detail" of implementation that helped carry into execution Congress's legislative programs in the absence of more specific direction from Congress, or whether the President was in fact making new law and encroaching on Congress's prerogatives. Chief Justice Vinson said the former; Justice Black the latter. Reasonable analysts can disagree on the answer, but the point remains that the President can only execute the laws – and prosecute wars – with the tools, officers, and armies that Congress provides. Seizing the steel mills seems like an attempt to raise and provide for the army and navy, which also would require just compensation and therefore appropriations. Those are not mere statutory details. That is new lawmaking.

8.3 A PROTECTIVE POWER

Although the Supreme Court rejected a claim of inherent or emergency powers in the *Steel Seizure Case*, the Court has upheld presidential authority in other cases where there was no clear statutory or constitutional power to act. Scholars have tended to try to find justifications for the results in these cases, as if the consequences of failing to recognize a presidential power to act would be impractical or dangerous. Let us analyze such claims.

The first case is *In re Neagle*.[28] The facts are rather astounding. Stephen Field, a Justice of the Supreme Court of the United States, when sitting as a circuit court judge in California, had ruled against David Terry and his wife, Sarah Terry. The two had concocted a scheme to forge a marriage certificate between Sarah and a wealthy decedent in order to collect money from the decedent's estate. Justice Field and the other judges sitting as a circuit court found the marriage certificate to be a forgery. When Justice Field delivered the judgment of the circuit court, violence erupted in the courtroom, and Field sentenced Terry and his wife to prison for contempt of court. Since that time, Terry made frequent and open threats against Justice Field's life.[29] Rather astonishingly, Terry had been a justice of the California Supreme Court some thirty years earlier.[30]

Because of the threats against Justice Field, the Attorney General of the United States assigned David Neagle, a deputy U.S. marshal, to accompany Justice Field as he rode circuit in California, even though there was no statute authorizing deputy U.S. marshals to accompany Supreme Court Justices while riding circuit. It was on a train from Los Angeles to San Francisco that David Terry accosted and struck Justice Field. Neagle allegedly shouted at Terry to stop, drew his revolver, and shot and killed Terry. Terry, however, had in fact been unarmed, and Sarah convinced the local county sheriff, Thomas Cunningham, to arrest Neagle on suspicion of murder.[31] Neagle then sued for a writ of habeas corpus which, if granted, would require his release from state authorities. A federal statute authorized the issuance of such a writ "for an act done or omitted in pursuance of a law of the United States," or if the petitioner "is in custody in violation of the constitution or of a law or treaty of the United States."[32]

The Supreme Court recognized that no specific law authorized Neagle to accompany Justice Field. Nevertheless, the Court held, "In the view we take of the Constitution of the United States, any obligation fairly and properly inferable from that instrument, or any duty of the marshal to be derived from the general scope of his duties under the laws of the United States, is a 'law,' within the meaning of" the habeas corpus statute. "It would be a great reproach to the system of government of the United States, declared to be within its sphere sovereign and supreme," the Court held, "if there is to be found within the domain of its powers no means of protecting the judges, in the conscientious and faithful discharge of their duties, from the malice and hatred of those upon whom their judgments may operate unfavorably." "We hold it to be an incontrovertible principle that the government of the United States may," the Court went on, "by means of physical force, exercised through its official agents, execute on every foot of American soil the powers and functions that belong to it. This necessarily involves the power to command obedience to its laws, and hence the power to keep the peace to that extent."[33]

The Court then sought to locate such a power to keep the "peace of the United States."[34] It found it in the duty of faithful execution. "Is this duty limited to the enforcement of acts of congress or of treaties of the United States according to their express terms," the Court asked, "or does it include the rights, duties, and obligations growing out of the constitution itself, our international relations, and all the protection implied by the nature of the government under the constitution?" The Court then suggested that surely if there were credible intelligence that United States mails containing treasure were to be robbed, the President would have authority to send the marshals or the armed forces to protect the mails.[35] And it cited a case in which the Court had upheld the power of land agents, without specific statutory authorization, to seize illegally cut timber from United States lands.[36] It is "the duty of the United States to protect its officers from violence . . . in discharge of the duties which its laws impose upon them."[37]

The late Henry Monaghan famously argued that *In re Neagle* is an example of the "protective power" of the presidency.[38] Monaghan rejected the proposition that this was an emergency power. Rather, it was a power that can be exercised as part of the more general duty of law execution. Monaghan summarized:

> [T]he constitutional conception of a Chief Executive authorized to enforce the laws includes a general authority to protect and defend the personnel, property, and instrumentalities of the United States from harm. While the occasion for exercise of this presidential authority will often arise in emergencies, some relatively small, such as assigning a marshal to protect the life of a judge, the protective power is, strictly speaking, not a doctrine of emergency power. For example, acting without statutory authority, the Executive has standing to enforce the contract or property rights of the United States.[39]

It is hardly clear that a general law enforcement authority must include the power to protect government instrumentalities, property, or personnel. Congress can provide for that protection, of course, but it does not follow that the President must have unilateral authority to provide such protection in the absence of congressional legislation. If Congress had never established and appropriated for the office of deputy marshal, the President and Attorney General could not have acted as they did to protect the life of Justice Field.

It is sensible to think that the President should have asked the California authorities to protect the life of Justice Field. If they refused, perhaps the President could have assigned Neagle in a private capacity. But whether he committed murder or acted in defense of the life of another would be determined under California law, which is what the dissenters in *In re Neagle* proposed. And whether Congress ended up appropriating funds to pay for Neagle's private services or to indemnify the officer for any financial loss would be entirely within its discretion. It is of no small significance that in more recent times, Congress has specifically legislated to provide protection for Supreme Court Justices and their families after an intruder was apprehended outside the home of Justice Brett Kavanaugh.

In all events, if a "protective power" is inferable from the Constitution's grant of the executive power to the President, which is not entirely implausible, such a power would at least be reasonably limited in its scope.

8.4 EXPANDING INHERENT POWER

Another case involving the so-called protective power is *In re Debs*, stemming from the Pullman Strike of 1894.[40] The case report does not give the full background, which is recounted in former President Grover Cleveland's series of essays published ten years after the events.[41] The strike began in Chicago by disgruntled employees of the Pullman Palace Car Company. The company manufactured and operated certain train cars. The strike spread when the American Railway Union decided to join in solidarity and its workers refused to handle any trains with Pullman cars. This paralyzed the railway network nationwide, such that the U.S. mails were no longer being delivered. "The same railroad companies which had contracted to use these Pullman cars upon their lines had contracts with the United States Government for the carriage of mails, and were, of course, also largely engaged in interstate commerce," Cleveland explained. "It need hardly be said that, of necessity, the trains on which the mails were carried and which served the purpose of interstate commerce were, very generally, those to which the Pullman cars were also attached."[42] It also appeared that the strikers were disabling trains and preventing other individuals from working the trains.

At this stage, what powers would the executive department have to suppress the strike to ensure the delivery of the mails and to remove the obstruction to interstate commerce? One would think very few in the absence of congressional legislation. Congress had authorized the Postmaster General to enter into contracts with railroad companies for the delivery of mail, but nothing guaranteed that such companies would not be subject to strikes. A contract to deliver mail cannot impress private citizens into service to ensure the contract is fulfilled. Congress, of course, could have enacted a law prohibiting strikes that impeded the mails or interfered with interstate commerce, and empowering the President to call forth the militia or armed forces to execute that law. But Congress had not done so. And Congress had historically enacted laws authorizing the removal of obstructions on navigable waters;[43] no similar law authorized the removal of obstructions to interstate railway traffic.

The Constitution also provides that the federal government shall protect each state "against domestic Violence," but only upon "application of the Legislature or of the Executive" of the state.[44] Not only had the state legislature and governor not called for assistance but the Governor of Illinois also specifically denounced President Cleveland for subsequently calling out the army when the state had not requested the assistance of the federal government.[45]

Perhaps recognizing these limitations, the Cleveland Administration did not initially call out the army. Instead, it sought a federal court injunction against the strikers. The circuit court that issued the injunction relied on the recently enacted Sherman Anti-Trust Act of 1890, which authorized injunctions to prevent any "contract, combination ..., or conspiracy, in restraint of trade or commerce."[46] This was a plausible but dubious use of the law, which was aimed at price-fixing and monopolization. It probably did not prohibit refusing to work.[47] The court nevertheless issued an injunction.

Once the circuit court issued the injunction to disperse the strike, the injunction was read to the strikers; it had no effect.[48] This was what allowed Cleveland to call out the army. Federal law provided that the President could call forth the armed forces if it was impracticable to enforce the laws "by the ordinary course of judicial proceedings," and when any combination of persons "opposes or obstructs the laws of the United States."[49] That includes opposing or obstructing a court injunction. President Cleveland's proclamation went further, stating military intervention was necessary "for the purpose of enforcing the faithful execution of the laws of the United States and protecting its property and removing obstructions to the United States mails."[50]

Eugene V. Debs, the leader of the strikers, was imprisoned for violating the injunction. He defended on the ground that the injunction was issued without legal authority. In a sweeping decision, the Supreme Court held that the President had even more power than Cleveland had attempted to exercise. The Court held that "under the constitution, power over interstate commerce and the transportation of the mails is vested in the national government," a power that Congress has exercised, and it therefore "follows that the national government may prevent any unlawful and forcible interference therewith."[51] Of course, no one disputed that, as the Court stated, "it is within the competency of congress to prescribe by legislation that any interferences with these matters shall be offenses against the United States, and prosecuted and punished by indictment in the proper courts."[52] The question was whether the President could take actions beyond those Congress had prescribed.

The Court said that even in the absence of any relevant laws, "[t]he entire strength of the nation may be used to enforce in any part of the land the full and free exercise of all national powers and the security of all rights intrusted by the constitution to its care," and the "strong arm of the national government may be put forth to brush away all obstructions to the freedom of interstate commerce or the transportation of the mails." The Court stated explicitly, "If the emergency arises, the army of the nation, and all its militia, are at the service of the nation, to compel obedience to its laws."[53]

This is an astonishing doctrine. Congress establishes and provides for the armed forces. Congress provides for when they shall be used to execute the national laws. And yet the Court seemed to say that the President had an inherent power – a protective power – to use the armed forces even in the absence of congressional legislation to protect the instrumentalities and property of the United States. The Court's decision went further still to suggest the President could unilaterally suppress any interference with interstate commerce whether federal instrumentalities are involved or not, and whether or not Congress had authorized their use in that situation.

At least President Cleveland had had the good sense to wait for the strikers to ignore a court injunction. But there was still the question of whether the President had properly applied for the injunction. If the Supreme Court agreed that the strikers were violating the Sherman Anti-Trust Act, that statute at least specifically authorized the granting of injunctions. The Court chose not to rest its decision on the basis of that Act (which, as noted, was of dubious usefulness to the government's argument), and instead decided the case on much more sweeping grounds. "Every government, intrusted by the very terms of its being with powers and duties to be exercised and discharged for the general welfare, has a right to apply to its own courts for any proper assistance in the exercise of the one and the discharge of the other." The "obligations which it is under to promote the interest of all and to prevent the wrongdoing of one, resulting in injury to the general welfare, is often of itself sufficient to give it a standing in court."[54]

The doctrine of the *In re Debs* case is therefore that the executive branch of the government has the authority to use the armed forces to suppress obstructions to the mails or interstate commerce even without statutory authorization, and to seek injunctions prohibiting such interferences even when no law prohibits them and certainly no law authorizes the United States to seek a court injunction. Congress, however, could have provided for all those circumstances given its power over the postal system and interstate commerce, as well as its power to establish (or not) a system of federal courts. There was little need to hold that any of these powers must somehow exist inherently in the President even if Congress has not acted.

8.5 HISTORICAL GLOSS

In the *Steel Seizure Case*, Justice Frankfurter voted against President Truman's seizure of the mills. But his opinion included an interesting reason for his doing so. "It is an inadmissibly narrow conception of American constitutional law to confine it to the words of the Constitution and to disregard the gloss which life has written upon them. In short," Justice Frankfurter opined, "a systematic, unbroken, executive practice, long pursued to the knowledge of the Congress and never before questioned, engaged in by Presidents who have also sworn to uphold the Constitution ... may be treated as a gloss on 'executive Power' vested in the President."[55] Frankfurter explained that in a prior case, "lands which Congress had opened for entry were, over a period of 80 years and in 252 instances, and by Presidents learned and unlearned in the law, temporarily withdrawn from entry so as to enable Congress to deal with such withdrawals."[56] The Court had therefore upheld such practices despite a lack of statutory authorization. Unlike in that situation, however, in the *Steel Seizure Case* there was "[n]o remotely comparable practice" that can vouch "for executive seizure of property."[57]

Justice Frankfurter thus suggested that an "unbroken" executive practice in which Congress has "acquiesce[d]"[58] can "gloss" the meaning of "executive power," authorizing the President to exercise the authority in question. This proposition has sometimes justified presidential foreign affairs powers, which Chapter 9 addresses. For present purposes, one should be skeptical of such reasoning. It has often been remarked that using historical gloss to justify presidential power is somewhat like adverse possession in property law,[59] and this adverse possession will systematically favor the aggrandizement of the presidency.[60]

Curtis Bradley, one of the leading contemporary scholars of presidential power and historical gloss, argues that gloss is justified in the sense that it rarely disables Congress from acting in response. Thus, it tends to operate only in the category where Congress has been otherwise silent.[61] Additionally, it is a "gloss" in the sense that the text is otherwise ambiguous with respect to the Constitution's distribution of powers.[62] Both points, however, are debatable.

On the first, gloss has hardly operated only when Congress has been silent. The very case Justice Frankfurter cited as the leading one on historical gloss, *United States v. Midwest Oil Co.*,[63] involved President Taft withdrawing certain public lands from oil exploration and extraction when Congress's statute had specifically provided that such lands shall be "free and open to occupation, exploration, and purchase by citizens of the United States ... under regulations prescribed by law."[64] Taft's excuse was that he thought the law unwise; he sought to afford Congress an opportunity to change the law before all of the oil was depleted (a quaint concern from the perch of a twenty-first-century reader). This was, at best, an invocation of "emergency" power to suspend the law. The reader will recall that such a power is incompatible with the Constitution and was arguably rejected by the Convention. And as Chapter 9 will demonstrate, historical gloss played a powerful role in supporting an exclusive presidential power to recognize foreign governments even though Congress had sought to establish a different policy pursuant to its own enumerated powers.

Regarding textual ambiguity, it is true that the word "gloss" implies the glossing of some text. Theoretically, the asserted presidential power does not come out of thin air. But in practice it often does. That is because usually the only text available for glossing is the vesting of "executive power" in the President, the very clause whose gloss Justice Frankfurter explored. That text is only ambiguous, however, if one accepts the residuum theory. But if this grant of power is merely an authorization to execute law, then of course Taft could not withdraw public lands that Congress had specifically provided would be open to the public. Gloss, in other words, only works to resolve textual ambiguity if there is some inherent or residual component to the grant of executive power, which is an invitation to those same emergency powers earlier rejected.

It is certainly possible that some amount of gloss is necessary. If one agrees that much of the President's foreign affairs powers cannot be explained without a residuum of power – something Chapter 9 will explore – then historical practice may very well be the best guide to those practices. But that premise is open to question. To the extent historical gloss merely elucidates the meaning of the Constitution's text, however, as Bradley recognizes, it could be perfectly consistent with an interpretive approach aimed at the original meaning of the Constitution.[65]

8.6 GENUINE EMERGENCIES

In the cases discussed in this chapter, there was no genuine emergency in which it would have been impossible to wait for Congress to act. The situation was very different when President Abraham Lincoln suspended the privilege of the writ of habeas corpus during the opening weeks of the Civil War. Lincoln authorized his generals to suspend the writ along the railway lines in Maryland, over which members of Congress would have to travel to convene in the extraordinary session that Lincoln had called, and over which Union troops would have to travel to reach the capital. Pursuant to that instruction, Major General Cadwalader arrested one John Merryman, a prominent local citizen and county commissioner, on suspicion of sabotaging railway lines. Merryman was held in Fort McHenry in Baltimore and somehow managed to file a petition for a writ of habeas corpus, which was heard by Chief Justice Roger Taney as the circuit justice for Maryland.[66]

Taney held Lincoln's suspension unconstitutional. He wrote that he had "supposed it to be one of those points of constitutional law upon which there was no difference of opinion, and that it was admitted on all hands, that the privilege of the writ could not be suspended, except by act of congress."[67] That is because the authorization to suspend the writ is found in the ninth section of the first article of the Constitution, which provides that "[t]he Privilege of the Writ of Habeas Corpus shall not be suspended, unless when in Cases of Rebellion or Invasion the public Safety may require it."[68] This placement suggests that the "suspension clause" is a limitation on the powers of Congress, and therefore only Congress has power to suspend the writ.

That argument is probably correct, although it is not entirely clear that Lincoln had no power to suspend the writ. The ninth section also contains a prohibition on withdrawing money from the Treasury without an appropriation made by law.[69] That would seem to be a limitation on the executive. And it is possible to think that Lincoln, who had the power under Article II "on extraordinary Occasions" to "convene both Houses, or either of them,"[70] could as a result suspend the writ narrowly to ensure that Congress could successfully convene for the extraordinary session.[71] As noted in an earlier chapter on the Necessary and Proper Clause, however, ordinarily such great powers are not left to implication. That argument, moreover, would not have applied to Lincoln's broader suspension of habeas corpus in September 1862 to suppress draft resistance.[72]

Although Lincoln denied that he had violated the Constitution, he defended his actions even on the ground that he might have technically violated the Suspension Clause. "The whole of the laws which were required to be faithfully executed were being resisted and failing of execution in nearly one-third of the States," Lincoln observed. "Are all the laws *but one* to go unexecuted, and the Government itself go to pieces lest that one be violated?" In such a case, Lincoln asked, "would not the official oath be broken if the Government should be overthrown when it was believed that disregarding the single law would tend to preserve it?"[73] Thus, an argument can be made that the suspension was necessary to ensure faithful execution of the laws generally, and to make good on Lincoln's oath as President to "preserve, protect, and defend the Constitution of the United States."[74] If the rebellion succeeded before Congress could safely assemble, there would be no more Union, and without a Union there would be no Constitution.

This defense was a claim to emergency power. If Lincoln was right to do what he did, can such a claim be supported here when it was rejected elsewhere? There are two alternatives one could take. The first is to adjust one's theory of the Constitution to account for Lincoln's actions. As one prominent scholar has written, "the residuum of 'executive Power' in the opening words of Article II surely encompassed Lincoln's mandate to save the Union."[75] It is dangerous, however, to adopt a theory of constitutional interpretation for the purpose of justifying actions one believes to be right and just, even necessary. The touchstone of a correct theory of presidential power is not one that justifies everything presidents have done throughout history.

The second, alternative route is to accept that sometimes presidents undertake unconstitutional but justified actions, and they must throw themselves upon the judgment of the country. That appears to have been the theory of emergency powers prevalent at the Founding. "The question you propose, whether circumstances do not sometimes occur, which make it a duty in officers of high trust, to assume authorities beyond the law," Thomas Jefferson wrote to a correspondent in 1810, "is easy of solution in principle, but sometimes embarrassing in practice. A strict observance of the written laws is doubtless *one* of the high duties of a good citizen," Jefferson continued, "but it is not *the highest*. The laws of necessity, of self-preservation, of saving our country when in danger, are of higher obligation. To lose our country by a scrupulous adherence to written law, would be to lose the law itself."[76]

Jefferson made clear that such a course of action should be reserved for truly emergency situations and that the officer who exceeds constitutional or legal authority acts at his own peril and must "throw himself on the justice of his country":

> From these examples and principles, you may see what I think on the question proposed. They do not go to the case of persons charged with petty duties, where consequences are trifling, and time allowed for a legal course, nor to authorize them to take such cases out of the written law. In these, the example of overleaping the law is of greater evil than a strict adherence to its imperfect provisions.
>
> It is incumbent on those only who accept of great charges, to risk themselves on great occasions, when the safety of the nation, or some of its very high interests are at stake. An officer is bound to obey orders; yet he would be a bad one who should do it in cases for which they were not intended, and which involved the most important consequences. The line of discrimination between cases may be difficult; but the good officer is bound to draw it at his own peril, and throw himself on the justice of his country and the rectitude of his motives.[77]

Andrew Jackson declared to have acted on similar principles when he imposed martial law in New Orleans as a commander in the War of 1812, going so far as to arrest a federal judge who had ordered the release of a state legislator whom Jackson had also arrested. Jackson also arrested the U.S. Attorney and a state judge for attempting to obtain the release of the federal judge in the state courts.[78] The prisoners were released after the treaty of peace, but the federal judge sought to hold Jackson in contempt. Jackson argued his actions could be justified only by "necessity" where the "permanent preservation of constitutional rights" is at risk; and the necessity must not be "doubtful." The judge imposed a fine, which Jackson paid. Jackson is then reported to have said that when the danger is "past," he should "submit cheerfully to the operation of the laws, when they punished acts which were done to preserve them," and that he should "undergo the penalty of the law, and find his indemnity in the approbation of his own conscience."[79]

Justice Joseph Story, in the case of *The Apollon*, explained why a private party injured by a governmental act done in an emergency situation, but which the laws did not authorize, was entitled to recover for the injury. "It may be fit and proper for the government, in the exercise of the high discretion confided to the executive, for great public purposes, to act on a sudden emergency, or to prevent an irreparable mischief, by summary measures, which are not found in the text of the laws," Story observed. "Such measures are properly matters of state, and if the responsibility is taken, under justifiable circumstances, the Legislature will doubtless apply a proper indemnity. But this Court can only look to the questions, whether the laws have been violated; and if they were, justice demands, that the injured party should receive a suitable redress."[80] In other words, a private party injured by an illegal act can recover in an appropriate case, but the legislature can always indemnify the officer who exceeded legal authority if there had been great justification for the officer having acted in that manner.

Even in England, emergency powers were understood to be extraconstitutional. Michael McConnell relates the story of the grain crisis of 1766. There was a severe shortage of grain but Parliament was out of session; King George III therefore imposed a forty-day embargo on shipping grain out of the kingdom without any statutory authority for doing so. The King had sought to justify his actions as constitutional on the grounds that he had power to act for the public safety during the recess of Parliament. When Parliament reconvened, it disagreed: It declared the embargo to have been unlawful, but indemnified the officers because the acts, although unlawful, had been "necessary for the safety and preservation" of the kingdom.[81]

Lucius Wilmerding Jr. summarized this doctrine of emergency powers in 1952, writing in the aftermath of the *Steel Seizure Case*. The Founders, Wilmerding wrote, "thought it incumbent on those who accept great charges to risk themselves on great occasions, when the safety of the nation or some of its very high interests were at stake." But, Wilmerding explained,

> they never confounded acts which the law says may be lawfully done in a case of necessity with acts done in violation of the law for the public good. They never pretended that acts of the latter type were legal acts. When, in some cases of urgent necessity, they ventured to act without law or against law, they boldly took a responsibility; they ran the risk of the law, sometimes the risk of their fortune in damages; then they hastened to acknowledge on the records of the legislature that they had done a thing, meritorious indeed, but illegal; and they asked the legislature to cover them with an indemnity.[82]

There is no better summary of the doctrine of emergency powers in the American constitutional system. It is a view that has been largely lost to modern generations, but one they would do well to recover.[83]

9

Foreign Affairs

Prominent scholars of constitutional law have observed that the Constitution "is strangely uninformative with respect to foreign affairs."[1] It is "laconic" on the topic and an "invitation to struggle" for primacy in the field.[2] Formalists have argued that several foreign affairs powers are not specified in the constitutional text, but that a residual grant of executive power authorizes the President to exercise them.[3] Functionalists and living constitutionalists, for their part, claim the President's unenumerated foreign affairs powers exist by virtue of necessity, inherent attributes of sovereignty, or historical gloss.[4]

This chapter dissents. It is true, as some scholars have observed, that Congress has most of the foreign affairs powers.[5] But it does not follow that the President only has cramped or narrow powers in the field. Both "congressional primacy" advocates and pro-executive formalists who have relied on a residuum of foreign affairs powers have taken unnecessarily stringent views of the President's granted powers. And, simultaneously, some in the latter group have presumed that the President has more power by virtue of the residuum than the constitutional text warrants.

Some have argued, for example, that without a residuum or historical gloss the President's right to communicate with foreign nations or instruct ambassadors, enter into non-treaty executive agreements, or set foreign policy would be unclear.[6] This chapter will show, however, that the power to appoint ambassadors covers much of the necessary ground. Ambassadors were understood under the law of nations to "manage" relations and communicate with foreign nations. It is absurd to suggest there is no power in the Constitution to manage such relations or communicate with foreign powers. It is also a mistake to suggest the President has a power to "set" foreign policy. The President can express a policy preference, but its efficacy depends on the Constitution's formal distribution of powers. The President can announce the Monroe Doctrine, but only Congress can impose consequences on a European nation for interfering in the American hemisphere. And whether executive agreements have any legal effect depends on powers that Congress has delegated to the President or that Congress subsequently chooses to exercise.

Simply put, a proper textual analysis of the Constitution accounts for all that is necessary in foreign affairs. And such an analysis reveals that both functionalists and formalists have sometimes defended historical practices that have unnecessarily aggrandized the President's powers. The President has ample powers over foreign affairs, but such powers must always be assessed in light of congressional prerogatives and the Constitution's separation of powers.[7]

The chapter begins with two early foreign affairs episodes: the neutrality proclamation and the Monroe Doctrine. It then jumps to a modern and prominent dispute in *Zivotofsky v. Kerry* involving passports, the legal status of Jerusalem, and whether the President has a unilateral power to "recognize" foreign governments. Finally, the chapter explores in more depth the treaty power and the distinction between treaties and executive agreements. It demonstrates how the Constitution's formal text can help resolve most questions about the distribution of foreign affairs powers between Congress and the President.

9.1 PACIFICUS AND HELVIDIUS

In 1793, war was spreading between England and France. The conflict raised a thorny problem: Was the United States obligated to come to the aid of France because of the mutual assistance treaty the two nations had signed when the United States needed France's aid in the Revolutionary War? Or was the treaty inapplicable because France's wars with European powers were offensive rather than defensive? Or because the treaty with King Louis XVI did not contemplate a war to perpetuate the revolutionary government that deposed and executed him? The new nation could add little to France's efforts, whereas an entanglement in these European disputes had significant risks. President Washington issued a proclamation of neutrality. Was it constitutional?[8]

A famous and pseudonymous debate ensued between Alexander Hamilton and James Madison on the constitutionality of Washington's proclamation. Hamilton, writing as "Pacificus," defended it.[9] He first argued that such a proclamation did not naturally fall within the power of the legislature. "The Legislative Department is not the organ of intercourse between the [United States] and foreign Nations. It is charged neither with making nor interpreting Treaties." Thus, it is "not naturally that Organ of the Government which is to pronounce the existing condition of the Nation, with regard to foreign Powers, or to admonish the Citizens of their obligations and duties as founded upon that condition of things."[10] Nor could the judicial department issue such a proclamation because "[t]he province of that Department is to decide litigations in particular cases," and the judiciary "has no concern with pronouncing upon the external political relations of Treaties between Government and Government."[11] Thus, Hamilton concluded,

> It appears to be connected with [the executive] department in various capacities, as the *organ* of intercourse between the Nation and foreign Nations – as the interpreter of the National Treaties in those cases in which the Judiciary is not

competent, that is in the cases between Government and Government – as that Power, which is charged with the Execution of the Laws, of which Treaties form a part – as that Power which is charged with the command and application of the Public Force.[12]

Because the President is the organ of intercourse between nations and can interpret treaties as part of executing those treaties, the President is the most natural person to issue a proclamation *declaring* the current condition of the nation with respect to other nations.

Hamilton could have stopped there. Although Madison, writing as Helvidius, charged that treatymaking and determining on war are more legislative decisions,[13] Hamilton was surely right that the President could declare a state of peace until Congress decided to go to war.[14] Hamilton, however, proceeded to make an additional argument that he admitted later in his essay was unnecessary. After concluding that the President was the most natural organ to issue a proclamation of neutrality, he quoted Article II's Vesting Clause and stated that the rest of Article II "designate[s] particular cases of Executive Power." He listed the commander-in-chief clause and the power to make treaties and appointments. "The general doctrine then of our constitution is," Hamilton advocated, "that the Executive Power of the Nation is vested in the President; subject only to the *exceptions* and *qualifications* which are expressed in the instrument." Among those qualifications and exceptions were the powers of appointment and treatymaking, which were shared with the Senate, and the power to declare war, which the Constitution assigned to Congress.[15]

Hamilton's essay was the genesis of the "residuum" theory of executive power.[16] He appeared to argue that there is a general, residual foreign affairs power that is part of the "executive power," and that this foreign affairs power might otherwise be absent from the Constitution. In other words, Hamilton articulated a substantive, residuum account of the Vesting Clause, and that account included not merely law execution authorities but apparently also any power in its nature "executive" or that had been exercised by the royal monarch by virtue of the royal prerogative. The power to manage foreign relations was among those powers.

Hamilton invoked the removal power debates in support of this residuum reading. Madison responded, however, that although "the executive power" included the power to oversee the execution of the laws, from which could be derived the power to remove, it did not follow that other substantive authorities like treatymaking or war could be similarly derived. "To justify any favourable inference from this case, it must be shewn, that the powers of war and treaties are of a kindred nature to the power of removal, or at least are equally within a grant of executive power," Madison explained. "[N]o analogy, or shade of analogy, can be traced between a power in the supreme officer responsible for the faithful execution of the laws, to displace a subaltern officer employed in the execution of the laws; and a power to make treaties, and to declare war . . . ."[17] Thus, both Madison and Hamilton agreed that

Article II's Vesting Clause was a substantive grant of power, but disagreed on whether it was a vesting of merely law-execution authorities or also other royal prerogatives.

Hamilton went on to say that his discussion of the Vesting Clause was unnecessary. He admitted that "though it has been thought adviseable to vindicate the authority of the Executive on this broad and comprehensive ground – it was not absolutely necessary to do so." He wrote that the "clause of the constitution which makes it [the President's] duty to 'take care that the laws be faithfully executed' might alone have been relied upon, and this simple process of argument pursued."[18] He explained:

> The President is the constitutional Executor of the laws. Our Treaties and the laws of Nations form a part of the law of the land. He who is to execute the laws must first judge for himself of their meaning. In order to the observance of that conduct, which the laws of nations combined with our treaties prescribed to this country, in reference to the present War in Europe, it was necessary for the President to judge for himself whether there was any thing in our treaties incompatible with an adherence to neutrality. Having judged that there was not, he had a right, and if in his opinion the interests of the Nation required it, it was his duty, as Executor of the laws, to proclaim the neutrality of the Nation, to exhort all persons to observe it, and to warn them of the penalties which would attend its non observance.
>
> The Proclamation has been represented as enacting some new law. This is a view of it entirely erroneous. It only proclaims a *fact* with regard to the *existing state* of the Nation, informs the citizens of what the laws previously established require of them in that state, & warns them that these laws will be put in execution against the Infractors of them.[19]

That is all there is to it. Both Madison and Hamilton exaggerated in these debates. Madison was surely right that warmaking and treatymaking are not executive powers, or at least that the Constitution gives the legislative branch a say in those powers. But it did not follow that the Neutrality Proclamation was an act of warmaking or treatymaking. At most, the President was interpreting an existing treaty and keeping the country in a state of peace until Congress chose to declare war. That is where Hamilton could have rested his argument. He did not need to make a gratuitous claim about the Vesting Clause. That claim was also dubious because no one doubted Congress's power to declare a state of neutrality, and so even granting the premise of a residuum would not have established that the power rested with the President.

9.2 ESTABLISHING FOREIGN POLICY

The Neutrality Proclamation illustrates an important insight about the President's powers over foreign affairs. Strictly speaking, the issuance of the proclamation was not the exercise of power at all. Anybody can speak. Anybody can write. The heart of the question is different: whether a particular constitutional actor has power to make good on what is said. The President, for example, could have declared that the United States was on the side of England; but only Congress could have declared war against France.

The Neutrality Proclamation nicely illustrates this point because Washington, in the proclamation, directed the criminal prosecution of individuals taking actions inconsistent with the United States' position of neutrality.[20] A prosecution was brought against an American citizen, Gideon Henfield, who had taken up arms on behalf of the French, but the jury refused to convict.[21] Apparently, the jury thought that without a congressional law on the question, there was no crime.[22] As Chief Justice John Marshall later wrote, "it was universally asked" in democratic papers at the time, "[W]hat law had been offended, and under what statute was the indictment supported? Were the American people already prepared to give to a proclamation the force of a legislative act, and to subject themselves to the will of the executive?"[23] The Constitution gives Congress the enumerated power "to define ...Offences against the Law of Nations."[24] Thus, Congress subsequently enacted the Neutrality Act of 1794;[25] it appears only one other prosecution was brought prior to Congress's enactment, which also resulted in acquittal.[26]

Moreover, the jury instruction in Henfield's case did not mention the proclamation;[27] Henfield's acts may have occurred before the proclamation was even issued, or at least before he had been aware of it.[28] The Attorney General had given an opinion to the Secretary of State that Henfield was punishable for violating various peace treaties and the "common law," not the proclamation.[29] The proclamation also did not purport to establish any law, but rather directed prosecutions for violations of the "law of nations."[30] The judges similarly instructed the jury that Gideon offended against the law of nations and existing treaties, making no mention of the proclamation.[31] Although in one grand jury instruction Chief Justice Jay mentioned the proclamation, he argued it was "consistent with and declaratory of the conduct enjoined by the law of nations."[32] The judicial department is "charged with the interpretation of treaties," Hamilton had said, "but it exercises this function only where contending parties bring before it a specific controversy."[33] That is exactly what happened in these prosecutions.

That is also what appears to have happened in the few reported cases involving maritime captures that occurred prior to the Act of 1794 and that potentially violated neutrality.[34] One federal district judge in South Carolina specifically mentioned the executive branch's instructions and regulations to the customs collectors regarding enforcing the proclamation of neutrality.[35] He stated that "these instructions were not binding on the court," although they were "entitled to attention as expressive of the wishes of the government founded upon the law of nations."[36] In another case, he observed that the Court "cannot notice" the "interference of the president of the United States" in the matter because the "constitution has wisely separated the judicial and executive departments."[37]

When it came to the question of whether prizes – the cargo of belligerent merchant ships captured by the other belligerent – could be sold in American cities, the State Department consulted the writers on the law of nations and could not find much precedent or consensus. The President did not act alone to prohibit prize sales and instead referred the issue to Congress.[38] The Senate passed a provision prohibiting such sales as part of the Neutrality Act, but it was struck by the more pro-French House. Eventually the Senate ratified the Jay Treaty, which prohibited the sale of captured British vessels in American ports.[39] In later years, Chief Justice Marshall, interpreting the law of nations for himself when sitting on a circuit court, held that such sales were unlawful under the law of nations without express authorization from the neutral nation.[40]

In none of these discussions or adjudications did anyone appear to argue that the President could on his own authority prohibit such sales. The President could only enforce a statute, a treaty, or the law of nations.[41] President Washington did forbid the French consuls from adjudicating prizes in American ports, but the only consequence for disobedience was revoking the credentials of the French ministers.[42] Such action was within the President's constitutional power to "receive Ambassadors and other public Ministers."[43]

The lesson of the foregoing materials is that the President could proclaim neutrality and announce his view of United States policy, but he could not alter existing legal relations. He could interpret existing treaties and the law of nations for himself in adopting his course of policy. The courts, however, would interpret those existing relations for themselves in cases that properly came before them. And it was up to Congress to alter them, or to make the law of nations binding in court through legislation defining offenses against it. As Washington explained when submitting to Congress his instructions to the customs collectors, by his proclamation he had hoped merely to declare "the existing legal state of things."[44]

One further example demonstrates the nature of the President's authority. When a French vessel seized an English merchant vessel in American waters, the administration demanded its release, and the French complied.[45] That, too, did not depend on any special power to set foreign policy, or on a residuum of power. Had the French refused, which they did on other occasions, that might have been cause for war with France; but the President could not have unilaterally ordered a military reprisal.[46] Nor could Washington unilaterally order financial restitution to the British. "[A]lthough the usage of other nations may be opposed to this practice" of referring such matters to Congress, Washington wrote, "the difference may result from the difference between their constitutions and ours, and from the prerogative of their Executives."[47] As the district judge in South Carolina noted, most complaints about vessels "improperly fitted out in our ports" had to "be made to the executive, who will proceed by negotiation to obtain the due redress."[48] That the President could negotiate with foreign powers was nothing new. Or as Hamilton had said, the President must interpret the treaties and the law of nations "in the cases between Government and Government."[49] That is what President Washington did, and the effect of his proclamation was limited to such cases.

To summarize: The President's proclamation had no domestic legal effect. The President could pursue the neutrality policy only through diplomatic channels and his other acknowledged powers, such as when he revoked consular credentials.[50] The courts would interpret any statutes, treaties, and the law of nations for themselves, without reference to the President's proclamation. And Congress had the power to define offenses against that law and would not be bound by the President's view. Similarly, the President might think a foreign nation has violated American neutrality, but only Congress can decide whether that is sufficient cause for war and whether the President's assessment is correct.

Nor did the President's proclamation appear to have any meaningful international legal effect. The proclamation announced the President's view that any hostile actions on the part of American citizens were unauthorized by the government and therefore ought not to give the other nation cause for war.[51] But the state of neutrality did not exist by virtue of the President's proclamation, which merely announced the President's view that the nation was in such a condition. Had Congress declared war, for example, no one would have doubted that the President's proclamation had no contrary international legal effect. And had Washington declared that, pursuant to some treaty, the United States had to support one belligerent over another, it is the treaty that would have created that legal state. There is no evidence suggesting that in the absence of treaties or congressional declarations, the President could have unilaterally proclaimed that the United States would support one belligerent over another. A statutory or constitutional grant of power would still be required to take any action consistent with such a proclamation, and the proclamation would arguably be unconstitutional for the additional reason that it would risk provoking war and usurping Congress's prerogatives.

In short, the neutrality episode does not compel the view that the President has unenumerated, inherent, or residual foreign affairs powers. One can understand the Monroe Doctrine in the same way. In 1823, President Monroe declared that it would be the policy of the United States to oppose any European interference in the Americas. He stated in his annual message to Congress that the United States "could not view any interposition" on the part of European powers "for the purpose of oppressing" or "controlling" their former dependencies in South America "in any other light than as the manifestation of an unfriendly disposition toward the United States."[52] Was the Monroe Doctrine constitutional? Where did the President get the power to declare a general "policy" of the United States with respect to foreign nations? Can this statement of policy be justified only by a general, residual foreign affairs power?

The better view is that the President's statement was not an exercise of power at all. If a European nation did interfere in the American hemisphere, the President still could not take military action without a declaration of war from Congress. Nor could the President unilaterally abrogate existing regulations of foreign commerce; only Congress could repeal its prior laws on such questions for the purpose of imposing penalties on European powers. That demonstrates once again that anyone can talk, and the President has the loudest megaphone. But whether anyone can make good on what one says depends on the Constitution's distribution of powers.[53]

The Monroe Doctrine presents a final wrinkle. The President declared that the United States would *not* be neutral if European powers took certain actions. David Currie argued that as a result the declaration was possibly unconstitutional because it effectively pre-committed the nation to go to war. Congress, Currie argued, would not truly be free to make an independent decision whether or not to declare war because the national honor would be at stake.[54] That may be the case, but the point remains: The President could not on his own authority send the army and navy to a South American country to stop European interference. Although the President could declare the sentiments of the nation, it was still up to Congress to authorize concrete actions.

9.3 RECOGNITION

The President's ability to set foreign policy was at issue more recently in the 2015 case *Zivotofsky v. Kerry*, involving the power to "recognize" foreign governments.[55] In 2002, Congress enacted a law requiring the Secretary of State to list "Israel," at the parents' request, as the country of birth for any American born in Jerusalem to U.S. citizen parents. This designation was to appear both on the individual's passport and on the consular report of birth abroad. The law was enacted in part to demonstrate Congress's support for Israel. The State Department, however, had for a long time provided that any American born in Jerusalem could not have the country "Israel" listed on these documents. That was consistent with the foreign policy of many U.S. presidents not to recognize any one nation's sovereignty over Jerusalem. When the law was enacted, President George W. Bush issued a signing statement asserting that if the statutory provision were mandatory, that would "impermissibly interfere with the President's constitutional authority to formulate the position of the United States, speak for the Nation in international affairs, and determine the terms on which recognition is given to foreign states."[56]

When the State Department refused to list Israel as the birthplace of Menachem Binyamin Zivotofsky, his parents sued. Thirteen years later, his case finally arrived on the merits at the Supreme Court of the United States. The majority of the Court correctly observed that the President's action in refusing to list Israel as the place of birth fell into Justice Jackson's third category in *Youngstown*; his power was therefore at its lowest ebb.[57] One would think that that would have resolved the case. After all, for the President's power to be *exclusive* and *preclusive* – for the President to be able to ignore a law of Congress – the relevant presidential power ought to be clearly derivable from the constitutional text.

The majority could point to no such text. It rightly observed that the President has the duty to "receive Ambassadors and other public Ministers."[58] But it is not entirely clear this duty implies a power to recognize governments at all, let alone an exclusive power to recognize governments for all purposes beyond simply accepting an ambassador's credentials. Hamilton wrote in *The Federalist* that this duty was "more a matter of dignity than of authority," given to the President simply because Congress would not always be in session.[59] And Michael McConnell has written that the clause implies the duty to receive ambassadors from nations already recognized under the law of nations, suggesting either that recognition flowed from facts and conditions in the other country or that the power to recognize must come from some other source.[60]

Hamilton somewhat changed his tune, writing later as Pacificus that the power to receive ambassadors "includes that of judging, in the case of a Revolution of Government in a foreign Country, whether the new rulers are competent organs of the National Will and ought to be recognised or not."[61] In the context of the neutrality debate and the existing treaty with France, the question thus became whether to give "operation or not" to that preexisting treaty. "For until the new Government is *acknowledged*, the treaties between the nations, as far at least as regards *public* rights, are of course suspended."[62] President Washington did receive Ambassador Genet, thereby recognizing the revolutionary French government. But Madison responded to Hamilton that under the law of nations, the question was simply whether the ambassador's "credentials [are] from the existing and acting government of his country[.]"[63] That was a question of fact. In only extraordinary circumstances might a government be so illegitimate that it ought not to be recognized; but that would be for the nation to decide, not for the executive department acting alone.[64]

Even if the Receptions Clause gives the President an incidental power to recognize foreign governments for the purpose of deciding whether to receive an ambassador, there was no question in *Zivotofsky* of receiving an ambassador. The United States had long ago received ambassadors from Israel and continued to do so. The question is entirely different: namely, the scope of Israel's recognized territory. The question is whether the Receptions Clause, even if it gives the President some power to recognize foreign governments for that purpose, implies the power to make any and all decisions related to recognition.

The Constitution's text suggests otherwise. The Constitution assigns many powers to Congress that might depend on Congress's recognition of foreign governments. Congress has the power to regulate foreign commerce; surely it has the right to decide whether to tax imports from Jerusalem the same way it taxes imports from Israel.[65] Or to break off trade with an illegitimate government. Or to impose economic sanctions. Or to recognize an insurgent group by authorizing war on their behalf.[66] Congress also has the power to establish and appropriate funds for embassies and ambassadorships; surely it can thereby decide whether to recognize foreign governments.[67] And the Senate can refuse to confirm an ambassador to a country whose government it believes is illegitimate.

Congress's power to make uniform rules of naturalization, in combination with the Necessary and Proper Clause, gave it the power to provide for consular reports of births abroad, which are evidence of citizenship, and to provide for passports. Congress's foreign commerce power similarly supported Congress's ability to prescribe regulations for passports, which authorize Americans to travel abroad to engage in commerce with foreign nations. If in so exercising its enumerated powers Congress also expresses a view about foreign policy, so be it; nothing would prevent Congress from doing so.

The majority's remaining textual analysis was similarly unpersuasive. The majority relied on the powers to make treaties and appoint ambassadors, but of course those are shared with the Senate.[68] And again, those powers would at most suggest that the President has a concurrent authority to recognize foreign governments for the President's purposes. The President can refuse to make treaties with illegitimate governments, just as the President's agreeing to negotiate may imply recognition. It hardly follows that Congress is thereby disabled from expressing its views on recognition through exercising its own powers, such as those over naturalization and foreign commerce. To take a contemporary example, President Obama could negotiate a nuclear agreement with Iran, but Congress could continue to impose economic sanctions or refuse to confirm an ambassador.

The majority in *Zivotofsky* danced around Congress's enumerated powers by rather limply and unpersuasively arguing that the President's recognition power was "exclusive." "The various ways in which the President may unilaterally effect recognition – and the lack of any similar power vested in Congress [!] – suggest that" the President's power is exclusive, the Court held.[69] It then added "functional considerations" to the mix, announcing that "the Nation must have a single policy regarding which governments are legitimate in the eyes of the United States and which are not." "Recognition," the Court added, "is a topic on which the Nation must 'speak . . . with one voice.' That voice must be the President's." That is so because "only the Executive has the characteristic of unity at all times."[70] The majority's opinion thus boiled down to functional considerations – and when the President's power was at its lowest ebb.

Properly analyzed, the Constitution demonstrates that both Congress and the President have powers over recognition. Each can incidentally recognize foreign governments through exercising their respective powers. Contrary to what most scholars of the presidency seem to believe, there is simply no free-floating "Recognition Power." The writers on international law do not even agree on the nature of such a power.[71] The central ramification of recognition appears to be the right to diplomatic relations,[72] which is precisely the ground the Constitution already covers with its rules relating to ambassadors. And even if international law today recognizes "recognition" as a discrete power, it hardly follows that that power, as defined under modern international law, is vested somewhere in a constitution written at a time when international law did not recognize such a power. Emerich de Vattel's treatise on the law of nations spoke of recognition in the context of receiving ambassadors; so did Hugo Grotius's prominent treatise.[73] Blackstone similarly made no special mention of recognition, although he did list the power to send and receive ambassadors as a principal foreign affairs prerogative.[74]

In sum, just as with the Neutrality Proclamation and Monroe Doctrine, whether Congress or the President can effectuate their views on recognition depends on the Constitution's distribution of powers. In *Zivotofsky*, Congress's law did not interfere with the President's reception of any ambassador or the negotiation of any treaty. Thus, the President had a duty to execute Congress's law, which was within its enumerated powers. In the absence of Congress's law, the President certainly had the concurrent power to decide whether Israel would be listed on the relevant documents because that would be a matter of interstitial detail necessary for executing Congress's existing laws respecting passports and consular reports. And in filling in that interstitial detail, the President could rely on his view of the international status of Jerusalem. But once Congress passed a law on point, a law within its enumerated powers, the President had to conform. Whatever concurrent power the President had in the absence of any statute should have given way to the President's duty to take care that the laws be faithfully executed.

9.4 TO TREAT AND MAKE TREATIES

One of the President's few enumerated foreign affairs powers is to make treaties with the advice and consent of the Senate. This power is not particularly controversial. President Washington took the text quite earnestly and presented himself to the Senate for advice in negotiating a treaty with southern Indian tribes. The experience was not promising. Never again did he, or any other President, attend the Senate in person to obtain advance advice about treaty negotiations.[75] The Senate's role has since been understood to be to advise and consent to a treaty mostly after it is negotiated. If the Senate confirms the treaty by a vote of two thirds of Senators present, the President can then officially ratify the treaty; the President can still withhold ratification after the Senate consents.[76]

Some formalists, however, have questioned whether the President has the power to negotiate and communicate generally with foreign nations without a residuum of power.[77] Not all interactions end in treaties. Some end in executive agreements, and some are merely about managing relations.

As an initial matter, it is unclear why speaking to foreign leaders or officials is considered a "power" at all. The significance of such communications derives from subsequent acts that might follow, for example, the making of a treaty. Only the President can "make" a treaty with the Senate, and so foreign leaders know that devising a successful treaty requires talking to the President or the President's ambassadors. These communications are not an exercise of power, but rather are conditions precedent to the subsequent exercise of power.

Even if a source of power were required for all communications and negotiations, the notion the President cannot manage relations without a residuum requires a cramped reading of the power to make treaties. That power implies *treating* with foreign nations.[78] What treating will result in treaties cannot be known in advance. It is not far-fetched to suggest that all presidential and ambassadorial treating therefore falls within the treatymaking power.

At a minimum, ambassadors should be able to communicate with foreign powers and manage foreign relations because that was their role under the law of nations. Vattel described the role of "public ministers," or ambassadors, as enabling nations "to treat and communicate together." Each nation is "possessed of the right to treat and communicate with others," which they do "by the agency of … public ministers."[79] These public ministers are "delegates charged with [the sovereigns'] commands, and vested with their powers," and are "intrusted with the management of public affairs … at a foreign court."[80] Vattel emphasized that such ministers are "representative of a foreign power, – a person charged with the commands of that power, and delegated to manage his affairs."[81] It follows that "[e]very sovereign state then has a right to send and to receive public ministers; for they are necessary instruments in the management of those affairs which sovereigns have to transact with each other, and the channels of that correspondence which they have a right to carry on."[82] The powers to manage foreign relations and communicate with foreign governments are not "missing" at all – at a minimum ambassadors possess them.[83]

The question then becomes whether the President can instruct those ambassadors. Vattel explained that ambassadors are "delegates charged with" the "commands" of the sovereign. An ambassador is "delegated" power to "manage *his* affairs" – that is, the sovereign's. McConnell explains that the power to "send" ambassadors included the power to instruct them.[84] McConnell argues, however, that the Constitution does not empower the President to send ambassadors; the President only appoints.[85] The reason the Convention altered this language was to share this power with other departments. Congress establishes offices, and therefore ambassadorships.[86] The President then nominates to the office, and the Senate advises and consents to the appointment.

This change in language notwithstanding, the treaty power suggests that the President must have the power to instruct ambassadors at least as to treaty negotiations. It is textually possible, although it would be rather surprising, if the President has the power to instruct only with respect to treaty negotiations and nothing else. The way out of the conundrum is to recognize once again that anyone can talk; the President can always instruct. The question is rather the constitutional obligation of ambassadors to obey. There are two possibilities.

The first is that ambassadors are inferior officers because they are not the head of any "department." They are at least plausibly inferior to the Secretary of State and have to follow the Secretary's orders. And the Secretary must follow the President's orders by statute.[87] Even if there were no statutory provision requiring the Secretary of State to follow the President's instructions, the President could always demand opinions and threaten removal if necessary.

The second is that, if ambassadors are principal officers as more commonly assumed, the President would be able to recall them because of the common law maxim that one who appoints also removes. The same arguments that justify the President's power to remove in the domestic context apply in the foreign affairs context. The President has the executive power and must be able to oversee law execution. Ambassadors engage in statutory duties, for example, those relating to consular reports of births abroad, just as domestic officers do. Additionally, to the extent they merely manage relations, the President can surely direct them if their work might lead to treaty negotiations. And if ambassadors have duties imposed upon them by the law of nations while managing their sovereign's relations abroad, the President can perhaps oversee the faithful execution of that body of law, too. As with other principal officers, a power to remove does not necessarily imply a power to interfere with statutory duties, but there would be nothing improper about removing an ambassador who neglected to follow orders when the ambassador does not otherwise have any independent duties under statutory law.

In sum, there are alternative ways to view the President's general management of foreign affairs. One possibility is that such management and communications are not an exercise of power at all and are imbued with significance only because of the subsequent exercises of statutory or constitutional power that they precede. Another possibility is that the President's power to appoint and recall ambassadors, and therefore to instruct them in their general ambassadorial duties, is the source of the President's power to treat with foreign nations and to act as the "organ of communication" between them and the United States.[88] Still another is that the President's treatymaking power implies treating with foreign nations generally.

The difference between these possibilities and the residuum theory should not be overstated. Most residual theorists reject the proposition that the President has independent lawmaking authority in foreign affairs by virtue of the residuum.[89] If the residuum is necessary only to engage in communications with foreign nations, or proclaim the nation's position in foreign affairs, or for the President to exercise other minor powers, then as noted previously not too much rides on the distinction between this and other theories of the executive power. Those differences might, however, be more pronounced in the context of treaty terminations and executive agreements, discussed presently.

9.5 TO UNMAKE TREATIES

A controversial question in this domain is whether the President may unilaterally terminate existing treaties. The most prominent modern example is President Jimmy

Carter's abrogating the United States' Mutual Defense Treaty with Taiwan as part of his recognition of the communist government of the People's Republic of China. Modern formalist scholars argue that the power to terminate treaties is part of the President's "residual" foreign affairs powers.[90] Some functionalists agree that the President must be able to terminate treaties.[91]

The Constitution's distribution of powers suggests that it is generally Congress that must terminate a treaty, although it depends on the precise treaty at issue. A non-self-executing treaty, for example, requires congressional legislation to implement. Congress can therefore breach the treaty by failing to pass implementing legislation or by repealing implementing legislation. Presumably, if Congress has the power to breach the treaty, it has the power to announce in advance that it is terminating the treaty. Or it can so announce as part of a repeal of implementing legislation. The President can claim to terminate such a treaty, but of course the President cannot repeal any of the laws Congress has passed to implement it. The President would have no constitutional power to back up such talk.

Congress also has several enumerated powers that may be relevant to a particular treaty. The President and the Senate can negotiate and make a commercial treaty, but Congress also has power to make regulations of foreign commerce. If Congress enacts such a regulation that is inconsistent with an existing commercial treaty, then Congress will have effectively required the United States to breach that treaty. Between treaties and laws of Congress, neither is "higher law" relative to the other; the ordinary rule that laws enacted later in time supersede prior inconsistent ones would apply. The historical record supports this conclusion because over the nineteenth century, Congress instructed the President on several occasions to withdraw from or terminate commercial treaties,[92] and occasionally Presidents have purported to terminate such treaties when inconsistent with Congress's statutes.[93]

Congress's declare war power may also be relevant. In 1798, Congress passed a resolution terminating the United States' treaty of alliance with France. If Congress can declare war, then surely it can take related actions short of a full-scale war – including abrogating a treaty, which would occur as a matter of course if war had been declared.[94] That is what happened in 1798: Congress abrogated the treaty as part of a series of measures authorizing military actions against France.[95] More generally, if it is up to Congress whether to authorize military action in fulfillment of a treaty obligation, as was the case with the U.S.–Taiwan Mutual Defense Treaty, then Congress can breach the treaty by refusing such authorization. And, to repeat, if it is within Congress's power to fulfill or breach a treaty commitment, then presumably it can announce in advance that it considers the treaty abrogated.

A self-executing treaty is more complicated. If one supposes there are treaties the President can, on independent authority, execute – an extradition treaty may be an example, or one involving matters over which Congress has delegated wide discretion to the President – then the President alone can breach the treaty by refusing to act. And if the President alone can breach the treaty, the President can presumably announce the treaty abrogated. The President's duty faithfully to execute the laws, however, may include treaties, which bind at least judges as the supreme "law of the land."[96] A duty of faithful execution might then preclude a right to abrogate such treaties unilaterally.

At best, the President would retain the right to terminate the treaty in only two circumstances. The President might conclude that the other party had already breached the treaty such that it was no longer binding, or that other circumstances exist where international law might permit withdrawal.[97] Or, if the treaty included a provision specifying conditions for its own termination, the President might announce those conditions had been met; but the President could not on independent initiative create such conditions if beyond the President's own statutory or constitutional powers. Both arguments are supportable under the President's power to execute the laws and treaties of the United States. Contrary to what some residual scholars have written, the Taiwan treaty termination would still be unconstitutional because even though the treaty provided that either party may give a notice of withdrawal, it does not follow that the President may unilaterally give such notice on behalf of the nation.[98]

The nineteenth-century historical record casts even more doubt on the President's power to abrogate a treaty unilaterally because the Senate or Congress generally authorized the President to terminate self-executing treaties as well.[99] It was not until 1909 that the State Department took the position that the President had a unilateral treaty termination authority.[100] It was not until the late 1930s that a President of the United States unilaterally abrogated a treaty that did not conflict with any U.S. statutes.[101] The presidential power of treaty termination was an invention of the mid twentieth century.

9.6 EXECUTIVE AGREEMENTS

Presidents of the United States have negotiated many agreements with foreign nations never submitted to the Senate for ratification. These have included postal conventions, trade agreements, and the Obama Administration's Iran nuclear agreement, to name a few prominent examples. The Constitution assumes a distinction between treaties and other agreements in the tenth section of Article I, where it provides that "No State shall enter into any Treaty, Alliance, or Confederation," and separately that "No State shall, without the Consent of Congress, . . . enter into any Agreement or Compact with another State, or with a foreign Power."[102] Emerich de Vattel's treatise on the law of nations appears to have guided the Founders on this distinction between treaties or alliances and agreements or compacts.[103] Vattel explained, "A treaty . . . is a compact . . . either for perpetuity, or for a considerable time."[104] In contrast, "compacts which have temporary matters for their objects are called agreements, conventions, and pactions," and "are perfected in their execution once for all," as opposed to requiring a "successive execution whose duration equals that of the treaty."[105] St. George Tucker's early commentary on the Constitution refers to Vattel on the question of the Constitution's distinction between treaties and compacts.[106]

Some scholars and commentators have argued that such agreements are end-runs around the Treaty Clause.[107] Others have prominently argued that the President does not have a textually enumerated power to enter into such non-treaty agreements, and that this is a "missing" foreign affairs power for which only a residuum can account.[108] Quite to the contrary, the Constitution's distribution of powers readily accounts for executive agreements. The insight is once again to recognize that anyone can talk.

As part of the power to treat, or to instruct ambassadors with respect to managing relations, the President can enter into an agreement with a foreign nation. Whether the President can make good on the agreement depends entirely on the Constitution's distribution of powers. The President can implement only few agreements on independent initiative. An armistice might fall into this category: The President, as commander in chief of the armed forces, can pause fighting if doing so is strategically wise or as a condition precedent to peace negotiations.[109] An armistice of this type does not derogate from any other actor's constitutional powers and seems to follow from the President's status as commander in chief and to make treaties.

An early example of a similar executive agreement was President Jefferson's agreement with Spain to create a neutral territory around the Red River to avoid an accidental conflict between the two nations. The agreement was within the power of the executive department because Jefferson could have unilaterally prohibited the army from entering that area of the Louisiana Purchase.[110] President Madison entered into an executive agreement with Great Britain over the treatment of prisoners of war, which also seems within the President's authority as commander in chief.[111]

There are other agreements the President can undertake because Congress has delegated broad powers. The Rush–Bagot agreement between the United States and Great Britain to reduce each country's naval presence on the Great Lakes is one early example: Congress had over one year prior to the agreement statutorily authorized the president to remove the armed vessels from the lakes.[112] More recently, President Obama could lift economic sanctions on Iran in exchange for promises that Iran would not develop nuclear weapons because Congress had delegated broad authority to vary sanctions on the basis of national security interests.[113] The President did not need a treaty because he could unilaterally take the relevant action under the statute. He could have reduced sanctions even if Iran promised nothing in return.[114]

Most agreements, however, require congressional participation. Postal conventions, for example, were among the earliest non-treaty agreements.[115] The President's agents negotiated these conventions, but the President could not personally deliver foreign mail into the United States. For that, Congress had to establish a postal system pursuant to its powers over post offices and post roads. To execute that agreement, the President needed an established postal system and funds from Congress to pay for international carriage. The same analysis explains trade agreements like the North Atlantic Free Trade Agreement. Congress can enact a law eliminating tariffs on Mexican and Canadian goods pursuant to its power to regulate commerce with foreign nations. It could do so without any agreement on the part of Canada and Mexico.

Two conclusions follow. First, there was no need for a treaty because Congress's enumerated powers were adequate to the task.[116] That is why Congress can often proceed by what has been called a "congressional-executive agreement," which is an international commitment that is simply enacted by Congress and the President as law. Second, most executive agreements require Congress. "Sole" executive agreements, or unilateral executive agreements, can have no legal effect unless Congress has delegated the relevant statutory authority or the President has an enumerated power to act alone.[117]

9.7 ARE TREATIES NECESSARY?

The previous discussion raises a final question: Is the treaty power even necessary? The answer may be surprising. Usually not. So long as Congress has an enumerated power to act, it can act with or without a treaty. It does not even have to wait for the foreign nation. There are important advantages to proceeding by treaty, however. One of the more important advantages is that it communicates to other nations that the terms are binding under U.S. domestic law.

It is true that under international law other nations might view an executive agreement as binding on the United States, but that is simply irrelevant for purposes of the U.S. Constitution: International law cannot assign the President powers not already possessed pursuant to the constitutional distribution of powers. Other nations rely on executive agreements at their own peril. Future Congresses and Presidents might choose to honor them because of other nations' reliance, but there would be no impropriety in their refusing to do so.[118] Even residual theorists accept at the very least that executive agreements cannot have any domestic legal effect, so it is simply irrelevant how other nations view the bindingness of executive agreements that purport to have such effect.[119]

To illustrate the relevance and importance of treaties, consider treaties of alliance. Congress could always come to the aid of another nation without a treaty. One might also hope that the other nation would come to the defense of the United States. But it is a treaty that obligates Congress to do so in the future, and that obligates the other nation; both nations know of this obligation in advance and rely on it. Resolving border disputes also usually requires treaties; Congress could on its own cede federal territory, but the only guarantee of an exchange is a treaty. The principal advantage of the treaty is thus the obligation it imposes on the other party.

Treaties are necessary when the United States seeks perpetual or long-term obligations on the part of another nation, in exchange for similar long-term obligations on the part of the United States. To return to the Rush–Bagot agreement, either country could remilitarize the Great Lakes in the future, and neither would have grounds to claim that the other violated a treaty.

As to subject matters outside of Congress's enumerated powers, treaties alone would be able to create national commitments. Treaties of peace, for example, often resolve the property or other legal claims of foreign nationals that would ordinarily be within a state's control. Extradition treaties might supply another example. It is difficult to locate a source of congressional power to provide for the extradition of persons in the United States to foreign countries. Perhaps that is why extradition agreements are still to this day almost entirely concluded by the Article II treatymaking process.[120]

There may, however, be structural limits to the scope of the treatymaking power. The President and Senate can enter into treaties exceeding Congress's enumerated powers when the matter genuinely involves both nations, such as the property and extradition treaties noted earlier.[121] Whether the President and Senate can enter into other international "conventions" that require the implementation of domestic policy outside of Congress's control is more controversial and possibly unconstitutional.[122]

Treaties, whether within or without Congress's enumerated powers, also have the advantage of being the supreme law of the land under Article VI of the Constitution.[123] Even if there is no congressional legislation implementing a treaty, the treaty can still bind state courts and supersede state law. Treaties of peace adjusting the property claims of foreign nationals, or settling related legal claims, fit that description. If such property or claims were at issue in state court, the treaty would control the outcome.

The Supreme Court's cases approving a presidential power to supersede state law through executive agreements are therefore mistaken.[124] In *United States v. Pink*, the Supreme Court declared that executive agreements have the same "dignity" as treaties and are binding on state courts.[125] It held that the Litvinov Agreement, which President Franklin Roosevelt negotiated with the Soviet Union as part of his recognition of the Soviet government, was binding in state court even though it adjusted existing state-law claims pending against Russian banks. Congress, if it had an appropriate enumerated power, could perhaps have enacted a law implementing such an agreement, which law would then be the supreme law of the land. But Congress did not do so. The Senate could have alternatively ratified the agreement as a treaty, but it did not do so. The Court nevertheless held that the Agreement was valid as part of the President's power to "recognize" the Soviet government. The President, however, has no freestanding recognition power, let alone a further incidental power to make mere executive agreements the supreme law of the land.[126]

In unjustifiably holding that the President had such powers, the Supreme Court did what it has done on many other occasions, with support of scholars of various political and methodological perspectives. It held that the President had more power in foreign affairs than the constitutional text can justify. There is no power to set foreign policy; each branch can announce its views and act according to those views when exercising its respective powers. There is no unitary power to recognize foreign governments; each branch can recognize a government for its own purposes and in pursuance of its own powers. Nor is there a unilateral power to abrogate treaties. And whether executive agreements have any binding effect depends entirely on the relevant constitutional and statutory distribution of powers. Certainly, such executive agreements are not the supreme law of the land, binding in state courts and superseding contrary state law. That status is reserved for treaties.

10

War

Intimately related to questions of foreign policy is the Constitution's distribution of war powers. Congress has power to "declare War, grant Letters of Marque and Reprisal, and make Rules concerning Captures on Land and Water."[1] It has a suite of other military-related powers that also historically belonged to the British monarch as part of the royal prerogative: the powers to "define and punish Piracies and Felonies committed on the high Seas, and Offences against the Law of Nations"; to "raise and support Armies" and "provide and maintain a Navy"; to "make Rules for the Government and Regulation of the land and naval Forces"; to "provide for calling forth the Militia to execute the Laws of the Union, suppress Insurrections and repel Invasions" and, with certain limitations, to "provide for organizing, arming, and disciplining" the militia; and lastly to exercise exclusive legislation over all places purchased from the states "for the Erection of Forts, Magazines, Arsenals, dock-Yards and other needful Buildings."[2] In contrast, the Constitution says about the chief executive only that the "President shall be Commander in Chief of the Army and Navy of the United States, and of the Militia of the several States, when called into the actual Service of the United States."[3]

The central question that arises from this distribution of power is the President's ability to engage in armed conflict without authorization from Congress. The delegates to the Constitutional Convention believed the President would have the power to repel sudden attacks. What is the source of this power? And if it exists, does it extend to other military actions, short of full-scale war, without congressional authorization? The administrations of President Barack Obama and President Donald J. Trump, channeling earlier administrations, officially promulgated the view that the President can engage, without congressional authorization, in any armed conflict short of "war," so long as doing so is in the "national interest." The Obama Administration invoked this rationale to justify bombing Libyan forces, contributing to the death of Libya's leader during an internal civil war. And the first Trump Administration similarly justified the bombing of Syrian targets after that country's leader used chemical weapons.

The power to repel sudden attacks derives from three propositions. First, the President's status as commander in chief permits the use and direction of armed forces if a state of war exists between the United States and another nation. Second, Congress can authorize such a state of war, or another nation can initiate it. Third, a state of war can be "imperfect," meaning any military conflict short of a full-scale, perfect war. Thus, although the academic literature has not been clear about the source of the President's defensive power,[4] when repelling invasions the President is simply using the armed forces to confront an "imperfect war" – any military hostilities short of a perfect war – thrust upon the nation or its people.

From these propositions it follows that the President cannot bomb another nation to protect rebels in an internal civil war or to punish the use of chemical weapons without authorization from Congress or an immediate risk to American lives or property. There may be "war" in those countries, but the President as commander in chief may confront an imperfect or perfect war thrust upon *the United States*; the President may not intervene in wars entirely between other nations without prior congressional approval.

Another important issue is how Congress's power to declare war otherwise limits the President's acknowledged powers. Supposing the President can deploy military forces around the world, take defensive actions, and undertake secret negotiations with foreign nations, what happens if those actions risk provoking war with other nations? At what point do the President's acknowledged powers trench on Congress's power to declare war? As will become clear, the President may only take genuinely defensive actions or proportionate offensive measures necessary to deter future hostilities. The President may not, in other words, escalate a defensive armed conflict without congressional authorization. Nor may the President engage in acts that would constitute acts of war under the law of nations or use otherwise acknowledged presidential powers in a way that creates a serious risk of provoking another nation into war. If a state of imperfect war exists, the President may confront that state of war but not expand it.

10.1 DECLARING WAR

Any discussion of the Constitution and war powers must begin with a short debate at the Constitutional Convention. The Committee of Detail had assigned to Congress the power to "make war."[5] Blackstone used this terminology in his *Commentaries* to describe one of the royal prerogatives.[6] On August 17, James Madison and Elbridge Gerry moved to strike the word "make" and insert "declare" instead, "leaving to the Executive the power to repel sudden attacks." Roger Sherman agreed that the Executive should "be able to repel and not to commence war," but worried that limiting Congress to "declaring" war might give too much power to the President. George Mason was also against "giving the power of war to the Executive," but preferred "declare" over "make."[7] The motion initially failed by a vote of five to four.[8]

One can see the confusion: No one wanted the President to initiate offensive wars, and restricting Congress's powers in any respect from the full prerogative of "making" war would enlarge the President's own war powers. It was not clear by how much. Madison and Gerry supposed the change would leave the President only a defensive power, but others feared it might imply more executive authority. When Rufus King suggested, however, "that 'make' war might be understood to 'conduct' it which was an Executive function," the delegates changed their minds and voted in favor of the substitution by a vote of eight to one.[9]

Two conclusions follow from this short debate. The first and more obvious is that the President was to have the power to conduct war once declared or begun in some other way. Hamilton's draft constitution had proposed that the Senate would have "the sole power of declaring war," and the executive would have "the direction of war when authorized or begun."[10] The change on August 17 suggested this exact division, although Congress and not the Senate alone had the power of declaring war. All the delegates surely recalled the experience of the Continental Congress attempting to conduct the Revolutionary War by committee; no one wanted to repeat it.[11] In fact, the Articles of Confederation had provided that the Confederation Congress had the power of "making rules for the government and regulation of the said land and naval forces, *and directing their operations.*"[12] The present Constitution conspicuously omits the latter power. The President's status as commander in chief, in other words, must authorize the conduct of war; otherwise, nothing in the Constitution gives the President any authority to command the armed forces.[13]

None of that is to say Congress has no authority over the military or grand strategy. Congress's powers to authorize hostilities and to support the military through appropriations include the power to permit or forbid certain military actions. For example, Congress can specify on what conditions to seize French ships, as it did in the 1790s,[14] or can authorize or prohibit the sending of army divisions to Europe, which was debated after World War II.[15] The power to raise armies would seem to include the power to establish bases and thereby to shape the global distribution of U.S. forces.[16] Nothing in the enumeration in the eighth section of Article I, however, suggests anything like a power to dictate specific tactical maneuvers. And the textual changes described earlier suggest that the President's tactical control, at least in wartime, is in any event exclusive.[17]

The second conclusion that follows from the change to "declare" war is that the President was to have some authority to engage in military activities without congressional authorization. It appears, at a minimum, that would include the ability to repel sudden invasions. But this raises further questions. What is the source of this defensive power? And is it limited to defense, or might it extend to other military actions short of full-scale war?

The answers to these questions may lie in an analysis of both the meaning of Congress's power to "declare" war, as well as the President's status as commander in chief. Under the law of nations, to "declare" war had a very specific meaning: to give an armed conflict the international *legal status* of war, thereby triggering the laws of wars. As Michael McConnell notes, a formal declaration of war "affects the treatment of aliens, the application of treason laws, the legitimacy of trade with the enemy nation, the legality of privateering," the confiscation of property, and the applicability of martial law.[18] A declaration, Blackstone explained, also signals to all sides that the public authorities, and not mere private persons, are engaged in hostilities.[19] Textually, Congress's power could be limited to declaring the legal status of wars, while leaving the President authority to commence wars; or, its power could include both declarations of war and the commencement of hostilities.

The narrower view of Congress's power is implausible for at least two reasons.[20] First, nothing in the Constitution gives the President the power to commence a war. The status as head of the armed forces hardly constitutes authorization to use those forces to engage in unauthorized wars. Blackstone described the king's prerogatives over war and peace as part of his powers over foreign intercourse, while the commander-in-chief powers were *domestic* prerogatives.[21] The President's command authority, therefore, does not include the power to commence a war, at least if Blackstone was the Founders' guide on prerogative power. Logically, the constitutional power to declare war must include the power to commence it; otherwise, no institution would possess that power.

Second, Charles Lofgren has shown that the Framers and ratifiers used "declare" essentially synonymously with "authorize."[22] James Wilson, for example, told the Pennsylvania ratifying convention that "[i]t will not be in the power of a single man" to "involve" the United States in war because "the important power of declaring war is vested in the legislature at large."[23] This usage presumes that to declare war is to "involve" the nation in war – that is, to commence it.

Hamilton, in *Federalist* No. 69, similarly explained that the President's power "would amount to nothing more than the supreme command and direction of the military and naval forces, as first general and admiral of the confederacy; while that of the British king extends to the DECLARING of war, and to the RAISING and REGULATING of fleets and armies."[24] The President had only command; Congress did the rest. Madison and Gerry's motion at the Convention reflected the same understanding: Congress would control any offensive use of force; the President would retain only the power to repel sudden attacks. In short, the power to declare war was understood to include the power to commence hostilities; the President as commander in chief would conduct any war authorized by Congress or initiated by an adversary.[25]

But what counts as war? Did Congress's power to commence war include the authorization of military actions short of war? And what in the Constitution's text authorizes the President to take any military actions, including defensive ones, without congressional authorization? To complete the analysis of these questions, it is necessary to understand the distinction between perfect and imperfect wars.

10.2 IMPERFECT WAR

The power to declare – that is, commence – war almost certainly empowered Congress to authorize military actions short of a full-scale war. The inclusion of a power to "grant Letters of Marque and Reprisal" put Congress's authority on this score beyond doubt. As Lofgren explains, such letters authorized individual naval forces to engage in limited hostilities. In the seventeenth century and before, such authorizations were often granted to private vessels for satisfaction of private claims; during the early eighteenth century, nation-states would use "both public naval forces and private ships sailing under private commissions or letters of marque and reprisal" to attack enemy ships.[26] Such authorizations often led to open war, but they were themselves more limited.[27] Blackstone's text supports Lofgren's analysis. The "prerogative of granting" letters of marque and reprisal "plainly derived from" the prerogative "of making war," Blackstone wrote, because such letters create "an incomplete state of hostilities, and generally end[] in a formal denunciation of war."[28]

Early Congresses authorized military hostilities short of war. During the Quasi-War with France in the late 1790s, Congress enacted measures allowing American naval vessels to engage French ships without declaring war outright. Two Supreme Court cases – *Bas v. Tingy* and *Talbot v. Seeman* – arose from this conflict, and in both the Court recognized Congress's power to authorize limited hostilities. These cases elucidate the now mostly forgotten distinction between perfect and imperfect wars.[29]

In *Bas v. Tingy*,[30] the commander of an American public armed ship liberated a merchant vessel that had been seized by a French privateer. A congressional law from 1799, enacted as part of the Quasi-War, allowed the commander of the public armed vessel to acquire one-half of a recaptured ship's property as a "prize," under certain conditions and for certain purposes. Most relevant here, such a vessel had to be retaken from "the enemy." The owner of the recaptured ship argued that because there was no declared war with France, the French were not "the enemy" within the meaning of the statute, and so he did not have to give up half his cargo to the liberating ship. The Justices of the Supreme Court, writing seriatim, rejected the argument.

Justice Alfred Moore wrote that "the relative situation of America and France could" only be communicated by the term "hostility, or war," and thus the parties were enemies.[31] Justice Samuel Chase wrote in more detail: "Congress is empowered to declare a general war, or congress may wage a limited war; limited in place, in objects, and in time," he explained. If Congress declares a "general" war, "its extent and operations are only restricted and regulated by the *jus belli*, forming a part of the law of nations; but if a partial war is waged, its extent and operation depend on our municipal laws."[32] In other words, a declared state of war triggers all the laws of war under the law of nations; but Congress may still authorize a limited state of war, to be governed by Congress's specific laws. In the context of the

Quasi-War, Congress authorized military action "only to citizens appointed by commissions, or exposed to immediate outrage and violence," which Justice Chase argued was a "public war," but only "a partial" one.[33]

Justice William Paterson argued similarly that there is a "public war" between the two nations, but an "imperfect" one – what Justice Chase called a partial or limited public war. The United States and France were "in a qualified state of hostility," and therefore "[a]n imperfect war, or a war, as to certain objects, and to a certain extent, exist[ed] between the two nations."[34] This "imperfect war" was authorized by Congress, suggesting its validity.[35]

Justice Bushrod Washington – George Washington's nephew – wrote the most comprehensive opinion. He argued that a state of war did exist between France and the United States, even if not declared. Washington wrote, of central importance here, that "*every* contention by force between two nations, in external matters, under the authority of their respective governments, is not only war, but public war." He then also distinguished between a declared or "perfect" war, and an "imperfect" war:

> If [a war] be declared in form, it is called *solemn*, and is of the perfect kind; because one whole nation is at war with another whole nation; and *all* the members of the nation declaring war, are authorised to commit hostilities against all the members of the other, in every place, and under every circumstance. In such a war all the members act under a general authority, and all the rights and consequences of war attach to their condition.
>
> But hostilities may subsist between two nations more confined in its nature and extent; being limited as to places, persons, and things; and this is more properly termed *imperfect war*; because not solemn, and because those who are authorised to commit hostilities, act under special authority, and can go no farther than to the extent of their commission. Still, however, it is *public war*, because it is an external contention by force, between some of the members of the two nations, authorised by the legitimate powers. It is a war between the two nations, though all the members are not authorised to commit hostilities such as in a solemn war . . . .[36]

Justice Washington then explained that Congress in 1798–1799 did not call the conflict a "war" because "[s]uch a declaration by congress, might have constituted a perfect state of war, which was not intended by the government."[37] The thrust of all these opinions was the same: Congress had authority to authorize war, both perfect wars and imperfect ones; that is, both complete and solemn wars under the law of nations as well as limited or partial wars.

In *Talbot v. Seeman*,[38] Chief Justice Marshall, then recently appointed to the Court, confirmed that "[t]he whole powers of war being by the constitution of the United States, vested in congress," it followed that "congress may authorize general hostilities, in which case the general laws of war apply to our situation; or partial hostilities, in which case the laws of war, so far as they actually apply to our situation, must be noticed."[39] Chief Justice Marshall then referred repeatedly to the ongoing hostilities with France as our "present war."[40] He again demonstrated that any state of hostilities between nations is a "war" within the meaning of the constitutional grant.

It may be concluded, then, that Congress has the power to commence war, not merely to declare its existence. If Congress declares its existence, or commences a perfect and solemn war through declaration, then all the laws of war apply. Congress can also, however, authorize limited, partial, or imperfect war through its powers to declare war or issue letters of marque and reprisal.

10.3 REPELLING ATTACKS

The distinction between perfect and imperfect war, and the President's status as commander in chief, now supply the answer to the motivating question: What is the source of the President's power to repel invasions?

As noted previously, the President's commander-in-chief status gives the President the power to direct the conduct of war. Being commander in chief therefore entails the power to *use* the armed forces *when a state of war exists* between the United States and other nations. Congress can authorize such a state of war, or other nations can initiate one. The state of war may consist in perfect war, which usually requires a declaration, or imperfect war. The power to repel sudden invasions derives from the now-evident proposition that attacks on the United States create a state of imperfect war. Once a state of imperfect war exists, the President can do what commanders in chief always do: use the armed forces to prosecute that partial, limited, imperfect war that others have thrust upon the nation.

The President cannot, however, go beyond defensive measures. Doing so would trench on Congress's powers to commence war. Defensive measures merely meet the contingencies of an imperfect war thrust upon the United States by an enemy; any other military measures, such as those of offense, which would either create a perfect war or expand the state of imperfect war, can only be authorized by Congress. The President's commander-in-chief status allows the use of force to confront an existing state of imperfect war. It does not allow for the commencement or expansion of that state of war.

10.4 THE FIRST THREE PRESIDENTS

Early constitutional history largely reflects and supports this interpretation of the President's limited unilateral ability to engage in defensive war. A starting point for analysis is the actions and statements of the first three American presidents.

The first military conflict under the Constitution occurred between the United States and the Indian tribes along the Wabash River in the Northwest Territory between 1790 and 1795.[41] Many scholars recognize that President George Washington engaged in at least some offensive expeditions against the tribes without explicit congressional authorization.[42] This precedent has been cited by numerous executive branch lawyers in recent decades to justify unilateral executive actions.[43] It is true that nothing in the existing statutes directly authorized the use of troops for any offensive expeditions, but they did presume that regular troops would "protect" the frontier. The Establishment Act of 1789 authorized the President to nationalize state militias "for the purpose of protecting the inhabitants of the frontiers," and the Establishment Act of 1790 provided the same authorization respecting the militia "for the purpose of aiding the troops now in service, or to be raised by this act, in protecting the inhabitants of the frontiers of the United States."[44] The latter statute presumed troops would be used to protect the frontier. That is consistent with Congress's statute in 1789 adopting the resolves of the Continental Congress respecting the raising of troops,[45] which had provided that several hundred troops "should be stationed on the frontiers to protect the settlers on the public lands from the depredations of the Indians."[46] One article argues that these statutes were tantamount to congressional authorization for the use of force;[47] at a minimum, they authorized the stationing of troops on the frontier to "protect" against the depredations on the part of the tribes.

Even if these statutes did not specifically authorize offensive measures, President Washington made clear in statements and letters that any expeditions into Indian territory were ultimately defensive. In a message to Congress in late 1790, he wrote that "it became necessary to put in force the Act which empowers the President to call out the Militia for the protection of the frontiers," and that he had also authorized the use of the regular troops for that purpose.[48] Thus, any "offensive" expeditions into enemy territory were purely for the "protection" of the frontier towns. In other letters, Washington confirmed that Congress had to authorize any offensive expeditions of importance. Writing to a state governor about a conflict with a different tribe, he averred, "The Constitution vests the power of declaring War with Congress, therefore no offensive expedition of importance can be undertaken until after they shall have deliberated upon the subject, and authorised such a measure."[49] In another letter, he wrote that "our hands are tied to defensive measures" against "Indian hostilities" on the frontiers; and, if treaty negotiations should fail and "if the Sword is to decide," then he hoped "that the arm of government *may be enabled* to strike home."[50]

In short, President Washington never maintained independent authority to engage in offensive hostilities of importance, that is, to expand the existing state of war. He instead affirmed that any offensive expeditions against the tribes were strictly necessary to defend the frontier settlements. It is also possible that Washington believed that Congress authorized the offensive expeditions against the tribes through the statutory authority to use the militia.[51]

President John Adams expressed similar views. In a 1797 message to Congress, he explained that he had forbidden armed vessels from voyages other than to the East Indies in order to "prevent collisions with the powers at war," per Congress's policy in the Neutrality Act of 1794. Adams did not doubt "the policy and propriety of permitting our vessels to employ means of defense while engaged in a lawful foreign commerce," but he feared that arming American vessels on the high seas might provoke war if they did not act strictly defensively. Thus, he argued, it was "for Congress to prescribe such regulations as will enable our seafaring citizens to defend themselves against violations of the law of nations, and at the same time restrain them from committing acts of hostility against the powers at war."[52] Although Adams was probably overly cautious in this episode, it again reflects a narrow view of unilateral executive authority.

Alexander Hamilton agreed. In a letter to the Secretary of War, James McHenry, he wrote that absent a statute, the Constitution empowered the President on the high seas only "to employ" any armed vessels approved by Congress "as convoys," which could "repel force by force." They could not, however, "capture" vessels, such actions falling within Congress's power to authorize reprisals and declare war. Within the jurisdictional waters of the United States, Hamilton argued, ships could more broadly "repress hostilities."[53] Adams' instructions to the naval officers tracked Hamilton's distinction,[54] which also aligned with Washington's treatment of the Wabash tribes along the frontier. Congress later authorized several offensive measures against France.

President Thomas Jefferson espoused a similarly narrow view. When a fifty-gun British vessel attacked a thirty-six-gun U.S. vessel departing Hampton Roads, Virginia, in search of British deserters, Jefferson took defensive measures "for preventing future insults within our harbors." But, he told the Governor of Virginia, he could do nothing that might commit Congress to war: "Whether the outrage is a proper cause of war, belonging exclusively to Congress, it is our duty not to commit [Congress] by doing anything which would have to be retracted."[55] During a border dispute with Spain over West Florida, he likewise wrote to Congress, "Considering that Congress alone is constitutionally invested with the power of changing our condition from peace to war, I have thought it my duty to await their authority for using force in any degree which could be avoided."[56]

Jefferson's actions and statements were more complicated respecting the Barbary States, which had been preying on American commerce in the Mediterranean and holding hundreds of Americans hostage. In the most famous episode, Jefferson reported to Congress an encounter between the schooner *Enterprise* and a Tripolitan vessel. "Unauthorized by the Constitution, without the sanction of Congress, to go beyond the line of defense, the vessel, being disabled from committing further hostilities, was liberated with its crew. The Legislature," he added, "will doubtless consider whether, by authorizing measures of offense also, they will place our force on an equal footing with that of its adversaries."[57] As Abraham Sofaer has noted, however, Tripoli had declared war, and the instructions to the naval commanders provided for more aggressive actions in that contingency.[58] Moreover, the reason the American ship did not capture the Tripolitan vessel was purely tactical.[59]

Jefferson deleted a similar request for congressional authorization after Morocco declared war the following year.[60]

Hamilton, responding to Jefferson's message, argued that Tripoli's declaration of war obviated the need for congressional authorization. "[I]t belongs to Congress only, *to go to War*," he wrote, "[b]ut when a foreign nation declares, or openly and avowedly makes war upon the United States, they are then by the very fact, already *at war*" and any declaration from Congress would be "unnecessary."[61] In this sentiment, Hamilton had an unusual ally: the staunch Jeffersonian Republican Albert Gallatin, who stated in a Cabinet meeting and in letters to Jefferson that "[t]he [executive] can not put us in a state of war, but if we be put into that state either by the decree of Congress or of the other nation, the command and direction of the public force then belongs to the [executive]."[62] The administration's instructions to the naval commanders and Jefferson's deletion of the Morocco request were more consistent with the Hamilton–Gallatin view than with what Jefferson had told Congress.

It later emerged that Morocco had been secretly violating the peace treaty, so an American naval commander captured and held a Moroccan frigate. Jefferson praised the move and made no suggestion that the American vessel had crossed the line from defense to offense.[63] But he asked for and received authorization from Congress to take additional and more significant offensive actions should Morocco's depredations continue.[64] Whatever exception Tripoli's or Morocco's unilateral declarations of war may have created, Jefferson's statements were consistent with the proposition that the President may, without Congress, take only defensive or limited offensive actions.

10.5 PROTECTING AMERICANS ABROAD

Another instructive set of precedents involves the use of force abroad against non-state actors to protect American persons or property. In the 1970s, historian Arthur M. Schlesinger Jr. wrote that such incidents "make up the bulk of the lists so often compiled in recent years to show that a President, when he sends the Army or Navy into combat without the benefit of Congress, does so with abundant historical precedent."[65] Executive-branch lawyers continue to invoke these precedents in this manner.[66] But as Schlesinger then wrote, drawing on the work of Abraham Sofaer, many such incidents were not really precedents at all: "A substantial number took place not only without congressional authorization but also without presidential authorization, very often the consequence of the individual initiative or short temper of lieutenants along the southern border or commodores on the high seas."[67]

Schlesinger described the "spectacular" example of Greytown, Nicaragua, where in 1854 "someone in an angry crowd threw a bottle at the American Minister to Central America, who was trying to save the property of a transit company in which American citizens owned shares." The Secretary of the Navy dispatched a ship with instructions to demand apology "without a resort to violence" if possible. The commander flattened the town.[68] Although the commander plainly exceeded instructions, President Franklin Pierce defended the action on the ground that Greytown was not an "organized political society" but rather a "camp of savages" and a "piratical resort of outlaws."[69]

When an American whose property was destroyed later sued the commander of the ship, Justice Samuel Nelson of the U.S. Supreme Court, sitting as a circuit justice, argued that "the question whether it was the duty of the president to interpose for the protection of the [American] citizens at Greytown against an irresponsible and marauding community ... belonged to the executive to determine; and his decision is final and conclusive."[70] He explained:

> [A]s it respects the interposition of the executive abroad, for the protection of the lives or property of the citizen, the duty must, of necessity, rest in the discretion of the president. Acts of lawles[s] violence, or of threatened violence to the citizen or his property, cannot be anticipated and provided for; and the protection, to be effectual or of any avail, may, not unfrequently, require the most prompt and decided action. Under our system of government, the citizen abroad is as much entitled to protection as the citizen at home. The great object and duty of government is the protection of the lives, liberty, and property of the people composing it, whether abroad or at home; and any government failing in the accomplishment of the object, or the performance of the duty, is not worth preserving.[71]

Setting aside whether the shelling of Greytown was defensive – as Schlesinger pointed out, it was more calculated punishment[72] – Justice Nelson's analysis raises more questions than it answers. True enough, the government of the United States is responsible for the protection of Americans abroad, not just those at home. Sometimes those Americans are subject to violence that requires "prompt and decided" action. That is another way of saying the President must occasionally repel attacks or take defensive measures. But does it matter that the actions are directed at a marauding community rather than an organized political society? And what is the source of the President's power to use force against such communities?

One possibility that scholars have argued for over a century is that international law is what empowers the President to protect American lives and property abroad.[73] That argument is entirely plausible, and perhaps even correct, although it is not without its problems. It is true that part of the executive power of law execution is preventing violations of the law. But even if it is a violation of international law for marauding communities to commit outrages against the lives or property of citizens of another nation, and even if international law is part of the law of the United States, it is nevertheless Congress, not the President, that has power under the Constitution to "define and punish Offences ... against the Law of Nations."[74] And if under international law or the customary practice of nations chief executives exercise a kind of protective military power abroad, that would be similar to claiming unenumerated or inherent powers.

The concept of imperfect war may prove more helpful. If an imperfect public war can exist between two sovereign nations, it is unclear why a similar state could not exist between a nation and a band of marauders, pirates, or brigands. Such a war could not be declared in the formal sense because the law of nations under a declared war presupposes two or more states. But if Congress can commence or authorize imperfect wars between nations without a declaration, it should likewise have the power to commence or authorize imperfect wars between the United States and non-state actors.[75] The Authorization for the Use of Military Force, enacted following the terrorist attacks on the United States on September 11, 2001, is an example of such authorization.

Once it is recognized that a state of imperfect war can exist between a nation or a portion of its people and non-state actors, then such a state thrust upon the United States by non-state actors can trigger the same defensive commander-in-chief powers. The President may therefore deploy the armed forces abroad to protect American lives and property without waiting for congressional authorization. The only limitation is that the President may not through such actions risk provoking a broader war or expanding the state of hostilities. The shelling of Greytown likely violated that principle. That limitation may also explain why many actors over time have distinguished between nations and non-state actors. Retaliating against sovereign nations for abuses committed against U.S. citizens is highly likely to provoke war and therefore calls for congressional judgment. Unilateral defensive actions against non-state actors are less likely to provoke wider wars. Such actions are within the commander-in-chief powers and are unlikely to trench on Congress's power to declare war.

Whether one adopts this account of presidential power abroad or the one based in international law, the President's power in this respect is limited to enforcing a state of peace in defense of American lives and property. As discussed later, executive-branch lawyers have invoked this aspect of presidential power in modern times to justify offensive but congressionally unauthorized military operations. The precedents do not justify such an extension.

10.6 THE CIVIL WAR

The Civil War was another conflict in which a declaration was unavailable. In the *Prize Cases*, the Supreme Court addressed whether President Abraham Lincoln could, without authorization from Congress, lawfully impose an embargo on the South that rendered any neutral vessel trading with seceded states liable to be seized.[76] The laws of war permitted such embargoes; but there was no declared war. Lincoln's theory of the conflict was that the South had never truly seceded; the states remained in the Union, and the national government could not declare war against an existing state. Had war been declared between two nations, the legitimacy of the embargo would have been unquestionable. Nor was there any doubt that

Congress could specifically authorize an embargo, which it eventually did, but Congress had not yet convened. Was the existing embargo constitutional, absent a declaration or specific authorization from Congress, in the context of an internal rebellion?

A closely divided Supreme Court upheld the embargo. The dissent would have held that without a declaration of war or other specific authorization, no war powers under the law of nations could vest in the President. "[B]efore this insurrection against the established Government can be dealt with on the footing of a civil war, within the meaning of the law of nations and the Constitution of the United States, and which will draw after it belligerent rights, it must be recognized or declared by the war-making power of the Government," the dissent maintained. "No power short of this can change the legal status of the Government or the relations of its citizens from that of peace to a state of war, or bring into existence all those duties and obligations of neutral third parties growing out of a state of war."[77] On this view, the President had to wait for congressional authorization. As Justice Chase had explained in *Bas v. Tingy*, when a "partial war is waged, its extent and operation depend on our municipal laws."[78] Here, there were as yet no applicable municipal laws.

The majority, however, held that a state of war already existed. That was nothing new; it was widely accepted that a state of war could exist without a declaration. The President could repel sudden attacks and defensively prosecute an imperfect war thrust upon the nation. The President could also prosecute an imperfect offensive war with congressional authorization, as in the Quasi-War with France. But here there was effectively a perfect war brought upon the nation before Congress had any time to convene to declare it or authorize other measures. The question was therefore whether the laws of war applied to this perfect war in the absence of legislative authorization.

The majority held that the President had authority to meet the conflict in its full scope: "This greatest of civil wars . . . sprung forth suddenly from the parent brain, a Minerva in the full panoply of war. The President was bound to meet it in the shape it presented itself, without waiting for Congress to baptize it with a name; and no name given to it by him or them could change the fact."[79] In other words, under the laws of war, the war powers typically do not vest in the commander in chief without a declaration. The majority held, however, that in this unique circumstance a perfect war existed even absent a declaration. All the attendant war powers therefore vested in the President. That makes good sense and would apply to any similar conflict in which Congress could not convene. The President should, and would, be able to prosecute such a conflict with the full war powers recognized by the law of nations.

Nothing about the *Prize Cases* undermines the general propositions that the war powers under the laws of war vest only with a declaration of war; that the President can act only defensively when an imperfect state of war exists by virtue of enemy attack; and that Congress generally must authorize offensive measures to commence or expand a state of war. But where a perfect state of war exists by virtue of rebellion and Congress either cannot declare war or convene, it is entirely reasonable to conclude that the full panoply of war powers vests in the commander in chief.

10.7 MODERN CONFLICTS AND INTERNATIONAL TREATIES

Although some public commentators like to observe that the last declaration of war occurred during World War II and that the United States has nevertheless continued to engage in many military conflicts, Congress has as a general matter authorized most of the military conflicts in which the country has engaged since 1945. For example, the Authorization for the Use of Military Force, employed against the Taliban after the attacks of September 11, was not a declaration of war but authorized hostilities much as Congress did during the Quasi-War with France.[80]

The United States has also deployed forces pursuant to various international treaties or United Nations (UN) Security Council resolutions. The constitutional question involved is whether the President may independently commit troops to fulfill treaty commitments or must first seek congressional authorization. The only major modern conflict in which the President did not obtain such authorization was the Korean War. It is a serious question whether the Korean War was a constitutionally authorized conflict. After North Korean forces crossed the thirty-eighth parallel into South Korea, the U.N. Security Council adopted resolutions requesting, recommending, and authorizing U.S. participation and command of the military effort.[81] In response, President Harry Truman dispatched troops to South Korea on his own initiative.[82]

An international obligation to commit troops does not, however, necessarily grant the President unilateral power to send them. Treaties bind *the nation*. It is true that the President, when exercising any Article II powers, must comply with treaties. But the President must be exercising Article II powers. Committing troops without congressional authorization, except for defensive operations when the United States is attacked, is not within the President's Article II powers. Only Congress, it would seem, may authorize the use of force to honor treaty commitments. If Congress refuses to do so, the United States may breach its obligations; but that is Congress's prerogative. An international treaty does not alter the constitutional distribution of powers. As the Supreme Court has explained, "The responsibility for transforming an international obligation arising from a non–self-executing treaty into domestic law falls to Congress."[83] Many treaties clarify the point and specify that states should commit troops "according to [their] constitutional processes."[84]

The Korean War proved the exception.[85] When Saddam Hussein invaded Kuwait in 1990, President George H. W. Bush unilaterally mobilized forces to defend Kuwait without waiting for congressional authorization. President Bush argued U.N. authorization sufficed and that he had inherent authority as commander in chief "to defend vital U.S. interests." Many in Congress contended legislative authorization was necessary. They had the better of the argument. Congress authorized the use of troops, averting a constitutional showdown.[86]

10.8 LIBYA AND SYRIA: THE MODERN FRAMEWORK

Since the 1990s, the executive branch has increasingly justified the use of military force around the world without congressional authorization, and even where the United States was not acting defensively and where state forces were involved. Arguably, the Kosovo intervention fit this description: President William Jefferson Clinton, on his own initiative, ordered air strikes against Yugoslavia to pressure its government to participate in peace talks with the Kosovo Albanians. Congress never authorized this use of force, although it routinely appropriated funds for operations in Kosovo to prevent the massacre of religious and ethnic minorities.[87]

An even clearer case of unauthorized military action was President Obama's intervention in the Libyan Civil War in 2011. The United States and North Atlantic Treaty Organization (NATO) allies launched a bombing campaign to prevent Libyan leader Muammar Gaddafi from massacring rebel forces and civilians. The bombing campaign substantially aided the rebels' success. More concerning, an American bomb likely destroyed a convoy in which Gaddafi was traveling, leading directly to his capture and execution by rebel forces.[88] What authorized such military intervention on the part of the United States?

The Office of Legal Counsel (OLC) within the Department of Justice issued a memorandum purporting to justify U.S. military involvement in Libya. The memorandum adopted a two-part analysis to determine the constitutionality of military actions that Congress has not authorized. The first question is whether the military action is in the "national interest." The second is whether the duration, nature, and scope of the military action constitute "war" within the meaning of the Constitution. If the action amounts to war, Congress must authorize it; if it does not, the President may proceed independently. In OLC's view, a no-fly zone and bombing campaign in Libya did not constitute "war" and was in the "national interest" because it would promote "regional stability."[89]

The OLC under the first Trump Administration adopted the same framework in a 2018 memorandum justifying airstrikes against Syrian targets after the regime used chemical weapons against rebel forces. "[T]he President could lawfully direct [the strikes] because he had reasonably determined that the use of force would be in the national interest and that the anticipated hostilities would not rise to the level of a war in the constitutional sense."[90] OLC likewise relied on this framework to conclude that President Trump could order the targeted killing of Qassem Suleimani, an Iranian military leader behind numerous attacks on U.S. forces throughout the Middle East.[91]

These OLC memoranda are inconsistent with the Constitution's text, structure, and history. Setting aside the infinitely malleable notion of the "national interest," the more fundamental issue is that no clause in the Constitution authorizes the President to use military force wherever and whenever the President believes it to be in the national interest. Put differently, even if not all military actions constituted "war," Article II would still need to contain a clause empowering the President to engage in such nonwar military actions. The commander in chief status authorizes the President to conduct military actions when authorized or begun. It does not authorize the President to take military actions in other nations without congressional authorization. The precedents on the question at most suggest the President has a power, whether under international law or otherwise, to protect American lives and property abroad against depredations and outrages of non-state actors.

A further problem with the "national interest" standard is that using force abroad for whatever presidents perceive to be in the national interest often risks provoking war. The lesson from Washington, Adams, and Jefferson is that the President may act defensively, or at most take proportionate, offensive military acts necessary to deter similar future attacks. If the President commits an act of war against another nation, or if the President takes some other action that risks provoking war such as sending troops to disputed territory and having them train their guns on foreign troops,[92] those acts intrude on Congress's war power.

It cannot be doubted that bombing the military forces of the Libyan and Syrian governments were acts of war. To be sure, those governments likely knew they would lose any conflict with the United States, and such hostile acts may not ultimately provoke wider war. But under the law of nations (now known as international law), those bombings remain acts of war.[93] If the President unilaterally and non-defensively commits an act of war against another country, which however likely or unlikely may provoke a retaliatory response and wider war, Congress's power would amount to nothing.

As for the second part of the OLC analysis, the claim that not all military actions are "war" within the meaning of Congress's declare-war power is historically untenable. As Justice Bushrod Washington said, "*every* contention by force between two nations, in external matters, under the authority of their respective governments, is not only war, but public war."[94] The United States was therefore engaged in imperfect wars against Libya, Syria, and Iran. Congress must authorize such wars unless an imperfect state of war already exists, permitting the commander in chief to act defensively. Such was arguably the case with the Suleimani strike; but it is more difficult to defend U.S. actions in Libya and Syria on those grounds. Presidents of both parties have, perhaps unsurprisingly, at times usurped Congress's constitutional authority over war.

10.9 IS THE EXECUTIVE ABOVE THE LAW?

Having analyzed several matters involving executive power and the separation of powers in this and preceding chapters, a few concluding observations are in order.

It is often said that an originalist interpretation of the Constitution would lead to a President who is "above the law." But as the preceding chapters have aimed to show, an originalist and formalist conception of the presidency need not produce such results. The President has no residuum of inherent power, and is under the law, not above it. But what is more, to the extent the President appears above the law, that is at best only partly due to mistaken formalist interpretations of presidential powers. The greater culprit is functionalist constitutional interpretation that has served as a one-way ratchet in favor of executive power.

In *Zivotofsky v. Kerry*, the Supreme Court held that the President has an exclusive recognition power implied from the power to receive ambassadors. The Court reasoned: "Recognition is a topic on which the Nation must speak with one voice. That voice must be the President's."[95] That reasoning is functionalist, not originalist. The Court did not say the Constitution requires the President to be the nation's sole voice in foreign affairs; it said there must be one voice on the topic of recognition. That is a policy judgment, and a questionable one. In *Youngstown*, Justice Jackson's functionalist tripartite framework provided that, even absent explicit constitutional power or congressional authorization, "contemporary imponderables and imperatives of events" may justify executive action. And it is a functionalist claim that whether a military action constitutes "war" for purposes of the declare-war clause depends on its nature, duration, and scope.

To these points one might add that it is a functionalist, not formalist, argument that society is too complex for Congress to make critical policy decisions and therefore broad delegations of power to the executive are justified[96] – a topic Chapter 11 addresses. And before the Supreme Court recently overturned the so-called *Chevron* deference doctrine, it was a functionalist, not formalist, argument that courts must defer to executive interpretations of law because the executive has superior interpretive competence.[97] If the President is above the law, it is not because of a catastrophic embrace of originalism or formalism. If the President is above the law, or wields too much power, it may instead be because the American people, or at least their legal officials, have embraced functionalism in disputes over the separation of powers.

PART V

Separation of Powers (II)

11

Nondelegation

Separation of powers disputes do not exclusively involve tension between the legislative and executive branches. The courts occasionally have had to police the boundaries between the two when they have worked in tandem. This and the next chapter deal with some of the central separation of powers questions that arise largely, although not entirely, in the domestic sphere; most revolve around what is known as the administrative state. The reader has already encountered this subject in the chapters on presidential control of administration. This chapter addresses the nondelegation doctrine: the rule of constitutional law that maintains that Congress cannot delegate its legislative responsibilities, including to the President or the executive branch agencies. This subject will then set the groundwork for the next: the "legislative veto" provisions of the twentieth century, including in the famous War Powers Resolution. Together, these two subjects will create important insights into the separation of powers, and into formalism and functionalism as methods of constitutional interpretation.

This chapter begins with the Constitution's text, structure, and history, all of which support the proposition that Congress cannot delegate its legislative power to the President or to subordinate administrative agencies. It then describes the evolution of the Supreme Court's doctrine, leading to the modern test: Congress's statutes must contain sufficiently intelligible principles to guide the executive branch in the exercise of that branch's law-execution duties. The challenge with the nondelegation doctrine is that every statute delegates authority to the executive, and so the question becomes, when does a delegation become so broad or vague – or flawed for some other reason – that it amounts to an impermissible delegation of the legislative power vested in Congress. The theory behind the intelligible principle test is that if a statute contains such a principle, then the President is merely executing the law when administering that statute; the President is merely carrying into execution the will of Congress. If the statute established no such principle, then the President would have discretion under the statute to establish one and the President would effectively become the lawmaker.

The doctrine, however, has become so flexible that courts have upheld the broadest of standards as intelligible, such as the power to regulate in the "public interest." That has led some modern scholars and judges to call for a revival of the nondelegation doctrine. Some revisionist scholars have responded to these revivalists and argue unconventionally that the Constitution contains no nondelegation principle at all. Others claim that the nondelegation doctrine, if it existed, was not particularly robust. These theories and arguments will be examined and compared to the historical evidence. The view presented here is that the Constitution's text and structure require a nondelegation doctrine, and moreover that the Constitution was historically understood to contain a nondelegation principle.

11.1 TEXT AND STRUCTURE

One must begin, as always, with the text of the Constitution. There is no nondelegation clause in the Constitution. Some pundits, at least, have suggested that as a result Congress may freely delegate its legislative power.[1] The reader knows better. Congress can only exercise powers the Constitution has granted. The absence of a nondelegation clause is immaterial because there is no delegation clause, either, and Congress must always point to an enumerated authorization for its actions.[2] At best, Congress could point to the Necessary and Proper Clause. That clause authorizes Congress to exercise incidental powers; it does not authorize the exercise of any great, substantive prerogatives. It is at best a dubious proposition that delegating to the executive branch legislative power the people have vested in Congress is merely an incidental, and not a great, power.

Other textual and structural inferences in the Constitution tend to support the proposition that if the people had intended to authorize Congress to delegate its legislative powers, the Constitution would have said so explicitly. One such textual inference is the *expressio unius est exclusio alterius* canon of construction with which the reader is already familiar: The expression of one item implies the exclusion of other, similar items not listed. That legislative power is assigned to *Congress* is some evidence that it is not assigned to *the President*; and that the Constitution assigns the President executive power is some evidence that it does not assign to that department legislative or judicial power.

The more general structural inference is that the Constitution separates power for a reason; allowing Congress to delegate its power to the President would allow the latter to exercise combined legislative and executive powers.[3] It is a commonplace to recognize that the Framers separated powers better to secure liberty. As James Madison wrote in *Federalist* No. 47,

> The accumulation of all powers, legislative, executive, and judiciary, in the same hands, whether of one, a few, or many, and whether hereditary, self-appointed, or elective, may justly be pronounced the very definition of tyranny. Were the federal

Constitution, therefore, really chargeable with this accumulation of power, or with a mixture of powers, having a dangerous tendency to such an accumulation, no further arguments would be necessary to inspire a universal reprobation of the system.[4]

Or in the words of the influential Montesquieu, "When legislative power is united with executive power in a single person or in a single body of the magistracy, there is no liberty, because one can fear that the same monarch or senate that makes tyrannical laws will execute them tyrannically."[5] That is not to say any blending of power is impermissible. The Constitution contains checks and balances by assigning the different branches some degree of powers appertaining to the other branches. As noted in previous chapters, the Constitution assigns some legislative power to the President, for example, the veto power and, arguably, treatymaking. It assigns some judicial power to the legislature (impeachment), and some executive power to the Senate (appointments). Those exceptions prove the general rule: Except where the Constitution specifically assigns legislative power to the President, the President enjoys no such power.

Moreover, delegating legislative power does not serve the same purpose as these other assignments of power, which require the coordinated actions of two branches. Once legislative power is delegated, the President can exercise legislative and executive power unilaterally. To be sure, Congress could always attempt to reclaim the delegation; but future presidents could veto any such attempt, and a mere one-third of a single House of Congress could sustain that veto. As Representative John Randolph said in 1803, cautioning against a broad delegation of power to President Jefferson to govern the Louisiana Territory: "If we give this power out of our hands, it may be irrevocable until Congress shall have made legislative provision; that is, a single branch of the Government, the Executive branch, with a small minority of either House, may prevent its resumption."[6]

There is a more affirmative explanation, however, for why the Framers separated powers.[7] When they created three distinct institutions to exercise three distinct powers, they did so because they believed the structure of each institution would make that institution uniquely suited to its task. They and the ratifying public would have understood that, as a consequence, no branch could delegate its own power, nor could Congress reassign any powers, without defeating the whole purpose of variously designing the three national institutions.

In *Federalist* No. 53, Publius ‡ describes the advantages representation brings to the legislative process. The "public affairs of the Union" are "diversified by the local affairs connected with them, and can with difficulty be correctly learned in any other place than in the central councils, to which a knowledge of them will be brought by the representatives of every part of the empire." Some knowledge of these

---

‡ These passages refer to Publius because although some of the following cited essays can be attributed to either Madison or Hamilton, the authorship of certain numbers remains disputed.

affairs "ought to be possessed by the members from each of the States." Publius goes on:

> How can foreign trade be properly regulated by uniform laws without some acquaintance with the commerce, the ports, the usages, and the regulations of the different States? How can the trade between the different States be duly regulated without some knowledge of their relative situations in these and other points? How can taxes be judiciously imposed and effectually collected if they be not accommodated to the different laws and local circumstances relating to these objects in the different States? How can uniform regulations for the militia be duly provided without a similar knowledge of some internal circumstances by which the States are distinguished from each other? These are the principal objects of federal legislation and suggest most forcibly the extensive information which the representatives ought to acquire. The other inferior objects will require a proportional degree of information with regard to them.[8]

The representative mechanism, which allows members of Congress to bring knowledge from all parts of the Union, is essential to the proper exercise of legislative power. If those members could delegate their power to the executive department, that would defeat the purpose of having an institution that can adequately represent the interests of the various parts of the nation and whose members would have the requisite local knowledge. Additionally, Publius wrote that one "advantage" stemming from the "constitution of the Senate" is that it can serve as an "additional impediment . . . against improper acts of legislation."[9] The advantage of bicameralism would also evaporate if Congress could freely delegate its legislative power to the executive.

The reader will recall that the presidency was also structured to be well suited to its functions. "Energy in the Executive," Publius wrote, "is essential to the protection of the community against foreign attacks," and is no less essential "to the steady administration of the laws; to the protection of property against those irregular and high-handed combinations which sometimes interrupt the ordinary course of justice; to the security of liberty against the enterprises and assaults of ambition, of faction, and of anarchy."[10] A key ingredient of energy is "unity": "Decision, activity, secrecy, and despatch will generally characterize the proceedings of one man in a much more eminent degree than the proceedings of any greater number; and in proportion as the number is increased, these qualities will be diminished."[11]

The judiciary, too, was structured suitably for its role. "The standard of good behavior for the continuance in office of the judicial magistracy, is certainly one of the most valuable of the modern improvements in the practice of government"; it is "the best expedient which can be devised in any government, to secure a steady, upright, and impartial administration of the law."[12] "The complete independence of the courts of justice is peculiarly essential in a limited Constitution" because constitutional limitations "can be preserved in practice no other way than through the medium of courts of justice, whose duty it must be to declare all acts contrary to the manifest tenor of the Constitution void."[3] "That inflexible and uniform adherence to the rights of the Constitution, and of individuals ... can certainly not be expected from judges who hold their offices by a temporary commission."[4] And "[next] to permanency in office, nothing can contribute more to the independence of the judges than a fixed provision for their support."[5]

The Framers thus created a constitution that structured each of the three branches of government in such a way that it would do its task well. The ratifying public would have understood that, by vesting legislative power in Congress, executive power in the President, and judicial power in the courts, the intention of the Framers was that each of these respective institutions would exercise its respective powers. Put another way, every statement to the effect that each institution was structured in a particular way includes within it a widely shared implication: that, therefore, these institutions and only these institutions can exercise their respective powers.

The best textual argument against a nondelegation doctrine turns on the definition of executive power. If the executive power is the power to execute Congress's statutes, then even if Congress instructed the President to make any regulation for the goodness or prosperity of the nation, the President would be "executing" that statute and thereby exercising executive power.[16] It is not at all obvious, however, that in executing such an instruction the President would be exercising "the executive power." When Congress executes the powers the people delegated to it in the eighth section of the first article, for example, Congress is not exercising executive power but rather legislative power.

Even the modern critics, relying on Montesquieu and Rousseau, agree that at a bare minimum the legislature reflected the "general will" of the state, and legislative power was the power to "determine" the "will of the state."[17] If Congress enacted a statute authorizing the President to make any regulation of interstate commerce that in the President's judgment will be in the public interest, the President would be exercising the exact same power that Congress exercises when it passes laws pursuant to its enumerated power over interstate commerce. They would both be exercising legislative power. In the absence of an intelligible principle, the "will of the state" is obscure; the legislative power has not yet been exercised. The legislative power that cannot be delegated is at least the power to establish such principles. That leads directly to the modern doctrine.

11.2 EARLY HISTORY

During and after ratification, members of the Founding generation involved in public life and government repeatedly argued that Congress could not delegate its legislative power to the executive. At times, their opponents argued that the occasion did not raise a nondelegation concern, and often Congress enacted the legislation in question. But no one appears to have controverted the nondelegation principle.[18]

There does not appear to have been much discussion of the nondelegation doctrine in the ratifying period, perhaps because the idea behind assigning powers would have been self-evident. But James Wilson once again provides some important insight. In the Pennsylvania ratifying convention, Wilson brought up Henry VIII's detested Statute of Proclamations of 1539, according to which Parliament purported to give the King's proclamations the force of law. Blackstone wrote that the statute "was calculated to introduce the most despotic tyranny; and which must have proved fatal to the liberties of this kingdom, had it not been luckily repealed . . . about five years after."[19] (The reader might recall that the Democratic Party newspapers would go on to argue that President Washington's Neutrality Proclamation could not have the force of law.)

Wilson alluded to the Statute of Proclamations to make the point with which the reader is already familiar: that under the British constitutional system, Parliament was supreme and could rearrange government institutions and powers as it pleased. Thus, the Statute of Proclamations was not unconstitutional, certainly not on the eighteenth-century British understanding. But Wilson then strongly hinted that a delegation of that type would be unconstitutional under the American systems of written constitutions. "The British constitution is just what the British Parliament pleases. When Parliament transferred legislative authority to Henry VIII, the act transferring it could not, in the strict acceptation of the term, be called unconstitutional," Wilson declared. "To control the power and conduct of the legislature by an overruling constitution, was an improvement in the science and practice of government reserved to the American states."[20] Wilson's statement powerfully suggested that the transference of authority in the Statute of Proclamations was permissible only because Parliament could alter the British constitution at will. In America, the legislatures could not alter the structure and assignment of powers made in constitutions supposed to control the actions of all departments of government.

After ratification, the first extensive debate over whether a particular law would violate the nondelegation principle occurred in 1791 over the establishment of the post roads.[21] A committee of the Second Congress introduced a bill that specified in great detail where the post roads would be.[22] Representative Sedgwick proposed an amendment to strike the enumerated routes and replace them with the provision "by such route as the President of the United States shall, from time to time, cause to be established."[23] That raised a nondelegation question: Can Congress simply give away its power to specify the roads to the President, or must Congress itself specify the roads?

Several prominent members argued that the amendment would create an impermissible delegation of legislative power. According to the summary of the reporter, Representative Livermore "observed that the Legislative body being empowered by the Constitution 'to establish post offices and post roads,' it is as clearly their duty to designate the roads as to establish the offices; and he did not think they could with propriety delegate that power, which they were themselves appointed to exercise."[24]

Representative Hartley argued, "The Constitution seems to have intended that we should exercise all the powers respecting the establishing [of] post roads we are capable of," and added, "We represent the people, we are constitutionally vested with the power of determining upon the establishment of post roads; and, as I understand at present, ought not to delegate the power to any other person."[25] Representative Page agreed:

> If the motion before the committee succeeds, I shall make one which will save a deal of time and money, by making a short session of it; for if this House can, with propriety, leave the business of the post office to the President, it may leave to him any other business of legislation; and I may move to adjourn and leave all the objects of legislation to his sole consideration and direction. . . . I look upon the motion as unconstitutional, and if it were not so, as having a mischievous tendency . . . .[26]

Representative White additionally "made several observations on the expediency and constitutionality of the measure," though the reporter highlighted only the policy arguments against the amendment.[27] Representative Vining added, "The Constitution has certainly given us the power of establishing posts and roads, and it is not even implied that it should be transferred to the President; his powers are well defined."[28] Regarding another representative's statements, the recorder simply wrote that Representative Gerry "took a general view of most of the arguments in favor of the motion; and replied to each."[29] One can surmise from this comment that Gerry likely agreed that the provision was unconstitutional. James Madison, then a representative in the House, also argued in opposition to Sedgwick's motion, stating that the establishment of post offices and post roads "is expressly committed to Legislative determination by the Constitution." He contended that "there did not appear to be any necessity for alienating the powers of the House; and that if this should take place, it would be a violation of the Constitution."[30]

Sedgwick's amendment was rejected.[31] Although it is impossible to know the motivations of every member voting, at least seven representatives seem to have thought the motion unconstitutional because it would amount to transferring, alienating, or delegating the House's legislative power. Importantly, not even the author of the proposed amendment denied the nondelegation principle; he simply argued that his motion did not violate it. Sedgwick did not wish "to resign all the business of the House to the President, or to any one else; but he thought that the Executive part of the business ought to be left to Executive officers."[32] He wanted to "leave the details of this business entirely to the supreme Executive" because "he thought it sufficient that the House should establish the principle, and then leave it to the Executive to carry it into effect."[33] This was not a higher-order dispute about the validity of nondelegation as a principle of constitutional law.

To be sure, the final language of the enacted statute provided that the Postmaster General could "enter into contracts, for a term not exceeding eight years, for extending the line of posts ... and the roads, therein designated, shall, during the continuance of such contract, be deemed and considered as post roads."[34] Perhaps the delegates were contradicting themselves. But it is one thing to establish an intricate network of post roads and grant the Postmaster General discretion to extend the specific roads if necessary; it is quite another to give the executive total discretion to decide where any and all the post roads should be.

The Act also delegated to the Postmaster General the question of where the post offices should be.[35] The delegation respecting post offices was not particularly significant, however, because the post offices would be on the post roads that Congress had established. Presumably, there would be at least one such office in every major town. The President's discretion was greatly cabined once Congress had established the roads, which was the important question for towns.[36] This seems to have been Representative Livermore's argument:

> The establishment of post roads [Livermore] considered as a very important object .... If the post office were to be regulated by the will of a single person, the dissemination of intelligence might be impeded, and the people kept entirely in the dark with respect to the transactions of Government; or the Postmaster, if vested with the whole power, might branch out the offices to such a degree as to make them prove a heavy burden to the United States .... The most material point, in his opinion, was to determine the road itself .... [37]

Livermore's statement suggests one possible test for the nondelegation doctrine. Every statute delegates authority to the President. The question is at what point does the President's authority become more than mere law execution and cross the line between execution and legislation. One possible test is that Congress must resolve the important policy details; it must make the important decisions. But it can leave the details up to the President and the executive branch agencies.

What is important may depend on the nature of the right or conduct at issue. During the Alien and Sedition Acts controversy, Madison raised the nondelegation principle. The Alien Friends Act authorized "the President of the United States ... to order all such aliens as he shall judge dangerous to the peace and safety of the United States" to depart the country.[38] In the Report of 1800, which Madison drafted on behalf of the Virginia legislature, he argued that the statute violated the nondelegation principle:

> However difficult it may be to mark, in every case, with clearness and certainty, the line which divides legislative power, from the other departments of power; all will agree, that the powers referred to these departments may be so general and undefined, as to be of a legislative, not of an executive or judicial nature; and may for that reason be unconstitutional. Details, to a certain degree, are essential to the nature and character of a law; and, on criminal subjects, it is proper, that details should leave as little as possible to the discretion of those who are to apply and to execute the law.

If nothing more were required, in exercising a legislative trust, than a general conveyance of authority, without laying down any precise rules, by which the authority conveyed, should be carried into effect; it would follow, that the whole power of legislation might be transferred by the legislature from itself, and proclamations might become substitutes for laws. A delegation of power in this latitude, would not be denied to be a union of the different powers.[39]

Here, Madison argued that a vague and undefined law could create an unconstitutional transfer of legislative power to another department. Some amount of specificity is required in laws.

More to the present point, there may be distinctions based on the nature of the subject at hand. In the very next sentence, Madison wrote that "it must be enquired whether" the Act "contains such details, definitions, and rules, as appertain to the true character of a law; especially, a law by which personal liberty is invaded, property deprived of its value to the owner, and life itself indirectly exposed to danger."[40] Put another way, all laws require sufficient detail and specificity such that they have the "true character" of laws, and those that involve particularly important criminal matters involving the life, liberty, or property of a person may require even more detail and specificity.[41]

At least two representatives made similar arguments during the legislative debates over the Alien Friends Act.[42] The Act was nevertheless enacted, but no one controverted the principle.[43] Over the next two decades, several laws were in fact modified or rejected entirely after nondelegation concerns were raised.[44]

11.3 EARLY CASES

Federal court cases have been largely consistent with these early nondelegation arguments. The Supreme Court announced its first nondelegation decision in 1813.[45] *Cargo of the Brig Aurora v. United States* involved the embargoes that Congress had imposed on Great Britain and France while the two countries were at war and had both been committing depredations against American commerce. In 1809, Congress imposed the embargo and provided that the President was authorized "to declare ... by proclamation" that "either France or Great Britain ... revoke[d] or modif[ied] her edicts" such "that they shall cease to violate the neutral commerce of the United States," in which case the embargo would be lifted and trade resumed with that country.[46] The embargo then expired, but in 1810 Congress provided that if either Great Britain or France "shall cease to violate the neutral commerce of the United States, which fact the President of the United States shall declare by proclamation," and the other country refused to do so, then the earlier embargo "shall ... be revived" against the country continuing to violate American commerce.[47]

The second statute explicitly stated Congress's opinion that the President was not exercising legislative power; the President was merely finding a "fact" upon which

Congress's policy choices regarding an embargo would then operate. The Supreme Court agreed. "[W]e can see no sufficient reason," the Court held, "why the legislature should not exercise its discretion in reviving the act of March 1st, 1809, either expressly or conditionally, as their judgment should direct." Congress had the power to extend the operation of the embargo "upon the occurrence of any subsequent combination of events."[48] The President was merely proclaiming a fact; Congress made the policy.

Even delegating this authority could be troubling: President Madison declared that France had ceased violating America's neutral commerce on the basis of letters and French decrees that he likely knew were fraudulent. When Britain refused to lift its decrees against American commerce without sufficient proof that the French had repealed theirs, Madison recommended, and Congress declared, war – and thus the War of 1812 began.[49] This episode is more a mark against Madison than against the constitutionality of the delegation. But it does evoke the possible dangers of delegating certain determinations to the executive department.

The Supreme Court's next case was *Wayman v. Southard*, decided in 1825. It involved the question whether Congress could delegate to the courts the power to alter their rules respecting proceedings at common law.[50] "It will not be contended that Congress can delegate to the Courts, or to any other tribunals, powers which are strictly and exclusively legislative," Chief Justice Marshall explained, but "Congress may certainly delegate to others, powers which the legislature may rightfully exercise itself."[51] "The line has not been exactly drawn," he continued, "which separates those important subjects, which must be entirely regulated by the legislature itself, from those of less interest, in which a general provision may be made, and power given to those who are to act under such general provisions to fill up the details."[52]

Chief Justice Marshall's dictum supplies two important insights. First, he suggested that there is a category of "exclusively" legislative power that Congress cannot delegate to the executive or the courts. There are certain things only Congress can do. But, he argued, there are things that could be done either by Congress, or by the executive or the courts. In other words, there are categories of functions or activities that can be reached by more than one branch exercising more than one type of power. Some functions can only be done by Congress exercising its legislative power; other functions can be accomplished by Congress exercising its legislative power, or by the President exercising executive power or the courts exercising judicial power. Chapter 12 returns to this insight.

Marshall next suggested that the difference between the two types of powers or functions is that Congress must decide upon the "important subjects": Congress must make the important policy decisions. But Congress can give other departments the power to "fill up the details" of a legislative program. Congress, for example, could certainly enact by statute all of the various administrative regulations promulgated by modern administrative agencies. It does not follow, however, that all such regulations must be promulgated by Congress. Some might be sufficiently detail oriented or interstitial to qualify as "executive power." And as in *Wayman* itself, Congress could establish all the procedures for the federal courts if it wanted to do so; but it could also establish the baseline and allow courts to modify them if necessary.

The Court reaffirmed the nondelegation doctrine over the next century in several cases involving tariffs. In *Marshall Field & Co. v. Clark*, Congress had enacted a statute establishing certain tariffs, but authorized the President to make a finding that the tariffs on like goods in foreign countries were "reciprocally unequal and unreasonable."[53] The statute itself directed what the alternative, higher tariffs would be. The Court upheld the law, observing, "What the president was required to do was simply in execution of the act of congress. It was not the making of law. He was the mere agent of the law-making department to ascertain and declare the event upon which its expressed will was to take effect."[54] "The legislature," the Court went on to say, "cannot delegate its power to make a law, but it can make a law to delegate a power to determine some fact or state of things upon which the law makes, or intends to make, its own action depend."[55]

The modern black-letter test comes from *J. W. Hampton Jr. & Co. v. United States*.[56] There, Congress had enacted a tariff statute that went a step farther than the statute at issue in *Clark*: It allowed the President to establish tariff rates that would "equalize . . . differences in costs of production" for certain products as compared to the costs of production in competing foreign countries after an administrative investigation into those costs.[57] Arguably, this statute, too, authorized merely the findings of fact. But undoubtedly much discretion could go into a finding regarding "costs of production."

In upholding the law, the Court did not rely on the distinction between policy-making and factual findings, and instead issued the following famous dictum: "If Congress shall lay down by legislative act an intelligible principle to which the person or body authorized to fix such rates is directed to conform, such legislative action is not a forbidden delegation of legislative power."[58] Under this test, even if the President or subordinate agencies make some amount of policy, such policy-making is merely executive power so long as Congress's statute gives the agencies sufficient "intelligible principles" to guide the exercise of their discretion. The difference between this test and one in which Congress must make important policy decisions does not seem too great; one could imagine that principles will only be intelligible if Congress has in fact made those decisions.

To reemphasize an important conclusion: The theory behind these various tests is that every statute delegates some authority to the President. The President has nothing to execute until Congress enacts laws. The question then becomes how to distinguish between mere delegations of authority and delegations of legislative power. The various tests propose related solutions. If the President is merely finding a fact, that is mere law execution; if the President is merely filling in details, that is mere law execution; if the President is merely following an intelligible principle, that is mere law execution. The idea behind all of these alternative formulations is that there comes a point at which the President may be "executing" Congress's statute, but that statute is so broad that the President is executing the statute effectively by exercising "legislative power" instead of "executive power."

11.4 FROM 1935 TO THE PRESENT

In 1935, the Court, for the first and so far last time, declared unconstitutional national legislation for having violated the nondelegation doctrine. In two separate cases, the Court considered two provisions of the National Industrial Recovery Act, enacted during the Great Depression. The first, *Panama Refining Co. v. Ryan*, involved the provision authorizing the President to interdict, or not, the interstate shipment of "hot oil," oil produced in violation of a state's production quota.[59] The statute, the Court held, "does not state whether or in what circumstances or under what conditions the President is to prohibit the transportation of the amount of petroleum or petroleum products produced in excess of the state's permission"; it contains "no criterion to govern the President's course" nor requires "any finding by the President as a condition of his action." The statute "thus declares no policy as to the transportation of the excess production," giving the President "an unlimited authority to determine the policy and to lay down the prohibition, or not to lay it down, as he may see fit."[60]

There was a "declaration of policy" at the beginning of the Act, but it contained many broad and general policies that often worked at cross-purposes. Congress declared the following objectives: "to remove obstructions to the free flow of interstate and foreign commerce which tend to diminish the amount thereof"; "to provide for the general welfare by promoting the organization of industry for the purpose of cooperative action among trade groups"; "to induce and maintain united action of labor and management under adequate governmental sanctions and supervision"; "to eliminate unfair competitive practices"; "to promote the fullest possible utilization of the present productive capacity of industries"; "to avoid undue restriction of production"; "to increase the consumption of industrial and agricultural products by increasing purchasing power"; "to reduce and relieve unemployment"; "to improve standards of labor"; and "otherwise to rehabilitate industry and to conserve natural resources."

The statute effectively authorized the President to do whatever he believed good and just. The policy goals were so general as to be what Congress itself should consider when making policy. It is not making policy to declare "Congress desires full employment" and "Congress desires to conserve natural resources." That is simply declaring the goals, not the policies necessary for achieving them. Those goals also worked at cross-purposes. Permitting the interstate shipment of hot oil would surely promote full productive capacities and would remove obstructions to the free flow of commerce. A prohibition might conserve natural resources and prevent unfair trade practices.

Another provision of the same statute authorized private industry groups to establish "codes of fair competition" for their industries, and for the President to approve them.[61] In *A.L.A. Schechter Poultry Corp. v. United States*, the Court addressed this provision and the "Live Poultry Code" for New York City. Part of the code prohibited poultry wholesalers from selling individual chickens to butchers and retailers, who were required to choose a coop or half-coop but not individual chickens within the coops. Joseph Schechter was criminally charged for violating the code when he allowed his retail buyers to purchase individual chickens. The code also had various wages and hours rules, required collective bargaining, and even specified the minimum number of employees that each slaughterhouse operator had to employ. It prohibited various other "unfair methods of competition" and required various recordkeeping.

"[T]he Constitution has never been regarded as denying to Congress the necessary resources of flexibility and practicality, which will enable it to perform its function in laying down policies and establishing standards," the Court insisted, "while leaving to selected instrumentalities the making of subordinate rules within prescribed limits and the determination of facts to which the policy as declared by the Legislature is to apply."[62] But there were limits. The statutory provision in *Schechter Poultry* was even more problematic than in *Panama Refining*: "There the subject of the statutory prohibition was defined" to a specific subject, hot oil; here, the subject was "fair competition" in many different industries, which could include almost any subject.[63] The Court observed that the statute "supplies no standards for any trade, industry, or activity" and "does not undertake to prescribe rules of conduct," but instead "authorizes the making of codes to prescribe them." "[T]he discretion of the President in approving or prescribing codes, and thus enacting laws for the government of trade and industry throughout the country," the Court concluded, "is virtually unfettered," and therefore "an unconstitutional delegation of legislative power."[64]

Justice Benjamin Cardozo had dissented in *Panama Refining* but agreed with the other Justices in *Schechter Poultry*. The act to be performed in the former case was "definite and single," and there had been "no grant to the Executive of any roving commission to inquire into evils and then, upon discovering them, do anything he pleases."[65] In the latter case, however, the delegation was "not confined to any single act," but was rather "a roving commission to inquire into evils and upon discovery correct them." There was "no standard, definite or even approximate, to which legislation must conform."[66] "What is fair . . . becomes as wide as the field of industrial regulation," and if such a delegation were upheld, then "anything that Congress may do within the limits of the commerce clause for the betterment of business may be done by the President upon the recommendation of a trade association by calling it a code." Such a provision "is delegation running riot," Cardozo wrote, and "[n]o such plenitude of power is susceptible of transfer."[67]

The Supreme Court has not declared unconstitutional any delegation since these cases in 1935. The composition of the Court changed and in a subsequent chapter it will be seen that the Court allowed Congress broader powers under the Commerce Clause. It is widely believed that the changing composition of the Court led it to uphold various statutes under the nondelegation doctrine. There may be at least some truth to that story. Some delegations appear hard to reconcile with the intelligible principle test.[68]

In 2001, a unanimous Supreme Court, in an opinion by Justice Antonin Scalia, rejected a nondelegation challenge to the Clean Air Act and explained the subsequent history:

> In the history of the Court we have found the requisite "intelligible principle" lacking in only two statutes, one of which provided literally no guidance for the exercise of discretion, and the other of which conferred authority to regulate the entire economy on the basis of no more precise a standard than stimulating the economy by assuring "fair competition."
>
> We have, on the other hand, upheld the validity of § 11(b)(2) of the Public Utility Holding Company Act of 1935, which gave the Securities and Exchange Commission authority to modify the structure of holding company systems so as to ensure that they are not "unduly or unnecessarily complicate[d]" and do not "unfairly or inequitably distribute voting power among security holders." We have approved the wartime conferral of agency power to fix the prices of commodities at a level that "will be generally fair and equitable and will effectuate the [in some respects conflicting] purposes of th[e] Act." And we have found an "intelligible principle" in various statutes authorizing regulation in the "public interest."
>
> In short, we have "almost never felt qualified to second-guess Congress regarding the permissible degree of policy judgment that can be left to those executing or applying the law."[69]

Thus things stood in 2001. In one of the Court's latest nondelegation cases, however, several current Justices have expressed a desire to revisit and revive a more robust version of the nondelegation doctrine. Their arguments have also engendered a significant scholarly response.

11.5 REVIVALISTS AND REVISIONISTS

Formalist and originalist judges have argued that something has gone awry. Justice Thomas, in a concurrence in a 2015 case, argued that "[u]nder the original understanding of the Constitution," the "formulation of generally applicable rules of private conduct ... requires the exercise of legislative power."[70] The modern Court, however, "has abandoned all pretense of enforcing a qualitative distinction between legislative and executive power." If "the 'intelligible principle' test was ever an adequate means of enforcing that distinction, it has been decoupled from the historical understanding of the legislative and executive powers and thus does not keep executive 'lawmaking' within the bounds of inherent executive discretion."[71]

In the more recent case *Gundy v. United States*,[72] Justice Gorsuch, writing in dissent for himself, Chief Justice Roberts, and Justice Thomas, would have found that the Sex Offender Registration and Notification Act constituted an unconstitutional delegation of legislative power when it delegated to the Attorney General the power to "specify the applicability" of its requirements to sex offenders who had committed their offenses before the law's enactment. The majority used statutory interpretation to narrow the delegation, holding that the statute required the Attorney General to apply the law's requirements to pre-enactment offenders as soon as feasible. The dissenters were not persuaded by the majority's interpretation of the statute.

The dissenters then observed three general rules about the historic nondelegation doctrine. First, "as long as Congress makes the policy decisions when regulating private conduct, it may authorize another branch to 'fill up the details.'"[73] "Second, once Congress prescribes the rule governing private conduct, it may make the application of that rule depend on executive fact-finding."[74] "Third, Congress may assign the executive and judicial branches certain non-legislative responsibilities."[75] Here, they pointed to the *Brig Aurora* case, which involved the "foreign affairs" powers of the President, and *Wayman*, which involved procedures for court proceedings. Many cases involving the intelligible principle test, they wrote, would also be consistent with these other tests. But the intelligible principle rule "eventually began to take on a life of its own," and its contemporary "mutated version . . . has no basis in the original meaning of the Constitution, in history, or even in the decision from which it was plucked."[76]

There is no denying the many delegations of authority the modern test has allowed. But the focus from those seeking to revive the doctrine on "private conduct" or "private rights" requires a bit of an explanation. Private rights and conduct are those freedoms individuals have by nature that do not depend on government. The rules governing private rights and conduct are what Blackstone described as the "rule[s] of civil conduct prescribed by the supreme power in a state, commanding what is right and prohibiting what is wrong."[77] Private rights tend to be distinguished from "public rights," like welfare benefits or government employment, that do not exist in the state of nature.[78]

Private rights and conduct are surely at the core of legislative power. But it hardly follows that Congress could freely delegate to the President the power to establish a social security program. To hark back to Chief Justice Marshall's test, and to James Madison's statement in the Report of 1800, private rules of conduct will undoubtedly be more important than rules that merely affect procedure, or that merely affect public rights. It does not follow that those other rules are unimportant. Conversely, it is hardly clear that Congress is prohibited from delegating some discretion over private rights and conduct, so long as it has resolved the important policy questions.[79]

To put a finer point on the discussion, the test for nondelegation ought to depend on the definition of legislative power. Fixing the rules of conduct is certainly at the core of that power. Regulating private rights such as contracts and wills is, too. But so is establishing a welfare program or a government department. The better definition of legislative power comes from *INS v. Chadha*, a case discussed in Chapter 12: it is the power of "altering the legal rights, duties and relations of persons."[80] The executive merely executes the existing state of legal relations, and the judiciary merely applies the existing rules surrounding those legal relations. Only the legislature can alter such relations.

The establishment of a welfare program or a government department or a post road all alter legal rights, duties, and relations and so would be included in the definition of legislative power. Thus, the private rights/conduct test for nondelegation cannot be correct; legislative power reaches beyond these. But since the details of legislation will often shape legal relations, too, there must be some way to distinguish between the kinds of rules or regulations that "alter" those relations, and those that merely sharpen or clarify them. Chief Justice Marshall's "important subjects" test starts to make a lot of sense: Congress must decide on the important policy questions, leaving to the executive department the power to fill up the details. Private rights and conduct may be more important, but legislative power reaches beyond them, too.

Another definition of legislative power comes from Rousseau and Montesquieu: It is the power to determine the "will" of the state, while the executive power is the power to execute that will. If that is correct, then the intelligible principle test makes good sense. Without such a principle, the will of the state would be obscure; the President would be making law in executing a vague statute. The problem with the modern nondelegation doctrine is not that this test is incorrect, but rather that the Supreme Court has upheld incredibly broad and vague, and often competing, standards as intelligible.

A reinvigorated nondelegation doctrine that retains the intelligible principle test could look not only to private rights, but also to the breadth of the statutory standards in light of the scope of the subject matter to which those standards apply. As both Justice Cardozo and the majority agreed in *Schechter Poultry*, there is a difference between delegating power over a defined subject and delegating power over the entire national economy. "[T]he degree of agency discretion that is acceptable," Justice Scalia wrote for the unanimous Court in the case cited earlier about the Clean Air Act, "varies according to the scope of the power congressionally conferred."[81]

As this portion of the study comes to a close, the reader should be aware that a burgeoning scholarship seeks to cast doubt on the nondelegation doctrine from the other direction. Some of the scholarship contends there was never any such thing as a nondelegation doctrine.[82] Others look at statutes from the First Congress and other early Congresses and conclude that the nondelegation doctrine cannot be very robust given the broad delegations found therein.[83] This author has responded to these claims.[84] The interested reader may consult this scholarship and the historical record directly.

Suffice it to say, it appears to the author that none of the evidence casts doubt on the proposition that there was a nondelegation doctrine. In contrast to the numerous statements in the historical record supporting such a doctrine, the opponents of the doctrine have been unable to locate a single statement in the historical record to the opposite effect. Many of the early statutes did delegate discretion to the executive. All statutes do. But none appears inconsistent with an intelligible principle or the important subjects theory of nondelegation. The historical record does cast doubt on a theory of nondelegation that focuses exclusively on private conduct. Formalists and originalists seeking to revive the doctrine may therefore have some rethinking to do. But nothing casts doubt on the fundamental principle of nondelegation.

The Legislative Veto

One consequence of increasingly broad delegations to Congress over the course of the twentieth century was the invention of the "legislative veto." Congress would delegate authority to an executive branch agency or to the President – say, to reorganize the executive departments, to promulgate regulations related to education policy, or to make individual immigration decisions – subject to a legislative override. The presidential veto mechanism comes at the beginning of the legislative process: Congress and the President both must agree to enact law. Once the law is enacted, it is the President's responsibility to execute that law. The legislative veto added a new, additional step: Even if the President executes the law, a legislative veto provision required the President or the executive agencies to submit their actions or decisions to one or both Houses of Congress, which could then choose to "veto" any of those decisions.

The Supreme Court quite rightly held legislative vetoes unconstitutional in the landmark case *INS v. Chadha*, decided in 1983.[1] That case is worth exploring because it starkly highlights the differences between formalism and functionalism as methods of constitutional interpretation in separation of powers disputes. It will help the student of constitutional law to evaluate whether the War Powers Resolution, enacted during the Vietnam War, is constitutional. And a close examination of the opinion also helps elucidate the nature of government power more generally. After examining these matters, the chapter concludes with an affirmative proposal. Although the legislative veto may be unconstitutional, it strikes this author as a good idea in a wide variety of cases in which the executive branch engages in regulatory rulemaking. The author has participated in a number of constitutional reform projects over the past several years, one of which included a proposal to amend the Constitution to give Congress the authority in certain contexts to implement legislative vetoes.

12.1 THE *CHADHA* DECISION

Jagdish Chadha was lawfully admitted to the United States on a nonimmigrant student visa in 1966. He overstayed. In 1973, the Immigration and Naturalization

Service (INS) instituted proceedings to have Chadha removed from the United States.[2] The Immigration and Nationality Act permitted the Attorney General to suspend the deportation of otherwise deportable individuals. The Attorney General exercised that discretion through immigration judges, who are called judges but are executive-branch officials.

The statute provided the conditions on which the Attorney General, acting through the immigration judges, could "in his discretion" allow the suspension of deportation. Such suspension was permissible only if the individual had been physically present in the United States for a continuous period of at least seven years and could prove that during that period "he was and is a person of good moral character." Moreover, the law allowed the suspension only if "in the opinion of the Attorney General" deportation would "result in extreme hardship to the alien or to his spouse, parent, or child, who is a citizen of the United States or an alien lawfully admitted for permanent residence."[3] The immigration judge concluded that these conditions were met: Chadha "had resided continuously in the United States for over seven years, was of good moral character, and would suffer 'extreme hardship' if deported."[4]

That did not end the matter. The statute provided that a report of the suspension had to be submitted to Congress and that either chamber could "veto" the decision to suspend deportation. The statute provided that in the case of a suspension, "a complete and detailed statement of the facts and pertinent provisions of law in the case shall be reported to the Congress with the reasons for such suspension."[5] It then stated that if during that or the next session of Congress "either the Senate or the House of Representatives passes a resolution stating in substance that it does not favor the suspension of such deportation, the Attorney General shall thereupon deport such alien."[6] Absent any disapproval by either the House or Senate, the deportation proceedings would be cancelled and the individual could remain in the United States pursuant to the suspension.

One and a half years after the immigration judge ordered the suspension of Chadha's deportation, Congress, at the last minute provided by law, acted to veto the suspension. The chairman of the immigration subcommittee of the House Committee on the Judiciary introduced a resolution to have Chadha and five other aliens deported. The full House of Representatives approved the resolution apparently on the basis of the chairman's statement that "[i]t was the feeling of the committee, after reviewing 340 cases, that the aliens contained in the resolution . . . did not meet these statutory requirements, particularly as it relates to hardship; and it is the opinion of the committee that their deportation should not be suspended."[7] After his deportation proceedings were reopened, Chadha sued the federal government, arguing that the legislative veto provision of the Immigration and Nationality Act was unconstitutional.

The Supreme Court agreed. The Court first held that the action of the House of Representatives was legislative in character. "Examination of the action taken here by one House . . . reveals that it was essentially legislative in purpose and effect," the Court declared. "[T]he House took action that had the purpose and effect of altering the legal rights, duties and relations of persons, including the Attorney General, Executive Branch officials and Chadha, all outside the legislative branch."[8] The Court elaborated that the one-House veto "mandate[d] Chadha's deportation," which thereby "altered Chadha's status."[9] And because the majority concluded that this veto was a legislative act, it was unconstitutional: The Constitution provides that all legislation must be enacted through bicameralism and presentment, that is, through the agreement of both Houses of Congress as well as that of the President.[10]

The Court's conclusion that the veto of the suspension of deportation was legislative in nature, however, raises a question. If that was legislative power, why was the Attorney General's suspension of deportation not an exercise of legislative power? The House of Representatives may have mandated Chadha's removal, altering his legal status. But before the immigration judge suspended deportation, Chadha was deportable. The suspension of deportation therefore altered Chadha's legal status, too. Why can the Attorney General exercise legislative power without bicameralism and presentment, but one House of Congress cannot?

The majority supplied the beginnings of an answer in the sixteenth footnote of its opinion, worth quoting at some length:

> To be sure, some administrative agency action – rule making, for example – may resemble "lawmaking." . . . Clearly, however, "[i]n the framework of our Constitution, the President's power to see that the laws are faithfully executed refutes the idea that he is to be a lawmaker." When the Attorney General performs his duties pursuant to [the statute], he does not exercise "legislative" power. The bicameral process is not necessary as a check on the Executive's administration of the laws because his administrative activity cannot reach beyond the limits of the statute that created it – a statute duly enacted pursuant to Art. I, §§ 1, 7 . . . .
>
> [T]he Attorney General acts in his presumptively Art. II capacity when he administers the Immigration and Nationality Act. Executive action under legislatively delegated authority that might resemble "legislative" action . . . is always subject to check by the terms of the legislation that authorized it; and if that authority is exceeded it is open to judicial review as well as the power of Congress to modify or revoke the authority entirely. A one-House veto is clearly legislative in both character and effect and is not so checked . . . . Congress' authority to delegate portions of its power to administrative agencies provides no support for the argument that Congress can constitutionally control administration of the laws by way of a Congressional veto.[11]

This explanation leaves something to be desired. It is true that in executing the statute, the Attorney General is limited by its terms. But so is the House of Representatives. The House of Representatives could only veto the specific acts that the statute allowed them to. Although there were no limits on the reasons the House could supply for its decision to veto a suspension of deportation, there were no real limits on the Attorney General either. The Attorney General in his discretion could suspend deportation under certain conditions but did not have to do so. The statute seemed to give the House a similar range of action as the Attorney General. One could in his "discretion" and "opinion" allow a deportable alien to stay, and the other in its "discretion" and "opinion" could require that alien to be deported.

It is often true that judicial review is available when the executive branch takes actions pursuant to a statute. But it is not always available. If Chadha had been allowed to stay in the United States, for example, it is not at all clear that anyone would have had standing to sue the Attorney General for improperly allowing him to stay; no one would have been injured by that decision.[12] And in certain "public rights" cases like immigration – more on this category of cases anon – sovereign immunity can shield Congress from lawsuits. If Chadha had been denied the right to stay in the United States, Congress would not have had to give him the right to sue to reverse that determination.

The Court's footnote does, however, point the way to an interesting insight. The Court said that when the Attorney General "administers" Congress's law, he is acting in a "presumptively" Article II capacity. That seems another way of saying that when the Attorney General executes Congress's statute, he is exercising executive power, not legislative power. When Congress enacted the Immigration and Nationality Act, it had free rein to decide on all the policies. There were no preexisting restrictions on what Congress could do, outside the prohibitions in the Bill of Rights or elsewhere in the Constitution. Congress thereby exercised legislative power in enacting the law. Once it enacted the law, however, anyone carrying that law into execution would be exercising executive power.

That is a good explanation for why the Attorney General's action was lawful, and perhaps also a good explanation for why the House's action was unlawful. The House was not exercising legislative power at all; in exercising the veto power that Congress had given to it, the House was exercising executive power. "It was the feeling of the committee," the chair of the subcommittee had stated, "that the aliens contained in the resolution did not meet these statutory requirements ...."[13] Deciding whether certain individuals meet statutory criteria is executive power. The House was purporting to carry into execution the statute that it had previously enacted.

That would also be unconstitutional. Although executive actions need not go through bicameralism or presentment, the Constitution says something else about them: Only the President can undertake them. Put another way, Congress has legislative power, not executive power. By applying its own statute to a specific individual, Congress was exercising executive power it did not have. Whether Congress was exercising legislative power or executive power, the Court arrived at the right outcome.

For that matter, perhaps the House's action was an exercise of judicial power. Justice Powell argued in his concurring opinion: "When Congress finds that a particular person does not satisfy the statutory criteria for permanent residence in this country it has assumed a judicial function in violation of the principle of separation of powers."[4] That raises another interesting question: What is the difference between executive power and judicial power? Was the House exercising one or the other?

Chief Justice Marshall observed, "It is the peculiar province of the legislature to prescribe general rules for the government of society; the application of those rules would seem to be the duty of other departments."[5] Both the executive and the judicial departments apply rules the legislature has enacted. The difference between the two in most cases is finality: A federal prosecutor, for example, applies the law to the facts of a particular case and decides whether to bring a prosecution, but only a judge or jury can determine with finality that the defendant has violated the law. That does not necessarily help resolve the question of what types of cases require the application of judicial power as opposed to those matters that the executive branch may conclusively and finally determine for itself, a subject deferred to the end of this chapter.

The central point is that it does not matter how one characterizes the House's action because neither Congress, nor the House of Representatives acting alone, has any judicial power outside the impeachment process. Whether its act was executive or judicial, it was unconstitutional for the House to undertake it.

12.2 FORMALISM AND FUNCTIONALISM

Congress's action was unconstitutional under a formalist interpretation of the Constitution. *Chadha* is a good illustration of how formalism operates. Formalism maintains that the Constitution recognizes three types of power – legislative, executive, and judicial – each of which can only be exercised according to the constitutional requirements for that type of power. Congress must exercise legislative power, and it must do so through bicameralism and presentment. The President must exercise executive power, whether personally or through supervision over subordinate officers. And only courts whose judges enjoy lifetime tenure and salary protections may exercise judicial power.

The majority in *Chadha* reached the correct result because a legislative veto is unconstitutional no matter how one characterizes it. If it is an exercise of legislative power, a legislative veto does not go through presentment, and usually not even bicameralism; if it is an exercise of executive or judicial power, the House is not subordinate to the President nor is it a court. Legislative vetoes are unconstitutional.

Justice White, however, took a different approach in dissent. His approach was functionalist. He argued that although the executive branch agencies theoretically exercise only executive power, they in fact exercise legislative power because of Congress's extraordinarily broad delegations of power. Although the nondelegation doctrine "formally" holds that Congress cannot delegate its legislative power,

White's view was that Congress routinely did precisely that and everyone knew it. "The Court's holding today that all legislative-type action must be enacted through the lawmaking process ignores that legislative authority is routinely delegated to the Executive branch," he asserted.[16] "This Court's decisions sanctioning such delegations make clear that Article I does not require all action with the effect of legislation to be passed as a law."[17]

Justice White accepted the theory of the nondelegation doctrine. But that theory did not reflect the reality on the ground:

> Theoretically, agencies and officials were asked only to "fill up the details," and the rule was that "Congress cannot delegate any part of its legislative power except under a limitation of a prescribed standard." . . . In practice, however, restrictions on the scope of the power that could be delegated diminished and all but disappeared. In only two instances did the Court find an unconstitutional delegation. In other cases, the "intelligible principle" through which agencies have attained enormous control over the economic affairs of the country was held to include such formulations as "just and reasonable," "public interest," "public convenience, interest, or necessity," and "unfair methods of competition."[18]

"[T]hese cases establish that by virtue of congressional delegation, legislative power can be exercised by independent agencies and Executive departments without the passage of new legislation," White summarized. "There is no question but that agency rulemaking is lawmaking in any functional or realistic sense of the term." And "[i]f Congress may delegate lawmaking power to independent and executive agencies, it is most difficult to understand Article I as forbidding Congress from also reserving a check on legislative power for itself."[19]

Justice White's argument is compelling. What good is formalism if it masks the underlying reality of the administrative state? The point is so attractive that this author once argued in a law journal that formalists should accept the functional reality that Congress routinely delegates legislative power to agencies, even though the doctrine pretends it does no such thing. Accepting that one formalist tool, the author argued, would allow a panoply of new formalist separation of powers tools, including a legislative veto.[20]

But the author's youthful exuberance for functionalism has long since passed. There are other, better ways to think about the problem Justice White posed. One is to reinvigorate the nondelegation doctrine. Another is to recognize that in many instances the three powers of government functionally overlap, a point addressed presently. Still a third way is to amend the Constitution to authorize legislative vetoes of certain types, which the author has also proposed.

The immediate point is that functionalism is an alternative, often attractive way to approach separation of powers problems. There is no one "functionalist" way to resolve such problems, but functionalism can be characterized as a series of related propositions. First, functionalism is more concerned with the underlying reality than formal categories. If the executive branch in fact exercises legislative power, then that reality should be recognized even if a formalist understanding of the Constitution dictates that that is not possible. Second, functionalism is concerned with making modern government work. Justice White's dissent detailed how the legislative veto arose from Congress's increasing, and arguably inevitable, delegations of power to agencies as a way to preserve its role in the lawmaking process. "It is an important if not indispensable political invention," White wrote, "that allows the President and Congress to resolve major constitutional and policy differences, assures the accountability of independent regulatory agencies, and preserves Congress' control over lawmaking."[21]

None of that, however, suggests a test functionalists should apply to determine whether any given arrangement should be held to violate the separation of powers. The third proposition develops something of a test: It maintains that so long as any given arrangement does not intrude on another branch's "core" functions, such that one branch is "aggrandizing" itself at the expense of another, then courts should generally uphold that arrangement. As Justice White stated in another case, "[T]he question is whether there is a genuine threat of 'encroachment or aggrandizement of one branch at the expense of the other.'"[22] Two further examples illustrate this approach.

12.3 THE INDEPENDENT COUNSEL

A poignant example of functionalism is the Supreme Court's decision in *Morrison v. Olson*, which upheld the independent counsel statute.[23] In the wake of the Watergate scandal, Congress enacted the Ethics in Government Act of 1978. It required the Attorney General to investigate the possibility of certain executive-branch misconduct, and unless there were "no reasonable grounds to believe that further investigation is warranted," to report the results of the investigation to a specially designated court. The court would then appoint an "independent counsel" to investigate and prosecute those government officials who may have committed crimes. The independent counsel could only be fired by the Attorney General for good cause.[24] Independent counsels were appointed to investigate the Iran-Contra affair and whether President Clinton lied under oath about his sexual relations. (Both parties, sensing the problem such independent counsels pose, have allowed the statute to lapse; Department of Justice regulations today provide instead for the appointment of "special counsels" with similar authorities.)[25]

Under a formalist interpretation of the Constitution, this scheme was unconstitutional for two reasons. First, under the Appointments Clause, and setting aside the question of interbranch appointments, a court can only appoint inferior officers. It is difficult to imagine how the independent counsel could be such an officer. The name – "independent" – demonstrates Congress's intent that the counsel be independent of any of the high-level government officials, including the Attorney

General and the President, whom the independent counsel might have to investigate and prosecute. The Supreme Court, over Justice Antonin Scalia's lone and now classic dissent, nevertheless ruled that the independent counsel was an inferior officer, incorrectly deploying the test for distinguishing officers from employees.[26]

As for the removal power, the law under *Humphrey's Executor* provided that Congress could insulate independent agencies with for-cause removal protections if they exercised "quasi-legislative" or "quasi-judicial" power. There was no question, however, that prosecution was a purely executive power. And yet the Supreme Court allowed for independence anyway:

> We undoubtedly did rely on the terms "quasi-legislative" and "quasi-judicial" to distinguish the officials involved in *Humphrey's Executor* . . ., but our present considered view is that the determination of whether the Constitution allows Congress to impose a "good cause"-type restriction on the President's power to remove an official cannot be made to turn on whether or not that official is classified as "purely executive." The analysis contained in our removal cases is designed not to define rigid categories of those officials who may or may not be removed at will by the President, but to ensure that Congress does not interfere with the President's exercise of the "executive power" and his constitutionally appointed duty to "take care that the laws be faithfully executed" under Article II.[27]

The Supreme Court accepted the proposition that prosecution was an executive function but held that the President did not need removal authority over the officer wielding that power. Because the independent counsel was an inferior officer (or so the Court had held), "we simply do not see how the President's need to control the exercise of that discretion is so central to the functioning of the Executive Branch."[28]

The Court's concession that prosecution was an executive power would have resolved the matter for a formalist. Once the function is recognized as executive, the Constitution provides for how that power is to be exercised: That power is vested in the President, who must therefore have the ability to oversee the execution of the laws through the power to remove.

Functionalist considerations, however, motivated the Court. The entire purpose of the Ethics in Government Act was to police the police and to prosecute the prosecutors. One cannot trust high-level government officials to investigate themselves; very few officials in the executive branch would be willing to investigate themselves or their colleagues. Few presidents would prosecute their own administration. One can see the appeal of functionalism.

But it has drawbacks. Any reader with a memory of any length understands that independent counsels are rarely truly independent. They have their own political loyalties and preferences. So-called independent counsels can do a lot of damage to a politician whom they oppose, all with the veneer of legitimacy and independence. To take one example, the independent counsel investigating the Iran-Contra affair prosecuted Caspar Weinberger, who had served in the Reagan-Bush Administration.

A mere four days before the 1992 election in which President George H. W. Bush was seeking reelection, the independent counsel filed a second indictment that also cast Bush in a poor light. That indictment was later thrown out. Who knows what effect that had on the 1992 presidential election.[29]

Nor does Congress have no recourse. Under the Constitution, Congress can investigate the executive branch. It can conduct impeachments. It is true that the conviction threshold is rather too high for impeachment to be an effective mechanism for removing a president from office. But a proper impeachment can help shift political sentiment and influence future elections. In short, functionalism may often seem attractive but has drawbacks, and formalism often has its own mechanisms for addressing the concerns motivating functionalism.

12.4 WAR POWERS RESOLUTION

The War Powers Resolution poses another case study in formalism and functionalism. The reader will recall from a previous chapter the Constitution's original division of war powers between Congress and the President. The President had some authority as commander in chief to repel invasions and otherwise confront an existing state of war thrust upon the United States. But it was up to Congress to create or expand a state of war. Yet, unilateral executive power reached a crescendo during the Vietnam War, in particular with the President's unilateral decision as part of the wider conflict to carry out bombing missions in Laos and Cambodia.[30] In more recent times, presidents of both political parties have engaged in bombing campaigns against foreign nations without congressional authorization and often when no American lives were at risk.

Congress tried to address its diminished role in decisions over military conflict with the War Powers Resolution of 1973, enacted over President Nixon's veto.[31] After correctly describing the Constitution's distribution of war powers, the law provides that "[t]he President in every possible instance shall consult with Congress before introducing United States Armed Forces into hostilities or into situations where imminent involvement in hostilities is clearly indicated by the circumstances."[32] It then provides that in "the absence of a declaration of war," the President must submit to Congress within 48 hours the relevant circumstances of any case into which armed forces are introduced into hostilities.[33] Such military action then terminates in one of two ways: automatically after sixty days, unless Congress approves the action, or at any time if Congress "so directs by concurrent resolution."[34]

Under formalism, both provisions are problematic. The second, legislative veto provision is more obviously so. If the decision to introduce military forces is legislative in nature, Congress cannot act on its own. Although the War Powers Resolution provides for bicameralism (a concurrent resolution), it does not provide for presentment to the President. And if the actions in question with respect to the military are executive in nature, Congress does not have the executive power, or more precisely the powers that come with being commander in chief. One can again see the functionalist appeal. The President should not be engaging in these military activities at all without congressional authorization. Yet, if the President is doing so – if the President is effectively usurping Congress's powers – it seems sensible to give a back-end check to Congress. It is the same insight that Justice White deployed in *Chadha*: Theoretically, the President is just exercising the executive power or the commander in chief powers, but everyone understands that the President in reality is exercising Congress's legislative power to declare or authorize war.

Here, too, functionalism has its risks. The War Powers Resolution can be understood as congressional approval of short-term military actions that have not been vetoed. Or it can be seen as a resignation to the fact that the President will exercise these powers. To be sure, the Resolution states that nothing in it is intended to "alter the constitutional authority of the Congress or of the President," or to "be construed as granting any authority to the President with respect to the introduction of United States Armed Forces into hostilities."[35] Still, that Congress included such a proviso is a good indication that it understood that that was precisely the risk. And formalism does offer some solutions to unilateral presidential warmaking, including Congress's power of the purse and the power of impeachment. Neither has proven particularly effective in restraining executive power in this regard, but the War Powers Resolution also has not.

The mechanism for automatic termination is more complicated. If such troop deployments are believed to be within the President's constitutional power, then requiring automatic termination of such deployments would be an unconstitutional usurpation of presidential prerogatives. But if the decision to deploy troops into military conflict is in fact legislative power – part of the power to declare war or authorize imperfect hostilities – then to that extent the War Powers Resolution can be understood as Congress limiting its authorization for military conflict. In other words, Congress is perfectly within its right to enact a declaration of war but provide that such declaration shall expire in sixty days. After that point, there would be no more declaration and no more war for the President to prosecute.

For this argument to work, however, it would require one to believe that Congress was granting authorization in the War Powers Resolution to the President in the first place to engage in military hostilities not lasting more than sixty days. But the Resolution says it is not in fact authorizing any such hostilities; and moreover, if it were so authorizing, that would be a potentially problematic delegation of Congress's war powers. Congress cannot give up its war powers so easily; it probably cannot pass a law that says "the President may declare war if in the President's opinion the national interest so requires." If such a delegation were constitutional, however, then certainly limiting that delegation to sixty days would be constitutional, too.

12.5 NONEXCLUSIVE FUNCTIONS

The discussion of the *Chadha* case left an important question unresolved. How should one characterize the power at issue? It did not matter for the outcome: Whether legislative, executive, or judicial, Congress could not have exercised the power it did in the manner it did. But the question still matters because formalism often requires distinguishing between acts of legislative, executive, and judicial power so that one knows which branch is supposed to exercise the function at issue. And the uncertainty about the nature of power in *Chadha* has created skepticism about formalism. If formalists cannot determine what kind of power was at issue in *Chadha*, how can formalism work? Elizabeth Magill has argued that "[t]he sporadic judicial efforts to identify the differences among the governmental power are nearly universally thought to be unhelpful," and *Chadha* was a central case in point.[36]

There is a solution to this problem, one that in fact helps solve many mysteries about separation of powers disputes.[37] The answer was described previously in the context of presidential power and the *Youngstown* framework: Sometimes the Constitution's three powers functionally overlap. Put another way, sometimes the government can achieve the exact same outcome through the exercise of legislative, executive, or judicial power, depending on the function at issue. As John Manning has written, "[M]ultiple branches can often bring about very nearly the same result, provided that they do so in a manner consistent with the operating procedures prescribed by the [Constitution]."[38] There is nothing about this idea inconsistent with formalism.

A few examples will now further illustrate this proposition. One of the nation's earliest statutes provided that the national government would assume the pension payments made to the invalid veterans of the Revolutionary War pursuant to legislation of the Confederation Congress, "under such regulations as the President of the United States may direct."[39] President Washington and Secretary of War Henry Knox's regulations provided that the sums were to be paid in "two equal payments," the first on March 5, 1790, and the second on June 5, 1790; and that each application for payment was to be accompanied by vouchers and affidavits proving eligibility.[40] Once Congress enacted the statute, President Washington could promulgate those regulations because doing so was merely an act of executive power carrying into execution Congress's law. But Congress itself could have provided in its legislation precisely the same regulations. Congress could have legislated such details, or it could have left those details to the President.

Another example occurs in *Wayman v. Southard*, the case involving a delegation of authority to courts to alter their rules of procedure. The reader will recall from Chapter 11 that Chief Justice Marshall wrote, "It will not be contended that Congress can delegate to the Courts, or to any other tribunals, powers which are strictly and exclusively legislative. But Congress may certainly delegate to others, powers which the legislature may rightfully exercise itself."[41] Congress could have written all the judicial procedures without leaving any discretion for the courts. Or it could have left some discretion, as it did in the statute there at issue. Some functions can be accomplished by an exercise of either legislative power or executive power, or by an exercise of either legislative power or judicial power.

A classic example of a government function that can be achieved through an exercise of any of the three powers is the resolution of public rights claims. Chapter 11 noted that the central example of public rights are government benefits, such as welfare benefits or public employment. These do not involve private rights to life, liberty, or property, but rather government entitlements. Congress historically resolved many such matters on its own by private bill: Congress could pass a law directing that a particular person be given a pension or a public land grant.[42] But Congress could also pass a law authorizing the executive branch to make such determinations, as long as Congress had provided sufficient standards for the executive branch to follow (and sufficient appropriations). In following Congress's law, the executive branch would then be exercising executive power. Congress does not have to provide judicial review over such matters because sovereign immunity would bar any lawsuit without Congress's consent. But Congress could assign such cases to the judiciary, too, because judicial power extends to the adjudication of any adversarial dispute under existing law. Such cases would fit that definition.

That explains *Chadha*: Historically, immigration was understood to be a public privilege, not a private right. Congress often admitted aliens or granted them citizenship through private bills.[43] And early on, Congress passed a general law authorizing courts to decide whether the citizenship requirements had been met.[44] Later, that task was transferred to executive branch agencies, namely, the INS at the time Chadha's case was decided – and Congress even provided that such decisions could be final.[45] That comported with the notion that immigration was a privilege, the denial of which is subject to sovereign immunity. In short, the decision whether or not to deport Chadha could be accomplished through legislation; through the President's carrying into execution Congress's immigration and naturalization law; or through judicial review if Congress had assigned such matters to courts. The same result can sometimes be accomplished by the exercise of more than one branch exercising its vested power.

None of that is to say that all government functions can be reached by an exercise of any of the three powers. There are some functions that are exclusive to one branch or another. Chief Justice Marshall hinted that there were powers "strictly and exclusively legislative." What is strictly and exclusively legislative depends on one's theory of the nondelegation doctrine. Under the modern doctrine, the establishment of intelligible principles is an exclusively legislative task that only Congress can undertake. If Congress's statute does not contain an intelligible principle, then the President cannot simply make one up; establishing such a principle is exclusively within Congress's domain.

There are also examples of exclusively executive power. No matter what Congress may desire, it cannot deprive the President of the power to supervise the principal officers through removal.[46] Congress cannot pass legislation specifying that a particular officer should be removed (other than by impeachment) or not removed. It cannot provide that Congress itself will bring criminal prosecutions in court.[47] Some things only the President can do because they require an exercise of what is strictly and exclusively executive power. Although the matter is a bit more advanced, certain matters are exclusively within the province of the judiciary, namely, the power to divest a person of life, liberty, or property.[48]

In sum, formalism stands for the proposition that the Constitution recognizes three types of power, and that each power must be exercised by the particular branch with which it is associated and according to the constitutional requirements for its exercise. And it stands, in this author's view, for the proposition that some government functions can only be reached by one type of power or another. But it does not follow that all government functions must always be characterized as one type of power or another. Sometimes the exact same result can be achieved through an exercise of two or all three of the powers that the Constitution vests in the respective departments of the national government.

12.6 A PROPOSED AMENDMENT

This chapter has established why the legislative veto, under a formalist approach to the separation of powers, is unconstitutional. But it still strikes this author as a good idea, at least when it comes to the administrative state's regulatory authorities. To be sure, as noted repeatedly, when an agency promulgates a regulation, it is exercising executive power, so long as Congress's statute does not violate the nondelegation doctrine, and even though Congress could have promulgated the exact same regulation through the legislative process. But it remains the case that today the administrative agencies exercise vast amounts of regulatory power that are unlikely to be much diminished even if the modern judiciary were to begin reinvigorating the nondelegation doctrine. Congress may not have the time or capacity to address and consider all the kinds of regulations that the myriad government agencies currently promulgate. So long as agencies continue to exercise such vast regulatory powers, giving Congress a say on the back end seems a sensible way to restore Congress's proper role in the constitutional system of government. That is the spirit in which the War Powers Resolution was enacted.

Nevertheless, the legislative veto seems inappropriate in certain types of cases. In Chadha's case, one wonders whether the Court's decision was motivated in part by the unseemliness of Congress deciding the fate of a particular individual. A legislative veto over general administrative regulations would be much more appropriate. To that end, as part of a constitutional reform project, the author has proposed an amendment to the Constitution that received the support of the conservative, progressive, and libertarian scholars participating in the project. It reads as follows:

> Congress may by law provide for a veto, by majority votes in each of the Houses of Congress, of actions taken by the executive department, except actions adjudicating the applicability of a statute or regulation to a person. A failure by Congress to act pursuant to such a law shall not affect any judicial determination as to whether any law, or any actions of the executive department, are valid or enforceable.[49]

This amendment would empower Congress to include legislative vetoes in legislation. Such vetoes would require the concurrence of both Houses of Congress rather than approval of a single House. And it would apply only to actions that are regulatory in effect, such as agency rulemakings. It would therefore also apply to other executive orders, such as one imposing conscription. But it would not apply to actions like those involving Chadha in which a statute or regulation is applied to a particular individual. The final clause ensures that Congress's failure to veto an executive action would not be interpreted to mean that Congress approves of the executive action. Nor would a failure to veto affect a court's determination as to whether the law violates the nondelegation doctrine in the first place, or the regulation otherwise violates the statute at issue. The author does not pretend that voters will rush to the polls to support such an amendment. But it is certainly one that many Americans could get behind, one that would be consistent with the original spirit of the Constitution.

PART VI

The Judicial Power

13

Article III and Judicial Review

The structure of the Constitution's third article is even more puzzling than that of its first two. Article III creates one Supreme Court and then leaves it up to Congress whether to create lower federal courts. Article III grants this single Supreme Court original jurisdiction to hear only a few matters – cases in which a state is a party, and those affecting ambassadors – leaving the rest of the federal judicial power to the Court's appellate jurisdiction "with such exceptions . . . as the Congress shall make." This combination of features might seem to render the federal judicial branch exceedingly weak: Congress need not create lower federal courts at all and perhaps it can make "exceptions" to the Supreme Court's appellate jurisdiction by removing it entirely. One might conclude that the federal judiciary would hardly be a "co-equal" branch of government if subject to such complete regulation by Congress.[1] On the other hand, Congress has always used the federal courts to vindicate federal interests, and there is little reason to think national lawmakers would have much incentive to eliminate the role of the federal courts in the federal system.

This puzzle of Article III's text has absorbed some of the most brilliant minds in constitutional law over the past century. This chapter will not resolve the debates but introduces them for three reasons. First, a comparison of the preceding two articles to Article III may help elucidate questions about the former, for example, whether "the executive power" is a substantive grant of authority. Second, the debates over Article III's structure suggest that perhaps courts were not intended to be as important as they are today in the constitutional system. Third, the structure of Article III was at issue in *Marbury v. Madison*, the case that affirmed – some say established – judicial review. Understanding that structure is, at a minimum, helpful for understanding the facts of that case.

Some still believe that Chief Justice Marshall invented the concept of judicial review, for which there is otherwise no support in the constitutional text.[2] That is incorrect. With the advent of written constitutions, judicial review became almost inevitable: It followed from well-established conflict-of-laws principles. Not a single Framer or member of Congress between 1787 and 1803 when *Marbury* was decided, at least none of which this author is aware, believed judicial review was unavailable under the Constitution.[3] Everyone expected the federal courts to review congressional legislation for consistency with the Constitution.

It does not follow, however, that the Supreme Court is the final arbiter of the Constitution's meaning. Chapter 14 addresses the notorious case of *Dred Scott v. Sandford*, in which the Supreme Court grievously erred and held that free persons of African descent were not "citizens of the United States" within the meaning of the Constitution entitled to any of the privileges and immunities of citizens. It examines whether Chief Justice Taney, the author of that opinion, was a true originalist, or whether Justice Benjamin Curtis in dissent had the better of the argument. It will explore whether the Founders, and the Constitution they bequeathed to future generations, were as proslavery as Taney asserted.

Chapter 15, the final chapter in this part of the study, will turn to the question of what to do when the Supreme Court grievously and momentously errs, as it did in *Dred Scott*. It explains Abraham Lincoln's response to that decision. Lincoln argued that although court judgments made with proper jurisdiction are binding on the parties to the suit, the legislative and executive departments of government need not follow what the courts say "as a political rule," at least not until the issue is finally "settled." Lincoln's "departmentalism" has important implications for the modern day. Today's "judicial supremacy," in which the Supreme Court acts as and is believed to be the final arbiter of the Constitution's meaning, does not reflect the role the original Constitution contemplated for the courts.

13.1 OVERVIEW OF ARTICLE III

The first sentence of Article III provides: "The judicial Power of the United States, shall be vested in one supreme Court, and in such inferior Courts as the Congress may from time to time ordain and establish." The next sentence establishes lifetime, "good Behavior" tenure and salary protections for judges. The first paragraph of Article III's next section then declares that "[t]he judicial Power shall extend to all Cases" arising under federal laws, treaties, or the Constitution; to all cases affecting ambassadors; and to all cases of admiralty and maritime jurisdiction. These are the three "subject matter" jurisdictional heads that Article III allows the federal courts to exercise. The judicial power then extends to six categories of "controversies" based on the parties to the suit, which may or may not involve federal law but which the Framers thought national courts would be better suited to resolve: those in which the United States is a party; those between two states, a state and a citizen of another state, citizens of different states, or citizens and foreign states/citizens; and finally controversies involving land grants from different states.[4]

The second paragraph of the second section takes some of these categories of federal judicial power and assigns them to the Supreme Court's original jurisdiction, meaning such lawsuits can be filed in the first instance in the Supreme Court and the Court can hold trials on those matters. Article III assigns only two of the abovementioned categories to the Court's original jurisdiction: "In all Cases affecting Ambassadors, other public Ministers and Consuls, and those in which a State shall be Party, the supreme Court shall have original Jurisdiction." As for the other categories, the Supreme Court is to have appellate jurisdiction. Congress can also make "exceptions" to that jurisdiction: "In all the other Cases before mentioned, the supreme Court shall have appellate Jurisdiction, both as to Law and Fact, with such Exceptions, and under such Regulations as the Congress shall make."[5] The meaning of this clause shall be investigated presently.

13.2 MADISONIAN COMPROMISE

By vesting the judicial power in "one supreme Court, and in such inferior Courts as the Congress may from time to time ordain and establish," Article III appears to give Congress discretion not to create any lower federal courts at all. The only court that is constitutionally required is the Supreme Court. The reason the Constitution gives Congress this discretion is well known: This provision was part of the "Madisonian Compromise" at the Constitutional Convention. The strong nationalists at the Convention wanted to make lower federal courts constitutionally required. But the more anti-nationalist delegates feared the power of the national courts. Would a local farmer have to travel to a far-away federal court to make or defend claims? The state courts would have more, and more local, branches. These delegates also thought that state courts would be more solicitous of state prerogatives; national courts would be favorable to the new national government and to commercial interests.[6]

The Convention compromised and left the creation of lower federal courts up to Congress. In the meantime, the state courts could hear any federal claims. Thus, it is often said that the state courts have concurrent jurisdiction with federal courts over matters involving federal law or controversies to which the federal judicial power might also extend. A party can always file a suit against the citizen of another state in that citizen's state court, for example.[7] And a litigant may bring federal claims in state courts, too. These cases might eventually end up in the one "supreme Court" of the United States on appeal, but they could all initially be heard in state courts.

Although Congress had discretion not to create lower federal courts, the Federalists in the First Congress immediately created a set of national courts. But this set of courts was nothing like the extensive network of lower federal courts of the present day. The Judiciary Act of 1789 only gave lower courts jurisdiction to hear admiralty and maritime cases, criminal cases arising under federal law, and otherwise a variety of "diversity" jurisdiction cases involving citizens of different states with high amounts-in-controversy.[8] Other statutes granted jurisdiction to the lower federal courts to hear specific matters such as those involving patents.[9] But it was not until 1875 that Congress created a general jurisdiction in the lower federal courts to hear all federal questions.[10] The standard story is that because Congress has discretion not to create lower federal courts, it has the lesser power to create only some lower federal courts or to create such courts for limited purposes.[11]

13.3 APPELLATE JURISDICTION

Congress might never have created any lower federal courts. In that case, the state courts would hear federal claims and the only federal court around, the "one supreme Court," would hear appeals directly from the state courts. But does not the Constitution also give Congress wide discretion over this appellate jurisdiction? "[T]he supreme Court shall have appellate Jurisdiction, both as to Law and Fact, with such Exceptions, and under such Regulations as the Congress shall make." The standard story is that this "exceptions clause" gives Congress the power to remove cases from the Supreme Court's appellate jurisdiction.[12] On this understanding, Congress could pass a law declaring, "The Supreme Court shall have no appellate jurisdiction."

If Congress refused to create lower federal courts and passed a law eliminating the Supreme Court's appellate jurisdiction, that would effectively neuter the federal judicial power. There would only be the Supreme Court, which could only hear matters within its original jurisdiction: those affecting ambassadors or in which a state is a party. Can it be that the Framers wrote Article III in a way that gave Congress the power to write the federal courts out of the constitutional system of separated powers? The question how far Congress can make such exceptions usually surfaces when Congress threatens to "strip" the federal courts of jurisdiction over certain matters. In recent years, Congress famously tried to strip the federal courts of jurisdiction to hear cases from detainees at the military prison in Guantanamo Bay, Cuba. The Supreme Court rebuffed the effort in an opinion that sidestepped the relevant questions.[13]

One response is that Congress can limit the jurisdiction of the inferior courts and remove any appellate jurisdiction it would like, but that that is nothing to worry about; the people ought to trust their democratically elected members of Congress to decide how much of the federal judicial power should be assigned to federal courts as opposed to state courts, which the Supremacy Clause expressly obligates to enforce the Constitution and federal laws.[14] And Congress has in fact always created a network of federal courts, demonstrating that there is not much to fear from the extreme possibilities. As noted previously, national lawmakers have historically been motivated to rely upon national courts to effectuate national interests. Tara Leigh Grove has also demonstrated how Congress has used the Exceptions Clause to promote, rather than hinder, the Supreme Court's role in the constitutional system by replacing mandatory appellate jurisdiction with discretionary certiorari jurisdiction, giving the Court far more control over its docket and the kinds of questions it will answer.[15]

Other scholars have argued that historical antecedents limit the kinds of exceptions Congress can make. Jim Pfander and Daniel Birk have argued, for example, that a similar clause in the Acts of Union governing judicial review in Scotland, which was similarly hierarchical with a "supream" and inferior courts, permitted only regulations that furthered the administration of justice.[16] Although the relevant article of Union did not include the term "exceptions," this precursor nevertheless strongly suggests that Congress may not be able to make exceptions that defeat the very purpose of Article III.

One reading of the Exceptions Clause that would allow it to serve this function is that it merely authorizes Congress to take cases from the Court's appellate jurisdiction and assign them to its original jurisdiction. This reading of the clause contradicts some evidence from the ratification debates: Several Anti-Federalists worried that by expanding the original jurisdiction of the Supreme Court, more trials would be held in a faraway national capital; prominent Federalists reassured them that the Court's original jurisdiction would only apply to the two limited sets of cases specified in the Constitution.[17] The "augmentation" reading of the clause, however, is certainly a natural one, and Laurence Claus has shown that the notes from the Constitutional Convention suggest the Framers appear to have intended precisely that reading.[18]

Steven Calabresi and Gary Lawson have relatedly argued that the power to regulate the Supreme Court's jurisdiction comes from the Necessary and Proper Clause. The Exceptions Clause simply recognizes that this power exists.[19] The phrase "under such Regulations as the Congress shall make" does not read like a grant of power; it reads more like the portion of the Appointments Clause that references offices "which shall be established by Law."[20] In either case, the Necessary and Proper Clause supplies the requisite congressional power to establish offices and to regulate the Court's jurisdiction. This is significant because under that clause, the reader will recall, Congress may only enact laws that carry into execution the powers of the other departments; it cannot write those departments out of existence.[21]

There are still other possibilities: Some scholars argue that lower federal courts exercising all of the federal judicial power are in fact mandatory, the Madisonian Compromise notwithstanding.[22] That is textually and historically implausible. Akhil Amar, following Justice Joseph Story, has advanced an alternative more consistent with historical practice: that there are two separate tiers of federal jurisdiction, one mandatory and one permissive. Both Story and Amar observed that the judicial power shall extend to "all" cases arising under federal law or admiralty, or those affecting ambassadors; but in the remaining jurisdictional heads based on the identity of the parties rather than the subject matter, the judicial power shall extend "to Controversies," not to "all" controversies. They argued that this means there must be a federal court, whether inferior or the one supreme Court, to hear at least cases arising under federal laws or admiralty or affecting ambassadors.[23]

Amar's and Story's argument has the virtue of being largely consistent with early drafts of Article III that did seem to divide these two tiers of jurisdiction.[24] As the

Constitution is written, however, there are more plausible textual reasons for including the word "all" in front of "cases," including to emphasize that cases can be civil or criminal whereas controversies are civil only.[25] In other words, there are two tiers of jurisdiction, but it does not follow that federal courts must be available to hear either type. It is just as likely, if not more likely, that judicial power is permissive for either type of jurisdiction and Article III merely specifies that the maximum extent of that power penetrates more deeply with respect to matters of federal law.[26]

For present purposes, it is sufficient to understand the standard picture, although some of that picture might be incorrect as a matter of original meaning: Congress's power not to create lower federal courts has been understood to give it the lesser power to create only some federal courts with authority to hear only some of the matters to which the federal judicial power "shall extend." Congress has always created lower federal courts, but it has never given them the full judicial power listed in Article III. More pertinent to the *Marbury* decision, the Supreme Court has original jurisdiction solely over two sets of cases or controversies, those affecting ambassadors or in which a state is a party, leaving the rest to its appellate jurisdiction as regulated by Congress.

13.4 THE ROAD TO *MARBURY*

Marbury v. Madison involved this very structure of Article III and the constitutionality of a portion of the Judiciary Act of 1789. The essential facts are these. After the Democratic-Republicans won the elections of 1800 and were soon to sweep the Federalists out of power, the lame-duck Federalist Congress and President John Adams enacted the Judiciary Act of 1801, creating a whole new set of federal judgeships, and an act concerning the District of Columbia that established offices for justices of the peace for the District.[27] The Federalists filled these new positions with the so-called midnight judges before Thomas Jefferson was inaugurated.

William Marbury was nominated and confirmed as a justice of the peace for the District of Columbia but had not yet received his commission. Adams signed Marbury's commission and gave it to interim Secretary of State John Marshall to deliver. Marshall had already been appointed to the Supreme Court and held both offices simultaneously. For reasons that will never be fully known, Marshall neglected to deliver the commission to Marbury. Thomas Jefferson then ordered his Acting Secretary of State Levi Lincoln, and subsequently Secretary of State James Madison, not to deliver the commission.[28]

Marbury sued for his commission and sought a writ of mandamus, an order commanding an executive or judicial officer to undertake a ministerial duty that the officer has no discretion under the law to refuse. The problem was that Marbury sued for the writ directly in the Supreme Court; that Court, however, only had original jurisdiction over the two sets of cases described earlier, those affecting ambassadors or in which a state was a party. Neither applied. William Marbury, however, claimed the authority of the Judiciary Act of 1789, which allowed parties to seek writs of mandamus in the Supreme Court. Did that provision of the Act unconstitutionally expand the Court's original jurisdiction?

In a decision famous for its judicial statesmanship, Marshall held that President Jefferson violated the law by refusing to deliver a commission already signed by the previous president, and further asserted the Court's power of judicial review by pronouncing the relevant provision of the Judiciary Act of 1789 unconstitutional. But because that provision was unconstitutional, Marbury had improperly sued directly in the Supreme Court. If Marbury wanted his commission, he would have to seek a writ of mandamus in a lower court first. The Court thus could not and would not force Jefferson to deliver the commission. The Court established all the principles it sought without forcing a showdown with the Jefferson Administration.

Most of Marshall's opinion was almost certainly legally wrong. First, it is not at all clear that Jefferson had to deliver the commission. If the Constitution leaves to the President the commissioning of officers,[29] presumably the President could have a change of heart. Perhaps new information about the would-be officer has come to light. Most legal documents, to be effective, must be not only signed and sealed but also delivered.[30] Moreover, holding that a commission has legal effect once signed overlooks the possibility that the commission might be lost. It is the delivery of the commission and its continued existence that gives an officeholder authority to act; others may not otherwise know that it had been signed and was effective.[31]

Second, for Marshall's holding about the commission to make sense, it must be presumed that Jefferson did not have the power to remove William Marbury from office. If Jefferson had that power, then Marshall's opinion was making much ado about nothing. The President would not need to deliver the commission because he simply could remove the officer. Marshall, however, presumed that the justice of the peace was not removable for the duration of the five-year term for which he had been appointed.

It is not entirely clear why he thought so. It is possible that William Marbury was not a federal officer at all, but rather a local officer of the District of Columbia, exercising local judicial or local executive power rather than the federal judicial or federal executive power.[32] Shortly after *Marbury* was decided, that is what one circuit court judge concluded, although his colleagues thought the justices of the peace were federal judicial officers requiring lifetime tenure under the Constitution.[33] President Jefferson, however, thought the justices of the peace were executive officers whom he could remove at pleasure; he in fact removed all of the justices of the peace from office prior to reappointing several of them.[34] If they were executive officers, Marshall was wrong to conclude that they were entitled to uninterrupted five-year terms. They would have been subject to presidential removal.

Third, Marshall may have misinterpreted the Judiciary Act of 1789. If that Act had in fact sought to expand the original jurisdiction of the Supreme Court, then perhaps that would have been unconstitutional. But that is not what the statute

seemed to do. The provision allowing the Supreme Court to issue writs of mandamus was in a section about the Court's appellate jurisdiction. Section 13 of the Act
provided in its first few sentences that the Supreme Court was to have original
jurisdiction over certain cases specified by the Constitution, namely, state-as-party
cases and those affecting ambassadors and consuls. It then provided,

> The Supreme Court shall also have appellate jurisdiction from the circuit courts
> and courts of the several states, in the cases herein after specially provided for; and
> shall have power to issue writs of prohibition to the district courts, when proceeding
> as courts of admiralty and maritime jurisdiction, and writs of mandamus, in cases
> warranted by the principles and usages of law, to any courts appointed, or persons
> holding office, under the authority of the United States.[35]

Standard tools of statutory interpretation suggest that the Supreme Court therefore had the power to issue writs of mandamus in cases otherwise within its appellate
jurisdiction. The grant of power to issue writs of mandamus did not create jurisdiction in the Supreme Court, but rather gave the Supreme Court a basic tool to use
when exercising whatever jurisdiction it already possessed. At least one scholar,
however, has argued that writs of mandamus were freestanding writs that could be
sought in a higher court in the first instance and that the version of the statute that
Marshall likely had before him suggested an independent grant of mandamus
jurisdiction.[36]

Fourth, earlier parts of this chapter suggest that Marshall was by no means
obviously correct about his interpretation of the Constitution, either. Even if the
Judiciary Act had expanded the Supreme Court's original jurisdiction, one reading
of the Exceptions Clause is that it permits Congress to take from the Court's default
appellate jurisdiction and assign it to the Court's original jurisdiction. That means
that the baseline of the Court's original jurisdiction comprises state-as-party cases
and those affecting ambassadors, but Congress could add to that baseline. To be
sure, Article III and the Exceptions Clause are, as noted, notoriously ambiguous on
this question and there are other ways to read the relevant provisions of the
Constitution. Marshall was probably right about this issue – it is unlikely Congress
can add to the original jurisdiction of the Supreme Court – but it is at least possible
that he also misinterpreted the relevant provision of the Constitution.

Whether or not Marshall misinterpreted the Constitution, the statute, or both, his
interpretations of the Judiciary Act and Article III created the conflict between
Congress's law and the Constitution.[37]

13.5 *MARBURY* AND JUDICIAL REVIEW

Because Marshall interpreted the statute and Article III in a manner that created a
conflict between the two, he was now in a position to declare the relevant section of
the Judiciary Act unconstitutional. This is the crux of *Marbury*'s enduring legacy.

Marshall refused to give legal effect to that provision of the Judiciary Act because it conflicted with the Constitution, and Marshall thereby asserted the power of judicial review. The question is whether Marshall was inventing a novel power or whether the Court genuinely had this power under the Constitution.

Marshall relied first on several suggestive but not dispositive arguments. He relied on the Oath Clause, which requires judicial and other officers to take an oath to support the Constitution.[38] "How immoral to impose [the oath] on [judges]," Marshall insisted, "if they were to be used as the instruments, and the knowing instruments, for violating what they swear to support?"[39] This argument cannot alone answer the question. If the Constitution does not give the Court the power of judicial review, then assuming that power would violate the oath. If the Constitution includes the power of judicial review, then certainly the oath would be a compelling argument for treating the Constitution as superior to ordinary legislation.

Marshall also relied on the Supremacy Clause:

> This Constitution, and the Laws of the United States which shall be made in Pursuance thereof; and all Treaties made, or which shall be made, under the Authority of the United States, shall be the supreme Law of the Land; and the Judges in every State shall be bound thereby, any Thing in the Constitution or Laws of any State to the Contrary notwithstanding.[40]

This clause mentions the Constitution first, Marshall noted, and provides that only those laws made in "pursuance" of the Constitution are the supreme law of the land.[41] Best read, however, the clause is not about the supremacy of the Constitution over contrary federal laws, but is rather a preemption clause: It declares that all federal laws, of whatever source, are supreme over contrary state law. That is why the clause says the judges in every state, and not the judges in federal territories or the District of Columbia, shall be bound by this federal law. If the Supremacy Clause were the source of judicial review, then it would appear that the Supreme Court itself, which sits in the District, would not have that power because it does not sit in a state.

When drafting the Supremacy Clause, the Framers were not concerned with establishing the supremacy of the Constitution over Congress's laws; they were concerned with establishing the supremacy of the national government over the state governments.[42] The most natural reading of the clause is that laws made in "pursuance" of the Constitution are those made consistently with the process of bicameralism and presentment, and that state judges in every state are bound both by the Constitution and these federal laws, notwithstanding anything to the contrary in their own states' laws.[43]

It is, of course, possible to read the phrase as requiring substantive compliance with the Constitution. Section Twenty-Five of the Judiciary Act of 1789 explicitly presumed that state courts would invalidate federal laws for repugnancy to the Constitution, authorizing Supreme Court review of such decisions.[44] It would certainly be odd to think that state courts had authority to evaluate federal laws for consistency with the Constitution but that federal judges did not. The Judiciary Act also assumed that at least the Supreme Court could evaluate federal statutes for repugnancy to the Constitution in those instances in which state courts first evaluated and found against them. None of this solves the problem that the Supremacy Clause seems directed to the issue of inconsistent state statutes or, if it extends to review of federal statutes, that it does not include judges in the territories or the federal district. The clause along with the Judiciary Act are, however, strongly suggestive that judicial review was presumed.

Marshall next relied on the grant of jurisdiction in Article III to hear cases "arising under the Constitution."[45] "Could it be the intention of those who gave this power, to say that, in using it, the constitution should not be looked into?" Marshall asked. "That a case arising under the constitution should be decided without examining the instrument under which it arises?"[46] Yet, the Supremacy Clause made clear that many cases involving a state's laws or actions could arise under the Constitution. Most of the litigation in the Supreme Court in the first century involved state laws and whether they impermissibly regulated interstate commerce, or whether they violated the Contracts Clause, which prohibits states from "impairing the Obligations of Contract."[47] The federal courts had plenty of cases "arising under the Constitution" to hear without having to consider the constitutionality of federal statutes. Moreover, William Marbury's lawsuit did not "arise" under the Constitution in that same sense; it arose under the laws of Congress that created his office.

Thus far, Marshall's arguments were suggestive but not dispositive. Nevertheless, he did ultimately make a compelling and decisive argument for judicial review. The argument is rooted in standard conflict-of-laws principles and the nature of written constitutions. Conflict-of-laws principles require courts to decide what law applies to a set of facts when more than one law might apply. If one Mississippi resident commits an assault against another such resident while both are in another state and a lawsuit were brought in Mississippi courts, those courts would have to decide whether Mississippi's tort law applied to the action or rather the tort law of the state in which the assault occurred. Similarly, when one state's citizen sues a citizen of another state in federal court under diversity jurisdiction, the courts must decide whether to apply the law of one state or the other, or perhaps a general common law.[48] When Congress enacts two laws that conflict, courts must decide which applies; some possible answers are those enacted later in time control, or a more specific statute controls a more general one.[49]

In short, when more than one law might apply to a situation, courts must decide what law governs the case. This is to what Marshall referred by his famous dictum, "It is emphatically the province and duty of the judicial department to say what the law is":

> It is emphatically the province and duty of the judicial department to say what the
> law is. Those who apply the rule to particular cases, must of necessity expound and

interpret that rule. If two laws conflict with each other, the courts must decide on the operation of each.

So if a law be in opposition to the constitution; if both the law and the constitution apply to a particular case, so that the court must either decide that case conformably to the law, disregarding the constitution; or conformably to the constitution, disregarding the law; the court must determine which of these conflicting rules governs the case. This is of the very essence of judicial duty.[50]

When both a congressional statute and the Constitution apply to a given situation, and each requires a different result such that there is an actual conflict between the two, the courts must decide which controls. That is part of their judicial power to decide cases under existing law, which requires determining what existing law is applicable to the case. A conflict between a congressional statute and the Constitution is like any other conflict-of-laws problem.

The nature of written constitutions leads to the resolution of this problem. The very purpose of having a written constitution establishes the Constitution as superior to ordinary legislation. "If ... the courts are to regard the constitution," Marshall wrote, "and the constitution is superior to any ordinary act of the legislature; the constitution, and not such ordinary act, must govern the case to which they both apply."[51] Marshall elaborated upon America's written Constitution:

> The powers of the legislature are defined, and limited; and that those limits may not be mistaken, or forgotten, the constitution is written. To what purpose are powers limited, and to what purpose is that limitation committed to writing, if these limits may, at any time, be passed by those intended to be restrained? The distinction, between a government with limited and unlimited powers, is abolished, if those limits do not confine the persons on whom they are imposed, and if acts prohibited and acts allowed, are of equal obligation. It is a proposition too plain to be contested, that the constitution controls any legislative act repugnant to it; or, that the legislature may alter the constitution by an ordinary act.
>
> Between these alternatives there is no middle ground. The constitution is either a superior, paramount law, unchangeable by ordinary means, or it is on a level with ordinary legislative acts, and like other acts, is alterable when the legislature shall please to alter it. ...
>
> Certainly all those who have framed written constitutions contemplate them as forming the fundamental and paramount law of the nation, and consequently the theory of every such government must be, that an act of the legislature, repugnant to the constitution, is void.
>
> This theory is essentially attached to a written constitution, and is consequently to be considered, by this court, as one of the fundamental principles of our society.[52]

To summarize: A written constitution defining and limiting the powers of the government is intended to control in the event of a conflict. Such constitutions would be futile if the government could transcend those limits. Under the British unwritten system, the constitution was whatever the particular government arrangements happened to be at any given time, an arrangement that Parliament itself could change.[53] The reader may recall from Chapter 1 that whereas most of the British "could not conceive of the constitution as anything anterior and superior to government and ordinary law, but rather regarded it as the government and ordinary law itself," the American colonists began to conceive of a constitution as "a written superior law set above the entire government against which all other law is to be measured."[54]

Numerous Founding-era writers assumed that judicial review of legislative acts followed from the nature of written constitutions. James Iredell, a future Justice of the Supreme Court, wrote that the Constitution was a fundamental law "limiting the powers of the Legislature, and with which every exercise of those powers must, necessarily, be compared."[55] Judges can and must make this comparison as part of their ordinary judicial duties because the Constitution was not "a mere imaginary thing, . . . but a written document to which all may have recourse, and to which, therefore, the judges cannot wilfully blind themselves."[56] James Wilson, another future Justice, stated that "the power of the Constitution was paramount to the power of the legislature acting under that Constitution," and when judges confront a statute they find "to be incompatible with the superior power of the Constitution, – it is their duty to pronounce it *void*."[57]

Similarly, in *Federalist* No. 78, Alexander Hamilton declared,

> The complete independence of the courts of justice is peculiarly essential in a limited Constitution. By a limited Constitution, I understand one which contains certain specified exceptions to the legislative authority; such, for instance, as that it shall pass no bills of attainder, no ex-post-facto laws, and the like. Limitations of this kind can be preserved in practice no other way than through the medium of courts of justice, whose duty it must be to declare all acts contrary to the manifest tenor of the Constitution void. Without this, all the reservations of particular rights or privileges would amount to nothing.[58]

Several of the first Supreme Court Justices, when sitting as circuit judges along with the various district judges, refused to implement a federal statute in 1792; no one in Congress questioned the Court's authority, but rather Congress amended the statute.[59] David Currie wrote in his magisterial study of Congress that "[r]epeatedly and without contradiction," members in the decade-and-a-half between the initiation of the Constitution in 1789 and the decision in *Marbury v. Madison* in 1803 expected their decisions to be reviewed by the courts for consistency with the Constitution.[60]

As for the Constitutional Convention, there was little explicit consideration of the issue, perhaps because the delegates all presumed that judicial review followed from the nature of written constitutions.[61] Their familiarity with judicial review would not have been surprising, as the Privy Council had reviewed colonial laws for repugnancy to British laws in litigated cases;[62] judges in both England and America reviewed corporate ordinances and bylaws for consistency with statute law;[63] and state courts had experimented with judicial review of legislation since at least 1780.[64]

The most explicit statement came in discussions of the proposed Council of Revision, in which judges would participate with the executive in a negative on national laws. Rufus King of Massachusetts, as recorded in the notes of William Pierce, argued against such a council "because the Judges will have the expounding of those Laws when they come before them; and they will no doubt stop the operation of such as shall appear repugnant to the constitution."[65] Elbridge Gerry stated similarly that judges "will have a sufficient check agst. encroachments on their own department by their exposition of the laws, which involved a power of deciding on their Constitutionality," and observed that state judges had "set aside laws as being agst. the Constitution," which had been done "with general approbation."[66] George Mason agreed that judges "could declare an unconstitutional law void," but argued in favor of a council because he worried about constitutional yet oppressive laws.[67]

The historian Paul Rahe has argued that such statements demonstrate that the Convention delegates widely presumed that judicial review would take the place of other, more radical proposals. If a Council of Revision had been adopted, judges would have assessed congressional legislation for constitutionality prior to enactment. Similarly, if a negative on state laws had been adopted, Congress would have assessed state legislation for, among other things, constitutionality. Both possibilities were fraught with peril; better to leave most constitutional questions to the ordinary course of judicial proceedings.[68]

Marshall's reasoning stands for nothing more nor less than the proposition that the writtenness of the Constitution makes it enforceable against the government. That is the simple, elegant case for judicial review. It is part of the judicial power, it is the very duty of judges, to ascertain what law applies to a given case and then to interpret and apply that law. When two laws conflict, a judge must decide which of the laws governs the case. When there is a congressional statute on point, and it requires a result at odds with the Constitution, the judge must decide whether the statute or the Constitution controls. As Marshall wrote, the very nature of a written constitution is that it is intended to be superior to the legislative power. In the event of a conflict between the Constitution and an act of the ordinary legislature, the Constitution must prevail.

14

Dred Scott, the Constitution, and Slavery

For the half century after *Marbury*, the Supreme Court only occasionally reviewed federal legislation for constitutionality and regularly upheld Congress's laws.[1] Almost all of the Court's cases involved judicial review of state legislation under the Supremacy Clause, usually for potential violations of the Commerce Clause or the Contracts Clause.[2] It was not until 1857, in the infamous case *Dred Scott v. Sandford*,[3] that the Supreme Court next invalidated a significant and politically salient federal law, the Missouri Compromise of 1820. The Court in that decision also held that any Americans of African descent, even if free, were not "citizens of the United States" within the meaning of the Constitution.

The *Dred Scott* case is important to examine for several reasons. It is, as noted, the first significant instance of judicial invalidation of a congressional law since *Marbury*. It raises questions about constitutional interpretation and particularly originalism. It poses others about whether the Founders, or the Constitution they framed, were irredeemably proslavery. And it necessitates consideration of the Court's role in a constitutional system of separated powers.

14.1 BLACK CITIZENSHIP

The facts of the *Dred Scott* case are notoriously complicated, but the relevant ones can be distilled as follows. Dred Scott was enslaved in Missouri to one Dr. Emerson, who took Scott to Upper Louisiana Territory where they resided for several years. The Missouri Compromise of 1820 prohibited slavery everywhere north of the 36° 30' parallel, excepting Missouri itself; this federal prohibition applied to the Upper Louisiana Territory. Under existing Missouri precedent, a sufficiently long stay in free states or territory would make a formerly enslaved person free, and so when Scott and Emerson returned to Missouri, Scott sued for his freedom in state court. Reflecting the changing tone of interstate relations and comity over the slavery issue in this period, the Missouri courts reversed their prior precedents and denied Scott his freedom. Before the judgment became final, Emerson sold Scott to another owner, John Sanford,[4] who was a citizen of New York. Scott then filed a new lawsuit in federal court against Sanford, again seeking his freedom.

The United States Supreme Court had to decide two issues. The first was whether Scott could even sue in federal court. Article III grants jurisdiction to the federal courts over controversies between "citizens" of different states. Was Scott, who purported to be a free person but was of African descent, a "citizen" within the meaning of the Constitution, entitling him to all the privileges and immunities that the Constitution affords to citizens? The second was on the merits of Scott's claim to his freedom. The Court had to address whether the Missouri Compromise was constitutional. If it was invalid and Congress's law prohibiting slavery north of the 36° 30′ parallel unconstitutional, then Upper Louisiana Territory had never been free territory. Scott's stay there would not have entitled him to his freedom even under earlier Missouri precedents.

It is the Court's answer to the first question for which it is most infamous. "Does the Constitution of the United States act upon [an enslaved person] whenever he shall be made free under the laws of a State, and raised there to the rank of a citizen, and immediately clothe him with all the privileges of a citizen in every other State, and in its own courts?" the Court asked. Chief Justice Roger Taney, writing for the majority, answered "no." Taney recognized that the answer to the question depended on whether free persons of African descent were citizens of the several states before the adoption of the Constitution, and thus whether they formed part of the political community that adopted the Constitution in 1787–1788. "[T]he personal rights and privileges guaranteed to citizens of this new sovereignty were intended to embrace those only who were then members of the several State communities, or who should afterwards by birthright or otherwise become members, according to the provisions of the Constitution and the principles on which it was founded."[5]

In answering this question, the majority of the Court looked to the history of the thirteen colonies at the time of Independence and whether the drafters of the Declaration of Independence intended to include persons of African descent in its famous dictum that all men are created equal. "[T]he legislation and histories of the times, and the language used in the Declaration of Independence," the majority concluded, "show that neither the class of persons who had been imported as slaves, nor their descendants, whether they had become free or not, were then acknowledged as a part of the people, nor intended to be included in the general words used in that memorable instrument."[6]

In reaching this conclusion also as to the meaning of the term "citizen" in the Constitution, the majority purported to apply what today would be labeled an originalist methodology. "It is difficult at this day to realize the state of public opinion in relation to that unfortunate race, which prevailed in the civilized and enlightened portions of the world at the time of the Declaration of Independence, and when the Constitution of the United States was framed and adopted."[7] The people of 1857 might be more enlightened, but the Founding generation was less so – or so the majority of the Court alleged. "No one, we presume, supposes that any change in public opinion or feeling, in relation to this unfortunate race, in the civilized nations of Europe or in this country," the Court later added, "should induce the court to give to the words of the Constitution a more liberal construction in their favor than they were intended to bear when the instrument was framed and adopted."[8] "Such an argument would be altogether inadmissible in any tribunal called on to interpret it," the Court explained, because "while it remains unaltered" by constitutional amendments, "it must be construed now as it was understood at the time of its adoption." As long as it remains unamended, the Constitution "speaks not only in the same words, but with the same meaning and intent with which it spoke when it came from the hands of its framers, and was voted on and adopted by the people of the United States."[9]

How then did the Founding generation consider free persons of African descent? The majority offered the following infamous observations:

> They [persons of the African race] had for more than a century before been regarded as beings of an inferior order, and altogether unfit to associate with the white race, either in social or political relations; and so far inferior, that they had no rights which the white man was bound to respect; and that the negro might justly and lawfully be reduced to slavery for his benefit. He was bought and sold, and treated as an ordinary article of merchandise and traffic, whenever a profit could be made by it. This opinion was at that time fixed and universal in the civilized portion of the white race. It was regarded as an axiom in morals as well as in politics, which no one thought of disputing or supposed to be open to dispute ...."[10]

The majority went on to illustrate the proposition with a variety of discriminatory laws throughout the colonies including anti-miscegenation laws prohibiting racial intermarriage. They then quoted the Declaration of Independence and observed that its general words "would seem to embrace the whole human family, and if they were used in a similar instrument at this day would be so understood." Taney and the majority again suggested that, although they may be more enlightened than the Founders, they had to adhere to the Founders' vision. "But it is too clear for dispute, that the enslaved African race were not intended to be included, and formed no part of the people who framed and adopted this declaration," the majority suggested, "for if the language, as understood in that day, would embrace them, the conduct of the distinguished men who framed the Declaration of Independence would have been utterly and flagrantly inconsistent with the principles they asserted." "[T]he men who framed this declaration," Taney asserted, "were great men ... incapable of asserting principles inconsistent with those on which they were acting."[11]

Chief Justice Taney and the majority then argued that the provisions of the Constitution proved that the status of persons of African descent had not changed by the time of the Constitution's adoption. The Court specifically pointed to the clause prohibiting Congress from abolishing the Atlantic Slave Trade before 1808,[12] and to the Fugitive Slave Clause,[13] which required free states to cooperate with slave states to return any escaped slaves. "[T]hese two provisions show conclusively that neither the description of persons therein referred to, nor their descendants, were embraced in any of the other provisions of the Constitution," the majority concluded, "for certainly these two clauses were not intended to confer on them or their posterity the blessings of liberty, or any of the personal rights so carefully provided for the citizen."[14] The majority then recited a few anti-marriage laws in Northern states enacted or persisting beyond 1787, as if one could not be a citizen because of discrimination in this one respect.[§]

That left one final secondary question. Could free persons of African descent be made citizens in some way, now that the Constitution was adopted? In an even more remarkably gerrymandered part of the opinion, the Court first held that states could not make such persons citizens because the Constitution granted Congress the naturalization power.[15] But neither could Congress make such free persons citizens because that power only applied to foreigners, not to descendants born here to persons brought as slaves.[16] The Court therefore had it every which way: Free persons of African descent were not citizens prior to the adoption of the Constitution; the states could not make them citizens; and Congress could not make them citizens, either.

The dissent by Justice Benjamin Curtis provided a satisfactory and unassailable[17] textual and historical response to the majority's arguments. Curtis pointed out that Article II's clause on presidential eligibility refers to "a Citizen of the United States, at the time of the Adoption of this Constitution." He agreed, then, that there could be citizens "of the United States" at the time of the Constitution's adoption by virtue of citizenship in one of the several states.[18] Curtis showed through citations to judicial decisions and state laws that at the time of the ratification of the Articles of Confederation, even well before the adoption of the Constitution, "all free native-born inhabitants" of five states, namely, New Hampshire, Massachusetts, New York, New Jersey, and North Carolina, "though descended from African slaves, were not only citizens of those States, but such of them as had the other necessary qualifications possessed the franchise of electors, on equal terms with other citizens."[19] He added that it was well known that there were non-white citizens in some of the states because Article IV of the Articles of Confederation had provided that the "free inhabitants" of each state shall enjoy a general citizenship in all the states, and a proposal to limit this clause to white persons had been rejected.[20]

[§] Indeed, Taney's arguments tend strongly to show why Loving v. Virginia, which in 1967 held that interracial marriage bans violated the equality guarantee of the Fourteenth Amendment, was correct. Anti-miscegenation laws had been the primary examples of the alleged inferiority of the African race.

The question then became whether anything in the Constitution stripped these free persons of their citizenship by mere virtue of their color. "Did the Constitution of the United States deprive them or their descendants of citizenship?" asked Curtis. He answered the obvious: "nothing in the Constitution," certainly nothing explicit, "deprives of their citizenship any class of persons who were citizens of the United States at the time of its adoption, or who should be native-born citizens of any State after its adoption."[21] Curtis then addressed whether Congress had power to deprive these individuals or their descendants of citizenship. He again pointed to the clause on presidential eligibility that refers also to "a natural-born citizen" and "thus assumes that citizenship may be acquired by birth."[22] He then observed that Congress's power "to establish a uniform rule of naturalization" is "a power to prescribe a rule for the removal of the disabilities consequent on foreign birth." Congress could make new citizens of foreigners, but it had no power to deprive of citizenship those who were born citizens.[23]

Curtis concluded and summarized: "[A]s free colored persons were then citizens of at least five States, and so in every sense part of the people of the United States, they were among those for whom and whose posterity the Constitution was ordained and established."[24]

14.2 THE CONSTITUTION AND SLAVERY

Justice Curtis's textual and historical analysis refuted Chief Justice Taney's majority opinion. It remains to address why Taney got the case so wrong and whether he was right about the Founders. "[T]his is not the place [to] vindicate their memory," Curtis had written of Taney's calumny. But his own opinion was that "a calm comparison of these assertions of universal abstract truths" in the Declaration of Independence, "and of their own individual opinions and acts, would not leave these men under any reproach of inconsistency." The "great truths they asserted on that solemn occasion, they were ready and anxious to make effectual," Curtis asserted, "wherever a necessary regard to circumstances, which no statesman can disregard without producing more evil than good, would allow." It "would not be just to them nor true in itself to allege that they intended to say that the Creator of all men had endowed the white race, exclusively, with the great natural rights which the Declaration of Independence asserts."[25]

In assessing whether Chief Justice Taney or Justice Curtis was right, it is important to separate the question of whether the Constitution itself condoned or sanctioned slavery, and whether the Founders themselves did. Beginning with the former question, the Constitution did have, as Taney had written, a clause that presumed there would be continued commerce in slaves, and further requiring states to cooperate in the returning of fugitive slaves. It had other notorious clauses, such as the Three-Fifth Clause.[26] Was then the Constitution proslavery as Chief Justice Taney and a modern segment of the American people today have alleged, but as Justice Curtis denied? Other scholars have done excellent work on this question, including most recently the historians Sean Wilentz and James Oakes.[27] Many of the following insights derive from their work and the work of others writing in a similar vein.

In assessing the Constitution's nature and effect, both what the Constitution replaced and what its principal alternative would have been must always be kept in view. The Constitution gave Congress extraordinary powers over slavery, powers that had not existed under the Articles of Confederation. It is true that the clause about the Atlantic Slave Trade prohibited abolishing the trade until 1808. But Congress did so immediately upon the arrival of that year.[28] And the Confederation Congress had had no power whatsoever over commerce, let alone the slave trade specifically. James Wilson, who the reader will recall had been at the Constitutional Convention and would later be a Supreme Court Justice, responded in the Pennsylvania ratifying convention to the argument Taney would make decades later:

> With respect to the clause restricting Congress from prohibiting the *migration or importation of such persons* as any of the states now existing shall think proper to admit, prior to the year 1808, the honorable gentleman says that this clause is not only dark, but intended to grant to Congress, for that time, the power to admit the importation of slaves. No such thing was intended.
>
> But I will tell you what was done, and it gives me high pleasure that so much was done. Under the present Confederation, the states may admit the importation of slaves as long as they please; but by this article, after the year 1808, the Congress will have power to prohibit such importation, notwithstanding the disposition of any state to the contrary. I consider this as laying the foundation for banishing slavery out of this country; and though the period is more distant than I could wish, yet it will produce the same kind, gradual change, which was pursued in Pennsylvania.[29]

Wilson also pointed out that the clause prohibited congressional interference prior to 1808 only in the original thirteen states.[30] Congress could thus prohibit the slave traffic in any newly admitted states, allowing it to effectuate the Northwest Ordinance of 1787, which forbade slavery and involuntary servitude in the Northwest Territory and any future states fashioned from it.[31]

Most of the Convention delegates did not intend for the clause to expand slavery, or condone it, but rather to empower Congress eventually to abolish it.[32] James Madison, in *Federalist* No. 42, emphasized a similar point and hinted at his own views on slavery. "It were doubtless to be wished that the power of prohibiting the importation of slaves had not been postponed until the year 1808," he wrote, but it "ought to be considered as a great point gained in favor of humanity that a period of twenty years may terminate forever, within these States, a traffic which has so long and so loudly upbraided the barbarism of modern policy." He described the slave trade as an "unnatural traffic," and concluded "[h]appy would it be for the unfortunate Africans if an equal prospect lay before them of being redeemed from the oppressions of their European brethren!"[33] So much for Roger Taney's backward interpretation of the clause.[34]

The Constitution also empowered Congress to prohibit slavery in the territories. Although the Confederation Congress enacted the famous prohibition on slavery in the Northwest Ordinance, readopted by the new Congress in 1789, it was not obvious that the Confederation had the power to so regulate the territories and otherwise prepare new states for admission.[35] The Northwest Ordinance may have inspired the Constitutional Convention in 1787 to include in Article IV of the present Constitution provisions respecting the admission of new states and regulating federal territory and property.[36] Exercising the latter power, Congress had prohibited slavery in many territories, most famously all territory north of the 36° 30′ parallel in the Missouri Compromise. Without this power to prohibit slavery in the territories, slavery could have existed anywhere in the territories where individual slave owners brought their slaves. The Constitution once again empowered Congress to act against slavery.

The Constitution thus empowered Congress to stop slavery from expanding from across the seas and to stop it from expanding westward within the continental United States. Equally importantly, Congress had no power to interfere with abolition within the states. About half the states abolished slavery or set a timetable for abolition between 1776 and 1789,[37] and Congress could not reestablish the institution in those states. In states as far south as Virginia, legislatures repealed laws against the private manumission of slaves.[38] To be sure, the Founders had not foreseen the invention of the cotton gin, which made slavery more profitable and prevented a more immediate extirpation of the institution. But even so, as Oakes has written, these mechanisms allowed Congress by the mid nineteenth century to create a policy by which freedom would be national and slavery only a local institution. "Freedom national, slavery local" was a rallying cry of the Republican Party; the idea was to create a "cordon of freedom" surrounding the remaining slave states and to make slavery unprofitable.[39]

Whether a cordon of freedom would have effected slavery's ultimate extinction in the absence of civil war and constitutional amendment is difficult to know with certainty. But scholars have not sufficiently appreciated that Congress did have one more tool in its arsenal, a tool that would have been unthinkable at the time but that could have been later used to deal slavery a fatal blow. Congress could have used its power over interstate commerce to prohibit the interstate sale of all goods made with enslaved labor. Although the Supreme Court struck down a law prohibiting the interstate sale of all goods made with child labor in the 1918,[40] that decision was soon overturned[41] and was probably wrong when it was decided. Chapter 16, on Congress's power under the Commerce Clause, explores that decision. It is sufficient at present to know that the Constitution empowered Congress to create the conditions for the eventual total abolition of slavery.

There remain, of course, the clauses respecting apportionment and fugitive slaves. These are the more odious of the provisions relating to slavery. They mar what otherwise should be considered a tremendous achievement. Two observations about these clauses are, however, warranted. The Three-Fifth Clause was undeniably odious, but not for the reason most think. The clause did not suggest that enslaved persons were somehow subhuman, or worth only three-fifths of white persons.[42] On the contrary. The clause increased the South's representation in the House of Representatives and the Electoral College; every five enslaved persons would be treated as if three free persons entitled to representation. The South's slaves increased the South's political power in Congress, all while the South denied slaves the right to vote and most other rights. From the South's perspective, a five-fifths clause would have been preferable. If enslaved persons counted as whole persons for purposes of representation, the South's political power would have further increased. That is likely why Chief Justice Taney did not even mention the Three-Fifth Clause in his *Dred Scott* opinion.[43]

The Three-Fifths Clause was odious not because it deemed slaves to be only partly human, which it did not do, but rather because it increased the political power of the South. The three-fifths bump in the Electoral College at least partly explains why four of the first six American presidents were from Virginia. To take the most famous example, John Adams would have won the election of 1800 if only free persons counted for representation in the electoral college.[44] The slavery bonus thereby also partly explains why many Southerners were appointed to the Supreme Court – including the majority that decided the *Dred Scott* case.[45] Despite its odiousness, however, the clause eventually became irrelevant because population growth in the North exploded with the industrial revolution while stagnating in the backward, slave-owning South.[46]

As for the Fugitive Slave Clause, it is hard to discern any redeeming value. But one must be wary of what the historian E. P. Thompson once described as the "enormous condescension of posterity."[47] In seeking to understand the past, modern analysts must try to perceive things as those then living did without the moral condescension of modern sensibilities. Without the guarantee that fugitive slaves would be returned, the South might not have agreed to the Constitution and there never would have been a Union.[48] And if there were no Union, and instead there were an independent, slaveholding confederacy in the southern portions of the continent, it is unclear how slavery would have ended. Separate confederacies would have also had other unthinkable consequences as the two vied for territory in the West. European powers would have taken advantage of the inevitable conflict.

So the Constitution did include a clause about fugitive slaves. But even here, the Framers studiously avoided any mention of slavery; the clause refers to persons "held to service or labour." As Madison wrote in his notes on the Constitutional Convention, and as Wilentz writes today, they likely chose their language to affirm their belief that there could be "no property in man."[49] And the final version was revised from "No person legally held to service or labour in one state" to "No person held to service or labour in one state, under the laws thereof." This change affirmed that slavery was a purely local institution.[50] They likely included the clause out of necessity, as the alternative would have been, from their perspective and to the best of their knowledge, worse. But even then the language they chose evinced their hope that slavery would someday pass away.

14.3 THE FOUNDERS AND SLAVERY

The relationship of the Constitution to slavery is therefore complicated. The matter is too nuanced to describe the Constitution as merely or entirely proslavery or antislavery.[51] The Constitution was a tremendous improvement over what had come before and its general tenor was "freedom national, slavery local." But the Founders had not anticipated the cotton gin or the practical effect of the three-fifths bump, which made the ultimate destruction of slavery more difficult to achieve. Still, on balance, Chief Justice Taney's assessment of the Constitution as a proslavery document should strike reasonable observers as being incorrect. It remains to be seen whether he was right about the Founders themselves, and, if he was wrong, how he could have gotten their views so wrong from his perch six decades later.

Taney claimed that the Founders all believed, along with the universal opinion of mankind, that persons of African descent were inferior beings and had no rights that the white man was bound to respect. One cannot deny that 250 years ago Americans had different views than their posterity about race. But one must again avoid posterity's enormous condescension. The question is rather whether the Framers believed in slavery and more specifically whether they believed Taney's claim that slavery was a "benefit" to the enslaved.

It has been noted that the Constitution itself for the most part did not condone slavery but rather empowered Congress to take actions to curb it; that is also largely consistent with what important Founders said.[52] George Washington wrote that "there is not a man living who wishes more sincerely than I do, to see a plan adopted for the abolition of [slavery] – but there is only one proper and effectual mode by which it can be accomplished, & that is by Legislative authority . . . ."[53] John Adams "held the practice of slavery in . . . abhorrence," and thought "every measure of prudence therefore ought to be assumed for the eventual total extirpation of Slavery from the US."[54] Benjamin Franklin thought slavery was "an atrocious debasement of human nature."[55] Alexander Hamilton wrote that because slaves were men, "by the laws of God and nature, they were capable of acquiring liberty."[56]

James Madison said in the Constitutional Convention, "We have seen the mere distinction of colour made in the most enlightened period of time, a ground of the most oppressive dominion ever exercised by man over man."[57] And Gouverneur Morris, who arranged and drafted the final language of the Constitution, called slavery a "nefarious institution": "It was the curse of heaven on the States where it prevailed."[58] Then there was Thomas Jefferson, principal author of the Declaration of Independence, who wrote the following in his Notes on the State of Virginia:

The whole commerce between master and slave is ... the most unremitting despotism. ... Can the liberties of a nation be thought secure when we have removed their only firm basis, a conviction in the minds of the people that these liberties are of the gift of God? That they are not to be violated but with his wrath? Indeed I tremble for my country when I reflect that God is just: that his justice cannot sleep for ever .... I think a change already perceptible, since the origin of the present revolution. The spirit of the master is abating, that of the slave rising from the dust, his condition mollifying, the way I hope preparing, under the auspices of heaven, for a total emancipation ....[59]

No one can charge Thomas Jefferson with sainthood. He may have fathered several children with his slave Sally Hemmings and is remembered as a great democratic figure despite having sat atop a plantation of slaves who funded his aristocratic lifestyle. But he did author the famous Declaration, the first foundational national document to assert that all men are created equal. He asserted that slavery was inconsistent with that principle in a draft of the Declaration, which passage alleged that the King "has waged cruel war against human nature itself" by "captivating and carrying ... into slavery" a distant people.[60] And he subsequently asserted that same inconsistency in the Notes on the State of Virginia. Jefferson was a hypocrite; that was better than what Taney would allege, that the Founders were incapable of hypocrisy and therefore must have been supporters of slavery. Hypocrisy is the tribute that vice pays to virtue.[61] It implies the existence of some principle, a principle that the Founding generation established for the first time and for the benefit of all posterity.[62]

One need not believe the Founders' own statements, of which there are many more.[63] On the eve of the Civil War, the Southerners themselves recognized that they had diverged from the Founders' principles.[64] A U.S. Senator from Virginia reportedly said the following on the floor of the Senate in 1860:

[W]e in Virginia have changed our ground; we do not stand where we stood anciently; we do not stand where our fathers stood upon this slavery question.... [W]e do not believe in what Washington believed and Jefferson believed and Madison believed and Monroe believed, and all the leading men of Virginia, for the first fifty years of our existence under the Constitution, believed; we have changed our opinions in Virginia, and instead of now admitting that slavery is an evil, to be restricted and discouraged, and which we may hope and pray may be someday entirely removed from the Republic, we now take the ground that it is a blessing, to be fostered, encouraged, and extended, as a benefit to the black man and a benefit to the white.[65]

Alexander Stephens, Vice President of the Confederacy of the newly seceded states, flatly and similarly conceded in his famous "cornerstone" speech that "[t]he prevailing ideas entertained by [Thomas Jefferson] and most of the leading statesmen at the time of the formation of the old constitution, were that the enslavement of the African was in violation of the laws of nature; that it was wrong in principle, socially, morally, and politically." To the Founders, slavery "was an evil they knew not well how to deal with, but the general opinion of the men of that day was that, somehow or other in the order of Providence, the institution would be evanescent and pass away." In contrast, the Confederacy's "foundations are laid, its corner-stone rests, upon the great truth that the negro is not equal to the white man; that slavery – subordination to the superior race – is his natural and normal condition."[66]

It is unquestionable that on the eve of the Civil War, the nigh universal opinion in the South was that slavery was a benefit to both the owner and the enslaved. That is the language Taney had used. It was not the language of the Founders. It was the language of the interbellum South, especially the deep South, whose leading writers like George Fitzhugh and John C. Calhoun developed the "positive good" theory of slavery between the 1820s and 1850s.[67]

When Taney and the *Dred Scott* majority argued that although their generation was more enlightened, they had to follow the views of the Founders, that was exactly backward. Taney and his brethren were adopting the prejudices and beliefs of their time and place and projecting them backward on the Founders to justify their decision. It is not unworthy of observation that Taney himself had manumitted his own slaves almost forty years earlier. Perhaps his own views had evolved along with those of the society in which he lived.[68]

The Taney Court's accusations against the Founders were both calumny and irony. They emphasize for modern Americans the risk of modern-day jurists similarly adopting their own prejudices and projecting them on the Founders. That is not a mark against originalism, which this author has defended in another work.[69] But the risk underscores the possibility that the Supreme Court will err and raises the question of what role the Supreme Court ought to play in a constitutional system of separated powers.

14.4 THE MISSOURI COMPROMISE

Before we turn to that issue in Chapter 15, to the role of the courts as originally understood and to Abraham Lincoln's response to the *Dred Scott* decision, a brief examination of *Dred Scott's* second holding is warranted. The majority declared the Missouri Compromise unconstitutional. Here, again, the Court gravely erred.

The issue was whether Congress could constitutionally prohibit slavery in the Upper Louisiana Territory, such that Scott had a plausible claim to freedom. The Court held that Congress could not prohibit slavery in any territories despite the clause empowering Congress "to dispose of and make all needful Rules and Regulations respecting the Territory or other Property belonging to the United States."[70] The majority held that the clause was limited to the territories *then existing* when the Constitution was adopted. In this instance, its interpretation, although hardly inevitable, was not implausible. The Territories Clause included a proviso that "nothing in this Constitution shall be so construed as to Prejudice any Claims of the United States, or of any particular State," suggesting that the clause may have been concerned only with existing territory.[71] And when the Constitution empowered Congress to make all laws for the District of Columbia, it empowered it to "exercise exclusive legislation" over the district. The power to make needful rules and regulations could be interpreted as a narrower power over a specific object, namely, rules and regulations for disposing of the public land by sale.[72]

Even Taney, however, recognized that a power to regulate subsequently acquired territories must exist somewhere. He accepted that "[t]he right to govern may be the inevitable consequence of the right to acquire territory."[73] Curtis had argued that the right to make laws for the government of the territories would be necessary and proper to prepare them for statehood; and Congress has explicit power to admit new states.[74] Taney appeared to agree: "[I]t is undoubtedly necessary that some Government should be established, in order to organize society, and to protect the inhabitants in their persons and property," he conceded, until the territory could be admitted as a state; "[t]he power to acquire necessarily carries with it the power to preserve and apply to the purposes for which it was acquired."[75]

But why could Congress not then prohibit slavery in the territory? Because, Taney argued, Congress was limited by the Constitution in the kind of discretion it could exercise over the territories. He cited various provisions of the first eight amendments. "[N]o one, we presume, will contend that Congress can make any law in a Territory respecting the establishment of religion, or the free exercise thereof, or abridging the freedom of speech or of the press," he wrote, "or the right of the people of the Territory peaceably to assemble, and to petition the Government for the redress of grievances."[76] It is hard to disagree with this strawman.[77] Taney then got to the nub of it:

> [T]he rights of property are united with the rights of person, and placed on the same ground by the fifth amendment to the Constitution, which provides that no person shall be deprived of life, liberty, and property, without due process of law. And an act of Congress which deprives a citizen of the United States of his liberty or property merely, because he came himself or brought his property into a particular Territory of the United States, and who had committed no offence against the laws, could hardly be dignified with the name of due process of law.[78]

That was the sum of it. The only reason Taney could cite for disabling Congress from prohibiting slavery in the territories was that it would violate "due process." The clause as written, however, does allow Congress to deprive someone of property so long as there is "due process of law." Historically, due process required established law and known procedures for adjudicating violations of the law.[79] Yet, Taney held that due process might have a "substantive" component; it might prevent Congress from depriving someone of a certain kind of property altogether. Taney, in a single sentence, invented the concept of "substantive due process," which allows courts to decide that some unwritten rights are so fundamental that no government can take them away, and further held there was a fundamental right to property in other human beings.

Both of the Court's holdings – that free persons of African descent could not be citizens of the United States, and that the Due Process Clause of the Fifth Amendment disabled Congress from prohibiting slavery in the territories despite Congress's having exercised such a power for the first seventy years of the Republic – were grievous errors as a matter of basic constitutional interpretation. And it is to both of those holdings that Abraham Lincoln had to respond in his famous debates with Stephen Douglas. It is to those debates, and what they teach about the role of the courts in a constitutional democracy, to which this study turns next.

15

Departmentalism

It is the nature of judicial power for judges to interpret and apply the law to cases properly before their courts. If two laws conflict, the judge must decide which one controls; in the case of a written constitution, that constitution prevails. That is the straightforward case for judicial review. Whether it follows that the Supreme Court is the final arbiter of the Constitution's meaning is the question now to be examined. Abraham Lincoln opposed the *Dred Scott* decision; he had to supply an answer. In his famous debates with Stephen Douglas, Lincoln offered an understanding of judicial power that diverges from the modern conception. That understanding was consistent with how judicial review operated at the Founding.

15.1 LINCOLN VERSUS DOUGLAS

In 1857, Abraham Lincoln ran for Senate in Illinois. He had been a one-term Congressman a decade earlier. The Kansas-Nebraska Act of 1854 spurred him back into the political arena; the Act allowed for slavery to expand north of the Missouri Compromise line, violating what antislavery and other Americans had viewed for three decades as a sacrosanct compact necessary to preserve the Union. At least the Kansas-Nebraska Act had had the pretended decency to allow the people of the respective territories to decide for themselves whether there shall be slavery or not, and the Act was limited in its geographic scope. The *Dred Scott* decision, however, invalidated the entire compromise, all the while holding that Americans of African descent could never be citizens. The *Dred Scott* decision annihilated the central tenet of the new Republican Party, that a cordon of freedom could surround the slave states and suffocate the institution into extinction.

Lincoln opposed the decision and sought to have it overturned. This led his rival, Stephen Douglas, to accuse Lincoln of seeking the rule of the mob and to defy judicial decisions. Douglas made an argument with strikingly modern overtones:

> I have never yet learned how or where an appeal could be taken from the Supreme Court of the United States! The Dred Scott decision was pronounced by the

highest tribunal on earth. From that decision there is no appeal, this side of Heaven. Yet, Mr. Lincoln says he is going to reverse that decision. By what tribunal will he reverse it? Will he appeal to a mob? Does he intend to appeal to violence, to Lynch law? Will he stir up strife and rebellion in the land and overthrow the court by violence? ... I will not be drawn off into an argument upon the merits of the Dred Scott decision. It is enough for me to know that the Constitution of the United States created the Supreme Court for the purpose of deciding all disputed questions touching the true construction of that instrument, and when such decisions are pronounced, they are the law of the land, binding on every good citizen.[1]

Douglas sounded like the modern Supreme Court often does. His sentiment is similar to that which many Americans share in the present day. Was not Douglas correct? Was it not the case that the Supreme Court was created "for the purpose of deciding," finally and ultimately, "all disputed questions" about the Constitution? Was it not correct that its decisions "are the law of the land, binding on every good citizen"?

Lincoln argued not. He never stated that he or anyone else could ignore the judgment in the *Dred Scott* case. It did not follow that the reasoning or principles of that decision had to be treated as binding. The Supreme Court's decisions were binding on the parties to the case; but its decisions were not the supreme law of the land. Lincoln explained the purposes of judicial decisions as follows: "Judicial decisions have two uses – first, to absolutely determine the case decided, and secondly, to indicate to the public how other similar cases will be decided when they arise. For the latter use, they are called 'precedents' and 'authorities.'"[2] Lincoln stated that he had as much obedience to and respect for the judiciary as did Douglas. He emphasized that he was not suggesting that anyone undermine the specific resolution of the case the Supreme Court decided: "[Douglas] denounces all who question the correctness of that decision, as offering violent resistance to it. But who resists it? Who has, in spite of the decision, declared Dred Scott free, and resisted the authority of his master over him?"[3]

Following the principle of the Supreme Court's decision was another matter. That would require treating the Court's decisions as part of the law of the land. The Constitution is the supreme law; the Court's decisions are not the Constitution. Courts have often reversed themselves and overturned prior decisions. Lincoln said: "[W]e think the Dred Scott decision is erroneous. We know the court that made it, has often over-ruled its own decisions, and we shall do what we can to have it to over-rule this. We offer no *resistance* to it."[4] The decision bound Dred Scott and his master, but the Court's reasoning ought not to be followed as a "political rule."[5] At least when courts make rulings on a particular issue for the first time, their decisions do not have to be treated as immediately settling the matter. Other cases can be brought to test the limits of the prior holdings or have them reconsidered.

Lincoln's understanding of judicial review and judicial power tracked the account of Alexis de Tocqueville in his famous antebellum study of democracy in

America. Tocqueville argued that judicial review conferred tremendous power on courts in America; but he also observed that the nature of the judicial role limited the extent of that power. Tocqueville appreciated that courts refuse to enforce laws inconsistent with the Constitution. "In the United States, the Constitution dominates legislators as it does plain citizens. It is therefore the first of laws, and it cannot be modified by a law. It is therefore just that the courts obey the Constitution in preference to all laws."[6] It did not follow that courts could opine at will about the constitutionality of laws. "The first characteristic of judicial power among all peoples is to serve as an arbiter. In order that action on the part of the courts take place, there must be a dispute. In order that there be a judge, there must be a case," Tocqueville wrote. "As long as a law does not give rise to a dispute, therefore, the judicial power has no occasion to occupy itself with it." It is "necessary" for a judge "to judge the law in order to come to judge the case," but if "he pronounces on a law without starting from a case, he goes outside his sphere completely and enters that of the legislative power."[7]

Tocqueville then explained what happens when a court refuses to enforce a law because of its unconstitutionality:

> When one invokes a law before the courts of the United States that the judge deems contrary to the Constitution, he can therefore refuse to apply it. This power is the only one that is particular to the American magistrate, but a great political influence flows from it.
>
> There are in fact very few laws of a nature to escape judicial analysis for long, for there are very few that do not hurt an individual interest and that litigants cannot or will not invoke before the courts.
>
> Now, on the day when the judge refuses to apply a law in a case, at that instant it loses a part of its moral force. Those whom it has wronged are then notified that a means exists of escaping the obligation of obeying it: cases multiply, and it falls into impotence. One of two things then happens: the people change their constitution or the legislature rescinds its law.
>
> Americans have therefore entrusted an immense political power to their courts; but in obliging them to attack the laws only by judicial means, they have much diminished the dangers of this power.[8]

Tocqueville offered a window into the antebellum concept of judicial review. Judges do not invalidate laws; they do not strike them down. They refuse to give them effect in particular cases if they are unconstitutional and instead give effect to the Constitution. But those laws are still on the statute books. The Supreme Court does not send a law clerk over to the U.S. Government Publishing Office to delete provisions of the United States Code. Those provisions remain there, waiting to be enforced; and they can be enforced in other cases, although the Supreme Court is likely to refuse to give them effect if it has already pronounced such provisions unconstitutional. But the issue is not necessarily settled until either Congress repeals the law or the people amend the Constitution; or, perhaps, until Congress appoints new judges who might overrule the Court's prior precedents.

15.2 DEPARTMENTALISM

Lincoln's view accorded with a proper understanding of judicial power. It may be added in support of Lincoln's position that Congress and the President might also engage in acts that courts will never review. When exercising their own functions, they need not consider themselves bound by the principles of Supreme Court decisions. For example, many public privileges in the 1850s depended upon the recipient's being a citizen. One could only get a coasting license to engage in trade and fishing along the United States coast, for example, if one was a "citizen of the United States."[9] The President could issue passports, but also only to "citizens of the United States."[10] Lincoln issued both licenses and passports to free persons of color, whom he considered to be citizens notwithstanding the Supreme Court's contrary pronouncement.[11] Such cases would never come before the courts because no one would be harmed by them; there was nothing the Supreme Court could do to reverse Lincoln's decisions.

Another example of this phenomenon is the appointment of Hiram Revels as the first African-American United States Senator.[12] Revels was appointed by the reconstructed Mississippi legislature in 1870. The problem was that the Constitution provides that no person may be a Senator who has not been a citizen of the United States for at least nine years.[13] *Dred Scott* had held that free persons of African descent were not citizens of the United States, and it was not until 1868 that the Fourteenth Amendment reversed that decision and specifically declared in the Citizenship Clause that all persons born or naturalized in the United States are citizens of the United States.[14] If *Dred Scott* had been the "supreme law of the land" until the Fourteenth Amendment was adopted, then Hiram Revels had only been a citizen of the United States for two years and therefore ineligible to be a U.S. Senator. The Senators debated the issue, including the validity or invalidity of the *Dred Scott* decision, and decided to seat Revels.[15] In exercising their own functions under the Constitution to "Judge of the Elections, Returns and Qualifications of its own Members,"[16] the Senate was not bound by the Supreme Court's erroneous interpretations of the Constitution.[17]

This understanding of the three departments' roles in interpreting the Constitution has been termed "departmentalism." The Supreme Court must interpret the Constitution when exercising its own function, the deciding of existing cases and controversies under existing law; it does not have a roving commission to examine and assess the constitutionality of government action. There must be a genuine private dispute involving a private injury to invoke the judicial power, a limitation enforced by the modern doctrine of standing.[18] The dispute must be amenable to resolution by the judiciary: There must be preexisting legal standards to apply, a limitation enforced by the modern political question doctrine.[19] And a court must typically limit any relief to the parties to the case, suggesting the impropriety of issuing what in modern times have been called universal or nationwide injunctions.[20]

The other departments must also then interpret the Constitution for their own purposes when exercising their own functions. President Lincoln could issue licenses and passports in the exercise of his functions, and the Senate could seat Revels in the exercise of its functions. And, as noted in prior chapters, the states and the people themselves, when exercising their own functions, can also interpret the Constitution – as perhaps the jury did in Gideon Henfield's case.[21]

Another example of departmentalism occurs when the courts uphold legislation as constitutional. Future Congresses or Presidents might still disagree and continue to insist that the law in question is unconstitutional. The courts' upholding the law would not prevent Congress from repealing the act, or the President from vetoing a similar act or exercising other acknowledged constitutional powers. Thomas Jefferson, for example, pardoned at least two individuals who had been convicted under the Sedition Act.[22] In a letter to Abigail Adams, he defended his approach. "You seem to think it devolved on the judges to decide on the validity of the sedition law. But nothing in the Constitution has given them a right to decide for the Executive, more than to the Executive to decide for them," he wrote. "Both magistracies are equally independent in the sphere of action assigned to them. The judges, believing the law constitutional, had a right to pass a sentence of fine and imprisonment; because that power was placed in their hands by the Constitution. But," he continued, "the Executive, believing the law to be unconstitutional, was bound to remit the execution of it; because that power has been confided to him by the Constitution."[23]

Andrew Jackson vetoed the rechartering of the Second Bank of the United States even though the Supreme Court had upheld its constitutionality in *McCulloch v. Maryland*. "It is maintained by the advocates of the bank that its constitutionality in all its features ought to be considered as settled by precedent and by the decision of the Supreme Court," Jackson stated in his veto message. "To this conclusion I can not assent. Mere precedent is a dangerous source of authority, and should not be regarded as deciding questions of constitutional power except where the acquiescence of the people and the States can be considered as well settled."[24] The Supreme Court's opinion "ought not to control the coordinate authorities of this Government," but rather "Congress, the Executive, and the Court must each for itself be guided by its own opinion of the Constitution" because "[e]ach public officer who takes an oath to support the Constitution swears that he will support it as he understands it, and not as it is understood by others." Thus, Jackson argued, "It is as much the duty of the House of Representatives, of the Senate, and of the President to decide upon the constitutionality of any bill or resolution which may be presented to them for passage or approval as it is of the supreme judges when it may be brought before them for judicial decision." He concluded: "The opinion of the judges has no more authority over Congress than the opinion of Congress has over the judges, and on that point the President is independent of both."[25]

15.3 LIQUIDATION AND POLITICAL SETTLEMENT

A more difficult question arises when the President continues to enforce a law previously declared to be unconstitutional, or when Congress enacts a law that would be squarely unconstitutional under a prior ruling of the Supreme Court. Those cases are bound to arrive at the Supreme Court again, and it may seem odd or inefficient to bring such cases repeatedly. Congress in 1862 abolished slavery in all the territories in violation of the holding of the *Dred Scott* decision.[26] Had the Civil War not been ongoing, enslaved persons may have continued to press for their freedom and the Supreme Court would have continued to hold as it did in *Dred Scott*.

Good faith may require that at some point the political branches treat a constitutional question as having been fully settled. Jackson suggested as much in his bank veto message: The Court's decisions "should not be regarded as deciding questions of constitutional power except where the acquiescence of the people and the States can be considered as well settled."[27] Lincoln, too, recognized that there comes a point at which good faith might require that a constitutional question be treated as "settled" by all the departments of the government and by the people. "We think," Lincoln argued, that the Court's "decisions on Constitutional questions, when fully settled, should control, not only the particular cases decided, but the general policy of the country, subject to be disturbed only by amendments of the Constitution as provided in that instrument itself."[28]

When has a constitutional decision been settled is the difficult question. Lincoln gave some guidance, again referring to the *Dred Scott* decision:

> If this important decision had been made by the unanimous concurrence of the judges, and without any apparent partisan bias, and in accordance with legal public expectation, and with the steady practice of the departments throughout our history, and had been in no part, based on assumed historical facts which are not really true; or, if wanting in some of these, it had been before the court more than once, and had there been affirmed and re-affirmed through a course of years, it then might be, perhaps would be, factious, nay, even revolutionary, to not acquiesce in it as a precedent.
>
> But when, as it is true we find it wanting in all these claims to the public confidence, it is not resistance, it is not factious, it is not even disrespectful, to treat it as not having yet quite established a settled doctrine for the country.[29]

Lincoln recognized that the Supreme Court's decisions must be respected at a certain point, lest the courts as an institution not have the necessary legitimacy to serve their proper functions in a constitutional scheme of separate powers. Continuous disobedience to the courts undermines the rule of law. Continually refusing to accept the Court's decision may also be inefficient; even if prior decisions technically bind only the particular parties, the lower courts follow the Supreme Court's decisions in similar cases.

A single decision of a single court, however, does not settle constitutional matters on which reasonable people might disagree. When Congress subsequently abolished slavery in all the territories, it is at least possible that the Supreme Court would have reconsidered its prior decision. Or the people will have disagreed with the Supreme Court and will have elected to national offices opponents of the Court's decision, as Lincoln was seeking to accomplish. Those opponents would then, over time, appoint judges more sympathetic to their own views, views which a newly constituted Supreme Court might vindicate in the future. Variations on this sequence of events occurred prior to the Supreme Court's overruling decisions like *Plessy v. Ferguson* and *Roe v. Wade*. In the meantime, departmentalism presumes that each department of government must interpret the Constitution for its own purposes and might disagree about what the Constitution means or requires. Over time, such disagreements might get resolved, but the Supreme Court does not get to resolve them with a single controversial decision. The other branches of the federal government have a say in this constitutional conversation.

So too do the states and the people themselves. James Madison anticipated as much in *Federalist* No. 46, as noted in Chapter 2: "[S]hould an unwarrantable measure of the federal government be unpopular in particular States," Madison argued, "[t]he disquietude of the people; their repugnance and, perhaps, refusal to co-operate with the officers of the Union; the frowns of the executive magistracy of the State; the embarrassments created by legislative devices," all would combine to form "very serious impediments" to the federal program. Any "ambitious encroachments of the federal government," moreover, "would be signals of general alarm": "Every government would espouse the common cause. A correspondence would be opened. Plans of resistance would be concerted. One spirit would animate and conduct the whole."[30]

This kind of process played out in the context of the Alien and Sedition Acts. Congress, the President, and the federal courts – including several Supreme Court Justices sitting as circuit judges – approved or upheld the Sedition Act. It did not violate the First Amendment because the freedom of press at common law was merely freedom from prior restraints. The government could not prohibit the publication of speech, but certain kinds of speech would nevertheless be subject to consequences once published. Various actors at the state level, however, pushed for another interpretation. Madison explained in his Report of 1800, which defended the earlier Virginia Resolutions of 1798, that the freedom of speech in the American context required much more than a mere a prohibition on prior restraints. Unlike the British system, where Parliament was the key protector of the people's rights, in America the Constitution was the protector of rights and directly bound the legislative power. Unlike Parliament, it was not Congress's role to decide what speech to punish. And in a more thoroughly electoral and republican system, the free flow of political opinions and sentiments was essential.[31]

Both the "Federalist" view and the "Republican" view of the First Amendment were therefore within the range of plausible original meanings. The Federalist view won temporarily in Congress, the executive department, and the lower federal courts. But the question was not yet fully settled. Madison and Jefferson sounded the general alarm and opened up committees of correspondence in Kentucky and Virginia to communicate their concerns to the other states. Their Resolutions contained a number of constitutional arguments against the Acts. When Jefferson became President soon thereafter, he exercised his constitutional powers to put into effect his understanding of the Constitution. Jefferson's party then controlled Congress and the White House for the next twenty-four years. It was not until 1964 that the Supreme Court of the United States weighed in, declaring that the Sedition Act had been overturned "in the court of history."[32]

This method of "settling" constitutional questions operated in the debates over the constitutionality of the Bank of the United States, discussed in Chapter 4. The Supreme Court's pronouncements in *McCulloch v. Maryland* came almost three decades after the bank issue had been debated in Congress and within the executive branch in 1791. When Madison became President years later and was confronted with legislation creating the Second Bank of the United States, he put aside his previous constitutional qualms. The issue, he argued, had become settled. His constitutional objections, he wrote, were "precluded in my judgment by repeated recognition under varied circumstances of the validity of such an institution in acts of the legislative, executive, and judicial branches of the Government, accompanied by indications, in different modes, of a concurrence of the general will of the nation."[33] Madison described the process by which constitutional questions become settled as a kind of "liquidation," that is, the meaning of the relevant provisions would become ascertained, determined, and fixed.[34]

This approach still raises the question of when exactly an issue becomes settled. Andrew Jackson vetoed the rechartering of the Second Bank in 1832, having at his disposal all the prior debates in Congress and within the executive branch, as well as the Supreme Court's pronouncements in *McCulloch v. Maryland*. Yet, Jackson said, even at that late date, it was still up to him to interpret the Constitution for the purposes of the executive department.[35] To be sure, Jackson was not exactly repudiating the Supreme Court's holding in *McCulloch*; he went on to say that a national bank was no longer "convenient" or "useful" or "necessary and proper," and therefore it was unconstitutional on the facts as he understood them.[36] Nor did Jackson disagree with the proposition that at some point open constitutional questions can become "settled"; he merely argued that the debate over the bank was not as fully settled as its proponents claimed. Lincoln appealed to Jackson's rejection of longstanding precedent, a rejection that at the time was supported by Stephen Douglas and his fellow Democrats, to advance his own argument about the viability of reversing the *Dred Scott* decision.[37]

Still, Jackson's veto perhaps ironically leaves unsettled the point at which a constitutional question becomes settled. Although the combined approach of departmentalism and liquidation may not be a perfect system, that system appears superior to alternatives. It is inconceivable that a single divided decision of the Supreme Court of the United States can determine constitutional law for decades to come no matter how erroneous the decision. Congress, the President, the states, and the people themselves must have a say along with the courts. The decisions of the courts bind the parties to the cases decided, but Congress and the President can disagree and act accordingly using their own constitutional powers. The states and the people themselves can make their sentiments known, too, as they arguably did in the elections of 1800 and 1860. Over time, new representatives and presidents come to power and appoint new judges whose views are more consonant with the constitutional understandings of these other constitutional actors. The Supreme Court might then also overturn its own prior precedents.[38] That system may not be perfect, but it has many virtues. Not the least of which is that it is the system the Founders established.

15.4 JUDICIAL SUPREMACY

Despite the virtues of departmentalism and the traditional understanding of judicial review, most Americans have become accustomed to thinking of the Court as the final arbiter of constitutional meaning. That is so even though for much of its history it has been wrong on important issues – from *Dred Scott* to *Plessy v. Ferguson*,[39] upholding "separate but equal," to *Korematsu v. United States*,[40] upholding the internment of Japanese-American citizens during World War II. In the mid twentieth century, with the incorporation of the Bill of Rights against the states, liberals began to view the Court as the savior and guardian of rights and as the ultimate arbiter of the Constitution's meaning.

The Court fueled this sentiment with its own pronouncements. In *Cooper v. Aaron* (1958),[41] the Court confronted state-level intransigence and resistance to the Court's prior desegregation holding in *Brown v. Board of Education* (1954).[42] A day before the African-American students were to attend Central High School in Little Rock, Arkansas, "the school authorities were met with drastic opposing action on the part of the Governor of Arkansas, who dispatched units of the Arkansas National Guard to the Central High School grounds and placed the school 'off limits' to colored students."[43] Eventually an injunction had been obtained against the Governor, Orval Faubus, and President Eisenhower dispatched federal troops to control the crowds and implement the desegregation order. Throughout the year, there was nevertheless "chaos, bedlam and turmoil" at the school, including acts of violence, such that a federal district court subsequently granted the school board's request to resegregate the high schools for the safety of the students and to re-enable the basic educational functions of Central High.[44]

The Supreme Court, quite rightly, invalidated the district court's order. But it went on to "answer the premise of the actions of the Governor and Legislature that they are not bound by our holding in the *Brown* case." In so answering, the Court claimed that it was "necessary only to recall some basic constitutional propositions which are settled doctrine."[45] The Court then quoted *Marbury* for its famous proposition that "[i]t is emphatically the province and duty of the judicial department to say what the law is." The Court then stated: "This decision declared the basic principle that the federal judiciary is supreme in the exposition of the law of the Constitution, and that principle has ever since been respected by this Court and the Country as a permanent and indispensable feature of our constitutional system."[46]

That is not what *Marbury* established. *Marbury* confirmed the principle that a judge, when confronting a genuine case, must give effect to the Constitution as the judge understands it in the event of a conflict between the Constitution and some other law. *Marbury* confirmed the principle of "judicial review"; *Cooper v. Aaron* announced a different principle, one in which the Supreme Court's interpretations of the Constitution are supreme. This might be termed "judicial supremacy." It was the line Stephen Douglas took in defense of *Dred Scott*.

The Court hardly needed to announce a doctrine of judicial supremacy to reach the correct result. What was very clear from the proceedings was that political actors in Arkansas sought to nullify federal law. As explained in Chapter 2, that was unconstitutional. If every state could decide what federal laws prevailed in their state, then there would be "four and twenty masters" – or today, fifty masters. To be sure, Faubus was not dealing with a federal law, but rather a Supreme Court decision. But he did not merely oppose the Court's ruling in *Brown*; he actively resisted a court judgment in the particular case requiring the desegregation of Central High School. Lincoln specifically disclaimed disturbing the judgment in *Dred Scott* itself. Faubus sought to disturb an actual court judgment.

The Court has continued to articulate visions of judicial supremacy. In *United States v. Windsor* (2013), the Court struck down the 1996 Defense of Marriage Act. Both the Obama Administration and the plaintiff Edith Windsor agreed that the law was unconstitutional and that the district court's order requiring the government to pay Windsor should be enforced.[47] Yet, the government appealed solely for the purpose of obtaining a favorable Supreme Court opinion, even though it refused to defend the law on appeal. It was argued that there was no real case or controversy because all the parties agreed with the lower court's ruling. The Court decided the case anyway, observing that "if the Executive's agreement with a plaintiff that a law is unconstitutional is enough to preclude judicial review, then the Supreme Court's primary role in determining the constitutionality of a law … would become only secondary to the President's."[48] That is an odd statement to make given that it was Abraham Lincoln – the soon-to-be President – who put in place policies disagreeing with the Supreme Court's constitutional interpretation in *Dred Scott*.

Another modern but more nuanced example of judicial supremacy famously occurred in the context of the Free Exercise Clause, which prohibits Congress (and, through the Fourteenth Amendment, the states) from "prohibiting the free exercise [of religion]."[49] Until 1990, the Supreme Court had interpreted the clause to require states and the federal government to make religious exemptions from generally applicable laws unless there was a compelling government interest counseling otherwise. For example, in *Sherbert v. Verner* (1963) the Court applied this test and held that Congress had to make religious exemptions allowing religious individuals to observe their Sabbaths without risking a loss of their unemployment benefits.[50]

In 1990, the Supreme Court reversed decades of precedent and held in *Employment Division v. Smith*, in which the Justices effectively divided five against four, that generally applicable and neutral laws do not violate the Free Exercise Clause even if the law impinges on religious practices. Only a law that specifically targets or discriminates against religion would be unconstitutional.[51] In that case, the Court held that Native Americans had no Free Exercise claim supporting their use of peyote, which was a controlled substance under the national drug laws but which this particular tribe had used in religious ceremonies. The federal government (and the states) could create exemptions if they wished, but they did not have to do so under the First Amendment.

Congress in response swiftly passed the Religious Freedom Restoration Act of 1993 (RFRA) by a voice vote in the House of Representative and ninety-seven against three in the Senate. This law required not only the federal government but also the states to restore the previous doctrine and to provide religious exemptions from generally applicable laws unless there was a compelling government interest not to do so.[52] The Fourteenth Amendment, which under modern doctrine incorporates the Bill of Rights against the states, gives Congress the power in its fifth section to enforce the amendment against the states by appropriate legislation.[53] Congress explicitly stated that RFRA reflected Congress's own considered views of the meaning of the First Amendment,[54] which it sought to enforce against the states via the Fourteenth Amendment.

Was RFRA a constitutional exercise of Congress's enforcement power if the states were not in fact violating the First Amendment according to the Supreme Court's holding in *Employment Division v. Smith*? The Fourteenth Amendment allows Congress the power to remedy constitutional violations by the states, but the Supreme Court had ruled that refusing to give religious exemptions from generally applicable laws was constitutional. On the other hand, Congress expressed its own views of the Constitution and explicitly disagreed with the Supreme Court. Whose view should prevail?

In *City of Boerne v. Flores* (1997), the Court considered Congress's power to enact RFRA. It held, correctly, that Congress could not define the scope of the Bill of Rights that it was tasked with enforcing against the states. After all, Congress would otherwise be able to define the scope of its own powers relative to the states. That would undermine the courts' role in ensuring that Congress stay within its proper legislative boundaries.[55] Many scholars have argued that *Boerne* was wrongly decided because Congress has special interpretive authority over the Fourteenth Amendment,[56] but that cannot be true. Congress can interpret the amendment when passing enforcement legislation just as it must interpret other constitutional provisions when enacting other laws, but the courts, too, must interpret the amendment when it comes before them. There is nothing special about the Fourteenth Amendment in this regard.

The problem is different. Justice Sandra Day O'Connor, in dissent, argued that the Supreme Court should have at least reconsidered its earlier ruling in *Employment Division v. Smith* in light of Congress's near-unanimous disagreement with the Court's decision. After all, *Smith* had overturned decades of precedent by a closely divided vote of the Court, and it was controversial on the day it was decided. "I remain of the view that *Smith* was wrongly decided," she wrote, "and I would use this case to reexamine the Court's holding there."[57] *Smith* "is a recent decision," and "it has not engendered the kind of reliance on its continued application that would militate against overruling it," she added.[58] Another way of making Justice O'Connor's point is that the issue in *Smith* had not yet been fully settled.

When a century of prior courts, half the Justices of the Supreme Court, a nearly unanimous Congress, and the President of the United States, all of different political parties, think the Supreme Court has made a mistake, surely Congress need not abide by the Court's decision as a "political rule" – at least not until that decision is fully settled. And that decision is not fully settled merely because one divided Supreme Court opinion held a particular way. The Court in *Boerne* missed an important modern-day opportunity to let the process of departmentalism and liquidation unfold. Instead, the Court continued to maintain that it had primacy in interpreting the Constitution, and that its own pronouncements were the supreme law of the land. That view is inconsistent with the Constitution and the separation of powers that it creates.

15.5 EXECUTIVE SUPREMACY

Equally troubling are assertions of executive supremacy in interpreting the Constitution. The judiciary, Hamilton wrote in *Federalist* No. 78, "must ultimately depend upon the aid of the executive arm even for the efficacy of its judgments."[59] But may the President legitimately refuse to carry the judgments of the courts into execution? May the President more generally refuse to enforce an act of Congress the President believes to be unconstitutional?

Whether the President may refuse to enforce a law believed to be unconstitutional arose early in constitutional history. President Jefferson not only exercised the pardon power to effectuate his constitutional views but also instructed federal prosecutors to cease existing prosecutions under the Sedition Act.[60] The argument in favor of Jefferson's instruction is that the Take Care Clause requires the President to see that the laws be faithfully executed, and the Constitution is also a law. Just as the courts must decide what to do when two laws operate but also conflict, so too must the President decide which law to execute when both are applicable and conflict. The law contrary to the Constitution is then treated as a nullity. As Jefferson articulated when he refused to enforce the Sedition Act: "[W]henever in the line of my functions I should be met by the Sedition law," he wrote, "I should treat it as a nullity" and "order a Nolle prosequi," an instruction to dismiss a prosecution.[61]

This view, however, contradicts other historical and structural evidence about the President's powers. The most prominent of which is the President's qualified veto. The reader will recall that the President may veto legislation, but Congress may override that veto. If the President vetoes legislation on constitutional grounds and that veto is overridden, it is difficult to accept that the President can nevertheless refuse to execute the law. That would convert the qualified veto into an absolute veto. To be sure, the qualified veto would still operate in situations in which the President vetoes legislation on mere policy rather than constitutional grounds, and so a power to refuse to execute unconstitutional laws would not entirely eliminate the purpose of the veto override. Nevertheless, allowing the President to ignore unconstitutional laws would be tantamount to a suspending power at least for these purposes, a power the Convention had rejected.

Allowing the President to refuse to execute laws merely because of constitutional misgivings would also lead to executive supremacy, which seems as problematic as judicial supremacy. If the President may refuse to execute laws that Congress believes to be constitutional, including those that the judiciary has upheld, then the President alone is supreme in interpreting the Constitution – at least for the duration of that term. There is no principled reason why the President would not also be able to refuse to enforce a particular court judgment if enforcing that judgment would violate the Constitution in the President's own view.

These textual and structural arguments suggest that the President does not have a general power to refuse to execute laws merely because of a difference of opinion about their constitutionality. Departmentalism means Congress can interpret the Constitution when passing laws or judging the qualifications of its members or impeaching a President; the courts can interpret the Constitution when exercising the power of judicial review in particular cases and controversies; and the President can interpret the Constitution when exercising the veto and pardon powers. But the President cannot refuse to enforce the laws generally because then the President would be supreme; nor can the President refuse to enforce court judgments because of a constitutional disagreement.

History, with only some exceptions, supports this distinction between vetoing and pardoning and refusing to enforce the laws generally. Presidents in the nineteenth century who vetoed legislation on constitutional grounds and whose vetoes Congress overrode always enforced the legislation once enacted. Christopher May, who has chronicled this history, concluded that President Franklin Pierce was the first president to have a constitutionally based veto overridden; he vetoed five river and harbor appropriation bills because of his view that Congress had no enumerated power to spend on internal improvements. Pierce faithfully executed all five statutes once Congress overrode his vetoes.[62] President Chester Arthur also enforced a river and harbors bill that he had vetoed on constitutional grounds, which veto Congress overrode.[63]

Chief Justice Taney, in 1860, wrote a letter to former president Martin Van Buren, vice president in the Jackson Administration, in which he argued that Andrew Jackson never maintained that he could refuse to enforce laws he believed to be unconstitutional. Taney distinguished between vetoing the reauthorization of the Second Bank of the United States and refusing to treat the bank's charter as law while it was in effect. In the letter, not quoted in over 100 years and therefore worth quoting at some length here,[64] Taney wrote that Jackson "has been charged with asserting that he, as an executive officer, had a right to judge for himself whether an act of Congress was Constitutional or not," and that he "was not bound to carry it into execution, if he believed it to be unconstitutional, even if the Supreme Court had decided otherwise." Taney described this charge as a "misrepresentation." When Jackson vetoed the bank bill, "[h]e was speaking of his rights and his duty when acting as part of the Legislative power – and not of his right or duty as an executive officer." That is, he could decide for himself whether to veto the legislation on constitutional grounds, "notwithstanding an opinion to the contrary had been pronounced by the Supreme Court." But, Taney continued,

> General Jackson never expressed a doubt as to the duty & the obligation upon him, in his executive character, to carry into execution any act of Congress regularly passed, whatever his own opinion might be of the constitutional question. And at the time this veto message was written & sent, he was carrying into execution all the provisions of the existing charter & continued to do so until it expired. And when the deposites [*sic*] were removed, they were not withdrawn upon the ground that the charter was unconstitutional and void – but expressly upon the ground that it was still in force & would continue to be so until the expiration of the time limitted [*sic*] by the law itself. It would make the president grossly & absurdly inconsistent with himself, if the language in the message, could with any justice or fairness be applied to his executive powers.[65]

Both Taney and Jackson favored great executive power to control law execution, and it is therefore quite significant that both seemed to believe that the President had to execute all the properly enacted laws of Congress despite any constitutional misgivings. The President could always exercise the veto power on constitutional grounds, and the President could exercise the pardon power when a criminal law was at issue, as Jefferson did. A general power to refuse to enforce the laws is another matter entirely. To be sure, all of these events occurred later in constitutional history than did Jefferson's pardons, and may not reflect original meaning as convincingly.

Jefferson's pardons and refusal to enforce the sedition law might also suggest that, at least as to criminal statutes, the President can refuse to enforce the laws because of the availability of the pardon power. This argument may depend on the President's power to direct subordinate prosecutors. As suggested in Chapter 7, it is entirely possible that the President can order federal prosecutors to cease enforcing certain laws but that the President's only mechanism of compliance would be the removal of disobeying officers and to pardon offenders. The exercise of both powers comes at higher political cost. Regardless, the President's power in this respect would be limited to criminal laws.

There may necessarily be a more general exception to the rule that the President must enforce properly enacted laws despite constitutional misgivings: when Congress interferes with the President's exclusive prerogatives. After Lincoln's assassination, Congress enacted the Tenure of Office Act over President Andrew Johnson's veto. The Act prohibited Johnson from removing any principal officer without the advice and consent of the Senate, apparently reversing the Decision of 1789. Congress worried that Johnson would not execute its Reconstruction policies and wanted to secure in office officials who had begun serving during the Lincoln Administration. Johnson nevertheless removed from office the Secretary of War, Edwin Stanton, in potential violation of the statute.[66]

The House voted to impeach Johnson, and former Justice Benjamin Curtis defended the President in the impeachment trial in the Senate on the ground that the law specifically invaded the President's exclusive prerogatives and that he could violate the law to bring a judicial test case. Justice Curtis argued that ordinarily the President does not have the power to refuse to execute law despite constitutional misgivings; private persons affected by the law would have to bring a suit. "He is not to erect himself into a judicial court and decide that the law is unconstitutional, and that therefore he will not execute it; for, if that were done, manifestly there never could be a judicial decision."[67] Curtis declared that Johnson's view was that "if a law is passed over his veto which he believes to be unconstitutional, and that law affects the interests of third persons, those whose interests are affected must take care of them," and further that if the public generally is affected, "the people must take care at the polls that it is remedied in a constitutional way."[68]

In contrast, only the President can see to the interests and rights of the executive department. When "a particular law has cut off a power confided to him by the people through the Constitution, and he alone can raise that question, and he alone can cause a judicial decision to come between the two branches of the Government to say which of them is right," Curtis argued, then to violate the law and bring about such a judicial decision is not a breach of the President's duty.[69] Johnson's practices were consistent with his lawyer's arguments. Congress overrode several of President Johnson's vetoes, but Johnson always enforced those other laws, including many relating to Reconstruction.[70]

There is further historical support for the Johnson position. A passage from a leading constitutional law treatise by John Pomeroy argued that the President must normally execute the law, even those believed to be unconstitutional, because "[i]f the President may determine for himself, and refuse to execute, his action would be final."⁷¹ No private person would be able to bring a judicial case to enforce the statute. To this general rule, however, Pomeroy included an exception: "A statute may be passed of such a form and character as to be addressed directly to the President; it assumes to regulate his official action; no private person and no subordinate officer is affected by its provisions. If the Chief Magistrate enforces this law," Pomeroy wrote, "no question as to its validity can be raised, no opportunity can be given to deny the power of the legislature."⁷² In such a case, the President "may plainly exercise an independent judgment, and act upon his own separate convictions."⁷³

Other examples illustrate the exception. If Congress purported to prohibit the President from issuing pardons or to deprive the President of command of the military, it is evident that the President should ignore those laws. One possible reason to allow this course of action is to force a judicial test case; that is the answer Curtis and Pomeroy offered. But if the courts, in a fit of partisan passion, uphold Congress's usurpations and the President were expected to abide by their judgments, that would revert to judicial supremacy.

Perhaps in such situations the President need not follow even the courts' contrary judgments. The structure of Article II may offer a reason why. When the President proceeds to pardon individuals or to remove an officer or to command the army, doing so is not ignoring a law of Congress at all. The President is not executing a law of Congress, nor is the President, strictly speaking, refusing to execute the law in such situations. The take care duty simply does not apply. The President is instead exercising a power under a different provision of the Constitution altogether. When the President pardons an offender despite a congressional prohibition, the President need only look to the first paragraph of the second section of Article II. Congress's law is irrelevant because the President need not even look to Congress's law unless the President is exercising the very different power of carrying law into execution. The same logic applies to exercising direction of the military. Congress's laws, to the extent they touch that subject, and whatever they may be, are simply irrelevant; the President need look only to the Constitution to mark out the lines of executive duty and power. The President's power to remove principal officers, similarly, can be derived by consulting the text of the Constitution without having to consider any law of Congress. When it comes to ordinary legislation, however, the only thing the Constitution says on the matter is that the President must take care that the laws be faithfully executed. Those laws might, in the President's opinion, exceed Congress's enumerated power, or perhaps violate one of the rights in the Bill of Rights. But the only role the Constitution assigns to the President is faithfully to oversee the execution of those laws.

To summarize, if the President has a general duty to execute the laws despite constitutional misgivings, there are two plausible exceptions. The first is the criminal laws. The President's power to pardon may include the lesser power to cease enforcement. This exception is by no means obvious, however, because as noted previously, the President may not have a constitutional right of direction. Still, to the extent Congress's laws authorize the President to direct criminal law enforcement, and certainly to the extent the President can enforce a constitutional understanding through removal and pardoning, the President can refuse to carry into effect federal criminal laws believed to be unconstitutional. The second exception is when Congress's laws target the President's exclusive prerogatives; there the President's powers and duties do not derive from the Take Care Clause, but rather from other parts of the Constitution to which the President can resort with no knowledge of any congressional laws at all. The general rule, however, that the President's qualified veto invites, is that the President does not have a power to suspend the laws; any alternative would lead to executive supremacy.

PART VII

Federalism

16

Commerce

The earlier chapters of this book examined the structure of legislative, executive, and judicial power in the Constitution. Chapters 2–4 demonstrated how the Constitution creates a national government of limited, enumerated legislative powers. A discussion of this structure, and particularly the role of the Necessary and Proper Clause, was necessary for comparison to the executive and judicial power provisions of the Constitution and for understanding Congress's role in regulating executive and judicial power. This part now returns to Congress's legislative powers and specifically to their scope relative to the powers of the state governments. If the earlier parts of this study dealt generally with the horizontal separation of powers among Congress, the executive branch, and the courts, this part concludes with the vertical separation of powers. This topic is often called federalism. At issue is the scope of Congress's specific powers and the resulting distribution between the national and state governments.

This topic remains of keen interest. Although Congress has only enumerated powers, the Supreme Court has interpreted many of Congress's key legislative authorities in a way that seems to give Congress general, plenary legislative control over even state and local matters. The Court's modern interpretation of Congress's power to "regulate Commerce . . . among the several States," for example, maintains that Congress can regulate any activity that, when done in the aggregate, substantially affects the economy. Thus, the Court has upheld Congress's power to set quotas on a farmer's wheat production, even though that farmer grew the wheat in question on his own farm for his own personal consumption, all within a single state. If this interpretation of the interstate commerce power is correct, then it would seem there is almost nothing Congress cannot reach with that power. Similarly, the Supreme Court has held that Congress possesses the independent powers not only to tax but also to spend, and that Congress's exercise of those powers need not be in furtherance of its other enumerated powers. The Court has upheld congressional efforts to accomplish indirectly through the taxing and spending powers what Congress could not accomplish directly through its regulatory powers. These interpretations, too, seem to give Congress significantly more control over national life than the Framers envisioned.

This chapter begins with the original meaning of the Commerce Clause and how that original meaning would apply to leading modern cases. Chapter 17 turns to the closely related topic of "state sovereignty," involving the issues of anti-commandeering and sovereign immunity. Chapter 18, the final chapter of this part, and of the book, explores Congress's powers to tax and to spend, powers through which Congress indirectly, but quite effectively, controls much of modern policy.

Turning now to commerce. The original understanding and implementation of Congress's power over interstate commerce was conceptually elegant. Commerce was understood to involve the exchange of goods, although early Congresses presumed that their power over interstate commerce included the ability to facilitate it by, for example, removing obstructions to navigation or building lighthouses. This interstate commerce power was also often thought to be exclusive, meaning the states themselves could not exercise any power over interstate commerce whatsoever. This lends significant support to the modern "dormant commerce clause" doctrine, which many originalists have questioned.

Even though the states could not make regulations of interstate commerce, they retained their police powers: their general, residual powers to regulate for the health, safety, morals, and welfare of their populations. When exercising this police power, for example, by quarantining interstate goods, the states might issue regulations that looked like regulations of interstate commerce; in fact, Congress often could have imposed the exact same regulations through an exercise of its power over interstate commerce. Such state regulations were constitutional, however, if they were genuinely made for a police-power purpose. If the state frankly exercised its police power, the regulation would stand even if it incidentally affected interstate commerce because it would be considered a regulation of police within the power of the state rather than a regulation of interstate commerce that only Congress could make.

Conversely, Congress might, under the guise of a regulation of interstate commerce, aim to interfere with the police powers of the states. So long as Congress's legislation directly regulated interstate commerce, it could thereby affect the police power of the states; that even could be Congress's primary goal, as was often the case when Congress sought to prohibit the interstate sale of or travel with certain goods. But sometimes legislation was too indirect from commerce itself, as when Congress aimed to regulate production or manufacturing, such that Congress's legislation was not a genuine regulation of interstate commerce but rather an interference with the police power of the states. In the late nineteenth century, the Supreme Court monitored both the states and Congress to ensure they were frankly exercising their respective powers and not impermissibly interfering with the power of the other.

Over the past century, the Court abandoned this elegant symmetry. That symmetry is worth recovering. It has surprising implications for debates old and new, such as whether Congress could have closed the channels of interstate commerce to traffic in goods produced by slave labor, and whether the states today can seek to impose their own moral vision on other states by closing their doors to commerce from those other states.

16.1 ORIGINAL MEANING OF "COMMERCE"

Although common today to think of the word "commercial" as synonymous with "economic," commerce in the eighteenth century was a subset of economics. Much economic activity such as agriculture or manufacturing was distinct from commerce, which was the exchange and sale of those commodities and services. Commerce was the field of merchants. Agriculture, manufacturing, mining, and labor, or collectively "production," all preceded commerce and became the objects of it. Randy Barnett has written what is perhaps the definitive article on the original meaning of the term commerce. After surveying every use of the word commerce in the various notes of the Constitutional Convention, the ratification debates, and *The Federalist* essays, Barnett found that not a single use of the word referred to all economic or "gainful" activity, but rather each referred strictly to the exchange of goods.[1]

Alexander Hamilton, for example, distinguished commerce from these other activities in numerous essays. In *Federalist* No. 11, he wrote that "[a]n unrestrained intercourse between the States themselves will advance the trade of each by an interchange of their respective productions"; in *Federalist* No. 12, he remarked upon the "often-agitated question between agriculture and commerce"; and in *Federalist* No. 35, he asked, "Will not the merchant understand and be disposed to cultivate, as far as may be proper, the interests of the mechanic and manufacturing arts to which his commerce is so nearly allied?"[2] Hamilton's use was consistent with the 1785 edition of Samuel Johnson's influential *Dictionary of the English Language*, which defined commerce as "Intercourse; exchange of one thing for another; interchange of any thing; trade; traffick," whereas it defined manufacturing as "the practice of making any piece of workmanship" and agriculture as "the art of cultivating the ground."[3]

Additional research confirms what Barnett's piece concluded a quarter century ago. The reader is already familiar with Giles Jacob's influential law dictionary. The 1782 edition defined commerce as "Traffick, trade, or merchandise in buying and selling of goods." Interestingly, Jacob explained that there was a distinction between "commerce" and "trade," the former relating to dealings with foreign nations, the latter relating to "mutual traffick and dealings among ourselves at home." Jacob used the term "commerce" as part of several other definitions, and all indicate barter or exchange. Under the entry for "exchange," he wrote that the "commerce of money" is the "bartering or exchanging" of one city's money for another's. Elsewhere he wrote that the "exchanges of goods and merchandise[w]ere the original and natural way of commerce" before the invention of money. An "embargo … [p]rohibit[s] commerce in the time of war," which obviously cannot mean production and manufacturing. There is more still in the dictionary that confirms this usage.[4]

In John Bouvier's 1856 edition of his influential American law dictionary, commerce is noted along with "trade" and "contracts" and is defined similarly: "The exchange of commodities for commodities," the "exchange of the products of the earth or industry of man," or any "sale" or "exchange or barter."[5]

Early on, Congress interpreted its power over interstate commerce somewhat more broadly than the mere exchange of goods across state lines. Congress interpreted its power to include the facilitation of commerce, and not merely its regulation, by clearing obstructions to commerce. Andrew Jackson, skeptical of Congress's power over such matters and over internal improvements more generally, accepted this longstanding interpretation of Congress's power: "The practice of defraying out of the Treasury of the United States the expenses incurred by the establishment and support of light-houses, beacons, buoys, and public piers within the bays, inlets, harbors, and ports of the United States, to render the navigation thereof safe and easy," he wrote, "is coeval with the adoption of the Constitution, and has been continued without interruption or dispute."[6] As David Currie explained, "Since 1790 Congress had consistently and without objection acted on the understanding that it was competent to facilitate as well as to regulate commerce."[7]

Early on, Congress also regulated the instrumentalities of commerce, the modes by which commerce was undertaken. The very first Congress enacted a comprehensive labor law for merchant seamen.[8] In 1819, Congress enacted safety legislation setting maximum passenger limits on ships sailing to or from the United States and requiring adequate provision for those on board.[9] In 1838, Congress enacted numerous regulations concerning steamboats after a series of fatal boiler explosions.[10] Although perhaps not, strictly speaking, regulations of trade or exchange, Congress would seem necessarily to have such power as an incident of regulating the exchange itself, particularly because otherwise no one state would have jurisdiction over such matters.

All this is quite consistent with what Chief Justice Marshall wrote in *Gibbons v. Ogden* in response to the argument that the term commerce should exclude "navigation":

> This would restrict a general term, applicable to many objects, to one of its significations. Commerce, undoubtedly, is traffic, but it is something more: it is intercourse. It describes the commercial intercourse between nations, and parts of nations, in all its branches, and is regulated by prescribing rules for carrying on that intercourse. The mind can scarcely conceive a system for regulating commerce between nations, which shall exclude all laws concerning navigation, which shall be silent on the admission of the vessels of the one nation into the ports of the other, and be confined to prescribing rules for the conduct of individuals, in the actual employment of buying and selling, or of barter.[11]

In sum, the core definition of commerce at the Founding and throughout the antebellum period was the exchange of goods. Commerce meant trade, barter, and exchange; it did not include every and any economic matter.[12] The objects of commerce, the articles to be traded, had to precede commerce; these were agriculture, manufacturing, and production more generally. And Congress, of course, could not regulate purely internal commerce (or trade), but only interstate commerce or commerce between the United States and foreign nations or the Indian tribes. Congress's power over interstate commerce, however, was understood to be somewhat broader than merely the exchange of goods and to encompass regulations of the instrumentalities and channels of commerce as well, such as clearing navigational obstructions or establishing labor or safety regulations for merchants and vessels engaged in commerce.

16.2 *GIBBONS V. OGDEN* AND EXCLUSIVITY

Almost all the early Commerce Clause cases did not involve the meaning of the term commerce and thus the scope of congressional power. They dealt instead with the question whether states could themselves regulate interstate commerce in the absence of congressional legislation, or whether the states could otherwise affect interstate commerce. The Commerce Clause says only that Congress shall have power to "regulate Commerce . . . among the several States." It does not say Congress must use that power, and it does not say the states cannot regulate interstate commerce in the absence of congressional legislation. The tenth section of the Constitution's first article specifies numerous powers prohibited to the states, many of which are within the enumerated powers of Congress, but that section does not mention commerce. It mentions treaties, letters of marque and reprisal, coining money, emitting bills of credit, impairing contractual obligations, laying duties on imports and exports, keeping troops and ships in peacetime, and engaging in war (unless actually invaded or in imminent danger). It says nothing else remotely relevant to commerce.[13]

In *Gibbons v. Ogden*, Chief Justice Marshall ultimately did not answer whether Congress's power over interstate commerce was exclusive, although he seemed to think it was. The issue in *Gibbons* was whether New York's exclusive license to Ogden to operate steamboat ferries in New York waters – ostensibly as a reward for innovations in steamboat technology – precluded Gibbons from operating his own ferry pursuant to a license issued under the federal coasting trade laws. Marshall avoided the question of whether the federal commerce power was exclusive by concluding there was in any event a direct conflict between the state statute and the federal law. The federal law controlled pursuant to the Supremacy Clause.[14]

But consider the powerful arguments made in favor of exclusivity by Daniel Webster in his advocacy for Gibbons. First, there is the central reason the Constitutional Convention convened. The Framers were concerned not only with the general government having to rely on requisitions for taxes and troops but also the burgeoning commercial rivalries among the states. Webster summarized this history:

> The leading state papers of the time are full of this topic. The New-Jersey reso-
> lutions complain, that the regulation of trade was in the power of the several States,
> within their separate jurisdiction, in such a degree as to involve many difficulties
> and embarrassments; and they express an earnest opinion, that the sole and
> exclusive power of regulating trade with foreign States, ought to be in Congress.
> Mr. Witherspoon's motion in Congress, in 1781, is of the same general character;
> and the report of a committee of that body, in 1785, is still more emphatic.
> It declares that Congress ought to possess the sole and exclusive power of regulating
> trade, as well with foreign nations, as between the States. The resolutions of
> Virginia, in January, 1786, which were the immediate cause of the convention,
> put forth this same great object. Indeed, it is the only object stated in those
> resolutions. There is not another idea in the whole document. The entire purpose
> for which the delegates assembled at Annapolis, was to devise means for the
> uniform regulation of trade. They found no means, but in a general government;
> and they recommended a convention to accomplish that purpose.[15]

Thus, Webster observed, "We do not find, in the history of the formation and
adoption of the constitution, that any man speaks of a general *concurrent power*, in
the regulation of foreign and domestic trade, as still residing in the States. The very
object intended, more than any other, was to take away such power."[16] As Webster
hinted, the Annapolis Convention of 1786 – the precursor to the Convention of
1787 – convened when several states empowered commissioners "to consider how
far a uniform system in their commercial intercourse and regulations might be
necessary to their common interest and permanent harmony."[17]

In his concurring opinion in *Gibbons*, Justice William Johnson explained, citing
many of Webster's sources:

> For a century the States had submitted, with murmurs, to the commercial restrictions
> imposed by the parent State; and now, finding themselves in the unlimited possession
> of those powers over their own commerce, which they had so long been deprived of,
> and so earnestly coveted, that selfish principle ... began to show itself in iniquitous
> laws and impolitic measures, from which grew up a conflict of commercial regula-
> tions, destructive to the harmony of the States, and fatal to their commercial interests
> abroad. This was the immediate cause, that led to the forming of a convention.[18]

Putting aside the reasons the Constitutional Convention formed, some originalists
nevertheless complain that there is no textual foundation for the proposition that the
commerce power is exclusive. To repeat, the tenth section of Article I prohibits the
states from exercising numerous powers, some explicitly within Congress's enumerated powers; it does not, however, mention commerce.

Webster and Johnson had a convincing answer to the textual question having to
do with the nature of the power over interstate commerce. They argued that what

Congress chooses not to regulate is as much part of the system of commercial regulations as what Congress chooses to regulate. Webster explained that even when Congress has left an object unregulated, it "has acted on this power" and "has done all that it deemed wise"; Congress, in short, "makes such rules as, in its judgment, the case requires; and those rules, whatever they are, constitute the *system*." He continued: "All useful regulation does not consist in restraint; and that which Congress sees fit to leave free, is a part of its regulation, as much as the rest."[19]

In his opinion, Justice Johnson put the matter as follows:

> The law of nations, regarding man as a social animal, pronounces all commerce legitimate in a state of peace, until prohibited by positive law. The power of a sovereign state over commerce, therefore, amounts to nothing more than a power to limit and restrain it at pleasure. And since the power to prescribe the limits to its freedom, necessarily implies the power to determine what shall remain unrestrained, it follows, that the power must be exclusive; it can reside but in one potentate; and hence, the grant of this power carries with it the whole subject, leaving nothing for the State to act upon.[20]

Put another way, commerce may be engaged in freely until a sovereign makes some regulation prohibiting some aspect of it. Prohibitory regulations imply that whatever is not prohibited shall remain free of restraint. Thus, Johnson reasoned, when the power to regulate commerce was given to Congress, that meant it would henceforth be up to Congress and no one else to decide what restrictions on commerce there would be.

Chief Justice Marshall was inclined to agree. The taxing power was not exclusive because each sovereign could raise and collect taxes for its own purposes, and thus when "each government exercises the power of taxation, neither is exercising the power of the other." But, he continued, "when a State proceeds to regulate commerce with foreign nations, or among the several States, it is exercising the very power that is granted to Congress, and is doing the very thing which Congress is authorized to do."[21] After registering this agreement with the exclusivity argument, Marshall immediately suggested that he may "dismiss the inquiry" from the present case because Congress had in fact exercised its commerce power by enacting coasting laws, and thus the state law could have no effect to the extent it conflicted with those laws.[22]

The view that the interstate commerce power was exclusive was shared by other prominent legal thinkers of the era. Attorney General William Wirt, who also argued in *Gibbons*, agreed that the commerce power was exclusive because commerce "was one undivided subject."[23] In his 1803 commentaries on the U.S. Constitution, St. George Tucker "repeatedly noticed the defect of the former confederation, in respect to the regulation of the commerce between the several states," and numbered commerce among Congress's exclusive powers.[24]

Justice Joseph Story's 1833 commentaries also observed that the "want of some uniform system to regulate" commercial relations "was early perceived," and that the "public papers of that period" are "crowded with complaints on this subject."[25] "The difference of regulations," Story wrote, "was a perpetual source of irritation and jealousy."[26] By the time he was writing, Story could cite to *Gibbons* for the proposition, although not strictly what the Court held, that the power to regulate interstate commerce "is exclusive in the government of the United States."[27] Relying on the reasoning already described, Story wrote, "Regulation is designed to indicate the entire result, applying to those parts, which remain as they were, as well as to those, which are altered."[28] The power to regulate "produces a uniform whole, which is as much disturbed and deranged by changing, what the regulating power designs to have unbounded, as that, on which it has operated."[29]

In sum, although what has been called the "dormant commerce clause doctrine" is often denounced by originalists, there are serious historical arguments in favor of exclusivity. One of the central purposes of the Convention was to give Congress the power to regulate commerce to avoid partial commercial regulations on the part of the states and all the rivalries and jealousies that would result. That objective helps one to understand what the Framers were seeking to accomplish with the language they used.

True, they did not say in express language that the interstate commerce power was exclusive, nor that it was prohibited to the states. And other textual provisions could be seen to hint that states continued to possess concurrent power over interstate commerce, although these arguments are, in this author's view, relatively weak.[30] Nevertheless, as Webster, Wirt, Marshall, Johnson, Tucker, and Story all argued, the very power to regulate commerce was understood to include whatever was left untouched by regulation. What Congress left unrestrained was a part of the commercial "system" of the United States. It may not have been necessary expressly to prohibit the states from regulating interstate commerce because any regulations of such commerce create a uniform system. There was no need to exclude what was already excluded by the nature of the congressional grant.

16.3 THE STATES' POLICE POWERS

Even though Congress's power over interstate commerce was generally understood to be exclusive, federal courts routinely upheld state regulations that had some connection with that commerce. The states retained their "police power" over the health, safety, morals, and welfare of the people within their borders, the residuum of regulatory power that the people did not delegate to the national government in the Constitution. It could be difficult to distinguish a regulation of police from a regulation of interstate commerce; if a state enacted regulations requiring the inspection and possible quarantining of goods coming into the state from another, those regulations would operate on the same subject that Congress's power of interstate commerce could reach. If Congress's power over interstate commerce was exclusive, then it was not immediately clear what ought to happen to these kinds of state regulations.

The early courts settled on an elegant solution. So long as a state regulation was genuinely enacted for a police-power purpose, the courts would deem it a regulation of police rather than a regulation of interstate commerce, even if Congress could have preempted that state regulation with one made pursuant to its interstate commerce power. This ensured that a state stayed within its proper boundaries and was not impermissibly attempting to interfere with interstate commerce.

All the parties and the Court itself adhered to this solution in *Gibbons*.[31] Webster argued that an exclusive interstate commerce power was not inconsistent with the state's recognized power over "pilot laws, the health laws, or quarantine laws; and various regulations of that class."[32] Webster thought that "all these things were, in their general character, rather regulations of police than of commerce, in the constitutional understanding of that term."[33] He recognized that such police regulations could affect interstate commerce, but argued that this effect did not make them by nature commercial regulations. "[G]enerally speaking," he explained, "roads, and bridges, and ferries, though, of course, they affect commerce and intercourse, do not obtain that importance and elevation, as to be deemed *commercial regulations* .... Quarantine laws, for example, may be considered as affecting commerce; yet they are, in their nature, *health laws*."[34]

To ensure that the states were not impermissibly seeking to interfere with interstate commerce, Webster argued, the constitutionality of such regulations must depend on the genuineness of the purposes for which they were enacted and the closeness of the relation between the regulation and those purported objects. "While a health law is reasonable, it is a health law; but if, under colour of it, enactments should be made for other purposes, such enactments might be void."[35] Thus, a state could not use its police power as a pretext for trying to regulate interstate commerce.

Ogden's counsel agreed that internal state regulations might "indirectly affect the right of commercial intercourse between the States," but so do "quarantine laws, inspection laws, duties on auctions, licenses to sell goods, &c," all of which "are acknowledged to be valid."[36] Whether such laws were reasonably calculated to advance a legitimate police-power purpose determined their validity: "They are passed, not with a view or design to regulate commerce, but to promote some great object of public interest, within the acknowledged scope of State legislation: such as the public health, agriculture, revenue, or the encouragement of some public improvement."[37] Thus, "[b]eing passed for these legitimate objects, they are valid as internal regulations, though they may incidentally restrict or regulate foreign trade, or that between the States."[38] William Wirt took a similar position.[39]

Chief Justice Marshall's opinion for the Court makes good sense in light of these arguments. After finding that the power over interstate commerce includes navigation and that Congress had exercised its power by providing for the licensing of the coasting trade, Marshall addressed the power of states to regulate on similar subjects. Marshall did not deny that inspection laws had a considerable impact on commerce, but their "object" was not commerce; their object was "to improve the quality of articles produced by the labour of a country; to fit them for exportation; or, it may be, for domestic use"; such regulations "act upon the subject before it becomes an article of foreign commerce, or of commerce among the States, and prepare it for that purpose."[40] Quarantine laws and "health laws of every description" were similar.[41]

Marshall agreed that so long as the state laws were passed for these purposes and had a reasonable relation to them, they could not be considered impermissible regulations of interstate commerce. "So, if a State, in passing laws on subjects acknowledged to be within its control, and with a view to those subjects, shall adopt a measure of the same character with one which Congress may adopt," Marshall explained, "it does not derive its authority from the particular power which has been granted [the interstate commerce power], but from some other [the police power], which remains with the State, and may be executed by the same means."[42] It was the purpose for which the laws were enacted that determined the source of the power.

Justice Johnson similarly wrote that the distinction between proper and improper state regulations touching on the same subjects of the commerce power was the purpose for which those state regulations were enacted. "It is no objection to the existence of distinct, substantive powers, that, in their application, they bear upon the same subject. The same bale of goods, the same cask of provisions, or the same ship, that may be the subject of commercial regulation, may also be the vehicle of disease."[43] Thus, "the health laws that require them to be stopped and ventilated, are no more intended as regulations on commerce, than the laws which permit their importation, are intended to innoculate the community with disease."[44] It is the purpose and frank exercise of power that mark a valid police regulation: "Their different purposes mark the distinction between the powers brought into action; and while frankly exercised, they can produce no serious collision."[45]

Numerous cases took this approach after *Gibbons*. In *Willson v. Black Bird Creek Marsh Co.*, decided in 1829, a unanimous Court permitted Delaware to construct a dam in a navigable stream because "[t]he value of the property on its banks must be enhanced by excluding the water from the marsh, and the health of the inhabitants probably improved." The Court held that "[m]easures calculated to produce these objects, provided they do not come into collision with the powers of the general government, are undoubtedly within those which are reserved to the states." Such laws cannot "be considered as repugnant to the power to regulate commerce in its dormant state."[46] In other words, as long as Congress has not enacted a contrary regulation, the state could act on the same subject so long as its regulation was legitimately "calculated to" advance a police-power purpose.

In the 1837 case of *Mayor of New York v. Miln*, the Court upheld a state law requiring ship captains to provide lists of their passengers, with the ostensible purpose of helping the state keep immigrants from becoming public charges. "To decide" whether the regulation was "not of commerce, but police," Justice Barbour wrote, the Court must "examine its purpose, the end to be attained, and the means of its attainment."[47] The Court summarized the doctrine:

> [W]hilst a state is acting within the legitimate scope of its power as to the end to be attained, it may use whatsoever means, being appropriate to that end, it may think fit; although they may be the same, or so nearly the same, as scarcely to be distinguishable from those adopted by congress acting under a different power: subject, only, say the Court, to this limitation, that in the event of collision, the law of the state must yield to the law of congress.[48]

As late as 1867 in *Steamship Co. v. Portwardens*,[49] the Court unanimously recognized that "some [state] powers, the exercise of which may, in various degrees, affect commerce, have always been held not to be within the grant to Congress," and "[t]o this class it is settled belong quarantine and other health laws, laws concerning the domestic police, and laws regulating the internal trade of a State."[50] All of these cases accorded with Justice Story's 1833 commentaries. Writing about the states' powers over "certain subjects, having a connexion with commerce," Story maintained that such powers "are entirely distinct in their nature from that to regulate commerce." Health, inspection, and pilotage laws "are not so much regulations of commerce, as of police."[51]

To summarize, the early commerce cases involved mostly state laws. The Supreme Court and other legal thinkers generally agreed that Congress's power over interstate commerce was exclusive, lending support to a "dormant" commerce doctrine. The textual argument is not foolproof, but, at a minimum, such a doctrine is supportable under plausible readings of the text, especially given the purposes for which the Framers convened in Philadelphia. And, as Justice Oliver Wendell Holmes said in another context, a page of history is worth a volume of logic.[52] Numerous litigants, Supreme Court Justices, and Supreme Court decisions presumed or upheld such a doctrine for the first several decades of the Republic.

The states still retained their police powers, however, and these powers could sometimes act on the subjects that Congress's own interstate commerce power could reach. In this respect, one might draw a parallel to the previous discussion of nonexclusive functions. Congress, the President, and the courts each have an exclusive power – legislative, executive, judicial – but functionally those powers sometimes overlap such that a similar result can be achieved through an exercise of more than one of these powers. So too here: Congress and the states have their respective, exclusive powers – interstate commerce and the police power – but functionally these powers could and did occasionally overlap.

What made state regulations constitutional in this context was the purpose for which they were enacted. If genuinely made for a police-power purpose, they were constitutional, although such constitutional laws would have to give way if Congress enacted a conflicting federal law. If the states used the police powers merely as a pretext to interfere impermissibly with interstate commerce, such laws were unconstitutional.

16.4 FEDERAL POWER, 1887–1937

Until 1887, most cases about the commerce power involved state regulations because the federal government did not assume a large role in regulating the national economy. The creation of the Interstate Commerce Commission in 1887 was a watershed. The next fifty years saw massive growth in national regulations concerning the economy. The courts had to confront the reach of Congress's affirmative power under the Commerce Clause.

In this era, the Supreme Court enforced something of a symmetry between the "dormant" and the "active" components of the commerce power. The national government could use its commerce power to affect matters traditionally within the states' police powers, such as agriculture, manufacturing, mining, or labor; but its regulation had to be one of interstate commerce, for example the closing down of the channels of interstate shipments or transactions. Congress could not otherwise regulate these articles of commerce because they were too indirect from Congress's power over interstate exchange. As shall be seen, the Court sometimes failed to implement correctly this original meaning and structure.

In this period, the Court affirmed Congress's powers over the instrumentalities of commerce, sustaining a federal regulation of intrastate shipping rates on the part of some railroads.[53] Earlier congressional laws had regulated the instrumentality itself, enacting labor laws for merchant seamen, safety laws for steamboats, and provisions requirements for sailing vessels. Never before had Congress assumed the power to regulate the intrastate commercial transactions of an instrumentality merely because that instrumentality also engaged in interstate commerce. Nevertheless, the Court was surely correct as a historical matter that Congress had some power not merely over interstate transactions but also over the instrumentalities of commercial exchange.

In two other cases, the Court upheld Congress's power to prohibit altogether interstate traffic in certain goods. In *Champion v. Ames* (1903), the Supreme Court in a split decision upheld a prohibition on the interstate shipping of lottery tickets. The Court reasoned that the power to "regulate" commerce included the power to "prohibit" traffic in at least "noxious" goods.[54] In *Caminetti v. United States* (1917), the Court upheld a federal prohibition on the interstate transportation of women engaged in sex work.[55] Congress, as far back as 1842, had prohibited the interstate shipment of "indecent and obscene prints, paintings, lithographs, engravings, and transparencies," although there had been no discussion of Congress's constitutional power to do so.[56]

Putting aside the matter of intrastate rates, these cases can be understood as standing for the historically accurate propositions that Congress can regulate the instrumentalities of interstate commerce such as ships and railroads and the channels of interstate commerce, which included removing obstructions to navigation and facilitating intercourse but also prohibiting interstate traffic altogether.

If Congress could prohibit interstate traffic altogether, it could also exercise that power to induce states to take actions that Congress could not have required directly.

The issue culminated in a series of cases involving child labor. In *Hammer v. Dagenhart* (1918), Congress had attempted to prohibit the interstate traffic in any goods that had been produced in a factory that employed child labor as defined by the federal statute.[57] This created a conundrum: The production of goods preceded commerce and was generally left to the states, but Congress could also prohibit the interstate traffic in goods like lottery tickets or obscene materials. In a split decision, the Court invalidated Congress's law on the ground that these latter items were inherently noxious, whereas the products at issue in *Hammer* were not. If such products were otherwise perfectly appropriate to sell in interstate commerce, the mere fact that they had been produced under conditions of child labor was insufficient to trigger Congress's power.

The Court's reasoning in *Hammer* was similar to its reasoning in the early dormant commerce cases. The Court's aim was to ensure that Congress did not trench on the powers of the states under the guise of regulating commerce. Recognizing that the line between commerce and that which precedes it – agriculture, manufacturing, production – can be blurry, the question was whether the real object of the legislation was commerce or those other things. The Court argued:

> The act in its effect does not regulate transportation among the states, but aims to standardize the ages at which children may be employed in mining and manufacturing within the states. The goods shipped are of themselves harmless . . . . [T]he mere fact that they were intended for interstate commerce transportation does not make their production subject to federal control under the commerce power . . . .
>
> The making of goods and the mining of coal are not commerce, nor does the fact that these things are to be afterwards shipped, or used in interstate commerce, make their production a part thereof . . . .
>
> If it were otherwise, all manufacture intended for interstate shipment would be brought under federal control to the practical exclusion of the authority of the states, a result certainly not contemplated by the framers of the Constitution when they vested in Congress the authority to regulate commerce among the States.[58]

Toward the end of the opinion, the Court emphasized that, although the Court may not inquire into the "motives" of Congress, "[t]he purposes intended must be attained consistently with constitutional limitations and not by an invasion of the powers of the states." The "necessary effect" of the act was "to regulate the hours of labor of children in factories and mines within the states, a purely state authority." If this were allowed, then "the power of the states over local matters may be eliminated, and thus our system of government be practically destroyed."[59]

The Court was concerned with maintaining the limits on Congress's enumerated powers. If Congress could prohibit the interstate transportation of any good not produced by a person or firm who had adopted federal standards, there would be no economic activity of any kind that Congress could not reach. Agriculture, manufacturing, and all production would be within Congress's grasp, undermining the intended division of power between Congress and the states. The way to determine whether a congressional regulation was impermissible was to judge, by its practical effects, its true intended purpose. In *Hammer*, the Court concluded that the law "aim[ed] to standardize" the child labor laws, and that its "necessary effect" showed that Congress's intended purpose was not to regulate commerce, but rather to regulate local matters reserved to the states.

Hammer was likely wrongly decided, but the correctness of this decision shall be deferred for the moment; the story of the Court's cases is not yet complete. *Hammer* involved a prohibition on interstate sales; Congress also attempted to regulate wages and hours directly. The Court initially invalidated these efforts.[60] Just as a state could not attempt to interfere with interstate commerce on the pretext that it was regulating local matters, neither could Congress interfere with these local matters on the pretext that it was regulating interstate commerce. The Court policed the line by examining whether Congress was regulating activity with a "direct" effect on interstate commerce, or merely an "indirect" effect.

In *A.L.A. Schechter Poultry Corp. v. United States*, famous for its separate non-delegation holding, the Court struck down federal wages and hours laws on the ground that wages and hours only "indirectly" affected interstate commerce. If Congress were allowed to regulate anything that eventually affected interstate commerce – wages and hours clearly affect the ultimate price a good will have in the interstate market – then there would be no separation between Congress and the states on matters of economic concern. Gesturing toward cases involving instrumentalities, the Court observed that Congress could prescribe safety appliances on railroads or could fix intrastate railroad rates, both of which "directly" affected commerce. "But where the effect of intrastate transactions upon interstate commerce is merely indirect," the Court went on to say,

> such transactions remain within the domain of state power. If the commerce clause were construed to reach all enterprises and transactions which could be said to have an indirect effect upon interstate commerce, the federal authority would embrace practically all the activities of the people, and the authority of the state over its domestic concerns would exist only by sufferance of the federal government.[61]

After surveying past decisions, the Court concluded that "the distinction between direct and indirect effects of intrastate transactions upon interstate commerce must be recognized as a fundamental one, essential to the maintenance of our constitutional system," otherwise "there would be virtually no limit to the federal power, and for all practical purposes we should have a completely centralized government."[62]

16.5 FEDERAL POWER EXPANDS, 1937–1942

Starting in 1937, the Court reversed course. In *National Labor Relations Board v. Jones & Laughlin Steel Corp.* (1937), the Supreme Court considered the constitutionality of the National Labor Relations Act and of the determination of the National Labor Relations Board that it was an "unfair trade practice" to discriminate in tenure and hiring against unionized workers. Historically, labor was a matter of production, which preceded commerce. But the Court repudiated both the direct–indirect effects test and the distinction between production and commerce. The sole question, according to the Court, was an object's "effect upon commerce." Thus, the Court held, intrastate, noncommercial activities could be regulated if they had "a close and substantial relation to interstate commerce that their control is essential or appropriate to protect that commerce from burdens and obstructions." The Court upheld the legislation on the grounds that it sought to prevent industrial strife, which undoubtedly would have a great effect upon interstate commerce.[63]

In *United States v. Darby* (1941), the Court reversed its decision in *Hammer*. It held that Congress could prohibit the interstate shipment of goods produced by a firm that used child labor. The Court held that the "motive and purpose" of Congress in making the regulation did not matter; as long as the regulation was of interstate commerce, it would be sustained even if Congress sought to affect commodities and activities traditionally within the purview of the states. The Court also overturned its holding in *Schechter Poultry* and expanded upon its decision in *Jones & Laughlin*. It upheld a federal minimum wage and maximum hours law, holding that the federal government could not only prohibit the interstate transportation of goods made in violation of federally prescribed standards but also directly impose those standards by regulating the wages and hours of workers.[64] Although the Court was not entirely clear about the matter, it appeared to rely more on the Necessary and Proper Clause than on the Commerce Clause itself.[65]

Finally, in *Wickard v. Filburn* (1942), the Court sustained federal quotas on the amount of wheat a farmer could grow on his own farm for his own consumption purely within the confines of his own state. The Court reasoned that by forestalling access to the interstate market for wheat by making his own wheat, the farmer was in effect reducing demand for interstate wheat. In "the aggregate," if done by many farmers, such self-production would affect interstate wheat prices, and thereby have a substantial effect on commerce.[66] The Court again appeared to rely on the Necessary and Proper Clause, although without doing so explicitly.[67] Thus, under the modern doctrine, Congress can regulate any intrastate matter that, "in the aggregate," substantially affects commerce.

Although in the past three decades the Court has sometimes sought to impose limits on Congress's power to regulate interstate commerce by insisting that the intrastate activity be economic in nature,[68] the problem is evident. By turning away from an inquiry into Congress's purpose, by abandoning the direct–indirect effects test, and by collapsing the distinction between articles of commerce and commerce itself, the Court has effectively given Congress plenary power to regulate intrastate activities. At least four Justices of the Supreme Court, at one time or another, even concluded that Congress's power over interstate commerce reached the carrying of guns near schools or extended to compelling individuals to engage in commercial transactions through penalties for inaction.[69]

16.6 THE ORIGINAL STRUCTURE RECONSIDERED

Recovering the original structure of the commerce power may help clarify the Court's turn-of-the-century cases. The Court had the right idea but often erred in the implementation. To start, the Court was likely wrong in *Hammer* to limit Congress's power over the interstate sale of goods. It is true that Congress can easily abuse that power to attempt to enforce uniformity among the states in matters outside of Congress's enumerated powers. It remains the case, however, that the regulation of interstate exchange is precisely the power the Constitution assigns to Congress. For better or worse, Congress can use its power over interstate commerce to prohibit all commercial intercourse among the states. That Congress might abuse its power in this manner is not evidence against the power's existence; all power can be abused.

The existence of such a power would also have allowed Congress eventually to smother slavery out of existence. The reader will recall that the rallying cry of abolitionists and Republicans was "freedom national," and their agenda was to create a "cordon of freedom" around the existing slave states and to make slavery unprofitable. The central question has always been how abolitionists expected to abolish slavery if there was no direct federal power on the subject within the states.[70] After abolishing the international slave trade, abolishing slavery in the territories, and even abolishing the interstate slave trade,[71] surely Congress could have prohibited the interstate shipment of all goods made with enslaved labor. That would have been the "nuclear option" of the era, but it was an option within Congress's power and would have almost certainly led to the abolition of slavery without constitutional amendment. The present point is only that Congress had (and has) the power to close the channels of interstate commerce and thereby to affect the internal police of the states. But that power comes at a high political cost, and a prohibition on interstate transportation is not as severe as a direct prohibition.

Hammer was also likely wrong because some sovereign power must have the authority to close the channels of interstate commerce. Every nation on earth has the power to close its commerce with foreigners. If Congress could not close the channels of interstate commerce among the states, then it would seem to follow that that power was reserved to the states themselves in the Constitution. That would lead precisely to the tempestuous commercial rivalries that it was a central purpose of the Constitution to avoid. One state could close its doors to the traffic of a neighboring state. The other would retaliate. Massachusetts could have prohibited within its border the sale of goods made with enslaved labor. The Civil War might have started decades earlier. Justice Holmes' dissent in *Hammer* was quite right to observe,

[The States] may regulate their internal affairs and their domestic commerce as they like. But when they seek to send their products across the State line they are no longer within their rights. If there were no Constitution and no Congress their power to cross the line would depend upon their neighbors. Under the Constitution such commerce belongs not to the States but to Congress to regulate.[72]

Simply put, just as the states have a power of police which, if frankly exercised, may affect commerce among the states, so too does Congress have a power over interstate commerce that could affect the same subjects that are within the police powers of the states. In *Gibbons*, Justice Johnson had explained, "It is no objection to the existence of distinct, substantive powers, that, in their application, they bear upon the same subject. The same bale of goods, the same cask of provisions, or the same ship, that may be the subject of commercial regulation, may also be the vehicle of disease."[73] And in *Darby*, the Court correctly observed, "It is no objection to the assertion of the power to regulate interstate commerce that its exercise is attended by the same incidents which attend the exercise of the police power of the states."[74] These ideas are perfectly symmetrical.

The Supreme Court was right, however, to insist on the distinction between direct and indirect effects upon interstate commerce. That was just another way of saying there is a distinction between commerce and articles of commerce. That distinction, as shown earlier, is rooted in the text and early history of the Commerce Clause. As soon as the distinction disappears, there is almost nothing Congress cannot directly regulate.

The original structure of Congress's power, then, can be summarized thus: Congress could indirectly affect matters of production, manufacturing, and so on, through a direct regulation of interstate commerce, including prohibitions on interstate exchange. But Congress could not directly regulate matters of production, manufacturing, and the like, on the theory that such matters indirectly have effects upon interstate commerce. As for state power, states could indirectly affect interstate commerce through a direct and genuine regulation of police, including genuine health and safety laws. But the states could not directly regulate interstate commerce on the theory that such matters indirectly affected matters of police.[75]

The original structure of the commerce power is both elegant and sound. Local matters and interstate commerce are intertwined; one could always affect the other. So long as a state genuinely exercised its police power over health, safety, morals, or welfare, it could thereby affect interstate commerce. Any effect would be only incidental to the police regulation. And so long as Congress genuinely exercised its interstate commerce power – and the closing down of interstate exchange is within the core of that power – it could thereby affect a state's regulations of police or the private behavior ordinarily regulated by such state laws. Such an effect could be great indeed, which was the point of prohibitions on interstate sale or transportation of certain goods. That does not, however, make Congress's law a direct regulation of police as opposed to a regulation of interstate exchange. And just as the states could not directly interfere with interstate commerce under a pretextual police regulation, Congress's regulation had to be directly related to interstate commerce itself; anything too indirect would be but an improper attempt at regulating those articles that precede commerce.

The doctrine was neat, elegant, and symmetrical. And it kept Congress, more or less, within proper bounds.

16.7 ON PORK AND POLICE

One piece of the doctrinal story remains to be told. The modern dormant commerce doctrine, often assailed by originalists, is surprisingly originalist. The modern doctrine maintains that even in the absence of any congressional legislation, the states cannot discriminate against the commerce of other states, and furthermore that any neutral law that unduly burdens interstate commerce is invalid unless the state can point to a compelling local interest.[76] That would seem to track the historic doctrine almost exactly. A state regulation that discriminates against the commerce of other states is a direct regulation of interstate commerce and nothing more; it is precisely that subject which the Constitution has assigned to Congress and prohibited to the states. An ostensibly neutral law with a great effect upon interstate commerce but little local benefit is a regulation of interstate commerce under the guise or pretext of a police regulation.

The original structure of the commerce power can provide an even clearer conceptual framework for addressing important dormant commerce questions. Most recently and prominently, the Supreme Court addressed the doctrine in *National Pork Producers Council v. Ross*.[77] California prohibited all sales within its borders of pork produced contrary to California's prescribed standards. Californians were concerned with the humane treatment of swine, and the effect of their regulation was to close their market to any producer that did not comply with their preferred standards. California has the biggest economy of all the states and the vast majority of impacted pork producers were out-of-state producers. The Supreme Court upheld California's law in a severely fractured series of opinions. Some Justices questioned the validity of balancing local interests against the interstate burden.[78] One Justice questioned whether the local benefit to Californians in this instance was even measurable against the economic impact on other states, and so declined to engage in judicial balancing.[79]

With some further elaboration, the original framework better answers this question. California's law was unconstitutional. It was a direct attempt at regulating the commerce coming in from other states. In the antebellum period, could Massachusetts have prohibited the sale in Massachusetts of all goods produced by enslaved labor? Such a law would have applied equally to producers in Massachusetts (none of whom had slaves) and to those of Virginia and South Carolina. Yet, it seems quite evident that the entire purpose of such a regulation would not have been to regulate Massachusetts' own citizens, but rather to affect the domestic practices of other states through otherwise prohibiting their commerce with Massachusetts. Congress could have prohibited the interstate traffic in such goods, just as Congress could have prohibited the interstate traffic in goods produced with child labor; but the states could do neither.

That is, the states could do neither unless they could demonstrate a valid police-power purpose. But there is none. The theory which led some Justices of the Supreme Court to uphold California's law is that that law reflected the moral views of the people of California. But that is not a police power. The police power includes the power to regulate the morals of Californians; it does not include the power to close its commerce to other states because it morally disapproves of the behavior of those other states. Just as a state could prohibit the interstate commerce of goods infected with disease, so too could a state prohibit the interstate commerce in lottery tickets, which affect the morals of the state's own citizenry. Or the interstate commerce in pornographic materials. But those matters directly affect the morals of the people within the state; they affect their conduct.

Put another way, the Supreme Court's now-discarded distinction in *Hammer* between goods noxious in themselves and those that are not noxious may not make sense in the context of federal power, because interstate commerce is interstate commerce that Congress can regulate regardless. The distinction makes a great deal of sense, however, in the context of a state's police power and its effect on interstate commerce. Goods that are noxious in themselves affect the morals of the people of the state directly. They affect their moral behavior and productivity and integrity as citizens. But prohibiting goods from other states not noxious in themselves because of a moral disapproval of the conditions in which those goods were produced does nothing to regulate the morals of the people of the state. That is the line Justice McLean took in the 1841 case *Groves v. Slaughter*: The states could prohibit the introduction of slavery, which was noxious in itself and could have an evil effect on the state's population, but they could not prohibit the sale of southern cotton or northern manufactures.[80]

The central insight is that most laws have a moral purpose, but if any such law could be conceptualized as affecting morals, then all the states would be allowed to regulate interstate commerce merely because of a moral disapproval of activities within other states. That would recreate the precise conditions the Constitution was designed to prevent. The state may have a moral purpose, but the regulation must also be one of *morals*, or of some other police power. Congress, similarly, can have a moral purpose, as it did in *Hammer*, so long as it is regulating interstate commerce itself and not directly regulating the morals of the people in the states. Once again, the true doctrine is perfectly symmetrical.

17

State Sovereignty

In a traditional constitutional law course, students encounter "state sovereignty" cases after completing their study of the commerce power. It is said that in these cases the Supreme Court sought to cabin the reach of Congress's broad and open-ended power over interstate commerce, a power the Supreme Court itself sustained in the New Deal, by giving legal effect to inchoate federalism values. The cases of enduring relevance are those involving sovereign immunity and anti-commandeering. In its sovereign immunity cases, the Court has held that Congress cannot abrogate a state's sovereign immunity and force the state to be sued by its own citizens for violating federal law. In the anti-commandeering cases the Court has held that Congress cannot compel state executive officers to help implement and enforce federal law.

A common theme in these cases is that the Supreme Court's conservative majority does not purport to rely on the text of the Constitution. For example, in *Printz v. United States*, Justice Scalia said the answer to the question whether Congress can commandeer state executive officers to implement federal law will not be found in the text, but rather "in historical understanding and practice, in the structure of the Constitution, and in the jurisprudence of this Court."[1] And in its sovereign immunity cases, the Court has said that its doctrine does not follow the text of the Eleventh Amendment – the only textual provision explicitly referencing sovereign immunity – but rather the amendment reflects a more general principle to which the Court is giving effect.[2] Scholars both non-originalist and originalist have condemned these cases for appearing to ignore the text of the Constitution and for inventing new law.

There is, however, a textual basis for the Court's holdings: the Necessary and Proper Clause. That is the only clause that plausibly gives Congress the power to abrogate a state's sovereign immunity or to commandeer state officials. If abrogating sovereign immunity or commandeering cannot be implied as merely incidental to other powers, but are rather great, substantive, and independent prerogatives, then Congress could not use those means to achieve its other enumerated ends. A great-powers analysis could easily lend itself to judicial lawmaking, however, and guard-rails must be sought to ensure any limitation on congressional power is rooted in text, structure, and history.

17.1 STATE COFFERS

A discussion of the modern state sovereignty cases often begins with the Supreme Court's decisions in *National League of Cities v. Usery* (1976)[3] and *Garcia v. San Antonio Metropolitan Transit Authority* (1985),[4] the latter of which overturned the former. In *National League of Cities*, the Court held that the Fair Labor Standards Act, which imposed minimum wage and overtime pay requirements upon employers, could not be applied to state government employees in areas of "traditional governmental functions" such as police and fire protection.[5]

The imposition of such regulations under Congress's expanded, modern commerce power would cost millions of additional dollars that states may not have, and which they would have to raise through the taxation of their own citizens. The Court did not deny that, by its own terms, the Commerce Clause is not restricted to private-sector employees. "This Court has never doubted that there are limits upon the power of Congress to override state sovereignty," the Court nevertheless held, "even when exercising its otherwise plenary powers to tax or to regulate commerce which are conferred by Art. I of the Constitution."[6]

The *Garcia* case overturned this holding within ten short years. It was, admittedly, difficult to distinguish between traditional and nontraditional government functions. The Court's ultimate holding, however, was based on its view that there was no Commerce Clause exception for state employees by the terms of the clause. "[I]t long has been settled that Congress' authority under the Commerce Clause extends to intrastate economic activities," such as the operation of a local transit authority, "that affect interstate commerce."[7] "Of course," the Court added, "the Commerce Clause by its specific language does not provide any special limitation on Congress' actions with respect to the States."[8]

The states do retain sovereignty, the Court insisted, but "only to the extent that the Constitution has not divested them of their original powers and transferred those powers to the Federal Government."[9] "With rare exceptions, ... the Constitution does not carve out express elements of state sovereignty that Congress may not employ its delegated powers to displace."[10] The majority declared that the protections for state sovereignty must be found in the political safeguards of the federalist structure.[11]

Justice O'Connor's dissent did not disagree with much of the majority's reasoning, but argued that the Court had to enforce "affirmative limits on federal regulation of the States to complement the judicially crafted expansion of the interstate commerce power."[12] It is quite clear that the Commerce Clause does not, by its terms, extend only to private individuals and exclude state employees; but it is also evident that the Commerce Clause has itself been extended to include intrastate activities that would not have originally been within the scope of national power. If the Court has indeed supported this expansion of the commerce power, then Justice O'Connor was surely correct that it would be up to the Court, and not the text of the Constitution, to find suitable limits on this "judicially crafted expansion."

More fundamentally, the text itself supplies a framework for answering these questions. Although as Chapter 16 noted the Court has not been entirely clear about the matter, the Court first supported the expansion of Congress's power over internal commerce and production under the Necessary and Proper Clause. Justice O'Connor's dissent in *Garcia* recognized this point, the only occurrence in all the opinions in both cases in which the clause is even cited.[13] If intrastate activities, such as controlling wheat production, are necessary and proper for effectuating a regulation of interstate commerce respecting interstate wheat prices, then perhaps the clause can justify national control over such local matters. It does not follow, however, that Congress could impose millions of dollars in costs on the states.

To be sure, a great-powers analysis under the Necessary and Proper Clause might call into question the extension of congressional power to internal commerce in the first place. After all, if the power over interstate commerce was a great, substantive, and important power, then surely the power over internal trade, and over production and manufacturing more generally, would have been understood as a great, substantive, and important power that could not have been left to implication. Such a grant would have extended to Congress something akin to a general police power.

Presuming that the clause can justify Congress's expansion into these areas, it would be a still greater power to impose direct regulations on state governments and their officers and employees. Such a power would effectively give Congress a means to eviscerate the states; all Congress would have to do is enact an inordinately expensive regulation of "commerce" and thereby bankrupt the states. Congress is unlikely to abuse the power in that manner, but given the ease of abuse and the tremendous burden on taxpayers, it is highly implausible that such a power would have been left to mere implication.

In sum, whether or not the traditional government functions test of *National League of Cities* was workable, what is clear is that the text of the Constitution, and particularly the Necessary and Proper Clause, provides a framework for answering the relevant questions about state sovereignty.

17.2 SOVEREIGN IMMUNITY

Another component of state sovereignty, sovereign immunity, is the notion that a state cannot be sued in court without its consent. It has a long history in the common law. Caleb Nelson has written that sovereign immunity was part of the common law of personal jurisdiction: A court simply could not exercise power over the body of the king or the state because there was no way to force them into court or to pay money from the treasury.[14] Blackstone wrote that the idea of a sovereign who was not immune from suit was an absurdity; that would require an entity more sovereign than the sovereign.[15] Government officers could be held personally liable for committing wrongs by exceeding their authority, and the state in its discretion might indemnify them.[16] But the state itself could not be sued without its consent.

Justice James Iredell in 1793 explained that sovereign immunity was part of the law of every state of the Union prior to the adoption of the Constitution.[17] Did the states retain this immunity when they adopted the Constitution?[18] The Supreme Court confronted this question in *Chisolm v. Georgia* (1793),[19] when a citizen of South Carolina sought to sue the state of Georgia. The plaintiff invoked the Supreme Court's diversity jurisdiction, which Article III grants as follows: "The judicial power shall extend ... to controversies ... between a state and citizens of another state."[20] Chisolm's case was certainly "between a state and [a] citizen[] of another state." The Supreme Court thus held that Chisolm could indeed sue Georgia in federal court. This caused a tremendous uproar, leading to the very first post-bill-of-rights amendment, the Eleventh Amendment, which overturned *Chisolm*: "The judicial power of the United States shall not be construed to extend to any suit in law or equity, commenced or prosecuted against one of the United States by citizens of another state, or by citizens or subjects of any foreign state."[21]

It would appear that, as a result of the Eleventh Amendment, the citizen of one state cannot sue another state in federal court; that, and foreign citizen suits, are the only circumstances the amendment addresses. Over the next 200 years, however, in cases ranging from *Hans v. Louisiana* (1890)[22] to *Seminole Tribe v. Florida* (1996),[23] the Supreme Court held that Congress did not have power under Article I of the Constitution to enact a federal law that imposes obligations on the states and allows one of that state's own citizens to sue the state in federal court for a violation. Congress cannot abrogate the state's sovereign immunity even if the matter involves a state dealing with one of its own citizens, a situation the text of the Eleventh Amendment does not contemplate. In *Alden v. Maine* (1999), the Court further held that Congress could not force a state to be sued by one of its own citizens in state courts.[24] This holding again seems beyond the scope of the Eleventh Amendment, which speaks only to suits in federal, not state, courts between a citizen of one state against another state.

It is often thought that these cases are hard to reconcile with original meaning. Nothing in the Constitution indicates expressly that the states keep their sovereign immunity. The only part of the Constitution bearing at all on the subject, the Eleventh Amendment, is inapplicable where citizens are seeking to sue their own states. Eric Segall has explained the conventional wisdom thus:

> There is no better example of how Justices Scalia and Thomas ignored clear text and relevant history when it suited their policy preferences than their interpretations of the Eleventh Amendment .... The Eleventh Amendment by its clear terms bars any suit, whether for damages or an injunction, against a state by citizens of "another" state. Both Justices Scalia and Thomas, however, have interpreted this language to bar lawsuits by citizens of the same state against their home state. They have taken the word *another* and twisted it to mean "the same." They engaged in this fancy word play despite the beliefs of four dissenting justices, and the views of

most scholars, that the Amendment only bars suits against states by citizens of a different state, consistent with the clear text.[25]

It is the critics who are in error and who get the Constitution exactly backward. It is true that nothing in the Constitution explicitly says that the states retain their sovereign immunity. But the states always had that immunity, as Caleb Nelson and Justice Iredell explained. The question is instead whether Congress has any power granted to it that in some way affects that sovereign immunity. Congress can only exercise those powers delegated and enumerated in the Constitution. Therefore, states lost or can lose their sovereign immunity only if the Constitution abrogates that immunity directly or delegates to Congress a power to abrogate it.

There were only two possible ways the original Constitution of 1789 could accomplish that abrogation. As Bradford Clark has written,[26] the first was the grant of jurisdiction in Article III referred to previously. The Court concluded in *Chisolm* that, by including that jurisdictional grant, the Framers must have intended to abrogate the sovereign immunity of the states in suits between them and citizens of other states.[27] That is, the very existence of jurisdiction in such cases was presumed to mean that the states would be amenable to suit in those cases. Whether or not that was correct as a matter of original meaning, the Eleventh Amendment quickly rendered that view obsolete. That amendment specifically targeted and rendered moot the argument that the diversity jurisdiction granted to federal courts in Article III presumed the abolition of sovereign immunity. And nothing else in the Constitution plausibly abrogates that sovereign immunity.

It could be, however, that Congress has the power to abrogate the states' sovereign immunity. There is no express enumerated authority to do so. The Necessary and Proper Clause could, perhaps, allow Congress to abrogate sovereign immunity if doing so is "necessary and proper for carrying into execution" its other enumerated powers. If Congress passes a law pursuant to its Article I powers, and that law obligates the states, it certainly seems plainly adapted to allow an injured citizen the right to sue the state for failing to abide by its obligations under federal law.

The inquiry under the Necessary and Proper Clause would once again be whether abrogating sovereign immunity is a great, substantive and independent power – like the power to tax or to declare war – that cannot be left to implication. Justice Iredell thought so in explicit terms:

> So much ... has been said on the Constitution, that it may not be improper to intimate that my present opinion is strongly against any construction of it, which will admit, under any circumstances, a compulsive suit against a State for the recovery of money. I think every word in the Constitution may have its full effect without involving this consequence, and that nothing but express words, or an insurmountable implication (neither of which I consider, can be found in this case) would authorise the deduction of so high a power.[28]

Although Iredell was in the minority in *Chisolm*, the reaction to the Court's decision and the subsequent adoption of the Eleventh Amendment suggest that the founding generation largely understood sovereign immunity to be one of the greatest attributes of sovereignty, which the people did not abrogate when they adopted the Constitution. Thus, the power to abrogate such immunity cannot be left to implication.

There is no need to go into great detail, but there is significant additional historical evidence for this understanding.[29] When George Mason worried that the grant of diversity jurisdiction might lead to states being "arraigned like a culprit, or private offender,"[30] James Madison responded that the clause would only apply to cases where the state "should condescend to be a party."[31] John Marshall stated in the same debate, "I hope no Gentleman will think that a State will be called at the bar of the Federal Court . . . . It is not rational to suppose, that the sovereign power shall be dragged before a Court."[32]

Discussions from more Federalist perspectives confirmed the consensus. In the Massachusetts Convention, everyone seemed to agree that a state could not be haled into federal court without its consent.[33] "Every person that attended the debates," according to one observer recalling events as of 1793, "knows that this question was agitated in the Convention, and . . . that both parties *mutually* and *cordially* consented, that the 'suability' of the States was not contemplated by the framers of the Constitution."[34] And Alexander Hamilton famously stated in *Federalist* No. 81, "It is inherent in the nature of sovereignty not to be amenable to the suit of an individual without its consent."[35]

Certainly the reaction to the *Chisolm* decision itself confirmed the view that sovereign immunity was a great prerogative of sovereignty and therefore Congress would be unable to abrogate that immunity absent express provision. As Aaron Coleman has recently written, it was two leading Federalists from Massachusetts, Theodore Sedgwick and Caleb Strong, who the day after the decision introduced amendments to see it reversed.[36] And not only Massachusetts and Georgia, but also Virginia, New York, Connecticut, and Maryland passed resolutions condemning the decision and calling for an amendment.[37] As Coleman explains, "opposition to state suability crossed geographic regions or partisan politics,"[38] suggesting the great importance of this state prerogative to the Founding generation.

In sum, the Court has not adequately defended its sovereign immunity decisions. But those decisions are supported by the Constitution's text and original meaning. Congress has only those powers specifically granted to it, and it does not have a power to abrogate a state's sovereign immunity. It could only have such a power by virtue of the Necessary and Proper Clause. It would appear, however, that abrogating sovereign immunity, which itself was one of the most important attributes of sovereignty, was understood to be a great, substantive, and independent power that could not be left to implication. Thus, Congress could not have exercised such a power under the Necessary and Proper Clause.

17.3 ANTI-COMMANDEERING

A similar analysis applies to the Supreme Court's anti-commandeering cases. As noted in the introduction to this chapter, the Court's originalists said in *Printz v. United States* that the answer to whether the Constitution allows Congress to coopt state executive officers into enforcing federal laws will not be found in its text, but rather in its history and structure and the Court's own jurisprudence. This is an issue of great importance today. In *Printz*, the federal government sought to use county officials to help create and enforce a nationwide system of background checks for firearms purchases. In the past few years, the federal government has sought to use local officials to help enforce immigration laws. Whether or not the federal actions in the two cases require the same result, the mode of analysis is the same: Is the federal government commandeering state officers, and if so, whether that is permissible under the Constitution.

Although the Court in *Printz* did not analyze it this way, the real analysis is under the Necessary and Proper Clause.[39] Is the commandeering of state executive officers "necessary and proper" to effectuating Congress's enumerated powers, or is it a great, substantive, independent power that would have to be explicitly enumerated? The structure of and the historical practice under the Constitution will be relevant to the analysis. Structure and history strongly suggested, for example, that commandeering state legislatures was impermissible, as that would recreate the precise problem under the Articles of Confederation of relying upon the state governments to raise taxes, troops, or to enact implementing legislation for any manner of national policies.[40] In contrast, deploying the state judiciaries to help implement federal law was contemplated by the Madisonian Compromise and the Supremacy Clause.[41] The matter of state executives was more ambiguous.

The majority and dissenting opinions in *Printz* deployed competing historical accounts. The majority emphasized the complete absence of any attempts to commandeer state executive officers in the first several decades after the Constitution was adopted. Justice Scalia argued that "the utter lack of statutes imposing obligations on the States' executive (notwithstanding the attractiveness of that course to Congress), suggests an assumed *absence* of such power."[42] Additionally, the Court noted that the federal government's power would be greatly increased if commandeering were allowed: "The power of the Federal Government would be augmented immeasurably if it were able to impress into its service – and at no cost to itself – the police officers of the 50 States."[43]

Yet, as legal historian Jud Campbell has written, the Court may have had this history exactly backward. The Anti-Federalists who feared federal power preferred state officers to enforce federal laws. They preferred state tax collectors, for example, who were attuned to local conditions and more familiar with the local populace, over the potential swarms of federal officers that might be required to enforce federal laws. Relying on state officers was one way to keep the federal government's power in check.[44] The Federalists even assured their opponents, in the words of Hamilton in *Federalist* No. 27, that "the Legislatures, Courts and Magistrates of the respective members will be incorporated into the operations of the national government, as far as its just and constitutional authority extends; and will be rendered auxiliary to the enforcement of its laws."[45] The absence of commandeering in the historical record might therefore reflect that once the Federalists assumed power, they created the national bureaucracy they had always wanted. A federal bureaucracy would give the national government more power and prestige than reliance on state officers.[46]

None of this early history suggests that the Anti-Federalists thought the federal government could compel a state's assistance. Perhaps they expected the states to assist willingly. The larger point is that this history is rather inconclusive. Structural considerations may therefore be more important to this specific inquiry. The commandeering of state officers raises several potential structural problems.

Gary Lawson and Guy Seidman have suggested, for example, that agency law principles may determine the commandeering question. The reader will recall that the doctrine of implied powers existed in the law of agency, which over time came to recognize that agents could undertake certain incidental powers to help carry into execution those powers expressly granted by the principal. One principle from agency law was that agents, to whom the principal had delegated power, could not subdelegate that power to someone else without express authorization. Commandeering improperly subdelegates the executive power of the laws to state officials.[47]

Perhaps subdelegation is not necessary for the argument because it may be that commandeering directly violates Article II's Vesting Clause. As previously established, the President is vested with the executive power to carry laws into execution. The President must have assistants, and therefore appoints and removes all principal officers; and the President and the principal officers appoint and remove inferior officers. State officers cannot be considered the President's assistants in this sense unless the President can oversee, control, or remove them. The President has no such power over state officers. Allowing Congress to derogate from the President's executive power and place the enforcement of federal laws in the hands of state officers may for that reason be too great and important a power to be left to implication.[48]

Another structural consideration relevant to the question was discussed in earlier chapters of this study on the nature of the Union. The Articles of Confederation operated on and through the states; the Confederation Congress could not operate directly on the people. That led to states' disobeying or ignoring the requests of the Confederation Congress; there was no way to compel obedience without resorting to force of arms. That is why the Constitution of 1789 was to operate directly on individuals. Federal officers would enforce federal law; no longer would the states be required. And that is why, as noted, Congress cannot commandeer state legislatures.

A law commanding state officers to enforce federal law would encounter at least similar difficulties as the national government encountered under the Articles of Confederation and that commandeering state legislatures would create. If a state executive officer refused to comply, whether on orders from the state legislature or other state officials or on independent initiative, there would be no way for the national government to enforce the obligation. The states, as noted earlier, could refuse consent to suit in federal tribunals. And even if the federal government could sue a state in federal court, the court would not be able to enforce its own judgments. The inevitable conclusion is that the only way to ensure compliance with such an obligation would be the threat of war against a state. As Anthony Bellia and Bradford Clark have written, "The central government could successfully commandeer state governments only if the Constitution also authorized it to use force against delinquent States – a power the Founders considered too dangerous to confer."[49] That applies to state legislatures and executive officers.

One final consideration is the parallel to sovereign immunity. Sovereign immunity was a great attribute of sovereignty. Bellia and Clark demonstrate that the right to command one's own officers was also a great attribute of sovereignty under the law of nations.[50] "Every nation that governs itself," according to Emerich de Vattel, "without any dependence on a foreign power, is a *sovereign state*. Its rights are naturally the same as those of any other state."[51] If another nation could command and control the officers of another, the latter would not be sovereign. And Bellia and Clark have further shown that nations could alienate their sovereign rights under the law of nations only "in clear and express terms or by unavoidable implication."[52] Clarity was essential in matters of treaty interpretation where a misinterpretation could give cause for war. Under this reasoning, for the same reason that abrogating sovereign immunity cannot be left to implication under the Necessary and Proper Clause, neither can commandeering a state's officers be left to implication. Each involves a great attribute of sovereignty and the Constitution's text and structure do not unavoidably require or permit their abrogation.

In sum, whether Congress can commandeer state officers is not as clearly answered by the historical record as is the question of abrogating sovereign immunity, on which there was a quite specific historical understanding. But numerous historical and structural reasons abound for treating commandeering as a great and important power that cannot be left to implication. Whatever the answer to the question, the Necessary and Proper Clause provides the relevant framework. Justice Scalia was wrong to purport to ignore the text. If one only knows where to look, the Constitution might provide answers to more questions involving the retained sovereignty of the states.

18

Taxing and Spending

The two powers of Congress of most consequence for the division of federal and state authority, besides that of regulating commerce among the states, are the powers to tax and to spend. It is through these powers, and especially the spending power, that Congress exerts much control over national life. Congress may not have the ability to control the content of educational standards directly, but it can promise states money for textbooks that meet certain curricular standards or, more aggressively, on condition that they adopt a nationwide curriculum. Congress may not be able to compel a nationwide homelessness policy directly, but it can offer municipalities "incentive payments" to adopt its preferred solution. And, to turn to the taxing power, Congress may not be able to compel individuals to purchase health insurance; but it can, apparently, tax them if they refuse to do so.

This chapter unravels the complexity of Congress's taxing and spending powers. As a doctrinal matter, these powers parallel Congress's power over the channels of interstate commerce. Just as Congress may close those channels with the motive of affecting matters within the traditional police power of the states – because interstate commerce is interstate commerce – so too can Congress tax and spend with similar motives. But Congress must in fact be taxing and spending. At some point, Congress's taxes may become so onerous and coercive that they are in fact "penalties," which is another way of saying regulatory. If outside the enumerated powers, such regulatory penalties are impermissible. Similarly, there may come a point where federal spending inducements are impossible to refuse such that they are similarly coercive and therefore regulatory, or where the attached conditions are so unrelated to the purpose of the spending program that those conditions are also regulatory.

As a historical and textual matter, however, the taxing and spending powers were even more limited. The first clause of the eighth section of Article I, from which both powers have been derived, is most naturally read as merely a power to tax for national purposes. That would suggest that having a regulatory motive beyond the enumeration of powers is impermissible. Even more consequentially, it would suggest that Congress does not have a freestanding power to spend for the "general welfare"; its only power to spend would be what can be derived from the Necessary and Proper Clause, which would have to be in furtherance of the enumeration.

This chapter begins with the debates over how to read the first grant of power in the enumeration and then examines the provision of the Articles of Confederation from which it derived, the records of the committee of detail, and the structural role of the Necessary and Proper Clause. This analysis concludes that the first clause in the eighth section of Article I is most naturally read as merely a power to tax for national purposes. That analysis is supported by significant historical evidence, although, to be sure, there is counterevidence. The chapter then pivots to an assessment of modern taxing power doctrine in light of this most likely original meaning of the clause.

Although under the best original meaning there is no freestanding power to spend, an independent power to spend for the general welfare may well be within the range of plausible original meanings. The Supreme Court weighed in on the matter in 1936, concluding that Congress does have an independent power to spend for the general welfare. The final part of the chapter assesses the modern spending power doctrine and particularly the permissibility of conditioning spending on regulatory changes. It proposes a better test than the existing doctrine for distinguishing between genuine exercises of the spending power and impermissibly purchasing compliance with regulatory requirements that otherwise would be beyond Congress's enumerated powers.

18.1 THE TEXT

The first grant of power in the Constitution's first article, eighth section, reads: "The Congress shall have Power To lay and collect Taxes, Duties, Imposts and Excises, to pay the Debts and provide for the common Defence and general Welfare of the United States; but all Duties, Imposts and Excises shall be uniform throughout the United States; . . ."[1] The punctuation and structure of the clause create some ambiguity: The clause could grant one, two, or even three separate powers to Congress. If a single power, Congress would have the power to raise taxes for national purposes, that is, for the purpose of paying the debts and providing for the common defense and general welfare of the United States. If the clause grants two powers, Congress would have the power to tax for any purpose, and another power to "spend" for national purposes, namely, to pay the national debt and to provide for the common defense and general welfare. It is further possible to read the clause as granting three powers: a power to tax, a power to pay the debts, and a power to regulate more broadly for the common defense and general welfare.

Textually, the single-power reading has the most to commend it. It would make sense for the Constitution to specify that if Congress has the power to impose taxes directly on the American people, a power concurrent with the states and which was lacking under the Articles of Confederation, that that power be limited to raising revenue for national purposes. Chief Justice Marshall explained in *Gibbons* why the taxing power was concurrent: "Congress is not empowered to tax for those purposes which are within the exclusive province of the States."[2] The requirement that taxes "shall be uniform," moreover, comes at the very end of the clause and modifies the power to tax. Although it would not be linguistically impossible to specify two powers and then to modify the first power, that the clause begins and ends with taxation strongly suggests the entire clause is about taxation. Finally, every other distinct power in the eighth section is set off by a semicolon or, if serially the last power among a series of related powers, by an Oxford comma and the conjunctive "and."[3] If the powers "to pay the debts" and "provide for the general welfare" were one or two additional powers, they would be the only ones in all of the eighth section to deviate from this grammatical structure.

The two-powers reading is also plausible, though more improbable as a textual matter. It is unclear why the Constitution would need to specify that Congress has the power "to pay the debts" of the United States. Congress is granted the power "[t]o borrow Money on the credit of the United States" in the very next grant,[4] which would naturally include the power to repay those debts. Otherwise, Congress would not be borrowing but rather stealing money. Specifying the power to pay the debts would be superfluous.

As for the common defense and general welfare, the words "provide for" can be understood as supplying or provisioning through the expenditure of money, in the sense that one provides for one's family. Yet, several of Congress's other regulatory powers are introduced with similar language, namely, the power to "provide for" the punishment of counterfeit securities,[5] calling forth the militia,[6] and organizing, arming, and disciplining the militia.[7] If the first grant is not merely a power to tax, it is unclear why the second power would be limited to spending. It would be more natural to read the clause as three powers: to tax, to pay the debts, and to regulate for ("provide for") the common defense and general welfare.

Yet, the three-powers reading is even more implausible. It has already been noted that specifying the power to pay the debts would be superfluous. A power to regulate for the common defense would render superfluous several of Congress's enumerated powers touching the militia, the army and navy, and war more generally. A power to regulate for the general welfare would similarly render the remainder of the enumeration superfluous. To the extent "provide for" could be read as granting a general regulatory power, that is all the more reason to read the entire clause as a single power to tax.

18.2 THE ORIGINS

The history of the clause provides further insight. The words "general welfare" and "common defense" appeared twice, both times together, in the Articles of Confederation. Article III had provided that the states "hereby severally enter into a firm league of friendship with each other, for their common defense, the security of their liberties, and their mutual and general welfare . . . ." Article VIII provided that "[a]ll charges of war, and all other expenses that shall be incurred for the common defense or general welfare, and allowed by the United States in Congress assembled, shall be defrayed out of a common treasury, which shall be supplied by the several States, in proportion to the value of all land within each State . . . ." Only in Article IX did the Articles enumerate the Confederation Congress's specific regulatory powers.[8]

Article VIII did not grant Congress a power to spend for the common defense and general welfare. It provided rather that any expenses that "shall be incurred for the common defense or general welfare" may be defrayed out of the national treasury. Congress's authorization to incur those expenses in the first place had to come from elsewhere, presumably its regulatory powers in Article IX. The phrase "common defense and general welfare" therefore seems to have referred to the national purposes for which Congress could incur expenses. The article then pivoted to its real significance, how money shall be raised for the purpose of defraying those national expenses: The treasury "shall be supplied by the several States in proportion to the value of all land within each State." This article, in other words, was a clause providing for the raising of money for the purpose of paying for, or defraying, the national expenses.

The Constitution of 1789 parallels the Articles. Just as the Articles included the common defense and general welfare in its preamble, the Constitution includes in its preamble the national objectives of promoting the general welfare and providing for the common defense. The subsequent occurrence of these words in the first grant in the eighth section of Article I then does work similar to Article VIII of the Articles of Confederation. The Articles specified that any expenses incurred for the general welfare and common defense shall be defrayed from a common treasury, and the states shall supply the necessary funds in proportion to their land. The Constitution takes this one step further and provides, unlike the Articles, that Congress may impose taxes directly on individuals for the purpose of defraying such expenses. Neither clause granted Congress the power to incur those costs in the first place. That power had to come from elsewhere. Roger Sherman and James Madison both confirmed that the language was taken from the Articles.[9]

The initial drafts of the constitution from the committee of detail support this interpretation of what one might now call the taxing clause. One early draft in the handwriting of Edmund Randolph, with emendations by John Rutledge, refers to "legislative powers; *with certain exceptions; and under certain restrictions.*" It then includes as the very first power: "*agrd.* 1. To raise money by taxation, unlimited as to sum, *for the (future) past (or)* ⟨&⟩ *future debts and necessities of the union* and to establish rules for collection."[10] (The words in parentheses were deleted by Randolph; the italicized words were added by Randolph; and those in the brackets were added by Rutledge.)

This draft makes the point unmistakably. There is no separate power to spend. There is no verb "to pay." The entire subordinate clause was intended as a limitation on the power to raise taxes. Taxes shall be laid "for the past & future debts and necessities of the union." Just as under the Articles of Confederation, those debts and the costs of those necessities would arise from Congress's exercise of its other enumerated powers such as the power to borrow money.

In a subsequent draft by James Wilson, the entire clause was replaced with merely the "Power to lay and collect Taxes, Duties, Imposts and Excises,"[11] with no proviso or limitation whatsoever; in this form, the power was presented to the full Convention.[12] Although one might interpret this revision in different ways, it seems reasonable to presume that Wilson understood the entire clause to have been about taxation. When the full Convention addressed this grant of power in Wilson's draft, it first resolved that a duty to pay the debts should be included.[13] The subsequent committee on postponed matters changed the language to its final form, reintroducing the original limitation from the Randolph and Rutledge draft. Roger Sherman, who advocated the rights of the states throughout the Convention, had insisted on this qualification, further suggesting that it was, indeed, a limitation.[14]

One final, interesting turn of events appears to have occurred. The committee of style tasked with finalizing the style and arrangement of the document changed the comma to a semicolon:

> The Congress may by joint ballot appoint a treasurer. They shall have power. ⟨(a)⟩ To lay and collect taxes, duties, imposts and excises; to pay the debts and provide for the common defence and general welfare of the United States. ⟨but all duties imposts & excises shall be uniform throughout the U. States.⟩[15]

There is no contemporaneous record explaining why the semicolon had been inserted, or why it was subsequently deleted. In 1798, Albert Gallatin alleged during a congressional debate that the committee of style, led by the great nationalist Gouverneur Morris, had tried to insert a semicolon to create independent taxing and spending powers, or perhaps even a regulatory power over the general welfare. Gallatin reported that the ever-watchful Roger Sherman caught wind of the change and had the semicolon removed.[16] Although it is difficult to know with certainty what led to these changes in punctuation, what seems clear from the relevant records is that the Convention never considered an independent power to spend or to regulate for the general welfare. The relevant words, when they first emerged and in their final form, appeared as limitations on the power to tax.

18.3 NECESSARY AND PROPER

Structural reasons support the single-power interpretation of the taxing clause. The first is that the Constitution would not have needed to specify Congress's power to spend. Congress's collection of revenues surely implied that those revenues would be spent on national purposes; otherwise, the monies would have remained in the treasury in perpetuity. The point was not left entirely to implication because the Necessary and Proper Clause specifically grants Congress the power to exercise incidental and implied powers. That would have included the power to spend money in pursuance of the enumerated powers.

The point may seem trivial when stated, but it powerfully undermines the two-powers reading of the taxing clause. Congress has the power to raise and provide for armies and navies, to establish post roads, and to purchase needful buildings, including forts, magazines, arsenals, and dockyards. It has the power to declare war, and the President has the power to prosecute war. Congress cannot achieve any of these purposes without spending money. Such a power is not only convenient but indispensably necessary to the functioning of the government. Congress cannot raise an army without paying soldiers. It cannot establish post offices without purchasing buildings or paying its postmasters. The power to spend on enumerated purposes is not a "great substantive and independent power"[7] that cannot be left to implication. The purposes for which the money may be spent must be enumerated, but spending for those purposes is merely incidental. "An express power to raise money, and an express power (for example) to raise an army, would surely imply a power to use the money for that purpose," Madison summarized in an 1830 letter. "And if a doubt could possibly arise as to the implication, it would be completely removed by the express power to pass all laws necessary and proper in such cases."[18]

On the other hand, taxing was considered a "great substantive and independent power" that could not have been left to implication. As Chief Justice Marshall famously said in *McCulloch v. Maryland*, the power to tax involves the power to destroy.[19] The rallying cry of the American colonists was no taxation without representation.[20] The power to tax is perhaps the most important, the most substantive, the greatest power any government can have. It makes eminent sense that the very first power among Congress's enumerated authorities is therefore the power to tax. Without specifying the power to tax, the government would have had (and still has) many methods of collecting money aside from taxation, including selling public lands, confiscating property in wartime, borrowing money, or imposing tariffs under Congress's commerce power.

Once delegated the power to tax, Congress might use that power for improper purposes. If the power to tax involves the power to destroy, then Congress could destroy anything it chose to tax, such as domestic agriculture, production, or manufacturing. The Framers would have been attuned to the risk of Congress seeking to accomplish indirectly through taxation what it could not achieve directly through regulatory legislation. They therefore granted Congress the great power to tax, but also limited it. Congress was prohibited from achieving indirectly what it could not achieve directly. Congress could raise taxes, but only for the purposes of paying the national debt or providing for the common defense or general welfare. If the Convention wanted to limit the power to tax solely to raise revenue for the purposes listed in the subsequent enumeration, it was natural as in the Articles of Confederation to refer to those purposes as providing for the common defense and general welfare, which collectively capture the full scope of Congress's enumerated powers.

The history of the sixth resolution of the Virginia Plan may shed further light. The reader will recall that the delegates agreed to give Congress the power to legislate on all matters over which the separate states were individually incompetent. The powers enumerated in the eighth section of Article I are precisely those the Framers believed had to be vested in the general government because they were matters of general, as opposed to local, welfare. The power to impose taxes "to pay the debts and provide for the common defense and general welfare of the United States" naturally limits the purpose of the taxation to the collection of revenue for spending on constitutionally enumerated objects.

18.4 CORROBORATING STATEMENTS

Although the matter was not free of doubt, most of the founding generation and early antebellum thinkers, with only a few though prominent exceptions, argued or presumed that the first grant in the eighth section of Article I was a power of taxation only. Even the Anti-Federalists, who had an incentive to exaggerate the scope of the clause (which they did on occasion), generally complained that the clause did not impose sufficient limits on federal taxation. As Theodore Sky has written in his book defending the spending power, the central Anti-Federalist concern was "an unlimited taxing power," one that would lead to a "potential loss of sources of revenues to state governments."[21] The Anti-Federalists "recognized" the clause "for what it was – an effort to limit the taxing power."[22] The complaint from the writer Centinel was illustrative: "The Congress may construe every purpose for which the state legislatures now lay taxes, to be for the *general welfare*, and thereby seize upon every object of revenue."[23]

As for the pro-Constitution writers, one of the most prominent treatments of the clause was the forty-first essay of *The Federalist*. In that paper, James Madison categorized the various enumerated powers according to their common purposes. For example, he began with the "[s]ecurity against foreign danger" and addressed the powers of war and raising fleets and armies.[24] He ended the essay with a discussion of the first grant of power. Here, Madison responded to the more exaggerated Anti-Federalist attack that had asserted that this power "amounts to an unlimited commission to exercise every power which may be alleged to be necessary for the common defense or general welfare."[25]

Madison called this interpretation a "misconstruction," and the language of the clause "so awkward a form of describing authority to legislate in all possible cases."[26] Madison explained that the plain language of the clause conveyed the power "to raise money for the general welfare."[27] In other words, some Anti-Federalists specifically alleged that this grant might give Congress a general legislative power to regulate for the common defense or general welfare, and, if so, few objects would escape the reach of national power. Madison made the sensible observation that the language naturally read as a power to tax for the purpose of raising money for national objects. The purposes for which those taxes can be laid, Madison added, were to effectuate the regulatory powers granted by the rest of the eighth section. "[A] specification of the objects alluded to by these general terms" in the first clause "immediately follows" in the rest of the enumeration.[28] Those regulatory powers all involved the common defense and general welfare – those subjects requiring national, as opposed to local, action.

Madison reiterated this position as President in his veto of an internal improvements bill in 1817. The proponents of appropriating money for internal improvements such as roads and canals argued that Congress could appropriate for "the general welfare" beyond any specific enumerated power. Madison responded by stating that such a reading would "render[] the special and careful enumeration of powers which follow the clause nugatory and improper."[29] Madison, to be sure, exaggerated; there is a difference between merely spending for the general welfare and a coercive power to regulate for the general welfare. The point remains, however, that Madison maintained throughout his life that the first grant was merely a taxing power.

Thomas Jefferson, in his opinion on the constitutionality of the Bank of the United States, similarly wrote the following about the clause:

> To lay taxes to provide for the general welfare of the United States, that is to say, "to lay taxes for *the purpose* of providing for the general welfare." For the laying of taxes is the *power* and the general welfare the *purpose* for which the power is to be exercised. They are not to lay taxes *ad libitum for any purpose they please*; but only *to pay the debts or provide for the welfare of the Union*. In like manner, they are not *to do anything they please* to provide for the general welfare, but only *to lay taxes* for that purpose. To consider the latter phrase, not as describing the purpose of the first, but as giving a distinct and independent power to do any act they please, which might be for the good of the Union, would render all the preceding and subsequent enumerations of power completely useless.[30]

St. George Tucker, in his 1803 commentaries on the Constitution, also said that the phrase "to pay for..." was "[t]he principle upon which the right of taxation is founded."[31] Roger Sherman argued during ratification that "[t]he objects of expenditure will be the same under the new constitution, as under the old."[32] Edmund Randolph, in response to Patrick Henry at the Virginia ratifying convention, specifically rejected the proposition that the subordinate clause was "an independent, separate, substantive power, to provide for the general welfare of the United States," but was rather "a power to lay and collect taxes, &c., *in order to* provide for the general welfare and pay the debts," an explicit endorsement of the one-power reading.[33]

Many Federalists made the exact same point. Oliver Ellsworth, in the Connecticut ratification convention, described the whole clause as dealing with the "power to lay taxes."[34] James Wilson breezily addressed this grant in his Lectures on Law after having discussed Congress's other powers. "For the exercise of the foregoing powers, and for the accomplishment of the foregoing purposes, a revenue is unquestionably indispensable. That congress may be enabled to exercise and accomplish them, it has power to lay and collect taxes, duties, imposts, and excises."[35] Here, Wilson made no mention of a power to regulate for the general welfare, nor even a power to spend for the general welfare beyond the enumeration. The first clause of the eighth section of Article I, he wrote, was merely a power to tax to raise money for national purposes; that money could then be spent in pursuance of the enumeration. And it will be recalled that Chief Justice Marshall explained that "Congress is not empowered to tax for those purposes which are within the exclusive province of the States,"[36] which implies the general welfare proviso limits the taxing power.

Alexander Hamilton was the most prominent thinker to advocate explicitly for an independent spending power. In his Report on Manufactures, Hamilton, to justify the right of Congress to provide financial support to domestic industry, dissected the clause in question and concluded, "It is therefore of necessity left to the discretion of the National Legislature, to pronounce, upon the objects, which concern the general Welfare, and for which under that description, an appropriation of money is requisite and proper."[37] The only "qualification" to this power was that "the object to which an appropriation of money is to be made be *General* and not *local*; its operation extending in fact, or by possibility, throughout the Union, and not being confined to a particular spot."[38]

Even Hamilton, it should be noted, thought that the clause was at most two powers. Almost no one seems to have thought the clause included a power to regulate for the general welfare, contrary to modern revisionist attempts to construct such an interpretation.[39]

18.5 HISTORICAL PRACTICE

Thus far, the evidence overwhelmingly favors a reading of the first clause of the eighth section as a power to tax for national purposes and nothing more. The record of historical practice post-Ratification is more equivocal. The power to spend money proved very tempting to members of Congress. Congress, for the first several years, found ways to spend money without confirming the existence of a power to spend for the general welfare, or used instead the taxing power to accomplish its objectives.

For example, in 1791, Congress wanted to give fishing vessels a "bounty" for the amount of codfish they caught, partly to offset the heavy duties against American codfish in other countries. Merely sending money to codfish fisheries would not be permissible without a power to spend for the general welfare; though to be sure, even with such a power it may have been less than clear that such spending was for the general, as opposed to local, welfare. After a debate about the constitutionality of the bounties, Congress instead created a subsidy or "allowance" for the reimbursement of sums paid on salt tariffs.[40] Thus, Congress early on learned to rely on its taxing power to benefit domestic industry.

In another example, Congress, in 1794, sought to give aid to French refugees from Saint Domingo, which was experiencing the fervor of the nascent French Revolution. There would be no justification for such foreign aid without a power to spend for the general welfare, and even then, one might question whether such spending was for the general welfare of Americans. Madison found a clever way around the problem. The United States owed money to France for assistance during the Revolutionary War; the money to refugees could be made in partial payment of this obligation.[41] A month later, Congress again used the tax code and, as David Currie explained, "forgave the tonnage duties assessed on the ship that had brought the refugees to this country."[42]

One of the most significant debates over the matter occurred in 1796 when much of Savannah, Georgia, was burned down by fire. The House of Representatives debated the constitutionality and propriety of sending federal dollars to the aid of Savannah and ultimately rejected appropriating the money. There were competing views, ranging from the position that Congress had already exercised a power to spend for the general welfare on other occasions, to the position that Congress had no such power, and including the intermediate position that even if Congress had the power it would not be for the general (as opposed to local) welfare to act as fire insurers to the people of Savannah.[43] In future disasters, Congress again resorted to the tax code. When fires burned through Norfolk and Portsmouth in the first decade of the following century, Congress extended by a year the time for discharging customs obligations.[44]

The most prominent and early example that may support an independent spending power was the assumption of state debts. The story is well known: In exchange for supporting Congress's assumption of the states' revolutionary war debts, Virginia, which had paid off most of its debt, would get the nation's new capital city.[45] Yet, Congress's power to assume state debts was unclear. Congress has the power to borrow money and therefore to repay the debts of the United States, but not the debts of the individual states. No other power seems relevant; the assumption could arguably be accomplished only if Congress could spend for the general welfare. Even here, supporters of assumption found a way around the problem: They argued that the state debts incurred during the war were in fact debts of the United States and certainly were incurred for the "common defense." The states had been the mere agents of the national government.[46]

Throughout the antebellum period, the debate over Congress's spending power centered on "internal improvements" such as roads, canals, and bridges entirely within individual states. It is necessary to recall that from early on Congress passed legislation for the removal of obstructions to navigation and to facilitate commerce more generally. "The practice of defraying out of the Treasury of the United States the expenses incurred by the establishment and support of light-houses, beacons, buoys, and public piers within the bays, inlets, harbors, and ports of the United States, to render the navigation thereof safe and easy," Jackson wrote in his second annual message to Congress, "is coeval with the adoption of the Constitution, and has been continued without interruption or dispute."[47]

Such appropriations would certainly be for the general welfare, but it is also possible to conceive of them as necessary and proper to make Congress's regulations of commerce effective. Although not the most natural reading of the power to "regulate commerce," if Congress can encourage navigation through regulations, then it can make such regulations more effective through the expenditure of funds.[48] Alternatively, Congress has the power to exercise exclusive legislation over land purchased with the consent of the states "for the Erection of Forts, Magazines, Arsenals, dock-Yards, and other needful Buildings,"[49] which could easily be read to include or at least imply a more general power to erect needful "buildings" such as lighthouses.

The question thus arises whether internal improvements such as roads, canals, and bridges are different in kind from lighthouses, piers, and buoys. James Madison's 1817 veto rejected any congressional power over such improvements, arguing they could only be justified under a power to spend for the general welfare, the existence of which Madison denied. At least certain internal improvements, however, could be justified under the Necessary and Proper Clause. Perhaps Congress can appropriate for the creation of a post road, or a road or canal convenient for military purposes.[50] That is how Madison justified appropriations for the Cumberland Road,[51] and the House of Representatives generally agreed in 1818 that it had the power to appropriate at least for such purposes.[52]

Chancellor Kent's commentaries, first published in 1826, argued that such improvements had been justified "under the power to establish post offices and post roads, and to raise moneys to provide for the general welfare."[53] This passage may suggest independent powers to raise money on the one hand and to provide for the general welfare through spending on the other. It is more natural, however, to interpret Kent as maintaining that Congress can raise funds through taxation, so long as the raising of funds is for the general welfare; the appropriation of such funds in pursuance of an enumerated power such as the postal power would of course satisfy the general welfare requirement. Thus, Kent added that Congress had also claimed "the power to open, construct, and improve military roads" and to "cut canals ... for promoting and securing internal commerce, and for the more safe and economical transportation of military stores in time of war."[54]

President Monroe eventually and nevertheless approved an internal improvements bill under a power to spend for the general welfare,[55] and Andrew Jackson would finally distinguish lighthouses and the like from internal improvements on the ground that the former were general in character but the latter local.[56] Although some Presidents, such as Tyler and Polk, tried again to deny the existence of a power over internal improvements, the matter died, at least in Congress, when Congress overrode five presidential vetoes of improvement bills in 1856.[57]

Joseph Story included several extensive discussions relevant to this debate in his 1833 commentaries. Those discussions are not entirely consistent. First, addressing the grammatical structure of the first grant of power in the eighth section of Article I, he rejected the view that the clause granted a power to regulate for the general welfare. If it were otherwise, he wrote, "then it is obvious, that under colour of the generality of the words to 'provide for the common defence and general welfare,' the government of the United States is, in reality, a government of general and unlimited powers, notwithstanding the subsequent enumeration of specific powers."[58] Story wrote that the alternative reading is that "the power of taxation only is given by the clause, and it is limited to objects of a national character, 'for the common defence and the general welfare.'"[59] Story admonished those holding the former view as having "minds of great ingenuity, and liberality of views." Fortunately, he said, the latter view "has been the generally received sense of the nation, and seems supported by reasoning at once solid and impregnable."[60] This was the majority view among both political parties at the Founding.[61] Story's commentaries are therefore powerful evidence that the taxing-only view was conventional.

In subsequent parts of his treatise, however, Story seemed to throw in his lot with Hamilton and Monroe. "Appropriations have never been limited by congress to cases falling within the specific powers enumerated in the constitution, whether those powers be construed in their broad, or their narrow sense," he wrote, and in particular "appropriations have been made to aid internal improvements of various sorts, in our roads, our navigation, our streams, and other objects of a national character and importance."[62] Story did not pause to consider whether his earlier discussion of the taxing power contradicted his assertion that Congress could make appropriations for the general welfare. In 1936, the U.S. Supreme Court finally agreed that Congress could spend not only in pursuance of the enumerated powers but also for the general welfare, relying largely on the authority of Story and Hamilton.[63]

Although the history of internal improvements provides some support for an independent power to spend for the general welfare, the better view seems to be that the erection of and spending on such improvements was incidental to several of Congress's enumerated powers. Aside from Hamilton, and subsequently Monroe and Story, that is how most members of Congress, presidents, and writers appear to have thought about the matter. An independent power to spend for the general welfare may well be within the range of plausible original meanings; but it is not the best reading of the clause. This should always be kept in view because Congress has greatly expanded, and one might say abused, its spending power in recent decades. Even if the courts and the people are prepared to accept an independent power to spend for the general welfare, that power should be carefully cabined better to comport with the original meaning of the Constitution.

18.6 TAXES, NOT PENALTIES

The modern doctrine surrounding taxing and spending is now to be considered. Beginning with the taxing power, the question is whether Congress may use that power indirectly to achieve regulatory objectives beyond the enumerated powers. The answer may depend on whether the first clause in the eighth section of Article I is only a grant of a taxing power, or also a grant of an independent spending power. Under the latter view, if the general welfare proviso does not modify the taxing power, that power is unlimited as to purpose.

Under the former view, Congress's taxing power would be limited to raising revenue for purposes of general welfare. That is not to say that taxes can never have a local, regulatory impact. Some of the earliest taxes were excise taxes, such as the tax on whiskey that led to the Whiskey Rebellion. These taxes to a certain degree have a regulatory purpose; Congress makes a conscious choice to tax whiskey rather than milk. By taxing whiskey, Congress not only raises revenue, which is its key motivation, but also discourages an activity it considers to be less desirable. Some line must therefore be drawn between permissible uses of the taxing power that happen to affect matters within a state's police powers, and those impermissible uses of the taxing power.

The solution is parallel to the solution in the context of the commerce power. So long as Congress's true object is to raise revenue, it is acceptable for Congress's tax to have an incidental regulatory purpose. Such incidental effects cannot be avoided. If Congress has the power to tax, it presumably must tax some article or object – and that article or object, whatever it is, will be discouraged because its price will increase. Because such effects are unavoidable, Congress stays within its proper bounds so long as such effects are truly incidental and Congress's primary objective is the raising of revenue.

By this reasoning, Congress can, and routinely did, impose tariffs on foreign goods for the purpose of promoting domestic manufactures – a matter within the cognizance of the states – because if it had to raise revenue it may as well also encourage domestic industries.[64] The southern constitutional opposition to tariffs during the nullification crisis of the 1820s and 1830s was that Congress sought to regulate beyond the enumerated powers, and that the tariffs promoted the regional, northern welfare rather the general welfare.[65] (Such tariffs may be separately justified, however, by Congress's power to regulate commerce with foreign nations, and early Congresses seem to have relied on this power in addition to the taxing power to impose tariffs.[66])

It was not until the progressive and New Deal eras that Congress began to use the taxing power more aggressively and the courts were confronted with serious attempts to circumvent the enumeration of powers. After the Supreme Court invalidated Congress's attempt under the Commerce Clause to prohibit child labor in *Hammer v. Dagenhart*, Congress made the same attempt under its taxing power. In *Bailey v. Drexel Furniture Co.* (1922),[67] the Court addressed congressional legislation imposing a 10 percent tax on all profits of any firm that employed child labor.

The Court began by explaining that it had often upheld taxes, even very prohibitive ones, out of solicitude for Congress. For example, the Court had previously upheld a tax on oleomargarine that was almost certainly enacted for the benefit of butter producers, the chief competitors to margarine producers, which suggests that Congress had had an impermissible regulatory motive.[68] But the Court could not extend such solicitude in *Bailey*:

> [I]n the act before us the presumption of validity cannot prevail, because the proof of the contrary is found on the very face of its provisions. Grant the validity of this law, and all that Congress would need to do, hereafter, in seeking to take over to its control any one of the great number of subjects of public interest, jurisdiction of which the states have never parted with, and which are reserved to them by the Tenth Amendment, would be to enact a detailed measure of complete regulation of the subject and enforce it by a so called tax upon departures from it. To give such magic to the word "tax" would be to break down all constitutional limitation of the powers of Congress and completely wipe out the sovereignty of the states.[69]

Here, as in the commerce context, the Court was properly concerned with maintaining limits on Congress's enumerated powers. The Court's language suggests that merely because Congress denominates an exaction a "tax" does not make that exaction a tax. It may have the form of a tax but in substance it is something quite different: It is a penalty for failing to abide by Congress's preferred regulations. The Court explained:

> Taxes are occasionally imposed in the discretion of the Legislature on proper subjects with the primary motive of obtaining revenue from them and with the incidental motive of discouraging them by making their continuance onerous. They do not lose their character as taxes because of the incidental motive. But there comes a time in the extension of the penalizing features of the so-called tax when it loses its character as such and becomes a mere penalty, with the characteristics of regulation and punishment. Such is the case in the law before us. Although Congress does not invalidate the contract of employment or expressly declare that the employment within the mentioned ages is illegal, it does exhibit its intent practically to achieve the latter result by adopting the criteria of wrongdoing and imposing its principal consequence on those who transgress its standard.[70]

The Court in *Bailey* nicely summarized the difference between constitutional and unconstitutional exercises of the taxing power, and it parallels the difference in the context of the commerce power. If the "primary motive" is to raise revenue and the regulatory effects are only "incidental," then the tax is constitutional. And

Congress can even have a regulatory objective, as when it taxes oleomargarine, so long as its tax is really a tax – just as Congress can have a regulatory objective when closing the channels of interstate commerce. But there comes a point at which the "so-called tax" really becomes a "penalty, with the characteristics of regulation and punishment."

Put differently, the tax in *Bailey* could hardly be expected to raise any revenue whatsoever. No sensible firm would accept a 10 percent tax on all of its profits; it would naturally seek to comply with the regulatory objective and avoid the tax altogether. That means the tax was not in fact a tax. Its objective was not to raise revenue at all, but rather to compel regulatory compliance. Congress therefore did not truly exercise its taxing power, but rather exercised a regulatory power in the guise of a tax. If the objective is outside of the enumeration, it would be an impermissible regulation.

The difficulty, of course, is determining the line between a tax imposed with a regulatory objective and a tax that is really not a tax at all, but rather a regulatory penalty. A comparison to *Steward Machine Co. v. Davis* (1937)[71] may prove instructive. The Court upheld provisions of the 1935 Social Security Act that imposed a payroll tax on employers. The Act provided that employers could avoid the tax almost entirely – they would receive up to a 90 percent credit – for contributions to a state unemployment fund that met federally prescribed standards. The tax clearly had a regulatory purpose: It was intended to encourage the states to create their own unemployment compensation systems. The Court, however, upheld the tax on the ground that its regulatory purpose was merely incidental. "Even if [the tax] were collected in the hope or expectation that some other and collateral good would be furthered as an incident, that without more would not make the act invalid."[72] So long as the tax and credit were not "weapons of coercion, destroying or impairing the autonomy of the states," the law was constitutional.[73] The state had not offered "a suggestion that in passing the unemployment law she was affected by duress."[74]

The tax was constitutional because it was truly a tax and therefore a proper exercise of Congress's taxing power. Unlike in the child labor tax case, the states and regulated parties had a legitimate choice. Congress sought to raise revenues and incidentally hoped to encourage states to create unemployment compensation systems. So long as the states or parties in question had a genuine choice in the matter, Congress's legislation was not a coercive regulation outside the scope of the enumerated powers. So long as Congress truly imposed a tax and not a penalty, Congress could have the motive of affecting the police powers of the states, just as Congress can close the channels of interstate commerce with that same motive.

Three-quarters of a century later, in 2012, the Supreme Court upheld as constitutional the Patient Protection and Affordable Care Act (ACA). The Act required individuals through an "individual mandate" to purchase health insurance or else pay a "penalty" to be collected by the Internal Revenue Service (IRS). In *NFIB v. Sebelius*,[75] the Court first held that Congress could not enact the individual mandate under the Commerce Clause. Congress's commerce power does not extend to compelling individuals to engage in commerce or to purchase a particular product. And such a power was too great and important to be left to implication under the Necessary and Proper Clause.[76]

Although the Court would not sustain the ACA under Congress's commerce power, it upheld that Act on the ground that the penalty for refusing to purchase insurance was, for constitutional purposes, a tax. The Court relied on *Bailey* and held that three non-exhaustive factors contribute to whether a financial exaction is a tax or penalty for constitutional purposes: the burden imposed by the exaction; whether the statute itself is punitive and has a scienter (mens rea) requirement for a violation; and whether the statute and exaction are enforced by the IRS or a different regulatory agency. A fourth factor is the extent to which the exaction can be expected to raise revenue. In *Bailey* the child-labor tax created a high burden, a violation required criminal intent, and the statute was enforced by the Department of Labor, all indicating that the so-called tax was in fact a penalty. In the ACA context, four million Americans were expected to pay the exaction, the statute was not criminal in nature, and the money was to be collected by the revenue service; the Court held that the so-called penalty was in reality a tax for purposes of the Constitution.[77]

In short, the modern doctrine has given Congress significant leeway to achieve indirectly through taxation regulatory objectives that it could not achieve directly through its other enumerated powers. But Congress must genuinely be exercising the taxing power, not a coercive regulation enforced by a penalty.

18.7 SPENDING, NOT REGULATION

Ninety years ago, the Supreme Court weighed in on the side of Hamilton, Story, and Monroe, and agreed that Congress had a freestanding power to spend for the general welfare. The requirement that such spending be for the general welfare is difficult to enforce, but there are serious questions as to whether that requirement has been violated in recent decades. The Obama Administration, for example, spent more discretionary spending delegated to it by Congress in competitive or "swing" states, and politically allied states, than in politically opposed states.[78] Swing states received more federal discretionary grant monies under the prior Bush and Clinton administrations, too.[79]

The Court in *Helvering v. Davis* (1937) held that whether spending was in the general as opposed to local welfare was a matter best left to the discretion of Congress "unless the choice is clearly wrong."[80] It is also difficult to imagine who would have standing to bring suit in the typical case involving federal grant monies. It is therefore generally up to the political branches to ensure that their spending programs comply with this constitutional requirement.

In this regard, President Jackson, in opposing various local internal improvement projects in 1830, remarked that "[t]he expenditures heretofore made for internal improvements ... have been distributed in very unequal proportions amongst the States," and that it is the duty of federal officials to make "the beneficial operation of the Federal Government as equal and equitable among the several States" as can be done consistently with its great ends.[81] He proposed "the adoption of some plan for the distribution of the surplus funds, which may at any time remain in the Treasury after the national debt shall have been paid, among the States, in proportion to the number of their Representatives, to be applied by them to objects of internal improvement."[82]

Another important and perhaps more judicially pressing matter is whether Congress, as with its interstate commerce and taxing powers, may seek to accomplish indirectly with its spending power what it cannot accomplish directly by regulation. The answer is once again parallel to that given in the commerce and taxing contexts.

In *United States v. Butler* (1936),[83] the Supreme Court held that "the power of Congress to authorize expenditure of public moneys for public purposes is not limited by the direct grants of legislative power found in the Constitution."[84] The Court, in other words, adopted the two-powers interpretation of the first grant in the eighth section of Article I. It is often thought that the Court then contradicted itself by saying that Congress nevertheless could not "indirectly accomplish" ends not authorized by the enumeration of powers "by taxing and spending to purchase compliance."[85]

The Court's holding, however, makes sense if the distinction between spending and regulation is to be maintained. Just as Congress might tax for a purpose beyond the enumerated powers, any exaction must still be a tax rather than a penalty. Similarly, even if Congress can *spend* beyond its enumerated powers, Congress must genuinely be exercising its spending power rather than imposing a regulation under the guise of spending.

Butler involved the Agricultural Adjustment Act of 1933, by which Congress sought to control agricultural production and output. At the time, such matters were beyond Congress's direct regulatory reach under the interstate commerce power. The Act sought a workaround in part by appropriating money to pay farmers for entering into contracts with the federal government in which they agreed to reduce their acreage or production.

It has been conceded that Congress can have a regulatory objective when it closes the channels of interstate commerce, or when it imposes taxes, and it can have regulatory objectives when it exercises the spending power. The Court in *Butler* acknowledged that Congress may "stat[e] the conditions upon which moneys shall be expended."[86] The difference in *Butler* was that the Agricultural Adjustment Act did not genuinely involve the spending power. Unlike social security payments or disaster relief, in no sense does the decision to produce less on the farm require the expenditure of funds. If Congress could have compelled production quotas directly, it would have done so, and without spending a single dollar. In contrast, Congress cannot accomplish the objectives of disaster relief or an old-age pension system without the expenditure of funds. The latter are exercises of the power held to be granted to Congress – the power to spend for the general welfare – whereas the Agricultural Adjustment Act was truly in the nature of a regulation the compliance with which Congress sought to purchase.

The act, in other words, did not merely specify "conditions" on which federal moneys shall be spent; rather, it was "a scheme for purchasing with federal funds submission to federal regulation of a subject reserved to the states."[87] To draw the analogy again to taxation, if Congress had sought to accomplish this objective with its taxing power, its exaction would have been considered an impermissible penalty rather than a tax.

More commonly, Congress achieves its objectives through conditional grants to the states. The same analysis can provide a framework for considering such grants. The leading case is *South Dakota v. Dole* (1987), but the Supreme Court muddled the analysis and incorrectly upheld the statute.[88] *Dole* involved congressional inducement to raise the drinking age. By 1984, every state but South Dakota had raised the minimum drinking age to twenty-one as part of their own, voluntary legislative processes. South Dakota permitted anyone as young as nineteen to purchase beer containing up to 3.2 percent alcohol. This was not good enough for Congress, which passed a law directing the Secretary of Transportation to withhold 5 percent of federal highway funds that would otherwise go to any state whose minimum drinking age was under twenty-one.

The Court explicitly found "this legislative effort within constitutional bounds even if Congress may not regulate drinking ages directly."[89] It explained that "objectives not thought to be within Article I's enumerated legislative fields may nevertheless be attained through the use of the spending power and the conditional grant of federal funds."[90] That is certainly correct as a general matter if Congress may spend beyond the enumeration for the general welfare, so long as that is the power Congress is in fact exercising. The question is whether the condition in *Dole* was in fact an exercise of the spending power.

The Court upheld the condition after analyzing a few factors, of which the most relevant to the present inquiry are that the condition must be sufficiently related or "germane" to the purpose of the spending program, and the amount of money to be withheld cannot be so great as to be "coercive."[91] It is these two factors that help determine whether Congress has in fact exercised its power to spend for the general welfare, or rather is seeking to purchase compliance with a federal regulatory scheme through federal dollars. One is the power granted to Congress, the other is a regulatory power beyond Congress's reach.

The central factor for present purposes is germaneness.[92] If a condition is so unrelated to the purpose of the spending program, then that is an indication that Congress is not exercising its spending power but is rather attempting to regulate. Justice O'Connor, in dissent in *Dole*, explained that the drinking age condition had nothing whatsoever to do with how the highway funds were to be spent. It was therefore unrelated altogether to the spending program. It was nothing but purchasing regulatory compliance with federal dollars. Congress could specify that its monies had to be spent on a certain kind of highway, but requiring the states to undergo regulatory changes was impermissible.

The majority, however, concluded that Congress's condition was germane because the drinking age also affected highway safety. Justice O'Connor quite rightly challenged this reasoning because many things might affect highway safety that are nevertheless completely unrelated to the spending of money.

There is another, simpler way to look at the matter, and it was suggested earlier in the discussion of *Butler*. If Congress could have ordered South Dakota to raise the drinking age directly, it would have done so, and without expending a single dollar. Therefore, that it induced the state to do so with federal dollars is not a genuine exercise of the spending power. The result in question can be achieved entirely without the receipt or payment of money at all, if only the regulatory power were available. Again, that contrasts with spending programs that truly require the expenditure of funds: disaster relief, social security, or even purchasing textbooks that meet certain curricular requirements. It is instead like the statute in *Butler*, in which Congress would have compelled production reductions directly without the expenditure of any funds if only it had the enumerated power to do so.

There is a real difference, in other words, between a law that offers money for textbooks that meet certain curricular requirements and one that offers money on the condition that the state adopt a particular curriculum. The latter does not require spending at all. Congress, if only it had the power, could simply impose a national curriculum directly without the expenditure of a single dollar. The former, in contrast, does require spending. And perhaps therein lies the real distinction between constitutional exercises of the power to spend for the general welfare and impermissible attempts to invade the prerogatives of the states.

It is worth recalling that the first grant of power in the eighth section of the Constitution's first article was almost certainly only the power to raise taxes for national purposes. Under the best reading of this clause, in relation to the remainder of the Constitution, Congress can spend only in pursuance of its enumerated powers. Although it is possible to interpret the clause as including a power to spend for the general welfare, such a reading not only contradicts the best reading of the text but also gives Congress a consequential power through which it can undermine the original division between federal and state power. The courts should therefore seek ways to cabin that power and to distinguish between genuine spending legislation and impermissible attempts at regulation beyond the scope of the enumerated powers.

The test here proposed may not be easy to apply in all cases, but it has the advantage of supporting clear exercises of the spending power such as the establishment of welfare programs and disaster relief while invalidating similarly clear attempts at national regulatory control. It would go a long way to sustaining the original division of federal and state power, a division that has played an important role in the success of the American Constitution over the previous 237 years.

Notes

CHAPTER 1

1 1 William Blackstone, Commentaries on the Laws of England 90 (Oxford: Clarendon Press 1765). Blackstone thus argued that one parliament could not bind a future parliament.

2 *Id.* at 156.

3 *See* Adam Tomkins, Public Law 7 (Oxford University Press 2003).

4 On the first point, *see generally* H. L. A. Hart, The Concept of Law (Oxford University Press, 3d ed. 2012). On the second, Viscount Bolingbroke wrote of the British Constitution in the early eighteenth century, "By constitution we mean, whenever we speak with propriety and exactness, that assemblage of laws, institutions and customs, derived from certain fixed principles of reason, directed to certain fixed objects of public good, that compose the general system, according to which the community hath agreed to be governed." 2 The Works of Lord Bolingbroke 88 (Philadelphia, PA: Carey & Hart 1841).

5 Prior to the eighteenth century, it was more common to think of the constitution as unwritten in the sense that some of the fundamental rules derived from immemorial custom. Parliament could then assert its prerogatives against the king by invoking this custom. But when Parliament abused its prerogative, the fundamental law itself, reflected in custom, could be invoked. *See* J. G. A. Pocock, The Ancient Constitution and the Feudal Law: A Study of English Historical Thought in the Seventeenth Century 32, 37, 46–52 (Reissue, Cambridge University Press 1987). As Pocock wrote, "One of the underlying themes in the history of seventeenth-century political thought is the trend from the claim that there is a fundamental law, with parliament as its guardian, to the claim that parliament is sovereign." The "Restoration and the Revolution of 1688 could" then "be represented as efforts to restore the fundamental law" rather than to establish Parliamentary sovereignty. *Id.* at 49–50. Importantly, these customs, too, would often be reduced to writing in the course of judicial decisions and in treatises, or in political documents such as the Petition of Right of 1628.

6 1 Blackstone, *supra* note 1, at 157. For his description of the institutional arrangements, *see id.* at 50–51:

[T]he British constitution has long remained, and I trust will long continue, a standing exception to the truth of this [previous] observation. For, as with us the executive power of the laws is lodged in a single person, they have all the advantages of strength and dispatch, that are to be found in the most absolute monarchy; and, as the legislature of the kingdom is entrusted to three distinct powers, entirely independent of each other; first, the king; secondly, the lords spiritual and temporal, which is an aristocratical assembly of persons.

7 "Through most of the seventeenth and eighteenth centuries," the historian Mary Sarah Bilder has summarized, the term constitution "did not refer to a specific document or even a specific, known set of laws," but rather to "that which is constituted," or "an almost anthropomorphic, organic body politic, with its history, geography, social and cultural composition, and well-being," or "to more specific laws, principles, customs, and institutions" but not to any discrete document. Mary Sarah Bilder, The Transatlantic Constitution: Colonial Legal Culture and the Empire 2 (Cambridge, MA: Harvard University Press 2004). It should be noted, however, that the American colonists did have more experience with written charters than did the English as written documents established many of their colonial governments, for example, the Fundamental Orders of Connecticut. *See* Aaron N. Coleman, The American Revolution, State Sovereignty, and the American Constitutional Settlement, 1765–1800, at 20–21 (Lanham, MD: Lexington Books 2016).

8 Bernard Bailyn, The Ideological Origins of the American Revolution 175 (Cambridge, MA: Belknap Press, Enlarged ed. 1992); for the original, *see* Charles Inglis, *The True Interest of America Impartially Stated, in* Certain Strictures on a Pamphlet Intitled Common Sense 18 (Philadelphia, PA: James Humphrey, 2d ed. 1776). Inglis appears to have been quoting Bolingbroke. *See supra* note 4.

9 Bailyn, *supra* note 8, at 179.

10 *Id.* at 176.

11 *Id.* at 181.

12 For this thesis, *see generally* the four volumes of John Philip Reid, Constitutional History of the American Revolution (Madison: The University of Wisconsin Press 1986–1993).

13 Gordon S. Wood, The Creation of the American Republic, 1776–1787, at 281 (Chapel Hill: University of North Carolina Press 1998) (1969).

14 Thomas Tudor Tucker, Conciliatory hints … 22 (Charleston: Printed for A. Timothy 1784). Part of this passage is quoted in Wood, *supra* note 13, at 281.

15 Wood, *supra* note 13, at 260–61.

16 Thomas Paine, The Crisis. Number XI, at 83 (Philadelphia, PA: Printed by Benjamin Towne, 1775).

17 *Id.* at 84. Both passages are quoted in Wood, *supra* note 13, at 266.

18 5 U.S. (1 Cranch) 137 (1803).

19 Future Supreme Court Justice James Iredell, who had been at the Constitutional Convention, argued that if the constitution was a fundamental law "limiting the powers of the Legislature, and with which every exercise of those powers, must necessarily be compared," then judges must make this comparison as part of their ordinary judicial duties. The Constitution was not "a mere imaginary thing, … but a written document to which all may have recourse, and to which, therefore, the judges cannot wilfully blind themselves." Wood, *supra* note 13 at 461–62 (quoting James Iredell to Richard Spaight, Aug. 26, 1787, and "To the Public," Aug. 17, 1789, *in* 2 Griffith John McRee, Life and

Correspondence of James Iredell 169–70, 172–76, 148 (New York: D. Appleton & Company 1857)). Alexander Hamilton in Federalist No. 78 assumed the same. "Limitations" of a written constitution, he wrote, "can be preserved in practice no other way than through the medium of courts of justice, whose duty it must be to declare all acts contrary to the manifest tenor of the Constitution void." The Federalist No. 78, at 466 (Clinton Rossiter ed. 1961). David Currie wrote that every member of the early Congresses assumed that their acts could be judicially reviewed. David P. Currie, The Constitution in Congress: The Federalist Period, 1789–1801, at 120 (University of Chicago Press 1997).

In a 1795 case in which Supreme Court Justice William Paterson actually assessed the constitutionality of a Pennsylvania statute, he explained that in England "the authority of the Parliament runs without limits, and rises above control" and that it "is difficult to say what the constitution of England is; because, not being reduced to written certainty and precision, it lies entirely at the mercy of the Parliament . . ." The "general position" in England was "that the validity of an act of Parliament cannot be drawn into question by the judicial department: It cannot be disputed, and must be obeyed." Besides, Patterson wrote, "in England there is no written constitution, no fundamental law, nothing visible, nothing real, nothing certain, by which a statute can be tested. In America the case is widely different: Every State in the Union has its constitution reduced to written exactitude and precision." Van Horne's Lessee v. Dorrance, 2 U.S. (2 Dall.) 304, 308 (C.C.D. Pa. 1795).

20 It is important to recognize recent scholarly work questioning whether the written nature of the Constitution fundamentally affected the Founding generation's understanding of constitutionalism. In Jonathan Gienapp's Second Creation: Fixing the American Constitution in the Founding Era (Cambridge, MA: Harvard University Press 2018), the author argues that whether the Constitution's meaning would be fixed and whether it would be confined to its words were widely contested and contingent propositions. It was not until the 1790s that the conventional view that the Constitution was a fixed, written document took hold. It is true that the nature of constitutionalism remained uncertain and contested throughout the 1770s and much of the 1780s – written constitutions were novelties, as noted – but Gienapp gives little reason to think that this uncertainty persisted beyond 1787 or that there was any doubt that the Constitution itself would be interpreted as any other written legal instrument. Constitutionalism "meant balancing powers and interests," not "policing linguistic barriers," Gienapp argues, but it is of course the written text of the Constitution that creates the relevant balance. Gienapp also relies on numerous debates in the First Congress – several of which are discussed in this book – to assert that the nature of the written Constitution remained contested. Yet, in these debates over the removal power or the incorporation of a national bank – discussed here in Chapters 4 and 6, respectively – the various parties argued over the meaning of the Constitution, not over its very nature. Gienapp, in sum, has not sufficiently established that the conventional accounts of constitutionalism in this period must be revised.

21 David Strauss, The Living Constitution 100–01 (Oxford University Press 2010).

22 Mark A. Graber, A New Introduction to American Constitutionalism 44 (Oxford University Press 2013).

23 *Id.* at 45 (quoting Stephen Holmes, *Precommitment and the Paradox of Democracy, in* Jon Elster & Rune Slagstad eds., Constitutionalism and Democracy 237 (New York: Cambridge University Press 1988).

24 To be sure, as noted, many of its rules were reduced to writing; but one can easily imagine a constitutional system in which oral traditions establish the rules of the game and distribution of powers and answer those questions that need settling. *See, e.g.*, Stephen E. Sachs, *Originalism without Text*, 127 Yale L.J. 156, 159–60 (2017). These rules could come from the customary law discussed in *supra* note 5.

25 Randy E. Barnett, Restoring the Lost Constitution: The Presumption of Liberty 102 (Princeton University Press 2004); Lon L. Fuller, *Consideration and Form*, 41 Colum. L. Rev. 799 (1941); John D. Calamari & Joseph M. Perillo, Contracts (St. Paul, MN: West Publishing Co., 3d ed. 1987).

26 Barnett, *supra* note 27, at 103.

27 The Federalist No. 1, *supra* note 19, at 33.

28 This point is the author's. Barnett argues that a written constitution and its amendment procedure channels parties to that procedure if they seek to amend the constitution. Barnett, *supra* note 27, at 102.

29 *Id.*

30 *See, e.g.*, Barnett, *supra* note 27; Richard A. Epstein, The Classical Liberal Constitution (Cambridge, MA: Harvard University Press 2014).

31 John Hart Ely, in his famous book *Democracy and Distrust*, proposed that judges use judicial review in a "representation-reinforcing" manner. Judges should "[clear] the channels of political change on the one hand," he wrote, and "[correct] certain kinds of discrimination against minorities on the other," for that would be "entirely supportive" of "the underlying premises of the American system of representative democracy." John Hart Ely, Democracy and Distrust: A Theory of Judicial Review 88 (Cambridge, MA: Harvard University Press 1980).

32 This paragraph borrows and adapts from Ilan Wurman, A Debt against the Living: An Introduction to Originalism 68–69 (Cambridge University Press 2017).

33 Edmund Burke, Reflections on the Revolution in France 243 (London: Printed at the Revived Apollo Press by John Bell 1814).

34 The political scientist Martin Diamond made this point about the amendment process, but it seems to this author to apply to ordinary legislation as well, although on a smaller scale. *See* Martin Diamond, *Democracy and the Federalist: A Reconsideration of the Framers' Intent, in* William A. Schambra ed., As Far as Republican Principles Will Admit: Essay by Martin Diamond 24 (Washington, DC: The AEI Press 1992). Of course, this principle does also undergird the Constitution's amendment process: Altering the Constitution requires even more enduring and geographically distributed majorities, as evidenced through two-thirds approval in both Houses of Congress and ratification by three-quarters of the states. U.S. Const., art. V.

35 Sanford Levinson, Our Undemocratic Constitution 6–7 (Oxford University Press 2006); *see also* Wurman, *supra* note 32, at 57–58.

36 The next two paragraphs are taken from Wurman, *supra* note 32, at 70–71.

37 The Federalist No. 39, *supra* note 19, at 240.

38 4 Robert J. Taylor ed., Papers of John Adams, February–August 1776, at 87 (Cambridge, MA: Harvard University Press 1979).

39 Wood, *supra* note 13, at 47.

40 1 Max Farrand ed., The Records of the Federal Convention of 1787, at 48 (1911).

41 *Id.* at 49.

42 *Id.* at 51.

43 The Federalist No. 78, *supra* note 19, at 471.

44 The Federalist No. 55, *id.* at 346.

45 The Federalist No. 10, *id.* at 84.

46 The author has already done so in another book. *See* Ilan Wurman, A Debt against the Living: An Introduction to Originalism (New York: Cambridge University Press 2017).

47 Trop v. Dulles, 356 U.S. 86, 101 (1958).

CHAPTER 2

1 Margaret Talev, *Two Americas Index: 20% Favor a 'National Divorce,'* Axios (Mar. 16, 2023), https://www.axios.com/2023/03/16/two-americas-index-national-divorce.

2 Ronald Reagan, First Inaugural Address (Jan. 20, 1981), https://www.reaganlibrary.gov/archives/speech/inaugural-address-1981 ("All of us need to be reminded that the Federal Government did not create the States; the States created the Federal Government.").

3 The Federalist No. 9, at 72 (Clinton Rossiter ed. 1961).

4 The Federalist No. 47, *id.* at 301.

5 James Madison, for example, said in the Virginia ratifying convention that "Blackstone's Commentaries" was a "book which is in every man's hand." Debates of the Virginia Convention (June 18, 1788) (statement of James Madison), *in* John P. Kaminski & Gaspare J. Saladino eds., 10 The Documentary History of the Ratification of the Constitution 1371, 1382 (Madison: State Historical Society of Wisconsin 1993). As for Coke, John Adams called him "our judicial oracle." Paul Wilstach ed., Correspondence of John Adams and Thomas Jefferson, 1812–1826, at 131 (Indianapolis, IN: The Bobbs-Merrill Company 1925). Thomas Jefferson wrote to Madison at the end of his life about the influence of both. "You will recollect that before the revolution, Coke Littleton was the universal elementary book of law students, and a sounder Whig never wrote," but then "the honied Mansfieldism of Blackstone became the Student's Hornbook," and "from that moment, that profession (the nursery of our Congress) began to slide into toryism." Letter from Thomas Jefferson to James Madison (Feb. 17, 1826), *in* Joyce Appleby & Terence Ball eds., Thomas Jefferson: Political Writings 57, 58 (New York: Cambridge University Press 2004). In a census of lawbooks from colonial Virginia, of 263 copies of 87 identified law reports, "the most popular of reporters was Sir Edward Coke," of which "18 copies of his reports" were found. William Hamilton Bryson, Census of Law Books in Colonial Virginia, at xii (Charlottesville: University Press of Virginia 1978). The census is based "on printed sources plus two manuscripts," principally inventories of decedent's estates. *Id.* at x. Unfortunately, the probate records of Williamsburg, the colonial capital and seat of the General Court, were lost to fire. *Id.* Presumably there would have been many more copies of Coke's reports found there.

6 Thomas Jefferson required Locke's essays on civil government and Sidney's discourses as part of the curriculum for the University of Virginia, noting they "may be considered as those generally approved by our fellow citizens of this, and of the US. and that on the distinctive principles of the gov[ernment] of our own state, and of that of the US. as understood and assented to when brought into union." Thomas Jefferson, Principles

of government for Uva, Feb. 1825, https://rotunda.upress.virginia.edu/founders/default
.xqy?keys = FOEA-print-04-02-02-5007. *See also* Bernard Bailyn, The Ideological
Origins of the American Revolution 27–28 (Cambridge, MA: The Belknap Press,
Enlarged Edition 1992) (1967) (influence of Locke); *id.* at 34–35 (influence of
Sidney). Other thinkers were of course studied and familiar. Several prominent founders studied James Harrington, and more studied his ideas as elaborated by Bolingbroke
and others. Forrest McDonald, Novus Ordo Seclorum: The Intellectual Origins of the
Constitution 76n (Lawrence: University Press of Kansas 1985). *See id.* at ix, 60 for more
on Locke's influence.

7 Bailyn, *supra* note 6, at 27–30; McDonald, *supra* note 6, at 80–85, 233–35; *see also* Jack N.
Rakove, *Fidelity through History (or to It)*, 65 Fordham L. Rev. 1587, 1598 (1997) ("There is
no question that politically articulate eighteenth-century Americans – and certainly
members of the political elite – were eclectically conversant with the works of luminaries
like Hobbes, Locke, Montesquieu, Hume, and Blackstone.").

8 Aristotle, The Politics, Bk 3, Ch. 7, at 95–96 (Carnes Lord trans., The University of
Chicago Press 1984).

9 Montesquieu, The Spirits of the Laws 21, 124–26 (Anne M. Cohler, Basia C. Miller, &
Harold S. Stone eds., Cambridge University Press 1989).

10 *Id.* at 124.

11 *Id.* at 126.

12 *Id.* at 131 ("If a republic is small, it is destroyed by a foreign force; if it is large, it is destroyed
by an internal vice.").

13 *Id.*

14 *Id.*

15 Gordon S. Wood, The Creation of the American Republic, 1776–1787, at 354–56 (Chapel
Hill: University of North Carolina Press 1998) (1969). The revolutionary era Americans
would also have been familiar with Emerich de Vattel's the *Law of Nations*, which stated
that "several sovereign and independent states may unite themselves together by a perpetual confederacy without each in particular ceasing to be a perfect state." *Id.* at 355; *see also*
Emmerich de Vattel, The Law of Nations, bk. I, § 10, at 3 (London: Printed for G.G. and
J. Robinson 1797).

16 Art. of Confed. art. IX (1777).

17 That is not to deny that the "Union" as such came into existence simultaneously with the
several independent states. *See, e.g.*, Craig Green, *United/States: A Revolutionary History of
American Statehood*, 119 Mich. L. Rev. 1–4 (2020) (describing literature). It is to say, however,
that the nature of that union was a confederation of the type described by Montesquieu and
Vattel. Although believing that the states or the union came first, prior to the other, may be
rhetorically helpful, it is constitutionally irrelevant. Moreover, describing the Union as
"sovereign" prior to the Constitution would be contrary to the entire colonial experience
in which the various colonies episodically failed to create more consolidated unions. *See*
Aaron N. Coleman, The American Revolution, State Sovereignty, and the American
Constitutional Settlement, 1765–1800, at 22 (Lanham, MD: Lexington Books 2016).

18 "The power of raising armies by the most obvious construction of the articles of the
Confederation is merely a power of making requisitions upon the States for quotas of
men," Hamilton wrote subsequently in Federalist No. 22, a "practice in the course of the

late war" that "was found replete with obstructions to a vigorous and to an economical system of defense." Rossiter, *supra* note 3, at 145. "The system of quotas and requisitions, whether it be applied to men or money, is in every view a system of imbecility in the Union, and of inequality and injustice among the members." *Id.* at 146.

19 Keith L. Dougherty, Collective Action under the Articles of Confederation 44 (Cambridge University Press 2001).

20 This episode is discussed in Coleman, *supra* note 17, at 50–54. For the conditions related to the appointment, removal, and supervision of the collectors, *see* Wesley J. Campbell, *Commandeering and Constitutional Change*, 122 Yale L.J. 1104, 1124 (2013) (describing how New York's condition "render[ed] it inadmissible by Congress") (quoting Letter from Henry Lee, Jr. to George Washington (Apr. 21, 1786), *in* W. W. Abbott et al. eds., 4 The Papers of George Washington: Confederation Series 26 (Charlottesville: University Press of Virginia 1995)).

21 The government of Massachusetts had no problem, however, recruiting a volunteer army to crush the rebellion. The rebellion also led Americans more generally to remark on the potential failure of republican governments in the states and the vices of the people, which they connected with the need for a stronger central government. McDonald, *supra* note 6, at 177–79. Shays's Rebellion must also be considered along with numerous other taxpayer and debtor revolts that shut down courthouses in several other colonies. *See* Coleman, *supra* note 17, at 73 (describing such actions in Maryland, South Carolina, Pennsylvania, and Virginia).

22 Commercial disputes led to a call for a convention of delegates at Annapolis, which itself called for a more general convention the following year; that meeting became the Constitutional Convention. John Ferling, A Leap in the Dark: The Struggle to Create the American Republic 275–76 (Oxford University Press 2003).

23 Coleman, *supra* note 17, at 55–61.

24 James Madison, *Vices of the Political System of the United States, in* Robert A. Rutland & William M. E. Rachal eds., 9 The Papers of James Madison: Congressional Series 9 April 1786–24 May 1787, at 351–52 (University of Chicago Press 1975).

25 *Id.* at 352.

26 1 Max Farrand ed., The Records of the Federal Convention of 1787, at 26 (New Haven, CT: Yale University Press 1911).

27 *Id.* at 122.

28 *Id.* at 356.

29 2 Farrand, *supra* note 26, at 88.

30 *Id.* at 92.

31 *Id.* at 93.

32 The Federalist No. 39, *supra* note 3, at 243–44.

33 The Federalist No. 43, *id.* at 279–80.

34 *Id.* at 279.

35 The Federalist No. 40, *id.* at 252.

36 *Id.* at 253.

37 The Federalist No. 22, *id.* at 152 (paragraph breaks added).

38 2 Jonathan Elliot ed., The Debates in the Several State Conventions, on the Adoption of the Federal Constitution 470 (Washington, DC: Printed for the Editor, 2d ed. 1836).

39 The writer "Alfredus," for example, asserted that the state constitution of New Hampshire is a compact between individuals; the federal Constitution, however, "is not a compact between individuals, but between several sovereign and independent political societies already formed and organized." "Alfredus" [Samuel Tenny], Essay: I, *Freeman's Oracle,* Exeter (Jan. 18, 1788), *in* Colleen A. Sheehan & Gary L. McDowell eds., Friends of the Constitution: Writings of the "other" Federalists, 1787–1788, at 252 (Indianapolis, IN: Liberty Fund 1998).

40 That is the point the Anti-Federalists were making when they argued the Constitution created a "consolidated" government, as opposed to a confederated one. They pointed particularly to the preamble's "We the People." *See* Andrew Coan & David S. Schwartz, *The Original Meaning of Enumerated Powers,* 971 Iowa L. Rev. 1011 (2024) (collecting quotations).

41 Tench Coxe stated, for example, that "[t]he contracting parties in the federal compact are the people of the several states and the federal state governments." "An American Citizen" [Tench Coxe], Thoughts on the Subject of Amendments II, Pa. Gazette, Philadelphia (Dec. 10, 1788), *in* Friends, *supra* note 39, at 259. Madison also suggested this view in Federalist No. 39, discussed in a prior paragraph. The Federalist No. 39, *supra* note 3, at 243–44 (writing that "the Constitution is to be founded on the assent and ratification of the people of America, given by deputies elected for the special purpose," but it is also derived from "the assent and ratification of the several States"). *See also* the discussion of interposition later in this chapter. Alison LaCroix has demonstrated that prominent antebellum thinkers including Justice William Johnson and Attorney General William Wirt viewed the Constitution as a "tripartite" contract. *See, e.g.,* Alison L. LaCroix, The Interbellum Constitution: Union, Commerce, and Slavery in the Age of Federalisms 60 (New Haven, CT: Yale University Press 2024) ("To me, the Constitution appears, in every line of it, to be a contract, which, in legal language, may be denominated tripartite. The parties are the people, the states, and the United States.") (quoting Martin v. Hunter's Lessee, 14 U.S. 304, 373 (1816) (Johnson, J., concurring)).

42 The Federalist No. 23, *supra* note 3, at 154.

43 The Federalist No. 15, *id.* at 109.

44 *Id.* at 110.

45 The Federalist No. 39, *id.* at 244–45.

46 *Id.* at 245.

47 *Id.*

48 The Federalist No. 23, *id.* at 155.

49 The Federalist No. 39, *id.* at 246.

50 U.S. Const. art. V ("[N]o state, without its consent, shall be deprived of its equal suffrage in the Senate."). The second mechanism was altered by the Seventeenth Amendment. *Id.* amend. XVII ("The Senate of the United States shall be composed of two Senators from each State, elected by the people thereof, for six years."). For the original language, *see id.* art. I, § 3, cl. 1 ("The Senate of the United States shall be composed of two Senators from each State, chosen by the Legislature thereof, for six Years; and each Senator shall have one Vote.").

51 *Id.* art. VI, cl. 2:

This Constitution, and the Laws of the United States which shall be made in Pursuance thereof; and all Treaties made, or which shall be made, under the Authority of the

United States, shall be the supreme Law of the Land; and the Judges in every State shall be bound thereby, any Thing in the Constitution or Laws of any State to the Contrary notwithstanding.

For a general discussion of these important structural features preserving the influence of the states on the national lawmaking processes, and the importance of the Supremacy Clause in this regard, *see* Bradford R. Clark, *Separation of Powers as a Safeguard of Federalism*, 79 Tex. L. Rev. 1321 (2001); Bradford R. Clark, *Constitutional Compromise and the Supremacy Clause*, 83 Notre Dame L. Rev. 1421 (2008). For an earlier famous statement on these important structural safeguards, *see* Herbert Wechsler, *The Political Safeguards of Federalism: The Role of the States in the Composition and Selection of the National Government*, 54 Colum. L. Rev. 543 (1954).

52 The Federalist No. 10, *id.* at 83–84.

53 Letter from Thomas Jefferson to James Madison, Apr. 27, 1809, *in* 1 J. Jefferson Looney ed., The Papers of Thomas Jefferson, Retirement Series, 4 March 1809 to 15 November 1809, at 168–70 (Princeton University Press 2004).

54 For a recent study on the contested understanding of "federalism" in the period between 1815 and 1861, *see* LaCroix, The Interbellum Constitution, *supra* note 41.

55 *See* David Hacket Fischer, Historians' Fallacies: Toward a Logic of Historical Thought 135–40 (New York: Harper Perennial 1970).

56 For a summary of these events, from the tariffs of 1828 to the compromise that ended the nullification crisis in 1833, *see* David P. Currie, The Constitution in Congress, Democrats and Whigs, 1829–1861, at 89–117 (University of Chicago Press 2005).

57 For their full speeches, as well as those of other senators, *see* Herman Belz ed., The Webster-Hayne Debate on the Nature of the Union (Indianapolis, IN: Liberty Fund 2000).

58 *Id.* at 79.

59 *Id.* at 125–26.

60 *Id.* at 126, 136–37.

61 *Id.* at 137.

62 Proclamation by Andrew Jackson, President of the United States, Dec. 10, 1832, *in* 2 James D. Richardson ed., A Compilation of the Messages and Papers of the Presidents, 1789–1897, at 643 (Washington, DC: Gov't Printing Off. 1896) (emphasis deleted).

63 *Id.* at 648–49.

64 For what is perhaps the most recent reminder of why secession was incompatible with the nature of the Union from two scholars who are nevertheless highly partial to state sovereignty, *see* Anthony J. Bellia Jr. & Bradford R. Clark, *Constitutional Federalism and the Nature of the Union*, 66 Wm. & Mary L. Rev. 281, 346–54 (2024) (explaining why, notwithstanding the states' retaining much of their sovereignty, nullification and secession are unconstitutional).

65 The Federalist No. 22, *supra* note 3, at 152.

66 Akhil Reed Amar, The Words That Made Us: America's Constitutional Conversation, 1760–1840, at 260–61 (New York: Basic Books 2021). For an extended discussion on the difference between a confederation and a constitution, and the impermissibility of secession under the latter, *see also* Akhil Reed Amar, America's Constitution: A Biography 21–39 (New York: Random House 2005) (drawing on many originalist sources).

67 1 Joseph Story, Commentaries on the Constitution of the United States §§ 321–22, at 289–90 (Boston: Hilliard, Gray, and Co.; Cambridge, MA: Brown, Shattuck, and Co. 1833).

68 James Buchanan, *Fourth Annual Message to Congress (Dec. 3, 1860), in* 5 James D. Richardson ed., A Compilation of the Messages and Papers of the Presidents, 1789–1897, at 630–31 (Washington, DC: Published by Authority of Congress 1899).

69 U.S. Const. art. I, § 8 ("Congress shall have the Power . . . To provide for calling forth the Militia to execute the Laws of the Union, suppress Insurrections and repel Invasions").

70 *Id.* art. II, § 3 ("he shall take Care that the Laws be faithfully executed").

71 For a discussion of the constitutionality of secession and the power of the federal government to suppress it, *see* David P. Currie, The Constitution in Congress, Descent into the Maelstrom, 1829–1861, at 228–50 (University of Chicago Press 2005).

72 An Act respecting Alien Enemies, July 6, 1798, 1 Stat. 577; An Act concerning Aliens, June 25, 1798, 1 Stat. 570.

73 An act in addition to the act, entitled, "An Act for the punishment of certain crimes against the United States," July 14, 1798, 1 Stat. 596.

74 U.S. Const. amend. I ("Congress shall make no law . . . abridging the freedom of speech, or of the press.").

75 4 William Blackstone, Commentaries on the Laws of England 151 (Oxford: Clarendon Press 1769).

76 U.S. Const. art. I, § 8 ("Congress shall have the Power . . . to make all Laws which shall be necessary and proper for carrying into Execution . . . all other Powers vested by this Constitution in the Government of the United States, or in any Department or Officer thereof.").

77 Jefferson's draft, as well as the final resolutions, can be found in 8 Paul Leicester Ford ed., The Works of Thomas Jefferson 458–79 and insert (New York: G. P. Putnam's Sons The Knickerbocker Press 1904), and in Ethelbert Dudley Warfield, The Kentucky Resolutions of 1798: An Historical Study 75–85 (New York: G. P. Putnam's Sons The Knickerbocker Press 1887).

78 Virginia Resolutions, Dec. 21, 1798, *in* David B. Mattern, J. C. A. Stagg, Jeanne K. Cross, & Susan Holbrook Perdue eds., 17 The Papers of James Madison: Congressional Series, 31 March 1797–3 March 1801 and supplement 22 January 1778–9 August 1795, at 189 (Charlottesville: University Press of Virginia 1991).

79 *Id.*

80 The Federalist No. 39, *supra* note 3, at 243–44.

81 Warfield, *supra* note 77, at 76.

82 Michael Stokes Paulsen, Michael W. McConnell, Samuel L. Bray, & William Baude, The Constitution of the United States 860 (Saint Paul, MN: Foundation Press, 5th ed. 2023); Ford, *supra* note 77, at 471.

83 Belz, *supra* note 57, at 79.

84 Currie, *supra* note 56, at 96 n.41. Currie explained that Madison had initially sought to limit "interposition" to "extreme cases only," but by 1830 stated unequivocally that nullification was unconstitutional. Only in extreme cases did states have the "extra & ultra constitutional right" of self-preservation and revolution. For Madison's 1830 essay on

the subject, *see* James Madison to Edward Everett, Aug. 28, 1830, The James Madison Papers at the Library of Congress, https://www.loc.gov/resource/mjm.23_0288_0294/.

85 The Federalist No. 46, *supra* note 3, at 298.

86 State legislatures, Hamilton wrote, "will constantly have their attention awake to the conduct of the national rulers, and will be ready enough, if any thing improper appears, to sound the alarm to the people . . . ." The Federalist No. 26, *id.* at 172.

87 Virginia's Remonstrance against the Assumption of State Debts, Dec. 16, 1790, *in* Lance Banning ed., Liberty and Order: The First American Party Struggle 68–69 (Indianapolis, IN: Liberty Fund 2004).

88 The Kentucky Resolutions specifically resolved, for example,

> That the Governor of this Commonwealth be, and is hereby authorized and requested to communicate the preceding Resolutions to the Legislatures of the several States, . . . and that the Co-states recurring to their natural right in cases not made federal, will concur in declaring these acts void and of no force, and will each unite with this Commonwealth in requesting their repeal at the next session of Congress.

Warfield, *supra* note 77, at 82, 85.

89 The people have always participated in acts of constitutional interpretation or principles, including over the Alien and Sedition Acts. Other examples include the Boston Tea Party and other acts of popular defiance in defense of constitutional principles. Still another example discussed later in this book (in Chapter 9) is the jury's acquittal of Gideon Henfield in part because the jury may have believed that Congress under the Constitution had to define and punish offenses against the law of nations before a punishment could be imposed. *See generally* Larry D. Kramer, The People Themselves: Popular Constitutionalism and Judicial Review (New York: Oxford University Press 2004).

90 New York Times Co. v. Sullivan, 376 U.S. 254, 276 (1964) ("Although the Sedition Act was never tested in this Court, the attack upon its validity has carried the day in the court of history.").

CHAPTER 3

1 U.S. Const. art. I, § 1.

2 *Id.* § 8, cl. 1 ("The Congress shall have Power To lay and collect Taxes, Duties, Imposts and Excises, to pay the Debts and provide for the common Defence and general Welfare of the United States; but all Duties, Imposts and Excises shall be uniform throughout the United States.").

3 *Id.* cl. 2 ("To borrow Money on the credit of the United States.").

4 *Id.* cl. 3 ("To regulate Commerce with foreign Nations, and among the several States, and with the Indian Tribes.").

5 *Id.* cl. 4 ("To establish an uniform Rule of Naturalization, and uniform Laws on the subject of Bankruptcies throughout the United States.").

6 *Id.* cl. 5 ("To coin Money, regulate the Value thereof, and of foreign Coin, and fix the Standard of Weights and Measures."); *Id.* cl. 6 ("To provide for the Punishment of counterfeiting the Securities and current Coin of the United States.").

7 *Id.* cl. 7 ("To establish Post Offices and post Roads.").

8 *Id.* cl. 8 ("To promote the Progress of Science and useful Arts, by securing for limited Times to Authors and Inventors the exclusive Right to their respective Writings and Discoveries.").

9 *Id.* cl. 9 ("To constitute Tribunals inferior to the supreme Court.").

10 *Id.* cl. 10 ("To define and punish Piracies and Felonies committed on the high Seas, and Offences against the Law of Nations.").

11 *Id.* cl. 11 ("To declare War, grant Letters of Marque and Reprisal, and make Rules concerning Captures on Land and Water.").

12 *Id.* cl. 12 ("To raise and support Armies, but no Appropriation of Money to that Use shall be for a longer Term than two Years."); *id.* cl. 13 ("To provide and maintain a Navy.").

13 *Id.* cl. 14 ("To make Rules for the Government and Regulation of the land and naval Forces.").

14 *Id.* cl. 15 ("To provide for calling forth the Militia to execute the Laws of the Union, suppress Insurrections and repel Invasions.").

15 *Id.* cl. 16 ("To provide for organizing, arming, and disciplining, the Militia, and for governing such Part of them as may be employed in the Service of the United States, reserving to the States respectively, the Appointment of the Officers, and the Authority of training the Militia according to the discipline prescribed by Congress.").

16 *Id.* cl. 17:

To exercise exclusive Legislation in all Cases whatsoever, over such District (not exceeding ten Miles square) as may, by Cession of particular States, and the Acceptance of Congress, become the Seat of Government of the United States, and to exercise like Authority over all Places purchased by the Consent of the Legislature of the State in which the Same shall be, for the Erection of Forts, Magazines, Arsenals, dock-Yards, and other needful Buildings.

17 *Id.* cl. 18.

18 *Id.* art. IV, § 1 ("Full Faith and Credit shall be given in each State to the public Acts, Records, and judicial Proceedings of every other State. And the Congress may by general Laws prescribe the Manner in which such Acts, Records and Proceedings shall be proved, and the Effect thereof.").

19 *Id.* § 3, para. 1 ("New States may be admitted by the Congress into this Union; but no new State shall be formed or erected within the Jurisdiction of any other State; nor any State be formed by the Junction of two or more States, or Parts of States, without the Consent of the Legislatures of the States concerned as well as of the Congress."); *id.* para. 2 ("The Congress shall have Power to dispose of and make all needful Rules and Regulations respecting the Territory or other Property belonging to the United States; and nothing in this Constitution shall be so construed as to Prejudice any Claims of the United States, or of any particular State.").

20 *Id.* § 4 ("The United States shall guarantee to every State in this Union a Republican Form of Government, and shall protect each of them against Invasion; and on Application of the Legislature, or of the Executive (when the Legislature cannot be convened) against domestic Violence.").

21 Other articles also contain some congressional powers. For example, Article III authorizes Congress to regulate the appellate jurisdiction of the Supreme Court. U.S. Const. art. III, § 2, para. 2.

22 Daniel Webster, Speech of Daniel Webster in Reply to Mr. Hayne, of South Carolina 58 (New York: Elliott & Palmer, 1830).

23 U.S. Const. amend X.

24 The Federalist No. 14, at 102 (Clinton Rossiter ed. 1961) (James Madison).

25 The Federalist No. 39, *id.* at 245 (James Madison).

26 The Federalist No. 41, *id.* at 256 (James Madison).

27 The Federalist No. 45, *id.* at 292–93 (James Madison).

28 Thomas Jefferson, Principles of Government for UVa, Feb. 1825. A transcription of this document has been made available in early access form at https://rotunda.upress.virginia .edu/founders/default.xqy?keys = FOEA-print-04-02-02-5007.

29 11 *Annals of Cong.* 679 (1802) (Washington, DC: Gales & Seaton 1851).

30 *See* Robert Bain, *The Federalist, in* Everett H. Emerson ed., American Literature, 1764–1789: The Revolutionary Years 260 (Madison: University of Wisconsin Press 1977), for a discussion of this edition. The translation of the relevant part of the introduction would be that the work represents "the imposing opinion of a nation already peaceful and strengthened in the exercise of its rights and of liberty." The full passage reads:

> D'ailleurs on m'auroit soupçonné peut-être d'avoir préparé ou ménagé des rapproche-ments qu'on ne pourra manquer de faire entre l'état politique des Américains & le nôtre, & les réflexions que je publie eussent perdu l'avantage de cette confiance qu'on ne peut refuser aux conseils impartiaux de l'experience étrangère, & à l'opinion imposante d'une Nation déjà paisible & affermie dans l'exercice de ses droits & de la liberté.

> C. M. Trudaine de la Sablière trans., Le Fédéraliste, ou Collection de quelques écrits en faveur de la constitution proposée aux États-Unis de l'Amérique, par la convention convoquée en 1787, at xxi (Paris: Chez Buisson 1792). I thank Carrie Henteleff, a research librarian at Arizona State University, for helping me locate the extant pages of this edition, which are available at https://id.lib.harvard.edu/alma/990039764070203941/catalog.

31 In the 1791 debate over the constitutionality of the Bank of the United States, it was referenced as an authority. 2 Annals of Cong. 1891 (1791) (Washington, DC: Gales & Seaton 1834). In 1789, the same member of Congress referenced the works of Publius in the debates over establishing the department of foreign affairs. 1 Annals of Cong. 530–31 (1789) (Washington, DC: Gales & Seaton 1834). And according to the historian Pauline Meier, during the ratification process itself, New Yorkers read the essays (which were prepared for them); some Massachusetts newspapers republished a handful of the essays; and several prominent indi-viduals possessed copies in Virginia during the ratifying convention there. Pauline Meier, Ratification: The People Debate the Constitution, 1787–1788, at 84, 257, 352–53 (New York: Simon & Schuster 2010). None of this evidence dispositively proves The Federalist reflected a consensus about the original public understanding. Still, there appears little reason to doubt Professor Abraham Sofaer's conclusion in the 1970s: "Whatever its specific impact, these papers are widely regarded by historians of all subsequent generations as having captured with a high degree of accuracy the spirit and intent of a broad spectrum of the Constitution's

draftsmen and advocates." Abraham D. Sofaer, War, Foreign Affairs and Constitutional Power: The Origins 39 (Cambridge, MA: Ballinger Publishing Company 1976).

32 Noah Webster, *"America," Daily Advertiser*, New York, Dec. 31, 1787, *reproduced in* Colleen A. Sheehan & Gary L. McDowell eds., Friends of the Constitution: Writings of the "Other" Federalists, 1787–1788, at 176 (Indianapolis, IN: Liberty Fund 1998).

33 "A Citizen of Philadelphia" [Peletiah Webster], "The Weakness of Brutus Exposed" (Philadelphia, PA 1787), reproduced in Sheehan & McDowell, *supra* note 32, at 185.

34 *Id.* at 186.

35 3 Max Farrand ed., The Records of the Federal Convention of 1787, at 99 (New Haven, CT: Yale University Press 1911).

36 Samuel Tenny of New Hampshire, writing as "Alfredus," said similarly: "These objects [in the Preamble] are all national and important. The powers vested in the supreme authority for the accomplishment of these purposes are accurately defined in the 8th section of the first article." "Alfredus" [Samuel Tenny], Essay: I, *Freeman's Oracle*, Exeter, Jan. 18, 1788, reproduced in Sheehan & McDowell, *supra* note 32, at 253. And Roger Sherman of Connecticut, who had been a delegate to the Constitutional Convention, wrote: "The powers vested in the federal government are clearly defined, so that each state still retain its sovereignty in what concerns its own internal government, and a right to exercise every power of a sovereign state not particularly delegated to the government of the United States." "A Citizen of New Haven" [Roger Sherman], The Letters: II, New Haven Gazette, Dec. 25, 1788, reproduced in *id.* at 267. He then summarized the powers in Article I, Section 8. Hugh Williamson, who had been a delegate to the Constitutional Convention from North Carolina, wrote that the national government's powers "are detailed in the 8th section of the first article," and these are a "small addition of power" over the existing Articles of Confederation. Hugh Williamson, "Remarks on the New Plan of Government," Daily Advertiser, New York, Feb. 25–27, 1788, reproduced in *id.* at 274–75.

37 It is, of course, difficult to prove a negative. None of the regularly cited statements, and none of the statements discovered from the author's own research, convey such a view.

38 To be sure, some statements reassured that the federal government would be limited to national objects, but did not explicitly convey that those objects were the powers enumerated in the Constitution. Fisher Ames, for example, stated in the Massachusetts Ratifying Convention that "the business of the federal government will be very different" from that of the state governments; "[t]he objects of their power are few and national." 2 Jonathan Elliot ed., The Debates in the Several State Conventions, on the Adoption of the Federal Constitution 10 (Washington, DC: Printed for the editor, 2d ed. 1836) [hereinafter Elliot's Debates]. That is not necessarily inconsistent with the view that the national government would have all powers over which the individual states were incompetent; but it is just as consistent with the proposition that the enumerated powers granted Congress all the necessary powers to effectuate national purposes.

39 "The documentary evidence suggests that the two principal draftsmen of the Constitution, who were responsible for the bulk of the specific language and structure of the final text, were [James] Wilson and [Gouverneur] Morris." David S. Schwartz & John Mikhail, *The Other Madison Problem*, 89 Fordham L. Rev. 2033, 2063 (2021). William Ewald explains that one dominant theory of the Committee of Detail "takes James Wilson to be the

Committee mastermind." William Ewald, *The Committee of Detail*, 28 Const. Comment. 197, 213 (2012). Other theories place Rutledge at the head, many accusing him of systematically favoring Southern slaveholding interests. *Id.* at 213–14. Ewald writes that "Wilson, far from being dominant, appears to have been outflanked by Rutledge and the others." *Id.* at 218. On Wilson's nationalism, *see* John Mikhail, *The Original Federalist Theory of Implied Powers*, 46 Harv. J.L. & Pub. Pol'y 57, 61 (2023).

40 2 Elliot's Debates, *supra* note 38, at 481.

41 2 Bird Wilson ed., The Works of the Honourable James Wilson 178 (Philadelphia, PA: Lorenzo Press 1804) [hereinafter Wilson, Works].

42 Mikhail, *Original Federalist Theory, supra* note 39, at 61:

The Preamble is not a grant of power itself. Rather, it is a statement of the purposes for which the Constitution was created. But the Necessary and Proper Clause authorizes Congress to make necessary and proper laws to execute all of the powers vested by the Constitution in the Government of the United States, or in any Department or Officer thereof. And one of the powers vested by the Constitution in the Government of the United States is the power to fulfill the purposes for which that government was formed.

Id. at 65 (claiming that this view is probably "what men like Wilson and [Gouverneur] Morris set out to achieve with the Constitution").

43 *See, e.g.*, the statement of Alfredus, *supra* note 36.

44 Wilson, Works, *supra* note 41, at 178–79.

45 Wilson said and wrote:

Another great end of the national government is, "to ensure domestick tranquillity." That it may be enabled to accomplish this end, congress may call forth the militia to suppress insurrections.

Again; the national government is instituted to "establish justice." For this purpose, congress is authorized to erect tribunals inferiour to the supreme court; and to define and punish offences against the law of nations, and piracies and felonies committed on the high seas . . . .

It is an object of the national government to "form a more perfect union." On this principle, congress is empowered to regulate commerce among the several states, to establish post offices, to fix the standard of weights and measures, to coin and regulate the value of money, and to establish, throughout the United States, a uniform rule of naturalization.

Once more, at this time: the national government was intended to "promote the general welfare." For this reason, congress have power to regulate commerce with the Indians and with foreign nations, and to promote the progress of science and of useful arts, by securing, for a time, to authors and inventors, an exclusive right to their compositions and discoveries.

Id. at 180.

46 As for the Necessary and Proper Clause, Wilson wrote: "The powers of congress are, indeed, enumerated; but it was intended that those powers, thus enumerated, should be effectual, and not nugatory." *Id.* at 181. Here, too, Wilson specifically connected the clause to the enumeration of powers, and not to the general ends of government.

47 This episode is retold in Richard Primus, *"The Essential Characteristic": Enumerated Powers and the Bank of the United States*, 117 Mich. L. Rev. 415, 434–35 (2018).

48 John P. Kaminski & Gaspare J. Saladino eds., 13 Documentary History of the Ratification of the Constitution [DHRC] 237 (Madison: Wisconsin Historical Society Press 1981).

49 *Id.*

50 Primus, *supra* note 47, at 436.

51 Referring specifically to the Necessary and Proper Clause, Madison argued that although the national government is limited to its enumerated powers, it also "has certain discretionary powers with respect to the means, which may admit of abuse to a certain extent, in the same manner as the powers of the State Governments under their constitutions may to an indefinite extent." Charles F. Hobson & Robert A. Rutland eds., 12 The Papers of James Madison: Congressional Series, 2 March 1789–20 January 1790, at 205 (Charlottesville: University Press of Virginia 1979).

52 3 Elliot's Debates, *supra* note 47, at 431 (June 14, 1788) (Statement of George Mason).

53 Primus also argues that Madison contradicted himself earlier that same day when he defended the Constitutional Convention arguably having exceeded its authority by pointing to the fact that the Confederation Congress had on previous occasions exceeded its powers. Primus, *supra* note 48 at 433–38. Primus concludes, correctly, that Madison's view was that "enumerating powers is not a practically reliable mechanism of limitation." *Id.* at 434. But that is another way of stating his point about many constitutional provisions, that they are mere "parchment barriers." Madison's point was *not* that the Confederation Congress could *constitutionally* exercise powers beyond the enumeration in the Articles. His argument was simply that sometimes government institutions exceed their powers for good reason. The reader will confront this argument again in the context of executive power in emergencies. Saying the President acted properly to save the nation is not the same thing as saying the President acted constitutionally.

54 The speech is reported at 13 DHRC, *supra* note 48, at 337–44. The text of the speech we have was reported by Alexander Dallas in the *Pennsylvania Herald*. According to Mr. Dallas, Wilson "delivered a long and eloquent speech," and noted that "[t]he outlines of this speech we shall endeavour to lay before the public, as tending to reflect great light upon the interesting subject now in general discussion." *Id.* at 337, 339. It must always be remembered that the reporter's version may not reflect the real speech; but it was that version that was widely circulated throughout the states.

55 *Id.* at 339.

56 *Id.* at 337.

57 Meier, *supra* note 31, at 77.

58 13 DHRC, *supra* note 48, at 340.

59 *Id.*

60 U.S. Const. art. I, § 9, cl. 1 ("The Migration or Importation of such Persons as any of the States now existing shall think proper to admit, shall not be prohibited by the Congress prior to the Year one thousand eight hundred and eight, but a Tax or duty may be imposed on such Importation, not exceeding ten dollars for each Person.").

61 *Id.* cl. 2.

62 *Id.* cl. 3.

63 *Id.* cl. 4.

64 *Id.* cl. 5.

65 *Id.* cl. 6.

66 *Id.* cl. 7.

67 *Id.* cl. 8.

68 Several of the prohibitions quite obviously related to taxing and commerce. The prohibition on titles of nobility presumably limits what Congress can do with its power to establish offices under the Necessary and Proper Clause. As for habeas corpus, securing the writ was necessary because Congress had power to call forth the militia to suppress insurrection and protect against invasion; presumably a suspension of habeas corpus might follow such actions. Additionally, courts traditionally issued the writs of habeas corpus, and Congress had power to make rules and regulations for the courts under the Necessary and Proper Clause.

69 2 Elliot's Debates, *supra* note 38, at 436 (Oct. 28, 1787).

70 *Id.*

71 "[A]n omission in the enumeration of the powers of government is neither so dangerous nor important as an omission in the enumeration of the rights of the people." *Id.* at 436–37.

72 "There are two kinds of government – that where general power is intended to be given to the legislature, and that where the powers are particularly enumerated," Wilson declared. "In the last case, the implied result is, that nothing more is intended to be given than what is so enumerated, unless it results from the nature of the government itself." Here is the first hint that Wilson believed there might be implied powers beyond the enumeration, but the thrust of his comments were undeniably enumerationist. Only "when general legislative powers are given, then the people part with their authority, and ... retain nothing," he went on to add. "[I]n a government like the proposed one," however, "there can be no necessity for a bill of rights, for, on my principle, the people never part with their power." *Id.* at 454.

73 The Federalist No. 84, *supra* note 24, at 513–14 (Alexander Hamilton).

74 Roger Sherman said, for example: "The liberty of the press can be in no danger, because that is not put under the direction of the new government." Sherman, *supra* note 36, *in* Sheehan & McDowell, *supra* note 32, at 268. For other examples, *see* Bradford R. Clark, *Unitary Judicial Review*, 72 Geo. Wash. L. Rev. 319, 340–41 (2003) (providing quotations from Thomas Hartley, Edmund Pendleton, Hugh Williamson, and newspaper essays).

75 From James Madison to Thomas Jefferson, Oct. 17, 1788, *in* Robert A. Rutland & Charles F. Hobson eds., 11 The Papers of James Madison, 7 March 1788–1 March 1789, at 295–300 (Charlottesville: University Press of Virginia 1977).

76 U.S. Const. amend. IX.

77 For a classic example of this argument, *see* Griswold v. Connecticut, 381 U.S. 479, 491 (1965) (Goldberg, J., concurring). For just two examples in the modern literature, *see* Christopher J. Schmidt, *Revitalizing the Quiet Ninth Amendment: Determining Unenumerated Rights and Eliminating Substantive Due Process*, 32 U. Balt. L. Rev. 169, 171 (2003); Louis Michael Seidman, *Our Unsettled Ninth Amendment: An Essay on Unenumerated Rights and the Impossibility of Textualism*, 98 Cal. L. Rev. 2129, 2151 (2010).

78 The first draft of the amendment had provided, "The exceptions here or elsewhere in the constitution, made in favor of particular rights, shall not be so construed as to diminish the just importance of other rights retained by the people, or as to enlarge the powers

delegated by the constitution." 1 Annals of Cong., *supra* note 31, at 435 (1789). Madison explained in a letter to Washington that the meaning of the final language was the same. Letter from James Madison to George Washington (Dec. 5, 1789), *in* 12 Hobson & Rutland, *supra* note 51, at 459 ("If a line can be drawn between the powers granted and the rights retained, it would seem to be the same thing, whether the latter be secured by declaring that they shall not be abridged, or that the former shall not be extended.").

79 Whether Congress has power to infringe unenumerated rights under the Necessary and Proper Clause may depend on whether power over such rights is too important to be left to implication. *See* Chapter 4. But that would be true regardless of the Ninth Amendment.

80 1 Annals of Cong., *supra* note 31, at 439.

81 *See, e.g.,* Michael W. McConnell, *The Ninth Amendment in Light of Text and History,* 2010 Cato Sup. Ct. Rev. 13, 18 (2010).

82 Henry Lee, Report of the Minority on the Virginia Resolutions, Jan. 22, 1799, J. House of Delegates (Va.) 6:93–95 (1798–99).

83 The Report of 1800, Jan. 7, 1800, *in* David B. Mattern, J. C. A. Stagg, Jeanne K. Cross, & Susan Holbrook Perdue eds., 17 The Papers of James Madison: Congressional Series, 31 March 1797–3 March 1801 and supplement 22 January 1778–9 August 1795, at 339 (Charlottesville: University Press of Virginia 1991).

84 Compare District of Columbia v. Heller, 554 U.S. 570 (2008), with *id.* at 645 (Stevens, J., dissenting).

85 U.S. Const. amend. II.

86 *Heller,* 554 U.S. at 641–43 (Stevens, J., dissenting).

87 *Id.* at 578 (majority opinion); *see also* Eugene Volokh, *The Commonplace Second Amendment,* 73 N.Y.U. L. Rev. 793, 795 (1998).

88 On June 8, 1789, Madison famously told the House of Representatives of his proposals, which he interlineated within the existing text of the Constitution. Most of the amendments he proposed to include within Article I, Section 9 of the Constitution. His draft of what would become the Second Amendment read: "The right of the people to keep and bear arms shall not be infringed; a well armed, and well regulated militia being the best security of a free country: but no person religiously scrupulous of bearing arms, shall be compelled to render military service in person." 12 Hobson & Rutland, *supra* note 51, at 201. The placement in Article I, Section 9 would have indicated a limitation on Congress's specific enumerated powers in Article I, Section 8. Madison's placement of what is now called the prefatory clause after the operative clause further suggests that the clause was not intended to limit the right, but merely explain its importance. The addition of a clause about military service of religiously scrupulous individuals further connects this right to Congress's military powers.

All of this also explains the likely meaning of the right itself: It is a right of the people to keep and bear arms typical in military service so that, in exigencies, the militia can be called to repel invasion, suppress insurrection, and execute the laws of the Union. *See* U.S. Const. art. I, § 8, cl. 15 ("Congress shall have Power … To provide for calling forth the Militia to execute the Laws of the Union, suppress Insurrections and repel Invasions").

89 *See, e.g.,* Andrew Coan & David S. Schwartz, *The Original Meaning of Enumerated Powers,* 109 Iowa L. Rev. 971, 983–92 (2024). "Nothing about a list is semantically, logically, or legally exhaustive – that is, preclusive of things not listed," these scholars

say, using the example of a grocery list. *Id.* at 984 & n.39. Whether a list is exhaustive depends on the nature of the list. Ordinary law works by specifying prohibitions ("thou shalt not steal"); everything else is permitted. Constitutions work by assigning powers: the government can do what we empower it to do, and nothing else. The reason the states have a general residuum of legislative powers is because the state constitutions do not as a general matter specify their powers; these constitutions vest the power to make any legislation so long as not prohibited elsewhere. In any case, the Tenth Amendment squarely disproves Coan and Schwartz; it specifically confirms that the delegated powers are exclusive.

90 *See, e.g., id.* at 997, 1011–12; David S. Schwartz, *A Question Perpetually Arising: Implied Powers, Capable Federalism, and the Limits of Enumerationism*, 59 Ariz. L. Rev. 573, 595 (2017); William Michael Treanor, *The Case of the Dishonest Scrivener: Gouverneur Morris and the Creation of the Federalist Constitution*, 120 Mich. L. Rev. 1, 49–59 (2021). These authors follow in the footsteps of William Crosskey. *See* 1 William W. Crosskey, Politics and the Constitution in the History of the United States 365–401 (University of Chicago Press 1953). Some revisionists argue that the preamble was concerning because it established a "consolidated" government of "we the people" rather than a league of states. *See, e.g.,* Jonathan Gienapp, *The Myth of the Constitutional Given: Enumeration and National Power at the Founding*, 69 Am. U. L. Rev. F. 183, 198–201 (2020). That was trivial; the parties all agreed that the new Constitution would bind and operate on the people directly, but that does not answer at all what its powers would be. The evidence for the revisionists' reading of the preamble is addressed later in this section.

91 John Mikhail, *Original Federalist Theory, supra* note 39, at 61; Treanor, *supra* note 90.

92 On Morris's role generally as the Constitution's "penman," *see* Dennis C. Rasmussen, The Constitution's Penman: Gouverneur Morris and the Creation of America's Basic Charter (Lawrence: University Press of Kansas 2023).

93 Chapter 4 addresses the argument that James Wilson drafted the Necessary and Proper Clause in a way that advanced his nationalist vision in which Congress would have power to make regulations in the general interest of the Union, despite all of his many public statements. For an initial account of the argument about the pro-nationalist reading of Wilson and the Necessary and Proper Clause, *see* Mikhail, *Original Federalist Theory, supra* note 39, at 61; Gienapp, *supra* note 90, at 201–04.

William Treanor, Dean of the Georgetown University Law Center, argues in a provocative article that Gouverneur Morris "covertly made fifteen substantive changes to the text" and that "[t]hese changes advanced ends that he had unsuccessfully fought for on the Convention floor." Treanor, *supra* note 90, at 6. Treanor argues:

Morris's changes established the basis for the Federalist Constitution. Morris crafted the Constitution to reflect his political ideals: a national government of broad powers (beyond those enumerated in Articles I and II), a strong executive, a broad conception of impeachment that included impeachment for nonofficial acts, a strong judiciary (involving both judicial review and a requirement that there be lower federal courts), and protection for public contracts against state interference.

Id. at 8.

Treanor's account is unpersuasive. Deferring for the moment the question of the relevance of any of this evidence, on the merits of the claim the evidence is weak. In one instance, there may be special pleading at work. Treanor suggests that the slight difference in the way the vesting clauses of Articles I and II are written, a result of Morris's revisions, was intended to make the argument for robust and unenumerated executive powers; or at least the difference opened the door for contestation about the scope of executive power. *Id.* at 59–67. That is because Article I specifies that Congress has all legislative powers "herein granted," but Article II merely grants "the executive power." Putting aside that there are simpler explanations for this difference (the executive power is merely the power to execute whatever laws Congress has enacted), it contradicts another of Treanor's argument that Morris sought to undermine the basis for the enumerated powers. After all, although it is true that many advocates of executive power have relied on the linguistic difference, many advocates of enumerationism have seized on the "herein granted" language of Article I. If the difference in language was intended to establish unenumerated executive power, then it follows the contrasting language of Article I must have been intended to establish enumerated legislative powers. Yet, Treanor's "Federalist reading" of the Constitution advocates the former but not the latter.

Other changes that Treanor highlights seem irrelevant rather than substantive, including the supposed changes to the power of the judiciary. Although Treanor argues that Morris's language in the Supremacy Clause "provide[d] a basis for judicial review of federal statutes by federal courts," *id.* at 94–96, it does no such thing. As the first chapter on the judiciary demonstrates, that clause merely confirmed that federal laws as well as the Constitution itself superseded contrary state laws. The ultimate case for judicial review in Marbury v. Madison did not depend on the Supremacy Clause. But there is also no evidence that this change was substantive. The Committee of Detail draft had provided that the Constitution and federal laws would be the "supreme law of the several states," which Morris changed to the "supreme law of the land." Both formulations described federal laws as well as the Constitution as supreme law; neither formulation answers the question whether federal judges could invalidate federal laws for inconsistency with the Constitution. Both versions provided that the "judges in every state" shall be bound thereby, which does not solve the question of federal judges in federal territories or enclaves. The Supremacy Clause was a preemption provision under both versions and nothing more. More still, almost everyone at the Convention supposed the federal courts would have this power of judicial review. *See* Rasmussen, *supra* note 92, at 141–42.

It is possible that Gouverneur Morris did make some minor changes with a substantive intent. But if so, in one of these efforts he was caught, and the language reverted; in the other two, he admitted he did not make his point expressly, and the language itself hardly supports his subsequent readings. Starting with the latter two changes, he wrote in a letter to Henry Livingston after the Louisiana Purchase that he had drafted the clause governing territories in such a way that would allow Congress to govern the territories as "provinces" and that they were barred from admitting them as new states. *See* Rasmussen, *supra* note 92, at 55–56; Treanor, *supra* note 90, at 14–15; *see also* 3 Farrand, *supra* note 35, at 404 (providing letter). But not only did Morris admit his attempt at deception – and the Constitution does not require that it be interpreted according to Morris's secret intent – he also admitted that the language was not clear because he did not want to raise alarm. He stated in the letter to Livingston that he "went as far as circumstances would permit" to craft the appropriate language without arousing a "strong opposition." Farrand, *supra* note

35, at 404. It is certainly unclear what about the Territories Clause would bar the admission of states out of acquired territory. Neither Rasmussen nor Treanor even attempts to explain how the clause might have been read to accomplish Morris's supposed objective. Although Jefferson initially took the view that the Constitution did not authorize acquiring foreign territory, let alone incorporating that territory into the Union, virtually no one else shared that view. Not even his staunch Republican and strict constructionist allies Madison and Gallatin agreed. *See, e.g.,* 1 Henry Adams ed., The Writings of Albert Gallatin 11–14 (Philadelphia, PA: J. B. Lippincott 1879).

In the debates over the repeal of the Judiciary Act of 1801, Morris argued that the Vesting Clause of Article III required Congress to establish lower federal courts. Rasmussen, *supra* note 92, at 55; Treanor, *supra* note 90, at 89–90. In a letter to Timothy Pickering in 1814, he wrote that he had chosen "select phrases" in Article III that would convey his "own notions" without alarming others. Rasmussen, *supra* note 92, at 55. But these were likely post hoc rationalizations for Morris's argument in 1801. The relevant linguistic change hardly conveys a requirement to establish inferior courts. The Committee of Detail draft provided that the judicial power "shall be vested in one Supreme Court, and in such inferior courts, as shall, when necessary, from time to time, be constituted by the Legislature of the United States." Morris revised the language: "The judicial Power of the United States shall be vested in one supreme Court, and in such inferior courts as the Congress may from time to time ordain and establish." Professor Rasmussen suggests that Morris "subtly shifted the language to suggest that Congress was *required* to establish lower federal courts, or at the very least that it could do so at its own discretion." Rasmussen, *supra* note 92, at 55; *see also* Treanor, *supra* note 90, at 89–90. Comparing the two versions, it is hardly clear how they are different. If anything, the first version stated that Congress *shall* establish such courts when necessary; Morris's revised version provided more explicitly that Congress "may" establish them.

The most public example of a stylistic change with substantive implications is the first clause of Article I, Section 8. The Committee of Style's draft provided a semicolon between the power to tax and the modifying phrase "to pay the debts" and "provide for the common defense and general welfare." This might have suggested two powers – a power to tax, and power to regulate for the general welfare. Representative Albert Gallatin asserted in 1798 that this semicolon had been a "trick" of Morris's, and that he was caught by Roger Sherman. Rasmussen, *supra* note 92, at 53–54; Treanor, *supra* note 90, at 22–24. Madison claimed it was a mere transcription error. Rasmussen, *supra* note 92, at 54; Treanor, *supra* note 90, at 24. Either way, if it was Morris's intent to alter the substantive scope of Congress's power, he was thwarted.

The preceding paragraphs are not intended to be a comprehensive examination of all the changes between the Committee of Detail and Committee of Style drafts. But the changes discussed appear to be some of the most consequential, and the evidence that any substantive change in meaning was in fact accomplished is quite thin. But even if Morris did attempt to make substantive changes, there is no methodological reason to prefer Morris's readings. The Constitution's words are binding, not the secret intent of one particular drafter – a point even Morris articulated. In his letter to Pickering, he wrote that the proceedings of the Convention were irrelevant to constitutional interpretation; what mattered was "the plain import of the words" and the "general tenor and object of the instrument."³ Jared Sparks ed., The Life of Gouverneur Morris, with Selections from His Correspondence and Miscellaneous Papers 322–23 (Boston: Gray & Bowen 1832). To be clear, Treanor claims not to rely on Morris's secret intent. Treanor, *supra* note 90, at 107. He positively asserts instead that "in most cases, the Federalist reading is . . . the superior reading of the text," *id.* at 104. That is hardly consistent with Treanor's own evidence. At most, Morris occasionally introduced ambiguity; but Treanor offers no reason to think the so-called Federalist Constitution is the best reading of the language. At best, his evidence suggests that occasionally some members of the Founding generation seized on the relevant language to make a particular argument. But as noted earlier, even that limited evidence is weak on its own terms.

94 Coan & Schwartz, *supra* note 89, at 1008.

95 *Id.*

96 They attempt an initial explanation in *id.* at 1021–22, but the attempt fails. They write, "Under modern public meaning originalism, it is the objective communicative content of the Constitution that is Supreme Law, not the subjective understandings or purposes or extratextual promises of the persons who supported it." But that misses the mark. Original meaning has an extremely close connection to public understanding; although it is possible, it is highly unlikely that the two would diverge greatly. Second, to the extent the public was persuaded to ratify the document on the basis of pro-ratification statements, it is reasonable to conclude that they were *persuaded* that that reading made sense of the Constitution's text. None of this is to say the Anti-Federalist views have zero probative value. But the probative value must be discounted not only by their incentive to exaggerate but also by their failure to persuade.

97 These statements are canvassed in *id.* at 1009–17. To name a few examples, Coan and Schwartz cite Richard Henry Lee's concern noted previously for the proposition that it was unlikely that the "distinction between federal and state constitutions was an article of faith broadly taken for granted among the ratifying public." *Id.* at 1009. But as also noted previously, Lee's point was not that Congress could exceed its enumeration; his point was that the implied powers granted to Congress could be interpreted to extend to the matters for which the Anti-Federalists generally sought protections in a bill of rights. Coan and Schwartz more generally assert, "One Anti-Federalist after another complained that the proposed Constitution needed, but lacked, such an express reservation of state sovereignty in order to create a national government governed by enumerationist principles." *Id.* For this, they cite three speeches or letters. But in each of those, too, the worry was that particular granted powers such as the Necessary and Proper Clause, or the treaty power, would allow Congress effectively to subsume the states. The enumeration was still taken as a given, as their own sources indicate. *See* John P. Kaminski & Gaspare J. Saladino eds., 10 The Documentary History of the Ratification of the Constitution [DHRC] 1325–26 (Madison: Wisconsin Historical Society Press 1993) (statement of George Mason on the first clause of Article I, Section 8); A Republican I: To James Wilson, Esquire, N.Y.J. (Oct. 25, 1787), *reprinted in* John P. Kaminski, Gaspare J. Saladino, Richard Leffler & Charles H. Schoenleber eds., 19 DHRC 130, 131–32 (2003) (statement about implied powers); Federal Farmer, Letters to the Republican, Letter IV (Oct. 12, 1787), *in* 19 *id.*, at 231, 233 (same).

That is not to say *no one* maintained the proposition that the federal government would have plenary power. The Anti-Federalist Agrippa certainly appears to have made the argument that all governments exercise all powers that are not expressly reserved. Agrippa XV, Mass. Gazette (Jan. 29, 1788), *reprinted in* John P. Kaminski, Gaspare J. Saladino, Richard Leffler & Charles H. Schoenleber eds., 5 DHRC 822, 824–25 (1998). But this was an exception; again, most homed in on specific enumerated powers. And others who spoke explicitly on the question disagreed with Agrippa, including the Federal Farmer. Federal Farmer: An Additional Number of Letters to the Republican, Letter XVI (Jan. 20, 1788), *in* John P. Kaminski, Gaspare J. Saladino, Richard Leffler & Charles H. Schoenleber eds., 20 DHRC 976, 1052 (2004):

> The supreme power is undoubtedly in the people, and it is a principle well established in my mind, that they reserve all powers not expressly delegated by them to those who govern; this is as true in forming a state as in forming a federal government. There is no possible distinction but this founded merely in the different modes of proceeding which take place in some cases.

98 Primus, *supra* note 47, at 462.

99 Treanor, *supra* note 90, at 59–67.

100 Primus, *supra* note 47, at 440.

101 *Id.* at 460–61.

102 *Id.* at 462.

103 *Id.* at 463.

104 2 Annals of Cong., *supra* note 31, at 1919–20 (1791).

105 *Id.* at 1921 (paragraph breaks added).

106 *Id.* at 1921–25.

107 Treanor, *supra* note 90, at 55.

108 Treanor writes that Elbridge Gerry "linked the Preamble and Congress's power under the Necessary and Proper Clause to 'carry[] [the powers specified in the Preamble] into effect.'" *Id.* The brackets are Treanor's, but they are inaccurate. Gerry never said the preamble specified powers, but rather the causes for abandoning the Articles of Confederation; the Constitution then specifies powers for removing those causes. Here is the passage Treanor quotes:

> The causes which produced the Constitution were an imperfect union, want of public and private justice, internal commotions, a defenceless community, neglect of the public welfare, and danger to our liberties. These are known to be the causes not only by the preamble of the Constitution, but also from our own knowledge of the history of the times that preceded the establishment of it. If these weighty causes produced the Constitution, and it not only gives power for removing them, but also authorizes Congress to make all laws necessary and proper for carrying these powers into effect, shall we listen to assertions that these words have no meaning, and that this Constitution has not more energy than the old?

> 2 Annals of Cong., *supra* note 31, at 1950 (1791). Treanor's gloss on the passage is not a necessary reading of the passage, and is not even the natural or best reading. The entire passage is introduced by a statement about the "spirit and reason of the law." *Id.*
> Treanor also writes that "Fisher Ames similarly argued that the Preamble 'vested Congress with the authority over all objects of national concern or of a general nature' and that 'a national bank undoubtedly came under this idea.'" Treanor, *supra* note 90, at

55. But this quote (as Treanor notes) is from William Crosskey; Ames's actual statement does not say the preamble "vests" Congress with "authority," but only that the preamble "warrants this remark, that a bank is not repugnant to the spirit and essential objects of that instrument." 2 Annals of Cong., *supra* note 31, at 1909 (1791). The closest statement comes from the reporter's summary of John Laurance's remarks. Laurance invoked the "context" of the Constitution and is reported to have said something along the lines of "[h]e ... inferred that every power necessary to secure these [objects] must necessarily follow." *Id.* at 1914–15. He added that because "a full uncontrollable power to regulate the fiscal concerns of this Union is a primary consideration in this Government," Congress "must possess the power to make every possible arrangement conducive to that great object." *Id.* at 1915. Although this summary of Laurance's statement could certainly be read for the proposition that Laurance argued the preamble was a grant of power, it could just as easily be read for the proposition that Laurance was resorting to the purposes of the Constitution to make a constructive argument about the scope of Congress's granted powers. Treanor highlights statements from other congressional debates, which the reader may consult; none definitively supports the proposition that anyone thought the preamble was a grant of power.

109 Coan & Schwartz, *supra* note 89, at 1011–12; *see also id.* at 997–98.

110 Speech of Gouverneur Morris, on the Judiciary Act, Jan. 14, 1802, *in* American Oratory, or Selections from the Speeches of Eminent Americans 134 (Philadelphia, PA: Edward C. Biddle 1840).

111 He argued that Article III's "extending" the federal judicial power to several jurisdictional heads, while also providing that the Supreme Court was to have only appellate jurisdiction over certain cases, required Congress to establish lower federal courts. *Id.* at 134–35. That is certainly a plausible reading of Article III, but hardly a necessary one – the state courts could hear them just as well with appellate jurisdiction in the Supreme Court, and thus the federal judicial power would still "extend" to those cases. Morris supported his argument by invoking the preamble's objectives of establishing justice and ensuring domestic tranquility. One can understand why James Madison wrote in 1824 that the preamble was "a source of so much constructive ingenuity." James Madison to Robert S. Garnett, Feb. 11, 1824, *in* David B. Mattern, J. C. A. Stagg, Mary Parke Johnson, & Katherine E. Harbury eds., 3 The Papers of James Madison: Retirement Series 216 (Charlottesville: University of Virginia Press 2016). Very few people, if any, appear to have disagreed with his earlier statement, however, that the preamble was merely a statement of "objects," whereas the specific clauses of the Constitution "designate the express powers by which those objects are to be obtained." 2 Annals of Cong., *supra* note 31, at 1957 (1791). For these citations, I am indebted to Rasmussen, *supra* note 92, at 164–73.

112 Primus, *supra* note 47, at 467.

113 He also cites representatives Fisher Ames and Elbridge Gerry, but it is unclear if Primus is relying on their statements to support the proposition. Ames, Primus writes, "argued explicitly against putting a thumb on the scale against federal legislation, contending that denying Congress a power that Congress should have would be just as bad as letting Congress exercise a power that Congress should not have." *Id.* at 468. As for Gerry, he "asked where the line marking the *minimum* that Congress was clearly authorized to do could be drawn if the power to create the Bank were denied." *Id.* Assuming these to be

accurate characterizations of their statements in the record, neither seems to support the proposition Primus seeks to establish.

114 Primus, *supra* note 47, at 468.

115 *Id.* at 467.

116 Sedgwick's statement upon which Primus relies was the following: "That all the different Legislatures in the United States had, and this [Congress], in his opinion, indispensably must construe the powers which had been granted to them, and they must assume such auxiliary powers as are necessarily implied in those which are expressly granted." 2 Annals of Cong., *supra* note 31, at 1910 (1791).

117 *Id.*

118 *Id.* at 468.

119 2 Annals of Cong., *supra* note 31, at 1925–26 (1791).

120 Of course, Primus's lengthy article adverts to many statements supporting various propositions. This is not the place to go through each one of them. Suffice it to say this author did not find these other statements to prove the propositions for which they were advanced. To take one other example, Primus argues that "Fisher Ames of Massachusetts also took the view that the government of the United States had inherent powers, independent of the Constitution's text, simply by virtue of its being the government of the United States." Primus, *supra* note 47, at 465. And specifically, "the inherent powers of Congress were not confined to minor matters," but "could be powers of the highest importance." Primus writes that Ames believed that "[i]f the Constitution had not enumerated a congressional power to raise armies," then "Congress would still obviously have that power, because national governments raise armies, and because the purposes of the Constitution require armies to be raised." *Id.*

But that is not what Ames said. Ames was pushing back against the argument that it was safer to ensure Congress stayed within the limits of its powers by denying Congress a power it might have than it would be to allow Congress a power that it might not have. 2 Annals of Cong., *supra* note 31, at 1905 (1791). "Why," he asked, "shall we be told that the negative is the safe side? Not exercising the powers we have, may be as pernicious as usurping those we have not." *Id.* It was at that point that Ames suggested first that if the Constitution did not specify that Congress could raise armies, Congress could still deduce that power "from other parts of the Constitution" – perhaps the power to declare war. But assume the power was omitted altogether, Ames said, and suppose the country were invaded.

[W]ould a decision in Congress against raising armies be safer than the affirmative? The blood of our citizens would be shed, and shed unavenged. He thought, therefore, that there was too much prepossession with some against the bank, and that the debate ought to be considered more impartially, as the negative was neither more safe, certain, nor conformable to our duty than the other side of the question. *Id.*

All Ames said was that denying Congress necessary powers is just as dangerous, if not more dangerous, than granting Congress powers it does not have; therefore, the participants in the debate should stop putting a thumb on the scale against national power. Nothing in his statement stands for the proposition that he believed Congress actually would have had the power to raise armies in the absence of any part of the Constitution from which such a power could be deduced.

121 The preceding section was not intended to deny that some Federalist and nationalist thinkers had a more capacious understanding of national power than did the Anti-Federalist and Republican thinkers and that they sometimes appealed to inherent powers and overarching national purposes. But as the preceding materials make clear, even the nationalist camp went to great lengths to justify its legislative program through a careful analysis of the Constitution's enumeration of powers. Chapter 4 will demonstrate that, too, with respect to the debate on the Bank of the United States.

122 2 Farrand, *supra* note 35, at 17.

123 *Id.*

124 *Id.* at 26; *Id.* at 131–32.

125 *Id.* at 303–33.

126 Gorham supported Resolution 6 only because "[w]e are now establishing general principles, to be extended hereafter into details which will be precise & explicit." *Id.* at 17. Rutledge had moved "that a specification of the powers comprised in the general terms, might be reported." *Id.* And Randolph had urged that the general language "involves the power of violating all the laws and constitutions of the States, and of intermeddling with their police." *Id.* at 26.

127 *Id.* at 17.

128 Most of the drafts to come out of the Committee of Detail are found in Wilson's papers and are in his handwriting. *Id.* at 129–75. Michael McConnell writes that Wilson was "long thought to be the Committee's dominant thinker." Michael W. McConnell, The President Who Would Not Be King: Executive Power under the Constitution 65 (Princeton University Press 2020). But Rutledge may have had more influence. *See supra* note 39.

129 1 Farrand, *supra* note 35, at 65.

130 *Id.* at 65–66.

131 Wilson, Works, *supra* note 41, at 179.

132 The idea that the enumeration of powers may have been a result of the desire to assign to Congress a variety of executive powers is attributed to William Crosskey. 1 Crosskey, *supra* note 90, at 428–29; *see also* McConnell, *supra* note 128, at 68.

133 Blackstone's treatise was "in every man's hand" at the founding. Debates of the Virginia Convention (June 18, 1788) (statement of James Madison), *in* 10 DHRC, *supra* note 97, at 1371, 1382. Jefferson wrote, "[T]he honied Mansfieldism of Blackstone became the Student's Hornbook, [and] from that moment, that profession (the nursery of our Congress) began to slide into toryism, and nearly all the young brood of lawyers now are of that hue." Letter from Thomas Jefferson to James Madison (Feb. 17, 1826), *in* Joyce Appleby & Terence Ball eds., Thomas Jefferson: Political Writings 57, 58 (New York: Cambridge University Press 1999). The fact that most, if not all, of the executive/prerogative powers that Blackstone describes in his *Commentaries* are specifically assigned somewhere in the Constitution suggests the Framers used Blackstone as a drafting guide.

134 1 William Blackstone, Commentaries on the Laws of England 242 (Oxford: Clarendon Press 1765).

135 *Id.* at 245.

136 *Id.* ("The king therefore, considered as the representative of his people, has the sole power of fending ambassadors to foreign states, and receiving ambassadors at home.").

137 *Id.* at 249 ("It is also the king's prerogative to make treaties, leagues, and alliances with foreign states and princes.").

138 *Id.* ("Upon the same principle the king has also the sole prerogative of making war and peace.").

139 *Id.* at 250:

> But, as the delay of making war may sometimes be detrimental to individuals who have suffered by depredations from foreign potentates, our laws have in some respect armed the subject with powers to impel the prerogative; by directing the ministers of the crown to issue letters of marque and reprisal upon due demand: the prerogative of granting which is nearly related to, and plainly derived from, that other of making war.

140 *Id.* at 251 ("Upon exactly the same reason stands the prerogative of granting safe-conducts, without which by the law of nations no member of one society has a right to intrude into another. And therefore Puffendorf very justly resolves, that it is left in the power of all states, to take such measures about the admission of strangers, as they think convenient.").

141 *Id.* at 253–57.

142 *Id.* at 261–62.

143 *Id.* at 263.

144 *Id.* at 263–68.

145 *Id.* at 269.

146 *Id.* at 257.

147 *Id.* at 259.

148 *Id.* at 261.

149 *Id.* at 257.

150 U.S. Const. art. II, § 2, para. 2 ("[A]nd he shall nominate, and by and with the Advice and Consent of the Senate, shall appoint Ambassadors, other public Ministers and Consuls . . . .").

151 *Id.* art. II, § 3 ("he shall receive Ambassadors and other public Ministers").

152 *Id.* art. II, § 2, para. 2 ("He shall have Power, by and with the Advice and Consent of the Senate, to make Treaties, provided two thirds of the Senators present concur . . . .").

153 *Id.* art. I, § 8, cl. 11 ("The Congress shall have Power . . . To declare War . . . ."); *id.* art. II, § 2, para. 1 ("The President shall be Commander in Chief of the Army and Navy of the United States, and of the Militia of the several States, when called into the actual Service of the United States . . . .").

154 *Id.* art. I, § 8, cl. 11 ("The Congress shall have Power . . . To . . . grant Letters of Marque and Reprisal, and make Rules concerning Captures on Land and Water.").

155 *Id.* art. I, § 7, para. 3:

> Every Order, Resolution, or Vote to which the Concurrence of the Senate and House of Representatives may be necessary (except on a question of Adjournment) shall be presented to the President of the United States; and before the Same shall take Effect, shall be approved by him, or being disapproved by him, shall be repassed by two thirds of the Senate and House of Representatives, according to the Rules and Limitations prescribed in the Case of a Bill.

156 *Id.* art. II, § 2, para. 1 ("The President shall be Commander in Chief of the Army and Navy of the United States, and of the Militia of the several States, when called into the actual Service of the United States . . . .").

157 *Id.* art. I, § 8, cls. 12–14 ("The Congress shall have Power . . . To raise and support Armies, but no Appropriation of Money to that Use shall be for a longer Term than two Years; To provide and maintain a Navy; To make Rules for the Government and Regulation of the land and naval Forces.").

158 *Id.* art. I, § 8, cl. 17 ("The Congress shall have Power . . . to exercise [exclusive] Authority over all Places purchased by the Consent of the Legislature of the State in which the Same shall be, for the Erection of Forts, Magazines, Arsenals, dock-Yards, and other needful Buildings.").

159 *Id.* art. I, § 9, cl. 8 ("No Title of Nobility shall be granted by the United States.").

160 *Id.* art. I, § 8, cl. 4 ("Congress shall have Power . . . To establish an uniform Rule of Naturalization.").

161 *Id.* art. I, § 8, cls. 3, 5 ("Congress shall have Power . . . To regulate Commerce with foreign Nations, and among the several States, and with the Indian Tribes; . . . To coin Money, regulate the Value thereof, and of foreign Coin, and fix the Standard of Weights and Measures.").

162 *Id.* art. I, § 8, cl. 9 ("Congress shall have Power . . . To constitute Tribunals inferior to the supreme Court.").

163 *Id.* art. II, § 2, para. 2 ("[The President] shall nominate, and by and with the Advice and Consent of the Senate, shall appoint . . . Judges of the supreme Court, and all other Officers of the United States.").

164 *Id.* art. I, § 8, cl. 18 ("Congress shall have Power . . . To make all Laws which shall be necessary and proper for carrying into Execution the foregoing Powers . . . ."); McCulloch v. Maryland, 17 U.S. 316 (1819) (holding that Congress has the power to incorporate a bank under the Necessary and Proper Clause).

165 U.S. Const. art. I, § 8, cl. 10.

166 Blackstone, *supra* note 134, at 251; *see also* Robert G. Natelson, *The Power to Restrict Immigration and the Original Meaning of the Constitution's Define and Punish Clause*, 11 Br. J. Am. Leg. Studies 209 (2022).

167 Many of these prerogatives were already vested in the national government under the Articles of Confederation. But as noted in Chapter 2, there was no separation of powers under the Articles; the United States acted in Congress assembled. The assignment of these powers to Congress as opposed to the presidency is thus still likely to have been motivated by a desire to limit the powers of the executive.

168 Mark A. Graber, *Enumeration and Other Constitutional Strategies for Protecting Rights: The View from 1787/1791*, 9 U. Pa. J. Const. L. 357, 374 (2007).

169 *Id.* at 375 (emphasis omitted); *see also* John P. Kaminski, Gaspare J. Saladino, Richard Leffler & Charles H. Schoenleber eds., 17 DHRC 111 (1995).

CHAPTER 4

1 U.S. Const. art. I, § 8, cl. 18.

2 Art. of Confed. art. II (1781).

3 David P. Currie, The Constitution in Congress: The Federalist Period, 1789–1801, at 14 (University of Chicago Press 1997). Congress also supplied the oaths for state officers, and there is some question as to whether it had authority to do so. Article VI, paragraph 3 of the

Constitution provides that state legislators, as well as state executive and judicial officers, "shall be bound by Oath or Affirmation, to support this Constitution." But the Necessary and Proper Clause granted Congress power for carrying into execution its powers or those the Constitution vests in the government *of the United States* or in any department or officer thereof. Many at the Founding believed the Necessary and Proper Clause simply stated what would follow from necessary implication in its absence. In other words, even without the clause there would still have been implied powers. Thus, one can understand Congress to have the implied power directly under Article VI to implement the oath for state officers. *See id.* at 14–15.

4 *Id.* at 19–20.

5 *Id.* at 36–47.

6 *Id.* at 82.

7 *Id.* at 96–97 (offenses against courts); *id.* at 150 (postal crimes).

8 *Id.* at 153 n.160.

9 *Id.* at 205 n.243. Though Congress, as Currie notes, may have believed it had inherent power to make a flag for the nation even in the absence of the Necessary and Proper Clause; the Continental Congress had provided for a flag in 1777. *Id.* at 204.

10 McCulloch v. Maryland, 17 U.S. (4 Wheat.) 316, 407 (1819).

11 John Mikhail, *The Necessary and Proper Clauses*, 102 Geo. L.J. 1045, 1071 (2014).

12 2 Max Farrand ed., The Records of the Federal Convention of 1787, at 615 (New Haven, CT: Yale University Press 1911).

13 Bray Hammond, Banks and Politics in America from the Revolution to the Civil War 54–55, 90, 116 (Princeton University Press 1957).

14 Some of the next paragraphs are taken or adapted from Ilan Wurman, *Importance and Interpretive Questions*, 110 Va. L. Rev. 909 (2024).

15 Charles F. Hobson & Robert A. Rutland eds., 13 The Papers of James Madison: Congressional Series, 20 January 1790–31 March 1791, at 374 (Charlottesville: University Press of Virginia 1981).

16 *Id.* at 378.

17 *Id.*

18 *Id.* at 379–80.

19 *Id.* at 378.

20 *Id.* at 379.

21 *Id.*

22 *Id.*

23 Edmund Randolph, Enclosure: Opinion on the Constitutionality of the Bank (Feb. 12, 1791), *in* 7 Jack D. Warren, Jr. ed., The Papers of George Washington, Presidential Series 331–37 (Charlottesville: University Press of Virginia 1998).

24 *Id.*

25 *Id.*

26 Edmund Randolph, Enclosure: Additional Considerations on the Bank Bill (Feb. 12, 1791), *in* Warren, *supra* note 23, at 337–40.

27 6 Paul Leicester Ford ed., The Works of Thomas Jefferson 200 (New York: The Knickerbocker Press 1904) [herein after Jefferson, Works].

28 As Hamilton responded,

[W]hatever may have been the intention of the framers of a constitution or of a law, that intention is to be sought for in the instrument itself, according to the usual and established rules of construction. Nothing is more common than for laws to *express* and *effect* more or less than was intended. If, then, a power to erect a corporation in any case be deducible, by fair inference, from the whole or any part of the numerous provisions of the Constitution of the United States, arguments drawn from extrinsic circumstances regarding the intention of the Convention must be rejected.

3 Henry Cabot Lodge ed., The Works of Alexander Hamilton 463 (New York: The Knickerbocker Press 1904) [hereinafter Hamilton, Works].

29 Jefferson, Works, *supra* note 27, at 201.

30 Hamilton, Works, *supra* note 28, at 450. The emphases in Hamilton's opinion have been deleted in the text.

31 *Id.*

32 *Id.* at 451.

33 *Id.*

34 *Id.* at 473–86.

35 *Id.* at 465 (emphases deleted).

36 *Id.* at 472 (emphases deleted).

37 McCulloch v. Maryland, 17 U.S. (4 Wheat.) 316 (1819).

38 *Id.* at 432.

39 *Id.* at 363 (argument of counsel).

40 *Id.* at 403.

41 *Id.* at 404–05.

42 *Id.* at 405.

43 *Id.* at 406.

44 *Id.* at 407 (emphasis in original).

45 *Id.*

46 *Id.* at 408–09.

47 *Id.* at 411.

48 *Id.* at 414.

49 *Id.*

50 *Id.* at 413; *see also* Hamilton, Works, *supra* note 28, at 452–53 ("necessary often means no more than needful, requisite, incidental, useful, or conducive to") (emphases deleted).

51 *McCulloch*, 17 U.S. at 415 (emphasis in original).

52 The misinterpretations of this passage, and Marshall's related passage that it is a constitution we are expounding, are legion. Chief Justice Earl Warren invoked both passages to defend his Court's efforts to "adapt our Constitution" to modern crises. Earl Warren, *Foreword: Current Constitutional Issues*, 9 Wm. & Mary L. Rev. xxi, xxi–xxii (1967). Chief Justice Hughes used the passage to disagree with Justice Sutherland's originalism. *See* Home Bldg. & Loan Ass'n v. Blaisdell, 290 U.S. 393, 442–43 (1934):

If by the statement that what the Constitution meant at the time of its adoption it means to-day, it is intended to say that the great clauses of the Constitution must be confined to the interpretation which the framers, with the conditions and outlook of their time, would have placed upon them, the statement carries its own refutation. It was to guard against such a narrow conception that Chief Justice Marshall uttered the memorable warning: "We must never forget, that it is a constitution we are expounding" ....

(quoting *McCulloch*, 17 U.S. at 407). Alexander Bickel, in his famous work, endorsed Hughes's misreading of Marshall's passage. Alexander M. Bickel, The Least Dangerous Branch: The Supreme Court at the Bar of Politics 106 (New Haven, CT: Yale University Press 1962). For two prominent academic examples invoking this dictum in support of living constitutionalism, *see* Erwin Chemerinsky, *The Price of Asking the Wrong Question: An Essay on Constitutional Scholarship and Judicial Review*, 62 Tex. L. Rev. 1207, 1256–57 (1984); Thomas C. Grey, *Do We Have an Unwritten Constitution?*, 27 Stan. L. Rev. 703, 710 (1975). For an example of misinterpretation of the related passage, *see* Mark A. Graber, A New Introduction to American Constitutionalism 5 (Oxford University Press 2013) (incorrectly suggesting the passage implies the Constitution should be interpreted differently than other legal texts).

53 *McCulloch*, 17 U.S. at 415. That is not to say, however, that Congress has unfettered discretion in choosing the relevant means. As Gary Lawson and Patricia Granger have shown, several other clauses of the Constitution provide that the President or Congress shall take an action as they "shall deem" or "shall think" proper. Gary Lawson & Patricia B. Granger, *The "Proper" Scope of Federal Power: A Jurisdictional Interpretation of the Sweeping Clause*, 43 Duke L.J. 267, 276–81 (1993).

54 *McCulloch*, 17 U.S. at 421. Hamilton had written, "If the *end* be clearly comprehended within any of the specified powers, and if the measure have an obvious relation to that *end*, and is not forbidden by any particular provision of the Constitution, it may safely be deemed to come within the compass of the national authority." Hamilton, Works, *supra* note 28 at 458.

55 *McCulloch*, 17 U.S. at 422.

56 Marshall did not explicitly connect the proposition about finances to specific enumerated powers, but Hamilton did in his opinion.

A bank relates to the collection of taxes in two ways – *indirectly*, by increasing the quantity of circulating medium and quickening circulation, which facilitates the means of paying directly, by creating a *convenient species* of medium in which they are to be paid. ... The appointment, then, of the *money* or *thing* in which the taxes are to be paid, is an incident to the power of collection.

Hamilton, Works, *supra* note 28 at 474–75. "A bank has a direct relation to the power of borrowing money, because it is an usual, and in sudden emergencies an essential, instrument in the obtaining of loans to government. A nation is threatened with war; large sums are wanted on a sudden to make the necessary preparations." *Id.* at 477–78. "The institution of a bank has also a natural relation to the regulation of trade between the States, in so far as it is conducive to the creation of a convenient medium of *exchange* between them ...." *Id.* at 480. Hamilton also argued that the national bank was convenient for the disposing of the property of the United States under Article IV. A national bank is useful for the "management of the moneys of the United States" because it gives one place to deposit them. *Id.* at 484.

To be sure, there is some ambiguity in Marshall's language; he may have relied on the part of the clause empowering Congress to make necessary and proper laws for carrying into execution the others powers vested by the Constitution in the government of the United States as a whole. *See* Mikhail, *supra* note 11, at 1062–63, 1062 n.71. Even if true, Marshall did not deny that those powers had to be specified somewhere; he could have had in mind Article IV's Property Clause, which Hamilton had explicitly invoked.

57 The Court's first case arising under the Necessary and Proper Clause was United States v. Fisher, 6 U.S. (2 Cranch) 358 (1805). Mikhail argues that Chief Justice Marshall's invocation of the "all other powers" provision of the clause suggested "the existence of implied or unenumerated powers of government under the Constitution" generally. Mikhail, *supra* note 11, at 1061–62, 1062 n.69; *see also* John Mikhail, *The Original Federalist Theory of Implied Powers*, 46 Harv. J. L. Pub. Pol'y 57, 59–63. But the Court's treatment of the clause in *Fisher* is perfectly consistent with every point that has been made about the bank debate. Congress enacted a law providing that the United States shall have a priority claim in bankruptcy against receivers of public money, such as revenue officers, who become indebted to the government. The idea was that if the government is to appoint officers to collect money, it can ensure the safety of the funds. That is obviously necessary and proper for the collection of taxes, to stay with the example of revenue officers. Justice Bushrod Washington would have limited the statute to public receivers of money; the majority of the Court interpreted it to reach any debts owed to the United States. That dispute is immaterial. Assuming the government had the power of granting a debt to a private citizen, it was obviously necessary and proper to protect that debt by creating a priority preference in bankruptcy. It is true that the Court's quotation of the Necessary and Proper Clause elides the "foregoing powers" language, but the significance is unclear; that part of the clause was likely understood to be superfluous since, of course, Congress is a department of the United States. *See* John Mikhail, *The Constitution and the Philosophy of Language: Entailment, Implicature, and Implied Powers*, 101 Va. L. Rev. 1063, 1087 (2015). Mikhail has suggested that the Court in *Fisher* recognized an implied power to pay the debts is an implied power vested in the national government as a whole. *See* Center for the Study of Constitutional Originalism at the University of San Diego Law School, Originalism Works-in-Progress Conference, at 57:00–58:30 (YouTube, Mar. 29, 2024), https://www.youtube.com/watch?v = 1SKCW-4900c. It is unclear why the enumerated power to borrow money would not include the power to repay the money borrowed; indeed, the first clause of Article I, Section 8, specifically states that Congress may tax for the purpose of raising money to pay for the national debt.

David Schwartz argues that Marshall never adopted a "great powers" limitation on the Necessary and Proper Clause, and never denied that the national government might have some great implied powers. *See* David S. Schwartz, *A Question Perpetually Arising: Implied Powers, Capable Federalism, and the Limits of Enumerationism*, 59 Ariz. L. Rev. 573, 616–17 (2017). But this one-paragraph argument is unpersuasive. Schwartz argues that Marshall's test for powers that were unimportant was that "it is not exercised for its own sake, or as an end in itself." *Id.* at 616. And, Schwartz notes, even the great power of war "is never an end in itself: it is a means of preserving national independence, acquiring territory, or promoting trade." *Id.* On this reading, however, *all* of the enumerated powers are but means to the ends listed in the preamble. No one borrows money for the sake of borrowing; raises taxes for the sake of raising taxes; and so on. Marshall's statement about how acts of incorporation are never ends in themselves must be interpreted along with his statement that this power "is not, like the power of making war, or levying taxes, or of regulating commerce, a great substantive and independent power, which cannot be implied as incidental to other powers." *McCulloch*, 17 U.S. at 411. While it is obviously true that war and taxes and even commerce are never ends in themselves – common defense, welfare, and liberty perhaps are – Marshall nevertheless understood them to be "ends" in the sense that they are great powers that could not be left to implication. The better explanation is found in Attorney General Randolph's opinion on the bank. He distinguished between incidental powers and "substantive and independant [sic]" powers, the latter of which are "capable of being used, independently of what is called the principal power." Randolph, *supra* note 26. Put another way, Congress does not need a reason to raise and support armies. Although it surely has motives for raising armies, it is a principal power granted expressly. But, Marshall suggested, Congress never incorporates for the sake of having corporations.

58 The Federalist No. 44, at 284 (Clinton Rossiter ed. 1961).

59 *Id.* at 284–85.

60 *Id.* at 285.

61 2 Jonathan Elliot ed., The Debates in the Several State Conventions, on the Adoption of the Federal Constitution 481 (Washington, DC: Printed for the editor, 2d ed. 1836).

62 *Id.* at 468. Of course, Wilson elided the remainder of the clause, which also granted Congress the power to carry into execution any of the other powers vested by the Constitution in the government of the United States or in any department or officer thereof. But there is no reason to think Wilson was dissimulating. The latter parts of the clause are not inconsistent with enumerationism.

63 2 Bird Wilson ed., The Works of the Honourable James Wilson, L.L.D. 181 (Philadelphia, PA: Lorenzo Press 1804).

64 2 Herbert J. Storing ed., The Complete Anti-Federalist 168 (University of Chicago Press 1981).

65 *Id.* at 2:247.

66 *Id.* at 2:365 (emphasis added).

67 *Id.* at 2:389.

68 *Id.* at 2:389–90.

69 *Id.* at 6:86.

70 Andrew Coan & David S. Schwartz, *The Original Meaning of Enumerated Powers*, 109 Iowa L. Rev. 971, 1013 (2024) (citing Richard Henry Lee, Patrick Henry, and George Mason).

71 Hence, David Schwartz relies on "The General Welfare and Necessary and Proper Clauses" together, and his non-enumerationist reading of the Constitution hinges mostly on the former. Schwartz, *supra* note 57, at 595–600. His reading of the second provision of the Necessary and Proper Clause relies on the work of John Mikhail, which shall be examined presently.

72 Thus, An Old Whig explained that by virtue of the clause, Congress would not be limited to powers expressly granted, which no one denied. That was the point. Storing, *supra* note 64, at 3:24–25.

73 Gary Lawson, Geoffrey P. Miller, Robert G. Natelson, & Guy I. Seidman, The Origins of the Necessary and Proper Clause (New York: Cambridge University Press 2010).

74 *Id.* at 4–5.

75 *Id.* at 6.

76 *Id.* at 7.

77 2 William Blackstone, Commentaries on the Laws of England 347 (Oxford: Clarendon Press 1766).

78 Sir Edward Coke, The First Part of the Institutes of the Laws of England 268b (London: William Rawlins et al., 9th ed. 1684).

79 *Id.* at 227b.

80 *Id.* at 151b.

81 Giles Jacob, A New Law-Dictionary (J. Morgan ed., London: W. Strahan and W. Woodfall, 10th ed. 1782). He wrote the first edition of the law dictionary in 1729, with several editions including the one in 1782. Giles Jacob, A New Law-Dictionary (London: E. and R. Nutt and R. Gosling 1729). The law dictionary was "the fourth most popular of all law books available" in colonial Virginia. Gary L. McDowell, The Language of Law and the Foundations of American Constitutionalism 172 (New York: Cambridge University Press 2010) (citing Herbert A. Johnson, Imported Eighteenth-Century Law Treatises in American Libraries 1700–1799, at 61 (Knoxville: University of Tennessee Press 1978)); and William Hamilton Bryson, Census of Law Books in Colonial Virginia, at xvii (Charlottesville: University of Virginia Press 1978). It appears to have been the "most widely used English law dictionary" of the period. Leonard W. Levy, *Origins of the Fifth Amendment and Its Critics*, 19 Cardozo L. Rev. 821, 854 (1997); Bryson, *supra*, at xvi, xvii. The dictionary has been found in the libraries of Francis Dana, John Mercer, Robert Treat Paine, St. George Tucker, Theophilus Parsons, and John Adams, among other luminaries. Johnson, *supra*, at 33.

82 Jacob (1782), *supra* note 81 (under entry for "incident").

83 126 Eng. Rep. 737 (1796); 2 H. Bl. 618.

84 *Howard*, 126 Eng. Rep. at 737 (this is the court's formulation).

85 *Id.* at 737–39.

86 *Id.* at 739–40.

87 *Id.* at 738.

88 *Id.*

89 Mikhail, *supra* note 11, at 1114–21. Mikhail correctly argues that the phrase "signal[ed] little more than an informal and flexible standard for exercising appropriate discretion in various contexts." *Id.* at 1121. One may consult his examples. What seems evident is that such clauses were always used in service of some other specified objective of importance. The question is in service of what objectives does Congress have its residual powers. The Necessary and Proper Clause answers the question: for carrying into execution power that the Constitution has already vested in the government of the United States or in one of its departments or officers.

90 William Baude, *Rethinking the Federal Eminent Domain Power*, 122 Yale L.J. 1738 (2013); *id.* at 1761–77 (demonstrating practice of using states).

91 Kohl v. United States, 91 U.S. 367, 370 (1875).

92 Pollard's Lessee v. Hagan, 44 U.S. 212 (1845).

93 *Id.* at 223–24.

94 *See* Coan & Schwartz, *supra* note 70, at 993–94; Mikhail, *Philosophy of Language*, *supra* note 57, at 1084–103.

95 As an initial matter, there might be three powers vested in the undifferentiated "government of the United States" specified in the Constitution: The United States has the duty to guarantee the states a republican form of government and to protect them against insurrection and invasion. U.S. Const. art. IV, § 4 ("The United States shall guarantee to every State in this Union a Republican Form of Government, and shall protect each of them against Invasion; and on Application of the Legislature, or of the Executive (when the Legislature cannot be convened) against domestic Violence."). To be sure, these provisions of Article IV do not expressly grant power; they impose duties, and imply the power to effectuate that duty already exists. Congress has the Article I power to call forth the militia to execute the laws of the union, repel invasions, and suppress insurrection. And the President, as the chapter on the war powers shall demonstrate, has authority as commander in chief at least to repel invasions. The revisionist argument therefore has some linguistic appeal. Surely, there must be some powers vested in the "government of the United States" if that part of the clause is to do any work.

Even if the language is technically superfluous, there is a natural explanation for it. Under the Articles of Confederation, "the United States in Congress assembled" was a common phrase. Mikhail, *Philosophy of Language, supra* note 57, at 1085. Although the rephrasing to "the government of the United States" could indicate a difference in intended meaning, it is just as plausible that it is a reference to Congress. After all, "the United States" must act through one of its departments. It either acts through Congress, or the executive or judiciary. It makes perfect sense to think that "the government of the United States" is therefore Congress, and "any department or officer" of the United States would capture other constitutional actors. To be sure, Congress is also a "department" of the government, and so Congress would be captured by both "government of the United States" and "any department thereof." But saying "or in any" of the departments seems a natural way of extending the scope of the clause. The upshot is that if the "government" of the United States was simply another phrase for Congress, then Articles II–V do in fact grant Congress several additional powers to which the phrase might refer.

It is also not clear why superfluity must be avoided at all costs. As Madison said in the bank debate, "not … every insertion or omission in the constitution is the effect of systematic attention." 2 Annals of Cong., *supra* note 31, at 1899 (1791). Sometimes, emphasis is also appropriate. For example, the prohibition on ex post facto laws is probably subsumed entirely within the Due Process Clause of the Fifth Amendment, although admittedly the latter was incorporated into the Constitution in 1791. Another example may be that the power to declare war subsumed the power to issue letters of marque and reprisal. As this author once heard from Randy Barnett of the Georgetown University Law Center, redundancy is good in airplanes, and it can be good in constitutions.

But, assuming superfluity must be avoided, the phrase could refer to shared powers: those vested in more than one department or officer. One obvious example is Congress's power to make rules for the government of the armed forces. It is at least conceivable that the President has this power, too, as part of the commander-in-chief status and can therefore act in the absence of contrary congressional legislation on the matter. And Congress can authorize military actions to repel invasions, but the President can also repel invasions without such authorization. That is getting ahead of things for the moment, but the important point is that the powers vested by this Constitution "in the government of the

United States" may simply capture the idea that some exercises of government power may be reached by more than one department.

96 Mikhail argues that corporations, including political corporations such as the United States, are "vested with the implied power to fulfill its purposes." Mikhail, *Philosophy of Language*, *supra* note 57, at 1098. Corporations were understood to have certain powers incidental to every corporation, namely the capacity to sue and be sued and to grant and possess property. As stated in Giles Jacob's influential law dictionary: "When a *Corporation* is duly created, all Incidents, as to purchase and grant, sue and be sued, *&c.* are tacitly annexed to it." *See, e.g.*, Jacob (1782), *supra* note 81 (entry for "corporation"). That was, after all, the point of incorporating: so that the corporation could take such actions on behalf of the individuals comprising it. But Mikhail has cited no authority for the proposition that a corporation can do anything whatsoever that advances its purposes, no matter how great or important are its acts. We already know from Jacob that an "incident" is a lesser power. Corporations may have necessary incidental powers, but deducing from that proposition that they may also exercise great powers by implication would undermine the entire purpose of having charters of incorporation that specify a corporation's powers.

97 Hobson & Rutland, *supra* note 15, at 374.

98 Mikhail, *supra* note 11, at 1121. Thus, he writes that the "and all other" language was a "common formula by which 'sweeping clauses' perform their essential function of canceling the implication that a given list of items is exhaustive." The language, he writes, "cancels the inference that Congress's other Article I powers are exhaustive." Mikhail, *Philosophy of Language*, *supra* note 57, at 1084. He summarizes: "[I]t seems clear that one of [the clause's] intended functions was to give Congress the instrumental power to carry into effect its own enumerated powers, while a second objective was to cancel the implication that these enumerated powers were exhaustive." *Id.* at 1088. None of this is surprising. As noted, the Constitution also vests Congress with powers in other articles, and vests the judiciary and executive with powers that Congress will need to help carry into execution. The most natural reading of the "and all other Powers" language is that it negates what otherwise would be the inference that the Necessary and Proper Clause is limited to carrying into execution "the foregoing powers." It says nothing at all about whether Congress has powers beyond those in Article I *and* those specified elsewhere in the Constitution.

99 *See* discussion *supra* note 98.

100 Mikhail, *supra* note 11, at 1122; Lessee of Moor v. Moor, 98 Eng. Rep. 714, 714 (1774).

101 There is a parenthetical in the report. The entire passage reads, "by which kind of sweeping clauses, conveyancers often take in every thing relative to what had been before recited, and which it was possible they might have omitted to enumerate precisely; (and besides it helps forwards a line,) but they never mean to pass any thing new." *Moor*, 98 Eng. Rep. at 714.

102 *Id.*

103 *See generally* Mikhail, *supra* note 11 (explaining Mikhail's view of what Wilson likely thought as he drafted the Necessary and Proper Clause).

104 *Id.* at 1123.

105 *Id.*

106 *Id.*

107 James Wilson, Considerations on the Bank of North America, published in the year 1785, *in* 3 The Works of the Honourable James Wilson 395 (Bird Wilson ed. 1804). Wilson recognized that the Articles of Confederation provided that "each state retains … every power, jurisdiction, and right, which is not, by the confederation, *expressly* delegated to the United States in congress assembled." *Id.* at 405 (quoting Art. of Confed. art. II). He argued, however, that this provision meant only that those powers the states had previously exercised had to be expressly delegated to Congress. It did not follow that Congress did not possess other powers from some other source. *Id.* at 406.

108 *Id.* at 406.

109 *Id.*

110 *Id.* at 406–07.

111 *Id.* at 407.

112 *Id.* at 407–11.

113 Hammond, *supra* note 13, at 53–54.

114 2 Farrand, *supra* note 12, at 188 (Document IX):

> New States lawfully constituted or established within the limits of the United States may be admitted, by the Legislature, into this Government; but to such admission the consent of two thirds of the members present in each House shall be necessary. If a new State shall arise within the limits of any of the present States, the consent of the Legislatures of such States shall be also necessary to its admission.

> U.S. Const. art. IV, § 3, cl. 1 ("New States may be admitted by the Congress into this Union; but no new State shall be formed or erected within the Jurisdiction of any other State; nor any State be formed by the Junction of two or more States, or Parts of States, without the Consent of the Legislatures of the States concerned as well as of the Congress.").

115 U.S. Const. art. IV, § 3, cl. 2 ("The Congress shall have Power to dispose of and make all needful Rules and Regulations respecting the Territory or other Property belonging to the United States; and nothing in this Constitution shall be so construed as to Prejudice any Claims of the United States, or of any particular State.").

116 Coan & Schwartz, *supra* note 70, at 994.

117 The Chinese Exclusion Case, 130 U.S. 581, 603–04 (1889).

118 U.S. Const. art. I, § 9.

119 Christopher R. Green, *Tribes, Nations, States: Our Three Commerce Powers*, 127 Penn. St. L. Rev. 643, 649–50 (2023); Edye v. Robertson, 112 U.S. 580, 595 (1884) ("The burden imposed on the ship-owner by this statute is the mere incident of the regulation of commerce – of that branch of foreign commerce which is involved in immigration.").

120 1 Blackstone, *supra* note 77, at 251.

121 Robert G. Natelson, *The Power to Restrict Immigration and the Original Meaning of the Constitution's Define and Punish Clause*, 11 Br. J. Am. Leg. Stud. 209, 214 (2022).

122 As explained in Chapter 9.

123 Only the strictest of constructionists such as Thomas Jefferson seem to have thought the Constitution denied the national government this power. Jefferson justified the purchase

as a matter of great good and necessity, but at least initially did not think it constitutional. Letter from Thomas Jefferson to John Dickinson, Aug. 9, 1803, *in* 10 Jefferson, Works, *supra* note 27, at 29:

> The general government has no powers but such as the constitution has given it; and it has not given it a power of holding foreign territory, & still less of incorporating it into the Union. An amendment of the Constitution seems necessary for this. In the meantime we must ratify & pay our money, as we have treated, for a thing beyond the constitution, and rely on the nation to sanction an act done for its great good, without its previous authority.

Not many agreed with him, and the Senate overwhelmingly approved the treaty. S. Exec. Journal, 8th Cong., 1st Sess. 450 (1803) [Executive Journal Twenty-Second Session 57–58]. The house debated the treaty at 13 Annals of Cong. 385–419, 432–89, 497–515 (1803) (Washington, DC: Gales & Seaton 1852). A few members did argue that the Constitution did not contemplate acquiring territory beyond the territory of the United States existing at the time of adoption, suggesting that the President and Senate could not incorporate a foreign people into the Union or give away a state. *See, e.g., id.* at 432–33, 454–55, 462. Several speakers responded that the right to acquire territory follows from the right of conquest and therefore the right to make treaties. Interestingly, several other speakers questioned the constitutionality of the provision in the treaty that would give favorable preferences to Spanish and French vessels in New Orleans and other ports in the ceded territory for a period of years. They argued that such a provision would be a "preference" to the port of New Orleans – encouraging trade therein – that was denied to other ports in the United States in violation of the first part of the Port Preference Clause. U.S. Const. art. I, § 9, cl. 6 ("No Preference shall be given by any Regulation of Commerce or Revenue to the Ports of one State over those of another: nor shall Vessels bound to, or from, one State, be obliged to enter, clear, or pay Duties in another."); 13 Annals of Cong. 433–34, 440–41, 442–43, 455–56.

124 Am. Ins. Co. v. Canter, 26 U.S. 511, 542 (1828).

125 The Supreme Court recently described the various bases of congressional power over Indian affairs, including the treaty power and the commerce power as well as constitutional structure and inherent powers. *See* Haaland v. Brackeen, 599 U.S. 255, 273–75 (2023). It is a somewhat dubious proposition that Congress's power to govern commerce with the native tribes includes the power to regulate their internal affairs, but it is certainly possible that the power to regulate commerce *with* the Indian tribes or *with* a foreign nation included the power to regulate all intrastate commercial activity. Green, *supra* note 119, at 662 (arguing that the commerce power does authorize such regulation).

126 Baude, *supra* note 90, at 1761–77.

CHAPTER 5

1 U.S. Const. art. II, § 1.

2 U.S. Const. art. II, § 2, para. 1:

The President shall be Commander in Chief of the Army and Navy of the United States, and of the Militia of the several States, when called into the actual Service of the United States; he may require the Opinion, in writing, of the principal Officer in each of the executive Departments, upon any Subject relating to the Duties of their respective Offices, and he shall have Power to grant Reprieves and Pardons for Offences against the United States, except in Cases of Impeachment.

3 U.S. Const. art. II, § 2, para. 2:

He shall have Power, by and with the Advice and Consent of the Senate, to make Treaties, provided two thirds of the Senators present concur; and he shall nominate, and by and with the Advice and Consent of the Senate, shall appoint Ambassadors, other public Ministers and Consuls, Judges of the supreme Court, and all other Officers of the United States, whose Appointments are not herein otherwise provided for, and which shall be established by Law: but the Congress may by Law vest the Appointment of such inferior Officers, as they think proper, in the President alone, in the Courts of Law, or in the Heads of Departments.

4 U.S. Const. art. II, § 2, para. 3 ("The President shall have Power to fill up all Vacancies that may happen during the Recess of the Senate, by granting Commissions which shall expire at the End of their next Session.").

5 U.S. Const. art. II, § 3:

He shall from time to time give to the Congress Information of the State of the Union, and recommend to their Consideration such Measures as he shall judge necessary and expedient; he may, on extraordinary Occasions, convene both Houses, or either of them, and in Case of Disagreement between them, with Respect to the Time of Adjournment, he may adjourn them to such Time as he shall think proper; he shall receive Ambassadors and other public Ministers; he shall take Care that the Laws be faithfully executed, and shall Commission all the Officers of the United States.

For one view on the importance of the division among these paragraphs, *see* Michael W. McConnell, The President Who Would Not Be King: Executive Power under the Constitution 267–74 (Princeton University Press 2020).

6 Edward S. Corwin, The President: Office and Powers, 1787–1957, at 3 (New York University Press, 4th rev. ed. 1957).

7 *Id.* at 3–4.

8 Myers v. United States, 272 U.S. 52, 128 (1926).

9 Theodore Roosevelt, An Autobiography 389 (New York: The Macmillan Co. 1913).

10 *Id.*

11 2 Max Farrand ed., The Records of the Federal Convention of 1787, at 52 (New Haven, CT: Yale University Press 1911).

12 Gordon S. Wood, The Creation of the American Republic, 1776–1787, at 136 (Chapel Hill: University of North Carolina Press 1998) (1969).

13 *Id.* at 137.

14 *Id.* at 139.

15 *Id.* at 138.

16 Va. Const. of 1776, *reprinted in* 7 Francis Newton Thrope ed., The Federal and State Constitutions 3812, 3816–17 (Washington, DC: Gov't Printing Off. 1909) [hereinafter Thorpe, Constitutions].

17 The Maryland Constitution provided,

the Governor, by and with the advice and consent of the Council, may embody the militia; and, when embodied, shall alone have the direction thereof; and shall also have the direction of all the regular land and sea forces, under the laws of this State . . . ; *and may alone exercise all other the executive powers of government, where the concurrence of the Council is not required, according to the laws of this State*; and grant reprieves or pardons for any crime, except in such cases where the law shall otherwise direct; and may, during the recess of the General Assembly, lay embargoes . . . ; but the Governor *shall not, under any pretence, exercise any power or prerogative by virtue of any law, statute, or custom of England or Great Britain.*

Md. Const. of 1776, art. XXXIII, *reprinted in* 3 Thorpe, Constitutions, *supra* note 16, at 1686, 1696 (emphasis added). The Delaware Constitution of 1776 declared that the president of the state had the power to lay embargoes, grant reprieves and pardons, and "may exercise all the other executive powers of government, limited and restrained as by this constitution is mentioned, and according to the laws of the State." Del. Const. of 1776, art. 7, *reprinted in* 1 Thorpe, Constitutions, *supra* note 16, at 562–63. And Georgia's 1777 constitution provided that the governor and council shall "exercise the executive powers of government, according to the laws of this State and the constitution thereof, save only in the case of pardons and remission of fines, which he shall in no instance grant." Ga. Const. of 1777, art. XIX, *reprinted in* 2 Thorpe, Constitutions, *supra* note 16, at 777, 781. North Carolina's 1776 constitution provided that the governor "may exercise all the other executive powers of government, limited and restrained as by this Constitution is mentioned, and according to the laws of the State." N.C. Const. of 1776, art. XIX, *reprinted in* 5 Thorpe, Constitutions, *supra* note 16, at 2787, 2791–92. I have previously discussed these provisions in Ilan Wurman, *In Search of Prerogative*, 70 Duke L.J. 93, 113–15 (2020).

18 Forrest McDonald, *Novus Ordo Seclorum*: The Intellectual Origins of the Constitution 175 (Lawrence: University Press of Kansas 1985).

19 *Id.* at 176.

20 *Id.* at 177.

21 *Id.* at 177–78.

22 2 Farrand, *supra* note 11, at 35.

23 *Id.*

24 1 Farrand, *supra* note 11, at 48.

25 *Id.* at 71.

26 2 Farrand, *supra* note 11, at 52.

27 Marshall's "A Friend of the Constitution" Essays, No. 7 (July 9, 1819), *reprinted in* Gerald Gunther ed., *John Marshall's Defense of McCulloch v. Maryland* 196, 199 (Stanford University Press 1969). For this citation I am indebted to Michael Stokes Paulsen, Michael W. McConnell, Samuel L. Bray, & William Baude, The Constitution of the United States 22 (Saint Paul, MN: Foundation Press, 5th ed. 2023).

28 Paulsen et al., *supra* note 27, at 22.

29 Charles C. Thach Jr., The Creation of the Presidency, 1775–1789: A Study in Constitutional History 57 (Baltimore: The Johns Hopkins Press 1922).

30 *Id.* at 62.

31 *Id.*

32 1 Farrand, *supra* note 11, at 65.

33 *Id.*

34 *Id.* at 66.

35 *Id.* at 66–67.

36 *Id.* at 67. Madison had also moved that the President "execute such other powers not Legislative nor Judiciary in their nature as may from time to time be delegated by the national Legislature," *id.* (brackets and quote marks omitted), but this was defeated as being superfluous. For a discussion of this episode, *see* McConnell, *supra* note 5, at 40–41.

37 1 Farrand, *supra* note 11, at 96–97.

38 *Id.* at 96.

39 *Id.*

40 *Id.* at 97.

41 *Id.*

42 *Id.* at 98–104.

43 *Id.* at 100.

44 *Id.* at 101.

45 *Id.* at 103; *see also* McConnell, *supra* note 5, at 46.

46 1 Farrand, *supra* note 11, at 175–76.

47 *Id.* at 68 (Wilson); 2 Farrand, *supra* note 11, at 29 (Morris); *id.* at 54 (Madison).

48 1 Farrand, *supra* note 11, at 80.

49 2 Farrand, *supra* note 11, at 29.

50 *Id.* at 31. For a general discussion, *see* McConnell, *supra* note 5, at 54–56.

51 *See, e.g.,* 1 Farrand, *supra* note 11, at 81; 2 Farrand, *supra* note 11, at 22.

52 Gouverneur Morris "saw no alternative for making the Executive independent of the Legislature but either to give him his office for life, or make him eligible by the people." 2 Farrand, *supra* note 11, at 54. James McClurg stated that "[i]t was an essential object with him to make the Executive independent of the Legislature," and that "the only mode left for effecting" such independence, after the vote rejecting the idea of making the President ineligible for additional terms, "was to appoint him during good behavior." *Id.* at 36.

53 The Federalist No. 68, at 412 (Clinton Rossiter ed. 1961) (Hamilton).

54 For the deliberations over impeachment, *see* McConnell, *supra* note 5, at 56–61.

55 2 Farrand, *supra* note 11, at 57.

56 The Federalist No. 68, *supra* note 53, at 411.

57 For a general discussion of the Committee and its work, *see* McConnell, *supra* note 5, at 62–74. The electoral college was adopted a bit later on.

58 1 Farrand, *supra* note 11, at 66.

59 On August 22, 1787, the *Pennsylvania Journal* addressed rumors about the goings on of the Convention. It was rumored that the Convention was seeking to establish a monarchy. "[I]t has been uniformly answered," the *Journal* reassured, "tho' we cannot, affirmatively, tell you what we are doing, we can, negatively, tell you what we are not doing – we never once thought of a king." Akhil Reed Amar, The Words That Made Us: America's Constitutional Conversation, 1760–1840, at 220 (New York: Basic Books 2021); 3

Farrand, *supra* note 11, at 73–74 (reprinting article). Suffice it to say, Saikrishna Prakash's thesis that the presidency was intended to be "imperial from the beginning" does not comport with the historical record. *See* Saikrishna Bangalore Prakash, Imperial from the Beginning: The Constitution of the Original Executive (New Haven, CT: Yale University Press 2015).

60 The Federalist No. 77, *supra* note 53, at 463 (Hamilton). Hamilton also said this in the Constitutional Convention. 1 Farrand, *supra* note 11, at 289 ("[W]e ought to go as far in order to attain stability and permanency, as republican principles will admit."). I am, ultimately, indebted to Martin Diamond's work for alerting me to the significance of Hamilton's phrase. *See* William A. Schambra ed., As Far as Republican Principles Will Admit: Essays by Martin Diamond (Washington, DC: AEI Press 1991).

61 2 Farrand, *supra* note 11, at 35.

62 The Federalist No. 10, *supra* note 53, at 84 (Madison).

63 These next sections borrow heavily from Ilan Wurman, *The Removal Power: A Critical Guide*, 2020 Cato Sup. Ct. Rev. 157, 159–67, and Wurman, *supra* note 17.

64 Youngstown Sheet & Tube Co. v. Sawyer, 343 U.S. 579, 641 (1952) (Jackson, J., concurring).

65 In 1994, Professors Calabresi and Prakash collected several examples of academic commentators taking this position. Steven G. Calabresi & Saikrishna B. Prakash, *The President's Power to Execute the Laws*, 104 Yale L.J. 541, 572 n.114 (1994). These included Bruce Ledewitz, *The Uncertain Power of the President to Execute the Laws*, 46 Tenn. L. Rev. 757, 797 (1979); Morton Rosenberg, *Congress's Prerogative over Agencies and Agency Decisionmakers: The Rise and Demise of the Reagan Administration's Theory of the Unitary Executive*, 57 Geo. Wash. L. Rev. 627, 634 (1989); A. Michael Froomkin, Note, *In Defense of Administrative Agency Autonomy*, 96 Yale L.J. 787, 799–800 (1987); and Charles L. Black Jr., *The Working Balance of the American Political Departments*, 1 Hastings Const. L.Q. 13, 14–15 (1974).

66 2 Farrand, *supra* note 11, at 163 ("The Government shall consist of supreme legislative, executive, and judicial Powers.").

67 *See* Calabresi & Prakash, *supra* note 65, at 570–71.

68 The student was Devin Gates of the Sandra Day O'Connor College of Law at Arizona State University.

69 *See* note 389 in Chapter 4.

70 Giles Jacob, A New Law-Dictionary [528] (J. Morgan ed., London: W. Strahan and W. Woodfall, 10th ed. 1782).

71 2 Farrand, *supra* note 11, at 172 ("The Jurisdiction of the Supreme (National) Court shall extend to . . . ."); *id.* at 173 (providing the legislature may "distribute" or "assign" part of this "jurisdiction" to the "inferior courts").

72 He had said, according to Madison's notes:

Suppose that the three powers, were to be vested in three persons, by compact; that one was to have the power of making – another of executing, and a third of judging, the laws. Would it not be very natural for the two latter after having settled the partition on paper, to observe, and would not candor oblige the former to admit, that as a security agst. legislative acts of the former which might easily be so framed as to undermine the powers of the two others, the two others ought to be armed with a veto for their own defence, or at least to have an opportunity of stating their objections agst. acts of encroachment?

Id. at 78–79. Morris was defending a Council of Revision. His statement suggests that the three powers "vest" in the respective bodies the power of making, executing, or judging laws.

73 *See, e.g.,* Pacificus No. 1 (Hamilton) (arguing as one possibility that Article II's Vesting Clause is a residuum of all executive powers); Helvidius No. 1 (Madison) (suggesting the Vesting Clause is a source of power to oversee the faithful execution of the laws, and thus requires the President to have the removal power). My student, Devin Gates, also nicely suggested that if both Madison and Hamilton agreed on at least this much, it would seem rather decisive evidence against the cross-reference theory.

74 *See, e.g.,* Akhil Reed Amar, America's Constitution: A Biography 133 (New York: Basic Books 2005) ("While later specific clauses of Article II clarified and qualified this opening grant of power in a variety of ways, . . . the first words of Article II themselves vested the president with a residuum of general authority . . . ."); Abraham D. Sofaer, War, Foreign Affairs and Constitutional Power: The Origins 37 (Cambridge, MA: Ballinger Publishing Co. 1976) (describing textual basis for this view).

75 McConnell, *supra* note 5, at 235. Other scholars have articulated this view similarly. Curtis A. Bradley & Martin S. Flaherty, *Executive Power Essentialism & Foreign Affairs*, 102 Mich. L. Rev. 545, 549 (2004) (the residual theory "reconciles the text of the Constitution with the breadth of presidential power by stipulating that the Article II Vesting Clause grants the President all powers that are in their nature 'executive,' subject only to the specific exceptions and qualifications set forth in the rest of the Constitution"); Saikrishna B. Prakash & Michael D. Ramsey, *The Executive Power over Foreign Affairs*, 111 Yale L.J. 231, 253 (2001):

[T]he President's executive foreign affairs power is residual, encompassing only those executive foreign affairs powers not allocated elsewhere by the Constitution's text. The Constitution's allocation of specific foreign affairs powers or roles to Congress or the Senate are properly read as assignments away from the President. Absent these specific allocations, by Article II, Section 1, all traditionally executive foreign affairs powers would be presidential.

76 1 William Blackstone, Commentaries on the Laws of England 180 (Oxford: Clarendon Press 1765) ("[A]s the king has the sole right of convening the parliament, so also it is a branch of the royal prerogative, that he may (whenever he pleases) prorogue the parliament for a time, or put a final period to its existence.").

77 *See, e.g.,* John Harrison, *The Constitution and the Law of Nations*, 106 Geo. L.J. 1659 (2018), 1676 & n.88; United States v. Smith, 27 F. Cas. 1192, 1203 (C.C.D.N.Y. 1806) (argument of United States Attorney Sanford):

When it has become a law, according to the forms of the constitution, it is his duty to take care that it be faithfully executed. He cannot suspend its operation, dispense with its application, or prevent its effect, otherwise than by the exercise of its constitutional power of pardoning, after conviction. If he could do so, he could repeal the law, and would thus invade the province assigned to the legislature, and become paramount to the other branches of the government.

Id. at 1214 (argument of United States Attorney Edwards) ("The president of the United States possesses no power to dispense with the laws, but, on the other hand, is bound by his official oath to preserve them inviolate, and to defend the constitution of the United States."); *id.* at 1229–30 (Patterson, Circuit Justice):

[T]he president of the United States is bound by the constitution to 'take care that the laws be faithfully executed.' These are the words of the instrument; and, therefore, it is to be presumed that he would not countenance the violation of any statute .... Who holds the power of dispensation? True, a nolle prosequi may be entered, a pardon may be granted; but these presume criminality, presume guilt, presume amenability to judicial investigation and punishment, which are very different from a power to dispense with the law .... The president of the United States cannot control the statute, nor dispense with its execution, and still less can he authorize a person to do what the law forbids. If he could, it would render the execution of the laws dependent on his will and pleasure; which is a doctrine that has not been set up, and will not meet with any supporters in our government. In this particular, the law is paramount.

78 For a general discussion, *see* McConnell, *supra* note 5, at 115–19.

79 An Act declareing the Rights and Liberties of the Subject and Setleing the Succession of the Crowne. 1688 (c. 2), 1 Will. & Mar. s. 2 (royal assent on Dec. 16, 1689).

80 1 Blackstone, *supra* note 76, at 138.

81 McConnell, *supra* note 5, at 117 & n.61. Here is McConnell's note in full:
Section 7 of the Virginia Declaration of Rights (1776) provided "[t]hat all power of suspending laws, or the execution of laws, by any authority without consent of the representatives of the people, is injurious to their rights, and ought not to be exercised."4 The Founders' Constitution 123 (Philip B. Kurland & Ralph Lerner eds., 1987). Section 7 of the Delaware Declaration of Rights and Fundamental Rules (1776) said "[t]hat no Power of suspending Laws, or the Execution of Laws, ought to be exercised unless by the Legislature." *Id.* at 124. Chapter 1, Article 17 of the Vermont Constitution (1786) declared that "[t]he power of suspending laws, or the execution of laws, ought never to be exercised, but by the Legislature, or by authority derived from it, to be exercised in such particular cases only as the Legislature shall expressly provide for." *Id.*

82 1 Farrand, *supra* note 11, at 103.

83 *Id.* at 104.

84 The dispensing power was not categorically rejected in the Bill of Rights of 1689 in the same way the suspending power had been; it was the abuse by James II that troubled his subjects. The power to "dispense" with the law on particular occasions, in the same way that courts of "equity" had the power to mitigate the rigors of the common law, could be an important tool of justice. Perhaps that leaves some room for prosecutorial discretion today, although, as McConnell explains, such discretion is not the same thing as the dispensing power, which gave legal authorization to violate the law. McConnell, *supra* note 5, at 119. But the Take Care Clause may have required vigorous prosecution of all offenses; certainly, the fee structure for early federal prosecutors incentivized vigorous and energetic execution. Zachary S. Price, *Enforcement Discretion and Executive Duty*, 67

Vand. L. Rev. 671, 719–20 (2014). And the line between dispensing and suspending can be thin indeed, as attested by the Obama Administration's "deferred action" programs for children unlawfully present in the United States, colloquially known as "dreamers," and their parents. These issues are beyond the scope of this book, but the reader may explore them through further reading. A good place to start would be Price, *supra*. The United States Court of Appeals for the Fifth Circuit also considered the nature of the DAPA program (deferred action for parents) in the context of administrative law in Texas v. United States, 809 F.3d 134 (5th Cir. 2015).

85 McConnell, *supra* note 5, 236.

86 *Id.* at 9.

87 Louis Henkin, Foreign Affairs and the United States Constitution 13–15 (Oxford: Clarendon Press, 2d ed. 1996).

88 Prakash & Ramsey, *supra* note 75, at 253:

> [T]he President's executive foreign affairs power is residual, encompassing … executive foreign affairs powers not allocated elsewhere by the Constitution's text. The Constitution's allocation of specific foreign affairs powers or roles to Congress or the Senate are properly read as assignments away from the President. Absent these specific allocations, by Article II, Section 1, all traditionally executive foreign affairs powers would be presidential.

Amar, *supra* note 74, at 191, 196 n.* (arguing various powers such as treaty abrogation and recognition are residually vested in the President).

89 John Hart Ely, On Constitutional Ground 149 (Princeton University Press 1996).

90 Corwin, *supra* note 6, at 171–72.

91 This issue is also discussed in Wurman, *supra* note 17, at 125. The Committee on Postponed Matters in the Constitutional Convention considered the following resolution: "The Senate shall have power to treat with foreign nations, but no Treaty shall be binding on the United States which is not ratified by a Law." 2 Farrand, *supra* note 11, at 382–83. Thus, the making of treaties required "treating" with foreign nations. And Samuel Johnson's 1755 dictionary defined "to treat" as "1. To discourse; to make discussions …. 2. To practice negotiation …. 3. To come to terms of accommodation …. 4. To make gratuitous entertainments." 1 Samuel Johnson, A Dictionary of the English Language 2092 (London: W. Strahan 1755).

92 2 Farrand, *supra* note 11, at 183

93 *Id.* at 235. *See id.* at 183 for the assignment of these powers to the Senate.

94 1 Blackstone, *supra* note 76, at 253. For a comparison of the powers listed in Blackstone and those in the Constitution, *see* Chapter 3, and also Wurman, *supra* note 17, at 122–24.

95 1 Farrand, *supra* note 11, at 67.

96 McConnell, *supra* note 5, at 73.

97 The next few paragraphs on John Locke are taken from Wurman, *supra* note 17, at 108–09. For Locke's influence, *see* Bernard Bailyn, The Ideological Origins of the American Revolution 27–30 (Cambridge, MA: Belknap Press, Enlarged Ed. 1992) (describing John Locke's influence on Founding-generation Americans); Alan Gibson, Interpreting the Founding 13–21 (Lawrence: University Press of Kansas 2006) (describing the prominent twentieth-century interpretation of the Founding "that the core of the Founders' political

thought is encapsulated in the Lockean variation of the principles of classical liberalism"); Jack N. Rakove, *Fidelity through History (or Do It)*, 65 Fordham L. Rev. 1587, 1598 (1997) ("There is no question that politically articulate eighteenth-century Americans – and certainly members of the political elite – were eclectically conversant with the works of luminaries like Hobbes, Locke, Montesquieu, Hume, and Blackstone.").

98 John Locke, Two Treatises of Government 382–83 (Peter Laslett ed., Cambridge University Press 1960) (1690).

99 *Id.* at 383 (emphasis omitted).

100 *Id.* at 383–84 (emphasis omitted).

101 Prakash & Ramsey, *supra* note 75, at 268.

102 1 Farrand, *supra* note 11, at 73–74. Professor McConnell suspects that William Pierce, who reported this remark from Wilson, may have misheard Wilson. McConnell, *supra* note 5, at 38. That seems unlikely. According to Madison,

> Wilson preferred a single magistrate, as giving most energy dispatch and responsibility to the office. He did not consider the Prerogatives of the British Monarch as a proper guide in defining the Executive powers. Some of these prerogatives were of a Legislative nature. Among others that of war & peace [etc.]. The only powers he conceived strictly Executive were those of executing the laws, and appointing officers, not ⟨appertaining to and⟩ appointed by the Legislature.

> 1 Farrand, *supra* note 11, at 65–66. McConnell believes that "among others" refers to powers *not* legislative in nature, McConnell, *supra* note 5, at 36–38, but it seems more natural to read it as saying "among other examples of legislative powers, that of war & peace [etc.]." This would be consistent with Pierce's note.

103 John Harrison, Executive Power 24 (June 3, 2019) (unpublished manuscript), https://ssrn.com/abstract = 3398427 [https://perma.cc/CXS2-J8MP]; *see also* Bradley & Flaherty, *supra* note 75, at 560 (arguing that Locke "distinguishes executive power from foreign relations power").

104 1 Blackstone, *supra* note 76, at 242.

105 *Id.* at 245.

106 *Id.* at 257.

107 Blackstone himself went on to say that "those branches of the king's prerogative" discussed in his chapter on the king's various powers and authorities "constitute the executive power of the government." *Id.* at 271. And Montesquieu, who was also deeply influential on the Framers, *see* Bailyn, *supra* note 97, at 27–30; Rakove, *supra* note 97, at 1598, famously described an "executive power over the things depending on the right of nations," and an "executive power over the things depending on civil right." Charles-Louis de Secondat & Baron de Montesquieu, The Spirit of the Laws 156 (Anne M. Cohler, Basia Carolyn Miller, & Harold Samuel Stone eds., Cambridge University Press 1989) (1748). By the former power, the magistrate "makes peace or war, sends or receives embassies, establishes security, and prevents invasions," and by the latter "he punishes crimes or judges disputes between individuals." *Id.* at 156–57. Montesquieu therefore called this last power "the power of judging," and the other "the executive power of the state." *Id.* at 157.

108 For further reading, *see* Wurman, *supra* note 17; *see also* Julian Davis Mortenson, *Article II Vests the Executive Power, Not the Royal Prerogative*, 119 Colum. L. Rev. 1169 (2019); Matthew Steilen, *How to Think Constitutionally about Prerogative: A Study of Early American Usage*, 66 Buff. L. Rev. 557 (2018); Seth Barrett Tillman, *The Old Whig Theory of the Executive Power*, New Reform Club (Jan. 18, 2019, 5:02 AM), https://reformclub .blogspot.com/2019/01/the-old-whig-theory-of-executive-power.html   [https://perma.cc/ J8NT-4LB9].

109 Recall particularly that Gouverneur Morris, the lead drafter on the Committee of Style, used the terms in these ways. Responding to objections about blending powers, Morris described "the three powers" as "the power of making[,] ... of executing, and ... of judging, the laws." 2 Farrand, *supra* note 11, at 79.

110 Montesquieu, *supra* note 107, at 157.

CHAPTER 6

1 Significant portions of this chapter are based on, and borrow heavily from, my prior work. *See* Ilan Wurman, *The Original Presidency: A Conception of Administrative Control*, 16 J. Legal Analysis 26–63 (2024); Ilan Wurman, *In Search of Prerogative*, 70 Duke L.J. 93 (2020); Ilan Wurman, *The Removal Power: A Critical Guide*, 2019–20 Cato. Sup. Ct. Rev. 157 (2020).

2 *See, e.g.,* Jeffrey Crouch, Mark J. Rozell, & Mitchel A. Sollenberger, The Unitary Executive Theory: A Danger to Constitutional Government (Lawrence: University Press of Kansas 2020); Robert V. Percival, *Presidential Management of the Administrative State: The Not-So-Unitary Executive*, 51 Duke L.J. 963 (2001). These are just two examples. The label for this theory is extremely common.

3 U.S. Const., art. II, § 2, para. 1.

4 Seila Law LLC v. Consumer Financial Protection Bureau, 591 U.S. 197, 266 n.3 (2020) (Kagan, J. dissenting); Lawrence Lessig & Cass R. Sunstein, *The President and the Administration*, 94 Colum. L. Rev. 1, 32 (1994) ("What possible reason could there be for providing the President with a constitutional power to demand written reports from officers over whom he already had an inherent power of control?"); *see also, e.g.,* A. Michael Froomkin, Note, In *Defense of Administrative Agency Autonomy*, 96 Yale L.J. 787, 800 (1987) (if the President can fire at will, "why put the power to request written opinions in the Constitution?"); Zachary J. Murray, *The Forgotten Unitary Executive Power: The Textualist, Originalist, and Functionalist Opinions Clause*, 39 Pace L. Rev. 229, 234 (2018) (making negative inference from the Opinions Clause that the President does not have unenumerated powers like the removal power); *cf. also* John F. Manning, *Separation of Powers as Ordinary Interpretation*, 124 Harv. L. Rev. 1939, 2035 (2011) (not weighing in on the merits of the unitary executive debates but pointing out that "[i]f the President can fire executive officers for any reason or no reason at all, then he or she can presumably get an opinion in writing without an express grant of constitutional power to do so."). This argument seems to have been first made in writing by Richard Henry Lee. Letter from Richard Henry Lee to Samuel Adams (Aug. 8, 1789), *printed in* 2 James Curtis Ballagh, The Letters of Richard Henry Lee, 1779–1794, at 495–97 (New York: Macmillan Press 1914).

5 Several scholars have observed that that Congress may by law create duties for officers and that absent statutory authorization, the President may only oversee but not control those officers in the exercise of those duties. Peter L. Strauss, *Foreword: Overseer, or "The Decider"? The President in Administrative Law,* 75 Geo. Wash. L. Rev. 696 (2007); Kevin M. Stack, *The President's Statutory Powers to Administer the Laws,* 106 Colum. L. Rev. 263 (2006); Elena Kagan, *Presidential Administration,* 114 Harv. L. Rev. 2245 (2001); Cynthia R. Farina, *The Consent of the Governed: Against Simple Rules for a Complex World,* 72 Chi.-Kent L. Rev. 987 (1997); Morton Rosenberg, *Congress's Prerogative over Agencies and Agency Decisionmakers,* 57 Geo. Wash. L. Rev. 627, 649–57 (1989). These and other scholars tend to accept that Congress can restrict removals, too. Strauss, *supra,* at 716 ("one cannot say that Congress is unable to limit the removal of Heads of Departments to 'cause'"); Rosenberg, *supra,* at 689 ("If the President was meant to have full control over the executive, including the power to discharge at will, why was the power to request written opinions put in the Constitution?"); Peter M. Shane, Democracy's Chief Executive 114–17 (Oakland: University of California Press 2022) (relying on the Opinions Clause not only to support the proposition that the President can oversee but not control law execution, but also to question the removal power); *Seila Law,* 591 U.S. at 266 (Kagan, J., dissenting). Heidi Kitrosser has written that the Opinions Clause "fits much more logically into a system whereby officers are not mere alter egos to the president but are subject to presidential oversight." Heidi Kitrosser, Reclaiming Accountability: Transparency, Executive Power, and the U.S. Constitution 148 (University of Chicago Press 2015). She then adds that there was a "lack of founding consensus on the scope of the president's removal power," and even on whether appointments were executive. *Id.* at 149.
6 Humphrey's Ex'r v. United States, 295 U.S. 602, 629 (1935).
7 Richard E. Neustadt, Presidential Power and the Modern Presidents 10–11, 29–32 (New York: The Free Press, 3d ed. 1990). Neustadt's study was not of the President's formal, legal powers, but rather of the President's personal influence. *See id.* at ix; 7, n*; 10–11. Neustadt's claim (simplified here) was that whatever formal powers of direction the President might have, formal powers are not enough to influence outcomes.
8 Kagan, *Presidential Administration, supra* note 5, at 2325.
9 Edward Corwin, The President: Office and Powers, 1787–1957, at 80–81 (New York University Press, 4th rev. ed. 1957).
10 John P. Kaminski & Gaspare J. Saladino eds., 9 The Documentary History of the Ratification of the Constitution 1098 (Madison: Wisconsin Historical Society Press 1990).
11 2 Jonathan Elliot ed., The Debates in the Several State Conventions on the Adoption of the Federal Constitution 513 (Washington, DC: Printed for the editor, 2d ed. 1836) [hereinafter Elliot's Debates].
12 4 Elliot's Debates, *supra* note 11, at 136.
13 4 *id.* at 106.
14 3 Max Farrand ed., The Records of the Federal Convention of 1787, at 111 (New Haven, CT: Yale University Press 1911).
15 Other writers agreed. The President had "mighty power[]" to "take care, that the laws be faithfully executed." John P. Kaminski & Gaspare J. Saladino eds., 8 The Documentary History of the Ratification of the Constitution 203 (Madison: Wisconsin Historical Society Press 1988) (Americanus). His power was "to see [the laws] duly executed." Merril Jensen

ed., 3 The Documentary History of the Ratification of the Constitution 149 (Madison: Wisconsin Historical Society Press 1978) (Jerseyman).

16 2 Herbert J. Storing ed., The Complete Anti-Federalist 310 (University of Chicago Press 1981).

17 The Federalist No. 72, at 436 (Clinton Rossiter ed. 1961) (Hamilton).

18 George Wilson ed., Twelfth Part of the Reports of Sir Edward Coke [64] (London: Printed for J. Rivington & Sons et al. 1777). What actually happened in 1607 or 1608 is discussed in Roland G. Usher, *James I and Sir Edward Coke*, 18 The English Hist. Rev. 664, 670 (1903).

19 Act of Settlement, 12 & 13 Will. 3 c. 2 (1701).

20 Coke, *supra* note 18, at [64].

21 *See also* Edward Bagshaw, The Rights of the Crown of England as It Is Established by Law 105 (London: Printed by A.M. for Simon Miller at the Starre in St Pauls Church-yard, 1660) ("[H]e neither speaketh, nor acteth, nor judgeth, nor executeth, but by his Writt, by his Laws, by his Judges, and Ministers, and both these sworne to him to judge a right, and to execute justice to his People."); Matthew Hale, The Prerogatives of the King 107 [146] (D.E.C. Yale ed., Selden Society 1976) ("[H]e neither speaks nor doth anything in the public administration of this realm but what he doth by these or some of these, especially the chancellor."). For these references, I am indebted to Julian Davis Mortenson, *The Executive Power Clause*, 168 U. Pa. L. Rev. 1269, 1325–26 n.299 (2020).

22 It is possible that the President can exercise duties if the relevant officer is absent, although it is not entirely clear how far this principle extends. President Washington wrote to Gouverneur Morris in October 1789 instructing him on several points of negotiation with England. In an accompanying letter setting out Morris's credentials and authorization to conduct diplomacy on behalf of the United States, Washington explained that "[t]his communication ought regularly to be made to you by the Secretary of State; but, that office not being at present filled, my desire of avoiding delays induces me to make it under my own hand." Letter from George Washington to Gouverneur Morris (Oct. 13, 1789), *in* 11 Worthington Chauncey Ford ed., Writings of George Washington 441 (G. P. Putnam's Sons 1891). Taking this principle too far may defeat the purpose of the Appointments Clause and Congress's role in establishing offices; on the other hand, perhaps those powers and limitations are based on the functionalist concern that the President cannot personally execute all the laws even if there were a desire to do so. But if the President does have the capacity to execute certain duties, it is at least not obvious that he cannot do so personally if the relevant officer is incapacitated or absent. This question may also depend on other presidential powers in the Constitution, such as the Commander-in-Chief power or the treatymaking power.

23 Corwin, *supra* note 9, at 80.

24 1 Annals of Cong. 474 (1789) (Washington, DC: Gales & Seaton 1834).

25 1 William Blackstone, Commentaries on the Laws of England 257 (Oxford: Clarendon Press 1765).

26 *Id.* at 259. Of course, after the Act of Settlement, the king could not remove them.

27 *Id.* at 262.

28 Henry Parker, Observations Upon Some of His Majesties Late Answers and Expresses 38 (1642). For this reference, the author is again indebted to Mortenson, *supra* note 21, at 1325.

29 Giles Jacob, A New Law-Dictionary 544 (J. Morgan ed., London: W. Strahan and W. Woodfall, 10th ed. 1782); Giles Jacob, A New Law-Dictionary 418 (London: E. and R. Nutt and R. Gosling, 3d ed. 1736). The author is indebted to the work of Jed Shugerman for this quotation.

30 Giles Jacob, Every Man His Own Lawyer 376 (London: E. and R. Nutt, and R. Gosling, 1736) ("And he names, creates, makes and removes the great Officers of the Government."); Giles Jacob, Every Man His Own Lawyer 239 (New York: Hugh Gaine 1768) (same). On the influence of this treatise, *see* William Hamilton Bryson, Census of Law Books in Colonial Virginia, at xv (Charlottesville: University Press of Virginia 1978).

31 Giles Jacob, Lex Constitutionis: Or, the Gentleman's Law 72 (London: Eliz. Nutt and R. Gosling 1719).

32 Mortenson, *supra* note 21, at 1325 (capitalization from heading altered).

33 George Mason, *Objections to the Constitution*, Mass. Centinel (Nov. 21, 1787), *reprinted in* John P. Kaminski & Gaspare J. Saladino eds., 4 The Documentary History of the Ratification of the Constitution 287, 289 (Madison: Wisconsin Historical Society Press 1997).

34 2 Farrand, *supra* note 14, at 538–39 (James Wilson) (also objecting "to the mode of appointing, as blending a branch of the Legislature with the Executive.").

35 1 Farrand, *supra* note 14, at 66–67 (reporting Wilson's second of Madison's proposal); *see id.* at 70 (noting Wilson's independent argument that "Extive. powers are designed for the execution of Laws, and appointing Officers not otherwise to be appointed").

36 Hampden, Pittsburgh Gazette, Feb. 16, 1788, *reprinted in* Merrill Jensen et al. eds., 2 The Documentary History of the Ratification of the Constitution 663, 667 (Madison: Wisconsin Historical Society Press 1976).

37 Mortenson, *supra* note 21, at 1329–30 & nn.315–20.

38 The Federalist No. 47, *supra* note 17, at 305 (Madison). Kenton Skarin, in a book manuscript on colonial executives, demonstrates that "[g]ubernatorial commissions, royal instructions, and royal charters" firmly established the appointment power in colonial executives and that the appointment of local functionaries such as justices of the peace and sheriffs "depended directly on the executive." Kenton J. Skarin, Our Captain General and Governor in Chief: Executive Power over Lower Officials in Colonial America 139 (manuscript on file with author).

39 Gordon Wood, The Creation of the American Republic, 1776–1787, at 145 (Chapel Hill: University of North Carolina Press 1998) (1969).

40 *Id.* at 148.

41 The strict textualist might argue that there are really three kinds of officers. The Opinions Clause identifies "the principal officer" of each executive department. U.S. Const. art II, § 2, para. 1 (the President "may require the Opinion, in writing, of the principal Officer in each of the executive Departments, upon any Subject relating to the Duties of their respective Offices."). This has led some scholars to suggest that there are really three kinds of officers: a principal officer who is also the head of the department, non-inferior officers who are not the principal, and then inferior officers. Jennifer Mascott & John Duffy, *Executive Decisions after Arthrex*, 2021 Sup. Ct. Rev. 225, 225–26 n.1 (2021).

This creates a series of problems too advanced for more than a brief summary of them. In particular, if there are truly three categories of officers, then can the President demand opinions from the non-inferior officers, given how the Opinions Clause is limited to principal officers? And if not, do the non-inferior officers answer to the principal officers? Presumably the answer is yes – but then they would be "inferior" to the principals, and thus inferior officers. It is possible that the principal officers are the heads of departments, and every other officer is inferior and subject to the control of the head. That is contrary to modern doctrine, however, which maintains that there can be many principal officers who are not the head of a department.

If Congress does establish an office within a department, but independent of the department head, then at a minimum Congress must make the officer controllable by the President. Otherwise, there would be no way for the President to control such officers because there would be no power to demand opinions, and such officers would not be subject to supervision from officers from whom the President can demand information. Such an office would not be "necessary and proper for carrying into execution" the President's law-execution powers, but rather would be a hindrance to them by interfering with the supervision of law execution. All of this presumes that the President cannot directly control officers in the absence of statutory authorization. That point is addressed more in Chapter 7.

42 Edmond v. United States, 520 U.S. 651 (1997); Kennedy v. Braidwood Management, Inc., 145 S.Ct. 2427 (2025). This author attempted a relatively comprehensive analysis of the term "inferior officer." Wurman, *Original Presidency*, *supra* note 1. That analysis generally supports the modern doctrine.

43 *Edmond*, 520 U.S. at 664–66.

44 To the extent the Supreme Court has recently suggested in United States v. Arthrex, 141 S. Ct. 1970 (2021), that all the decisions of inferior officers must be subject to review by a principal, that cannot be right. Justice Thomas correctly noted in dissent that some decisions are irreversible. It must be sufficient to allow independent judgment with the check of removal.

45 Buckley v. Valeo, 424 U.S. 1 (1976); Lucia v. SEC, 585 U.S. 237 (2018).

46 As the Supreme Court concluded. *Lucia*, 585 U.S. at 247.

47 *See* Jennifer L. Mascott, *Who Are "Officers of the United States"?*, 70 Stan. L. Rev. 443 (2018).

48 Steamboat Act of 1852, ch. 106, 10 Stat. 61, § 9 (Aug. 30, 1852) (providing that the collector, supervising inspector, and U.S. district judge together "shall designate two inspectors, of good character and suitable qualifications," and that "the two persons thus designated, if approved by the Secretary of Treasury," shall be appointed inspectors for the district).

49 A separate line of cases deals with the question of whether entities exercising no government power – such as Amtrak, the Smithsonian, or the Bank of the United States – should be treated as government entities. *See, e.g.*, Lebron v. Nat'l R.R. Pass. Corp., 513 U.S. 374 (1995).

50 Jacob (1782), *supra* note 29, at 544.

51 1 Blackstone, *supra* note 25, at 327:

And herein we are not to investigate the powers and duties of his majesty's great officers of state, the lord treasurer, lord chamberlain, the principal secretaries, or the like; because I do not know that they are in that capacity in any considerable degree the objects of our laws, or have any very important share of magistracy conferred upon them: except that the secretaries of state are allowed the power of commitment, in order to bring offenders to trial.

Although taken literally, Blackstone is expressing doubt or uncertainty, the best sense of the passage is that he does not believe the great officers of state to be subject to removal restrictions.

52 Michael W. McConnell, The President Who Would Not Be King: Executive Power under the Constitution 162 (Princeton University Press 2020).

53 Jed H. Shugerman, *The Indecisions of 1789: Inconstant Originalism and Strategic Ambiguity*, 171 U. Pa. L. Rev. 753, 820 (2023) (citing various sources).

54 Bryson, *supra* note 30, at xvii (noting that in colonial Virginia, almost as many people had this treatise as had Coke's reports); *see also* Herbert A. Johnson, Imported Eighteenth-Century Law Treatises in American Libraries, 1700–1799, at 17 (Knoxville: University of Tennessee Press 1978) (noting prominent Americans that had the volume).

55 Michael Dalton, The Countrey Justice: Containing the Practice of the Justices of the Peace 49 (London: Printed by John Streater, James Flesher, and Henry Twyford 1666). Other variants of the maxim included, *"quo ligatur, eo dissolvitur"* and *"eodem modo, quo aliquid constituitur, destruitur,"* both appearing under the list of maxims in Henry Rolle's reports from 1676, although not in the context of appointments. Un Continuation des Reports de Henry Rolle 19, 39 (London: Printed for Francis Tyton, Thomas Basset, John Leigh 1676). The list of maxims is contained in the back of the volume in an unpaginated table. Shugerman highlights still another formulation, "eodem modo quo oritur, eodem modo dissolvitur," which translates to, "[i]n the manner in which . . . a thing is constituted, is it dissolved," which is found in some modern legal dictionaries and some nineteenth-century cases. Shugerman, *supra* note 53, at 820 & nn.375–76 (citing sources).

56 Letter from Thomas Jefferson to Unknown (Dec. 25, 1779), *in* 3 Julian P. Boyd ed., The Papers of Thomas Jefferson: Main Series 242, 242 (Princeton University Press 1951).

57 Skarin, *supra* note 38, at 144 & nn.486–88. For example, in one illustrative episode, the council "Ordered That a New Commission of the Peace Issue for the County of Lancaster and that Nicholas Martin & Henry Lawson who have refused to act be left out of the said Commission & that Abraham Currell & Thomas Pinckard be added in their Room." Virginia Council Journals 105 (Oct. 29, 1742).

58 Note Concerning the Right of Removal from Office (1780), *in* 4 The Papers of Thomas Jefferson, *supra* note 56, at 281, 281. Daniel Webster stated the view forcefully in an 1835 speech on the spoils system. He said that as far as he was aware, removals were always effected by new appointments. Edwin P. Whipple ed., The Great Speeches and Orations of Daniel Webster 400 (Boston: Little, Brown, & Co 1895):

The power of placing one man in office necessarily implies the power of turning another out. If one man be Secretary of State, and another be appointed, the first goes out by the mere force of the appointment of the other, without any previous act of removal whatever. And this is the practice of the government, and has been, from the first. In all the removals which have been made, they have generally been effected simply by making other appointments.

59 2 Farrand, *supra* note 14, at 183, 185.

60 *Id.* at 495; McConnell, *supra* note 52, at 79–80.

61 1 Annals of Cong., *supra* note 24, at 370–72.

62 *Id.* at 381, 484 (1789). Also, some representatives argued that impeachment was the only mode of removing officers – an argument that was not seriously advanced because, as Madison pointed out, impeachment is a method by which Congress can remove officers. It says nothing of the president's power. *Id.* at 374–75. I take the labels senatorial, presidentialist, and congressionalist from Shugerman, *supra* note 53, at 759.

63 1 Annals of Cong., *supra* note 24, at 495–96.

64 *Id.* at 496.

65 *Id.*

66 272 U.S. 52, 247 (1926) (Brandeis, J., dissenting).

67 *See, e.g.,* 1 Annals of Cong., *supra* note 24, at 506, 512 (discussing this argument).

68 *Id.* at 496. Madison earlier said, "The Constitution affirms, that the Executive power shall be vested in the President. Are there exceptions to this proposition? Yes, there are. The Constitution says, that in appointing to office, the Senate shall be associated with the President, unless in the case of inferior officers . . . . Have we a right to extend this exception? I believe not." *Id.* at 463.

69 *Id.* at 463.

70 *Id.* at 500.

71 Professors Bradley and Flaherty have made this point. "Instead of seeing the Vesting Clause as conveying a package of foreign affairs powers, the House members who invoked the Clause may have simply believed that the Clause gave the President a general power to execute the laws, and that removal of subordinate executive officers was included within such a power." Curtis A. Bradley & Martin S. Flaherty, *Executive Power Essentialism and Foreign Affairs*, 102 Mich. L. Rev. 545, 661 (2004).

72 1 Annals of Cong., *supra* note 24, at 371, 383.

73 *Id.* at 382.

74 *Id.* at 578.

75 *Id.* at 505.

76 *Id.* at 580.

77 William Maclay, Journal of William Maclay, United States Senator from Pennsylvania, 1789–1791, at 116 (Edgar S. Maclay ed., 1890), https://memory.loc.gov/ammem/amlaw/lwmj.html.

78 *See, e.g.,* Humphrey's Ex'r, 295 U.S. 602, 630 (1935).

79 1 Annals of Cong., *supra* note 24, at 495.

80 *See* 15 Harold C. Syrett ed., Alexander Hamilton, The Papers of Alexander Hamilton 40 (Columbia University Press 1969); 5 John Marshall, The Life of George Washington 200 (Philadelphia, PA: C.P. Wayne 1807).

81 *Myers*, 272 U.S. at 285 n.75 (Brandeis, J., dissenting); Edward S. Corwin, *Tenure of Office and the Removal Power under the Constitution*, 27 Colum. L. Rev. 353, 362–63 (1927); David P. Currie, The Constitution in Congress: The Federalist Period, 1789–1801, at 40–41 (University of Chicago Press 1997); Shugerman, *supra* note 53.

82 116 U.S. 483 (1886).

83 *Id.* at 483.

84 *Id.* at 483–84.

85 *Id.* at 485.

86 At least in theory, civil service protections do not apply to persons "whose position has been determined to be of a confidential, policy-determining, policy-making or policy-advocating character."[5] U.S.C. § 7511(b)(2). And the Administrative Procedure Act allows agency heads to overturn the adjudicatory decisions of their hearing officers. 5 U.S.C. § 557(b). And "[m]ost regulatory statutes specify that agency heads rather than the President shall make regulatory decisions." Robert V. Percival, *Who's in Charge? Does the President Have Directive Authority over Agency Regulatory Decisions?*, 79 Fordham L. Rev. 2487, 2487 (2011) (citing Clean Air Act § 109, 42 U.S.C. § 7409).

87 272 U.S. 52 (1926).

88 William Howard Taft, Our Chief Magistrate and His Power 144 (Columbia University Press 1916).

89 *Id.* at 139–40.

90 *Myers*, 272 U.S. at 117.

91 *Id.* at 163–64.

92 He did say, as quoted earlier, "The executive power was given in general terms strengthened by specific terms where emphasis was regarded as appropriate, and was limited by direct expressions where limitation was needed, and the fact that no express limit was placed on the power of removal by the executive was convincing indication that none was intended." *Id.* at 118; *see also id.* at 128 (similar). This passage does not necessarily reference executive authorities beyond the execution of the laws.

CHAPTER 7

1 Humphrey's Ex'r v. United States, 295 U.S. 602 (1935).

2 Federal Trade Commission Act, Pub. L. No. 63-203, ch. 311, § 1, 38 Stat. 717, 717–18 (1914).

3 *Id.* at 718. The next few paragraphs are taken from Ilan Wurman, *The Removal Power: A Critical Guide*, 2020 Cato Sup. Ct. Rev. 157, 184–85 (2020).

4 *Humphrey's Ex'r*, 295 U.S. at 620; Federal Trade Commission Act § 5, 38 Stat. at 719.

5 *Humphrey's Ex'r*, 295 U.S. at 619.

6 *Id.* at 624.

7 *Id.* at 625–26 (emphasis omitted).

8 *Id.* at 627–28.

9 *Id.* at 628.

10 *Id.*

11 *Id.* at 624.

12 *Id.* at 630.

13 As discussed in Chapter 5. *See also* 2 Max Farrand ed., The Records of the Federal Convention of 1787, at 23 (New Haven, CT: Yale University Press 1911) (resolution granting national executive "power to carry into effect the national laws" passed unanimously).

14 In the first instance of for-cause removal, President Taft removed two members of the Board of Appraisers for self-dealing and incompetence after having appointed a board of inquiry to investigate the matter. *See* Aditya Bamzai, *Taft, Frankfurter, and the First Presidential For-Cause Removal*, 52 U. Rich. L. Rev. 691 (2018). President Trump recently

removed for cause a governor of the Federal Reserve upon learning of allegations of mortgage fraud. The removal is moving through the courts as this book goes to press.

15 Charles Bangs Bickford, Kenneth R. Bowling, & Helen E. Veit eds., 11 The Documentary History of the First Federal Congress 897 (Baltimore: The Johns Hopkins University Press 1992) [hereinafter DHFFC].

16 *Ex parte Hennen*, 38 U.S. 230, 259–60 (1839) ("The tenure in those cases depends, in a great measure, upon ancient usage. But with us, there is no ancient usage which can apply to and govern the tenure of offices created by our Constitution and laws."); *see also* Jane Manners & Lev Menand, *The Three Permissions: Presidential Removal and the Statutory Limits of Agency Independence*, 121 Colum. L. Rev. 1, 20 (2021) ("In Revolutionary America, the idea of offices as property was roundly rejected."). Certainly, by the middle of the nineteenth century, this was the common view. *See* Caleb Nelson, *Vested Rights, "Franchises," and the Separation of Powers*, 169 U. Pa. L. Rev. 1429, 1472 & n.250 (2021) (citing cases).

17 Taylor v. Beckham, 178 U.S. 548, 577 (1900).

18 This section borrows heavily from, and summarizes the argument from, Ilan Wurman, *The Original Presidency: A Conception of Administrative Control*, 16 J. Legal Analysis 26–63 (2024).

19 Bickford et al., DHFFC, *supra* note 15, at 725.

20 *Id.* at 726.

21 *Id.*

22 An Act for establishing an Executive Department, to be denominated the Department of Foreign Affairs, 1 Stat. 28, 29 (July 27, 1789).

23 An Act to establish an Executive Department, to be denominated the Department of War, 1 Stat. 49, 50 (Aug. 7, 1789) (the principal officer "shall perform and execute such duties as shall from time to time be enjoined on, or entrusted to him by the President of the United States," and "the said principal officer shall conduct the business of the said department in such manner as the President of the United States shall from time to time order or instruct").

24 An Act for the temporary establishment of the Post Office, 1 Stat. 70 (Sept. 22, 1789) ("The Postmaster General to be subject to the direction of the President of the United States in performing the duties of his office, and in forming contracts for the transportation of the mail.").

25 A prominent example is found in Kendall v. United States ex rel. Stokes, 37 U.S. (12 Pet.) 524 (1838), in which the Supreme Court ordered the Postmaster General to make a payment as specifically directed by Congress.

26 Bickford et al., DHFFC, *supra* note 15, at 1083.

27 *Id.* at 1081; *see also* 1 Joseph Gales ed., Annals of Cong. 612 (1789) (Washington, DC: Gales & Seaton 1834).

28 Letter from George Washington to William Tatham (Apr. 14, 1791), *in* 8 Mark A. Mastromarino ed., The Papers of George Washington, Presidential Series, 22 March 1791–22 September 1791, at 103–04 (Charlottesville: University Press of Virginia 1999).

29 Letter from George Washington to Charlotte S. Hazen (Aug. 31, 1795), *in* 18 Carol S. Ebel ed., The Papers of George Washington, Presidential Series, 1 April–30 September 1795, at 500–01 (Charlottesville: University of Virginia Press 2015). In a letter from March 6, 1790, Washington's personal secretary, Tobias Lear, wrote to a supplicant that "in obedience to"

Washington's command, he was to "inform you that it is not of the line of his official duty to take any part in the settlement of accounts." "[T]he impropriety of his interfering in any degree with the claims of individuals upon the public is too obvious to escape observation," Lear explained, "to say nothing of the impracticability of his attending to all the applications which would appear equally meritorious." *Quoted in* Dorothy Twohig, Dorothy, Mark A. Mastromarino, & Jack D. Warren, eds., 5 The Papers of George Washington: Presidential Series, January–June 1790, at 134 n.2 (Charlottesville: University Press of Virginia 1996).

30 Letter from Thomas Jefferson to Benjamin Latrobe (June 2, 1808). The Thomas Jefferson Papers at the Library of Congress. Series 1: General Correspondence. 1651–1827. Microfilm Reel: 041. http://hdl.loc.gov/loc.mss/mtj.mtjbib018649. For Jefferson's letter and the Washington letters, I am indebted to Saikrishna Bangalore Prakash, Imperial from the Beginning 189–90 (New Haven, CT: Yale University Press 2015).

31 The President & Acct. Offs., 1 U.S. Op. Atty. Gen. 624, 625–26 (1823).

32 *Id.* at 626

Yet, in this case, the power of correction which the President holds is not to supersede such appointment by one made by himself; for the law gives him no such power of appointment. He is to take care, in such a case, that the Postmaster General be punished for this violation of the law: he has power to remove him – to appoint a successor; and through the medium of such successor, and by his instrumentality, to remove the deputy, and to see that his place be honestly supplied.

There is some suggestion in Wirt's opinion that perhaps Congress can limit this removal power. He wrote earlier in the opinion,

The constitution of the United States requires the President, in general terms, to take care that the laws be faithfully executed; that is, it places the officers engaged in the execution of the laws under his general superintendence: he is to see that they do their duty faithfully; and on their failure, to cause them to be displaced, prosecuted, or impeached, according to the nature of the case.

Id. at 625. This does suggest that there may be specific statutory limitations on how certain officers can be removed, perhaps gesturing to inferior officers.

33 Myers v. United States, 272 U.S. 52, 135 (1926).

34 *Id.*

35 *Id.*

36 William Howard Taft, Our Chief Magistrate and His Powers 81 (Columbia University Press 1916); *see also id.* at 125–26 (similar).

37 *See* Robert V. Remini, Andrew Jackson and the Bank War: A Study in the Growth of Presidential Power 109–53 (New York: W. W. Norton & Co. 1967).

38 3 James D. Richardson, A Compilation of the Messages and Papers of the Presidents 19 (Washington, DC: Published by Authority of Congress 1898).

39 As quoted in Daniel Webster, Mr. Webster's speech on the President's protest: delivered in the Senate of the United States, May 7, 1834, at 4 (Gales and Seaton 1834).

40 President Jackson's Message of Protest to the Senate, Apr. 15, 1834, *in* 3 Julius W. Muller ed., Presidential Messages and State Papers 1112–19 (New York: The Review of Reviews Company 1917).

41 Webster, *supra* note 39.

42 *Id.* at 4.

43 *Id.*

44 *Id.* at 4–5 (emphasis added).

45 *Id.* at 5.

46 *Id.*

47 *Id.* at 5–6 (emphasis added).

48 *Id.* at 6.

49 *Id.*

50 *See, e.g.,* Peter L. Strauss, *Foreword: Overseer, or "The Decider?" The President in Administrative Law,* 75 Geo. Wash. L. Rev. 696 (2007); Kevin M. Stack, *The President's Statutory Powers to Administer the Laws,* 106 Colum. L. Rev. 263, 295 (2006) ("Firing typically has a much higher political cost to the President than (successfully) directing an official's exercise of discretion.").

51 Webster, *supra* note 39, at 5.

52 Lawrence Lessig & Cass R. Sunstein, *The President and the Administration,* 94 Colum. L. Rev. 1, 21 (1994) ("There is an important difference between the power not to prosecute and the power to pardon – for the latter is much more likely than the former to incur significant political costs.").

53 Michael D. Shear & Matt Apuzzo, "F.B.I. Director James Comey Is Fired by Trump," N.Y. Times (May 9, 2017).

54 Strauss, *supra* note 50, at 706–07. Taney, of course, would later become Chief Justice of the United States.

55 *Id.* at 708.

56 *See, e.g.,* Justin Miller, "Napolitano Won't Go," The Atlantic (Dec. 30, 2009); Chris Cillizza, "Why Donald Trump might not fire Rod Rosenstein," CNN (Sept. 25, 2018).

57 Devan Cole & Marshall Cohen, "Trump says he didn't fire Mueller because firings 'didn't work out too well' for Nixon," CNN (June 16, 2019).

58 H.R. Doc. No. 93-339, art. II, para. 5, at 4 (1974).

59 Zachary S. Price, *Congress's Power over Military Offices,* 99 Tex. L. Rev. 491, 508–10 (2021).

60 Am. State Papers, 6 Foreign Relations 1067 (Jan. 20, 1827) (Buffalo, NY: William S. Hein & Co. 1998).

61 The Federalist No. 74, at 447 (Alexander Hamilton) (Clinton Rossiter ed., 1961).

62 Relation of the President to the Executive Departments, 7 Op. Att'y Gen. 453, 469–70 (1855).

63 Prakash, *supra* note 30, at 186–89.

64 *Id.* at 186; *see also* The Federal Farmer No. XIV (Jan. 17, 1788), *in* 2 Herbert J. Storing ed., The Complete Anti-Federalist 310 (University of Chicago Press 1981) ("Reason. and the experience of enlightened nations. seem justly to assign the business of making laws to numerous assemblies; and the execution of them. principally. to the direction and care of one man."); James Wilson, Lectures on Law (1790), *in* Kermit L. Hall & Mark David Hall eds., 1 Collected Works of James Wilson 703 (Indianapolis, IN: Liberty Fund 2007) ("the executive power of government is placed in the hands of one person, who is to direct all the subordinate officers of that department").

65 1 William Blackstone, Commentaries on the Laws of England 260–61 (Oxford: Clarendon Press 1765).

66 *Id.* at 261.

67 *Id.*

68 Michael W. McConnell, The President Who Would Not Be King: Executive Power under the Constitution 114 (Princeton University Press 2020).

69 Ilan Wurman, *In Search of Prerogative*, 70 Duke L.J. 93, 153–55 (2020).

70 Edward Corwin, The President: Office and Powers, 1787–1957, at 80–81 (New York University Press, 4th rev. ed. 1957).

CHAPTER 8

1 Youngstown Sheet & Tube Co. v. Sawyer (Steel Seizure Case), 343 U.S. 579 (1952).

2 As the *Youngstown* majority explained,

> There are two statutes which do authorize the President to take both personal and real property under certain conditions. However, the Government admits that these conditions were not met and that the President's order was not rooted in either of the statutes. The Government refers to the seizure provisions of one of these statutes (§ 201(b) of the Defense Production Act) as "much too cumbersome, involved, and time-consuming for the crisis which was at hand."
>
> Moreover, the use of the seizure technique to solve labor disputes in order to prevent work stoppages was not only unauthorized by any congressional enactment; prior to this controversy, Congress had refused to adopt that method of settling labor disputes.

> *Id.* at 585–86 (footnote omitted).

3 *Id.* at 635–38 (Jackson, J., concurring).

4 That is the opposite of how laws work for ordinary people, who are free to do anything not specifically prohibited.

5 *Youngstown*, 343 U.S. at 640.

6 *Id.* at 644.

7 U.S. Const. art. I, § 8, cls. 12–13.

8 *Youngstown*, 343 U.S. at 631 (Douglas, J., concurring).

9 *Id.* at 646–51 (Jackson, J., concurring).

10 *Id.* at 649.

11 *Id.* at 650.

12 *Id.*

13 *Id.* at 650–51.

14 *Id.* at 629 (Douglas, J., concurring).

15 *Id.* at 585 (Black, J.).

16 *Id.* at 637 (Jackson, J., concurring).

17 U.S. Const. art. I, § 8, cl. 14.

18 U.S. Const. art. IV, § 3, cl. 2.

19 On this point, both Thomas Jefferson and John Marshall agreed. *See* Letter from Thomas Jefferson to William H. Cabell (Aug. 11, 1807), *in* 10 Paul Leicester Ford ed., The Works of Thomas Jefferson 441n (New York: G. P. Putnam's Sons; London: The

Knickerbocker Press 1905) ("[T]he Constitution gives the executive a general power to carry the laws into execution. If the present law had enacted that the service of 30,000 volunteers should be accepted, without saying anything of the means, those means would, by the Constitution, have resulted to the discretion of the executive."); 10 Annals of Cong. 613–14 (1800) (Washington, DC: Gales & Seaton 1851) (noting that an extradition "treaty, which is a law, enjoins the performance of a particular object" and that the President may "perform the object, although the particular mode of using the means has not been prescribed").

20 Chevron U.S.A., Inc. v. Natural Resources Defense Council, Inc., 467 U.S. 837 (1984).

21 *Id.* at 846.

22 In Loper Bright Enterprises v. Raimondo, 603 U.S. 369 (2024), the United States Supreme Court overturned the central holding of the *Chevron* case that courts must defer to reasonable agency interpretations of law, even if those interpretations were not the best interpretations at which the courts themselves would have arrived. In the view of this author, the holding of *Loper Bright* was correct. Courts must interpret law for themselves in actual cases or controversies that come before them. But statutes often leave gaps, or details to fill, which are not matters of interpretation but rather interstitial gap-filling. In such situations, the President can fill those gaps until Congress specifies otherwise.

23 *Youngstown*, 343 U.S. at 587 (Black, J.).

24 *Id.*

25 *Id.* at 588 ("The President's order does not direct that a congressional policy be executed in a manner prescribed by Congress – it directs that a presidential policy be executed in a manner prescribed by the President.").

26 *Id.* at 667–69, 671–72 (Vinson, C.J., dissenting).

27 *Id.* at 672.

28 In re Neagle, 135 U.S. 1 (1890).

29 *Id.* at 42–46.

30 J. Edward Johnson, *David S. Terry*, 22 J. St. B. of Cal. 516 (1947).

31 *Neagle*, 135 U.S. at 52–54.

32 *Id.* at 40–41, 58.

33 *Id.* at 58–60.

34 *Id.* at 69.

35 *Id.* at 64–65.

36 *Id.* at 65–66 (discussing Wells v. Nickles, 104 U.S. 444 (1881)).

37 *Id.* at 72.

38 Henry P. Monaghan, *The Protective Power of the Presidency*, 93 Colum. L. Rev. 1 (1993).

39 *Id.* at 11.

40 In re Debs, 158 U.S. 564 (1895).

41 Grover Cleveland, Presidential Problems 79–117 (New York: The Century Co. 1904).

42 *Id.* at 85.

43 *See, e.g.*, David P. Currie, The Constitution in Congress: Democrats and Whigs, 1829–1861, at 13–14 (University of Chicago Press 2005).

44 U.S. Const. art. IV, § 4.

45 Cleveland, *supra* note 41, at 93–94, 112–13.

46 Sherman Anti-Trust Act, 26 Stat. 209, § 1 (codified at 15 U.S.C. § 1).

47 To be sure, some activities, such as disabling trains or acts of violence against willing workers, were probably illegal whether under this or other federal laws, including laws against interfering with the mails. The point is that an injunction could only be issued under the Sherman Act to prevent price-fixing combinations, not to prevent workers from striking.

48 Cleveland, *supra* note 41, at 99–100.

49 *Id.* at 94–95 (quoting Revised Statutes § 5298 and § 5299).

50 *Id.* at 105–06.

51 In re Debs, 158 U.S. 564, 581 (1895).

52 *Id.*

53 *Id.* at 582.

54 *Id.* at 584.

55 Youngstown Sheet & Tube Co. v. Sawyer, 343 U.S. 579, 610–11 (1952) (Frankfurter, J., concurring).

56 *Id.* at 611 (discussing United States v. Midwest Oil Co., 236 U.S. 459 (1915)).

57 *Id.*

58 *Id.* at 613.

59 *See, e.g.*, NLRB v. Noel Canning, 573 U.S. 513, 570 (2014) (Scalia, J., concurring in the judgment) ("The majority justifies those atextual results on an adverse-possession theory of executive authority: Presidents have long claimed the powers in question . . . .").

60 *Id.* at 593 (such a theory "will systematically favor the expansion of executive power at the expense of Congress").

61 Curtis A. Bradley, Historical Gloss and Foreign Affairs: Constitutional Authority in Practice 12, 32, 148 (Cambridge, MA: Harvard University Press 2024).

62 *Id.* at 12–13, 23.

63 236 U.S. 459 (1915).

64 *Id.* at 466.

65 Bradley, *supra* note 61, at 20–24.

66 The facts are recited in Seth Barrett Tillman, Ex Parte Merryman: *Myth, History, and Scholarship*, 224 Military L. Rev. 481, 483–88 (2016). As Tillman notes, although Taney found Lincoln's actions to be contrary to the Constitution, he did not order Lincoln to release Merryman. *Id.* at 495–98.

67 Ex parte Merryman, 17 F. Cas. 144 (C.C.D. Md. 1861).

68 U.S. Const. art. I, § 9, cl. 2.

69 U.S. Const. art. I, § 9, cl. 7.

70 U.S. Const. art. II, § 3.

71 Lincoln made the argument in his special message to Congress. Abraham Lincoln, Special message to Congress, July 4, 1861, *in* 6 James D. Richardson, A Compilation of the Messages and Papers of the Presidents, 1789–1897, at 25 (Washington, DC: Gov't Printing Off. 1898).

72 *Id.* at 98–99.

73 *Id.* at 25.

74 U.S. Const. art. II, § 1, para. 8.

75 Akhil Reed Amar, America's Constitution: A Biography 196 (New York: Random House 2005).

76 Letter from Thomas Jefferson to John B. Colvin (Sept. 20, 1810), *in* 11 Paul Leicester Ford ed., The Works of Thomas Jefferson 146 (New York: The Knickerbocker Press 1905).

77 *Id.* at 149 (paragraph breaks added). It appears that Jefferson employed this principle on more than one occasion, including when he spent unappropriated funds on unauthorized defensive measures after the British vessel *Leopard* attacked the American vessel *Chesapeake*. Abraham D. Sofaer, War, Foreign Affairs, and Constitutional Power: Origins 172–73 (Cambridge, MA: Ballinger Publishing Co. 1976).

78 The episode is retold in Sofaer, *supra* note 77, at 333–36.

79 *Id.* at 333–34. Sofaer could not locate the original source for this "undoubtedly biased version of Jackson's speech," but other versions "confirm that Jackson acknowledged the propriety of submitting to the legal process when the emergency was over." *Id.* at 478 n.509.

80 22 U.S. (9 Wheat.) 362, 366–67 (1824). Both this case and Jefferson's letter are discussed in Monaghan, *supra* note 38, at, 24–26.

81 Michael W. McConnell, The President Who Would Not Be King: Executive Power under the Constitution 111–12 (Princeton University Press 2020). John Locke had written in the seventeenth century that the executive had the "prerogative" to act beyond or contrary to law in cases of emergency. He suggested that the people would decide in cases of abuse. [John Locke], Two Treatises of Civil Government 291–93 (London: Printed for Awnsham and John Churchill 1698).

82 Lucius Wilmerding Jr., *The President and the Law*, 67(3) Poli. Sci. Q. (Sept. 1952), at 322–23.

83 For a modern assessment of the various models of emergency powers that defends the Founders' view, *see* Oren Gross, *Chaos and Rules: Should Responses to Violent Crises Always Be Constitutional?*, 112 Yale L.J. 1011 (2003). Gross concludes that "[g]oing completely outside the law in appropriate cases may preserve, rather than undermine, the rule of law in a way that constantly bending the law to accommodate emergencies will not." *Id.* at 1097. Under this model, ex-post ratification of the otherwise unconstitutional act, either by the legislature or by the people through reelection, is critical. *Id.* at 1111–15.

CHAPTER 9

1 David P. Currie, *Foreign Affairs: Presidential Initiative and Congressional Control*, 101 Mich. L. Rev. 1453, 1453 (2003) (reviewing H. Jefferson Powell, The President's Authority over Foreign Affairs: An Essay in Constitutional Interpretation (Durham: Carolina Academic Press 2002)).

2 Louis Henkin, Foreign Affairs and the U.S. Constitution 13–15 (New York: Columbia University Press, 2d ed. 1996); Edward S. Corwin, The President: Office and Powers, 1787–1957, at 171 (New York University Press, 4th rev. ed. 1957).

3 *See, e.g.*, Saikrishna B. Prakash & Michael D. Ramsey, *The Executive Power over Foreign Affairs*, 111 Yale L.J. 231, 258 (2001):

Many key foreign affairs powers that surely would have been known to the Framers cannot be encompassed by an ordinary reading of the specific provisions of the

Constitution: among others, the power to set foreign policy and speak internationally on behalf of the United States, the power to direct and to recall ambassadors, [and] the power to enter into nontreaty agreements, the power to terminate treaties[.]

Michael W. McConnell, The President Who Would Not Be King: Executive Power under the Constitution 178, 183–84 (Princeton University Press 2020).

4 See, e.g., Curtis A. Bradley, Historical Gloss and Foreign Affairs: Constitutional Authority in Practice (Cambridge, MA: Harvard University Press 2024) (arguing that much of the President's foreign affairs powers comes from historical gloss); id. at 39–44 (explaining accounts of presidential power rooted in sovereignty and other functional considerations); Andrew Coan & David S. Schwartz, The Original Meaning of Enumerated Powers, 109 Iowa L. Rev. 971, 994 (2024) (conducting foreign affairs is an inherent attribute of sovereignty); H. Jefferson Powell, The Founders and the President's Authority over Foreign Affairs, 40 Wm. & Mary L. Rev. 1471, 1474 (1999) (arguing that early history suggests the Founders thought the President had "inherent constitutional powers" in foreign affairs); David P. Currie, The Constitution in Congress: The Federalist Period, 1789–1801, at 178 (University of Chicago Press 1997) (suggesting on functionalist ground that the president has "broad implicit authority over foreign affairs"). The idea of inherent powers seems to have originated in the late nineteenth century. See Sarah H. Cleveland, Powers Inherent in Sovereignty: Indians, Aliens, Territories, and the Nineteenth Century Origins of Plenary Power over Foreign Affairs, 81 Tex. L. Rev. 1 (2002). The literature is vast; the above-mentioned is a small smattering. For the most recent defense of this view, Curtis A. Bradley, Sovereign Power Constitutionalism, 92 U. Chi. L. Rev. 1807 (2025).

5 The literature is again vast. See Powell, supra note 4, at 1471–72 & n.2 (citing vast literature for congressional primacy view as of 1999); see also Patricia L. Bellia, Executive Power in Youngstown's Shadows, 19 Const. Comment. 87, 117–18 (2002).

6 See supra note 3 for sources making the residuum claim. Bradley has made the point with respect to historical gloss. Bradley, Historical Gloss, supra note 4, at 37 (noting that "managing diplomacy, declaring neutrality, issuing passports, recognizing foreign governments, acquiring territory, concluding non-treaty international agreements, withdrawing from treaties, waging undeclared war, and regulating immigration" are not "mentioned" in the constitutional text). Bradley is careful, however, to observe that the Constitution does not "specifically" or "precisely" speak to the question, appearing to leave open the possibility that one can rely on textual analysis.

7 This chapter agrees generally with what Professor Corwin argued many decades ago. See Corwin, supra note 2, at 171:

What the Constitution does, and all that it does, is to confer on the President certain powers capable of affecting our foreign relations, and certain other powers of the same general kind on the Senate, and still other such powers on Congress; but which of these organs shall have the decisive and final voice in determining the course of the American nation is left for events to resolve. . . . The verdict of history, in short, is that the power to determine the substantive content of American foreign policy is a divided power, with the lion's share falling usually, though by no means always, to the President.

However, Corwin argued that the Constitution was largely silent on many specific foreign affairs powers. Id. at 172 ("To assume, however, that these powers are sufficient, either separately or together, to meet all the requirements of an expedient and just foreign policy would be entirely gratuitous; and, as a matter of fact, many powers have been asserted both by the President and by Congress in the field of foreign relations as to which the Constitution is completely silent."). This chapter disagrees. Corwin's account takes an unduly cramped view of both congressional and presidential powers specified in the Constitution itself.

8 Details of the episode are recounted in Ron Chernow, Alexander Hamilton 431–47 (New York: The Penguin Press 2004); Charles S. Hyneman, The First American Neutrality 11–19 (Urbana: University of Illinois 1934); Abraham D. Sofaer, War, Foreign Affairs and Constitutional Power: The Origins 103–16 (Cambridge, MA: Ballinger Publishing Co. 1976). The proclamation is available at Walter Lowrie & Matthew St. Claire Clarke eds., American State Papers, Foreign Relations, vol. I, at 140 (Washington, DC: Gales & Seaton 1833). William Casto also provides an excellent treatment in William R. Casto, Foreign Affairs and the Constitution in the Age of Fighting Sail (Columbia: University of South Carolina Press 2006). Casto observes that the French never expected the Americans to come to France's aid. Rather, they were hoping to accelerate payment of loans and to use the American seacoast to launch its commercial maritime campaigns. Casto, *supra*, at 14–25.

9 4 Henry Cabot Lodge ed., The Works of Alexander Hamilton 432–89 (New York: The Knickerbocker Press 1904).

10 Pacificus No. 1, *id.* at 436.

11 *Id.* at 436–37.

12 *Id.* at 437.

13 James Madison, Helvidius No. 1 (Aug. 24, 1793), *in* Thomas A. Mason, Robert A. Rutland, & Jeanne K. Sisson eds., 15 The Papers of James Madison: Congressional Series 68–69 (Charlottesville: University Press of Virginia 1985).

14 Pacificus No. 1, *in* Lodge, *supra* note 9, at 443.

15 *Id.* at 437–39.

16 *See, e.g.,* Corwin, *supra* note 2, at 181. In the removal power debate, Fisher Ames stated that as a result of Article II's vesting clause "all the powers properly belonging to the executive department of the government are given, and such only taken away as are expressly excepted." 1 Annals of Cong. 539 (1789) (Washington, DC: Gales & Seaton 1834). But that is similar to what Madison said in the debate and, as noted, these statements are consistent with the proposition that the executive power is merely the power to execute law. Ames's statement can certainly be interpreted, however, to refer to royal prerogative powers too.

17 Helvidius No. 1, *in* Mason et al., *supra* note 13, at 72.

18 Pacificus No. 1, *in* Lodge, *supra* note 9, at 443–44.

19 *Id.* at 444.

20 *See* Neutrality Proclamation, *in* Am. State Papers, *supra* note 8, at 140.

21 Hyneman, *supra* note 8, at 130.

22 Jules Lobel, *The Rise and Decline of the Neutrality Act: Sovereignty and Congressional War Powers in United States Foreign Policy*, 24 Harv. Int'l L.J. 1, 14 (1983); Hyneman, *supra* note 8, at 128–31; Charles Marion Thomas, American Neutrality in 1793: A Study in Cabinet Government 175 (New York: Columbia University Press 1931); 5 John Marshall,

The Life of George Washington 435 (Philadelphia, PA: Printed and published by C. P. Wayne 1807). It is also possible, of course, that this was simply an exercise of jury nullification on the part of pro-French juries. Currie, *supra* note 4, at 181. William Casto offers several explanations supported by contemporaneous accounts. Attorney General Randolph told President Washington that the "leading man among" the jury was persuaded by Henfield's claim that he had joined prior to the President's proclamation and had no knowledge of it. Casto, *supra* note 8, at 99. Others thought Henfield could expatriate himself and become a French citizen through his actions. *Id.* at 97, 102.

23 Marshall, *supra* note 22, at 435.

24 U.S. Const. art. I, § 8, cl. 10.

25 In addition to the act for the punishment of certain crimes against the United States, 1 Stat. 381 (June 5, 1794).

26 Casto, *supra* note 8, at 100–02 (describing the prosecution and acquittal of Joseph Rivers in Georgia); *see also* Sofaer, *supra* note 8, at 110; Hyneman, *supra* note 8, at 131.

27 *Henfield's Case*, 11 F. Cas. 1099 (C.C.D. Pa. 1793); Francis Wharton, State Trials of the United States during the Administrations of Washington and Adams 49 (Philadelphia, PA: Carey and Hart 1849) [hereinafter Whart. St. Tr.].

28 Marshall, *supra* note 22, at 435; Hyneman, *supra* note 8, at 130; *see also Henfield's Case*, Whart St. Tr., *supra* note 27, at 49 (argument of defense counsel). Henfield boarded the French cruiser *Citizen Genet* on May 1, and attacked the merchant ships of allied countries on May 5, two weeks after Washington's proclamation.

29 Am. State Papers, *supra* note 8, at 151.

30 *Id.* at 140.

31 *Henfield's Case*, Whart. St. Tr., *supra* note 27, at 49 (petit jury charge).

32 Reported in *id.* Jay would have had some incentive to mention the proclamation since he apparently submitted a first draft of the proclamation to Hamilton. 3 Henry P. Johnston ed., The Correspondence and Public Papers of John Jay, 1782–1793, at 474–77 (New York: The Knickerbocker Press 1891). Two grand jury charges and the petit jury charge are reported in *Henfield's Case*. Chief Justice Jay, Justice Wilson, and Justice Iredell all participated in either the grand jury or trial proceedings. A second grand jury charge by Jay is found in his papers. Johnston *supra*, at 478–85. In the latter, Jay instructed the grand jury that the "Constitution, the statutes of the United States, the laws of nations, and treaties constitutionally made compose the laws of the United States." *Id.* at 479. There is no mention of the proclamation having any legal effect. He made the same instruction in the other grand jury instruction, reported in *Henfield's Case*. 11 F. Cas. 1099. The grand jury instruction by Justice James Wilson also did not mention the proclamation.

33 Pacificus No. 1, *in* Lodge, *supra* note 9, at 437.

34 Talbot v. Jansen, 3 U.S. (3 Dall.) 133 (1795), involved privateering and captures in late 1793 and early 1794 prior to the Neutrality Act. Even though counsel had mentioned the President's proclamation, *id.* at 133, none of the Justices relied on Washington's proclamation. They relied instead on existing treaties and the law of nations generally. *See, e.g., id.* at 161 (Iredell, J.):

This is so palpable a violation of our own law (I mean the common law, of which the law of nations is a part, as it subsisted either before the act of Congress on the subject, or since that has provided a particular manner of enforcing it,) as well as of the law of nations generally; that I cannot entertain the slightest doubt, but that upon the case of the libel, prima facie, the District Court had jurisdiction.

Talbot is the only reported case the author could locate involving prizes and captures made in violation of neutrality prior to the Neutrality Act. It appears that some district judges believed they did not have jurisdiction under the Judiciary Act of 1789 to hear cases of capture, but the Supreme Court held that there was jurisdiction in The Betsey, 3 U.S. (3 Dall.) 6 (1794). *See generally* Hyneman, *supra* note 8, at 89–91.

35 Hyneman, *supra* note 8, at 77–82, discusses these regulations. The regulations are found in Am. State Papers, *supra* note 8, at 140–41.

36 The Mermaid, 4 F. Cas. 169, 170 (D.S.C. 1795).

37 Castello v. Bouteille, 5 F. Cas. 278, 279 (D.S.C. 1794).

38 Hyneman, *supra* note 8, at 122, 126–27. The issue arose because Article XXII of the Treaty of Amity and Commerce with France prohibited British ships from being fitted or from selling their prizes or cargo in American ports, but it was silent on whether French ships could do so.

39 Casto, *supra* note 8, at 159–62.

40 Consul of Spain v. Consul of Great Britain, 6 F. Cas. (C.C.S.C 1808).

41 This inference is further supported by the fact that Vice President Adams broke the tie in the Senate in favor of the provision prohibiting such sales. Casto, *supra* note 8, at 159. It was evidently the President's position that such sales should be prohibited. Yet, he took no action on his own authority.

42 Hyneman, *supra* note 8, at 118–20. Washington revoked the credentials of at least one British consul for fitting out a privateer. Sofaer, *supra* note 8, at 94 & n. 140.

43 U.S. Const. art. II, § 3.

44 Am. State Papers, *supra* note 8, at 140.

45 Sofaer, *supra* note 8, at 106 & n. 195. *See also* Hyneman, *supra* note 8, at 54–98, for other similar determinations.

46 Indeed, it is unclear whether President Washington believed he had any authority to seize ships militarily that had been captured in violation of neutrality. When a British ship *Little Sarah* had been captured by a privateer outfitted in Charleston harbor and brought into Philadelphia herself to be fitted out into a privateer – both in violation of neutrality – the British foreign minister demanded restitution of the ship. Jefferson wrote that an attack on the French ship to recapture *Little Sarah* would be a "reprisal," which the Constitution required Congress to authorize. *See* Thomas Jefferson, Opinion on "The Little Sarah," May 16, 1793, *in* 7 Paul Leicester Ford ed., The Works of Thomas Jefferson 332, 335 (New York: G. P. Putnam's Sons The Knickerbocker Press 1904). Washington seems to have followed this advice, although some military measures were prepared in coordination with state governors. Sofaer, *supra* note 8, at 108–11. Ultimately, Congress enacted as part of the neutrality law of 1794 some authorization for the use of military force in these circumstances. Casto, *supra* note 8, at 159–62.

47 George Washington to the Secretary of the Treasury, July 2, 1794, *in* 33 John C. Fitzpatrick ed., The Writings of George Washington, July 1, 1793–October 9, 1794, at 420, 422 (Washington, DC: Gov't Printing Off. 1940). Washington wrote this passage to explain Congress's refusal to make the necessary appropriations.

48 *Castello*, 5 F. Cas. at 279.

49 Pacificus No. 1, *in* Lodge, *supra* note 9, at 437.

50 The administration also decided it could not generally enter into new treaty obligations that benefited one of the belligerents. Hyneman, *supra* note 8, at 41–46. That also did not alter the legal state of things because the President always had discretion as to what treaties to make (as long as he could obtain Senate consent).

51 This is perhaps what Washington meant when he explained that the proclamation would allow the nation to obtain "an easier admission of our right to the immunities belonging to our situation." *Id.*

52 2 James D. Richardson ed., A Compilation of the Messages and Papers of the Presidents 218 (Published by the authority of Congress 1896).

53 As Jean Galbraith observes, the President has an undoubted power to *negotiate* with foreign governments, but that is not the same thing as the power to decide what the foreign *policy* of the nation shall be. Jean Galbraith, *The Runaway Presidential Power over Diplomacy*, 108 Va. L. Rev. 81, 119–23 (2022).

54 David P. Currie, The Constitution in Congress: The Jeffersonians, 1801–1829, at 207–10 (University of Chicago Press 2001).

55 Zivotofsky v. Kerry, 576 U.S. 1 (2015).

56 *Id.* at 5–8.

57 *Id.* at 10.

58 U.S. Const. art. II, § 3.

59 *Federalist* No. 69, at 420 (Clinton Rossiter ed. 1961) (Hamilton).

60 McConnell, *supra* note 3, at 186–88. McConnell argues that the recognition power therefore comes from the Vesting Clause, but that begs the whole question. It is not clear that recognition is a "power" at all. As the discussion will make clear, the President and Congress can each "recognize" a government in pursuance of their respective powers.

61 Pacificus No. 1, *in* Lodge, *supra* note 9, at 441.

62 *Id.*

63 James Madison, Helvidius No. 3 (Sept. 7, 1793), *in* Mason et al., *supra* note 13, at 97.

64 *Id.* at 97–98. As Curtis Bradley has recently written, this "de facto recognition" doctrine was arguably mandated by international law and became the policy of the United States "until at least the Civil War." Bradley, Historical Gloss, *supra* note 4, at 53.

65 *Zivotofsky*, 576 U.S. at 74, 76 (Scalia, J., dissenting).

66 As happened with Cuba and the Spanish–American War. See Corwin, *supra* note 2, at 189 (discussing this episode and Congress's recognition through its authorization to use force).

67 *See id.* at 75–76; *see also* the discussion in Currie, *supra* note 54, at 200–05; Corwin, *supra* note 2, at 187–88.

68 *Zivotofsky*, 576 U.S. at 13.

69 *Id.* at 14.

70 *Id.*

71 For example, there is a debate over whether recognition is a duty under the law of nations, is a matter of policy discretion that is nevertheless declarative of actual conditions in the other community, or is a matter of policy discretion that is constitutive of that community's statehood. *See, e.g.,* Hersch Lauterpacht, *Recognition of States in International Law*, 53 Yale L.J. 385, 386–87 (1944).

72 Hans Kelsen wrote, for example,

The political act of recognition of a state or government means that the recognizing state is willing to enter into political and other relations with the recognized state or government, relations of the kind which normally exist between members of the family of nations. Since a state according to general international law is not obliged to entertain such relations with other states, namely, to send or receive diplomatic envoys, to conclude treaties, etc., political recognition of a state or a government is an act which lies within the arbitrary decision of the recognizing state.

Hans Kelsen, *Recognition in International Law: Theoretical Observations*, 35 Am. J. Int'l L. 605, 605 (1941). Thus, one who receives ambassadors and makes treaties, as the President does, can recognize nations in that manner. It does not follow that other actors cannot have different views when not interfering with these ordinary diplomatic relations.

73 Emmerich de Vattel, The Law of Nations, bk. IV, § 78, at 461–62 (London: Printed for G. G. and J. Robinson 1797); Hugo Grotius, The Rights of War and Peace 379–80 (London: Printed for W. Innys et al. 1738). Both treatises support Hamilton's observation that the power to receive ambassadors is more a matter of dignity than authority, with which Madison agreed as Helvidius. There appears to be no right to refuse to accept ambassadors unless there is a question as to who possesses actual sovereign authority over a territory, although some powers refused to accept ambassadors due to external circumstances having little to do with recognition of sovereignty.

74 1 William Blackstone, Commentaries on the Laws of England 245 (Oxford: Clarendon Press 1765).

75 Currie, *supra* note 4, at 24–26. An attempt was made by a committee of the Senate personally to interview President Madison on the question of Albert Gallatin's nomination as minister to negotiate with Britain and Russia during the War of 1812, while he was simultaneously serving as Secretary of Treasury. Madison refused the interview, citing constitutional scruples. "[T]he Executive and Senate, in the cases of appointments to office and of treaties, are to be considered independent and coordinate with each other," Madison wrote to the Senators. The Executive Branch will supply all the relevant information, and the Senate may interview the relevant department heads. But "[t]he appointment of a committee of the Senate to confer immediately with the Executive himself, appears to lose sight of the co-ordinate relation between the Executive and the Senate, which the Constitution has established, and which ought therefore to be maintained." 26 Annals of Cong. 95–96 (1813) (Washington, DC: Gales & Seaton 1854); *see also* Sofaer, *supra* note 8, at 240–42.

76 Currie, *supra* note 4, at 22.

77 *See*, again, Prakash & Ramsey, *supra* note 3, at 258; McConnell, *supra* note 3, at 241.

78 A potentially useful data point is that the Committee on Postponed Matters in the Constitutional Convention considered a resolution that "[t]he Senate shall have power to treat with foreign nations, but no Treaty shall be binding on the United States which is not ratified by a Law." 2 Farrand at 382–83. There is any number of reasons this might not have been adopted – it would seem to give Congress as a whole a power to ratify – but the ultimate retention of the language to "make treaties" rather than "to treat" presumed the power to treat generally with foreign nations already existed somewhere. And that power must have been the President's because the President has the power to make treaties.

79 Vattel, *supra* note 73, at 453 (book IV, ch. v, §§ 55–56).

80 *Id.* (§ 56).

81 *Id.*

82 *Id.* (§ 57).

83 At a time when the draft Constitution provided that the Senate was to have power to "appoint" ambassadors and to make treaties, Charles Pinckney spoke of the Senate as having the "power of making treaties & managing our foreign affairs." 2 Max Farrand ed., The Records of the Federal Convention of 1787, at 183 (New Haven, CT: Yale University Press 1911) ("The Senate of the United States shall have power to make treaties, and to appoint Ambassadors, and Judges of the supreme Court."); *id.* at 235 (Pinckney statement).

84 McConnell, *supra* note 3, at 176–77.

85 *Id.* at 180.

86 Some scholarship has suggested that the President can send ambassadors without Congress having established the office. *See, e.g.*, E. Garrett West, *Congressional Power over Office Creation*, 128 Yale L.J. 166, 196–99 (2018). And it is true that until 1855, Congress did not establish ambassadorial offices, although it has done so since then. Corwin, *supra* note 2, at 205. The First Congress did, however, provide that "a sum not exceeding forty thousand dollars annually" was to be appropriated and paid "for the support of such persons as [the President] shall commission to serve the United States in foreign parts." An Act providing the means of intercourse between the United States and foreign nations, 1 Stat. 128 (July 1, 1790). Professor West and a coauthor have acknowledged the possibility that this was authorization. James Durling & E. Garrett West, *Appointments without Law*, 105 Va. L. Rev. 1281, 1290 n.27 (2019). To be sure, authorization to pay for those who shall have been commissioned does not naturally indicate whom the President has authority to appoint. Nevertheless, it is possible to read the statute as establishing these offices, and a reading of the Appointments Clause that allows ambassadors to be appointed without having an office established by law would require the President to be able to appoint Supreme Court Justices without limit, and that has never been the understanding. It is also possible to read the Appointments Clause as not requiring Congress to establish offices of ambassadors or judges of the Supreme Court, such that the President can appoint these officers in the absence of congressional legislation, but Congress has since 1789 specifically provided for the number of judges of the Supreme Court. For a summary of early debates over Congress's power to establish ambassadorial offices, *see* Sofaer, *supra* note 8, at 138.

87 Recall that the very first statute establishing the Department of Foreign Affairs provided that the said principal officer "shall conduct the business of the said department in such manner as the President of the United States shall from time to time order or instruct." An Act for establishing an Executive Department, to be denominated the Department of Foreign Affairs, 1 Stat. 28, 29 (1789).

88 For early evidence that President Washington and Congress thought that Washington was to be the sole organ of communication, *see* Sofaer, *supra* note 8, at 94.

89 *See* Prakash & Ramsey, *supra* note 3, at 340–46; *see also, e.g.*, Michael D. Ramsey, *The Vesting Clauses and Foreign Affairs*, 91 Geo. Wash. L. Rev. 1513, 1518–23 (2023); Michael D. Ramsey, The Constitution's Text in Foreign Affairs 91–106 (Cambridge, MA: Harvard University Press 2007).

90 Prakash & Ramsey, *supra* note 3, at 265.

91 Henkin, *supra* note 2, at 212.

92 Bradley, Historical Gloss, *supra* note 4, at 102.

93 *Id.* at 105–07.

94 *See also* S. Rep. No. 34-97, at 5 (1856) (Senate Foreign Relations Committee describing the 1798 treaty abrogation statute as a "rightful exercise of the war power, without viewing it in any manner as a precedent establishing in Congress alone, and under any circumstances, the power to annul a treaty."). I am indebted to the Library of Congress for this citation. Constitution Annotated, Art. II § 2, cl. 2.10, Breach and Termination of Treaties, https://constitution.congress.gov/browse/essay/artII-S2-C2-1-10/ALDE_00012961/.

95 *See* Bas v. Tingy, 4 U.S. (4 Dall.) 37, 40 (1800) (making this point).

96 U.S. Const. art. VI, para. 2. Additionally, both laws and treaties are understood to be legislative acts, and it would defeat the purpose of either legislative process if the President were allowed to ignore the laws after they were enacted.

97 This may explain President Grant refusing to enforce an extradition treaty that he believed Great Britain had already violated, at least until Congress expressed its sentiments on the question. Bradley, Historical Gloss, *supra* note 4, at 104.

98 Contra Ramsey, Constitution's Text in Foreign Affairs, *supra* note 89, at 172 (arguing that President Carter's abrogation can be justified on the ground that the treaty had a withdrawal clause).

99 Bradley, Historical Gloss, *supra* note 4, at 101–05.

100 *Id.* at 106.

101 *Id.* at 107. As Professor Bradley notes, some earlier terminations could be understood as necessary because otherwise the treaty provisions would conflict with other congressional statutes.

102 U.S. Const. art. I, § 10.

103 As demonstrated in Abraham C. Weinfeld, *What Did the Framers of the Federal Constitution Mean by "Agreements or Compacts"?*, 3 U. Chi. L. Rev. 453, 458–59 (1936). For an argument that Vattel was not particularly influential on the Founders generally, *see* Brian Richardson, *The Use of Vattel in the American Law of Nations*, 106 Am. J. Int'l L. 547 (2012). But *see* Robert G. Natelson, *The Power to Restrict Immigration and the Original Meaning of the Constitution's Define and Punish Clause*, 11 Br. J. Am. Leg. Studies 209, 218 (2022) (showing that Vattel was on a list of books on the law of nations recommended by a three-man committee of the Confederation Congress comprising James Madison, Hugh Williamson, and Thomas Mifflin).

104 Vattel, *supra* note 73, at 192 (bk. II, ch. xii, § 152).

105 *Id.* (§ 153).

106 Weinfeld, *supra* note 103, at 461–62; 1 St. George Tucker, Blackstone's Commentaries with Notes of Reference to the Constitution and Laws of the Federal Government of the United States and of the Commonwealth of Virginia, app. 310 (Philadelphia, PA: Published by William Young Birch, and Abraham Small 1803).

107 *See, e.g.*, Bradford R. Clark, *Domesticating Sole Executive Agreements*, 93 Va. L. Rev. 1573, 1579 (2007) (making this observation).

108 *See, e.g.*, Prakash & Ramsey, *supra* note 3, at 248–49; McConnell, *supra* note 3, at 241.

109 Bradley, Historical Gloss, *supra* note 4, at 87.

110 For this episode, *see* Sofaer, *supra* note 8, at 198, 204; 5 Dumas Malone, Jefferson and His Time 246–47 (Boston: Little, Brown and Company 1974). As Malone recounts, the agreement was entered into by General Wilkinson before even receiving instructions from Jefferson, but the agreement was ultimately consistent with those instructions.

111 Bradley, Historical Gloss, *supra* note 4, at 86.

112 Sofaer, *supra* note 8, at 260–61.

113 Samuel Estreicher & Steven Menashi, *Taking* Steel Seizure *Seriously: The Iran Nuclear Agreement and the Separation of Powers*, 86 Fordham L. Rev. 1199 (2017) (demonstrating this point but arguing that the agreement nevertheless violated Congress's statutory policy). The author takes no position on whether the President followed the sanctions laws or violated them. The point is only that the President understood he had no power to override those statutes and pursued an executive agreement within the bounds of possible interpretations of the statutory framework.

114 Though some of the sanctions statutes did tie sanctions to Iran's nuclear program. *See id.* at 1231.

115 Currie, *supra* note 4, at 151–52; Sofaer, *supra* note 8, at 97.

116 Corwin came to the same conclusion. Corwin, *supra* note 2, at 215 ("[I]f the subject matter to be regulated falls within the powers of Congress, the latter may constitutionally authorize the President to deal with it by negotiation and agreement with other governments, the treatymaking power to the contrary notwithstanding.").

117 This further suggests that there is no legitimate distinction, frequently drawn in the literature, between "unilateral" or "sole" executive agreements and "congressional-executive agreements" where the President is acting pursuant to congressional authorization or where Congress approves the agreement after the fact by joint resolution. *See, e.g.*, Henkin, *supra* note 2, at 215–24. The President can implement an executive agreement only if the constitutional or statutory power to do so already exists. Outside agreements like armistice agreements that can be accomplished by the President's preclusive and exclusive powers, all executive agreements, properly understood, if they are to have any actual effect, are congressional-executive agreements. *See also, e.g.*, Michael D. Ramsey, *Executive Agreements and the (Non)treaty Power*, 77 N.C.L. Rev. 133, 136–37 (1998) (concluding that executive agreements require "legislative enactment for domestic implementation"). Thus, an ex post approval by Congress of an executive agreement can be understood as Congress passing the agreement as a statute. Any ex ante approval to enter into agreements must be analyzed under the nondelegation doctrine.

118 Some scholars have argued that treaties and congressional-executive agreements are completely interchangeable; others that the rise of congressional-executive agreements reflects an illegitimate usurpation of the treaty power. *See* Oona A. Hathaway, *Treaties' End: The Past, Present, and Future of International Lawmaking in the United States*, 117 Yale L.J. 1236, 1244–48 (2008) (canvassing the debate). As this section will show presently, however, treaties are at least necessary to create national commitments beyond Congress's enumerated powers. *See* John C. Yoo, *Laws as Treaties?: The Constitutionality of Congressional-Executive Agreements*, 99 Mich. L. Rev. 757 (2001).

119 *See, e.g.*, Ramsey, *supra* note 117, at 136.

120 Bradley, Historical Gloss, *supra* note 4, at 83 (observing that extradition is still almost entirely governed by treaties). There is a debate whether Congress has the power to

implement a non–self-executing treaty beyond its enumerated powers. *See* Missouri v. Holland, 252 U.S. 416 (1920) (holding that Congress can implement treaties otherwise exceeding the enumerated powers); Nicholas Quinn Rosenkranz, *Executing the Treaty Power*, 118 Harv. L. Rev. 1867 (2005) (disagreeing with Missouri v. Holland); Jean Galbraith, *Congress's Treaty-Implementing Power in Historical Practice*, 56 Wm. & Mary L. Rev. 59 (2014) (disagreeing with Rosenkranz).

121 This view could also support environmental and migratory bird treaties, as in Missouri v. Holland, that affect more than one nation.

122 Thus, for example, it is highly unlikely that the President and Senate can enter into a convention requiring the implementation of domestic policies relating to violence against women, if such a subject matter is otherwise outside the scope of Congress's power. *See* United States v. Morrison, 529 U.S. 598 (2000) (holding invalid the Violence Against Women Act). The literature on the scope of the treatymaking power is vast. For a sampling, *see* sources cited in Galbraith, *supra* note 120, at 68 n.27.

123 Article VI provides, "This Constitution, and the Laws of the United States which shall be made in Pursuance thereof; and all Treaties made, or which shall be made, under the Authority of the United States, shall be the supreme Law of the Land; and the Judges in every State shall be bound thereby, any Thing in the Constitution or Laws of any State to the Contrary notwithstanding." U.S. Const. art. VI, cl. 2.

124 *See, e.g.*, Am. Ins. Ass'n v. Garamendi, 539 U.S. 396 (2003) (holding that executive agreement preempted contrary state law).

125 United States v. Pink, 315 U.S. 203, 231 (1942). It built on a prior case involving the same agreement. *See* United States v. Belmont, 301 U.S. 324 (1937).

126 Presidents have concluded executive agreements respecting settlement of claims arising out of activities on the high seas and that did not involve any state law, for example, when privateers seized vessels or when damage occurred as a result of a foreign blockade. The claimants' only recourse in such situations is whatever they can extract from the foreign nation through negotiation. The President can act as negotiator. It was purely voluntary whether American claimants would accept the terms; but they had no other viable alternatives. To the extent foreigners made claims against Americans, Congress would have to appropriate for their settlement, as George Washington had noted during the neutrality controversy. *See generally* Bradley, Historical Gloss, *supra* note 4, at 84–86 (describing such claims settlement practices).

CHAPTER 10

1 U.S. Const. art. I, § 8, cl. 11.

2 U.S. Const. art. I, § 8, cls. 10, 12–17.

3 U.S. Const. art. II, § 2, para. 1.

4 For an excellent short account that is largely consistent with what this chapter argues, *see* Michael D. Ramsey, *The President's Power to Respond to Attacks*, 93 Cornell L. Rev. 169 (2007).

5 2 Max Farrand ed., The Records of the Federal Convention of 1787, at 318 (New Haven, CT: Yale University Press 1911).

6 1 William Blackstone, Commentaries on the Laws of England 249 (Oxford: Clarendon Press 1765) ("[T]he king has also the sole prerogative of making war and peace.").

7 2 Farrand, *supra* note 5, at 318–19.

8 *Id.* at 314 (journal of the Convention). Madison's notes do not record this initial vote.

9 *Id.* at 314, 319.

10 1 Farrand, *supra* note 5, at 292.

11 *See* Charles C. Thach Jr., The Creation of the Presidency, 1775–1789: A Study in Constitutional History 55–75 (Baltimore: Johns Hopkins Press 1922) (describing the general transition of committee governance to standing departments including for military matters).

12 Articles of Confed. art. IX, para. 4 (emphasis added).

13 Michael W. McConnell, The President Who Would Not Be King 206 (Princeton University Press 2020). In Blackstone's *Commentaries*, the powers of commander in chief ("generalissimo") included the powers to raise troops and make rules and regulations for the armed forces, both of which the U.S. Constitution assigns to Congress. 1 Blackstone, *supra* note 6, at 254.

14 Little v. Barreme, 6 U.S. 170, 177 (1804). Congress's role in authorizing specific military measures during the Quasi-War with France is discussed later in this chapter.

15 For a discussion of this episode, *see* Jane E. Stromseth, *Rethinking War Powers: Congress, the President, and the United Nations*, 81 Geo. L.J. 597, 635–37 (1993). President Truman sent the divisions to Europe without congressional approval, but no one doubts that Congress could have prohibited his doing so. In the Quasi-War with France, Congress specified what ships could be used for, including limiting them to the jurisdictional waters of the United States. *See* Abraham D. Sofaer, War, Foreign Affairs and Constitutional Power: The Origins 147–48 (Cambridge, MA: Ballinger Publishing Company 1976). And Congress in 1789 adopted the resolves of the Continental Congress that troops shall be "stationed" on the frontier. *See infra* notes 45– 46 and accompanying text. For the full range of constitutional positions taken in the late 1790s, *see* Sofaer, *supra*, at 147–54.

16 As Saikrishna Prakash has written, "If Congress decreed that a militia could be stationed in one location, the president lacked the constitutional authority to deploy it elsewhere. If Congress dictated that the navy could attack only certain enemy ships, those ships were the only lawful targets." Saikrishna Bangalore Prakash, The Living Presidency: An Originalist Argument against Its Ever-Expanding Powers 151 (Cambridge, MA: Harvard University Press 2020); *see also id.* at 157 (similar).

17 But *see* David J. Barron & Martin S. Lederman, *The Commander in Chief at the Lowest Ebb – Framing the Problem, Doctrine, and Original Understanding*, 121 Harv. L. Rev. 689, 750–61 (2008) (disagreeing with the proposition that Congress cannot control tactics). For other accounts of this division of authority, *see* McConnell, *supra* note 13, at 208–12; John Harrison, *Executive Power* 44–45 (working paper June 2019), https://perma.cc/36YT-Q669.

18 McConnell, *supra* note 13, at 192. Among the excellent sources McConnell relies upon for this proposition are John Yoo, *War and the Constitutional Text*, 69 U. Chi. L. Rev. 1639, 1666–67 (2002), and Nathan Chapman, *Due Process of War*, 94 Notre Dame L. Rev. 639 (2018).

19 1 Blackstone, *supra* note 6, at 250.

20 For a summary of the contrary view, *see* Curtis A. Bradley & Jack L. Goldsmith, *Congressional Authorization and the War on Terrorism*, 118 Harv. L. Rev. 2047, 2058–59 (2005).

21 1 Blackstone, *supra* note 6, at 249, 254.

22 Charles A. Lofgren, War-Making under the Constitution: The Original Understanding, 81 Yale L.J. 672, 680–81, 685, 693–96 (1972).

23 *Id.* at 685 (quoting 2 Jonathan Elliot ed., The Debates in the Several State Conventions on the Adoption of the Federal Constitution 528 (1888)).

24 The Federalist No. 69, at 417–18 (Clinton Rossiter ed. 1961).

25 This is Saikrishna Prakash's conclusion as well. *See* Saikrishna Prakash, *Unleashing the Dogs of War: What the Constitution Means by "Declare War,"* 93 Cornell L. Rev. 45 (2007).

26 Lofgren, *supra* note 22, at 693.

27 *Id.*

28 1 Blackstone, *supra* note 6, at 250.

29 The distinction was recently discussed by another scholar, who describes its origins in the work of Burlamaqui, an influential writer on the law of nations. *See* Kenneth B. Moss, Marque and Reprisal: The Spheres of Public and Private Warfare 183 (Lawrence: University Press of Kansas 2019); *see also* Jean-Jacques Burlamaqui, The Principles of Political Law: Being a Sequel to the Principles of Natural Law 258, part IV, ch. 3, para. XXX (Thomas Nugent trans., London: J. Nourse 1752).

30 Bas v. Tingy, 4 U.S. (4 Dal.) 37 (1800).

31 *Id.* at 39 (Moore, J.).

32 *Id.* at 43 (Chase, J.).

33 *Id.*

34 *Id.* at 45 (Patterson J.).

35 *Id.*

36 *Id.* at 40–41 (Washington, J.).

37 *Id.* at 41.

38 Talbot v. Seeman, 5 U.S. (1 Cranch) 1 (1801).

39 *Id.* at 28.

40 *Id.* at 31, 32, 33, 34,

41 William Hall & Saikrishna Bangalore Prakash, *The Constitution's First Declared War: The Northwestern Confederacy War of 1790–1795*, 107 Va. L. Rev. 119 (2021). For a fuller historical account of the conflict with the tribes along the Wabash River, *see* Richard H. Kohn, Eagle and Sword: The Federalists and the Creation of the Military Establishment in America, 1783–1802, at 95–157 (New York: The Free Press 1975).

42 The Hall and Prakash article helpfully collects much of the relevant literature. *See* Hall & Prakash, *supra* note 41, at 126–30. For example, Professor John Yoo has written that President Washington "decided to escalate with a large, professional army that could permanently defeat the tribes," including incursions into enemy territory, but "Washington did not seek statutory authorization for offensive operations or a declaration of war." John Yoo, *George Washington and the Executive Power*, 5 U. St. Thomas J.L. & Pub. Pol'y 1, 20–21. (2010). Michael Ramsey writes that Congress's laws "empowered the President generally to call the militia to defend the frontier (without mentioning offensive measures or particular locations) and said nothing at all about how to use the regular Army." Ramsey, *supra* note 4, at 180. For related discussions, *see* David P. Currie, The Constitution in Congress: The Federalist

Period, 1789–1801, at 81–84 (University of Chicago Press 1997); Sofaer, *supra* note 15, at 119–24.

43 *See* Hall & Prakash, *supra* note 41, at 128–30.

44 Act of Sept. 29, 1789, ch. 25, 1 Stat. 95; Act of Apr. 30, 1790, ch. 10, 1 Stat. 119.

45 Act of Sept. 29, 1789, 1 Stat. 95.

46 33 Roscoe R. Hill ed., Journals of the Continental Congress 1774–1789, at 602 (Oct. 3, 1787) (Washington, DC: Gov't Printing Off. 1936).

47 Hall & Prakash, *supra* note 41, at 124.

48 George Washington, Address to the United States Senate and House of Representatives (Dec. 8, 1790), *in* 7 Jack D. Warren, Jr. ed., The Papers of George Washington: Presidential Series 45, 47 (Charlottesville: University Press of Virginia 1998).

49 Letter from George Washington to William Moultrie (Aug. 28, 1793), *in* Christine Sternberg Patrick eds., 13 The Papers of George Washington: Presidential Series, 1 June–31 August, 1793, at 570 (Charlottesville: University of Virginia Press 2007).

50 Letter from George Washington to Henry Lee (May 6, 1793), *in* Christine Sternberg Patrick & John C. Pinheiro eds., 12 The Papers of George Washington: Presidential Series, 16 January 1793–31 May 1793, at 533 (Charlottesville: University of Virginia Press 2005).

51 That is Hall and Prakash's interpretation. *See supra* note 41, at 163–71.

52 John Adams, Special Message to the Senate and the House (May 16, 1797), *in* 1 James D. Richardson ed., A Compilation of the Messages and Papers of the Presidents 237 (Published by Authority of Congress 1899).

53 10 Henry Cabot Lodge ed., The Works of Alexander Hamilton 281–82 (New York: G. P. Putnam's Sons The Knickerbocker Press 1904) (emphases deleted).

54 Sofaer, *supra* note 15, at 155–56.

55 10 Paul Leicester Ford ed., The Works of Thomas Jefferson 433 (New York: G. P. Putnam's Sons The Knickerbocker Press 1905). He wrote in another letter, "[T]he power of declaring war being with the Legislature, the executive should do nothing, necessarily committing them to decide for war in preference of non-intercourse." *Id.* at 449.

56 15 Annals of Cong. 19 (1805) (Washington, DC: Gales & Seaton 1852). Jefferson added: "I have barely instructed the officers stationed in the neighborhood of the aggressions, to protect our citizens from violence, to patrol within the borders actually delivered to us, and not to go out of them, but, when necessary, to repel an inroad, or to rescue a citizen or his property[.]" *Id.*

57 Thomas Jefferson, First Annual Message to the Senate and the House (Dec. 8, 1801), *in* 1 Richardson, *supra* note 52, at 326–27.

58 Sofaer, *supra* note 15, at 209–13; *see also* David P. Currie, The Constitution in Congress: The Jeffersonians, 1801–1829, at 127–28 (University of Chicago Press 2001). It is possible, however, to interpret those instructions as largely defensive. If Tripoli alone had declared war, which was the case, the instructions provided to the commander were that "you will then proceed direct to that Port, where you will lay your ships in such a position as effectually to prevent any of their Vessels from going in or out." 1 Naval Documents Related to the United States War with the Barbary Powers 467 (Washington, DC: Gov't Printing Off. 1939). If Algiers, the most powerful of the Barbary States, or all of them, had

declared war, the instructions provided that the fleet was to "sink burn, or otherwise destroy their ships & Vessels, wherever you find them." *Id.* This instruction could be interpreted as limited to destroying any vessels that the fleet should "find" while otherwise lawfully defending American commerce.

59 Sofaer, *supra* note 15, at 211–13. The instructions given by Captain Dale to Lieutenant Sterrett (commander of the *Enterprise*) were to capture any vessels on the way back from Malta after having secured water supplies, but merely to disable the vessels if encountered on the way to Malta. *See also* 1 Naval Documents, *supra* note 58, at 535.

60 Sofaer, *supra* note 15, at 222–23.

61 Currie, *supra* note 58, at 125–26 (quoting The Examination No. 1 (Dec. 17, 1801), *in* Harold C. Syrett & Jacob E. Cooke eds., 25 The Papers of Alexander Hamilton 444, 454–55 (Columbia University Press 1977)).

62 1 Paul Leicester Ford, The Works of Thomas Jefferson 365–66 (New York: G. P. Putnam's Sons The Knickerbocker Press 1904). Jefferson's notes from the Cabinet meeting suggest that only Attorney General Levi Lincoln though they must await congressional authorization, although Madison expressed some hesitation as to whether American ships could enter into enemy harbors if not in hot pursuit of a vessel. Gallatin repeated the point in other letters to Jefferson. *See* 1 Henry Adams ed., The Writings of Albert Gallatin 89 (Philadelphia, PA: J. B. Lippincott 1879):

> The Executive cannot declare war, but if war is made, whether declared by Congress or by the enemy, the conduct must be the same, to protect our vessels, and to fight, take, and destroy the armed vessels of that enemy. The only case which admits of doubt is whether, in case of such war actually existing, we should confine our hostilities to their armed vessels or extend them by capture or blockade to the trade.

Id. at 105:

> Authority for our vessels to act offensively in case of war declared or waged by other Barbary powers. I do not and never did believe that it was necessary to obtain a legislative sanction in the last case: whenever war does exist, whether by the declaration of the United States or by the declaration or act of a foreign nation, I think that the Executive has a right, and is in duty bound, to apply the public force which he may have the means legally to employ, in the most effective manner to annoy the enemy.

63 Sofaer, *supra* note 15, at 223–24.

64 *Id.*; 13 Annals of Cong. 564 (1803) (Washington, DC: Gales & Seaton 1852) (legislation).

65 Arthur M. Schlesinger Jr., The Imperial Presidency 51 (New York: Houghton Mifflin 1973).

66 *See, e.g.*, Office of Legal Counsel, April 2018 Airstrikes against Syrian Chemical-Weapons Facilities, 42 Op. O.L.C. (May 31, 2018), slip op. at 6–7; Office of Legal Counsel, Proposed Deployment of United States Armed Forces into Bosnia, 19 Op. O.L.C. 327, 331 (Nov. 30, 1995). The examples appear first to have been collected by the executive branch in Authority of the President to Repel the Attack in Korea, 23 Dep't State Bull. 173 (July 3, 1950). The full memorandum is available at H. Rep. 2495, 81st Cong., 2d Sess., at 61–68. It includes an appendix of all the supposedly unilateral presidential actions. *Id.* at 67–68.

67 Schlesinger, *supra* note 65, at 51. For examples, *see id.* at 52–56. Sofaer's account of the evidence is provided in Sofaer, *supra* note 15, at 276–79. Sofaer notes nevertheless that oftentimes presidential instructions were intentionally vague and the commanders had given the executive sufficient time to disapprove of planned actions. "[T]he executive, during this period," Sofaer concludes, "may have wanted officers in the field to undertake projects that would have been beyond what were then perceived to be the constitutional limits of the President's authority." *Id.* at 279.

68 Schlesinger, *supra* note 65, at 55.

69 5 Richardson, *supra* note 52, at 282.

70 Durand v. Hollins, 8 F. Cas. 111, 112 (C.C.S.D.N.Y. 1860).

71 *Id.*

72 *See* Schlesinger, *supra* note 65, at 56 ("It was not a question of emergency intervention to save American citizens; it was rather calculated retaliation after the fact.").

73 In 1912, J. Reuben Clark famously argued that such actions were permitted by international law, and that international law was part of the law of the United States. *Id.* at 132; *see also* Memorandum of the Solicitor for the Department of State Oct. 5, 1912, Right to Protect Citizens in Foreign Countries by Landing Forces (Washington, DC: Gov't Printing Off., 3d rev. ed. 1934). The Clark memorandum maintained not only that the President had this international police power but also that Congress could not "direct the President in the employment of forces" in nonwar police actions because "the grant of a large power does not carry with it the grant of other smaller or inferior powers merely because they are inferior." Memorandum, *supra*, at 40–42.

74 U.S. Const. art. I, § 8, cl. 10.

75 *See also, e.g.*, Bradley & Goldsmith, *supra* note 20, at 2066–72 (observing that both historical precedent and modern international law support treating armed conflict with non-state actors as "war" in the constitutional sense).

76 *Prize Cases*, 67 U.S. (2 Black) 635 (1863).

77 *Id.* at 688–89 (Nelson, J., dissenting).

78 Bas v. Tingy, 4 U.S. (4 Dal.) 37, 43 (1800) (Chase, J.).

79 *Prize Cases*, 67 U.S. at 669 (majority opinion).

80 Bradley and Goldsmith explain that declarations of war "serve little purpose" under modern international law, which recognizes and governs "armed conflicts" irrespective of a declaration of war by any of the parties. *See* Bradley & Goldsmith, *supra* note 20, at 2061–62.

81 United Nations Security Council Resolutions 83 [S/1511] & 84 [S/1588].

82 Harry S. Truman, Statement by the President on the Situation in Korea, June 27, 1950, https://perma.cc/Y6RM-D3FM.

83 Medellin v. Texas, 552 U.S. 491, 525–26 (2008).

84 For example, the Mutual Defense Treaty between the United States and the Republic of China (later Taiwan) of Dec. 2, 1954, provided that each party "would act to meet the common danger in accordance with its constitutional processes."[6] UST 433–38, art. V. The North Atlantic Treaty of Apr. 4, 1949, provides that "its provisions" shall be "carried out by the Parties in accordance with their respective constitutional processes."[4] Charles I. Bevins, Treaties and Other International Agreements of the United States of America, 1776–1949, at 830 (Department of State Publication, released June 1970).

Although never implemented, Article 43 of the U.N. Charter provides for Member Nations to enter into agreements with the U.N. Security Council to provide armed forces to implement the directives of the Council. Although Congress authorized the President to enter into such agreements in the United Nations Participation Act of 1945, it was never implemented. James E. Rossman, *Article 43: Arming the United Nations Security Council*, 27 N.Y.U. J. Int'l L. & Politics 227, 227 (1994); United Nations Participation Act, 59 Stat. 619 (1945). It is, however, questionable whether Truman's actions would have been constitutional had there been such agreements in place. As noted in Chapter 9, it is highly unlikely that a non–self-executing treaty can expand the powers of the national government or alter the distribution of powers. The treaty effectively required Congress to delegate its declare-war power to the President (or the United Nations). In any event, because no such agreements had ever been implemented, Truman could not have relied on this argument.

85 As Stephen Griffin argues, every U.S. president since Truman has maintained the position that the president can commit troops without congressional authorization. Griffin argues that this paradigm shift occurred as a result of the exigencies of the Cold War and the ongoing national security and foreign policy objectives of the nation. *See* Stephen M. Griffin, Long Wars and the Constitution 31–35 (Cambridge, MA: Harvard University Press 2013) (describing this "1950 Thesis"); *but see* Bradley, Historical Gloss, *supra* note 4, at 144–45 (arguing that the 1950 Thesis is wrong because modern unilateralism can best be traced to the aftermath of the Spanish-American War and because the Korean War remains an aberration).

86 For a general discussion of this episode, *see* Peter M. Shane, Harold H. Bruff, & Neil J. Kinkopf, Separation of Powers Law: Cases and Materials 1077–85 (Carolina Academic Press, 4th ed. 2018).

87 For this episode, *see id.* at 1022–25.

88 Human Rights Watch, Death of a Dictator: Bloody Vengeance in Sirte (2012), available at https://www.hrw.org/sites/default/files/reports/libya1012webwcover_0_0.pdf; Thomas Harding, "Col Gaddafi killed: convoy bombed by drone flown by pilot in Las Vegas," The Telegraph (Oct. 20, 2011).

89 Office of Legal Counsel, Authority to Use Military Force in Libya, 35 Op. O.L.C. 20 (Apr. 1, 2011).

90 Office of Legal Counsel, April 2018 Airstrikes against Syrian Chemical-Weapons Facilities, 42 Op. O.L.C. 1, 1 (May 31, 2018).

91 Office of Legal Counsel, Memorandum for John A. Eisenberg Legal Advisor to the National Security Council Re: January 2020 Airstrike in Iraq against Qassem Soleimani (Mar. 10, 2020), https://www.justice.gov/d9/2023-04/2020-03-10_soleimani_airstrike_redacted_2021.pdf.

92 As occurred in the lead-up to the Mexican-American War. *See* David P. Currie, The Constitution in Congress: Descent into the Maelstrom, 1829–1861, at 102 (University of Chicago Press 2005).

93 To repeat, committing an act of war under international law and thereby risking war would be unconstitutional. But so, too, would be committing other acts without congressional approval that seriously risk provoking war.

94 Bas v. Tingy, 4 U.S. (4 Dal.) 37, 40 (1800) (Washington, J.).

95 Zivotofsky ex rel. Zivotofsky v. Kerry, 135 S. Ct. 2076, 2086 (2015) (quotation marks, alterations, and citations omitted).

96 *See* Mistretta v. United States, 488 U.S. 361, 372 (1989) ("[O]ur jurisprudence has been driven by a practical understanding that in our increasingly complex society, replete with ever-changing and more technical problems, Congress simply cannot do its job absent an ability to delegate power under broad general directives.").

97 *See* Chevron v. Nat. Res. Def. Council, 467 U.S. 837 (1984). That decision was recently overturned in Loper Bright Enterprises v. Raimondo, 603 U.S. 369 (2024).

CHAPTER 11

1 Mark Joseph Stern, *Brett Kavanaugh Is Ready to Join the Supreme Court's Conservatives to Tear Down Key Federal Regulations*, Slate (Nov. 25, 2019), https://perma.cc/Y7K6-U22K. Scholars tend to be more careful, but similar themes sound in the leading critics of the nondelegation doctrine. Professors Julian Mortenson and Nicholas Bagley write that the nondelegation doctrine must depend significantly on history because otherwise it is a mere "inference from the text and structure of the Constitution." Julian Davis Mortenson & Nicholas Bagley, *Delegation at the Founding: A Response to Critics*, 122 Colum. L. Rev. 2323, 2325 (2022). But, of course, the view that delegation is permissible must then be equally an inference; that is not stated explicitly.

2 *See also* Gary Lawson & Guy Seidman, The Constitution of Empire: Territorial Expansion and American Legal History 128 (New Haven, CT: Yale University Press 2004) (Congress "generally cannot delegate legislative power for the simple reason that the Constitution does not affirmatively authorize such delegations").

3 Much of the following discussion is taken or adapted from Ilan Wurman, *Nondelegation at the Founding*, 130 Yale L.J. 1490 (2021).

4 The Federalist No. 47, at 301 (Clinton Rossiter ed., 1961) (James Madison).

5 Charles-Louis de Secondat, Baron de Montesquieu, The Spirits of the Laws 156 (Anne M. Cohler, Basia C. Miller, & Harold S. Stone eds., Cambridge University Press 1989) (1748).

6 13 Annals of Cong. 498 (1803) (Washington, DC: Gales & Seaton 1852).

7 Wurman, *supra* note 3, at 1523–24.

8 The Federalist No. 53, *supra* note 4, at 333 (James Madison).

9 The Federalist No. 62, *id.* at 378 (Alexander Hamilton or James Madison).

10 The Federalist No. 70, *id.* at 423 (Alexander Hamilton).

11 *Id.* at 424.

12 The Federalist No. 78, *id.* at 465 (Alexander Hamilton).

13 *Id.*

14 *Id.* at 470–71.

15 The Federalist No. 79, *id.* at 472 (Alexander Hamilton).

16 *See* Eric A. Posner & Adrian Vermeule, *Interring the Nondelegation Doctrine*, 69 U. Chi. L. Rev. 1721 (2002); Julian Davis Mortenson & Nicholas Bagley, *Delegation at the Founding*, 121 Colum. L. Rev. 277, 313–24 (2021).

17 Mortenson & Bagley, *supra* note 16, at 294 n.92 (citing Montesquieu, *supra* note 5, at 201); *id.* at 294 & n.93 (quoting Jean-Jacques Rousseau, The Social Contract 101 (Maurice Cranston trans., Penguin 1968)).

18 In the Post-Roads Debate of 1791, there is one reported statement by Representative Bourne that could be interpreted as the single exception. He is reported to have said that the Constitution "speaks in general terms" of establishing post offices and post roads, and that "[t]he Constitution meant no more than that Congress should possess the exclusive right of doing that, by themselves or by any other person, which amounts to the same thing."[3] Annals of Cong. 232 (1791) (Washington, DC: Gales & Seaton 1849). For a fuller analysis of the relevant historical data and episodes, *see* Wurman, *supra* note 3, at 1504–18.

19 1 William Blackstone, Commentaries on the Laws of England 261 (Oxford: Clarendon Press 1765).

20 James Wilson, Speech at the Pennsylvania Ratifying Convention (Nov. 24, 1787), *in* 2 Jonathan Elliot ed., The Debates in the Several State Conventions, on the Adoption of the Federal Constitution 432 (Washington, DC: Printed for the editor, 2d ed. 1836).

21 For a fuller analysis of the relevant historical data and episodes, *see* Wurman, *supra* note 3, at 1504–18. There were some earlier mentions of the principle, but the matter was not extensively discussed.

22 The statute enacted in its very first section:

That from and after the first day of June next, the following roads be established as post roads, namely: From Wisscassett in the district of Maine, to Savannah in Georgia, by the following route, to wit: Portland, Portsmouth, Newburyport, Ipswich, Salem, Boston, Worcester, Springfield, Hartford, Middletown, New Haven, Stratford, Fairfield, Norwalk, Stamford, New York, Newark, Elizabethtown, Woodbridge, Brunswick, Princeton, Trenton, Bristol, Philadelphia, Chester, Wilmington, Elkton, Charlestown, Havre de Grace, Hartford, Baltimore, Bladensburg, Georgetown, Alexandria, Colchester, Dumfries, Fredericksburg, Bowling Green, Hanover Court House, Richmond, Petersburg, Halifax, Tarborough, Smithfield, Fayetteville, Newbridge over Drowning creek, Cheraw Court House, Camden, Statesburg, Columbia, Cambridge and Augusta; and from thence to Savannah, and from Augusta by Washington in Wilkes county to Greenborough and from thence . . . .

Act of Feb. 20, 1792, ch. 7, § 1, 1 Stat. 232, 232.

23 3 Annals of Cong., *supra* note 18, at 229.

24 *Id.*

25 *Id.* at 231.

26 *Id.* at 233–34.

27 *Id.* at 233.

28 *Id.* at 235.

29 *Id.* at 236.

30 *Id.* at 238–39.

31 *Id.* at 241.

32 *Id.* at 230.

33 *Id.* at 229.

34 Act of Feb. 20, 1792, ch. 7, § 2, 1 Stat. 232, 233.

35 *Id.* §§ 3–7 (authorizing the Postmaster General "to appoint ... deputy postmasters, at all places where such shall be found necessary," and directing "[t]hat every deputy postmaster shall keep an office").

36 As scholars have noted, the post roads were the pork barrel or water projects of the day. Gary Lawson, *Delegation and Original Meaning*, 88 Va. L. Rev. 327, 403 (2002) ("Postal routes were the eighteenth-century equivalent of water projects."); Mortenson & Bagley, *supra* note 16, at 350 & n.389 (citing *id.*); David P. Currie, The Constitution in Congress: The Federalist Period, 1789–1801, at 149 (University of Chicago Press 1997) (speculating that "the House's zest for detail" was attributable "to a taste for pork").

37 3 Annals of Cong., *supra* note 18, at 230.

38 An Act Concerning Aliens, ch. 58, § 1, 1 Stat. 570, 571 (1798).

39 James Madison, *The Report of 1800*, *in* David B. Mattern, J. C. A. Stagg, Jeanne K. Cross, & Susan Holbrook Perdue eds., 17 The Papers of James Madison 303, 324 (Charlottesville: University Press of Virginia 1991) (paragraph break added).

40 *Id.* at 325.

41 This principle may also explain why both the Federalists and the Jeffersonians generally accepted broader delegations in the context of appropriations, which required flexibility and did not involve private rights. *See, e.g.*, Michael B. Rappaport, *The Selective Nondelegation Doctrine and the Line Item Veto*, 76 Tul. L. Rev. 265 (2001) (arguing that the nondelegation doctrine does not apply to the appropriations context). As Rappaport argues, appropriations were historically annual, which diminishes the risk of delegating more broadly. The point is that the nondelegation doctrine should be attuned to the type of right at issue and other structural considerations. *Cf. also* Chad Squitieri, *Towards Nondelegation Doctrines*, 86 Mo. L. Rev. 1239 (2021) (proposing the nondelegation doctrine should modulate depending on the congressional power at issue).

42 *See* 8 Annals of Cong. 1963, 2008 (1798) (Washington, DC: Gales & Seaton 1851) (reporting on statements by Representatives Williams and Livingston criticizing the Alien Friends Act); *see also* Wurman, *supra* note 3, at 1513–14 (quoting *id.*).

43 Over the next decade, other laws raised some nondelegation concerns, and although they were enacted, again no one controverted the principle. Wurman, *supra* note 3, at 1514–16.

44 Abraham Sofaer identified several such instances. Abraham D. Sofaer, War, Foreign Affairs and Constitutional Power: The Origins 76 (Cambridge, MA: Ballinger Publishing Co. 1976) (citing Act of July 1, 1790, ch. 22, 1 Stat. 128, 129; 2 Annals of Cong. 1873–75, 1884, 1965, 1971 (1790–91) (Washington, DC: Gales & Seaton 1834)). He recounts how the House of Representatives "succeeded in deleting" from an "excise tax bill a grant of power to the President to set the salaries of revenue officers, partly on the ground that Congress should 'retain the power of disposing of their own money.'" *Id.* (quoting 2 Annals of Cong., *supra*, at 1923 (statement of Representative Burke)). The Senate amendment did allow him to set salaries but limited that discretion substantially. *Id.* In another instance, the power to call forth the militia was more narrowly cabined after similar opposition. *Id.* at 77. And in a debate over delegating to President Adams the discretion to raise an army, Congress narrowed the discretion to the circumstance if war were declared against the United States while Congress was not in session. *Id.* at 144–45. Congress similarly granted discretion to President Adams to provide a navy if there were a danger to the coast and Congress was not in session. *Id.* at 147. Sofaer also described how,

in the lead-up to the War of 1812 when the Senate wanted to give the President broad discretion to employ armed vessels to protect American commerce whenever he deemed it "expedient," the House rejected the amendment after several voiced concerns that it would effect an unlawful delegation of legislative power. *Id.* at 281 (quoting 20 Annals of Cong. 673 (1810) (Washington, DC: Gales & Seaton 1853)).

45 Cargo of the Brig Aurora v. United States, 11 U.S. (7 Cranch) 382 (1813).

46 An Act to interdict the commercial intercourse between the United States and Great Britain and France, and their dependencies; and for other purposes, § 11, 2 Stat. 528, 530–31 (Mar. 1, 1809).

47 An Act concerning the commercial intercourse between the United States and Great Britain and France, and their dependencies, and for other purposes, § 4, 2 Stat. 605, 606 (May 1, 1810).

48 *Brig Aurora*, 11 U.S. at 388.

49 Sofaer, *supra* note 44, at 279–91.

50 23 U.S. (10 Wheat.) 1 (1825).

51 *Id.* at 42–43.

52 *Id.* at 43.

53 143 U.S. 649, 680 (1892).

54 *Id.* at 693.

55 *Id.* at 694.

56 276 U.S. 394 (1928).

57 *Id.* at 400.

58 *Id.* at 409.

59 293 U.S. 388, 418 (1935).

60 *Id.* at 415.

61 295 U.S. 495 (1935).

62 *Id.* at 530.

63 *Id.* at 530–31.

64 *Id.* at 541–42.

65 *Id.* at 551 (Cardozo, J., concurring) (quoting *Panama Refining*, 293 U.S. at 435 (Cardozo, J., dissenting)).

66 *Id.* at 551–52.

67 *Id.* at 553.

68 For example, in Yakus v. United States, 321 U.S. 414 (1944), the statute authorized a wartime price administrator to set prices for commodities that in the judgment of the Administrator would be "fair and equitable," and which would effectuate the purposes of the Act. *Id.* at 420. There were quite broad and often competing standards, including "to stabilize prices," "to eliminate and prevent profiteering," "to assure that defense appropriations are not dissipated by excessive prices," "to protect persons ... from undue impairment of their standard of living," and "to assist in securing adequate production of commodities and facilities." *Id.* Because this delegation of authority was upheld, it is hard to imagine what kind of delegation would not be.

69 Whitman v. Am. Trucking Ass'ns, 531 U.S. 457, 474–75 (2001) (paragraph breaks added) (first quoting *Panama Refining*, 293 U.S. 388; then Am. Power & Light Co. v. SEC, 329

U.S. 90, 104 (1946); then *Yakus*, 321 U.S. at 420, 423–26; then Nat'l Broad. Co. v. United States, 319 U.S. 190, 225–26 (1943); and then Mistretta v. United States, 488 U.S. 361, 416 (1989) (Scalia, J., dissenting)).

70 Dep't of Transp. v. Ass'n of Am. RRs, 575 U.S. 43, 70 (2015) (Thomas, J., concurring in the judgment).

71 *Id.* at 84.

72 588 U.S. 128 (2019).

73 *Id.* at 157 (Gorsuch, J., dissenting) (quoting Wayman v. Southard, 23 U.S. 43 (1825)).

74 *Id.* at 157–58.

75 *Id.* at 159.

76 *Id.* at 163–64.

77 1 Blackstone, *supra* note 19, at 44.

78 On the distinction between public and private rights, *see* Caleb Nelson, *Adjudication in the Political Branches*, 107 Colum. L. Rev. 559 (2007); Crowell v. Benson, 285 U.S. 22, 51 (1932) (stating that a case "of private right" is one "of the liability of one individual to another under the law as defined," and listing examples of public rights).

79 For example, as Professor Nicholas Parrillo has pointed out, Congress in the Direct Tax legislation of 1798 authorized a board of assessors to adjust the tax assessments for entire tax districts if doing so was "just and equitable." Nicholas R. Parrillo, *A Critical Assessment of the Originalist Case against Administrative Regulatory Power: New Evidence from the Federal Tax on Private Real Estate in the 1790s*, 130 Yale L.J. 1288, 1304 (2021) (quoting Act of July 9, 1798, ch. 70, § 22, 1 Stat. 580, 589). The idea appears to have been to equalize tax assessments across different districts and to prevent local assessors from favoring their locality. Wurman, *supra* note 3, at 1552. Obviously, as a result, the statute delegated authority to the assessors to affect private rights. But Congress had decided all the important questions: How much should be raised; how the tax was to be raised (first by a tax on enslaved persons, next a tax on houses, and finally a tax on land to make up any shortfall); whether houses should be taxed separately from land to favor rural farmers; and finally how to equalize the assessments to ensure fairness.

To take another example from a bit later in American history, the steamboat legislation of 1852 authorized the steamboat inspection service to impose passenger limits on ships and to make rules for the passing of ships; both would affect private rights and conduct, although it can certainly be argued that access to public waterways is a public right. Act of Aug. 30, 1852, ch. 106, §§ 10, 29, 10 Stat. 61, 69, 72. Wurman, *supra* note 3, at 1554–55. Regardless of the nature of the right, it hardly seems like the kind of thing one would expect Congress to have to specify. Congress decided all the important questions: that steamboats should be regulated to reduce accidents, and the methods of ensuring such a reduction (uniform rules for passenger limits and the passing of ships). It seems implausible to suggest that Congress must immerse itself in the details of the particular rules, though to be sure, nothing would stop Congress from approving proposals from the agency.

80 INS v. Chadha, 462 U.S. 919, 952 (1983).

81 Whitman v. Am. Trucking Associations, 531 U.S. 457, 475 (2001).

82 Mortenson & Bagley, *supra* note 16, at 279.

83 Kevin Arlyck, *Delegation, Administration, and Improvisation*, 91 Notre Dame L. Rev. 1 (2021); Christine Kexel Chabot, *The Lost History of Delegation at the Founding*, 56 Geo. L. Rev. 81 (2021); Parrillo, *supra* note 79.

84 Wurman, *supra* note 3.

CHAPTER 12

1 Immigr. & Naturalization Serv. v. Chadha, 462 U.S. 919 (1983).

2 *Id.* at 923.

3 *Id.* at 923–24 (quoting 8 U.S.C. § 1254 (repealed 1996)).

4 *Id.* at 924.

5 *Id.* at 924–25 (quoting 8 U.S.C. § 1254(c)(1) (repealed 1996)).

6 *Id.* at 925 (quoting 8 U.S.C. § 1254(c)(2) (repealed 1996)).

7 *Id.* at 926 (quoting H.R. Res. 926, 94th Cong., 1st Sess.; 121 Cong. Rec. 40800 (1975)).

8 *Id.* at 952.

9 *Id.*

10 U.S. Const. art. I, § 7.

11 *Chadha*, 462 U.S. at 953 n.16 (citations omitted).

12 As Justice White pointed out and the majority also recognized. *Id.* at 988 (White, J., dissenting); *Id.* at 957 n.22 (majority opinion) ("We are aware of no decision ... where a federal court has reviewed a decision of the Attorney General suspending deportation of an alien pursuant to the standards set out in § 244(a)(1). This is not surprising, given that no party to such action has either the motivation or the right to appeal from it.").

13 *Id.* at 926 (majority opinion) quoting 121 Cong. Rec. 40800).

14 *Id.* at 960 (Powell, J., concurring).

15 *Id.* at 967 (quoting Fletcher v. Peck, 6 Cranch 87, 136 (1810)).

16 *Id.* at 984 (White, J., dissenting).

17 *Id.* at 985.

18 *Id.* (citations omitted).

19 *Id.* at 985–86.

20 *See* Ilan Wurman, *Constitutional Administration*, 69 Stan. L. Rev. 359 (2017).

21 *Chadha*, 462 U.S. at 972–73 (White, J., dissenting).

22 Bowsher v. Synar, 478 U.S. 714, 770 (White, J., dissenting) (quoting Buckley v. Valeo, 424 U.S. 1, 122 (1976)).

23 Morrison v. Olson, 487 U.S. 654 (1988).

24 *Id.* at 660–61.

25 *See generally* 28 C.F.R. §§ 600.1–600.10.

26 *Morrison*, 487 U.S. at 670–73. There was also the question of whether cross-branch appointments were constitutional, but that is not a topic addressed in this study.

27 *Id.* at 689–90.

28 *Id.* at 691.

29 David Johnston, *Charge in Weinberger Case That Caused Furor before Election Is Thrown Out*, N.Y. Times (Dec. 12, 1992).

30 For a summary and analysis of the air war over South Vietnam, Laos, and Cambodia, *see* Bernard C. Nalty, Air War over South Vietnam, 1968–1975 (2000). One could argue that

such campaigns were authorized by the Gulf of Tonkin Resolution, which authorized the President "to take all necessary measures to repel any armed attack against the forces of the United States and to prevent further aggression." Pub. L. 88-408 (1964).

31 War Powers Resolution, 87 Stat. 555 (Nov. 7, 1973), codified at 50 U.S.C. §§ 1541–50.

32 *Id.* § 3, 5 U.S.C. § 1542.

33 *Id.* § 4, 5 U.S.C. § 1543.

34 *Id.* § 5, 5 U.S.C. § 1544.

35 *Id.* § 8(d), 5 U.S.C. § 1547.

36 M. Elizabeth Magill, *Beyond Powers and Branches in Separation of Powers Law*, 150 U. Pa. L. Rev. 603, 612 (2001). Victoria Nourse has written that commentators have been "mystified by *Chadha* and its categories." Victoria Nourse, *Toward a New Constitutional Anatomy*, 56 Stan. L. Rev. 835, 858 (2004).

37 The author developed this theory in a prior law review article, and in his administrative law casebook. Ilan Wurman, *Nonexclusive Functions and Separation of Powers Law*, 107 Minn. L. Rev. 735 (2022); Ilan Wurman, Administrative Law Theory and Fundamentals: An Integrated Approach (Foundation Press, 2d ed. 2024).

38 John F. Manning, *Separation of Powers as Ordinary Interpretation*, 124 Harv. L. Rev. 1939, 2019 (2011). Others have made similar observations without fully developing the theory or applying it very widely. Steven Calabresi has written that "[t]here are certain kinds of actions . . . which can be undertaken by the executive, but which can also be undertaken by Congress or by the Article III federal courts." Steven G. Calabresi, *The Vesting Clauses as Power Grants*, 88 Nw. U. L. Rev. 1377, 1390 n.46 (1994). And Gary Lawson has written that "an activity is not exclusively judicial merely because it is adjudicative." Gary Lawson, *The Rise and Rise of the Administrative State*, 107 Harv. L. Rev. 1231, 1246 (1994). Justice Thomas, in a concurring opinion, has written as follows:

The allocation of powers in the Constitution is absolute, but it does not follow that there is no overlap between the three categories of governmental power. Certain functions may be performed by two or more branches without either exceeding its enumerated powers under the Constitution. Resolution of claims against the Government is the classic example. At least when Congress waives its sovereign immunity, such claims may be heard by an Article III court, which adjudicates such claims by an exercise of judicial power. But Congress may also provide for an executive agency to adjudicate such claims by an exercise of executive power. Or Congress may resolve the claims itself, legislating by special Act. The question is whether the particular function requires the exercise of a certain type of power; if it does, then only the branch in which that power is vested can perform it. For example, although this Court has long recognized that it does not necessarily violate the Constitution for Congress to authorize another branch to make a determination that it could make itself, there are certain core functions that require the exercise of legislative power and that only Congress can perform.

Dep't of Transp. v. Ass'n of Am. R.Rs., 575 U.S. 43, 69 (2015) (Thomas, J., concurring) (citations omitted).

39 Act of Sept. 29, 1789, ch. 24, 1 Stat. 95.

40 Wurman, *Nonexclusive Functions, supra* note 37, at 791.

41 Wayman v. Southard, 23 U.S. (10 Wheat.) 1, 42–43 (1825).

42 For an excellent summary of "private bills" or "private law," *see* Matthew Mantel, *Private Bills and Private Law*, 99 Law Libr. J. 87 (2007).

43 *See generally* Bernadette Maguire, Immigration: Public Legislation and Private Bills (1997).

44 Act of Mar. 26, 1790, 1 Stat. 103.

45 On statutes that bar judicial review of immigration decisions, *see* Laura E. Dolbow, *Barring Judicial Review*, 77 Vand. L. Rev. 307, 353–57 (2024).

46 *See* Chapter 6 of this book.

47 Even the Court in *Morrison* recognized that prosecution was a "purely executive" function. Morrison v. Olson, 487 U.S. 654, 689–90 (1988).

48 *See, e.g.*, United States v. Lee, 106 U.S. 196, 220 (1882):

> [I]t is absolutely prohibited, both to the executive and the legislative, to deprive any one of life, liberty, or property. .... These provisions for the security of the rights of the citizen stand in the constitution in the same connection and upon the same ground as they regard his liberty and his property. It cannot be denied that both were intended to be enforced by the judiciary.

49 The entire project may be viewed at National Constitution Center, The Constitution Drafting Project: The Proposed Amendments, https://perma.cc/K7WQ-5H2M.

CHAPTER 13

1 For a view skeptical of the assumption that the federal government's departments were intended to be "co-equal," and that Congress was supposed to be preeminent, *see* David J. Siemers, The Myth of Coequal Branches: Restoring the Constitution's Separation of Functions (Columbia: University of Missouri Press 2018).

2 Alexander Bickel may have written the definitive modern account of the argument for why the Constitution's text does not compel judicial review. Alexander Bickel, The Least Dangerous Branch: The Supreme Court at the Bar of Politics 1–14 (New Haven, CT: Yale University Press 1962). *See also* Learned Hand, The Bill of Rights: The Oliver Wendell Holmes Lectures, 1958 (Cambridge, MA: Harvard University Press 1958).

3 Even the Anti-Federalists objected to the Constitution *because* it would allow judges to enforce the Constitution over contrary legislation. As Brutus wrote,

> The cases arising under the constitution must include such, as bring into question its meaning, and will require an explanation of the nature and extent of the powers of the different departments under it. This article, therefore, vests the judicial with a power to resolve all questions that may arise on any case on the construction of the constitution, either in law or in equity.

Brutus No. XI, *in* 2 Herbert J. Storing ed., The Complete Anti-Federalist 419 (University of Chicago Press 1981). Randy Barnett has similarly observed that there was opposition to judicial review, not doubts that it would exist under the new Constitution. Randy E. Barnett, *The Original Meaning of the Judicial Power*, 12 Sup. Ct. Econ. Rev. 115 (2004). For additional evidence and discussion, *see infra* notes 53– 65 and accompanying text toward the end of this chapter.

4 Here is the full text of these two paragraphs:

The judicial Power of the United States, shall be vested in one supreme Court, and in such inferior Courts as the Congress may from time to time ordain and establish. The Judges, both of the supreme and inferior Courts, shall hold their Offices during good Behaviour, and shall, at stated Times, receive for their Services, a Compensation, which shall not be diminished during their Continuance in Office.

The judicial Power shall extend to all Cases, in Law and Equity, arising under this Constitution, the Laws of the United States, and Treaties made, or which shall be made, under their Authority; – to all Cases affecting Ambassadors, other public Ministers and Consuls; – to all Cases of admiralty and maritime Jurisdiction; – to Controversies to which the United States shall be a Party; – to Controversies between two or more States; – between a State and Citizens of another State; – between Citizens of different States; – between Citizens of the same State claiming Lands under Grants of different States, and between a State, or the Citizens thereof, and foreign States, Citizens or Subjects.

U.S. Const. art. III, §§ 1–2.

5 *Id.* § 2, para. 2.

6 On the Madisonian Compromise, *see* Richard H. Fallon, Jr., John F. Manning, Daniel J. Meltzer, & David L. Shapiro, Hart and Wechsler's The Federal Courts and the Federal System 7–8 (St. Paul: Foundation Press, 7th ed. 2015) [hereinafter Hart & Wechsler]; 1 Max Farrand ed., The Records of the Federal Convention of 1787, at 124–25 (New Haven, CT: Yale University Press 1911). On the point about traveling to faraway courts, Madison countered in the Convention that without federal district courts with final decision-making authority in many cases, the only appeal from the state courts would be to the federal supreme court in the faraway national capital. Hart & Wechsler, *supra* at 7; 1 Farrand, *supra* at 124 (Madison "observed that unless inferior tribunals were dispersed throughout the Republic with *final* jurisdiction in *many* cases, appeals would be multiplied to a most oppressive degree").

7 28 U.S.C. § 1441(b)(2) (providing that diversity cases brought in state court in a defendant's home state are not removable to federal court).

8 Judiciary Act of 1789, 1 Stat. 73. For a description of the district courts' jurisdiction, *see* Akhil Reed Amar, *A Neo-Federalist View of Article III: Separating the Two Tiers of Federal Jurisdiction*, 65 B.U. L. Rev. 205, 260–62 (1985).

9 Act of Feb. 21, 1793, ch. 11, § 5, 1 Stat. 318, 322.

10 Act of Mar. 3, 1875, ch. 137, § 1, 18 Stat. 470, 470.

11 Hart & Wechsler, *supra* note 6, at 25–26, 307–08; Sheldon v. Sill, 49 U.S. (8 How.) 441 (1850).

12 Hart & Wechsler, *supra* note 6, at 314–19 (canvassing debate).

13 Boumediene v. Bush, 553 U.S. 723 (2008) (holding somewhat implausibly that Congress's attempt to strip the courts of jurisdiction was a suspension of habeas corpus and that such suspension was unconstitutional).

14 *See, e.g.,* Herbert Wechsler, *The Courts and the Constitution*, 65 Colum. L. Rev. 1001, 1005–06 (1965); Martin H. Redish, *Congressional Power to Regulate Supreme Court*

Appellate Jurisdiction under the Exceptions Clause: An Internal and External Examination, 27 Vill. L. Rev. 900, 927 (1982).

15 Tara Leigh Grove, *The Exceptions Clause as a Structural Safeguard*, 113 Colum. L. Rev. 929 (2013).

16 James E. Pfander & Daniel D. Birk, *Article III and the Scottish Judiciary*, 124 Harv. L. Rev. 1613 (2011).

17 Akhil Reed Amar, America's Constitution: A Biography 231–32 (New York: Random House 2005); *id.* at 580 n.55 (citing original sources).

18 Laurence Claus, *The One Court That Congress Cannot Take Away: Singularity, Supremacy, and Article III*, 96 Geo. L.J. 59, 81–87 (2007). Consider the first draft from the Committee of Detail. It provided, "But this supreme jurisdiction shall be appellate only, except in . . . those instances, in which the legislature shall make it original[] and the legislature shall organize it." 2 Farrand, *supra* note 6, at 147.

19 Steven G. Calabresi & Gary Lawson, *The Unitary Executive, Jurisdiction Stripping, and the Hamdan Opinions: A Textualist Response to Justice Scalia*, 107 Colum. L. Rev. 1002, 1007–08 (2007).

20 This is a point supplied by the present author, although it is consistent with what Calabresi and Lawson write.

21 It would also be very surprising if the Constitution empowered Congress effectively to eliminate the Supreme Court's role in the constitutional system through an obscure part of a rather obscure sentence about appellate jurisdiction. As Professor David Engdahl has written,

> For persons committed both to the separation of powers and to the principle of enumerated powers, it would have been remarkably offhanded to grant to one branch hegemony over another by two words placed as subordinate terms in prepositional phrases. The framers were otherwise careful to articulate grants of power in straightforward, unequivocal terms; for them to bestow by such indirection a power sufficient to cripple a coordinate branch would have been very peculiar.

> David E. Engdahl, *Intrinsic Limits of Congress' Power Regarding the Judicial Branch*, 1999 BYU L. Rev. 75, 125 (1999).

22 *See, e.g.,* Julius Goebel, History of the Supreme Court of the United States: Antecedents and Beginnings to 1801, at 246–47 (New York: The Macmillan Company 1971).

23 Amar, *supra* note 8; Martin v. Hunter's Lessee, 14 U.S. (1 Wheat.) 304, 331–32 (1816); 3 Joseph Story, Commentaries on the Constitution of the United States § 1696 (Boston: Hilliard, Gray, and Co.; Cambridge, MA: Brown, Shattuck, and Co. 1833).

24 2 Farrand, *supra* note 6, at 146–47.

25 John Harrison, *The Power of Congress to Limit the Jurisdiction of Federal Courts and the Text of Article III*, 64 U. Chi. L. Rev. 203, 210 (1997).

26 *See generally id.* at 212–47.

27 An Act to provide for the more convenient organization of the Courts of the United States, 2 Stat. 89 (Feb. 13, 1801); An Act concerning the District of Columbia, 2 Stat. 103 (Feb. 27, 1801).

28 For a general background on the decision and what we know about what led to it, *see* Michael W. McConnell, "The Story of *Marbury v. Madison*: Making Defeat Look Like

Victory," in Michael C. Dorf ed., Constitutional Law Stories 13–31 (New York: Foundation Press, 2d ed. 2009).

29 U.S. Const. art II, § 2, para. 3.

30 The rule had long been, for example, that deeds required signature and delivery. *See, e.g.*, 2 William Blackstone, Commentaries on the Laws of England 306 (Oxford: Clarendon Press 1766) ("A seventh requisite to a good deed is that it be *delivered*[.]").

31 On the other hand, Marshall may have been right because the Commissions Clause is framed as a duty, declaring that the President "shall commission Officers of the United States." One could argue that the President must deliver a commission after a nominee has been confirmed. Whether this argument has merit may depend on one's view of the President's power to remove the officer once confirmed, a point addressed later.

32 That is what the Supreme Court at one point concluded. Parsons v. United States, 167 U.S. 324, 335–36 (1897); *see also* Aditya Bamzai & Saikrishna Bangalore Prakash, *The Executive Power of Removal*, 136 Harv. L. Rev. 1756, 1804 (2023).

33 United States v. More, 7 U.S. (3 Cranch) 159, 160 n.2 (1805) (providing the circuit court opinions in the margin); Bamzai & Prakash, *supra* note 32, at 1810–13.

34 Bamzai & Prakash, *supra* note 32, at 1805–07.

35 Judiciary Act of 1789, 1 Stat. 73, 81 § 13.

36 James E. Pfander, *Marbury, Original Jurisdiction, and the Supreme Court's Supervisory Powers*, 101 Colum. L. Rev. 1515, 1523–46 (2001). That version of the statute read in relevant part,

> The supreme court shall also have appellate jurisdiction from the circuit courts and courts of the several states, in the cases herein after specially provided for : And shall have power to issue writs of prohibition to the district courts, when proceeding as courts of admiralty and maritime jurisdiction, and writs of mandamus, in cases warranted by the principle and usages of law, to any courts appointed, or persons holding office, under the authority of the United States.

> *Id.* at 1540 (quoting Judiciary Act of 1789 § 13, *reprinted in* 1 Laws of the United States 58 (Philadelphia, PA: Richard Folwell 1796)). The colon and capitalization do suggest a more independent grant.

37 Calabresi and Lawson have made this observation about *Marbury*'s holding. Calabresi & Lawson, *supra* note 19, at 1042–44.

38 U.S. Const. art. VI, para. 3 ("The Senators and Representatives before mentioned, and the Members of the several State Legislatures, and all executive and judicial Officers, both of the United States and of the several States, shall be bound by Oath or Affirmation, to support this Constitution.").

39 Marbury v. Madison, 5 U.S. 137, 180 (1803).

40 U.S. Const. art. VI, para. 2.

41 Marshall seems aware that it is a weak argument. He says: "It is also not entirely unworthy of observation, that in declaring what shall be the *supreme* law of the land, the *constitution* itself is first mentioned; and not the laws of the United States generally, but those only which shall be made in *pursuance* of the constitution, have that rank." *Marbury*, 5 U.S. at 180.

42 However, it should be said that the Supremacy Clause was proposed by the New Jersey Plan, which was favored by the small states. The clause was proposed in lieu of proposals to

coerce the states through force of arms or through a negative on state laws. *See* Bradford R. Clark, *The Supremacy Clause as a Constraint on Federal Power*, 71 Geo. Wash. L. Rev. 91, 106–07 (2003).

43 That is not to say the state judges cannot evaluate Congress's laws for consistency with the Constitution, but it does illustrate that the Supremacy Clause is irrelevant to the question of whether either state or federal judges have that power of judicial review.

44 Judiciary Act of 1789, 1 Stat. 73, 85–86 § 25:

> That a final judgment or decree in any suit, in the highest court of law or equity of a State in which a decision in the suit could be had, where is drawn in question the validity of a treaty or statute of, or an authority exercised under the United States, and the decision is against their validity; or where is drawn in question the validity of a statute of, or an authority exercised under any State, on the ground of their being repugnant to the constitution, treaties or laws of the United States, and the decision is in favour of such their validity, ... may be re-examined and reversed or affirmed in the Supreme Court of the United States upon a writ of error.

45 U.S. Const. art. III, § 2, para. 1 ("The judicial Power shall extend to all Cases, in Law and Equity, arising under the Constitution, the Laws of the United States, and Treaties made, or which shall be made, under their Authority.").

46 *Marbury*, 5 U.S. at 179.

47 U.S. Const. art. I, § 10, para. 1. David Currie explained that the "largest single group of [substantive] cases" in the Marshall period involved the Contracts Clause. David P. Currie, The Constitution in the Supreme Court: The First Hundred Years, 1789–1888, at 128 (University of Chicago Press 1985). Most other cases seem to have involved the states' power over commerce. *Id.* at 168–83.

48 Erie R.R. Co. v. Tompkins, 304 U.S. 64 (1938) (holding that in diversity actions federal courts must apply the substantive law of the states).

49 As for the priority between these two rules, it has been held that a more general later enacted statute does not supersede a more specific, earlier statute. *See, e.g.*, Radzanower v. Touche Ross & Co., 426 U.S. 148, 153 (1976) ("It is a basic principle of statutory construction that a statute dealing with a narrow, precise, and specific subject is not submerged by a later enacted statute covering a more generalized spectrum. 'Where there is no clear intention otherwise, a specific statute will not be controlled or nullified by a general one, regardless of the priority of enactment.'") (citation omitted).

50 *Marbury*, 5 U.S. at 177–78.

51 *Id.* at 178.

52 *Id.* at 176–77.

53 The reader may refer back to Chapter 1.

54 Gordon S. Wood, The Creation of the American Republic, 1776–1787, at 260–61 (Chapel Hill: University of North Carolina Press 1998) (1969).

55 Letter from James Iredell to Richard Spaight, Aug. 26, 1787, *in* 2 Griffith J. McRee ed., Life and Correspondence of James Iredell 172 (New York: D. Appleton and Company 1857).

56 *Id.* at 174.

57 2 Jonathan Elliot ed., The Debates in the Several State Conventions, on the Adoption of the Federal Constitution 445–46 (Washington, DC: Printed for the editor, 2d ed. 1836).

58 The Federalist No. 78, at 466 (Clinton Rossiter ed., 1961).

59 *Hayburn's Case*, 2 U.S. (2 Dall.) 409, 410 n.† (1792); David P. Currie, The Constitution in Congress: The Federalist Period, 1789–1801, at 155–56 (University of Chicago Press 1997).

60 Currie, *supra* note 59, at 120.

61 *See* Dennis C. Rasmussen, The Constitution's Penman: Gouverneur Morris and the Creation of America's Basic Charter 141–42 (Lawrence: University Press of Kansas 2023). Rasmussen, citing Michael Klarman, notes that of the delegates who mentioned the practice of judicial review generally, including in the states, eight favored the practice and two opposed. *Id.* at 141 (citing Michael J. Klarman, The Framers' Coup: The Making of the United States Constitution 160–61 (Oxford University Press 2016)).

62 Mary Sarah Bilder, The Transatlantic Constitution: Colonial Legal Culture and the Empire 186–96 (Cambridge, MA: Harvard University Press 2004).

63 Mary Sarah Bilder, *The Corporate Origins of Judicial Review*, 116 Yale L.J. 502 (2006). More generally, Philip Hamburger shows there was a robust practice of judicial review of governmental acts, including legislation, for consistency with higher law in England, the colonies, and the American states, even though no judge could overturn the high court of Parliament. Philip Hamburger, Law and Judicial Duty 393–94 (Cambridge, MA: Harvard University Press 2008) (summarizing).

64 Paul D. Moreno, How the Court Became Supreme: The Origins of American Juristocracy 35–37 (Baton Rouge: Louisiana State University Press 2022); William Michael Treanor, *Judicial Review before* Marbury, 58 Stan. L. Rev. 455, 474–97 (2005). To be sure, many of the state cases involved institutional self-defense.

65 1 Farrand, *supra* note 6, at 109.

66 *Id.* at 97.

67 2 Farrand, *supra* note 6, at 78.

68 Paul A. Rahe, *Background to* Marbury v. Madison: *The Debate Concerning Judicial Review at the Federal Convention and during the Ratification Period, in* Marbury v. Madison: 1803–2003: A French-American Dialogue 19–30 (Paris: Dalloz 2003).

CHAPTER 14

1 Keith E. Whittington, Repugnant Laws: Judicial Review of Acts of Congress from the Founding to the Present 62–63 (Lawrence: University Press of Kansas 2019).

2 The Contracts Clause provides, "No State shall … pass any … Law impairing the Obligation of Contracts." U.S. Const. art. I, § 10. AsChapter 16 shall explain, the Commerce Clause was understood to disable the states from regulating interstate commerce. For an analysis of the Court's early cases under these clauses, and others limiting state power, *see* David P. Currie, The Constitution in the Supreme Court: The First Hundred Years, 1789–1888, at 127–93 (University of Chicago Press 1985).

3 Dred Scott v. Sandford, 60 U.S. 393 (1857).

4 The owner's name was Sanford, not Sandford, which was misreported by the court reporter. Don E. Fehrenbacher, The Dred Scott Case: Its Significance in American Law and Politics 2 & n* (Oxford University Press 1978).

5 *Dred Scott*, 60 U.S. at 406.

6 *Id.* at 407.

7 *Id.* at 407.

8 *Id.* at 426.

9 *Id.*

10 *Id.* at 407.

11 *Id.* at 410.

12 U.S. Const. art. I, § 9, cl. 1 ("The Migration or Importation of such Persons as any of the States now existing shall think proper to admit, shall not be prohibited by the Congress prior to the Year one thousand eight hundred and eight, but a Tax or duty may be imposed on such Importation, not exceeding ten dollars for each Person.").

13 U.S. Const. art. IV, § 2, cl. 3 ("No Person held to Service or Labour in one State, under the Laws thereof, escaping into another, shall, in Consequence of any Law or Regulation therein, be discharged from such Service or Labour, but shall be delivered up on Claim of the Party to whom such Service or Labour may be due.").

14 *Dred Scott*, 60 U.S. at 411.

15 *See* U.S. Const. art. I, § 8, cl. 4 ("The Congress shall have Power ... To establish an uniform Rule of Naturalization.").

16 *Dred Scott*, 60 U.S. at 418.

17 That is the author's considered opinion. The most sophisticated treatment of the *Dred Scott* decision in modern scholarship that argues the majority opinion was correct as a matter of antebellum jurisprudence is Mark A. Graber, *Dred Scott and the Problem of Constitutional Evil* 28–33, 46–47 (New York: Cambridge University Press 2006). Graber makes a herculean effort to reconstruct the jurisprudential environment in which *Dred Scott* was decided, but it remains the case that the vast majority of antebellum jurisprudence involved cases *denying* free black persons rights, hence raising the question of their citizenship. These cases arose overwhelmingly in the South. There were only two notable cases in the North. One was Crandall v. State, 10 Conn. 339 (1834), involving the denial of the right of black persons from other states to come to Connecticut to be educated. One judge on the state's high court had concluded when sitting as a trial judge that free black persons were not citizens. The case was reversed on a technicality. As Graber notes, after the Civil War, the state court observed on the basis of notes in their possession that the rest of the justices at the time had disagreed with the trial court's conclusion on the merits. Opinion of the Judges of the Supreme Court, 32 Conn. 565 (1865). Then, in Massachusetts, the question arose only when free black persons were denied the right to integrated public schools, and the court confirmed their citizenship while nevertheless sustaining segregation. Roberts v. City of Boston, 59 Mass. 198 (1849).

18 *Dred Scott*, 60 U.S. at 571–72 (Curtis, J., dissenting).

19 *Id.* at 572–73.

20 *Id.* at 575.

21 *Id.* at 576.

22 *Id.*

23 *Id.* at 578.

24 *Id.* at 582.

25 *Id.* at 574–75.

26 U.S. Const. art. I, § 2, cl. 3 ("Representatives and direct Taxes shall be apportioned among the several States which may be included within this Union, according to their respective

Numbers, which shall be determined by adding to the whole Number of free Persons, including those bound to Service for a Term of Years, and excluding Indians not taxed, three fifths of all other Persons.").

27 Sean Wilentz, No Property in Man: Slavery and Antislavery at the Nation's Founding (Cambridge, MA: Harvard University Press 2018); James Oakes, Freedom National: The Destruction of Slavery in the United States, 1861–1865 (New York: W. W. Norton & Co. 2014).

28 An Act to prohibit the importation of slaves into any part or place within the jurisdiction of the United States, from and after the first day of January, in the year of our Lord one thousand eight hundred and eight, ch. 22, 2 Stat. 426 (Mar. 2, 1807).

29 2 Jonathan Elliot ed., The Debates in the Several State Conventions, on the Adoption of the Federal Constitution 452 (Washington, DC: Printed for the editor, 2d ed. 1836) (paragraph break added).

30 *Id.* ("and in the mean time, the *new* states which are to be formed will be under *the control* of Congress in this particular, and slaves will never be introduced amongst them."); *see also* U.S. Const. art. I, § 9, cl. 1 ("The Migration or Importation of such Persons as any of the States *now existing* shall think proper to admit, shall not be prohibited by the Congress prior to the Year one thousand eight hundred and eight, but a Tax or duty may be imposed on such Importation, not exceeding ten dollars for each Person.") (emphasis added).

31 An Ordinance for the Government of the Territory of the United States, North-West of the River Ohio, § 14, art. 6 (July 13, 1787):

It is hereby ordained and declared by the authority aforesaid, That the following articles shall be considered as articles of compact between the original States and the people and States in the said territory and forever remain unalterable, unless by common consent, to wit: ... There shall be neither slavery nor involuntary servitude in the said territory, otherwise than in the punishment of crimes whereof the party shall have been duly convicted: Provided, always, That any person escaping into the same, from whom labor or service is lawfully claimed in any one of the original States, such fugitive may be lawfully reclaimed and conveyed to the person claiming his or her labor or service as aforesaid."). Even fugitive slaves had to be returned under the ordinance only if they escaped from one of the original states.

32 For a balanced and careful analysis of the motives of various framers as to this clause, *see* Fehrenbacher, *supra* note 4, at 23–24.

33 The Federalist No. 42, at 266 (Clinton Rossiter ed., 1961).

34 To be sure, these advocates all would have preferred to abolish the trade immediately. They did worry about the impact of even two more decades of slave importation. They were not wrong to worry. The enslaved population of the United States grew tremendously in this period. Paul A. Rahe, Republics Ancient and Modern: Inventions of Prudence: Constituting the American Regime 87–99 (Chapel Hill, NC: The University of North Carolina Press 1994).

35 James Wilson, Considerations on the Bank of North America, published in the year 1785, *in* 3 The Works of the Honourable James Wilson 395, 407–11 (Bird Wilson ed. 1804) (arguing that nothing explicit in the Articles of Confederation allowed Congress to regulate territories and prepare them for statehood); The Federalist No. 38, *supra* note 33, at 239 (James Madison) (the creation of territorial governments has been done "without

the least color of constitutional authority"). Article XI of the Articles did provide that Canada may join the Union, "but no other colony shall be admitted into the same, unless such admission be agreed to by nine States."

36 U.S. Const. art. IV, § 3, cl. 1 ("New States may be admitted by the Congress into this Union."); *id.* cl. 2 ("Congress shall have Power to dispose of and make all needful Rules and Regulations respecting the Territory or other Property belonging to the United States.").

37 Wilentz, *supra* note 27, at 5. Wilentz argues that this emancipation was "to that point the largest emancipation in modern history and the crucial departure from which all later antislavery activity would follow." *Id.*

38 Fehrenbacher, *supra* note 4, at 18. Manumissions continued to occur further South, too, where the laws did not restrict such manumissions at all. But manumissions quickly came to be restricted with suspicion of the free black population. *Id.* at 49–50.

39 Oakes, *supra* note 27, at 1–48; *see* particularly *id.* at 32–33, 44.

40 Hammer v. Dagenhart, 247 U.S. 251 (1918).

41 United States v. Darby Lumber Co., 312 U.S. 100 (1941).

42 In Federalist No. 54, Madison, summarized the *Southern* position on the compromise, stating that it "regards the *slave* as divested of two fifths of the *man*." The Federalist No. 54, *supra* note 33, at 339 (James Madison). Yet, even here, Madison was hardly saying that enslaved persons were in fact less than human, only that the laws under which they lived treated them also as property.

43 Fehrenbacher, *supra* note 4, at 22.

44 Akhil Reed Amar, America's Constitution: A Biography 345–46 (New York: Basic Books 2005).

45 *See, e.g.,* Wilentz, *supra* note 27, at 58; Michael L. Rosin, *The Three-Fifths Rule and the Presidential Elections of 1800 and 1824,* 15 U. St. Thomas L. J. 159 (2018); Earl M. Maltz, *The Presidency, the Electoral College, and the Three-Fifths Clause,* 43 Rutgers L.J. 439 (2013). Both of the journal articles cite additional sources. It is impossible to know who would have been elected in an alternate universe without such a clause, but it is certainly possible that not much would have changed. Still, the effect of the bump was not insignificant at first, although it became insignificant over time.

46 Wilentz, *supra* note 27, at 187, 243.

47 E. P. Thompson, The Making of the English Working Class 12 (New York: Pantheon Books 1963).

48 However, despite this oft-made claim, Fehrenbacher pointed out that the clause was introduced late in the Convention and produced little debate. Fehrenbacher, *supra* note 4, at 25. He wrote that there is "little evidence to support the assertion frequently made in later years that without the clause the Constitution would have failed." *Id.* But as Fehrenbacher himself stated, all three of the Constitution's clauses dealing with slavery embodied "no ruling principle except compromise for the sake of union." *Id.* at 26. And one reason there may have been little debate is that everyone understood the importance of the clause to the Southern states insisting on it. For the short discussion, *see* 2 Max Farrand ed., The Records of the Federal Convention of 1787, at 443, 446 (New Haven, CT: Yale University Press 1911).

49 2 Farrand, *supra* note at 48, at 417; Wilentz, *supra* note 27.

50 Fehrenbacher, *supra* note 4, at 27; 2 Farrand, *supra* note 48, at 601, 628.

51 It is difficult to improve upon Fehrenbacher's sober assessment. *See* Fehrenbacher, *supra* note 4, at 26–27. He has stated that Abraham Lincoln "was perhaps overreaching the evidence when he declared that the fathers of the government intended to put the institution 'in the course of ultimate extinction,'" but "he may have been much closer to the mark than the Southerners who insisted that the right to hold slaves as property was 'distinctly and expressly affirmed in the Constitution.'" His own assessment was, "It is as though the framers were half-consciously trying to frame two constitutions, one for their own time and the other for the ages, with slavery viewed bifocally – that is, plainly visible at their feet, but disappearing when they lifted their eyes." *Id.* at 27.

52 For a good summary which also includes several of the passages to be quoted, *see* Thomas G. West, Vindicating the Founders 1–36 (Lanham, MD: Rowman & Littlefield 1997).

53 Letter from George Washington to Robert Morris, Apr. 12, 1786, *in* W. W. Abbot & Dorothy Twohig eds., The Papers of George Washington, 4 Confederation Series, 2 April 1786–31 January 1787, at 15 (Charlottesville: University Press of Virginia 1995).

54 Letter from John Adams to Robert J. Evans, June 8, 1819, *in Founders Online*, National Archives, https://founders.archives.gov/documents/Adams/99-02-02-7148.

55 Benjamin Franklin, An Address to the Public from the Pennsylvania Society for Promoting the Abolition of Slavery, and the Relief of Free Negroes Unlawfully Held in Bondage (Philadelphia, Nov. 9, 1789), *in* 12 John Bigelow ed., The Works of Benjamin Franklin 157–58 (New York: The Knickerbocker Press 1904).

56 "Philo Camillus No. 2," Aug. 7, 1795, *in* 19 Harold C. Syrett ed., The Papers of Alexander Hamilton, July 1795–December 1795, at 101 (New York: Columbia University Press 1973).

57 1 Farrand, *supra* note 48, at 135 (June 6). Mary Sarah Bilder argues that the sheet of Madison's notes containing his June 6 speech was likely from 1790. No other speaker recorded Madison making such a statement; Bilder speculates that the language paralleled anti-slavery petitions in Congress in 1790. Mary Sarah Bilder, Madison's Hand: Revising the Constitutional Convention 199–200 (Cambridge, MA: Harvard University Press 2015). Yet, that does not detract from the significance of the statement. Madison wanted posterity to know that that was his thinking. If he believed it in 1790 and stated as much, that would also be probative of his and the Founders' general views on slavery.

As suggested earlier, Madison also famously said on Aug. 25 that he "thought it wrong to admit in the Constitution the idea that there could be property in men." 2 Farrand, *supra* note 48, at 417. Bilder has suggested that Madison's statement would have been written after 1787, possibly in 1789, because Madison had ceased taking more than rough notes at this point in the Convention. Bilder, *supra*, at 108–13. Again, even if Madison revised the notes to include such statements in 1789, it would remain key evidence of how a leading Founder thought about slavery. *But see infra* note 62 (noting Madison's weaknesses in regard to slavery).

58 2 Farrand, *supra* note 48, at 221.

59 Thomas Jefferson, Notes on the States of Virginia 270–72 (London: Printed for John Stockdale 1787).

60 1 Julian P. Boyd ed., The Papers of Thomas Jefferson, 1760–1776, at 243–47 (Princeton University Press, 1950) (original rough draft reconstructed by editor).

61 This saying is attributed to Francois Duc De La Rochefoucauld, Reflections or Sentences and Moral Maxims. *See, e.g.*, p. 66 of the 1775 edition published by Alexander Donaldson in Edinburgh.

62 Neither Madison nor Jefferson is the model delegate in this regard; however. Mary Sarah Bilder has shown how Madison was willing to increase the political power of the South and to count enslaved persons fully for purposes of representation to induce the Southern States to join the larger states in favor of proportional representation in both branches of the legislature. *See* Bilder, *supra* note 57, at 108–13. Madison appears to have thought it better to give the South some additional political power than it was to give states equal representation in the national legislature. Of course, history would turn out quite differently: Equal representation in the Senate turned out to be the great protector of slavery. More decisively, neither Madison nor Jefferson freed his slaves upon death. And by the 1820s, both were alarmed by the rising abolitionist sentiments in Congress and throughout the nation. Jefferson even called the Missouri Compromise a "fire bell in the night." *See* Fehrenbacher, *supra* note 4, at 110–11.

63 Including from Southern delegates. Luther Martin of Maryland stated that the slave trade was "inconsistent with the principles of the revolution and dishonorable to the American character." 2 Farrand, *supra* note 48, at 364. George Mason of Virginia declared, "Every master of slaves is born a petty tyrant. They bring the judgment of heaven on a Country." *Id.* at 370. As Professor Rasmussen has correctly noted, "[n]o one at the Convention defended slavery as a positive moral good" as the Southerners would start to do around the 1830s. They defended slavery on the basis of their economic interests and the reality that the Constitution would not be ratified in the Southern states without it. Dennis C. Rasmussen, The Constitution's Penman: Gouverneur Morris and the Creation of America's Basic Charter 152–53 (Lawrence: University Press of Kansas 2023).

64 For a more general discussion, *see* Bradley Rebeiro, A *Tale of Two Declarations*, 25 Pa. J. Const. L. 915, 932–33 (2023).

65 Cong. Globe, 36th Cong., 1st Sess. App. 98–99 (Jan. 3, 1860). For this quotation, I am indebted to Forrest Nabors, From Oligarchy to Republicanism: The Great Task of Reconstruction 169 (Columbia: University of Missouri Press 2017).

66 Alexander H. Stephens, *Cornerstone Speech*, Mar. 21, 1861, *in* Stanley Harrold ed., The Civil War and Reconstruction: A Documentary Reader 59, 61 (Malden, MA: Blackwell Publishing 2008).

67 George M. Fredrickson, The Black Image in the White Mind: The Debate on Afro-American Character and Destiny, 1817–1914, at 43–51 (New York: Harper & Row 1971); Eugene D. Genovese, The World the Slaveholders Made: Two Essays in Interpretation (Hanover: University Press of New England 1988); Fehrenbacher, *supra* note 4, at 12; Nabors, *supra* note 65, at 165–72. The author uses the term "interbellum" to refer the period between the end of the War of 1812 and the Civil War. *See* Alison L. LaCroix, The Interbellum Constitution: Union, Commerce, and Slavery in the Age of Federalisms (New Haven, CT: Yale University Press 2024).

68 On Taney's manumissions, and for an argument that he went from being "a moderately antislavery lawyer" to a "zealous proslavery judge," see Timothy S. Huebner, *Roger B. Taney and the Slavery Issue: Looking Beyond – and Before – Dred Scott*, 97 J. Am. Hist. 17, 18–20 (2010).

69 Ilan Wurman, A Debt against the Living: An Introduction to Originalism (New York: Cambridge University Press 2017).

70 U.S. Const. art. IV, § 3, cl. 2.

71 *Id.*

72 *Dred Scott*, 60 U.S. at 514.

73 *Id.* at 442–43 (quoting Atlantic Insurance Company v. Canter, 26 U.S. (1 Pet.) 511, 542 (1828)).

74 *Id.* at 609 (Curtis, J., dissenting).

75 *Id.* at 448 (majority opinion).

76 *Id.* at 450.

77 At least if one puts aside the question whether Congress may perpetually govern territory in an unincorporated manner with no intent to admit such territory to statehood as in the *Insular Cases. See, e.g.,* DeLima v. Bidwell, 182 U.S. 1 (1901); Goetze v. United States, 182 U.S. 221 (1901); Dooley v. United States, 182 U.S. 222 (1901); Armstrong v. United States, 182 U.S. 243 (1901); Downes v. Bidwell, 182 U.S. 244 (1901), all of which were decided on the same day.

78 *Dred Scott*, 60 U.S. at 450.

79 For a more in-depth discussion of due process, *see* Ilan Wurman, The Second Founding: An Introduction to the Fourteenth Amendment (New York: Cambridge University Press 2020).

CHAPTER 15

1 Stephen Douglas, Speech at the Sixth Lincoln-Douglas Debate, Oct. 13, 1858, *in* Edwin Erle Sparks ed., The Lincoln-Douglas Debates of 1858, at 418–19 (Springfield: Illinois State Historical Library 1908).

2 Abraham Lincoln, Speech at Springfield, Illinois, June 26, 1857, *in* Roy P. Basler, Marion Dolores Pratt, & Lloyd A. Dunlap eds., 2 The Collected Works of Abraham Lincoln, Sept. 3, 1848–Aug. 21, 1858, at 400–01 (New Brunswick, NJ: Rutgers University Press 1953).

3 *Id.* at 400.

4 *Id.* at 401.

5 Abraham Lincoln, Sixth Joint Debate at Quincy, Illinois, Oct. 13, 1858, *in* Political Debates between Abraham Lincoln and Stephen A. Douglas 299 (Cleveland, OH: The Arthur H. Clarke Co., 1902).

6 Alexis de Tocqueville, Democracy in America 96 (Harvey C. Mansfield & Debra Winthrop trans., eds., The University of Chicago Press 2000).

7 *Id.* at 94.

8 *Id.* at 96.

9 An Act for enrolling and licensing ships or vessels to be employed in the coasting trade and fisheries, and regulating the same, ch. 8, 1 Stat. 305 (Feb. 18, 1793).

10 An Act to regulate the Diplomatic and Consular System of the United States, ch. 127, § 23, 11 Stat. 52 (Aug. 18, 1856).

11 As the Indiana Supreme Court stated in 1866 in reference to the *Dred Scott* decision, "That case was determined in 1856, and although never formally overruled, it is now disregarded by every department of the government. Passports are granted to free men of color, of African descent, by the executive department." Smith v. Moody, 26 Ind. 299, 304 (1866). An opinion for Lincoln's Attorney General Edward Bates held that such persons are

citizens of the United States eligible for coasting licenses. Citizenship, 10 Op. Att'y Gen. 382 (1862).

12 Richard A. Primus, *The Riddle of Hiram Revels*, 119 Harv. L. Rev. 1680 (2006).

13 U.S. Const. art. I, § 3, para. 3.

14 U.S. Const. amend. XIV, § 1.

15 Primus, *supra* note 12, at 1685–91.

16 U.S. Const. art. I, § 5, para. 1.

17 When the House of Representatives later excluded a member based on conduct outside the Constitution's list of qualifications, the Supreme Court did weigh in and hold the exclusion unconstitutional. Powell v. McCormack, 395 U.S. 486 (1969). Congress could have expelled the member by a two-thirds vote, but could not in the circumstance refuse to seat him by a mere majority vote.

18 The basic requirements of standing are an injury caused by the defendant that is redressable by a court. *See, e.g.*, Lujan v. Defs. of Wildlife, 504 U.S. 555, 560–61 (1992):

First, the plaintiff must have suffered an 'injury in fact' – an invasion of a legally protected interest which is (a) concrete and particularized and (b) actual or imminent, not conjectural or hypothetical. Second, there must be a causal connection between the injury and the conduct complained of – the injury has to be fairly traceable to the challenged action of the defendant, and not the result of the independent action of some third party not before the court. Third, it must be likely, as opposed to merely speculative, that the injury will be redressed by a favorable decision. (cleaned up)

19 Although the courts have used the political question doctrine to avoid resolving questions that are arguably amenable to judicial resolution, at a minimum the doctrine applies to those cases in which there are no ascertainable preexisting legal standards to apply. In one famous antebellum case involving the Dorr Rebellion in Rhode Island, in which a private dispute raised the question whether the acts of the defendant were authorized by the act of the legitimate government of the state, the Supreme Court declined to resolve the dispute. The Court concluded that there was no judicial standard by which it could determine which of the two governments of the state was the legitimate one, and that it had to defer to the executive department's prior determination of the question. *See* Luther v. Borden, 48 U.S. 1, 41 (1849) ("[I]f the Circuit Court had entered upon this inquiry, by what rule could it have determined the qualification of voters upon the adoption or rejection of the proposed constitution, unless there was some previous law of the State to guide it? It is the province of a court to expound the law, not to make it.").

20 The Supreme Court was therefore correct to hold recently that it was impermissible for courts to issue universal injunctions applicable to nonparties and that purport to bind the executive department to act a certain way with respect to those nonparties. Trump v. CASA, Inc., 606 U.S. 831 (2025). Its decision was based on its interpretation of courts' equitable powers under the Judiciary Act of 1789, but would seem to generally apply under the principles of Article III itself.

21 For the discussion of interposition and popular constitutionalism generally, see Chapter 2; for the discussion of Henfield's case, see Chapter 9.

22 He explained in a letter to Spencer Roane in 1819:

A legislature had past the Sedition law. the federal courts had subjected certain individuals to it's penalties, of fine and imprisonment. on coming into office I released these individuals by the power of pardon committed to Executive discretion, which could never be more properly exercised than where citizens were suffering without the authority of law, or, which was equivalent, under a law unauthorised by the constitution, & therefore null.

Letter from Thomas Jefferson to Spencer Roane, Sept. 6, 1819, *in* 15 J. Jefferson Looney ed., The Papers of Thomas Jefferson, Retirement Series, 1 September 1819 to 31 May 1820, at 17 (Princeton University Press 2018). In an 1802 letter to Albert Gallatin, however, Jefferson recollected only two pardons. Letter from Thomas Jefferson to Albert Gallatin, Oct. 6, 1802, *in* 38 Barbara B. Oberg ed., The Papers of Thomas Jefferson, 1 July to 12 November 1802, at 452 (Princeton University Press 2011); *see also* Letter from Albert Gallatin to Thomas Jefferson, Oct. 5, 1802, *in id.* at 448.

23 Letter from Thomas Jefferson to Abigail Adams, Sept. 11, 1804, *in* 44 James P. McClure ed., The Papers of Thomas Jefferson, 1 July to 10 November 1804, at 380 (Princeton University Press 2019). The capitalization has been corrected and modernized in the quoted passages.

24 Veto Message, July 10, 1832, *in* 2 James D. Richardson ed., A Compilation of the Messages and Papers of the Presidents, 1789–1897, at 581–82 (Washington, DC: Gov't Printing Off. 1896).

25 *Id.* at 582.

26 An Act for the Release of certain Persons held to Service or Labor in the District of Columbia, ch. 54, 12 Stat. 376 (Apr. 16, 1862); An Act to secure Freedom to all Persons within the Territories of the United States, ch. 111, 12 Stat. 432 (June 19, 1862).

27 See *supra* note 24 and accompanying text.

28 Abraham Lincoln, Speech at Springfield, Illinois, June 26, 1857, *in* Basler et al. eds., *supra* note 2, at 401.

29 *Id.*

30 The Federalist No. 46, at 297–98 (Clinton Rossiter ed. 1961).

31 *See* James Madison, Report of 1800, *in* David B. Mattern, J. C. A. Stagg, Jeanne K. Cross, & Susan Holbrook Perdue eds., 17 The Papers of James Madison: Congressional Series 336–45 (Charlottesville: University Press of Virginia 1991).

32 New York Times Co. v. Sullivan, 376 U.S. 254, 276 (1964) ("Although the Sedition Act was never tested in this Court, the attack upon its validity has carried the day in the court of history.") (footnote omitted). The House of Representatives had concluded as much in 1840 when Congress many years later paid the fines of Matthew Lyons, who had been imprisoned for violating the act. The House reported that the constitutional question was "conclusively settled by the concurring opinions of all parties, after the heated political contests of the day had passed away." H.R. Rep. No. 86, 26th Cong., 1st Sess. 2–3 (Mar. 5, 1840); Act of July 4, 1840, ch. 45, 6 Stat. 802.

33 James Madison, Veto Message, *in* 1 James D. Richardson ed., A Compilation of the Messages and Papers of the Presidents, 1789–1897, at 555 (Washington, DC: Gov't Printing Off. 1896).

34 In Federalist No. 37, Madison wrote, "All new laws, though penned with the greatest technical skill and passed on the fullest and most mature deliberation, are considered as

more or less obscure and equivocal, until their meaning be liquidated and ascertained by a series of particular discussions and adjudications." The Federalist No. 37, *supra* note 30, at 229; *see also* William Baude, *Constitutional Liquidation*, 71 Stan. L. Rev. 1 (2019).

35 *See supra* notes 24– 25 and accompanying text.

36 Veto Message, *supra* note 24, at 582–83.

37 Abraham Lincoln, Speech at the Sixth Lincoln-Douglas Debate, Oct. 13, 1858, *in supra* note 1, at 430 ("Did not [Douglas] and his political friends find a way to reverse the decision of that same court in favor of the constitutionality of the National Bank? Didn't they find a way to do it so effectually that they have reversed it as completely as any decision ever was reversed, so far as its practical operation is concerned?").

38 Developing a theory of precedent that is consistent with Article III of the Constitution is beyond the scope of this study. The literature is vast. The reader could consult, to start, John O. McGinnis & Michael B. Rappaport, *Originalism and Precedent*, 34 Harv. J.L. Pub. Pol'y 121 (2010); John O. McGinnis & Michael B. Rappaport, *Reconciling Originalism and Precedent*, 103 Nw. U. L. Rev. 803 (2009); Michael Stokes Paulsen, *The Intrinsically Corrupting Influence of Precedent*, 22 Const. Comment. 289 (2005); Gary Lawson, *Mostly Unconstitutional: The Case against Precedent Revisited*, 5 Ave Maria L. Rev. 1 (2007); Thomas Merrill, *Originalism, Stare Decisis and the Promotion of Judicial Restraint*, 22 Const. Comment. 271 (2005); Henry Paul Monaghan, *Stare Decisis and Constitutional Adjudication*, 88 Colum. L. Rev. 723 (1988). These latter citations are collected in McGinnis & Rapport's 2009 article. For more recent treatments, *see* Randy J. Kozel, *The Scope of Precedent*, 113 Mich. L. Rev. 179 (2014); Randy J. Kozel, *Precedent and Constitutional Structure*, 112 Nw. U. L. Rev. 789 (2017).

The author's own current view is that following precedent is consistent within the scope of Madison's theory of liquidation. If a matter has been settled within the range of ambiguous constitutional meanings, the courts ought to follow such liquidated settlements. If a prior precedent is outside the range of permissible meanings – it is clearly erroneous – it should be overturned. If a court's prior precedent is within the range of original meanings but the matter has not been fully settled, the question is more difficult. The Supreme Court should be free to overturn that prior precedent in favor of the best answer, but there is nothing illegitimate about following a prior precedent that is within the range of original meanings. Perhaps such precedents ought generally to be followed absent special reasons for overturning them.

39 Plessy v. Ferguson, 163 U.S. 537 (1896).

40 Korematsu v. United States, 323 U.S. 214 (1944).

41 Cooper v. Aaron, 358 U.S. 1, 18 (1958).

42 Brown v. Board of Education of Topeka, 347 U.S. 483 (1954).

43 *Cooper*, 358 U.S. at 9.

44 *Id.* at 13.

45 *Id.* at 17.

46 *Id.* at 18.

47 United States v. Windsor, 570 U.S. 744 (2013).

48 *Id.* at 762.

49 U.S. Const. amend. I.

50 Sherbert v. Verner, 374 U.S. 398 (1963).

51 Emp. Div. v. Smith, 494 U.S. 872 (1990). Justice O'Connor filed an opinion concurring in the judgment but disagreeing with the majority's new test.

52 107 Stat. 1488, §§ 3, 5(1) (1993).

53 U.S. Const. amend XIV, §§ 1, 5.

54 § 2(a), 107 Stat. at 1488.

55 City of Boerne v. Flores, 521 U.S. 507, 529 (1997).

56 *See, e.g.,* Michael W. McConnell, *Institutions and Interpretation: A Critique of* City of Boerne v. Flores, 111 Harv. L. Rev. 153 (1997).

57 *Boerne,* 521 U.S. at 544–45 (O'Connor, J., dissenting).

58 *Id.* at 548.

59 The Federalist No. 78, *supra* note 30, at 465.

60 Jefferson affirmed this position in several letters, but the clearest statement of his view that the Sedition Act was a nullity that he need not enforce was in a first draft of his first annual message to Congress, although the relevant passages did not make it into the final message. Fair Copy, First Annual Message (by Nov. 27, 1801), *in* 35 Barbara B. Oberg ed., The Papers of Thomas Jefferson: Main Series, 1 August 30–30 November 1801, at 647–48 (Princeton University Press 2008).

61 Letter from Thomas Jefferson to William Duane, May 23, 1801, *in* 34 Barbara B. Oberg ed., The Papers of Thomas Jefferson: Main Series, 1 May–31 July 1801, at 169–70 (Princeton University Press 2007). James Wilson also states at the Pennsylvania Ratifying Convention that the President may be able to ignore an unconstitutional law. 2 Jonathan Elliot ed., The Debates in the Several State Conventions, on the Adoption of the Federal Constitution 446 (Washington, DC: Printed for the editor 1836) (suggesting that because of an independent presidential salary "the President of the United States could shield himself, and refuse to carry into effect an act that *violates* the Constitution").

62 Christopher N. May, *Presidential Defiance of "Unconstitutional" Laws: Reviving the Royal Prerogatives,* 21 Hastings Const. L. Q. 865, 908 (1994).

63 *Id.* at 920–21.

64 It does not appear to have been quoted since 1 Charles Warren, The Supreme Court in United States History 763–64 (Boston: Little, Brown, and Company, rev. ed. 1926).

65 Letter from Roger Brooke Taney to Martin Van Buren, June 30, 1860. The letter is available courtesy of the Primary Source Cooperative of the Massachusetts Historical Society. https://www.primarysourcecoop.org/publications/rbt/document/RBT01356?doci = undefined.

66 There was some question as to whether the statute successfully secured Lincoln's appointments because it provided that these officers shall hold their office "during the term of the President by whom they may have been appointed," and of course Lincoln's term arguably ended with his assassination. Still, it is easy enough to read the statute to allow the officers to hold office for what would have been the entire presidential term, which would be consistent with Congress's stated intention. An Act regulating the Tenure of certain Civil Offices, ch. 154, 14 Stat. 430 (Mar. 2, 1867). Additionally, before the Twenty-Fifth Amendment, the language of the Constitution suggested that if the President dies, the Vice President is merely "acting" as President, further supporting the proposition that Lincoln's cabinet members would hold over by the terms of the statute. I am indebted to William Baude for this point. *See also* David P. Currie, The Constitution in Congress: Democrats and Whigs, 1829–1861, at 177–81 (University of Chicago Press 2005).

67 Cong. Globe, 40th Cong., 2d Sess. supp. 126 (1868).

68 *Id.*

69 *Id.* at 126–27.

70 May, *supra* note 62, at 909–10.

71 John N. Pomeroy, An Introduction to the Constitutional Law of the United States 444 (New York: Hurd & Houghton 1868). The author is indebted to May, *supra* note 62, for this passage.

72 *Id.* at 444.

73 *Id.* at 445.

CHAPTER 16

1 Randy E. Barnett, *The Original Meaning of the Commerce Clause*, 68 U. Chi. L. Rev. 101, 104 (2001).

2 The Federalist No. 11, at 89 (Clinton Rossiter ed. 1961); The Federalist No. 12, *id.* at 91; The Federalist No. 35, *id.* at 216. All of these passages are quoted in Barnett, *supra* note 1, at 115–16.

3 Samuel Johnson, A Dictionary of the English Language (London: Printed for J. F. and C. Rivington et al., 6th ed. 1785). The respective definitions are in volumes 1 and 2. These, too, are quoted in Barnett, *supra* note 1, at 113–14.

4 Giles Jacob, A New Law-Dictionary (London: W. Strahan and W. Woodfall, 10th ed. 1782). Under the entry for "bond," Jacob noted that an alien may be an "obligee" for "since he is allowed to trade and traffick with us, it is but reasonable to give him all ... which will the better enable him to carry on his commerce and dealings amongst us." The institution of "fairs and markets," he wrote, "seems plainly to be for the better regulation of trade and commerce."

5 1 John Bouvier, A Law Dictionary, Adapted to the Constitution and Laws of the United States of America 245 (Philadelphia, PA: Childs & Peterson, 6th ed. 1856).

6 Andrew Jackson, Second Annual Message to Congress, *in* 2 James D. Richardson, A Compilation of the Messages and Papers of the Presidents, 1789–897, at 508 (Washington, DC: Gov't Printing Off. 1896).

7 David P. Currie, The Constitution in Congress: The Jeffersonians, 1801–1829, at 275 (University of Chicago Press 2001).

8 1 Stat. 131 (July 20, 1790); *see also* David P. Currie, The Constitution in Congress: The Federalist Period, 1789–1801, at 65 (University of Chicago Press 1997).

9 3 Stat. 488 (Mar. 2, 1819); *see also* Currie, *supra* note 7, at 301.

10 5 Stat. 304 (July 7, 1838).

11 Gibbons v. Ogden, 22 U.S. 1, 189–90 (1824).

12 That is not to say the word commerce could never be used more broadly. Akhil Amar has suggestively argued, based on a few examples, that commerce among the states could be read to mean any interstate affairs or interactions. *See* Akhil Reed Amar, America's Constitution: A Biography 107–08 (New York: Random House 2005). He relies on the passage from Bolingbroke's influential work, *The Idea of a Patriot King*, in which the author discussed the "free and easy commerce of social life." *Id.* at 107; Henry St. John Bolingbroke, Letters, on the Spirit of Patriotism: On the Idea of a Patriot King 218

(London: A. Millar 1749). Bolingbroke's use of the term is obviously literary. His work has an entire section devoted to "trade and commerce," in which the pair is used at least nine times. Bolingbroke, *supra*, at 184–89. Commerce could mean affairs in this pairing, but it is unlikely to carry that extensive meaning. Amar's two other cited references also seem literary, as in "domestic animals which have the greatest Commerce with mankind" and "our Lord's commerce with his disciples." Amar, *supra*, at 107. Perhaps for this reason Amar writes in an endnote that his argument is that the term "may" have the broader reading, not that it "must." *Id.* at 542 n.16.

It is, however, useful to observe that Congress's power over *relations* with the native tribes, and with foreigners, may be broader. Christopher Green argues that the terms commerce "with" the Indian tribes or "with" foreign nations had a broader meaning than simply the term "commerce." *See* Christopher R. Green, *Tribes, Nations, States: Our Three Commerce Powers*, 127 Penn State L. Rev. 643 (2023). Even here, however, Green limits the reach of the clauses to "commercial interactions" that are economic in nature, albeit local. That would also be generally consistent with Congress's early regulation of all affairs with the Indian tribes. *See also, e.g.*, Gregory Ablavsky, *The Original Meaning of Commerce in the Indian Commerce Clause*, 56 Conn. L. Rev. 1013 (2024).

13 U.S. Const. art. I, § 10.

14 *Gibbons*, 22 U.S. at 209–10:

> Since, however, in exercising the power of regulating their own purely internal affairs, whether of trading or police, the States may sometimes enact laws, the validity of which depends on their interfering with, and being contrary to, an act of Congress passed in pursuance of the constitution, the Court will enter upon the inquiry, whether the laws of New-York, as expounded by the highest tribunal of that State, have, in their application to this case, come into collision with an act of Congress, and deprived a citizen of a right to which that act entitles him. Should this collision exist, it will be immaterial whether those laws were passed in virtue of a concurrent power "to regulate commerce with foreign nations and among the several States," or, in virtue of a power to regulate their domestic trade and police. In one case and the other, the acts of New-York must yield to the law of Congress; and the decision sustaining the privilege they confer, against a right given by a law of the Union, must be erroneous.

15 *Id.* at 12 (argument of Daniel Webster) (footnotes omitted). For Witherspoon's motion, and the discussions in the Confederation Congress, for the resolution of Virginia, and for the resolution of the Annapolis Convention, *see* 1 Jonathan Elliot ed., The Debates in the Several State Conventions, on the Adoption of the Federal Constitution 92–120 (Washington, DC: Printed for the editor, 2d ed. 1836).

16 *Gibbons*, 22 U.S. at 13.

17 Address of the Annapolis Convention, Sept. 14, 1786, *in* Harold C. Syrett & Jacob E. Cooke eds., 3 The Papers of Alexander Hamilton, 1782–1786, at 687 (New York: Columbia University Press 1962). This address is also presented in Elliot, *supra* note 15, at 116–19. This language is present in both the Annapolis resolutions as well as the resolutions calling for that convention.

18 *Gibbons*, 22 U.S. at 224 (Johnson, J., concurring).

19 *Id.* at 17–18 (argument of Daniel Webster).

20 *Id.* at 227 (Johnson, J., concurring).

21 *Id.* at 199–200 (Marshall, C.J., opinion for the court).

22 *Id.* at 200:

> In discussing the question, whether this power is still in the States, in the case under consideration, we may dismiss from it the inquiry, whether it is surrendered by the mere grant to Congress, or is retained until Congress shall exercise the power. We may dismiss that inquiry, because it has been exercised, and the regulations which Congress deemed it proper to make, are now in full operation. The sole question is, can a State regulate commerce with foreign nations and among the States, while Congress is regulating it?

23 *Id.* at 177 (argument of Attorney General William Wirt).

24 1 St. George Tucker, Blackstone's Commentaries: With Notes of Reference to the Constitution and Laws of the Federal Government of the United States; and of the Commonwealth of Virginia, app'x 249 (Philadelphia. PA: William Young Birch and Abraham Small 1803). For the exclusivity of the commerce power, see *id.* at app'x 180.

25 1 Joseph Story, Commentaries on the Constitution of the United States 239 (Boston: Hilliard, Gray, and Co.; Cambridge, MA: Brown, Shattuck, and Co. 1833).

26 *Id.* at 240.

27 2 Story, *supra* note 25, at 513.

28 *Id.*

29 *Id.*

30 For example, the Atlantic Slave Trade Clause presumes that states have power over the migration and importation of persons. U.S. Const. art. I, § 9, cl. 1. Even if the migration and importation of persons can be reached by the commerce power, however, it is unclear why it could not also be reached by a state's reserved police powers over health and safety, for example, or by a power over immigration, which surely is something other than merely commerce. The Import-Export Clause provides, "No State shall, without the Consent of the Congress, lay any Imposts or Duties on Imports or Exports, except what may be absolutely necessary for executing it's inspection Laws . . . ." *Id.* art. I, § 10, cl. 2. It could be argued that this clause presumes that states would otherwise possess a power to regulate interstate commerce through the imposition of duties. That is not, however, a necessary reading. The clause is just as naturally read to empower the states to regulate interstate commerce only in this one respect. Indeed, the clause seems to confirm the conclusions of this section and the next that the states retain their police powers only, which would include health and safety regulations such as inspection laws, but not a power to interfere with or harass commerce from other states. Finally, even if the foreign commerce power authorizes Congress to regulate intrastate commercial interactions with foreigners, and that power was exclusive, it would not follow that the states were entirely disabled from regulating intrastate interactions with foreigners pursuant to their police powers over health, safety, welfare, and morals, as discussed in Section 16.3.

31 As the author has written elsewhere. Ilan Wurman, *The Origins of Substantive Due Process*, 87 U. Chi. L. Rev. 815, 837–41 (2020).

32 Gibbons v. Ogden, 22 U.S. (9 Wheat.) 1, 3, 18 (1824).

33 *Id.* at 19.

34 *Id.* at 20.

35 *Id.*

36 *Id.* at 71–72.

37 *Id.* at 72.

38 *Id.* Mr. Emmett, also arguing for Ogden, made the less persuasive argument that these police powers were also regulations of commerce and thus the power over interstate commerce must be concurrent. *Id.* at 112–13.

39 Importantly, the case was also litigated under the patent clause, which grants Congress the power "[t]o promote the Progress of Science and useful Arts, by securing for limited Times to authors and inventors the exclusive right to their respective writings and discoveries." U.S. Const. art. I, § 8, cl. 8. New York had justified its monopoly on the ground that it was granting an exclusive privilege to an inventor of a novel and useful method of steam engine. *Gibbons*, 22 U.S. at 5–6. The same arguments about exclusivity were made about this clause. The Attorney General argued:

> It might be admitted, that the State had authority to prohibit the use of a patented machine on that ground, or of a book, the copy-right of which had been secured, on the ground of its impiety or immorality. But the laws which are now in judgment were not passed upon any such ground. The question raised by them is, can the States obstruct the operation of an act of Congress, by taking the power from the National Legislature into their own hands? Can they prohibit the publication of an immoral book, licensed by Congress, *on the pretext of its immorality*, and then give an exclusive right to publish the same book themselves?

> *Id.* at 176 (emphasis added). Wirt thus implied that if the state regulation were genuinely for the purpose of suppressing immorality, within the traditional police power, then it could have been valid even if it affected or interfered with Congress's power over discoveries and inventions. Although he did not make the point explicitly in the context of the commerce power, there, too, he argued that "quarantine laws, and other regulations of police, respecting the public health in the several States," are not truly commercial regulations, suggesting again that so long as the intent is not to regulate commerce under pretext of such regulation, it would be valid. *Id.* at 178.

40 *Id.* at 203.

41 *Id.*

42 *Id.* at 204.

43 *Id.* at 235 (Johnson, J., concurring).

44 *Id.*

45 *Id.*

46 Willson v. Black Bird Creek Marsh Co., 27 U.S. (2 Pet.) 245, 251–52 (1829).

47 Mayor, Aldermen & Commonalty of City of New York v. Miln, 36 U.S. (11 Pet.) 102, 132–33 (1837).

48 *Id.* at 137.

49 Steamship Co. v. Portwardens, 73 U.S. (6 Wall.) 31 (1867).

50 *Id.* at 33.

51 2 Story, *supra* note 25, at 514–15.

52 New York Tr. Co. v. Eisner, 256 U.S. 345, 349 (1921).

53 Houston E. & W. T. Ry. Co. v. United States (The Shreveport Rate Case), 234 U.S. 342 (1914).

54 Champion v. Ames (The Lottery Case), 188 U.S. 321 (1903).

55 Caminetti v. United States, 242 U.S. 470 (1917).

56 David P. Currie, The Constitution in Congress: Democrats and Whigs, 1829–1861, at 124 (University of Chicago Press 2005).

57 Hammer v. Dagenhart, 247 U.S. 251 (1918).

58 *Id.* at 271–73.

59 *Id.* at 276.

60 A.L.A. Schechter Poultry Corp. v. United States, 295 U.S. 495 (1935); Carter v. Carter Coal Co., 298 U.S. 238 (1936).

61 *Schechter Poultry*, 295 U.S. at 546.

62 *Id.* at 548.

63 Nat'l Lab. Rel. Bd. v. Jones & Laughlin Steel Corp, 301 U.S. 1, 22, 37, 40, 42–44 (1937).

64 United States v. Darby, 312 U.S. 100 (1941). Technically, the statute applied only to workers employed in firms that transported goods in interstate commerce.

65 *Id.* at 124–25 ("From the beginning and for many years, the amendment has been construed as not depriving the national government of authority to resort to all means for the exercise of a granted power which are appropriate and plainly adapted to the permitted end.").

66 Wickard v. Filburn, 317 U.S. 111 (1942).

67 *Id.* at 121.

68 *See* United States v. Lopez, 514 U.S. 549 (1995) (invalidating the Gun-Free School Zones Act of 1990 on the ground that guns near schools were noneconomic activities, and areas of traditional state concern); Nat'l Fed'n of Indep. Bus. v. Sebelius, 567 U.S. 519 (2012) (holding the Patient Protection and Affordable Care Act of 2010 invalid under the Commerce Clause for requiring individuals to engage in commercial transactions, but upholding the law under Congress's taxing power). In Gonzalez v. Raich, 545 U.S. 1 (2005), the Supreme Court also seemed to suggest that noneconomic activity could be regulated under the Necessary and Proper Clause if necessary to effectuate a federal regulatory scheme.

69 *Lopez*, 514 U.S. at 615–31 (Breyer, J., dissenting); *Sebelius*, 567 U.S. at 599–618 (Ginsburg, J., dissenting in relevant part).

70 *See* James Oakes, Freedom National: The Destruction of Slavery in the United States, 1861–1865, at 5–8 (New York: W. W. Norton & Co. 2013) (raising this question, but not providing any suggestion about interstate commerce).

71 There seems little doubt that both Congress and the states could prohibit the interstate slave trade, the former as an exercise of the power to regulate interstate commerce, the latter as a regulation of police. For more on this latter point, *see infra* notes 77–80 and accompanying text.

72 Hammer v. Dagenhart, 247 U.S. 251, 281 (Holmes, J., dissenting).

73 Gibbons v. Ogden, 22 U.S. (9 Wheat.) 1, 235 (1824) (Johnson, J., concurring).

74 United States v. Darby, 312 U.S. 100, 114 (1941).

75 There may, however, be some exception to the rule that Congress cannot regulate production. United States v. E.C. Knight is often criticized, perhaps rightly so, for disabling Congress from disbanding a sugar monopoly, which the Court held involved production and not commerce. United States v. E.C. Knight Co., 156 U.S. 1 (1895). Surely Congress has the power to prohibit the interstate acquisition of companies that would

create a monopoly; that would be merely regulating interstate commerce itself. If it transpires that all production of a particular commodity is situated within a single state, even then it was widely recognized that Congress could remove obstructions to interstate commerce. A nationwide monopoly would at least arguably be such an obstruction. As Justice Harlan pointed out in dissent, restraints of trade, including monopolization, were understood to be "obstructions" to trade at the common law. *Id.* at 24 (Harlan, J., dissenting). "Whatever improperly obstructs the free course of interstate intercourse and trade, as involved in the buying and selling of articles to be carried from one state to another, may be reached by congress under its authority to regulate commerce among the states," Harlan wrote. "The exercise of that authority so as to make trade among the states in all recognized articles of commerce absolutely free from unreasonable or illegal restrictions imposed by combinations is justified by an express grant of power to congress." *Id.* at 37.

76 For some classic cases, *see* Pike v. Bruce Church, Inc., 397 U.S. 137 (1970); Hunt v. Washington Apple Advert. Comm'n, 432 U.S. 333 (1977); Kassel v. Consol. Freightways Corp. of Delaware, 450 U.S. 662 (1981).

77 Nat'l Pork Producers Council v. Ross, 598 U.S. 356 (2023).

78 *Id.* at 377–89 (questioning but not overturning the existing balancing test).

79 *Id.* at 393–94 (Barrett, J., concurring in part).

80 Groves v. Slaughter, 40 U.S. 449, 507–08 (1841) (McLean, J., concurring).

CHAPTER 17

1 Printz v. United States, 521 U.S. 898, 905 (1997).

2 *E.g.*, Alden v. Maine, 527 U.S. 706, 728–29 (1999) ("The Eleventh Amendment confirmed, rather than established, sovereign immunity as a constitutional principle; it follows that the scope of the States' immunity from suit is demarcated not by the text of the Amendment alone but by fundamental postulates implicit in the constitutional design."); Seminole Tribe of Fla. v. Fla., 517 U.S. 44, 54 (1996) ("Although the text of the Amendment would appear to restrict only the Article III diversity jurisdiction of the federal courts, 'we have understood the Eleventh Amendment to stand not so much for what it says, but for the presupposition . . . which it confirms.'") (quoting Blatchford v. Native Village of Noatak, 501 U.S. 775, 779 (1991)).

3 Nat'l League of Cities v. Usery, 426 U.S. 833 (1976).

4 Garcia v. San Antonio Metro. Transit Auth., 469 U.S. 528 (1985).

5 Nat'l League of Cities, 426 U.S. at 852.

6 *Id.* at 842. For the other assertions in this paragraph, *see id.* at 845–46.

7 *Garcia*, 469 U.S. at 537.

8 *Id.* at 547.

9 *Id.* at 549.

10 *Id.* at 550.

11 *Id.* at 550–51.

12 *Id.* at 587 (O'Connor, J., dissenting).

13 *Id.* at 584.

14 Caleb Nelson, *Sovereign Immunity as a Doctrine of Personal Jurisdiction*, 115 Harv. L. Rev. 1559 (2002).

15 1 William Blackstone, Commentaries on the Laws of England 237 (Oxford: Clarendon Press 1765):

> For, wherever the law expresses its distrust of abuse of power, it always vests of superior coercive authority in some other hand to correct it; the very notion of which destroys the idea of sovereignty …. The supposition of law therefore is, that neither the king nor either house of parliament (collectively taken) is capable of doing any wrong; since in such cases the law feels itself incapable of furnishing any adequate remedy.

see also id. at 238–39.

16 *Id.* at 237 (describing liability of officers); Little v. Barreme, 6 U.S. (2 Cranch) 170 (1804) (holding office liable in trespass despite instructions from the President).

17 Chisolm v. Georgia, 2 U.S. (2 Dall.) 419, 435–40 (1793) (Iredell, J., dissenting).

18 Some pieces of this discussion appeared in Ilan Wurman, "Originalism and Sovereign Immunity," Law & Liberty (May 24, 2019), https://www.lawliberty.org/2019/05/24/original ism-and-sovereign-immunity/.

19 *Chisolm*, 2 U.S. at 419.

20 U.S. Const., art. III, § 2, para. 1.

21 U.S. Const. amend. XI.

22 Hans v. Louisiana, 134 U.S. 1 (1890).

23 Seminole Tribe of Fla. v. Fla., 517 U.S. 44 (1996).

24 Alden v. Maine, 527 U.S. 706 (1999).

25 Eric Segall, Originalism as Faith 133 (Cambridge University Press 2018). Akhil Amar makes the same point, arguing that under the terms of the Eleventh Amendment, a state could still be sued for violating federal law. Akhil Reed Amar, America's Constitution: A Biography 334–36 (New York: Random House 2005).

26 Bradford R. Clark, *The Eleventh Amendment and the Nature of the Union*, 123 Harv. L. Rev. 1817 (2010).

27 *See, e.g., Chisolm*, 2 U.S. at 452 (opinion of Blair, J.); *id.* at 456–57 (opinion of Wilson, J.).

28 *Id.* at 449–50 (Iredell, J., dissenting).

29 Much of the relevant evidence is discussed in *Chisolm*, of course, but also in Professor Nelson's piece. Nelson, *supra* note 14, at 1592–601.

30 Debates of the Virginia Convention (June 19, 1788), *in* John P. Kaminski & Gaspare J. Saladino eds., 10 The Documentary History of the Ratification of the Constitution 1406 (Madison: State Historical Society of Wisconsin 1993).

31 *Id.* at 1414.

32 *Id.* at 1433. All of these citations are in Nelson, *supra* note 14, at 1592–93.

33 Nelson, *supra* note 14, at 1593–94.

34 A Republican, *The Crisis, No. XIII*, Indep. Chron. (July 25, 1793), *reprinted in* 5 Maeva Marcus ed., The Documentary History of the Supreme Court of the United States, 1789–1800, at 396 (New York: Columbia University Press 1994).

35 The Federalist No. 81, at 487 (Clinton Rossiter ed. 1961).

36 Aaron N. Coleman, The American Revolution, State Sovereignty, and the American Constitutional Settlement, 1765–1800, at 191–92 (Lanham, MD: Lexington Books 2016).

37 *Id.* at 193.

38 *Id.*

39 The majority did address the Necessary and Proper Clause at the end of its opinion, arguing the clause was "the last, best hope of those who defend ultra vires congressional action." Printz v. United States, 521 U.S. 898, 923 (1997). What Justice Scalia missed was that the clause was the crux of the analysis.

40 *See, e.g.,* New York v. United States, 505 U.S. 144, 162–63 (1992) (holding in part on this basis that the commandeering of state legislatures is beyond Congress's power).

41 *See, e.g.,* Testa v. Katt, 330 U.S. 386 (1947) (holding that the state judiciaries could not close their doors to federal claims similar to state claims for which their doors were open). For a discussion of the Madisonian Compromise and the Supremacy Clause, *see* Chapter 13.

42 *Printz,* 521 U.S. at 907–08.

43 *Id.* at 922.

44 Wesley J. Campbell, *Commandeering and Constitutional Change,* 122 Yale L.J. 1104, 1107–08, 1128–29 (2013).

45 Federalist No. 27, *supra* note 35, at 177.

46 Campbell, *supra* note 44, at 1109.

47 Gary Lawson & Guy Seidman, "A Great Power of Attorney": Understanding the Fiduciary Constitution 100 (Lawrence: University Press of Kansas 2017).

48 That Hamilton thought state officers would assist in enforcing federal laws is perhaps evidence against an indefeasible presidential removal power. It could be argued, however, that other means of accountability existed over state officers. They were closer to the people, which was the reason the Anti-Federalists preferred enforcement by such officers. That would not derogate from the proposition that as to federal officers the President must have control through removal.

49 Anthony J. Bellia Jr. & Bradford R. Clark, *State Sovereign Immunity and the New Purposivism,* 65 Wm. & Mary L. Rev. 485, 497 (2024); *see also* Anthony J. Bellia Jr. & Bradford R. Clark, *The International Law Origins of American Federalism,* 120 Colum. L. Rev. 835, 875–76 (2020).

50 Bellia & Clark, *International Law Origins, supra* note 49, at 847, 849.

51 Emmerich de Vattel, The Law of Nations, bk. I, ch. 1, § 4, at 2 (London: Printed for G.G. and J. Robinson 1797).

52 Bellia & Clark, *New Purposivism, supra* note 49, at 500.

CHAPTER 18

1 U.S. Const. art. I, § 8, cl. 1.

2 Gibbons v. Ogden, 22 U.S. 1, 199 (1824).

3 U.S. Const. art. I, § 8, cl. 3 ("To regulate Commerce with foreign Nations, and among the several States, and with the Indian Tribes"); *id.* cl. 4 ("To establish an uniform Rule of Naturalization, and uniform Laws on the subject of Bankruptcies throughout the United States"); *id.* cl. 5 ("To coin Money, regulate the Value thereof, and of foreign Coin, and fix the Standard of Weights and Measures"); *id.* cl. 11 ("To declare War, grant Letters of

Marque and Reprisal, and make Rules concerning Captures on Land and Water"); *id.* cl. 17:

To exercise exclusive Legislation in all Cases whatsoever, over such District (not exceeding ten Miles square) as may, by Cession of particular States, and the Acceptance of Congress, become the Seat of Government of the United States, and to exercise like Authority over all Places purchased by the Consent of the Legislature of the State in which the Same shall be, for the Erection of Forts, Magazines, Arsenals, dock-Yards, and other needful Buildings.

4 *Id.* cl. 2.
5 *Id.* cl. 6.
6 *Id.* cl. 15.
7 *Id.* cl. 16.
8 Art. of Confed. arts. III, VIII, IX (1781).
9 Roger Sherman, who was the leading advocate for this limitation on the taxing power in the Constitutional Convention, explicitly connected the two provisions in a letter to the Governor of Connecticut enclosing the new draft constitution. "The objects, for which congress may apply monies, are the same mentioned in the eighth article of the confederation, viz. for the common defence and general welfare, and for payment of the debts incurred for those purposes."³ Max Farrand ed., The Records of the Federal Convention of 1787, at 99 (New Haven, CT: Yale University Press 1911). True, in the letter, Sherman described it as a power to "apply monies," but that only suggests even more strongly that the taxing and spending powers were to be commensurate with the national objects that Sherman made clear in the same letter the Constitution specifically enumerated. Madison also connected the two. In a letter to Edmund Pendleton, responding to Hamilton's Report on Manufactures, Madison explained that the phrase "is copied from the old Articles of Confederation, where it was always understood as nothing more than a general caption to the specified powers, and it is a fact that it was preferred in the new instrument for that very reason, as less liable than any other to misconstruction." Letter from James Madison to Edmund Pendleton, Jan. 21, 1792, *in* Robert A. Rutland & Thomas A. Mason eds., 14 The Papers of James Madison: Congressional Series, 6 April 1791–16 March 1793, at 195–96 (Charlottesville: University Press of Virginia 1983).
10 2 Farrand, *supra* note 9, at 142.
11 *Id.* at 167.
12 *Id.* at 181.
13 *Id.* at 382 ("The Legislature shall fulfil the engagements and discharge the debts of the United-States, and shall have the power to lay and collect taxes, duties, imposts, and excises.").
14 The eleven-member committee reported on Sept. 4. *Id.* at 493. Sherman had asked to reintroduce a limitation when the Convention debated Wilson's draft, although it was rejected at the time. Sherman had suggested the clause parallel the Articles of Confederation: Congress shall have power to lay and collect taxes "for the payment of said debts and for the defraying the expences that shall be incurred for the common defense and general welfare." *Id.* at 414. Although the change in language may create some ambiguity, it remains the case that all proponents of the subordinate clause understood that clause as a limitation on the power to tax, and no one proposed an independent power

to spend for the general welfare. On Sherman's role, see also Theodore Sky, To Provide for the General Welfare: A History of the Federal Spending Power 43 (Newark: University of Delaware Press 2003) ("One may speculate that [Sherman] particularly wanted language that would limit the taxing power by differentiating federal from state functions . . . . [I]t should not be surprising to see Sherman picking up the phrase and attaching it to the taxing power, as a phrase of *limitation* . . . .").

15 2 Farrand, *supra* note 9, at 594.

16 Sky, *supra* note 14, at 51; 3 Farrand, *supra* note 9, at 379. For an account that is skeptical of Gallatin's and Sherman's claims, see David S. Schwartz, *The Committee of Style and the Federalist Constitution*, 70 Buff. L. Rev. 781, 834–39 (2022).

17 McCulloch v. Maryland, 17 U.S. (4 Wheat.) 316, 411 (1819).

18 James Madison to Andrew Stevenson, Nov. 17, 1830, *in* 3 Farrand, *supra* note 9, at 493.

19 *McCulloch*, 17 U.S. at 431.

20 James Otis was the leading pamphleteer on this issue. *See* James Otis, The Rights of the British Colonies Asserted and Proved (Boston: Edes and Gill 1764). The point, however, goes back to constitutional battles with Charles I over taxation. *See* Petition of Right, paras. I, X (1628).

21 Sky, *supra* note 14, at 58–60.

22 *Id.* at 61.

23 *Id.* at 59; Centinel I, *in* 2 Herbert J. Storing ed., The Complete Anti-Federalist 140 (University of Chicago Press 1981).

24 The Federalist No. 41, at 256 (Clinton Rossiter ed. 1961).

25 *Id.* at 262.

26 *Id.* at 262–63.

27 *Id.* at 263.

28 *Id.*

29 James Madison, Veto Message on the Bonus Bill, Mar. 3, 1817, *in* 1 James D. Richardson, A Compilation of the Messages and Papers of the Presidents, 1789–1897, at 584–85 (Washington, DC: Published by the Authority of Congress 1899).

30 Thomas Jefferson, Opinion on the Bank Bill, Feb. 15, 1791, *in* 6 Paul Leicester Ford ed., The Works of Thomas Jefferson 199–200 (New York: The Knickerbocker Press 1904). In another letter to George Washington, Jefferson described limiting (but really expanding) the clause to spending as a "sham." Letter from Thomas Jefferson to George Washington, Sept. 9, 1792, *in* John Catanzariti et al. eds., 24 The Papers of Thomas Jefferson: Main Series, 1 June to 31 December 1792, at 353 (Princeton University Press 2010).

31 1 St. George Tucker, Blackstone's Commentaries with Notes of Reference to the Constitution and Laws of the Federal Government of the United States; and of the Commonwealth of Virginia, app'x 231 (Philadelphia, PA: William Young Burch and Abraham Small 1803).

32 Roger Sherman, A *Citizen of New Haven: Observations on the New Federal Constitution, Connecticut Courant*, 7 Jan. 1788, *in* John P. Kaminski & Gaspare J. Saladino eds., 15 Documentary History of the Ratification of the Constitution 281 (Madison: State Historical Society of Wisconsin 1984).

33 3 Jonathan Elliot ed., The Debates in the Several State Conventions, on the Adoption of the Federal Constitution 466 (Washington, DC: Printed for the Editor, 2d ed. 1836) (emphasis added).

34 2 Elliot, *supra* note 33, at 190; *see generally id.* at 190–97.

35 2 Bird Wilson ed., The Works of the Honourable James Wilson, L.L.D. 181 (Philadelphia, PA: Lorenzo Press 1804).

36 Gibbons v. Ogden, 22 U.S. 1, 199 (1824).

37 10 Alexander Hamilton, *Report on Manufactures, Dec. 5, 1791, in* Harold C. Syrett ed., The Papers of Alexander Hamilton 303 (New York: Columbia University Press 1966).

38 *Id.* Theodore Sky intriguingly observes that in multiple statements to Congress, President Washington recommended that they promote learning and manufactures through "affording aids," but was otherwise quite vague as to how Congress could or should encourage these activities. Sky, *supra* note 14, at 80–81, 105–07.

39 Allison LaCroix demonstrates that Pennsylvania judge Alexander Addison adopted the three-powers view, but no one else of prominence seems to have done so. *See* Alison LaCroix, *The Shadow Powers of Article I*, 123 Yale L.J. 2044, 2082–83 & n.162. It was noted in Chapter 3 that modern revisionist scholars have sought to undermine that idea that Congress was limited to the enumeration of power. They rely in part on the so-called general welfare clause. It was noted in that previous chapter that, as an initial matter, this power would be enumerated, even if it granted Congress a general regulatory power. This chapter has now, it is hoped, established why the revisionist scholars are wrong. Their view has almost zero support in the text, structure, or history of the Constitution. They rely mostly on pre-ratification exaggerations by Anti-Federalists who sought to defeat the Constitution's adoption. Those who supported ratification were consistent both before and after adoption: The clause granted merely a power to tax. *See also, e.g.*, William Baude & Stephen E. Sachs, *The "Common-Good" Manifesto*, 136 Harv. L. Rev. 861, 869 & n.31 (2023) (noting this debate and citing some literature challenging the revisionist accounts of the "general welfare clause") (reviewing Adrian Vermeule, Common Good Constitutionalism (Medford, MA: Polity Press 2022)).

40 David P. Currie, The Constitution in Congress: The Federalist Period, 1789–1801, at 168–69 (University of Chicago Press 1997). At least some members in the debate took the two-power view that Congress could spend for the general welfare.

41 *Id.* at 188–89. Though it appears that France may have rejected the ruse, requiring the United States to pay the full amount it still owed. 6 Annals of Cong. 1724 (1796) (Washington, DC: Gales & Seaton 1849) (statement of W. Smith) (suggesting as much).

42 Currie, *supra* note 40, at 189 n.121.

43 *Id.* at 224–25 & n.149; 6 Annals of Cong., *supra* note 41, at 1712–27.

44 David P. Currie, The Constitution in Congress: The Jeffersonian, 1801–1829, at 91 n.35 (University of Chicago Press 2001).

45 Currie, *supra* note 40, at 76–77.

46 *Id.* at 77 & nn. 173–74. James Madison devoted much attention to responding to this argument, suggesting it was the leading constitutional ground in favor of assumption. Charles F. Hobson & Robert A. Rutland eds., 13 The Papers of James Madison, Congressional Series, 20 January 1790–31 March 1791, at 163–74 (Charlottesville: University Press of Virginia 1981). Further supporting this argument is the proposal of

the Committee of Eleven, which had proposed at the Constitutional Convention giving Congress a power "to discharge as well the debts of the United States, as the debts incurred by the several States during the late war, for the common defence and general welfare." 2 Farrand, *supra* note 9, at 352. The language is a bit hard to parse but seems to suggest that the state debts were incurred for the common defense.

It should be clear from this discussion that the constitutionality of assumption is a serious question with serious implications for understanding of the first grant of power in the eighth section. The constitutional arguments against assumption were therefore not "gibberish," as one prominent scholar has recently suggested. *See* Akhil Reed Amar, The Words That Made Us: America's Constitutional Conversation, 1760–1840, at 427 (New York: Basic Books 2021). Amar suggests, without pointing to any specific text, that assumption must have been constitutional because assumption was consistent with the "biggest and most obvious reasons why Americans had knowingly ratified" the Constitution, and points to the amorphous concepts of "common defense, national security, and international respectability." *Id.* at 362. Amar also suggests that assuming the debts fell within Congress's interstate commerce power, but it is hard to see how assumption was a "regulation" of interstate commerce, or necessary and proper for the creation of a single currency.

47 Andrew Jackson, *Second Annual Message to Congress, in* 2 James D. Richardson, A Compilation of the Messages and Papers of the Presidents, 1789–1897, at 508 (Washington, DC: Gov't Printing Off. 1896).

48 At the Convention, after the Taxing Clause took shape with its general welfare language, James McHenry wrote himself the following note: "Upon looking over the constitution it does not appear that the national legislature can *erect light houses* or *clean out or preserve the navigation of harbours* – This expence ought to be borne by commerce – of course by the general treasury into which all the revenue of commerce must come." 2 Farrand, *supra* note 9, at 504; Sky, *supra* note 14, at 48. This suggests that McHenry did not think the Taxing Clause included a general power to spend, and that he thought lighthouses and the like were intimately connected to commerce. On the other hand, his note suggests that he also did not think the commerce power itself sufficient to authorize funding for such projects. McHenry raised the suggestion to Morris, who thought it could be accomplished by the subordinate clause within the taxing power, but McHenry seemed to express skepticism. 2 Farrand, *supra* note 9, at 529–30.

49 U.S. Const. art. I, § 8, cl. 17.

50 However, James Monroe, in his famous memorandum on internal improvements, rejected this argument in favor of a power to appropriate for the general welfare. Richardson, *supra* note 47, at 157–60.

51 Currie, *supra* note 44, 271–74.

52 *Id.* at 277–78.

53 1 James Kent, Commentaries on American Law 250 (New York: O. Halsted 1826).

54 *Id.* at 251.

55 Currie, *supra* note 44, at 280–82; Richardson, *supra* note 47, at 144–83.

56 Richardson, *supra* note 47, at 511; *see also* David P. Currie, The Constitution in Congress: Democrats and Whigs, 1829–1861, at 11 & n.9 (University of Chicago Press 2005).

57 Currie, *supra* note 56, at 25.

58 2 Joseph Story, Commentaries on the Constitution of the United States 367, § 904 (Boston: Hilliard, Gray, and Co.; Cambridge, MA: Brown, Shattuck, and Co. 1833).

59 *Id.*

60 *Id.* at 368, § 905.

61 *Id.* at 368, § 905 n.1

62 *Id.* at 457, § 988; *see also* 3 Story, *supra* note 58, at 149–53, §§ 1268–72. In volume 3, Story suggests that Congress can erect and regulate internal improvements as incidental to enumerated powers. In section 1268, however, he took the position that its appropriations were not so limited.

> So far, as regards the right to appropriate money to internal improvements: generally, the subject has already passed under review in considering the power to lay and collect taxes. The doctrine there contended for, which has been in a great measure borne out by the actual practice of the government, is, that congress may appropriate money, not only … for … purposes allied to some of the enumerated powers; but may also appropriate it in aid of canals, roads, and other institutions of a similar nature …. The only limitations upon the power are those prescribed by the terms of the constitution, that the objects shall be for the common defence, or the general welfare of the Union. The true test is, whether the object be of a local character, and local use; or, whether it be of general benefit to the states.

> *Id.* at 149, § 1268. Story appears to conflate the powers to tax, and the power to spend the money raised. There is no other apparent explanation for the inconsistency between this discussion and his conclusion that the clause is only a taxing power.

63 United States v. Butler, 297 U.S. 1, 67 (1936).

64 Justice Story suggested that using taxation to support manufactures would be an unconstitutional usurpation of the taxing power. 2 Story, *supra* note 58, at 432–33, § 959. Congress, in other words, could only structure taxation in a way that supported the general welfare more broadly rather than the local welfare. As noted previously, however, Congress regularly used the taxing power rather than a spending power to support the codfish industry or to achieve other regulatory objectives.

65 See, for example, the South Carolina Ordinance of Nullification, Nov. 24, 1832, entitled "An ordinance to nullify certain acts of the Congress of the United States, purporting to be laws laying duties and imposts on the importation of foreign commodities." Reprinted in 9 Register of Debates in Congress, 22d Cong., 2d sess., App'x 162 (Washington, DC: Gales and Seaton 1838).

66 Currie, *supra* note 40, at 57, 60. The distinction between revenue-raising laws (taxation) and trade regulations that incidentally raise revenues can be traced back at least to John Dickinson's explanation for why the Stamp Act of 1765 was unconstitutional but imports on duties may not be. However, this distinction was not necessarily widely shared in the colonies. For a discussion, see Amar, *supra* note 46, at 66–67.

67 Bailey v. Drexel Furniture Co., 259 U.S. 20 (1922).

68 McCray v. United States, 195 U.S. 27 (1904).

69 *Bailey*, 259 U.S. at 37–38.

70 *Id.* at 38 (paragraph breaks supplied).

71 Steward Mach. Co. v. Davis, 301 U.S. 548 (1937).

72 *Id.* at 585.

73 *Id.* at 586.

74 *Id.* at 589.

75 Nat'l Fed'n Indep. Bus. v. Sebelius, 567 U.S. 519 (2012).

76 *Id.* at 548–61.

77 *Id.* at 561–74.

78 *See* Andy Sullivan, "Spending – Why 'Red' States Shoulder Deepest Cuts under Obama," Reuters (Jan. 28, 2015).

79 John Hudak, Presidential Pork: White House Influence over the Distribution of Federal Grants (Washington, DC: Brookings Press, 2014). This proposition holds after controlling for statistical outliers such as New York, California, and disaster years for certain states, as explained in *id.* at 32–67.

80 Helvering v. Davis, 301 U.S. 619, 640 (1937).

81 2 Richardson, *supra* note 47, at 513.

82 *Id.* at 514.

83 United States v. Butler, 297 U.S. 1 (1936).

84 *Id.* at 66.

85 *Id.* at 74.

86 *Id.* at 73.

87 *Id.* at 72. A related way to see the problem, which the Court did address, is the coerciveness of the program. No one is coerced to accept emergency relief dollars or social security benefits. Most persons are likely to accept such funds, but there is no coercive element because no behavioral or regulatory changes are required. That is the hallmark of a genuine spending program. In Butler, the Court argued that although the farmer "may refuse to comply," the "amount offered is intended to be sufficient to exert pressure on him to agree to the proposed regulation." This was "coercion by economic pressure" and "[t]he asserted power of choice [was] illusory." *Id.* at 70–71. In other words, there comes a point where the financial pressure induces or coerces an individual (or a state) to undergo a regulatory change and to take actions to receive the money that Congress could not have regulated or compelled directly. That is not an exercise of the spending power, but rather a regulatory power that Congress does not possess.

88 South Dakota v. Dole, 483 U.S. 203 (1987).

89 *Id.* at 206.

90 *Id.* at 207 (internal citation and quote marks omitted).

91 *Id.* at 207–08, 211.

92 As for coerciveness, if a spending program is so coercive that the states have no choice but to comply with the attached conditions, then Congress is not spending for the general welfare but rather regulating and purchasing compliance. Although the Court conducted this analysis in *Butler* as well, it is unclear why any amount of financial inducement should be constitutional if its purpose is nothing other than inducing compliance with a federal regulatory program otherwise beyond the enumeration of power. *See supra* note 87.

Index

For EU product safety concerns, contact us at Calle de José Abascal, 56–1°, 28003 Madrid, Spain or eugpsr@cambridge.org.

www.ingramcontent.com/pod-product-compliance
Ingram Content Group UK Ltd.
Pitfield, Milton Keynes, MK11 3LW, UK
UKHW022037310526
471684UK00010B/384